BARRON'S

How to Prepare for the
GED® TEST
CANADIAN
EDITION

Chris Smith, M.A.

Karen Sansom, B. Comm., M.Ed.

BARRON'S

About the Authors

Chris Smith is a community college instructor, e-learning designer, and writer in Saint John, New Brunswick. For twenty-five years, he has taught various levels of Adult Basic Education, including literacy, GED® test preparation, and high school English.

Karen Sansom works for Okanagan College in Salmon Arm, British Columbia, and has taught Adult Basic Education Mathematics courses for the past thirteen years.

Acknowledgements

Thanks to family members and friends for their patience and support during the long process of developing this book. Thanks to Barron's Educational Series, Inc. for their continued commitment to this project. Thanks to fellow instructors for insights and suggestions. In particular, thanks to you, the learners, for your hard work and dedication, which are the inspiration for this book.

All inquiries should be addressed to:
Barron's Educational Series, Inc.
250 Wireless Boulevard
Hauppauge, New York 11788
www.barronseduc.com

ISBN: 978-1-4380-0180-7

Library of Congress Control Number: 2014939350

PRINTED IN THE UNITED STATES OF AMERICA
9 8 7 6 5 4 3 2 1

10% POST-CONSUMER WASTE
Paper contains a minimum of 10% post-consumer waste (PCW). Paper used in this book was derived from certified, sustainable forestlands.

CONTENTS

LANGUAGE ARTS, WRITING, PART 2

LANGUAGE ARTS, READING

SCIENCE

SOCIAL STUDIES

MATHEMATICS

Introduction

▰▰▰▰▰▰▰▰▰▰▰▰▰▰▰▰

The General Educational Development (GED)® tests have changed the lives of thousands of Canadians. Across the country, successfully completing the GED® tests is recognized as equivalent to a high school diploma by many employers, colleges, and universities. The GED® test originated in the United States and was initially designed for American Servicemen who were returning from World War II. As adults who wanted to resume their lives and pursue careers and education, they could not return to the school system with high school students. The GED® tests were designed to recognize their life experience and their learning.

The GED® tests are designed for adults. The tests recognize that adults continue to learn throughout their lives. Whether reading the newspaper, watching television news, making a family budget, working as a cashier, or doing home renovations, adults continue to learn and develop new skills. The GED® tests are an evaluation of skills, not specific knowledge. You do not have to remember all the specific information from school, such as Shakespeare's birthday or the atomic weight of hydrogen. The GED® tests examine your skills in reading and applying scientific and social studies information, in solving problems using math, in reading and interpreting literature and practical documents, and in communicating ideas through writing.

When you successfully pass all five of the GED® tests, you earn a high school equivalency certificate or diploma that is accepted by most employers, colleges, and universities in every province and territory. However, you should be aware that some post-secondary programs may have additional requirements. For example, some college or university programs may require high school or equivalent and grade 11 math, grade 12 English, or specific science courses. These requirements would be the same for any high school graduate. If you plan to seek further education, you should check the entrance requirements for programs you want to study.

The GED® test has been very successful for many people. More than 600,000 people each year write the GED® test in North America. For adults, it is often the best option to move forward in achieving their goals.

This book was written to help you prepare for the GED® tests. It can be used as part of a class or to study and practice on your own or with the help of family members and friends. The book has information and exercises to help you learn about each of the five test areas, as well as practice tests to evaluate your skills. Barron's Educational Series books have been used for decades by test-takers like you to prepare for success on the Canadian GED® tests.

THE FIVE TEST AREAS

The GED® consists of five tests. If writing the paper tests, they are usually administered in a two-day session, including a Friday evening and a Saturday. Paper tests in Canada are not usually given individually, and you must sign up and write all the tests. Tests taken on a computer can be written individually.

All of the questions on the GED® test are multiple-choice, with two exceptions:

1. Language Arts Writing Part II consists of an essay to be written in 45 minutes
2. Mathematics Alternative Answer Types are some questions on the mathematics test that require you to write your answer and shade it on a corresponding grid, or to shade in a point on a graph

Your results on the GED® test will be reported as a standard score between 200 and 800. You must achieve a minimum score of 450 on each of the five tests to successfully pass the GED® and earn a high school equivalency certificate.

Test	Test Area	Time	Questions	Description
Test 1	Part 1: Language Arts, Writing	75 minutes	50	Sentence Structure 30% Usage 30% Mechanics 25% Organization 15%
	Part 2: Essay	45 minutes		Essay on a given topic
Test 2	Social Studies	70 minutes	50	History 40% (Canadian 25%, World 15%) Civics and Government 25% Economics 20% Geography 15%
Test 3	Science	80 minutes	50	Life Science 45% Physical Science 35% Earth and Space Science 20%
Test 4	Language Arts, Reading	65 minutes	40	Literature 75% Nonfiction 25%
Test 5	Part 1: Mathematics (calculator)	45 minutes	25	Number Operations and Number Sense 20–30% Measurement and Geometry 20–30%
	Part 2: Mathematics (no calculator)	45 minutes	25	Data Analysis 20–30% Algebra 20–30%

GED® TEST CHANGES

The GED® tests are changing. In the United States, a new series of the GED® tests began in January 2014. In Canada, the new tests are expected to be available in 2017. This means that if you are preparing for the GED® tests now or have already written some of the tests, you should set a goal to complete all the tests before the new testing series begins.

One change in the Canadian GED® tests has already begun. In some provinces, the tests can now be written on computers at GED® testing centres. Paper tests are still available, but computerized testing is expected to expand. Most GED® tests will soon be written on computers. When the new tests come out in 2017, all tests will be written on computers.

To find information about availability of computer testing centres in your province or territory, visit *GED.com*. To find information about tests on paper, accommodations, or test dates in your province or territory, contact your GED Administrator or local community college or high school. For general information about the GED® tests, visit *GEDtestingservice.com*.

Initial experience of computer-based testing in Canada has been favourable. Candidates have actually had a slightly higher success rate than on the paper tests. An additional advantage is that you do not have to write all the tests at one time. You can study for and take the tests one at a time with computer-based testing. Computer testing may not yet be available in all provinces and territories.

TO THE STUDENT

People write the GED® tests for many different reasons. As you begin your study, think about your reasons and your goals. Preparing for the GED® is not easy. As you study, remember your reasons and goals and use them as motivation to keep you on track.

Is your reason one of these?

- Personal accomplishment
- To get a job or a better job
- Further education
- Family members

Whatever your reasons, you have already taken the first step by beginning your preparation for the GED® test.

Study Strategies

Here are some strategies that can help you succeed:

1. **HAVE A REGULAR STUDY TIME**—Set aside the days of the week and times of day that you will study, then stick to the schedule. If you have family members who live with you, discuss the times with them so that they will know they can help you by respecting the study times.

2. **HAVE A REGULAR STUDY PLACE**—Choose a specific area where you can study. It should have good light and study supplies and be away from distractions. It should be a comfortable place where you can relax and concentrate.

3. **SET GOALS**—Make timelines for chapters or topics you wish to finish. These can change, but setting goals can help you to stay motivated and track your progress.

4. **SPEND TIME ON DIFFICULT SUBJECTS**—It can be hard to spend time with subjects you find difficult. For example, students who are good at math, but not good at writing, may spend most of their time practicing math. Divide up your study time by spending a set amount of time on subjects that are difficult or you don't like. Then reward yourself by spending some time on the subjects you do like.

5. **DISCUSS YOUR LEARNING**—Talk with family members or friends about topics you are studying. Sometimes, explaining things to other people or hearing other opinions can give different perspectives. Others might not always understand or agree with your perspective, but that's okay, and often greater understanding comes from different opinions.

How to Use this Book

If you are using this book to study at home, there are three primary strategies you can use. Pick the best method to match your learning needs:

1. **BRUSH UP**—If you are almost ready to write and only need to refresh your knowledge, this may be the approach for you. Complete the diagnostic practice test for a topic. Check your results. Review chapters or topics that gave you trouble. Repeat the process for other topics.

2. **SELECTIVE STUDY**—If you feel you are close to being ready to write, but you need some work in specific test areas, this may be the approach for you. Browse the table of contents to find topics you want to review. Read those sections and do the practice exercises. Complete challenge exercises to deepen your knowledge. Do chapter check-ups, progress checks, and practice tests to evaluate your learning.

3. **COVER-TO-COVER**—If you need more practice or just like an organized and orderly approach, you can work through the book from beginning to end. The skills in this book are meant to be incremental. For example, the skills in the social studies and science sections build on skills learned in the reading section. Begin with the diagnostic tests and then work through the chapters and exercises. Finally, complete each practice test to evaluate your progress. Remember that the diagnostic and practice tests are primarily intended as learning and self-evaluation tools. They are not official GED® tests.

TO THE INSTRUCTOR

As instructors ourselves, we have designed this book to support classroom and individual learning. A lot of research went into the design. This included interviews with several GED instructors from different parts of Canada, as well as research into methods of universal design to appeal to multiple learning styles. When asked what features would result in a better learning tool for their students, instructors identified the following: correct answers, visual appeal, ample practice, Canadian literature, and expanded social studies. We have tried to give you all of these while keeping the book a manageable size. In addition, you will find graphics, side notes, challenge exercises, and other features designed to present content in different ways and provide learners with alternative means of expression and engagement in a group setting.

Features

Features of this book include the following:

- More practice
- More social studies
- Designed for multiple learning styles
- Diagnostic practice tests (answers reference future chapters to identify topics of study)
- Think About It—stimulus to start each chapter
- In This Chapter—objectives or outcomes for each chapter
- Side notes to reinforce key concepts
- More graphics
- Challenge exercises
- Chapter check-ups
- Progress checks in selected sections
- Section practice tests (a full-length practice test at the end of each section)

Teaching Strategies

As experienced instructors, you already have many strategies to help your students achieve their goals. We offer a few ideas from our own experience.

- **START WITH SUCCESS**—Return to school can be intimidating. Start learners off with exercises that are achievable before moving on to more challenging topics.
- **SELECTIVELY CORRECT**—New writers often have many errors. When evaluating writing, consider being selective about what you correct. Set priorities, such as complete sentences or organization, for your students to accomplish first. Once they get stronger with these basic skills, move on to other issues.
- **BE CREATIVE**—Some of the best programs run on a shoestring budget. Make creative use of resources to minimize expense and develop inventive study activities and approaches to learning.
- **BE PRACTICAL**—Whenever possible, relate topics to prior learning or real-world situations.
- **MULTIPLE EXPRESSION**—In addition to practice exercises, provide other ways to express learning: add challenge exercises and research; create a class magazine; or make a video to illustrate Newton's laws—activities involving reading, communicating, and key concepts.
- **MULTIPLE ENGAGEMENT**—Everyone learns differently. Although the GED® test is a written test, media and interaction with others can help in learning to interpret text.
- **BE ENCOURAGING**—For adults, even more than young people, academic success is closely tied to self-esteem.

Diagnostic Tests

LANGUAGE ARTS, WRITING—DIAGNOSTIC TEST

Directions: The Language Arts, Writing Test contains two parts. **The first part includes 50 multiple-choice questions. Do not spend more than 75 minutes on Part 1.** When you finish the multiple-choice questions, you can immediately begin working on Part 2, the essay, even if your time is not over. You can use any time you have left over plus an additional 45 minutes to work on the essay.

The Language Arts, Writing Test evaluates your knowledge of standard written English. Remember that accepted standards for writing are different from those for speaking. You do not need to memorize rules of grammar or punctuation to do well on the test, but you do need to be a good writer and be able to recognize and correct errors in writing.

The diagnostic test includes written passages in which paragraphs are identified by letters and sentences are numbered. The passages include errors in sentence structure, organization, mechanics, and usage. After reading a passage, answer the multiple-choice questions that follow. Questions will ask you to identify and correct errors in writing. Some questions may refer to sentences that are already correct as written. In every case, the right answer will be one that is correct within the sentence and in the context of the passage as a whole.

Record your responses on the answer sheet that follows. For each question, mark the numbered space that corresponds with your answer choice.

EXAMPLE

Sentence 1: A new physician at the hospital is doctor Charles.

What correction should be made to this sentence?
(1)   Insert a comma after <u>physician</u>
(2)   Change the spelling of <u>new</u> to <u>knew</u>
(3)   Change <u>doctor</u> to <u>Doctor</u>
(4)   Replace <u>is</u> with <u>were</u>
(5)   No correction is necessary

In this example the word "Doctor" should be capitalized as part of the name Doctor Charles. Fill in answer space 3 on the answer sheet.

ANSWER SHEET
Diagnostic Test
Language Arts, Writing Test, Part 1

1. ① ② ③ ④ ⑤
2. ① ② ③ ④ ⑤
3. ① ② ③ ④ ⑤
4. ① ② ③ ④ ⑤
5. ① ② ③ ④ ⑤
6. ① ② ③ ④ ⑤
7. ① ② ③ ④ ⑤
8. ① ② ③ ④ ⑤
9. ① ② ③ ④ ⑤
10. ① ② ③ ④ ⑤
11. ① ② ③ ④ ⑤
12. ① ② ③ ④ ⑤
13. ① ② ③ ④ ⑤
14. ① ② ③ ④ ⑤
15. ① ② ③ ④ ⑤
16. ① ② ③ ④ ⑤
17. ① ② ③ ④ ⑤
18. ① ② ③ ④ ⑤
19. ① ② ③ ④ ⑤
20. ① ② ③ ④ ⑤

21. ① ② ③ ④ ⑤
22. ① ② ③ ④ ⑤
23. ① ② ③ ④ ⑤
24. ① ② ③ ④ ⑤
25. ① ② ③ ④ ⑤
26. ① ② ③ ④ ⑤
27. ① ② ③ ④ ⑤
28. ① ② ③ ④ ⑤
29. ① ② ③ ④ ⑤
30. ① ② ③ ④ ⑤
31. ① ② ③ ④ ⑤
32. ① ② ③ ④ ⑤
33. ① ② ③ ④ ⑤
34. ① ② ③ ④ ⑤
35. ① ② ③ ④ ⑤
36. ① ② ③ ④ ⑤
37. ① ② ③ ④ ⑤
38. ① ② ③ ④ ⑤
39. ① ② ③ ④ ⑤
40. ① ② ③ ④ ⑤

41. ① ② ③ ④ ⑤
42. ① ② ③ ④ ⑤
43. ① ② ③ ④ ⑤
44. ① ② ③ ④ ⑤
45. ① ② ③ ④ ⑤
46. ① ② ③ ④ ⑤
47. ① ② ③ ④ ⑤
48. ① ② ③ ④ ⑤
49. ① ② ③ ④ ⑤
50. ① ② ③ ④ ⑤

ANSWER SHEET
Diagnostic Test
Language Arts, Writing Test, Part 2

Directions: Please record your answer for the GED Language Arts, Writing Test, Part 2 here in the space provided. You may organize your thoughts and make notes on scrap paper. The scrap paper must be turned in with this answer sheet at the end of the test; however, the scrap paper will not be marked. Only the essay written on the official answer sheet will be marked.

_____

_____

_____

_____

_____

_____

_____

_____

_____

_____

_____

Language Arts, Writing, Part 1

Directions: Complete the diagnostic test, and then check the answers and analysis that follow. After you mark your work, review any topics you had trouble with or did not understand.

Questions 1–10 are based on the following passage.

How Can You Protect Your Mental Health?

(A)

(1) As a society, we are very aware of the importance of physical health. (2) There is little recognition of the importance of mental health. (3) Mental health is not just the avoidance of mental illness. (4) It is our overall emotional and mental well-being. (5) Our feelings about ourselves and others, how we cope with stress in life and work, how we make decisions and face problems. (6) Every aspect of our lives reflects our mental health.

(B)

(7) Most techniques for maintaining mental health are simple principle's for healthy and happy living. (8) There are also medical conditions, such as depression, that impact millions of Canadians. (9) These are real medical issues that can be treated, if you feel you may suffer from a mental illness, there is help available. (10) Contact your doctor or local mental health association.

(C)

(11) All of us need to take steps to protect our mental health. (12) One thing you can do is take care of yourself physically. (13) Studies have shown a strong correlation between physical and mental health, so you should exercise, eat good, and get sufficient rest. (14) Maintaining a balance between life and work is also important. (15) Spend time relaxing with family and friends. (16) Find hobbies or recreational activities, that help you unwind.

(D)

(17) Another aspect of mental health was maintaining a positive attitude. (18) It is easy to complain about people and situations at home or work and to find others who will do so as well. (19) A good job is hard to find these days. (20) Try to say positive things and surround yourself with positive people. (21) Attitude is infectious, so there positive attitude will help you stay positive as well.

(E)

(22) Financial problems are one of the biggest causes of stress. (23) Face financial issues directly and make a realistic budget. (24) Avoiding money problems doesn't make them go away or reduce the stress.

1. Sentences 1 and 2: As a society, we are very aware of the importance of physical health. There is little recognition of the importance of mental health.

   The best way to combine the sentences would include which of the following?

   (1) health; however, there
   (2) health. However there
   (3) health and there
   (4) health but there
   (5) health so there

2. Sentences 4 and 5: It is our overall emotional and mental well-being. Our feelings about ourselves and others, how we cope with stress in life and work, how we make decisions and face problems.

   The best way to write the underlined portion is which of the following? (If you think the original is the best way, choose option 1.)

   (1) well-being. Our feelings
   (2) well-being; our feelings
   (3) well-being our feelings
   (4) well-being, our feelings
   (5) well-being: our feelings

3. Sentence 7: Most techniques for maintaining mental health are simple principle's for healthy and happy living.

   Which correction should be made to the sentence?

   (1) Insert a comma after maintaining
   (2) Insert a comma after healthy
   (3) Capitalize Mental Health
   (4) Change are to is
   (5) Change principle's to principles

4. Sentence 9: These are real medical issues that can be treated, if you feel you may suffer from a mental illness, there is help available.

   The best way to write the underlined portion of the sentence is which of the following? (If you think the original is the best way, choose option 1.)

   (1) treated, if you
   (2) treated. If you
   (3) treated; if you
   (4) treated, when you
   (5) treated because you

5. Sentence 13: Studies have shown a strong correlation between physical and mental health, so you should exercise, eat good, and get sufficient rest.

   Which correction should be made to the sentence?

   (1) replace correlation with link
   (2) insert a comma after physical
   (3) change good to well
   (4) remove the comma after good
   (5) Start a new sentence after health

6. Sentence 16: Find hobbies or recreational activities, that help you unwind.

   Which correction should be made to the sentence?

   (1) Remove the comma after activities
   (2) Change hobbies to a hobby
   (3) Change help to helped
   (4) Insert a comma after you
   (5) Change that to that will

7. Sentence 17: Another aspect of mental health was maintaining a positive attitude.

   The best way to write the underlined portion of the sentence is which of the following? (If you think the original is the best way, choose option 1.)

   (1) health was maintaining
   (2) health. Was maintaining
   (3) health, was maintaining
   (4) health is maintaining
   (5) health maintained

8. Sentence 21: Attitude is infectious, so there positive attitude will help you stay positive as well.

   Which correction should be made to the sentence?

   (1) Delete the comma after infectious
   (2) Change infectious, so to infectious. So
   (3) Change there to their
   (4) Insert a comma after positive attitude
   (5) Change as well to also

9. To improve the organization of paragraph D
   (1) Move sentence (21) to the beginning
   (2) Move sentence (17) to the end
   (3) Delete sentence (20)
   (4) Move sentence (18) to the end
   (5) Delete sentence (19)

10. To improve the organization of the passage
    (1) Move paragraph B after paragraph E
    (2) Move paragraph A after paragraph D
    (3) Move paragraph C before paragraph A
    (4) Move paragraph C before paragraph B
    (5) Move paragraph E before paragraph C

Questions 11–20 are based on the following passage.

(A)

(1) One key to success in learning for students of any age, is knowing how to study. (2) For adults especially, having good study habits and making effective use of study time is essential. (3) Adults have families and careers and other responsibilities, so it is often at a premium. (4) It is, therefore, necessary to use the available time to the utmost advantage.

(B)

(5) The first step in developing good study habits is to take ownership of your studies. (6) What does this mean. (7) You must also recognize that the responsibility for success lies with you. (8) You may have books or teachers to provide information and guidance but these are only resources you make use of as you take charge of your learning.

(C)

(9) Establishing a study schedule is one way. (10) There are two approaches to choose from. (11) One is to set a regular time aside for studying. (12) For example, you may study every Monday, Wednesday, and Friday from 8 to 10 p.m. (13) A second approach is to make a daily schedule each week. (14) This is a schedule on which you plan all your activities for the week. (15) Mark in time to take the kids to the dentist, time to work, and other activities as well as study time. (16) This type of scheduling is very flexible if something comes up, you can easily reschedule. (17) Make a new schedule every week, and schedule you're study at the most convenient times.

(D)

(18) Preparing and being organized is how you take charge of your studies and start yourself on the way to success.

11. Sentence 1: One key to success in learning for students of any age, is knowing how to study.

    Which correction should be made to the sentence?

    (1) Insert a comma after key
    (2) Remove the comma after age
    (3) Change is knowing to to know
    (4) Change students to student's
    (5) Insert a period after knowing

12. Sentence 3: Adults have families and careers and other <u>responsibilities, so it</u> is often at a premium.

    The best way to write the underlined portion of the sentence is which of the following? (If you think the original is the best way, choose option 1.)

    (1) responsibilities, so it
    (2) responsibilities. So it
    (3) responsibilities so it
    (4) responsibilities, so time
    (5) responsibilities; so it

13. Sentence 4: It <u>is, therefore, necessary</u> to use the available time to the utmost advantage.

    The best way to write the underlined portion of the sentence is which of the following? (If you think the original is the best way, choose option 1.)

    (1) is, therefore, necessary
    (2) is; therefore, necessary
    (3) is. Therefore, necessary
    (4) is therefore necessary
    (5) is, therefore; necessary

14. Sentence 6: What does this mean.

    Which correction should be made to the sentence?

    (1) Insert a comma after <u>does</u>
    (2) Change <u>does</u> to <u>did</u>
    (3) Use a question mark after <u>mean</u>
    (4) Change <u>this</u> to <u>that</u>
    (5) Change <u>mean</u> to <u>Mean</u>

15. Sentence 8: You may have books or teachers to provide information and guidance but these are only resources you make use of as you take charge of your learning.

    Which correction should be made to the sentence?

    (1) Insert a comma after <u>information</u>
    (2) Insert a comma after <u>guidance</u>
    (3) Insert a comma after <u>resources</u>
    (4) Insert a comma after <u>books</u>
    (5) Insert a comma after <u>make use of</u>

16. Sentence 9: Establishing a study schedule is one way.

    Which is the best way to write the sentence for a smooth transition between paragraphs B and C?

    (1) Establishing a study schedule is one way you take control.
    (2) To establish a study schedule is one way.
    (3) Therefore, you should establish a study schedule.
    (4) However, establishing a study schedule is one way.
    (5) In the event that you establish a study schedule, it will help.

17. Sentence 13: <u>A second approach</u> is to make a daily schedule each week.

Which is the best way to write the underlined portion to improve the cohesion of the paragraph? (If you think the original is the best way, choose option 1.)

(1) A second approach
(2) One approach
(3) There is another approach
(4) One other way
(5) Another

18. Sentence 16: This type of scheduling is <u>very flexible if something</u> comes up, you can easily reschedule.

Which is the best way to write the underlined portion of the sentence? (If you think the original is the best way, choose option 1.)

(1) very flexible if something
(2) very flexible. If something
(3) very flexible, if something
(4) very flexible. Something
(5) very flexible if, something

19. Sentence 17: Make a new schedule every week, and schedule you're study at the most convenient times.

Which correction should be made to the sentence?

(1) Remove the comma after <u>week</u>
(2) Change <u>study</u> to <u>studying</u>
(3) Insert a comma after <u>study</u>
(4) Change <u>you're</u> to <u>your</u>
(5) Change <u>times</u> to <u>time's</u>

20. Sentence 18: <u>Preparing and being organized</u> is how you take charge of your studies and start yourself on the way to success.

Which is the best way to write the underlined portion of the sentence? (If you think the original is the best way, choose option 1.)

(1) Preparing and being organized
(2) To be prepared and being organized
(3) Being prepared and organized
(4) Preparing and to be organized
(5) Being prepared and organization

Questions 21–30 are based on the following memorandum.

To all employees:

(A)

(1) A person`s financial well-being depends on the ability to work. (2) Mortgages, bill payments, and children's education. (3) All depend on continued income. (4) Losing the ability to work for a period of time because of accident or illness places your economic health and that of their family in jeopardy. (5) To protect their financial security, the company now offers insurance coverage to employees.

(B)

(6) All employees are now protected by accidental death and dismemberment and short-term disability insurance. (7) Cost of premiums are covered in whole by the employer. (8) The policy provides insurance for accidental death in addition to existing benefits. (9) Accidents which result in loss of limb or other specified injury, such as brain injury or paralysis, are compensated as indicated in the attached table of benefits. (10) The policy also provides income protection for a period of three weeks beyond existing sick leave in the event the employee is unable to work as a result of accident or devastating illness. (11) Employees now have access to long-term disability insurance. (12) This optional coverage is purchased by employees through payroll deduction. (13) Long-term disability insurance gives income protection for them if they become disabled and unable to work. (14) Cost of the plans, underwritten by CG Insurance, varies based on duration and level of benefit. (15) For a detailed informational brochure and application form, contact human resources.

Yours truly,
Director of Human Resources

21. Sentence 1: A person`s financial well-being depends on the ability to work.

    Which correction should be made to the sentence?

    (1) Change person's to persons
    (2) Change person's to persons'
    (3) Replace well-being with well being
    (4) Insert a comma after depends
    (5) No correction necessary

22. Sentences 2 and 3: Mortgages, bill payments, and children's education. All depend on continued income.

    Which is the best way to write the underlined portion of the sentence? (If you think the original is the best way, choose option 1.)

    (1) education. All depend
    (2) education all depend
    (3) education; all depend
    (4) education, all depend
    (5) education? All depend

23. Sentence 4: Losing the ability to work for a period of time because of accident or illness places your economic health and that of their family in jeopardy.

Which correction should be made to the sentence?

(1) Insert a comma after work
(2) Change your to you're
(3) Change places to place's
(4) Change their to your
(5) Insert a period after illness

24. Sentence 5: To protect their financial security, the company now offers insurance coverage to employees.

Which is the best way to write the sentence? (If you think the original is the best way, choose option 1.)

(1) To protect their financial security, the company now offers insurance coverage to employees.
(2) The company now offers insurance to protect employee financial security.
(3) The company now offers insurance coverage, to protect their financial security, to employees.
(4) To protect financial security, the company now offers employee insurance.
(5) For protection of financial security, the company now offers insurance to employees.

25. Sentence 7: Cost of premiums are covered in whole by the employer.

Which is the best way to write the sentence? (If you think the original is the best way, choose option 1.)

(1) Cost of premiums are covered in whole by the employer.
(2) The cost of the premiums are covered in whole by the employer.
(3) Cost of premiums is covered in whole by the employer.
(4) By the employer, cost of premiums are covered in whole.
(5) Premiums cost are covered in whole by the employer.

26. Sentence 9: Accidents which result in loss of limb or other specified injury, such as brain injury or paralysis, are compensated as indicated in the attached table of benefits.

Which correction should be made to the sentence?

(1) Change which to that
(2) Change injury to injuries
(3) Change paralysis to being paralyzed
(4) Change are to is
(5) Change indicated to indicates

27. Sentence 10: The policy also provides income protection for a period of <u>three weeks beyond</u> existing sick leave in the event the employee is unable to work as a result of accident or devastating illness.

Which is the best way to write the underlined portion of the sentence? (If you think the original is the best way, choose option 1.)

(1) three weeks beyond
(2) three weeks; beyond
(3) three weeks. Beyond
(4) three weeks: beyond
(5) three weeks? Beyond

28. Sentence 13: Long-term disability insurance gives income protection for them if they become disabled and unable to work.

Which correction should be made to the sentence?

(1) Change <u>they</u> to <u>you</u>
(2) Insert a comma after <u>disability</u>
(3) Change <u>for them</u> to <u>to them</u>
(4) Insert a comma after <u>disabled</u>
(5) Change <u>them</u> to <u>employees</u>

29. Sentence 14: Cost of the plans, underwritten by CG Insurance, varies based on duration and level of benefit.

Which correction should be made to the sentence?

(1) Insert a period after <u>plans</u>
(2) Delete the comma after <u>plans</u>
(3) Delete the comma after <u>insurance</u>
(4) Change <u>CG</u> to <u>C.G.</u>
(5) Change <u>Cost</u> to <u>Costs</u>

30. The organization of the passage could be improved by beginning a new paragraph with
(1) Sentence 4
(2) Sentence 8
(3) Sentence 10
(4) Sentence 11
(5) Sentence 14

Questions 31–40 are based on the following information.

(A)

(1) Acupuncture is a form of medical treatment that had been practiced in China for thousands of years. (2) It involves the insertion of extremely fine needles into the skin at various points on the body. (3) Acupuncture points are located at specific points that are thought to follow the natural flow of energy through the body. (4) To cure a variety of ailments, stimulation of the points is believed to correct imbalances in the energy. (5) Another theory is that acupuncture has worked by stimulating nerve centres. (6) This activates the central nervous system to release hormones, improve circulation, and increase body temperature.

(B)

(7) Acupuncture is safe when performed with clean needles by a qualified professional. (8) It is generally considered a complementary treatment in conjunction with contemporary medicine. (9) It has been recognized by the World Health organization. (10) Advocates of acupuncture claim that it can be used for a wide variety of purposes, including treatment of pain, nausea, headache, arthritis, carpal tunnel syndrome, irregular menstrual cycles, lower back pain, stroke, and sciatica. (11) Acupuncture recipients, also report an overall feeling of wellness after treatment.

(C)

(12) The miracle of modern medicine has revolutionized society. (13) We are healthy and live longer than ever before. (14) New medicine and technology offers cures for conditions unimagined a decade ago. (15) Advances in medicine have changed our lives but other forms of medicine are very old. (16) Acupuncture is one form of ancient treatment that is gaining increased exceptance in a modern world.

(D)

(17) Critics of acupuncture claim that the practice has no real benefit. (18) They point to studies that show acupuncture produces no greater results with needles placed in real acupuncture points than placebo points. (19) In spite of the fact that it receives mixed reviews, acupuncture is widely accepted and treatments are covered by many employee health plans.

31. Sentence 1: Acupuncture is a form of medical treatment that had been practiced in China for thousands of years.

    Which correction should be made to the sentence?

    (1) Change is to was
    (2) Change had been to has been
    (3) Insert a comma after practiced
    (4) Change that to which
    (5) Change China to china

32. Sentence 4: To cure a variety of ailments, stimulation of the points is believed to correct imbalances in the energy.

The best way to write the sentence would include which of the following?

(1) points to cure a variety of ailments
(2) to cure imbalances in the energy
(3) imbalances in the energy to cure
(4) stimulation of imbalances in the energy
(5) stimulation of the points to cure

33. Sentence 5: Another theory is that acupuncture has worked by stimulating nerve centres.

Which is the best way to write the sentence? (If you think the original is the best way, choose option 1.)

(1) Another theory is that acupuncture has worked by stimulating nerve centres.
(2) Another theory is that acupuncture worked by stimulating nerve centres.
(3) By stimulating nerve centres is another theory about how acupuncture works.
(4) Acupuncture has worked by stimulating nerve centres.
(5) Another theory is that acupuncture works by stimulating nerve centres.

34. Sentence 11: Acupuncture recipients, also report an overall feeling of wellness after treatment.

Which correction should be made to the sentence?

(1) Delete the comma after recipients
(2) Change recipients to recipient's
(3) Insert a comma after feeling
(4) Insert a comma after wellness
(5) Change report to have reported

35. Sentence 14: New medicine and technology offer cures for conditions unimagined a decade ago.

Which is the best way to write the sentence? (If you think the original is the best way, choose option 1.)

(1) New medicine and technology offers cures for conditions unimagined a decade ago.
(2) Unimagined a decade ago, new medicine and technology offer cures for conditions.
(3) New medicine and technology offer cures unimagined a decade ago.
(4) Conditions unimagined a decade ago can be cured by new medicine and technology.
(5) Cures, unimagined a decade ago, are offered by new medicines and technologies.

36. Sentence 15: Advances in medicine have changed <u>our lives but other</u> forms of medicine are very old.

Which is the best way to write the underlined portion of the sentence? (If you think the original is the best way, choose option 1.)

(1) our lives but other
(2) our lives, and other
(3) our lives. And other
(4) our lives; but other
(5) our lives, but other

37. Sentence 16: Acupuncture is one form of ancient treatment that is gaining increased exceptance in a modern world.

Which correction should be made to the sentence?

(1) Change <u>treatment</u> to <u>treatments</u>
(2) Change <u>exceptance</u> to <u>acceptance</u>
(3) Change <u>increased</u> to <u>increasing</u>
(4) Change <u>modern</u> to <u>contemporary</u>
(5) Change <u>that</u> to <u>which</u>

38. Sentences 17 and 18: Critics of acupuncture claim that the practice has no real benefit. They point to studies that show acupuncture produces no greater results with needles placed in real acupuncture points than placebo points.

The best combination of the sentences includes which of the following?

(1) benefit. Although they
(2) benefit although they
(3) benefit until they
(4) benefit, and they
(5) benefit, they

39. Sentence 19: In spite of the fact that it receives mixed reviews, acupuncture is widely accepted and treatments are covered by many employee health plans.

Which correction should be made to the sentence?

(1) insert a comma after <u>fact that</u>
(2) change <u>In spite of the fact that</u> to <u>Although</u>
(3) delete <u>widely</u>
(4) change <u>treatment</u> to <u>treatments</u>
(5) change <u>are covered</u> to <u>is covered</u>

40. To improve the organization of the passage
(1) Move paragraph C before paragraph A
(2) Move paragraph D before paragraph B
(3) Move paragraph A after paragraph D
(4) Move paragraph B before paragraph A
(5) Move paragraph B after paragraph C

Questions 41–50 are based on the following information.

(A)

(1) What makes a good book it would probably be difficult to get people to agree. (2) Everyone has different tastes and a different viewpoint. (3) Some people prefer biographies, some like historical fiction, and some enjoy a crime thriller. (4) Magazines also sell quite well. (5) Given the differences in what people like, is there any way to agree on the qualities that make a book good?

(B)

(6) A critic often looks for qualities of literary merit. (7) Exactly they mean by "literary merit" is hard to say. (8) Critics may comment on a writer's skill, which could include the following: elegance of language, use of imagery, plot structure, and development of character. (9) The view of a critic is based on the work itself and has little to do with sales. (10) One objection to the judgment of critics about whether a book is good is that it is entirely subjective. (11) Ultimately, what makes their opinion any more valuable than that of anyone else's except that they may have read more books?

(C)

(12) A good book is one that lasts, one that endures. (13) It is enjoyed by new generations of readers year after year. (14) By that standard, good books would be those like J.D. Salinger's 1951 *The Catcher in the Rye* or Charles Dickens' 1838 *Oliver Twist*, which are great books as they continue to be read decades or even a century later. (15) But is a great book the same thing as a good book, one that you will enjoy reading today?

(D)

(16) What makes a good book may vary for different people, but here are some qualities to look for. (17) A good book should be a genre you enjoy, whether western adventure, romance, or non-fiction. (18) The style of writing should of kept your interest. (19) If the book is a novel, the characters should be ones that you can care about. (20) Most important, for a novel, is the willing suspension of disbelief. (21) Novels should enable readers and critics to temporarily withhold your rejection of improbable events to be immersed in the story.

41. Sentence 1: What makes a good book it would probably be difficult to get people to agree.

    Which correction should be made to the sentence?

    (1) Insert a comma after <u>makes</u>
    (2) Insert a question mark after <u>book</u>
    (3) Insert a comma after <u>probably</u>
    (4) Insert a period after <u>difficult</u>
    (5) Insert a question mark after <u>agree</u>

42. The organization of paragraph A could be improved by deleting
    (1) Sentence 1
    (2) Sentence 2
    (3) Sentence 3
    (4) Sentence 4
    (5) Sentence 5

43. Sentence 6: A critic often looks for qualities of literary merit.

    Which is the best way to write the sentence? (If you think the original is the best way, choose option 1.)

    (1) A critic often looks for qualities of literary merit.
    (2) A critic often look for qualities of literary merit.
    (3) A critic, looks for qualities, of literary merit.
    (4) Critics often looks for qualities of literary merit.
    (5) Critics often look for qualities of literary merit

44. Sentence 8: Critics may comment on a writer's skill, which could include <u>the following: elegance</u> of language, use of imagery, plot structure, and development of character.

    Which is the best way to write the underlined portion of the sentence? (If you think the original is the best way, choose option 1.)

    (1) the following: elegance
    (2) the following: Elegance
    (3) the following elegance
    (4) the following, elegance
    (5) the following. Elegance

45. Sentence 10: One objection to the judgment of <u>critics about whether</u> a book is good is that it is entirely subjective.

    Which is the best way to write the underlined portion of the sentence? (If you think the original is the best way, choose option 1.)

    (1) critics about whether
    (2) critics, about whether
    (3) critics. About whether
    (4) critics; about whether
    (5) critics? About whether

46. Sentence 11: Ultimately, what makes their opinion any more valuable than that of any-one else's except that they may have read more books?

    Which correction should be made to the sentence?

    (1) Remove the comma after <u>Ultimately</u>
    (2) Change <u>than</u> to <u>then</u>
    (3) Change <u>else's</u> to <u>else</u>
    (4) Insert a comma after <u>except that</u>
    (5) Change <u>they</u> to <u>he</u>

47. Sentences 12 and 13: A good book is one that lasts, one that endures. It is enjoyed by new generations of readers year after year.

An effective combination of sentences 12 and 13, beginning with "Because," would continue with what words?

(1) a good book
(2) one that lasts
(3) one that endures
(4) new generations of readers
(5) it is enjoyed

48. Sentence 15: But is a great book the same thing as a good book, one that you will enjoy reading today?

Which correction should be made to the sentence?

(1) Change But to However,
(2) Insert a comma after great book
(3) Insert a period after good book
(4) Change that to which
(5) Replace the question mark with a period

49. Sentence 18: The style of writing should of kept your interest.

Which is the best way to write the sentence? (If you think the original is the best way, choose option 1.)

(1) The style of writing should of kept your interest.
(2) The writing style should of kept your interest.
(3) The style of writing should have kept your interest.
(4) The style of writing should keep your interest
(5) Writing should of been in a style to keep your interest.

50. Sentence 21: Novels should enable readers and critics to temporarily withhold your rejection of improbable events to be immersed in the story.

What is the best way to write the underlined part above? (If you think the original is the best way, choose option 1.)

(1) withhold your rejection
(2) withhold rejection
(3) withhold our rejection
(4) withhold rejecting
(5) withhold. Rejection

Language Arts, Writing, Part 2

This part of the Language Arts, Writing Test includes an essay on the prompt and topic below to be completed in 45 minutes. When you finish the multiple-choice questions on Part 1, you can immediately begin working on the essay, which will give you additional time. Do not spend more than 75 minutes on Part 1 and 45 minutes on Part 2.

PROMPT

Every year, thousands of families go to the zoo to see all manner of exotic and domestic animals. However, there is debate about whether zoos are good things or bad. Proponents say that zoos are important to giving young people firsthand knowledge of the diversity of earth's animal population and help them understand the importance of conservation. They also provide an environment in which endangered species can be bred and protected. Opponents say that zoos are cruel because they keep animals that are not naturally domesticated, even those born in captivity, in a virtual prison for their entire lives.

In an essay, identify whether you think zoos are good or bad and what should be done according to your viewpoint. Use personal observations, experience, and knowledge to support your essay.

> **Directions:** Please record your answer for the GED Language Arts, Writing Test Part 2 on the answer sheet provided. You may organize your thoughts and make notes on scrap paper. The scrap paper must be turned in with the answer sheet at the end of the test; however, the scrap paper will not be marked. Only the essay written on the official answer sheet will be marked.

ANSWER KEY
Diagnostic Test

LANGUAGE ARTS, WRITING, PART 1

1. (1)	**11.** (2)	**21.** (5)	**31.** (2)	**41.** (2)
2. (4)	**12.** (4)	**22.** (2)	**32.** (3)	**42.** (4)
3. (5)	**13.** (1)	**23.** (4)	**33.** (5)	**43.** (5)
4. (2)	**14.** (3)	**24.** (2)	**34.** (1)	**44.** (1)
5. (3)	**15.** (2)	**25.** (3)	**35.** (3)	**45.** (1)
6. (1)	**16.** (1)	**26.** (1)	**36.** (5)	**46.** (3)
7. (4)	**17.** (5)	**27.** (1)	**37.** (2)	**47.** (5)
8. (3)	**18.** (2)	**28.** (5)	**38.** (4)	**48.** (1)
9. (5)	**19.** (4)	**29.** (4)	**39.** (2)	**49.** (4)
10. (1)	**20.** (3)	**30.** (4)	**40.** (1)	**50.** (2)

Interpret Your Results

Test Area	Questions	Recommended Minimum Score	Your Score
Sentences	1, 2, 4, 15, 18, 20, 22, 24, 27, 32, 36, 38, 45, 47, 48	11	
Organization	9, 10, 16, 17, 30, 40, 42	5	
Mechanics	3, 6, 11, 13, 14, 19, 21, 29, 34, 37, 41, 44, 46	9	
Usage	5, 7, 8, 12, 23, 25, 26, 28, 31, 33, 35, 39, 43, 49, 50	11	
Total		36	

Check your answers and calculate how you scored in each test area. If you scored less than the recommended minimum score in any test area, you should review topics in the relevant chapters.

ANSWER ANALYSIS

1. **(1)** Make a compound sentence with a conjunctive adverb, using a semi-colon before and a comma after.

2. **(4)** Sentence 5 is a sentence fragment. Use a comma to create a list of things that describe mental health and correct the fragment.

3. **(5)** The word is plural, not possessive.

4. **(2)** Use a period to begin a new sentence and correct the run-on.

5. **(3)** Use the adverb *well* to describe how one should eat.

6. **(1)** A comma is not needed before the relative pronoun *that*.

7. **(4)** To be consistent with the passage, the verb should be in the present tense.

8. **(3)** Be careful of the homophones *there*, *their*, and *they're*.

9. **(5)** The sentence is not related to the topic of the paragraph, which is "maintaining a positive attitude."

10. **(1)** The paragraph is clearly a conclusion, adding information about medical conditions and available help to wrap up the tips about mental health.

11. **(2)** Do not separate the subject and predicate of a sentence.

12. **(4)** It is unclear what the pronoun *it* refers to. Replace it with *time* to clarify the sentence.

13. **(1)** The word *therefore* is an interjection here, not a conjunctive adverb, so it should be set off by commas in the sentence.

14. **(3)** End a question with a question mark.

15. **(2)** Use a comma and coordinating conjunction to make a compound sentence.

16. **(1)** The reference to *take control* repeats the idea of taking charge from the previous paragraph and makes the transition.

17. **(5)** The passage says there are two approaches. There is one and another.

18. **(2)** Start a new sentence to correct the run-on.

19. **(4)** Use the possessive *your* rather than the homophone *you're*, the conjunction for *you are*.

20. **(3)** Parallel construction requires that both items listed have the same structure.

21. **(5)** The sentence is correct as written. There are no punctuation errors.

22. **(2)** Sentence 2 is a fragment that should be combined with the following sentence to be complete. No punctuation is needed.

23. **(4)** Pronouns must be consistent. *Your economic health* should be followed by *your family*.

24. **(2)** Correct the misplaced modifier. The initial sentence sounds like the company is protecting their own financial security.

25. **(3)** The singular subject *cost* requires a singular verb.

26. **(1)** The kind of accidents that are compensated are only those that result in loss of limb or other specified injury, so the clause requires the restrictive pronoun *that*.

27. **(1)** Although it is a long sentence, this is one sentence. No punctuation or division is required.

28. **(5)** It is unclear who *them* refers to, so it should be replaced with *employees* for clarity.

29. **(4)** Use periods after initials and abbreviations.

30. **(4)** Sentence 11 begins the new topic of long-term disability insurance.

31. **(2)** Correct the verb shift so that the tenses fit together.

32. **(3)** Move the dangling modifier to the end: correct imbalances in the energy to cure a variety of ailments.

33. **(5)** Ensure that the tense of verbs is consistent with the rest of the passage.

34. **(1)** Do not separate the subject and verb.

35. **(3)** Correct the misplaced modifier, which says that conditions—not cures—were unimagined a decade ago.

36. **(5)** Use a comma and conjunction to make a compound sentence.

37. **(2)** Use accept, not except.

38. **(4)** Use a comma and conjunction to form a compound sentence. While some other options could be grammatically correct, they do not have the correct meaning.

39. **(2)** Eliminate the overly wordy phrase *In spite of the fact that*.

40. **(1)** Paragraph C is clearly the introduction. It introduces the topic of acupuncture and ends with the thesis statement of the passage, that acupuncture is an ancient technique that is gaining modern acceptance.

41. **(2)** Correct the run-on sentence by adding a question mark to end the interrogative sentence.

42. **(4)** The sentence is not related to books, the topic of the passage.

43. **(5)** To be consistent with the rest of the paragraph, use the plural form *critics*.

44. **(1)** Use a colon to precede a list.

45. **(1)** The sentence is complete and correct as written.

46. **(3)** There is no reason for *else* to be possessive.

47. **(5)** The reason that the book lasts is that it is enjoyed by new generations of readers.

48. **(1)** A sentence cannot begin with a conjunction. It can begin with a conjunctive adverb, preceded by a semi-colon or period and followed by a comma.

49. **(4)** *Should of* is incorrect. It should be *should have*. In this sentence, changing to the present tense with *should keep your interest* is better, so *have* is not needed.

50. **(2)** Readers and critics are plural. The pronoun would be *their*, but in this sentence the pronoun is not needed.

LANGUAGE ARTS, WRITING TEST, PART 2—ANSWERS AND ANALYSIS

If self-evaluating your essay, put the essay aside for at least one day before reviewing it. Use the Essay Self-Scoring Guide below to assess your writing.

ESSAY SELF-SCORING GUIDE

Read your essay, and then answer each question about the essay with "Yes," "Fair," or "No."

	Yes	Fair	No
1. Is the essay all about the topic that was given and only about the topic that was given?			
2. Is the essay appropriate length (200–300 words)?			
3. Does the essay have an introduction, body, and conclusion?			
4. Does the introduction contain a clear thesis statement of your position on the topic?			
5. Is the essay divided into paragraphs of about 3–6 sentences, each paragraph being about only one main point in the essay?			
6. Does the essay give details and examples from your personal experience that support your points?			
7. Is the essay written in complete sentences with no sentence fragments or run-ons?			
8. Does the essay use correct spelling and capitalization?			
9. Does the essay use punctuation correctly, including apostrophes, commas, question marks, periods, semi-colons, exclamation marks, and quotation marks?			
10. Does the essay use an effective word choice to communicate your meaning clearly?			
11. Is the essay easy to read, flowing smoothly from sentence to sentence and paragraph to paragraph?			
12. Is your essay convincing; would it persuade a reader that your position on the topic is reasonable?			

Scoring: Give yourself 2 points for every "Yes," 1 point for every "Fair," and 0 for every "No" to get a total mark out of 24. Divide the total by 6 to find your GED essay score out of 4.

Total = ___ /24 ÷ 6 = ___ /4

INTERPRETING RESULTS

Less than 2	Complete chapters and exercises about writing skills in this book, including the challenge exercises, which will help you build your writing skills.
2–3	Complete chapters and exercises about writing skills in this book. Focus on the areas to which you responded "Fair" or "No." Complete challenge exercises to continue building your writing skills.
3–4	Continue to write practice essays as you prepare for the GED®. Focus on areas to which you responded "Fair" or "No."

LANGUAGE ARTS, READING—DIAGNOSTIC TEST

Directions: The Language Arts, Reading Test includes **40 multiple-choice questions. Do not spend more than 65 minutes on the test.**

The practice test includes multiple-choice questions based on reading passages that are excerpts from fiction, non-fiction, poems, and plays. Literature passages are drawn from significant works of world literature from pre-1920, 1920–1960, and post-1960. Non-fiction passages include articles about literature and the arts and at least one business document. Each reading section is preceded by a purpose question to help you focus your reading.

The Language Arts, Reading Test does not require specific knowledge of authors or literature. The questions test your ability to read and interpret information, including skills in comprehension, application, analysis, and synthesis.

Record your responses on the answer sheet that follows. For each question, mark the numbered space that corresponds with your answer choice.

EXAMPLE

Should We Be More Like a Stone?
How happy is the little Stone
That rambles in the Road alone,
And doesn't care about Careers
And Exigencies never fears.

by Emily Dickinson

Based on this excerpt from a poem, why is the stone happy?
(1)   It is on the road
(2)   It has places to go
(3)   It has no worries
(4)   It has no direction
(5)   It is small

In this example, you need to apply reading comprehension skills to recognize that the stone has no worries about careers or exigencies. Fill in answer space 3 on the answer sheet.

ANSWER SHEET
Diagnostic Test
Reading

1. ① ② ③ ④ ⑤
2. ① ② ③ ④ ⑤
3. ① ② ③ ④ ⑤
4. ① ② ③ ④ ⑤
5. ① ② ③ ④ ⑤
6. ① ② ③ ④ ⑤
7. ① ② ③ ④ ⑤
8. ① ② ③ ④ ⑤
9. ① ② ③ ④ ⑤
10. ① ② ③ ④ ⑤
11. ① ② ③ ④ ⑤
12. ① ② ③ ④ ⑤
13. ① ② ③ ④ ⑤
14. ① ② ③ ④ ⑤
15. ① ② ③ ④ ⑤

16. ① ② ③ ④ ⑤
17. ① ② ③ ④ ⑤
18. ① ② ③ ④ ⑤
19. ① ② ③ ④ ⑤
20. ① ② ③ ④ ⑤
21. ① ② ③ ④ ⑤
22. ① ② ③ ④ ⑤
23. ① ② ③ ④ ⑤
24. ① ② ③ ④ ⑤
25. ① ② ③ ④ ⑤
26. ① ② ③ ④ ⑤
27. ① ② ③ ④ ⑤
28. ① ② ③ ④ ⑤
29. ① ② ③ ④ ⑤
30. ① ② ③ ④ ⑤

31. ① ② ③ ④ ⑤
32. ① ② ③ ④ ⑤
33. ① ② ③ ④ ⑤
34. ① ② ③ ④ ⑤
35. ① ② ③ ④ ⑤
36. ① ② ③ ④ ⑤
37. ① ② ③ ④ ⑤
38. ① ② ③ ④ ⑤
39. ① ② ③ ④ ⑤
40. ① ② ③ ④ ⑤

Language Arts, Reading

> **Directions:** Complete the diagnostic test, and then check the answers and analysis that follow. Identify any topics you had trouble with or did not understand. Focus on these chapters or topics in the study section to continue preparing for the GED Language Arts, Reading Test.

Questions 1–5 are based on the following passage.

Can Little Things Make a Difference?

For Hush Puppies—the classic American brushed-suede shoes with the lightweight crepe sole—the tipping point came somewhere between late 1994 and early 1995. The brand had been all but dead until that point. Sales were down to 30,000 pairs a year, mostly to back-woods outlets and small-town family stores. Wolverine, the company that makes Hush Puppies, was thinking of phasing out the shoes that made them famous. But then something strange happened. At a fashion shoot, two Hush Puppies executives—Owen Baxter and Geoffrey Lewis—ran into a stylist from New York who told them that the classic Hush Puppies had suddenly become hip in the clubs and bars of downtown Manhattan. "We were being told," Baxter recalls, "that there were resale shops in the Village, in Soho, where the shoes were being sold. People were going to the Ma and Pa stores, the little stores that still carried them, and buying them up...."

By the fall of 1995, things began to happen in a rush. First the designer John Bartlett called. He wanted to use Hush Puppies in his spring collection. Then another Manhattan designer, Anna Sui, called, wanting shoes for her show as well. In Los Angeles, the designer Joel Fitzgerald put a twenty-five foot inflatable basset hound—the symbol of the Hush Puppies brand—on the roof of his Hollywood store and gutted an adjoining art gallery to turn it into a Hush Puppies boutique. While he was still painting and putting up shelves, the actor Pee-wee Herman walked in and asked for a couple of pairs. "It was total word of mouth," Fitzgerald remembers.

In 1995, the company sold 430,000 pairs of the classic Hush Puppies and the next year it sold four times that, and the year after that still more, until Hush Puppies were once again a staple of the wardrobe of the young American male....

How did that happen? Those first few kids, whoever they were, weren't deliberately trying to promote Hush Puppies. They were wearing them precisely because no one else would wear them. Then the fad spread to two fashion designers who used the shoes to peddle something else—haute couture. The shoes were an incidental touch. No one was trying to make Hush Puppies a trend. Yet, somehow, that's exactly what happened.

—From Gladwell, Malcom. *The Tipping Point.*
Boston: Little, Brown and Company, 2000. p. 3–5.

1. Which of the following is the most likely reason young people started buying Hush Puppies before 1995?
   (1) popularity
   (2) out of fashion
   (3) promote the brand
   (4) comfort
   (5) price

2. The writer reasons that the re-emergence of Hush Puppies was a result of
   (1) many small occurrences
   (2) fashion shows
   (3) marketing campaigns
   (4) actor endorsement
   (5) clubs and bars

3. Which actor purchased Hush Puppies shoes?
   (1) Owen Baxter
   (2) Geoffrey Lewis
   (3) John Bartlett
   (4) Anna Sui
   (5) Pee-wee Herman

4. The theory expressed in Gladwell's book is that change in business and other fields is similar to a disease epidemic. Which statement best summarizes the theory?
   (1) ideas can be contagious
   (2) planning has no benefit
   (3) marketing has positive and negative qualities
   (4) young people determine what is popular
   (5) change happens slowly

5. Based on information in the passage, a *tipping point* is a
   (1) beneficial social change
   (2) business strategy for increasing sales of goods
   (3) method of popularizing fashion
   (4) critical threshold where change becomes unstoppable
   (5) point at which products are discontinued

Questions 6–11 refer to the following poem.

What Do the Roads Represent?
Two roads diverged in a yellow wood,
And sorry I could not travel both
And be one traveler, long I stood
And looked down one as far as I could
To where it bent in the undergrowth;

Then took the other, as just as fair,
And having perhaps the better claim,
Because it was grassy and wanted wear;
Though as for that the passing there
Had worn them really about the same.

And both that morning equally lay
In leaves no step had trodden black.
Oh, I kept the first for another day!
Yet knowing how way leads on to way,
I doubted if I should ever come back.

I shall be telling this with a sigh
Somewhere ages and ages hence;
Two roads diverged in a wood, and I –
Took the one less traveled by,
And that has made all the difference.

—Robert Frost. *The Road Not Taken.* 1915

6. The poem is a metaphor in which the two roads represent
    (1) scenic and well-travelled highways
    (2) environmentally friendly and unfriendly actions
    (3) the gap between youth and age
    (4) possible careers
    (5) choices in life

7. People influenced by the message in this poem are likely to make decisions based on
    (1) what is popular
    (2) what is unpopular
    (3) their own minds
    (4) financial gain
    (5) natural beauty

8. The word *diverged* in this poem probably means
    (1) separated
    (2) passed through
    (3) unused
    (4) disappeared
    (5) endured

9. Which line from the poem describes one road as less travelled?
    (1) And both that morning equally lay
    (2) To where it bent in the undergrowth;
    (3) Had worn them really about the same.
    (4) Because it was grassy and wanted wear;
    (5) And be one traveler, long I stood

10. The attitude of the speaker at the end of the poem could be described as
    (1) regret
    (2) satisfaction
    (3) enthusiasm
    (4) anger
    (5) sadness

11. The organization of this poem is based on a description of
    (1) a series of events in the past
    (2) a single incident in the past
    (3) an unresolved situation in the past
    (4) a difficult decision for the future
    (5) an event that is happening now

Questions 12–17 refer to the following extract.

What Brings Happiness and Luck?

The New Year approached and in every house in the village there were preparations. Wang Lung went into the town to the candle maker's shop and he bought squares of red paper on which were brushed in gilt ink the letter for happiness and some with the letter for riches, and these squares he pasted upon his farm utensils to bring him luck in the New Year. Upon his plow and upon the ox's yoke and upon the two buckets in which he carried his fertilizer and his water, upon each of these he pasted a square. And then upon the doors of his house he pasted long strips of red paper brushed with mottoes of good luck, and over his doorway he pasted a fringe of red paper cunningly cut into a flower pattern and very finely cut. And he bought red paper to make new dresses for the gods, and this the old man did cleverly enough for his old shaking hands, and Wang Lung took them and put them upon the two small gods in the temple to the earth and he burned a little incense before them for the sake of the New Year. And for his house he bought also two red candles to burn on the eve of the year upon the table under the picture of a god, which was pasted on the wall of the middle room above where the table stood.

And Wang Lung went again into the town and he bought pork fat and white sugar and the woman rendered the fat smooth and white and she took rice flour, which they had ground from their own rice between their millstones to which they could yoke the ox when they needed to do so, and she took the fat and the sugar and she mixed and kneaded rich New Year's cakes, called moon cakes, such as were eaten in the House of Hwang.

When the cakes were laid out upon the table in strips, ready for heating, Wang Lung felt his heart fit to burst with pride. There was no other woman in the village able to do what his had done, to make cakes such as only the rich ate at the feast. In some of the cakes she had put strips of little red haws and spots of dried green plums, making flowers and patterns.

—Buck, Pearl S. *The Good Earth*. New York: Washington Square Press, 1931.

12. The setting of the extract is a
    (1) village in modern China
    (2) Chinese city a hundred years ago
    (3) rural China a hundred years ago
    (4) farm in pioneer Canada
    (5) farm in modern Canada

13. The celebration that is about to take place is
    (1) the New Year
    (2) Christmas
    (3) a wedding
    (4) Lung's birthday
    (5) the Feast of Riches

14. Based on the information in this passage, if his wife were to get sick, Wang Lung would probably
    (1) hire the best doctors
    (2) move into town
    (3) cook a special meal
    (4) make offerings to gods
    (5) ask neighbours for help

15. The *House of Hwang* probably refers to a
    (1) religious group
    (2) local landmark
    (3) poor neighbour
    (4) town hall
    (5) rich family

16. Based on information in this passage, the character of Wang Lung
    (1) is envious of the rich
    (2) is cold and hard
    (3) works hard all the time
    (4) wants a good life
    (5) is selfless and dedicated to others

17. The style of writing in the excerpt is
    (1) flowing
    (2) ornate
    (3) choppy
    (4) comic
    (5) harsh

Questions 18–22 refer to the following extract.

What Woke Him Up?

The door buzzer rang downstairs. Pushing the blankets off his head, Jack squinted at the alarm clock. 7:55. The real estate agent wasn't due till nine. Must be someone at the wrong house. He closed his eyes and tried not to think about the size of the rat droppings he'd found in the cellar the day before. At least as big as the leavings in Mrs. Brady's litter box. Maybe bigger.

It buzzed again, this time in quick, staccato beats.

"All right," he called, jumping up and pushing his legs into rumpled pants from the floor.

The buzzing beat changed now, to three long, three short, three long. Like SOS. Swearing silently, Jack hopped in place, trying to push a foot through the stubborn right leg hole, and crashed against his dresser. "I'm coming!"

He tore down the last staircase and across the black-and-white floor to the door, angry words already forming on his tongue. He yanked the door open.

There, on the stoop, was a tiny woman in a huge red blazer.

Barely acknowledging Jack, she marched inside. "I know just what you're going to say – I'm way on the worm's side of early! It's just that I was so excited to meet you and see the house for myself, I just couldn't sit home one more second waiting until the clock crept closer to nine." Deep inside the foyer now, she turned to face him and sucked in a breath. "Oh!" Coloring, laughing, she pushed a strand of bent hair behind her ear only to have it fall back again. "Dave didn't mention…"

Jack waited, "Yes?"

"Nothing. Look how rude I am." She held out her hand, which barely poked out of the long sleeve of her red jacket. "Doreen Allsop. But everyone calls me Dorrie."

Allsop? Jack knew that name. She was the one with the terrible real estate flyer. What was it? *Whatever you're selling, I'll show you my dwelling?*

"Jack Madigan," he said, shaking her narrow hand. She couldn't be much more than thirty, with flyaway blond hair half in, half out of a muddled ponytail, a Heritage Estates blazer with inventory tag still attached to the sleeve, and a smear of lipstick across one of her teeth. He wanted his hand back.

Eventually, she released it.

—From Cohen, Tish. *Town House*. Toronto: Harper Collins, 2007. p. 50–51.

18. The mood of the excerpt could be described as
    (1) unemotional
    (2) dark
    (3) chaotic
    (4) passionate
    (5) happy

19. Mrs. Brady is a
    (1) real estate agent
    (2) wife
    (3) landlady
    (4) cat
    (5) visitor

20. Based on the information in the passage, we can conclude that Dorrie is
    (1) in love with Jack
    (2) angry with Jack
    (3) highly organized
    (4) late for an appointment
    (5) a poor real estate agent

21. What is the effect of the following simile? "The buzzing beat changed now, to three long, three short, three long. Like SOS."
    (1) urgency
    (2) resolve
    (3) patience
    (4) tolerance
    (5) strength

22. Jack and Dorrie could both be described as
    (1) intelligent
    (2) disarrayed
    (3) desperate
    (4) friendly
    (5) neat

Questions 23–27 refer to the following information.

How Do You Write for Business?

When writing for a business environment, as with all other types of writing, it is necessary that you always consider your purpose and audience, your reason for writing and to whom. The tone you adopt when writing may depend in part on how well you know the recipient and on that individual's position. In addition, business people do not have the time or the inclination to read unnecessarily long communications, so your purpose must be clear. Come straight to the point; be direct. Avoid meaningless introductions like "The purpose of this letter is..." or "I am writing to inform you...."

To overcome the difficulty many people have in being direct, Ron S. Blicq in his text *Technically-Write!* recommends the "I want to tell you that..." method. He suggests that writers begin rough drafts of communications with the words "I want to tell you that" and then complete the sentence with the issue of the letter. Once the initial clause is removed, the letter or memo begins with a clear and direct statement.

Remember, however, that there is a difference between being clear and direct and being blunt and offensive. Business writing requires a degree of tact and diplomacy, particularly when you are sending bad news (rejecting an application for employment, for example). When writing bad news, you must be clear and direct, but you must also consider the reader's feelings.

To begin, avoid openings like "We regret to inform you..." This is immediately negative. The "negative news" letter begins with a buffer, then states the news in a positive way, and ends with a good will wish. In addition, negative news letters are often written in the passive voice giving a softer tone.

23. Based on information in the passage, writing for company executives and for staff would have different
    (1) information
    (2) length
    (3) tone
    (4) initial clause
    (5) buffers

24. The purpose of this passage is to
    (1) entertain
    (2) persuade
    (3) inform
    (4) motivate
    (5) instruct

25. A long and detailed report would be improved by a(n)
    (1) appendix
    (2) executive summary
    (3) detailed chart or graph
    (4) supplement
    (5) financial outlook

26. Based on the suggestions in this passage, the best sentence to begin a letter rejecting an offer of employment is which of the following?
    (1) I cannot accept the position that you have offered.
    (2) I want to tell you that I cannot accept your offer.
    (3) The offer of employment has not been accepted.
    (4) I regret to inform you.
    (5) Thank you for your offer of employment.

27. Many people have difficulty
    (1) writing introductions
    (2) being direct
    (3) speaking in public
    (4) writing in passive voice
    (5) giving advice

Questions 28–32 refer to the following extract from a play.

Who Is Hedda Gabler?

MISS TESMAN: [Takes both his hands and looks at him.] What a delight it is to have you again, as large as life, before my very eyes, George! My George—my poor brother's own boy!

TESMAN: And it's a delight for me, too, to see you again, Aunt Julia! You, who have been father and mother in one to me.

MISS TESMAN: Oh yes, I know you will always keep a place in your heart for your old aunts.

TESMAN: And what about Aunt Rina? No improvement—eh?

MISS TESMAN: Oh, no—we can scarcely look for any improvement in her case, poor thing. There she lies, helpless, as she has lain for all these years. But heaven grant I may not lose her yet awhile! For if I did, I don't know what I should make of my life, George—especially now that I haven't you to look after any more.

TESMAN: [Patting her back.] There there there—!

MISS TESMAN: [Suddenly changing her tone.] And to think that here are you a married man, George!—And that you should be the one to carry off Hedda Gabler—the beautiful Hedda Gabler! Only think of it—she, that was so beset with admirers!

TESMAN: [Hums a little and smiles complacently.] Yes, I fancy I have several good friends about town who would like to stand in my shoes—eh?

MISS TESMAN: And then this fine long wedding-tour you have had! More than five—nearly six months—

TESMAN: Well, for me it has been a sort of tour of research as well. I have had to do so much grubbing among old records—and to read no end of books too, Auntie.

MISS TESMAN: Oh yes, I suppose so. [More confidentially, and lowering her voice a little.] But listen now, George,—have you nothing—nothing special to tell me?

TESMAN: As to our journey?

MISS TESMAN: Yes.

TESMAN: No, I don't know of anything except what I have told you in my letters. I had a doctor's degree conferred on me—but that I told you yesterday.

MISS TESMAN: Yes, yes, you did. But what I mean is—haven't you any—any—expectations?

TESMAN: Expectations?

MISS TESMAN: Why you know, George—I'm your old auntie!

TESMAN: Why, of course I have expectations.

MISS TESMAN: Ah!

TESMAN: I have every expectation of being a professor one of these days.

MISS TESMAN: Oh yes, a professor—

—From *Hedda Gabler* by Henrik Ibsen

28. Based on the information in this excerpt, Tesman was
 (1) raised by his aunt
 (2) depressed by Rina's illness
 (3) recovering from illness
 (4) jealous of his wife
 (5) a medical doctor

29. Tesman's wife was
    (1) unfaithful
    (2) dejected
    (3) a student
    (4) a recluse
    (5) popular

30. When his aunt asks about Tesman's expectations, she probably thinks he has
    (1) received a degree
    (2) not listened to her
    (3) come into money
    (4) plans for another tour
    (5) knowledge of Rina's illness

31. Tesman's character could be described as
    (1) self-important
    (2) naïve
    (3) detached
    (4) calculating
    (5) intelligent

32. Hedda Gabler was the daughter of General Gabler and grew up in wealth and luxury.
    Based on the passage, her feeling toward her current situation might be
    (1) dissatisfied
    (2) enthusiastic
    (3) nostalgic
    (4) detached
    (5) romantic

Questions 33–36 refer to the following extract.

Who Did He Meet?

The second planet was inhabited by a conceited man.

"Ah! Ah! I am about to receive a visit from an admirer!" he exclaimed from afar, when he first saw the little prince coming.

For, to conceited men, all other men are admirers.

"Good morning," said the little prince. "That is a queer hat you are wearing."

"It is a hat for salutes," the conceited man replied. "It is to raise in salute when people acclaim me. Unfortunately, nobody at all ever passes this way."

"Yes?" said the little prince, who did not understand what the conceited man was talking about.

"Clap your hands, one against the other," the conceited man now directed him.

The little prince clapped his hands. The conceited man raised his hat in a modest salute.

"This is more entertaining than the visit to the king," the little prince said to himself. And he began again to clap his hands, one against the other. The conceited man again raised his hat in salute.

After five minutes of this exercise the little prince grew tired of the game's monotony. "And what should one do to make the hat come down?" he asked.

—From *The Little Prince* by Antoine de Saint Exupéry

33. Why did the man raise his hat?
    (1) he was embarrassed
    (2) to wave
    (3) he was surprised
    (4) the little prince applauded
    (5) in admiration of the prince

34. The tone of the passage could be described as
    (1) light
    (2) dark
    (3) gloomy
    (4) critical
    (5) accusing

35. In comparison with the conceited man, the Little Prince could be described as
    (1) morose
    (2) understanding
    (3) proud
    (4) foolish
    (5) innocent

36. Based on the passage, we can conclude that the Little Prince is a
    (1) statesman
    (2) child
    (3) politician
    (4) soldier
    (5) grown-up

Questions 37–40 refer to the following newspaper article.

Why Beware of Dogs?

THERE is sorrow enough in the natural way
From men and women to fill our day;
And when we are certain of sorrow in store,
Why do we always arrange for more?
Brothers and sisters, I bid you beware
Of giving your heart to a dog to tear.

Buy a pup and your money will buy
Love unflinching that cannot lie
Perfect passion and worship fed
By a kick in the ribs or a pat on the head.
Nevertheless it is hardly fair
To risk your heart for a dog to tear.

When the fourteen years which Nature permits
Are closing in asthma, or tumour, or fits,
And the vet's unspoken prescription runs
To lethal chambers or loaded guns,
Then you will find—it's your own affair,—
But ... you've given your heart to a dog to tear.

When the body that lived at your single will,
With its whimper of welcome, is stilled (how still!),
When the spirit that answered your every mood
Is gone—wherever it goes—for good,
You will discover how much you care,
And will give your heart to a dog to tear!

We've sorrow enough in the natural way,
When it comes to burying Christian clay.
Our loves are not given, but only lent,
At compound interest of cent per cent,
Though it is not always the case, I believe,
That the longer we've kept 'em, the more do we grieve;
For, when debts are payable, right or wrong,
A short-time loan is as bad as a long—
So why in—Heaven (before we are there)
Should we give our hearts to a dog to tear?

—*The Power of the Dog* by Rudyard Kipling published in 1909
in his book of short stories and poems *Actions and Reactions.*

37. The attitude of the poem toward dogs is
    (1) loving
    (2) grave
    (3) ambivalent
    (4) threatening
    (5) warning

38. The best summary of the poem is
    (1) dogs are often abused
    (2) dogs are the most loving animals
    (3) a dog will not return your love
    (4) loving a dog will break your heart
    (5) debts must be paid

39. "By a kick in the ribs or a pat on the head." This line means that dogs
    (1) are often mistreated
    (2) are sometimes vicious
    (3) love their masters if well treated
    (4) love their masters regardless of treatment
    (5) repay affection with affection

40. The sorrow from men and women and from dogs is the same because they
    (1) all die
    (2) are unfaithful
    (3) love unconditionally
    (4) do not return love
    (5) whimper

ANSWER KEY
Diagnostic Test
Reading

1. (2)	**11.** (2)	**21.** (1)	**31.** (2)
2. (1)	**12.** (3)	**22.** (2)	**32.** (1)
3. (5)	**13.** (1)	**23.** (3)	**33.** (4)
4. (1)	**14.** (4)	**24.** (5)	**34.** (1)
5. (4)	**15.** (5)	**25.** (2)	**35.** (5)
6. (5)	**16.** (4)	**26.** (5)	**36.** (2)
7. (3)	**17.** (1)	**27.** (2)	**37.** (1)
8. (1)	**18.** (3)	**28.** (1)	**38.** (4)
9. (4)	**19.** (4)	**29.** (5)	**39.** (4)
10. (2)	**20.** (5)	**30.** (3)	**40.** (1)

Interpret Your Results

Test Area	Questions	Recommended Minimum Score	Your Score
Comprehension	3, 8, 13, 19, 27, 29, 30, 37	6	
Application	7, 14, 23, 25, 26, 28, 36	5	
Analysis	2, 4, 5, 6, 9, 10, 15, 16, 20, 21, 31, 33, 39	10	
Synthesis	1, 11, 12, 17, 18, 22, 24, 32, 34, 35, 38, 40	9	
Total		30	

Check your answers and calculate how you scored in each test area. If you scored less than the recommended minimum score in any test area, you should review topics in the relevant chapters.

ANSWER ANALYSIS

1. **(2)** Of the reasons given, this is most likely. The passage says they wore them because no one else would.

2. **(1)** The writer describes a string of small things that led to the re-emergence.

3. **(5)** The fact is stated in paragraph 2.

4. **(1)** Choices of a few young people spread to the club scene, designers, actors, and the public.

5. **(4)** The fashion grew through small changes to a critical threshold. The passage states the tipping point came in 1994-95, but later shows continued increase in sales.

6. **(5)** Many clues show the roads represent a moment of decision with two choices.

7. **(3)** The speaker took the road less travelled, following his own inclination instead of the more popular choice.

8. **(1)** The road separates into different directions.

9. **(4)** The poet can tell it is less travelled because it is grassy and doesn`t show use.

10. **(2)** The sigh is one of satisfaction and shows no regret about his choice.

11. **(2)** The poem is organized around one metaphorical choice between two roads.

12. **(3)** Descriptions are of Asian customs and a farm with an ox and buckets to carry fertilizer.

13. **(1)** Wang Lung is preparing for the New Year.

14. **(4)** Wang Lung is clearly not rich, but he makes offerings to his gods to make requests.

15. **(5)** It is probably a rich family as the cakes are such as only rich people eat.

16. **(4)** Athough he asks for luck and riches, he also asks for happiness. He is proud of his wife. He would probably like to be rich, but he does not seem envious.

17. **(1)** Sentences are long and flowing, almost poetic.

18. **(3)** The mood of the passage is rushed and disorderly like the characters.

19. **(4)** The passage mentions Mrs. Brady's litterbox.

20. **(5)** An hour early for her appointment, wearing a blazer with the tag still on, and with a terrible flyer, we can conclude that Dorrie is a new and unsuccessful agent.

21. **(1)** The simile compares the buzzer to a Morse Code emergency signal, conveying a sense of urgency.

22. **(2)** Jack is asleep with the blanket over his head, pants are rumpled and he falls trying to get them on. Dorrie wears a blazer with the label still on, has flyaway hair and lipstick on her teeth.

23. **(3)** The passage says that the tone will vary based on the recipients and their position.

24. **(5)** The purpose of this passage is to instruct business writers.

25. **(2)** The passage says that business people do not read long communications. A summary is more likely to be read than the whole report.

26. **(5)** Avoid opening with negative news and start with a buffer.

27. **(2)** The passage states that many people have difficulty being direct and offers advice.

28. **(1)** He says that she has been a father and mother to him, and she says she will have nothing left when Rina is gone, now that she doesn't have him to look after.

29. **(5)** He says that some of his friends would like to be in his place with the beautiful Hedda Gabler.

30. **(3)** She has commented on the expense of his trip and clearly thinks there is something more when she asks if he has something special to tell her. Her comment *Ah* when he says that he does have expectations suggests that she suspects more than a professorship.

31. **(2)** Although Tesman is a scholar, he seems innocent in his comments about his wife's popularity and doesn't understand his aunt's questions about his expectations.

32. **(1)** Although we see nothing of Hedda Gabler in the passage, the prompt suggests that she might be dissatisfied as Tesman is clearly not wealthy nor employed.

33. **(4)** The conceited man wanted praise. He raised his hat when the little prince clapped his hands one against the other.

34. **(1)** The writing is light, almost like a children's story.

35. **(5)** The little prince seeks no admiration for himself, does as he is asked, and asks innocent questions.

36. **(2)** He is a little prince and the last question especially is typical of a child.

37. **(1)** The poem describes dogs as loving and worshipful.

38. **(4)** The poem is about how a dog will eventually break your heart because you will love it and it will die.

39. **(4)** Dogs worship their masters whether patted or kicked.

40. **(1)** The poem says that there will be enough sorrow from men and women, but that dogs will also break your heart by dying after about fourteen years.

SCIENCE—DIAGNOSTIC TEST

Directions: The Science Test **includes 50 multiple-choice questions. Do not spend more than 80 minutes on the test.**

The practice test includes multiple-choice questions based on reading passages, graphics, and diagrams about science topics in physical science, life science, and earth and space science. The Science Test does not require specific knowledge of science. The questions test your ability to read, interpret, and apply information.

Record your responses on the answer sheet that follows. For each question, mark the numbered space that corresponds with your answer choice.

EXAMPLE

Bacteria cells are different from plant and animal cells because bacteria cells do not have
(1) membranes
(2) ribosomes
(3) a nucleus
(4) a cell wall
(5) cytoplasm

In this example, almost all cells have a nucleus, but the diagram illustrates that bacteria cells do not. Fill in answer space 3 on the answer sheet.

① ② ● ④ ⑤

ANSWER SHEET
Diagnostic Test
Science

1. ① ② ③ ④ ⑤
2. ① ② ③ ④ ⑤
3. ① ② ③ ④ ⑤
4. ① ② ③ ④ ⑤
5. ① ② ③ ④ ⑤
6. ① ② ③ ④ ⑤
7. ① ② ③ ④ ⑤
8. ① ② ③ ④ ⑤
9. ① ② ③ ④ ⑤
10. ① ② ③ ④ ⑤
11. ① ② ③ ④ ⑤
12. ① ② ③ ④ ⑤
13. ① ② ③ ④ ⑤
14. ① ② ③ ④ ⑤
15. ① ② ③ ④ ⑤
16. ① ② ③ ④ ⑤
17. ① ② ③ ④ ⑤
18. ① ② ③ ④ ⑤
19. ① ② ③ ④ ⑤
20. ① ② ③ ④ ⑤

21. ① ② ③ ④ ⑤
22. ① ② ③ ④ ⑤
23. ① ② ③ ④ ⑤
24. ① ② ③ ④ ⑤
25. ① ② ③ ④ ⑤
26. ① ② ③ ④ ⑤
27. ① ② ③ ④ ⑤
28. ① ② ③ ④ ⑤
29. ① ② ③ ④ ⑤
30. ① ② ③ ④ ⑤
31. ① ② ③ ④ ⑤
32. ① ② ③ ④ ⑤
33. ① ② ③ ④ ⑤
34. ① ② ③ ④ ⑤
35. ① ② ③ ④ ⑤
36. ① ② ③ ④ ⑤
37. ① ② ③ ④ ⑤
38. ① ② ③ ④ ⑤
39. ① ② ③ ④ ⑤
40. ① ② ③ ④ ⑤

41. ① ② ③ ④ ⑤
42. ① ② ③ ④ ⑤
43. ① ② ③ ④ ⑤
44. ① ② ③ ④ ⑤
45. ① ② ③ ④ ⑤
46. ① ② ③ ④ ⑤
47. ① ② ③ ④ ⑤
48. ① ② ③ ④ ⑤
49. ① ② ③ ④ ⑤
50. ① ② ③ ④ ⑤

Science

Questions 1–3 are based on the following paragraph.

Over 97% of water on Earth is the salt water of the sea. Salt water cannot sustain life in plants or humans, but could be a source of nourishing water if there were some way to separate the water and salt. In fact, there are a number of ways to do this. Although salt water looks like a uniform substance, it is a mixture. Molecules of salt are dissolved in the water, but the water and salt remain physically separate substances, and are not chemically bonded. One way to separate pure water from the salt is through evaporation. Water vapour that evaporates from a container of salt water can be recaptured as pure drinking water. Another method is filtration (sometimes called reverse osmosis), which uses filters so fine that water molecules can pass through but larger salt molecules cannot.

1. A mixture is a combination of substances by
   (1) chemical means
   (2) reverse osmosis
   (3) physical means
   (4) nature
   (5) electricity

2. Wine is a mixture composed primarily of two compounds: water and ethanol. The boiling point of water is 100°C and the boiling point of ethanol is 78°C. If an open container of wine were heated to 78°C, which of the following would occur?
   (1) Wine would vaporize.
   (2) Water would vaporize.
   (3) Neither water nor ethanol would vaporize.
   (4) Ethanol would vaporize.
   (5) Both water and ethanol would vaporize.

3. Water is not a mixture, but a compound. Atoms of hydrogen and oxygen combine to form new molecules of H_2O. A compound is a combination of substances by
   (1) chemical means
   (2) reverse osmosis
   (3) physical means
   (4) nature
   (5) electricity

Questions 4–6 are based on the following information.

All cancers begin in cells, the body's basic unit of life. To understand cancer, it's helpful to know what happens when normal cells become cancer cells.

The body is made up of many types of cells. These cells grow and divide in a controlled way to produce more cells as they are needed to keep the body healthy. When cells become old or damaged, they die and are replaced with new cells.

However, sometimes this orderly process goes wrong. The genetic material (DNA) of a cell can become damaged or changed, producing mutations that affect normal cell growth and division. When this happens, cells do not die when they should and new cells form when the body does not need them. The extra cells may form a mass of tissue called a tumour.

Source: The website of the National Cancer Institute (*http://www.cancer.gov*)

Loss of Normal Growth Control

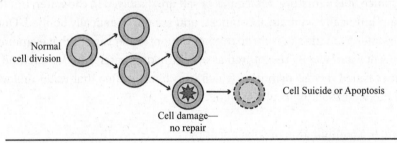

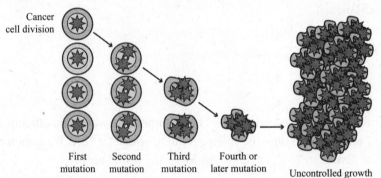

4. Cancer occurs when
    (1) cells divide
    (2) damaged cells divide uncontrollably
    (3) cells become old or damaged
    (4) cells form body tissue
    (5) cells do not divide

5. In a healthy body, cells that are damaged
    (1) continue to divide
    (2) mutate
    (3) continue to function
    (4) are cancerous
    (5) die and are replaced

6. Some contributing causes of cancer include tobacco use, genetics, UV exposure, radiation, environmental pollutants, and certain infections. These factors probably result in
   (1) cell division
   (2) cell mutation
   (3) tumours
   (4) DNA
   (5) new cells

Questions 7–9 are based on the following information.

Our sun began billions of years ago as a nebula, a huge cloud of hydrogen gas and dust in space. About 5 billion years ago, some of the gas came together into a clump. Its own gravity caused it to grow, drawing in more of the cloud and forming a protostar. After millions of years, internal temperature and pressure reached a point where nuclear fusion began, and the sun was formed. The sun has now burned for approximately 4.6 billion years and will burn for 5 billion more. As it burns, the sun consumes hydrogen gas at its core, converting it into helium. In approximately 5 billion years, it will have exhausted the supply of hydrogen in the core. It will expand to many times its current size to become a red giant, consuming hydrogen in a shell around the core instead of at the centre. Long before this occurs, the Sun will have already become too hot to support life on Earth. In approximately 6 billion years, hydrogen will be consumed and helium will ignite. The Sun will expand again, casting off much of its mass. In a much larger star, this would be a massive explosion called a supernova. The remaining core, called a white dwarf, will gradually cool and become a black dwarf.

Life Cycle of the Sun	
Nebula	
Protostar	5 billion years ago
Sun	Now
Red Giant	5 billion years from now
White Dwarf	6 billion years from now
Black Dwarf	10 billion years from now

7. The sun is composed primarily of
   (1) helium
   (2) dust
   (3) hydrogen
   (4) protostar
   (5) fusion

8. What is the life span of the sun from the time it forms a protostar until becoming a white dwarf?
   (1) 1 billion years
   (2) 5 billion years
   (3) 6 billion years
   (4) 10 billion years
   (5) 11 billion years

9. Which of the following is the smallest?
   (1) White dwarf
   (2) Nebula
   (3) Sun
   (4) Red Giant
   (5) Milky Way

Questions 10–12 are based on the following information.

Mass is a quality of matter that remains constant, regardless of location, whether on Earth, under the sea, or in space. The weight of an object is equal to its mass times the acceleration of the force of gravity, which at sea level on Earth is approximately $9.8 m/s^2$. Gravity on the Moon is approximately 1/6th that of Earth.

10. If a baseball, with a mass of 142.5g on Earth, were on the Moon, it would have a
    (1) greater mass
    (2) lesser mass
    (3) greater weight
    (4) lesser weight
    (5) greater density

11. If a baseball, with a mass of 142.5g, were hit with the same amount of force on Earth and on the Moon
    (1) the ball would travel a greater distance on the Earth
    (2) the ball would travel a greater distance on the Moon
    (3) the force would be greater the Moon
    (4) the force would be greater on the Earth
    (5) the ball would fall more quickly on the Moon

12. If 1kg of water is heated and becomes steam, the steam will have
    (1) greater density
    (2) less volume
    (3) less weight
    (4) less mass
    (5) the same mass

Questions 13–15 are based on the following information.

In thermodynamics, the study of heat and energy, the term *entropy* describes heat energy in a closed system that is not available to perform the desired work, but becomes more evenly spread out or disordered. The second law of thermodynamics says that entropy in a system continually increases. In other words, potential energy of a ball on top of a hill is greater than kinetic energy of the ball rolling down the hill, as some energy is "lost" as heat due to friction with the ground.

13. An example of entropy is
    (1) heat generated by a car engine
    (2) an object at rest
    (3) law of the conservation of matter
    (4) friction
    (5) electricity

14. Based on the concept of entropy, we know that
    (1) energy in a system can be destroyed
    (2) energy in a system can be created
    (3) a perpetual motion machine can never exist
    (4) energy efficiency is not important
    (5) heat is not a type of energy

15. The amount of energy in a system could be defined as the
    (1) sum of heat plus work done
    (2) difference between heat and work done
    (3) sum of mass and energy
    (4) difference between mass and energy
    (5) sum of mass and heat

Questions 16–18 are based on the following information.

Carbon dioxide (CO_2) is the most significant factor in greenhouse gas emissions worldwide, and levels in the atmosphere today are higher than at any time in the past 800,000 years. All living things are made of carbon. In the natural carbon cycle, it is released into the air by respiration of animals, ocean release, and the respiration of microorganisms. Carbon dioxide is absorbed by plants during photosynthesis. When plants die and decompose, carbon returns to the soil. Fossil fuels, such as oil, coal, and natural gas, are made of dead plant material that was buried millions of years ago. They are, therefore, rich in carbon. When fossil fuels are burned, carbon dioxide is released into the atmosphere. The burning of fossil fuels is the primary cause of increasing CO_2 levels in the atmosphere. As a greenhouse gas, CO_2 is a necessary part of our atmosphere, tapping sunlight that strikes the Earth to maintain a temperature that sustains life. Rising CO_2 levels, however, continue to raise the average temperature, threatening polar ice caps, raising water levels, playing havoc with weather, and threatening ecosystems.

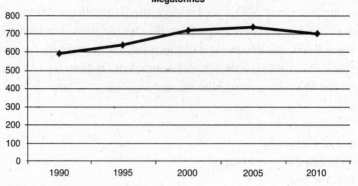

Greenhouse Gas Emissions Canada
Megatonnes

16. Greenhouse gas emissions in Canada
    (1) increased every year since 1990
    (2) reached a peak in 2000
    (3) were at the same level in 2000 and 2010
    (4) were highest in 2005
    (5) increased at the greatest rate between 1990 and 1995

17. Carbon dioxide in fossil fuels originates from
    (1) soil
    (2) photosynthesis
    (3) cell respiration
    (4) animal respiration
    (5) greenhouse gases

18. Carbon dioxide in the atmosphere is a result of
    (1) a natural cycle
    (2) human activity
    (3) industrial accident
    (4) photosynthesis
    (5) a natural cycle and human activity

Questions 19–20 are based on the following information.

The orbit of Jupiter, like that of all the planets, is elliptical instead of circular. At perihelion (closest approach) Jupiter comes within 741 million km, or 4.95 astronomical units (AU), of the Sun. Jupiter is the fifth planet from the Sun, but it is the third brightest object in the night sky here on Earth. Since Jupiter is farther from it, you would expect it to take longer to orbit the Sun, but did you know that it takes 11.86 Earth years, or 4331 Earth days for Jupiter to complete one orbit? Jupiter travels at 47,002 km/h through its orbit. Its orbit is inclined 6.09 degrees from the Sun's equator. Several of the planets have seasons, similar to Earth's, but Jupiter does not. It rotates too fast for seasonal variations (Jupiter rotates every 10 hours). Jupiter has several companions in its orbit. There are 64 known moons in orbit around Jupiter with a few more being suspected.

Source: Originally published in *Universe Today*

19. Jupiter is probably visible in the night sky because it
    (1) is the largest planet
    (2) is a gas giant
    (3) is close to Earth
    (4) reflects light from the sun
    (5) has a similar orbit to Earth's

20. A similarity between Earth and Jupiter is their
    (1) distance from the Sun
    (2) number of moons
    (3) speed of rotation
    (4) seasonal variation
    (5) elliptical orbit

Question 21 is based on the following information.

Symbiosis is a relationship between organisms that live together in the same environment and that depend on one another. There are three types of symbiosis:

1. Commensalism—one organism benefits, with little effect on the other
2. Mutualism—both organisms benefit
3. Parasitism—one organism benefits, but the other is harmed

21. Which of the following is an example of mutualism?
    (1) Toxoplasma organism infects mice, causing them to lose their fear of cats
    (2) Barnacles attach to whales to travel to new habitats
    (3) Bees take nectar from flowers and aid in pollination
    (4) Hookworm feeds in small intestine of mammals, host may experience inflammation
    (5) Cattle egrets feed on insects stirred up by feet of grazing cattle

Questions 22–24 are based on the following information.

Calories are units of heat that are used to measure the amount of energy in food. The number of calories that people need to eat each day varies by age, gender, and activity level. The following table shows recommended daily intakes for males of various ages and activity levels. Recommendations for females are lower. All values are approximate and individual requirements will differ.

Males (Calories per day)			
Age	Sedentary Level	Low Active Level	Active Level
2–3 y	1000	1000	1000
4–5 y	1200	1400	1600
6–7 y	1400	1600	1800
8–9 y	1600	1800	2000
10–11 y	1700	1900	2200
12–13 y	1900	2200	2500
14–15 y	2200	2500	2900
16–18 y	2400	2800	3200
19–35 y	2400	2800	3000
36–45 y	2400	2600	2800
46–60y	2200	2400	2800
66–75 y	2000	2200	2600
76 y+	2000	2200	2400

—Adapted from Information from the United States Department of Agriculture
http://www.cnpp.usda.gov/Publications/USDAFoodPatterns/EstimatedCalorieNeedsPerDayTable.pdf

22. Information in this table shows that calorie requirements
    (1) continue to increase throughout life
    (2) increase during development and then decrease
    (3) are greater for growing children than adults
    (4) fluctuate throughout life
    (5) are lowest in old age

23. Calorie requirements increase most rapidly
    (1) from 2–7
    (2) from 19–35
    (3) from 6–10
    (4) from 46–75
    (5) from 11–16

24. In which age group is there the greatest difference between calorie requirements for a sedentary lifestyle and active lifestyle?
    (1) 16–18y
    (2) 36–45y
    (3) 14–15y
    (4) 4–5y
    (5) 19–35y

Questions 25–27 are based on the following information.

A weather map contains much information. Pressure areas are indicated with an L in the middle for a low pressure system or an H for a high pressure system. Low pressure usually means an increase in temperature, cloudiness, and precipitation. A high pressure system brings clear skies, reduced wind and precipitation, and a wider range of warm or cool temperatures. Around each system are lines called isobars that show points of equal atmospheric pressure. The more lines and the closer they are together, the windier the conditions. Numbers on the isobars show air pressure in millibars. Fronts, which are warm or cold air boundaries between systems, are coloured lines with triangle and half circle shapes. A red line is warm, a blue line is cool, and a purple line is occluded (a cold front that has caught up to a warm front). The shapes show the direction the front is moving.

25. The weather map shows
    (1) a stationary low pressure system
    (2) high pressure moving out to sea
    (3) warm weather conditions
    (4) a storm moving inland from the sea
    (5) cold winter weather

26. The highest air pressure indicated on the map is
    (1) 953
    (2) 1025
    (3) 999
    (4) 1030
    (5) 1008

27. A front that moves towards you can be expected to bring
    (1) change in weather
    (2) increased temperature
    (3) colder temperature
    (4) storm
    (5) increase in air pressure

Questions 28–29 are based on the following information.

A father has blue eyes, which means that he has two blue eye genes (b). A mother has brown eyes (B), which is dominant trait, but she also has a blue eye gene (b), which is recessive. The four shaded boxes in the middle represent the children.

		Mother	
		B	b
Father	b	BB	bb
	b	Bb	bb

28. What is the percentage chance that a child of these parents will have blue eyes?
    (1) 0%
    (2) 25%
    (3) 50%
    (4) 75%
    (5) 100%

29. If both parents had blue eyes, two blue eye genes (b), what is the percentage change that the child would have blue eyes?
    (1) 0%
    (2) 25%
    (3) 50%
    (4) 75%
    (5) 100%

Questions 30–32 are based on the following information.

If a block is sitting on a flat table there are two forces acting on it. Gravity acting on the mass of the block is pulling it down. The force of the table acting on the block (the normal force) holds the block up. The forces are equal and balanced. The block will not move.

If the table were tilted to form an inclined plane, the same forces would act on the block. The normal force from the table holds the block. The normal force of the table pushes directly against the block, so it is perpendicular to the table. The force of gravity still pulls down on the block. As the block is on an inclined plane, the force of gravity is split, part balancing the normal force (B) and part accelerating the block down the incline (D).

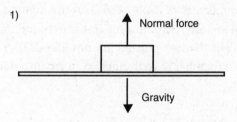

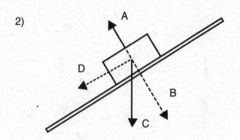

30. In graphic 2, which two forces are equal?
     (1) B and C
     (2) C and D
     (3) A and B
     (4) A and C
     (5) B and D

31. In graphic 2, which is the unbalanced force?
     (1) A
     (2) B
     (3) C
     (4) D
     (5) C and D

32. If the table were tilted to a steeper angle, which force would increase?
    (1) A
    (2) B
    (3) C
    (4) D
    (5) C and D

Questions 33–35 are based on the following information.

All living things are made of cells, and all cells reproduce by dividing in half. There are two ways that this can happen. Mitosis is the method by which most cells divide. In this process, a cell creates two exact duplicates of itself. Meiosis is the method by which sex cells, called germ cells, are formed. In meiosis, chromosomes cross over and mix together before the cells divide, so the daughter cells that are created are not identical to the parent. The resulting cells, sperm and eggs, join together in reproduction to create a new organism with chromosomes from both parents.

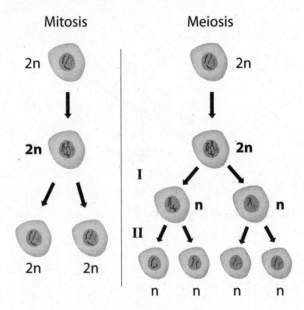

33. Meiosis is the process that creates which of the following types of cells?
    (1) Skin tissue
    (2) Spermatozoa
    (3) Muscle tissue
    (4) Blood cells
    (5) Embryos

34. Based on the information in the passage and graphic, we can see that
    (1) mitosis creates one cell from one parent cell
    (2) mitosis creates four cells from one parent cell
    (3) mitosis has fewer steps than meiosis
    (4) meiosis creates four cells from two parent cells
    (5) meiosis creates four cells from one parent cell

35. Based on the information in the passage and graphic, we can see that daughter cells produced in
    (1) meiosis have double the chromosomes of parent cells
    (2) mitosis have double the chromosomes of parent cells
    (3) meiosis have half the chromosomes of parent cells
    (4) mitosis have half the chromosomes of parent cells
    (5) meiosis are identical to the parent cells

Questions 36–37 are based on the following information.

An eclipse occurs when one celestial body passes between another celestial body and an observer, blocking its light. For example, a solar eclipse occurs when the Moon passes between the Sun and Earth, blocking or partly blocking the Sun from the view of the Earth. During a total eclipse, when the Moon passes completely in front of the Sun, the outer plasma layer of the Sun, called the corona, is visible to the human eye like a halo around the Moon.

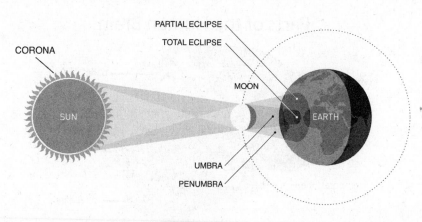

Solar Eclipse

36. In a solar eclipse, the umbra is the
    (1) shadow of the Moon
    (2) shadow of the Sun
    (3) shadow of the Earth
    (4) corona of the Sun
    (5) corona of the Moon

37. The graphic depicts a solar eclipse. During a lunar eclipse, which of the following occurs?
    (1) The Moon passes between the Sun and Earth
    (2) The Earth passes between the Sun and Moon
    (3) The Sun passes between the Moon and Earth
    (4) The Sun is in Earth's penumbra
    (5) The Earth is in the Moon's penumbra

Questions 38–40 are based on the following information.

The human brain has three main parts: the brain stem, cerebellum, and cerebrum. The brain stem is very important because it forms the connection to the spinal cord, which sends and receives information to and from all parts of the body. It is also responsible for controlling heart rate and respiration. The cerebellum is the centre of motor and fine motor control and balance. It also plays a role in language and attention. The cerebrum is separated from the top down into two hemispheres, each of which is divided into four lobes. The occipital lobe is primarily responsible for receiving and processing visual information. The parietal lobe plays a role in language, understanding numbers, and spatial awareness. It coordinates sensory information, in particular, the physical sensations, such as touch and pain. The frontal lobe is important to reasoning, figurative language, imagination, problem solving, emotion, and movement. At the base of the frontal lobe is the olfactory bulb, which processes smell. Finally, the temporal lobe processes auditory information, and plays and important role in memory and language.

Parts of the Human Brain

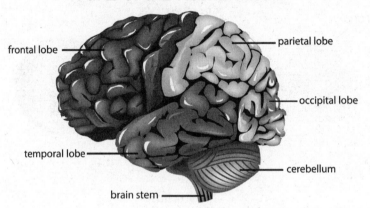

38.   The three main parts of the brain are the
      (1) frontal lobe, parietal lobe, occipital lobe
      (2) brain stem, cerebellum, cerebrum
      (3) temporal lobe, brain stem, cerebellum
      (4) spinal cord, brain, nerves
      (5) brain stem, cerebellum, occipital lobe

39.   Which structure processes visual information?
      (1) Cerebellum
      (2) Temporal lobe
      (3) Frontal lobe
      (4) Parietal lobe
      (5) Occipital lobe

40. According to the passage, which of the following is processed in more than one part of the brain?
    (1) Memory
    (2) Balance
    (3) Smell
    (4) Language
    (5) Reasoning

Questions 41–43 are based on the following information.

A 2011 aerial survey of polar bear populations in western Hudson Bay shows no significant decline. This and other studies have created some confusion. Are polar bears truly endangered?

Canada, which is home to 60% of the world's polar bears, entered into an international agreement in 1973 to conserve polar bears and their habitat. The agreement curbed over a century of unsustainable hunting, but new dangers have arisen. While some populations are stable and a few even increasing, others are declining and the overall size and weight of polar bears is also deteriorating.

To hunt and catch their prey, polar bears depend on sea ice, which is disappearing at a rate of 11% a decade. In more southern regions, such as Ontario's southern Hudson Bay the effect of climate change is most dramatic. The rapid decline of sea ice, especially the earlier spring melt, has caused well-documented problems for numerous species that depend on predictable sea ice, including polar bear, seal, and narwhal.

These are the effects of rapid climate change. They are fueled by our greenhouse gas emissions, an important reminder that we all have a global responsibility to address that while we still can and to shift towards a renewable energy-powered society. One troubling fact of the recent aerial survey is that, of 701 bears actually seen, only 22 were yearling cubs, a surprisingly low number compared to previous studies.

41. Based on information in this passage,
    (1) polar bears face an uncertain future
    (2) polar bears are no longer threatened
    (3) countries are successfully protecting polar bears
    (4) polar bear populations are increasing
    (5) the number of polar bears is not known

42. Which of the following is currently the greatest danger to polar bears?
    (1) hunting
    (2) over fishing
    (3) changing habitat
    (4) energy exploration
    (5) decreasing size and weight

43. Which fact is evidence that polar bear populations in western Hudson Bay may be in decline?
    (1) Canada is home to 60% of the world's polar bears.
    (2) An international agreement was signed in 1973.
    (3) Sea ice is disappearing at a rate of 11% per decade.
    (4) 701 bears were seen.
    (5) Only 22 yearling cubs were seen.

Questions 44–46 are based on the following information.

Canadians are among the largest consumers of electricity in the world, having a higher per capita consumption even than the United States. As a result, Canada employs many different technologies to meet our energy needs. Each technology has its own environmental impact. Some technologies produce carbon emissions through the burning of fossil fuels or waste. Hydroelectric power requires the damming of rivers and flooding large tracts of land. Nuclear power, which now meets a significant portion of our energy needs, presents the problem of disposing of spent fuel, as well as the danger of accidents. Even alternative energy sources have potential environmental consequences.

The most common methods of electric generation involve turbines. For example, water from a hydroelectric dam turns large turbines, inside of which are magnets inside of wire coils. The water moves the turbines, which in turn, rotate the magnet inside the wire coil to produce electricity. Fuel burning plants use a similar process in which water is heated to create steam, which moves the turbines. In windmills, the rotating blades turn a magnet inside a generator.

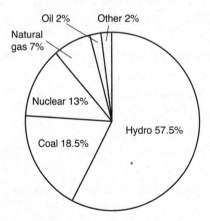

Electric Energy Generation

Oil 2% Other 2%
Natural gas 7%
Nuclear 13%
Hydro 57.5%
Coal 18.5%

44. Which technology is the third largest electrical energy producer in Canada?
    (1) Coal
    (2) Nuclear
    (3) Hydro
    (4) Oil
    (5) Natural gas

45. Coal generating stations produce power by converting
    (1) mechanical energy
    (2) sound energy
    (3) heat energy
    (4) light energy
    (5) potential energy

46. All of the technologies for creating electricity demonstrate which of the following scientific principles?
    (1) Energy can be created from nothing
    (2) An object in motion stays in motion, and an object at rest stays at rest
    (3) The buoyant force of a fluid in liquid is equal to the weight of the fluid it displaces
    (4) All energy moves in waves
    (5) Energy is not created or destroyed, but can be converted from one form to another

The term *phase transition* refers to the change in matter from one state to another: solid, liquid, or gas. For most substances, the molecules of the substance are closest together in a solid state. The molecules become farther apart in a liquid state and a gaseous state. One exception is water, which reaches its greatest density at 4°C.

47. If water at 4°C in a glass container were frozen, the glass might break because
    (1) ice expands
    (2) ice shrinks
    (3) the water evaporates
    (4) the glass expands
    (5) atoms stop moving

48. The cells that make up plants and animals are very similar and have similar structures. Some differences include the cell wall that gives plants their rigid structure and chloroplasts, which are used in photosynthesis and give plants their green colour. In the winter, there is insufficient water and sunlight for photosynthesis to occur. In autumn, leaves change colour because

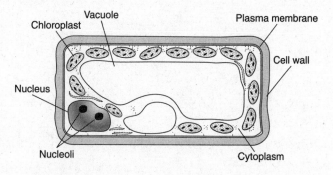

    (1) cell walls become less rigid
    (2) cells lose cytoplasm
    (3) chloroplasts change colour
    (4) photosynthesis stops
    (5) the cell has no nucleus

49. The acceleration of gravity is constant at approximately 9.8 m/s/s. If a bowling ball with a mass of 5 kg and a golf ball with a mass of 0.2 kg were released simultaneously at the top of a ramp
    (1) the bowling ball will reach the bottom first
    (2) the golf ball will reach the bottom first
    (3) the balls will reach the bottom at the same time
    (4) the golf ball will not roll
    (5) the bowling ball will roll faster

50. The equation to calculate force is mass times acceleration. If the bowling ball and golf ball were to strike another object at the bottom of the ramp the
    (1) golf ball would have greater force
    (2) golf ball would have greater mass
    (3) bowling ball would stop moving
    (4) bowling ball would have greater force
    (5) golf ball would have greater acceleration

ANSWER KEY
Diagnostic Test
Science

1. (3)	**11.** (2)	**21.** (3)	**31.** (4)	**41.** (1)
2. (4)	**12.** (5)	**22.** (2)	**32.** (4)	**42.** (3)
3. (1)	**13.** (1)	**23.** (5)	**33.** (2)	**43.** (5)
4. (2)	**14.** (3)	**24.** (1)	**34.** (5)	**44.** (2)
5. (5)	**15.** (1)	**25.** (4)	**35.** (3)	**45.** (3)
6. (2)	**16.** (4)	**26.** (2)	**36.** (1)	**46.** (5)
7. (3)	**17.** (2)	**27.** (1)	**37.** (2)	**47.** (1)
8. (5)	**18.** (5)	**28.** (3)	**38.** (2)	**48.** (4)
9. (1)	**19.** (4)	**29.** (5)	**39.** (5)	**49.** (3)
10. (4)	**20.** (5)	**30.** (3)	**40.** (4)	**50.** (4)

Interpret Your Results

Test Area	Questions	Recommended Minimum Score	Your Score
Physical Science	1, 2, 3, 10, 11, 12, 13, 14, 15, 30, 31, 32, 44, 45, 46, 47, 49, 50	13	
Life Science	4, 5, 6, 16, 17, 18, 21, 22, 23, 24, 28, 29, 33, 34, 35, 38, 39, 40, 41, 42, 43, 48	16	
Earth and Space Science	7, 8, 9, 19, 20, 25, 26, 27, 36, 37	7	
Total		36	

Check your answers and calculate how you scored in each test area. If you scored less than the recommended minimum score in any test area, you should review topics in the relevant chapters.

ANSWER ANALYSIS

1. **(3)** The mixture of water and salt can be separated by the physical means of evaporation.

2. **(4)** As the boiling point of ethanol in the mixture is lower, it would evaporate at a lower temperature, leaving the water behind.

3. **(1)** A compound is formed through a chemical combination of atoms.

4. **(2)** The graphic shows uncontrolled growth of cancer cells.

5. **(5)** The passage states that normally, when cells become old or damaged, they die and are replaced with new cells.

6. **(2)** The passage and graphics both show that cancer cells have mutations.

7. **(3)** The passage states that the sun was formed from a cloud of hydrogen gas and dust.

8. **(5)** The protostar was formed about 5 billion years ago and the sun will burn another 6 billion years before becoming a white dwarf.

9. **(1)** The Sun will cast off much of its mass before becoming a white dwarf.

10. **(4)** Mass is constant; however, weight equals mass times acceleration of gravity, which is lower on the Moon.

11. **(2)** As gravity is less on the Moon, the ball would travel further.

12. **(5)** Although the molecules spread out and the volume increases, the actual mass stays the same.

13. **(1)** Some energy in a car engine is transformed into heat instead of making the car go.

14. **(3)** A perpetual motion machine can never exist because some energy will always go to purposes other than the desired work.

15. **(1)** As *entropy* describes energy that does not perform the desired work, but is transformed into heat, the total amount of energy must be the heat energy plus work done.

16. **(4)** The graph clearly shows highest levels in 2005.

17. **(2)** The passage says that carbon dioxide is absorbed by photosynthesis.

18. **(5)** Carbon dioxide exists naturally in the atmosphere, but excessive quantities are a result of human activity.

19. **(4)** Although Jupiter is large, it has no light of its own, like our moon, and only reflects light from the sun.

20. **(5)** The passage states that all planets have an elliptical (oval) orbit.

21. **(3)** Both the bees and flowers benefit.

22. **(2)** The table shows that calorie requirements continue to increase for all activity levels until age 18, at which point they begin to decline.

23. **(5)** The table shows the largest increases in these periods of rapid growth.

24. **(1)** For 16–18 year olds, the difference between requirements of a sedentary and active lifestyle is 800 calories.

25. **(4)** Close isobars in the bottom left of the map show windy conditions, while the arrow shows the system moving toward land.

26. **(2)** The highest air pressure number written on the map is at the centre of the high pressure area beside the H.

27. **(1)** A front shows a boundary between systems, so it will bring a change of weather.

28. **(3)** As brown is dominant, only the combinations of two blue genes will result in a blue eyed child.

29. **(5)** If both parents had only blue eye genes, the child would have blue eyes.

30. **(3)** The normal force and force of the block against the table are always equal or else the block will be lifted up or fall through the table.

31. **(4)** Objects move in the direction of the unbalanced force.

32. **(4)** If the incline is steeper, less of the weight of the book is pushing against the table. This means that more of the force of gravity is used to accelerate the block down the incline.

33. **(2)** Meiosis is the method by which sex cells, such as sperm and eggs, are formed.

34. **(5)** The graphic clearly shows that meiosis results in 4 new cells from one parent.

35. **(3)** Looking at the graphic, you can see that there are two chromosomes inside each of the four daughter cells and four chromosomes inside the parent cell.

36. **(1)** The Moon comes between the Earth and Sun, casting a shadow on the Earth.

37. **(2)** The Moon rotates around the Earth, so the Sun cannot come between them. In a lunar eclipse, Earth casts its shadow across the Moon.

38. **(2)** The passage states that the three main parts are the brain stem, cerebellum, and cerebrum.

39. **(5)** The passage states that the occipital lobe receives and processes visual information.

40. **(4)** In the passage, language is mentioned in connection with the cerebellum, parietal lobe, frontal lobe, and temporal lobe.

41. **(1)** The passage clearly shows that, despite the aerial survey and restrictions on hunting, polar bears still face dangers.

42. **(3)** The polar bears' sea ice habitat is disappearing at a rate of 11% per decade.

43. **(5)** The population may be declining if polar bears are not producing enough young.

44. **(2)** Nuclear power produces 13% of Canada's electricity, which is third after hydro and coal generating power.

45. **(3)** The passage states that fuel burning plants heat water to move the turbines.

46. **(5)** In all of the examples, energy is not created but converted from mechanical energy, heat energy, or radiation energy to electricity.

47. **(1)** Water is most dense at 4°C, so it expands when it freezes and may break the glass.

48. **(4)** Plants are green because of the chloroplasts used in photosynthesis. When photosynthesis stops, the plants lose their colour.

49. **(3)** Acceleration of gravity is constant, so they will roll at the same rate.

50. **(4)** Force is equal to mass times acceleration, so the larger ball will have more force although the two are travelling at the same speed.

SOCIAL STUDIES—DIAGNOSTIC TEST

Directions: The GED Social Studies Test includes 50 multiple-choice questions. **Do not spend more than 70 minutes on the test.**

The practice test includes multiple-choice questions based on reading passages, maps, cartoons, photographs, tables, charts, and graphs. The information on the test represents global social studies topics. Some questions are about specifically Canadian topics.

The Social Studies Test does not require specific knowledge of nations, political figures, or world events. The questions test your ability to read and interpret information, including skills in comprehension, application, analysis, and synthesis. A good general knowledge of social studies can also help you to interpret the information on the test.

Record your responses on the answer sheet that follows. For each question, mark the numbered space that corresponds with your answer choice.

EXAMPLE

Top 5 Nickel-Producing Countries 2011

■ Nickel Production 2011
(In thousands of metric tonnes)

Source: U.S. Geological Survey

Based on this graphic, which country is the fourth-largest producer of nickel?
(1) Russia
(2) Philippines
(3) Canada
(4) Indonesia
(5) Australia

In this example, apply your ability to interpret the bar graph to recognize that Canada has the fourth-highest level of production. Fill in answer space 3 on the answer sheet.

ANSWER SHEET
Diagnostic Test
Social Studies

1. ① ② ③ ④ ⑤
2. ① ② ③ ④ ⑤
3. ① ② ③ ④ ⑤
4. ① ② ③ ④ ⑤
5. ① ② ③ ④ ⑤
6. ① ② ③ ④ ⑤
7. ① ② ③ ④ ⑤
8. ① ② ③ ④ ⑤
9. ① ② ③ ④ ⑤
10. ① ② ③ ④ ⑤
11. ① ② ③ ④ ⑤
12. ① ② ③ ④ ⑤
13. ① ② ③ ④ ⑤
14. ① ② ③ ④ ⑤
15. ① ② ③ ④ ⑤
16. ① ② ③ ④ ⑤
17. ① ② ③ ④ ⑤
18. ① ② ③ ④ ⑤
19. ① ② ③ ④ ⑤
20. ① ② ③ ④ ⑤

21. ① ② ③ ④ ⑤
22. ① ② ③ ④ ⑤
23. ① ② ③ ④ ⑤
24. ① ② ③ ④ ⑤
25. ① ② ③ ④ ⑤
26. ① ② ③ ④ ⑤
27. ① ② ③ ④ ⑤
28. ① ② ③ ④ ⑤
29. ① ② ③ ④ ⑤
30. ① ② ③ ④ ⑤
31. ① ② ③ ④ ⑤
32. ① ② ③ ④ ⑤
33. ① ② ③ ④ ⑤
34. ① ② ③ ④ ⑤
35. ① ② ③ ④ ⑤
36. ① ② ③ ④ ⑤
37. ① ② ③ ④ ⑤
38. ① ② ③ ④ ⑤
39. ① ② ③ ④ ⑤
40. ① ② ③ ④ ⑤

41. ① ② ③ ④ ⑤
42. ① ② ③ ④ ⑤
43. ① ② ③ ④ ⑤
44. ① ② ③ ④ ⑤
45. ① ② ③ ④ ⑤
46. ① ② ③ ④ ⑤
47. ① ② ③ ④ ⑤
48. ① ② ③ ④ ⑤
49. ① ② ③ ④ ⑤
50. ① ② ③ ④ ⑤

Social Studies

Questions 1–3 are based on the following article.

On November 26, 2006, Prime Minister Stephen Harper introduced a surprise motion into the House of Commons to recognize the province of Quebec as a nation within Canada. The government Conservatives received support for the motion from the Bloc Quebecois, NDP, and most Liberals in a vote of 266 to 16 in favour.

Despite the overwhelming support, some Liberal MPs voted against the motion and Michael Chong, Minister of Intergovernmental Affairs, resigned over the issue and abstained from the vote. The motion recognizes "that the Quebecois form a nation within Canada." The word "nation" is intended in a cultural rather than a legal sense. Mr. Chong explained to the press that he supports a united Canada built on sound government, not ethnic division. In his words, "Based on civic and not ethnic nationalism."

Prime Minister Harper said that it "was an historic night." He felt that it was an important step forward for national unity and reconciliation.

1. The person who resigned over the legislation was a member of the
   (1) Conservative Party
   (2) Liberal Party
   (3) New Democratic Party
   (4) Bloc Quebecois
   (5) Canadian Press

2. The motion approved by the House of Commons
   (1) separates Quebec from Canada
   (2) confers special powers on Quebec
   (3) acknowledges Quebec as a separate country
   (4) recognizes the people of Quebec as distinct
   (5) recognizes the unique culture of French Quebecers

3. The photograph that accompanies the article is probably of
   (1) Michael Chong
   (2) premier of Quebec
   (3) Prime Minister Harper
   (4) leader of the Liberal Party
   (5) leader of the Bloc Quebecois

Questions 4–6 are based on the following information.

For several years, economists, credit counsellors, and the Bank of Canada have been warning consumers to reduce spending and household debt. But most Canadians aren't listening. Prompted by low interest rates, Canadians continue to borrow and spend, despite predictions that rates may soon rise. In the final quarter of 2012, the ratio of household debt to income (not including mortgage debt) peaked at 163%. This means that for every dollar that Canadians earn, they have $1.63 in debt.

   More than 20% of Canadians are now debt-free, but those who do have debt are digging deeper, prompted by low-interest car loans and a rebounding housing market. Debt levels now surpass those that resulted in a recent United States financial crisis. Despite the concerning news, there are some positive signs. People are moving debt from high-interest credit cards to lower interest lines of credit. In addition, household net worth is also increasing.

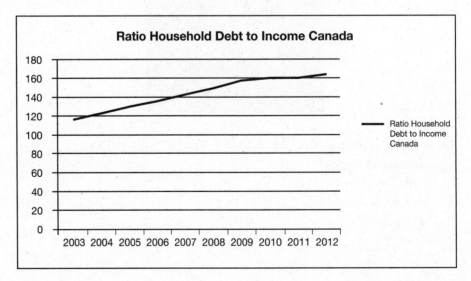

—Source: *Statistics Canada*

4. Consumers are likely to borrow money instead of saving because of
   (1) low interest rates
   (2) high interest rates
   (3) high unemployment
   (4) warnings from the Bank of Canada
   (5) being debt-free

5. During which period did the ratio of household debt to income rise the most?
   (1) 2005–2006
   (2) 2007–2008
   (3) 2008–2009
   (4) 2010–2011
   (5) 2011–2012

6. We can conclude that an increase in interest rates could mean that households with high debt may
   (1) stop spending and start saving
   (2) increase borrowing
   (3) be unable to meet debt payments
   (4) pay off debt more quickly
   (5) demand government intervention

Questions 7–9 are based on the following information.

Two bodies of water in North America bear the name of Henry Hudson, an English explorer who was searching for the extremely elusive Northwest Passage to Asia. In 1609, Hudson sailed his ship west across the Atlantic Ocean from England, hoping to find a sea route to the Pacific. Entering a river on the east coast, he travelled in northward until he realized that it was not a passage that would allow him to cross the continent. The river in today's New York State still bears his name, the Hudson River.

After returning to England, Hudson set out again in 1610 taking a more northerly route into Arctic waters. Finding a strait filled with ice, he eventually entered a large, open body of water and thought that he had reached the west coast of North America. He sailed south along the coast, eventually discovering that it was a bay. During winter, the ship was trapped in ice and the crew were forced to camp on shore. It was a difficult winter, with bitter weather, scurvy, and food and supplies running low. The ship was freed in spring, and the crew demanded to go home. When Hudson insisted on continuing to seek passage westward, the crew mutinied and set Hudson, his teenage son, and seven loyal crewmen adrift in a small boat. They were never seen nor heard from again..

Although he did not find the Northwest Passage, Hudson's discovery of the bay that bears his name was vital to British interests in North America. The French controlled Quebec and the St. Lawrence Seaway. Hudson Bay provided the British with a route to the interior of the continent and access to the fur trade. The British later granted all of the land around Hudson Bay, called Rupert's Land, to the Hudson's Bay Company.

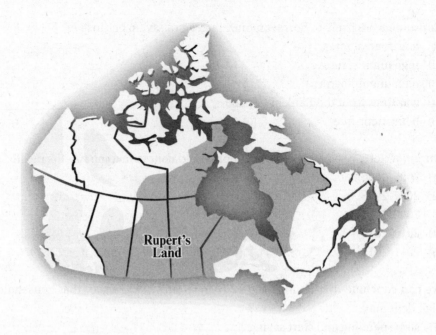

Rupert's Land

7. Henry Hudson was a(n)
   (1) British admiral
   (2) English explorer
   (3) North American captain
   (4) French politician
   (5) Canadian navigator

8. The region of Rupert's Land included
   (1) New Brunswick
   (2) British Columbia
   (3) Yukon
   (4) Southern Ontario
   (5) Northern Quebec

9. Based on information in the passage, we can conclude that Hudson Bay is located in
   (1) Europe
   (2) Northern Canada
   (3) Southern Canada
   (4) Eastern Canada
   (5) Western Canada

Questions 10–12 are based on the following information.

Canada is one of the most water-rich countries and has Earth's largest supply of fresh water, yet we also have a desert: the Arctic. A desert is a region receiving less moisture in precipitation than it loses through evaporation. It has sparse vegetation and gets less than 25 centimetres of rain annually. In contrast, the city of Vancouver, British Columbia, receives over 145 centimetres a year. Although deserts are generally thought of as hot, the largest desert in the world is Antarctica, followed by the Arctic. Fully one-third of land on Earth is desert.

The Sahara, covering most of northern Africa, is the largest non-polar desert, covering 9.4 million km^2 and large parts of Algeria, Chad, Egypt, Libya, Mali, Mauritania, Morocco, Niger, Sudan, Tunisia, and the region known as Western Sahara. Almost as large as the United States, the Sahara is the world's hottest desert, reaching temperatures as high as 58°C. In some regions, it receives less than 10 centimetres of rain yearly and in the central Sahara, less than three. Deserts are imagined as seas of flowing sand, but only the Arabian Desert, covering most of the Arabian Peninsula is primarily dunes. The Sahara, like most deserts is about 25% sand. There are also gravel plains, expanses of rock, and mountain ranges.

Life is sparse in the Sahara, but there is life. In the north, near the Mediterranean there are dry woods and shrublands sustained by winter rain. To the south is a narrow strip that receives summer rain and has seasonal watercourses and grassy plains. The Sahara is home to species of scorpions, snakes, rodents, foxes, and gazelle, as well as domesticated dromedaries and goats. Major cities in the Sahara include Cairo and Tripoli.

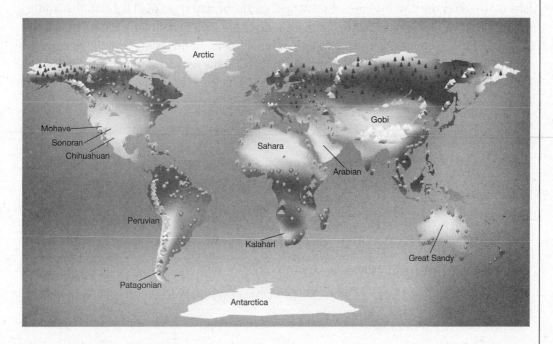

10. The largest desert in the world is
    (1) Sahara
    (2) Gobi
    (3) Great Sandy
    (4) Antarctica
    (5) Arctic

11. A desert located in Australia is
    (1) Great Sandy
    (2) Mohave
    (3) Gobi
    (4) Arabian
    (5) Kalahari

12. Which of the following is true of the Sahara?
    (1) There is a wide variety of wildlife
    (2) It receives no precipitation
    (3) The landscape is flat
    (4) It has a similar climate to Vancouver
    (5) It is home to major cities

Questions 13–16 are based on the following excerpt from a speech by British Prime Minister Winston Churchill to the Parliament of the United Kingdom on June 4, 1940.

Even though large tracts of Europe and many old and famous States have fallen or may fall into the grip of the Gestapo and all the odious apparatus of Nazi rule, we shall not flag or fail. We shall go on to the end, we shall fight in France, we shall fight on the seas and oceans, we shall fight with growing confidence and growing strength in the air, we shall defend our Island, whatever the cost may be, we shall fight on the beaches, we shall fight on the landing grounds, we shall fight in the fields and in the streets, we shall fight in the hills; we shall never surrender, and even if, which I do not for a moment believe, this Island or a large part of it were subjugated and starving, then our Empire beyond the seas, armed and guarded by the British Fleet, would carry on the struggle, until, in God's good time, the New World, with all its power and might, steps forth to the rescue and the liberation of the old.

13. The speech by Winston Churchill was given during
    (1) The Great Depression
    (2) World War I
    (3) World War II
    (4) The Vietnam War
    (5) The Cold War

14. The reference to "our Island" means
    (1) Ireland
    (2) England
    (3) Prince Edward Island
    (4) Europe
    (5) Rhode Island

15. In the extract, Churchill expresses that his country
    (1) will fight to the end
    (2) will not win
    (3) surrender to the enemy
    (4) ask for help from the colonies
    (5) is starving

16. According to the extract, Churchill believed that if his country were defeated, it would eventually be freed by
    (1) Canada
    (2) Australia
    (3) the colonies
    (4) the United States
    (5) Russia

Questions 17–19 are based on the following excerpt from the Constitution Act of 1867 (British North America Act), Section 145:

Inasmuch as the Provinces of Canada, Nova Scotia, and New Brunswick have joined in a Declaration that the Construction of the Intercolonial Railway is essential to the Consolidation of the Union of British North America, and to the Assent thereto of Nova Scotia and New Brunswick, and have consequently agreed that Provision should be made for its immediate Construction by the Government of Canada; Therefore, in order to give effect to that Agreement, it shall be the Duty of the Government and Parliament of Canada to provide for the commencement, within Six Months after the Union, of a Railway connecting the River St. Lawrence with the City of Halifax in Nova Scotia, and for the Construction thereof without Intermission, and the Completion thereof with all practicable Speed.

17. Based on the extract, construction of an Intercolonial Railway was
    (1) required by New Brunswick and Nova Scotia to enter confederation
    (2) needed for trade with the United States
    (3) needed by Quebec to access Atlantic ports
    (4) an impossible project to complete
    (5) provided by the British government

18. The purpose of the Intercolonial Railway was to
    (1) enable settlement of the west
    (2) create employment for eastern Canadians
    (3) enable movement of Canadian troops
    (4) link the provinces of Canada
    (5) motivate Canadian patriotism

19. The deadline for completion of the railway was
    (1) six months after confederation
    (2) to be completed before confederation
    (3) immediately
    (4) ten years after confederation
    (5) as soon as possible

Questions 20–22 are based on the following passage.

To become citizens, immigrants to Canada must meet certain requirements. To apply for citizenship, they must be between the ages of 18–54, permanent residents of Canada for at least three years, able to communicate in one of Canada's official languages, and not be convicted or currently under investigation for a serious crime. In addition, candidates for citizenship must pass a citizenship test to make sure that they know about Canada and their rights and responsibilities as citizens.

Canadians have rights and freedoms that are guaranteed under the Charter of Rights and Freedoms and principles of common law, which include freedom of speech, religion, and peaceful assembly, as well as freedom from unlawful detention and freedom of the press. With rights, there are also responsibilities specified by law or expectations of Canadian society. Among other responsibilities, Canadian citizens are expected to obey the law, vote in elections, take responsibility to support themselves and their families, help others in the community, and preserve the diversity of Canadian culture.

20. This passage is primarily about
    (1) Canadian rights and freedoms
    (2) principles of common law
    (3) the Charter of Rights and Freedoms
    (4) requirements for new Canadians
    (5) responsibilities of citizenship

21. Freedoms in Canada are protected by
    (1) freedom of speech
    (2) Canadian society
    (3) the Charter of Rights and Freedoms
    (4) the citizenship test
    (5) freedom of assembly

22. The responsibility to vote is a requirement of
    (1) Canadian law
    (2) Canadian constitution
    (3) Canadian citizenship
    (4) common law
    (5) not a legal requirement

Questions 23–25 are based on the following information.

The Consumer Price Index (CPI) is a way of measuring economic effects on Canadian families based on alterations in prices of a fixed basket of goods. The prices are collected at the beginning of each month for consistency and include approximately 600 goods in 175 categories. Categories are weighted as they represent the degree of a household's total expenditures. For example, a change in heating oil prices would have a greater impact on the average family than a change in the cost of a bag of French fries. The index is calculated both nationally and by province. It is a good indicator of inflation and cost of living, and changes in the CPI are often used to make adjustments in private and public pension plans, as well as the Old Age Security pension and Canada Pension Plan. The following chart shows changes in the Consumer Price Index for eight major categories over a 12 month period from October 2012 to October 2013.

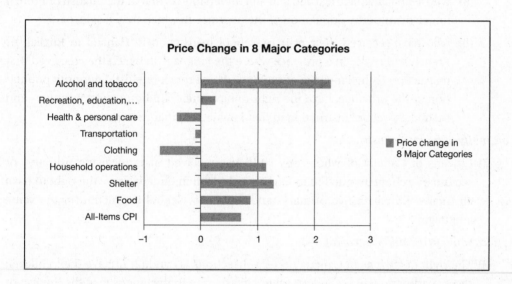

—Source: *Statistics Canada*

23. A large increase in the CPI would be an indication of
    (1) high inflation
    (2) low inflation
    (3) high consumer confidence
    (4) low consumer confidence
    (5) high unemployment

24. Based on the chart, prices in which category changed the least?
    (1) Alcohol and tobacco
    (2) Clothing
    (3) Food
    (4) Transportation
    (5) Health and personal care

25. An overall reduction in the Consumer Price Index would probably mean that pensions
    (1) stay the same
    (2) increase
    (3) decrease
    (4) be suspended
    (5) increase substantially

Questions 26–29 are based on the following extract from the Canadian Charter of Rights and Freedoms in the Constitution Act of 1982.

Minority Language Educational Rights

Language of instruction

23. (1) Citizens of Canada

    (a) whose first language learned and still understood is that of the English or French linguistic minority population of the province in which they reside, or

    (b) who have received their primary-school instruction in Canada in English or French and reside in a province where the language in which they received that instruction is the language of the English or French linguistic minority population of the province, have the right to have their children receive primary- and secondary-school instruction in that language in that province.

Continuity of language instruction

  (2) Citizens of Canada of whom any child has received or is receiving primary- or secondary-school instruction in English or French in Canada, have the right to have all their children receive primary- and secondary-school instruction in the same language.

Application where numbers warrant

  (3) The right of citizens of Canada under subsections (1) and (2) to have their children receive primary- and secondary-school instruction in the language of the English or French linguistic minority population of a province

    (a) applies wherever in the province the number of children of citizens who have such a right is sufficient to warrant the provision to them out of public funds of minority language instruction; and

    (b) includes, where the number of those children so warrants, the right to have them receive that instruction in minority-language educational facilities provided out of public funds.

26. This section of the Charter of Rights and Freedoms is primarily about rights of Canadians to
    (1) education in their native language
    (2) receive services in both official languages
    (3) responsibilities of provincial governments
    (4) minority English or French education
    (5) public funding of education

27. According to section 1(b), people in Quebec who received primary education in English
    (1) must have their children educated in French
    (2) have the right for their children to be educated in English
    (3) have no choice about their children's education
    (4) are the linguistic majority of that province
    (5) must receive secondary education in French

28. According to section 2, a family may have all of their children educated in English or French if
    (1) the oldest child is receiving education in that language
    (2) the parents were educated in that language
    (3) one child is receiving education in another language
    (4) one child is receiving education in that language
    (5) they will pay for private schooling

29. According to the extract, the right of Canadians to receive education in English or French is subject to
    (1) the availability of public funds
    (2) ethnic origin of their parents
    (3) increased taxation
    (4) income of the families
    (5) enough children desiring education in that language

Questions 30–31 are based on the following map.

GDP by Country

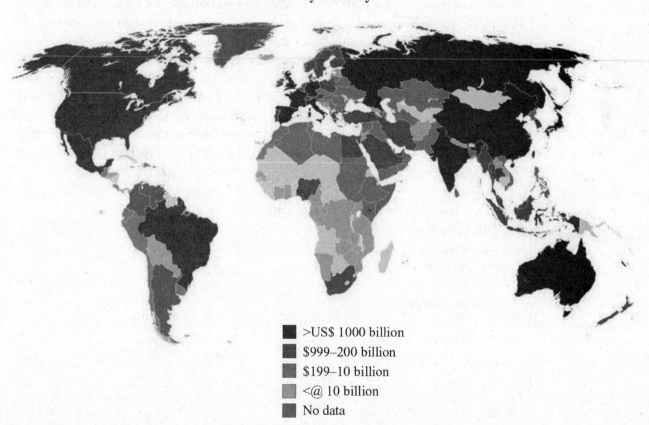

- ■ >US$ 1000 billion
- ■ $999–200 billion
- ■ $199–10 billion
- ■ <@ 10 billion
- ■ No data

30. Based on the map, the poorest continent in the world is
    (1) Asia
    (2) Africa
    (3) Australia
    (4) North America
    (5) South America

31. Based on the map, the GDP of Canada is
    (1) over $1000 billion
    (2) $999–200 billion
    (3) $199–10 billion
    (4) less than $10 billion
    (5) not given

Questions 32–34 are based on the following passage.

In 1980, Canadian embassy personnel, in cooperation with the CIA, rescued six American diplomats from Iran. The operation, known popularly as the *Canadian Caper*, took place during the Iranian hostage crisis, when 52 American hostages were held captive in the U.S. Embassy in Iran.

The Iranian Revolution took place in February of 1979. The Shah of Iran, a long-time ally of the United States and the last monarch of Persia, was overthrown by forces loyal to the Ayatollah Khomeini. A new government was established under a theocratic constitution and responsible to religious leaders, headed by Khomeini. In October, the United States allowed the Shah, who was ill, to enter the country for medical treatment. The move caused protest in Iran. In November, student supporters of Khomeini overran the U.S. Embassy in the capital, Tehran. Originally planned as a short-term occupation, the crisis lasted four hundred and forty-four days, despite diplomatic efforts and a failed military rescue.

Six American diplomats avoided capture and were hidden by Canadian Ambassador Ken Taylor in the Canadian embassy. In January 1980, the six were issued Canadian passports. Posing as members of a film crew on location, they were able to pass through airport security and leave the country. The Canadian embassy was closed on the same day. The staff returned to Canada where the leaders of the rescue received the Order of Canada. Ambassador Taylor was also later awarded the Congressional Gold Medal by the U.S. Congress for his assistance to the United States.

32. The hostages in the Iranian hostage crisis were
    (1) Canadians
    (2) Iranians
    (3) Persians
    (4) Americans
    (5) film makers

33. Based on information in the passage, we conclude that theocratic means government ruled by
     (1) the people
     (2) the poor
     (3) religious leaders
     (4) ambassadors
     (5) elected representatives

34. A good title for this passage would be
     (1) Canadian Heroes
     (2) Persian Monarch Overthrown
     (3) Diplomatic Efforts Fail
     (4) The Ayatollah and the Shah
     (5) 52 Hostages

Questions 35–36 are based on the following graphic.

35. This graphic, which compares Prime Minister Stephen Harper to Napoleon, suggests that he is a
     (1) dictator
     (2) military leader
     (3) poor leader
     (4) lazy person
     (5) religious person

36. The attitude expressed by the creator towards Prime Minister Harper is
    (1) positive
    (2) tentative
    (3) critical
    (4) indifferent
    (5) sympathetic

Questions 37–39 are based on the following passage.

The Canadian constitution details the powers of the provincial and federal levels of government; however, there are three levels of government in Canada: federal, provincial, and municipal. The third level is the elected councils that look after local affairs of cities, towns, and villages. The constitution does not list the powers of municipal governments, but states that each provincial or territorial legislature has the exclusive authority to make laws regulating municipalities.

Municipal governments generally consist of a mayor and a council. The mayor is the elected head of a municipality and chief executive. Duties of the mayor vary among municipalities, but the mayor is generally the public spokesperson of the municipality and the chairperson of the council. As chairperson, the mayor may not get to vote on issues except to break a tie. Although the mayor does not generally have authority to make independent decisions on topics that should come before council, he or she provides leadership and has a great deal of influence on municipal government.

Municipal governments are elected. The manner of the election may vary. In some cases, councillors are elected at large. This means that candidates are voted for by all voters in any part of the municipality. The candidates with the most votes form the council. Some municipalities are divided into wards. This means that candidates run to represent particular areas and are voted for only by the people of that area. Some municipal councils are composed of a combination of councillors at large and wards.

37. Powers of municipal governments are determined by
    (1) the constitution
    (2) the federal government
    (3) provincial governments
    (4) voters
    (5) councillors

38. Which of the following is likely a responsibility of municipal government?
    (1) criminal law
    (2) provincial courts
    (3) healthcare
    (4) taxation
    (5) local parks

39. A "ward" could be defined as a(n)
    (1) municipality
    (2) electoral district
    (3) a municipal election
    (4) candidate for election
    (5) candidate at large

Questions 40–42 are based on the following passage.

Canada became a sovereign country in 1867, but it was still, in some respects, a colony of Great Britain. Although Britain generally adopted a position of non-interference in Canadian Affairs, Canada did not have complete authority over its foreign policy and the British monarch, through his/her representative the Governor General, was the head of state. The King-Byng Affair of 1926 was a controversial episode in the story of Canadian independence that forever changed the role of the Governor General in Canada.

The situation was an unusual one. In the September 1925 election, the Conservative Party under Arthur Meighen won more seats than the Liberals under William Lyon McKenzie King. Counting on support from the Progressive Party (which was a separate party at the time), Prime Minister King did not resign. In 1926, a bribery scandal rocked King's government. Fearing that his government would be defeated, King asked Governor General Lord Byng of Vimy to dissolve Parliament and call an election. The Governor General refused and instead asked Meighen's Conservatives to form a government. It was the first and only time a Governor General refused to act on the advice of the prime minister.

The new government was short lived. After surviving a vote of non-confidence by one vote, Meighen asked the Governor General to call an election. Byng agreed and King's Liberals won a majority government in the ensuing election. Immediately on regaining power, King went to London to ask for changes in the role of the Governor General, who would remain the sovereign's representative in the Canadian government but no longer be a representative of British government. The changed paved the way for the 1931 Statute of Westminster, which recognized Canada and other colonies as independent, self-governing countries of equal status with Britain.

40. The election of 1925 was unusual because
    (1) the party with most seats did not form the government
    (2) the Liberal party won a majority government
    (3) the Governor General refused a request of the Prime Minister
    (4) there was a bribery scandal
    (5) the Progressive Party formed a government

41. The King-Byng affair was controversial because
    (1) McKenzie King lost the election
    (2) McKenzie King won the election
    (3) it led to a bribery scandal
    (4) the King, George V, interfered directly in Canadian politics
    (5) British authority overruled the elected Canadian Prime Minister

42. Canada achieved full independence through
    (1) the Constitution Act of 1867
    (2) the King-Byng Affair
    (3) the election of 1925
    (4) a vote of non-confidence
    (5) the Statute of Westminster

Questions 43–46 are based on the following information.

Pension plans across Canada are in trouble because of increased life expectancy and sustained low interest rates. As a result of the crisis, many public and privately funded pension plans are being renegotiated to ensure that they will be sustainable. It is estimated that new employees beginning in the workforce will have a life expectancy well into their nineties.

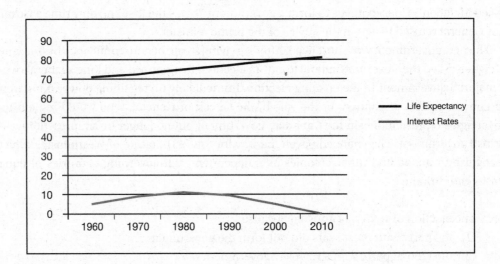

43. Based on this information, we can conclude that interest rates
    (1) remain constant over time
    (2) fluctuate widely from year to year
    (3) decrease each year
    (4) decreased steadily since 1980
    (5) were at the lowest level in 2000

44. One fact revealed in this information is that
    (1) people are living longer
    (2) people do not save enough money
    (3) companies are morally obligated to provide pensions
    (4) government should increase the Canada Pension Plan
    (5) new employees will live into their 90s

45. Based on information in the passage, we can conclude that traditional pension plans are now
    (1) bankrupt
    (2) underfunded
    (3) sustainable
    (4) more common
    (5) non-negotiable

46. If employees entering the workforce today were to retire at age sixty and live well into their nineties, it is likely they would
    (1) be more successful than previous generations
    (2) contribute less to pension plans
    (3) experience higher interest rates
    (4) spend more time in retirement than in careers
    (5) have more rewarding careers

Questions 47–48 are based on the following information.

The smallest country in the world, other than Vatican City, is the Principality of Monaco. Located on the Mediterranean Sea at the southeast corner of France, it has a total area of two square kilometres and a population just over 30,000.

Monaco is a popular resort, attracting tourists to its casinos and pleasant climate. The principality also is a banking centre and has successfully sought to diversify into services and small, high-value-added, nonpolluting industries. The country has no income tax, and low business taxes and thrives as a tax haven both for individuals who have established residence and for foreign companies that have set up businesses and offices. Monaco, however, is not a tax-free shelter; it charges nearly 20% value-added tax, collects stamp duties, and companies face a 33% tax on profits unless they can show that three-quarters of profits are generated within the principality. Monaco's reliance on tourism and banking for its economic growth has left it vulnerable to a downturn in France and other European economies, which are the principality's main trade partners. Monaco has a labour force of over fifty thousand, principally in the tourism industry.

Monaco is a constitutional monarchy. The head of state is Prince Albert II of the house of Grimaldi, which has ruled the country since 1297. The head of government is the Minister of State, who is appointed by the monarch from a list of French candidates that is prepared by the government of France. The nation also has an elected national council.

47. The primary industry of Monaco is
    (1) transportation
    (2) non-polluting industries
    (3) tourism
    (4) banking
    (5) services

48. Monaco collects tax on all of the following EXCEPT
    (1) stamps
    (2) sale of goods
    (3) company profits
    (4) local business profits
    (5) companies that earn profits from foreign sales

Questions 49–50 are based on the following information.

   Settlement of the prairies was unique in the Canadian experience. The eastern provinces had grown slowly over many years, predominately through British and French immigration. At the time of confederation, the prairies had less than one percent of Canada's population. Encouraging settlement became a priority for the central government to protect the territories from United States encroachment and to expand Canada's economic potential. In 1872, Ottawa passed the Dominion Lands Act, granting 160 acres of land to homesteaders who paid a ten dollar fee, lived on the property for three years, and built a house. Still, settlement was not practical until completion of the national railway in 1885 and did not begin in earnest until the late 1890s.

   Settlers who came to the Prairie Provinces were different from those before. Although some came from Eastern Canada, Ontario, and Britain, many came from Russia, Ukraine, Germany, Iceland, and elsewhere. Settlers included Mennonites and Doukhobors, seeking religious freedom, as well as the poor, enticed by the promise of free land.

   Challenges faced by newcomers included a long ocean voyage, often on crowded ships filled with disease. After a long journey by rail, the gruelling work began as settlers dealt with harsh winters and the work of tilling soil and constructing a house. A typical first home, called a *soddy*, was constructed from clumps of prairie sod.

   Immigrants came by the tens of thousands. They tended to establish themselves in areas with others of the same ethnicity, giving the prairies a diversity of culturally rich communities that continue to enrich the nation today. By 1920, the prairies had almost two million inhabitants and accounted for more than twenty percent of the population of Canada. The Dominion Lands Act was repealed in 1930.

49. Settlers were attracted to the Prairie Provinces by
    (1) free land
    (2) the railway
    (3) Canadian patriotism
    (4) overcrowding in eastern Canada
    (5) sod houses

50. Settlement of the Prairie Provinces was different from the rest of Canada because
    (1) settlers came from Europe
    (2) it happened quickly
    (3) settlers arrived by ship
    (4) it was a new frontier
    (5) settlers faced challenges

1. (1)	**11.** (1)	**21.** (3)	**31.** (1)	**41.** (5)
2. (5)	**12.** (5)	**22.** (5)	**32.** (4)	**42.** (5)
3. (3)	**13.** (3)	**23.** (1)	**33.** (3)	**43.** (4)
4. (1)	**14.** (2)	**24.** (4)	**34.** (1)	**44.** (1)
5. (3)	**15.** (1)	**25.** (1)	**35.** (1)	**45.** (2)
6. (3)	**16.** (4)	**26.** (4)	**36.** (3)	**46.** (4)
7. (2)	**17.** (1)	**27.** (2)	**37.** (3)	**47.** (3)
8. (5)	**18.** (4)	**28.** (4)	**38.** (5)	**48.** (4)
9. (2)	**19.** (5)	**29.** (5)	**39.** (2)	**49.** (1)
10. (4)	**20.** (4)	**30.** (2)	**40.** (1)	**50.** (2)

Interpret Your Results

Test Area	Questions	Recommended Minimum Score	Your Score
History	1, 2, 3, 7, 8, 9, 13, 14, 15, 16, 17, 18, 19, 32, 33, 34, 40, 41, 42	13	
Geography	10, 11, 12, 30, 31, 47, 48	5	
Civics and Government	20, 21, 22, 26, 27, 28, 29, 35, 36, 37, 38, 39	10	
Economics	4, 5, 6, 23, 24, 25, 43, 44, 45, 46	7	
Total		35	

Check your answers and calculate how you scored in each test area. If you scored less than the recommended minimum score in any test area, this will help you to identify topics for further study.

ANSWER ANALYSIS

1. **(1)** The Minister of Intergovernmental Affairs would be a member of the government party.

2. **(5)** The motion recognizes Quebec as a nation in a cultural sense.

3. **(3)** The passage is about a motion introduced by Prime Minister Harper.

4. **(1)** Low interest rates mean a low cost of borrowing and low return on savings.

5. **(3)** The line rises most steeply in the period from 2008–2009.

6. **(3)** Higher interest means higher payments.

7. **(2)** The passage states Hudson was an English explorer.

8. **(5)** The area corresponding to Northern Quebec is shaded on the map, as are Northern Ontario, Manitoba, and parts of Saskatchewan, Alberta, Nunavut, and the Northwest Territories.

9. **(2)** Hudson was seeking the Northwest Passage in North America.

10. **(4)** The passage states that Antarctica is the largest desert.

11. **(1)** The continent of Australia is located in Oceania.

12. **(5)** Major cities in the Sahara include Cairo and Tripoli.

13. **(3)** 1940 was during World War II. The passage also speaks of Nazis, who ruled Germany during that time.

14. **(2)** As Prime Minister of Britain, Churchill was referring to England.

15. **(1)** He says they will never surrender.

16. **(4)** Churchill says that the British Empire beyond the seas, Canada and other members of the Commonwealth, would continue the fight until the power of the New World, the United States, comes to the rescue.

17. **(1)** The extract says the Intercolonial Railway is essential to the Assent, or agreement, of Nova Scotia and New Brunswick to confederation.

18. **(4)** The purpose of the railway was the union or linking of British North America.

19. **(5)** Construction was to begin in six months and be completed with all possible speed.

20. **(4)** All topics are mentioned in the context of the citizenship test for new Canadians.

21. **(3)** Rights and freedoms are guaranteed under the Charter.

22. **(5)** The responsibility to vote is an expectation of Canadian society.

23. **(1)** An increase in the CPI means higher prices, which is inflation.

24. **(4)** Other categories went either up or down by a greater amount.

25. **(1)** Pension amounts seldom go down. If tied to the CPI, a reduction would probably mean they stay the same.

26. **(4)** The section is titled Minority Language Education Rights.

27. **(2)** People who received education in English or French in a province have the right to have their children educated in the same language in that province.

28. **(4)** If any of the children is receiving instruction in French or English, the family has the right for all their children to be educated in that language.

29. **(5)** The section is applicable where numbers warrant.

30. **(2)** The map shows the continent of Africa with the most countries that have a low GDP.

31. **(1)** All of North America has a GDP over $1000 billion.

32. **(4)** The hostages were from the United States Embassy.

33. **(3)** The theocratic constitution made the government responsible to religious leaders.

34. **(1)** Although all are topics in the passage, it is primarily about the Canadian rescue of American diplomats.

35. **(1)** Napoleon was the dictator of the French empire.

36. **(3)** Depicting the prime minister as an emperor is critical.

37. **(3)** The constitution states that each provincial or territorial legislature has the exclusive authority to make laws regulating municipalities.

38. **(5)** Municipal governments look after local affairs.

39. **(2)** Candidates run to represent a particular ward and are elected by the people of that ward.

40. **(1)** Although the Meighen's Conservatives won more seats than the Liberals, King did not resign but remained as prime minister.

41. **(5)** The appointed representative of the British government denied the request of the elected prime minister.

42. **(5)** The passage states that the Statute of Westminster recognized Canada as independent from and of equal status with Britain.

43. **(4)** The graph shows interest rates rising from 1960 to 1980 and declining thereafter.

44. **(1)** The graph shows life expectancy rising steadily.

45. **(2)** If people are living longer, they will collect more pension benefits; but if interest rates are low, money in the funds will increase only slightly. There will not be enough money.

46. **(4)** Entering a career after college or university, employees who retire at sixty could spend more time in retirement than working.

47. **(3)** Monaco is a popular resort and relies heavily on tourism.

48. **(4)** Companies do not pay tax on profits if three-quarters are generated within the principality.

49. **(1)** Based on the passage, we can conclude that settlers came because of land offered by the Dominion Lands Act.

50. **(2)** The passage says that settlement of the East happened gradually over many years, while the prairie population increased from a few thousand to almost two million in a few decades.

MATHEMATICS—DIAGNOSTIC TEST

Directions: The Mathematics Test has two parts, each with twenty-five multiple-choice and alternate-format questions for a total of **50 questions. Do not spend more than 90 minutes on the test.**

The Mathematics Test consists of multiple-choice and alternate-format questions intended to measure general mathematics skills and problem-solving abilities. The questions are based on short readings that often include a graph, chart, table, or diagram. Work carefully, but do not spend too much time on any one question. Be sure to answer every question. You will not be penalized for incorrect answers.

Formulas you may need are given on the next pages. Only some of the questions will require you to use a formula. Not all formulas given will be needed.

Some questions contain more information than you will need to solve the problem. Other questions do not give enough information to solve the problem. If the question does not give enough information to solve the problem, the correct answer is "Not enough information is given."

You may use a Casio fx-260 solar calculator on Part 1. Do not use a calculator for Part 2. When you write the GED® test, the calculator will be provided for you.

To record your answers, mark the numbered space on the answer sheet beside the number that corresponds to the question in the test.

EXAMPLE

If a grocery store bill totaling $15.75 is paid with a $20.00 bill, how much change should be returned?
(1) $5.26
(2) $4.75
(3) $4.25
(4) $3.75
(5) $3.25

The correct answer is $4.25; therefore, answer space 3 would be marked on the answer sheet.

FORMULA SHEET

AREA (A) FORMULAS

Square	$A = s^2$	Where s = side
Rectangle	$A = lw$	Where l = length, w = width
Parallelogram	$A = bh$	Where b = base, h = height
Triangle	$A = \frac{1}{2}bh$	Where b = base, h = height
Trapezoid	$A = \frac{1}{2}(b_1 + b_2)h$	Where b_1 and b_2 = base, h = height
Circle	$A = \pi r^2$	Where π = 3.14, r = radius

PERIMETER (P) FORMULAS

Square	$P = 4s$	Where s = side
Rectangle	$P = 2l + 2w$	Where l = length, w = width
Triangle	$P = a + b + c$	Where a, b, and c are the sides
Circle	$C = \pi d$	Where π = 3.14, d = diameter, and C = circumference (perimeter of a circle)

VOLUME (V) FORMULAS

Cube	$V = s^3$	Where s = side
Rectangular Container	$V = lwh$	Where l = length, w = width, and h = height
Cylinder	$V = \pi r^2 h$	Where π = 3.14, r = radius and h = height
Square Pyramid	$V = \frac{1}{3}b^2 h$	Where b = area of the base, h = height
Cone	$V = \frac{1}{3}\pi r^2 h$	Where π = 3.14, r = radius, and h = height

GRAPHING

Distance between two points	$d = \sqrt{(x_2 - x_1)^2 + (y_2 - y_1)^2}$	
Slope of a line	$m = \dfrac{y_2 - y_1}{x_2 - x_1}$	Where (x_1, y_1) and (x_2, y_2) are two points in a plane.

PROBABILITY

Mean	$mean = \dfrac{x_1 + x_2 + \ldots + x_n}{n}$	Where x's are the numbers in a series and where n = total number of values in the series.
Median	The point in an ordered set of numbers at which half of the numbers are above and half of the numbers are below this value.	

MISCELLANEOUS

Pythagorean Theorem	$c^2 = a^2 + b^2$	Where c = hypotenuse and a and b are the legs of a right triangle.
Simple Interest	$i = prt$	Where i = interest, p = principal, r = rate, and t = time
Distance/Rate/Time	$d = rt$	Where d = distance, r = rate, and t = time

1. ① ② ③ ④ ⑤
2. ① ② ③ ④ ⑤
3. ① ② ③ ④ ⑤
4. ① ② ③ ④ ⑤
5. ① ② ③ ④ ⑤
6. ① ② ③ ④ ⑤
7. ① ② ③ ④ ⑤
8. ① ② ③ ④ ⑤
9. ① ② ③ ④ ⑤
10. ① ② ③ ④ ⑤

11. [grid-in response: / / / with columns of 0–9]

12. [grid-in response: / / / with columns of 0–9]

13. ① ② ③ ④ ⑤
14. ① ② ③ ④ ⑤
15. ① ② ③ ④ ⑤
16. ① ② ③ ④ ⑤
17. ① ② ③ ④ ⑤
18. ① ② ③ ④ ⑤
19. ① ② ③ ④ ⑤
20. ① ② ③ ④ ⑤
21. ① ② ③ ④ ⑤
22. ① ② ③ ④ ⑤
23. ① ② ③ ④ ⑤
24. ① ② ③ ④ ⑤
25. ① ② ③ ④ ⑤
26. ① ② ③ ④ ⑤
27. ① ② ③ ④ ⑤
28. ① ② ③ ④ ⑤
29. ① ② ③ ④ ⑤
30. ① ② ③ ④ ⑤
31. ① ② ③ ④ ⑤

32. [grid-in response: / / / with columns of 0–9]

33. ① ② ③ ④ ⑤
34. ① ② ③ ④ ⑤

35. [grid-in response: / / / with columns of 0–9]

36. ① ② ③ ④ ⑤
37. ① ② ③ ④ ⑤
38. ① ② ③ ④ ⑤
39. ① ② ③ ④ ⑤
40. ① ② ③ ④ ⑤
41. ① ② ③ ④ ⑤
42. ① ② ③ ④ ⑤
43. ① ② ③ ④ ⑤
44. ① ② ③ ④ ⑤
45. ① ② ③ ④ ⑤
46. ① ② ③ ④ ⑤
47. ① ② ③ ④ ⑤
48. ① ② ③ ④ ⑤

49. [grid-in response: / / / with columns of 0–9]

50. ① ② ③ ④ ⑤

Mathematics, Part 1

1. Susan has 2.5 metres of fabric. She cuts off a piece that is 60 centimetres in length and gives it to her quilting friend. How much fabric is Susan left with?
   - (1) 190 m
   - (2) 190 cm
   - (3) 3.1 m
   - (4) 1.8 m
   - (5) 140 cm

2. A sporting goods store sells tennis rackets for $199.00 each or on promotion as "two rackets for $349.00." If John bought seven rackets for his tennis club, how much would he pay before taxes?
   - (1) $1426
   - (2) $1396
   - (3) $2443
   - (4) $1393
   - (5) $1246

3. The diagram below shows the dimensions of a cylindrical water container. Which expression represents the maximum volume, in cubic centimetres, of water it can hold?

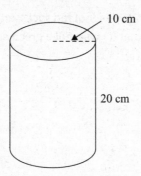

   - (1) 6280 cm^3
   - (2) 628 cm^3
   - (3) 62800 cm^3
   - (4) 2000 cm^3
   - (5) 20000 cm^3

4. There are seventy-five questions on a test. Richard only completed two-thirds of the questions. How many questions did Richard not complete?

    (1) 50

    (2) $74\frac{1}{3}$

    (3) 45

    (4) $20\frac{1}{2}$

    (5) 25

5. Susan's total monthly expenses are $3200. Given the pie chart below, determine how much Susan spends on food each month.

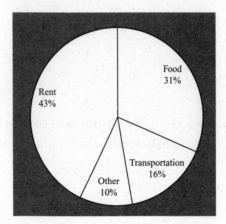

    (1) $900

    (2) $3100

    (3) $2208

    (4) $992

    (5) $310

6. Jeff throws 6 pair of green socks, 3 pair of red socks, and 2 pair of blue socks in a laundry bag. What is the probability that he will pull a green sock from the bag?

    (1) $\dfrac{6}{11}$

    (2) $\dfrac{1}{22}$

    (3) $\dfrac{1}{11}$

    (4) $\dfrac{3}{11}$

    (5) $\dfrac{3}{22}$

7. Debbie takes one week of vacation in January, two weeks of vacation in March, and five weeks of vacation over the months of July and August. Given there are 52 weeks in a year, what fractional part of the year did Debbie spend on vacation?

(1) $\dfrac{52}{8}$

(2) $\dfrac{3}{52}$

(3) $\dfrac{4}{13}$

(4) $\dfrac{2}{13}$

(5) There is not enough information given.

8. Moriah receives the following scores on four Math quizzes. What is the correct order ranked from lowest to highest?

$$72.5\% \qquad \dfrac{11}{15} \qquad 72\dfrac{1}{4}\% \qquad \dfrac{21}{30}$$

(1) 72.5% $\qquad$ $\dfrac{11}{15}$ $\qquad$ $72\dfrac{1}{4}\%$ $\qquad$ $\dfrac{21}{30}$

(2) $72\dfrac{1}{4}\%$ $\qquad$ $\dfrac{11}{15}$ $\qquad$ 72.5% $\qquad$ $\dfrac{21}{30}$

(3) 72.5% $\qquad$ $\dfrac{21}{30}$ $\qquad$ $72\dfrac{1}{4}\%$ $\qquad$ $\dfrac{11}{15}$

(4) $\dfrac{11}{15}$ $\qquad$ $72\dfrac{1}{4}\%$ $\qquad$ $\dfrac{21}{30}$ $\qquad$ 72.5%

(5) $\dfrac{21}{30}$ $\qquad$ $72\dfrac{1}{4}\%$ $\qquad$ 72.5% $\qquad$ $\dfrac{11}{15}$

9. Cheryl's gross salary is $1225 per week. Her salary is taxed at 14%. What is her net salary per week?

(1) $171.50

(2) $1396.50

(3) $1053.50

(4) $1053

(5) $171

Question 10 refers to the following figure.

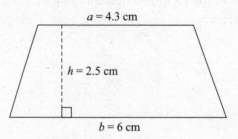

10. What is the area to the nearest cm^2 of the trapezoid shown above?
    (1) 7 cm^2
    (2) 9 cm^2
    (3) 11 cm^2
    (4) 13 cm^2
    (5) 15 cm^2

Questions 11 and 12 refer to the following figure.

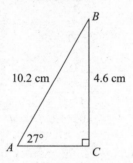

11. What is the measurement of $\angle B$? Mark your answer in the circles on the grid on the answer sheet.

12. What is length $\overline{CA}$ to the nearest tenth of a centimetre? Mark your answer in the circles on the grid on the answer sheet.

13. Evaluate $2x^2 - 3xy + 10$ when $x = -2$ and $y = -1$.
    (1) −24
    (2) −12
    (3) 20
    (4) 24
    (5) 12

14. Given the equation $2y - 16 \geq 46$, find y.
    (1) All numbers greater than 31
    (2) All numbers greater than or equal to 31
    (3) All numbers less than 15
    (4) All numbers less than or equal to 15
    (5) All numbers greater than 2

15. Given the equation $x^2 - 7x + 12 = 0$, what are the solutions for x?
    (1) 3, –4
    (2) 2, –6
    (3) –3, –4
    (4) 3, 4
    (5) 2, 6

16. Two times a number plus ten is equal to four times the original number. What is the number?
    (1) 2.5
    (2) 4
    (3) 1.5
    (4) 5
    (5) 1

17. In the line segment AC below, the ratio of $AB:BC = 5:2$. If $AB = 22$ centimetres, what is the length of BC?

                  A B C

    (1) 11 cm
    (2) 9.8 cm
    (3) 10 cm
    (4) 8 cm
    (5) 8.8 cm

18. Devin earns $140 for shoveling 8 driveways. At the same rate, what would Devin earn if he shoveled 10 driveways?
    (1) $175
    (2) $200
    (3) $180
    (4) $160
    (5) $195

19. What is the area of the rectangle shown below?

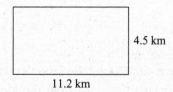

11.2 km

4.5 km

    (1) 15.7 km^2
    (2) 31.4 km^2
    (3) 55.0 km^2
    (4) 50.4 km^2
    (5) 47.5 km^2

20. There are 160 seats in a movie theatre. Three-quarters of the seats are filled at a Saturday matinee. Only 45 adults attended the matinee; the rest were children. The number of children that attended the matinee is

   (1) $160 - 45$

   (2) $\frac{3}{4}(160 - 45)$

   (3) $\frac{3}{4}(160) - 45$

   (4) $160 + \frac{3}{4} - 45$

   (5) $160 - 45 - \frac{3}{4}$

21. Jennifer is a hairdresser. She receives, on average, a 12% tip on all services. In one week, Jennifer completed 15 haircuts at $45 per cut and 5 colours at $120 per colour. How much did Jennifer earn in tips that week?

   (1) $1275
   (2) $153
   (3) $675
   (4) $1122
   (5) $828

22. Three friends are saving money to travel to Europe in the summer. Cherie saves twice as much as Jason. Jason saved $750 more than Jane. How much money did Cherie save?

   (1) $1500
   (2) $750
   (3) $850
   (4) $1200
   (5) Not enough information is given.

23. Carrie is a competitive swimmer. She swam 1.5 km on Monday, 2.7 km on Tuesday, 3.7 km on Thursday, and 2.5 km on Saturday. What is the mean distance she swam during those days?

   (1) 2.6 km
   (2) 10.4 km
   (3) 2.5 km
   (4) 1.8 km
   (5) 2.0 km

24. The Earth's circumference is 40,075 km. The Moon's circumference is 10,921 km. How much bigger is the Earth's circumference than the Moon's? Express your answer in scientific notation.

   (1) 2.9×10^4 km
   (2) 4.0×10^4 km
   (3) 1.0×10^4 km
   (4) 2.9×10^3 km
   (5) 4.0×10^2 km

25. Use the graph below to answer question 25.

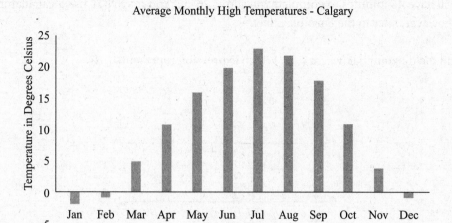

Average Monthly High Temperatures - Calgary

From March to August, the temperature increased by
(1) Between 5 and 8 degrees
(2) Between 10 and 13 degrees
(3) Between 15 and 18 degrees
(4) Between 20 and 23 degrees
(5) Not enough information given.

Mathematics, Part 2

You will have 45 minutes to complete questions 26–50. You may NOT use a calculator. You may, however, refer to the Formula Sheet.

26. In the diagram below, $\angle a = 3x$. Which expression represents $\angle d$?

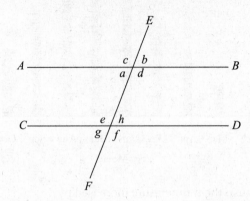

   (1) $3x + 180°$
   (2) $3x - 180°$
   (3) $180° - 3x$
   (4) $\dfrac{180°}{3x}$
   (5) $3x(180°)$

27. The sum of three consecutive numbers is 36. What are the numbers?
   (1) 10, 12, and 14
   (2) 11, 12, and 13
   (3) 2, 3, and 6
   (4) −11, −12, and −13
   (5) −10, −12, and −14

28. The ratio of boys to girls at a private school was 7:4. If there were 120 girls at the school, which equation could be used to find the number of boys at the school?

   (1) $\dfrac{7}{4} = \dfrac{x}{120}$

   (2) $\dfrac{7}{4} = \dfrac{120}{x}$

   (3) $(7)(4) = 120x$

   (4) $28x = 120$

   (5) $\dfrac{7}{120} = \dfrac{4}{x}$

29. The square root of 20 is between which of the following pairs of numbers?
    (1) 1 and 2
    (2) 2 and 3
    (3) 3 and 4
    (4) 4 and 5
    (5) 5 and 6

30. A boy purchases y kilograms of bananas at c cents per kilogram. He gives the grocery clerk a \$10 bill. The change he receives, in cents, is
    (1) $10 - cy$
    (2) $yc - 10.00$
    (3) $1000 - yc$
    (4) $y + c + 10$
    (5) $1000 / y - c$

31. Use the line graph below to answer the following question.

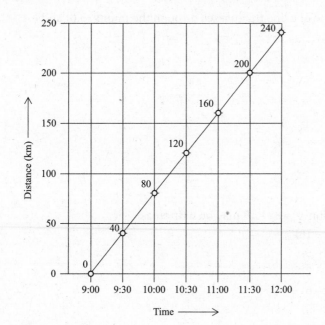

    In kilometres per hour, what is the rate of travel represented by the diagonal line?
    (1) Between 60 and 70 km/hr
    (2) Between 75 and 85 km/hr
    (3) Between 90 and 100 km/hr
    (4) Between 105 and 110 km/hr
    (5) Not enough information is given.

32. Identify the coordinates of the point on the grid below. Mark your answer in the circles on the grid on the answer sheet.

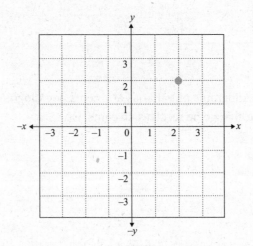

33. Find the slope of a line that passes through the points (3,6) and (–1,–4).

    (1) $1\frac{2}{5}$

    (2) $\frac{5}{2}$

    (3) $-\frac{5}{2}$

    (4) $\frac{2}{5}$

    (5) $-\frac{2}{5}$

34. The expression $x^2 + 3x - 18$ may be written as

    (1) $(x + 3)(x - 18)$
    (2) $(x + 2)(x - 9)$
    (3) $(x + 9)(x - 2)$
    (4) $(x + 3)(x - 6)$
    (5) $(x + 6)(x - 3)$

35. Use the figure below to answer question 35.

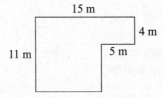

Irene plans to carpet her living room and den as shown above. How many square metres of carpet does she need to purchase? Mark your answer in the circles on the grid on the answer sheet.

36. Which of the following is not equal to 2.7?

    (1) $2\frac{7}{10}$

    (2) 270%

    (3) 2.7%

    (4) 2.700

    (5) $2\frac{70}{100}$

37. Sharon is in charge of ensuring that there are enough cookie dozens for the school bake sale. There are seven classes in the school. If six parents from every class prepares cookies for the sale, what expression represents the total number of cookies prepared?

    (1) (7×6)

    (2) $7(6 \times 12)$

    (3) $7(6 \times 2 \times 12)$

    (4) $6 \times 7(12)$

    (5) There is not enough information given.

38. Travelling at 105 kilometres per hour, approximately how long will it take Susan to drive the 1000 km between Vancouver and Calgary?

    (1) Between 7 and 8 hours

    (2) Between 8 and 9 hours

    (3) Between 9 and 10 hours

    (4) Between 10 and 11 hours

    (5) There is not enough information given.

39. If $x = 7$ which of the following equations is not true?

    (1) $2x - 4 = 10$

    (2) $x^2 - 7 = 40$

    (3) $3x + 2 \geq 23$

    (4) $\frac{x}{3} - \frac{1}{3} = 2$

    (5) $1.5x = 10.5$

40. Joe weighed 200 pounds. After following a strict diet Joe weighed 180 pounds. The percent of decrease in Joe's weight is

    (1) 20%

    (2) 15%

    (3) 10%

    (4) 5%

    (5) 2%

41. Rod had a package of 24 Oreos. He gave half the package to Adrian and divided the remaining cookies equally among David, Chris, and Colleen. How many cookies did David get?

(1) 4
(2) 8
(3) 12
(4) 2
(5) None

42. *ABCD*, shown in the diagram below, is a rectangle. The ratio of the area of △*EDC* to the area of the rectangle *ABCD* is

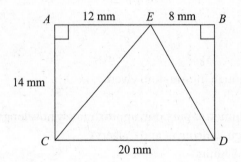

(1) 1:4
(2) 1:3
(3) 1:2
(4) 3:5
(5) 3:4

43. One number is five more than the other. Together they add to 43. What are the numbers?

(1) 5 and 38
(2) 20 and 25
(3) 24 and 29
(4) 19 and 24
(5) 5 and 43

44. A tree is 6 metres tall and casts a shadow of 3 metres. At the same time a tower casts a shadow of 8 metres. What is the height, in metres, of the tower?

(1) 12 m
(2) 5 m
(3) 11 m
(4) 16 m
(5) 4 m

45. Sharon had x dollars. She bought y things for z dollars each. The number of dollars Sharon has left is

    (1) $x - yz$
    (2) $x - y - z$
    (3) $y + z - x$
    (4) $x + yz$
    (5) $xy - z$

46. On the number line below, $\sqrt{25}$ is located at point

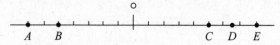

    (1) A
    (2) B
    (3) C
    (4) D
    (5) E

Questions 47 and 48 are based on the following chart.

Breakfast Menu

Item	Calories	Price
Latte	150	$5
Muffin	275	$1.75
Tea/Milk	75	$1.50
Cereal/Milk	250	$2.50
Banana	110	$1.25

47. How many calories would be consumed if a customer had a latte, banana, and muffin?

    (1) 500
    (2) 425
    (3) 510
    (4) 525
    (5) 535

48. If the customer used a $10 bill for the latte, banana, and muffin, how much change would she get?

    (1) $2
    (2) $2.50
    (3) $8
    (4) $7.50
    (5) $1.50

Questions 49 and 50 refer to the diagram below.

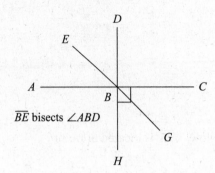

$\overline{BE}$ bisects $\angle ABD$

49. What is the measurement of $\angle CBG$. Mark your answer in the circles on the grid on the answer sheet.

50. Which expression is true?
    (1) $\angle DBC = 2(\angle ABH)$
    (2) $\angle ABC = \frac{1}{2}(\angle CBH)$
    (3) $\angle DBH = \frac{1}{2}(\angle ABH)$
    (4) $\angle DBC = \angle ABH$
    (5) $\angle ABC = \angle DBC$

ANSWER KEY
Diagnostic Test
Mathematics

1. (2)	**11.** 63°	**21.** (2)	**31.** (2)	**41.** (1)
2. (5)	**12.** 9.1 cm	**22.** (5)	**32.** (2, 2)	**42.** (3)
3. (1)	**13.** (5)	**23.** (1)	**33.** (2)	**43.** (4)
4. (5)	**14.** (2)	**24.** (1)	**34.** (5)	**44.** (4)
5. (4)	**15.** (4)	**25.** (3)	**35.** 130 m^2	**45.** (1)
6. (1)	**16.** (4)	**26.** (3)	**36.** (3)	**46.** (3)
7. (4)	**17.** (5)	**27.** (2)	**37.** (5)	**47.** (5)
8. (5)	**18.** (1)	**28.** (1)	**38.** (3)	**48.** (1)
9. (3)	**19.** (4)	**29.** (4)	**39.** (2)	**49.** 45°
10. (4)	**20.** (3)	**30.** (3)	**40.** (3)	**50.** (4)

SCORE YOURSELF

Number correct:

Excellent   _____ (40–50)

Good   _____ (32–49)

Fair   _____ (28–31)

EVALUATE YOUR SCORE

Did you get at least 28 correct answers? If not, you need more practice for the Mathematics test. You can improve your performance to Excellent or Good by analyzing your errors.

ANALYZE YOUR ERRORS

To determine your specific weaknesses, list the number of correct answers you had under each of the following skill areas and compare your score with the average scores specified in the right-hand column. After studying the answer analysis section beginning on page 126 for each of the questions you got wrong, give yourself more practice in your weak areas with the appropriate material in Chapters 22–34 before attempting Practice Exam One.

Content Areas	Items	Your Score	Average Score
Numbers & Basic Operations	2, 20, 22, 24, 27, 29, 30, 37, 41, 43, 46		7
Fractions & Measurements	1, 4, 7, 28, 38, 44		4
Decimals & Percents	5, 8, 9, 17, 18, 21, 36, 40		5
Data Analysis	6, 23, 25, 31, 47, 48		4
Algebra	13, 14, 15, 16, 32, 33, 34, 39, 45		5
Geometry	3, 10, 11, 12, 19, 26, 35, 42, 49, 50		6

ANSWER ANALYSIS

1. **(2)** Convert 2.5 m to cm by multiplying by 100 = 250 cm. Subtract: 250 cm − 60 cm = 190 cm.

2. **(5)** To buy seven rackets, John would purchase six on the promotion price and purchase one additional racket.

$$(3)(\$349) + \$199 = \$1246$$

3. **(1)** Refer to the Volume of a cylinder formula on the formula sheet. $V = \pi r^2 h$

$V = \pi r^2 h$
$V = 3.14(10)^2(20)$
$V = 6280 \text{ cm}^3$

4. **(5)** First determine how many questions Richard *did* complete. Multiply two-thirds by seventy-five $\left(\frac{2}{3} \times 75 = 50\right)$. Richard completed 50 questions; therefore he did not complete the difference between 75 and 50 = 25 questions.

5. **(4)** Find 31% of 3200.

$$\frac{31}{100} = \frac{?}{\$3200}$$
$$(31)(3200) \div 100 = \$992$$

6. **(1)** Determine the total number of socks in the bag. $6 + 3 + 2 = 11$ pairs which is equivalent to 22 socks. 6 pairs, or 12 socks, are green. The probability expressed as a fraction can also be simplified.

$$\frac{12}{22} = \frac{6}{11}$$

7. **(4)** Determine the total number of weeks of vacation taken. $1 + 2 + 5 = 8$. Express as a fraction and simplify.

$$\frac{8}{52} = \frac{2}{13}$$

8. **(5)** Convert each expression to a percent and order from lowest to highest.

$$\frac{11}{15} = 11 \div 15 \times 100 = 73.3\%$$

$$\frac{21}{30} = 21 \div 30 \times 100 = 70\%$$

9. **(3)** First find 14% of $1225.

$$\frac{14}{100} = \frac{?}{1225}$$
$$(14)(1225) \div 100 = \$171.50$$

Next, to determine net salary subtract the deductions from the gross salary.

$$\$1225 - \$171.50 = \$1053.50$$

10. **(4)** Refer to the Area formula of a trapezoid on the formula sheet.

$$A = \frac{1}{2}(a+b)h$$
$$A = \frac{1}{2}(4.3+6)(2.5)$$
$$A = 12.875 \text{ cm}^2$$

Round to the nearest whole number = 13 cm^2

11. Subtract. $90° - 27° = 63°$

12. Solve using the Pythagorean theorem (on the formula sheet).

$$c^2 = a^2 + b^2$$
$$10.2^2 = 4.6^2 + b^2$$
$$104.04 - 21.16 = b^2$$
$$82.88 = b^2$$
$$b = \sqrt{82.88} = 9.1 \text{ cm}$$

13. **(5)** Substitute into the expression, given $x = -2$ and $y = -1$, and simplify.

$$2x^2 - 3xy + 10$$
$$2(-2)^2 - 3(-2)(-1) + 10$$
$$2(4) - 6 + 10$$
$$8 - 6 + 10$$
$$12$$

14. **(2)** Solve for y and interpret the inequality.

$$2y - 16 \geq 46$$
$$2y \geq 46 + 16$$
$$2y \geq 62$$
$$\frac{2y}{2} \geq \frac{62}{2}$$
$$y \geq 31$$

15. **(4)** Either work backwards or solve by factoring.

$$x^2 - 7x + 12 = 0$$
$$(x-3)(x-4) = 0$$
$$x - 3 = 0 \text{ and } x - 4 = 0$$
$$x = 3, \ x = 4$$

16. **(4)** Let x represent the unknown number and solve the equation.

$$2x + 10 = 4x$$
$$2x - 4x = -10$$
$$-2x = -10$$
$$\frac{-2x}{-2} = \frac{-10}{-2}$$
$$x = 5$$

17. **(5)** Solve the proportion.

$$\frac{5}{2} = \frac{22}{?}$$

$$(2)(22) \div 5 = 8.8$$

18. **(1)** Solve the proportion.

$$\frac{\$140}{8} = \frac{?}{10}$$

$$(\$140)(10) \div 8 = \$175$$

19. **(4)** Refer to the Area formula of a rectangle on the formula sheet.

$$A = lw$$
$$A = (11.2)(4.5)$$
$$A = 50.4 \text{ km}^2$$

20. **(3)** First determine the number of filled seats by finding three-quarters of 160. Next subtract 45 from this total to determine the number of children attending. Keeping order of operations in mind, the expression $\frac{3}{4}(160) - 45$ satisfies this problem.

21. **(2)** First determine Jennifer's total income (15 × \$45 = \$675 plus 5 × \$120 = 600 for a total of \$1275). Next, find 12% of \$1275.

$$\frac{12}{100} = \frac{?}{\$1275}$$
$$(12)(1275) \div 100 = \$153$$

22. **(5)** We cannot calculate the proportion each person paid if we don't know the total amount of savings. This total is not given.

23. **(1)** Find the mean using the formula on the formula sheet.

$$\frac{1.5 + 2.7 + 3.7 + 2.5}{4} = 2.6$$

24. **(1)** Find the difference between 40,075 km and 10,921 km (40,075 − 10,921 = 29,154 km). Round and express in scientific notation by moving the decimal place four places to the left: 2.9×10^4 km.

25. **(3)** Use the graph to determine the average temperature in March (5 degrees) and in August (About 21 degrees). Next find the difference in temperatures (21 − 5 = 16). Temperature increased by about 16 degrees.

26. **(3)** $\angle a$ and $\angle d$ are supplementary. Subtract: $180° − 3x$

27. **(2)** Consecutive numbers go up by one digit. $11 + 12 + 13 = 36$

28. **(1)** Set up a proportion comparing boys to girls:

$$\frac{7 \text{ boys}}{4 \text{ girls}} = \frac{?}{120 \text{ girls}}$$

29. **(4)** 20 is between 16 and 25 which both have perfect square roots of 4 and 5. Therefore, the square root of 20 would be between 4 and 5.

30. **(3)** Read carefully. The price per unit is in *cents* per kilogram. Convert $10 to cents by multiplying by 100 = 1000 cents. Next, find the difference between the amount paid and the total cost which would be a product of the number of kilograms and the unit price $(1000 − yc)$.

31. **(2)** To determine rate, one must calculate the slope of the line. Using the data of both the first and last point, we can see that 240 km were travelled over a 3 hour time period (9:00 to 12:00). Slope is a ratio of rise over run.

$$240 \div 3 = 80 \text{ km/hr.}$$

32. The first coordinate measures how far the point is to the right of center and the second coordinate measures how far the point is above center. (2,2)

33. **(2)** Solve using the slope formula on the formula page.

$$m = \frac{y_2 − y_1}{x_2 − x_1}$$
$$m = \frac{−4 − (6)}{−1 − (3)}$$
$$m = \frac{−10}{−4}$$
$$m = \frac{5}{2}$$

34. **(5)** Work backwards or factor the constant (−18) to find two numbers that add to the coefficient of the linear term (+3). Note that $6 \times −3 = −18$ and $6 + −3 = 3$.

35. Determine the dimensions of the two rectangular rooms and combine the areas using the Area for a rectangle formula on the formula page.

$A = lw$ $A = lw$
$A = (4)(5)$ $A = (11)(10)$
$A = 20 \text{ m}^2$ (Den) $A = 110 \text{ m}^2$ (Living Room)

$20 \text{ m}^2 + 110 \text{ m}^2 = 130 \text{ m}^2$

36. **(3)** 2.7% is equivalent to 0.027 as a decimal (to convert % to a decimal, divide by 100).

37. **(5)** We are not given the number of dozens of cookies each parent prepares.

38. **(3)** Distance ÷ Rate = Time. Divide: $1000 \div 105 = 9.5$ hours

39. **(2)** Work backwards.

$$2x - 4 = 10? \qquad x^2 - 7 = 40?$$
$$2(7) - 4 = 10? \qquad (7)^2 - 7 = 40?$$
$$14 - 4 = 10? \qquad 49 - 7 = 40?$$
$$\textit{Yes} \qquad\qquad \textit{No}$$

40. **(3)** To find percentage decrease, first find the difference. 200 lbs – 180 lbs = 20 lbs difference. Next solve the proportion, comparing the difference to the original weight.

$$\frac{20}{200} = \frac{?}{100}$$

$$(20(100) \div 200 = 10\%$$

41. **(1)** First, calculate ½ of 24 = 12. Rod gave 12 cookies to Adrian so he has 24 – 12 = 12 left to share amongst his three friends. 12 ÷ 3 = 4 cookies each.

42. **(3)** The triangle and rectangle have the same height and base measurements. When you compare the Area formulas on the formula page, notice that the Area of a triangle is one-half the Area of a rectangle. One-half can be expressed as a ratio 1:2.

43. **(4)** Let x represent the first number. The second number would then be expressed as $x + 5$. Set up and solve the equation:

$$x + x + 5 = 43$$
$$2x = 43 - 5$$
$$2x = 38$$
$$\frac{2x}{2} = \frac{38}{2}$$
$$x = 19$$

If the first number is 19, the second number, which is five more than the first, would be 24.

44. **(4)** Set up and solve the proportion.

$$\frac{\text{height}}{\text{shadow}} = \frac{6}{3} = \frac{?}{8}$$

$$(6)(8) \div 3 = 16$$

45. **(1)** Determine the expression that represents the difference between what Sharon had to start (x) less the product of the number of things purchased and their unit price $(y)(z)$.

46. **(3)** $\sqrt{25} = 5$

47. **(5)** Add the calories of each item together: 150 (latte) + 110 (banana) + 275 (muffin) = 535 calories.

48. **(1)** First, add the cost of these three items: $5 + $1.25 + $1.75 = $8. Next, subtract this total from $10: $10 – $8 = $2

49. We are told line *BE bisects* ∠ABD which means it cuts the angle in half. As both ∠ABD and ∠CBH are 90° angles, 90° ÷ 2 = 45°.

50. **(4)** Both ∠DBC and ∠ABH are 90º angles so they are equivalent.

Language Arts

WRITING, PART 1

Overview of the Writing Test

Part 1 of the Language Arts, Writing Test includes:

- 50 multiple-choice questions
- 75 minute time limit

To succeed on Part 1 of the GED writing skills test does not require that you know all the rules of English grammar, punctuation, and spelling. It is a practical examination of your ability to identify errors in written work and the best way to correct them.

WRITING IS A SKILL

Writing is a skill, like playing guitar or many other things in life. As with any skill, improvement comes through practice. Whenever you write an email, send a text message, compose a letter to a friend, or fill out a form or a report at work, you are practicing writing. However, you also need to practice doing it correctly.

Famous basketball player Michael Jordan once said, "You can practice shooting eight hours a day, but if your technique is wrong, then all you become is very good at shooting the wrong way." From now on, whenever you write anything in everyday life, focus on doing so correctly.

- Use complete sentences
- Use correct spelling
- Use correct punctuation
- Use correct capitalization

WHAT'S ON THE TEST?

The Language Arts, Writing Test, Part 1, has questions in four different areas:

1. Sentence Structure
2. Organization
3. Mechanics
4. Usage

SENTENCE STRUCTURE—Recognize and correct sentence fragments, run-on sentences, and other sentence errors.

ORGANIZATION—Make documents more effective by revising sentences or paragraphs.

TIP

From now on, whenever you write *anything*, focus on doing it correctly.

MECHANICS—Recognize and correct mistakes in capitalization and punctuation, as well as common spelling errors.

USAGE—Recognize and correct mistakes in the way words are used within sentences or paragraphs.

HOW THE TEST WORKS

On the Language Arts, Writing Test, Part 1, there are written passages of 200–300 words. All sentences in the passages are numbered. All paragraphs are labelled with a letter. Each passage is followed by multiple-choice questions about the sentences and paragraphs.

Parts of a Sentence

1

THINK ABOUT IT

Imagine if an auto mechanic were not to know the names for the parts of a car. Every occupation has its own terminology. The same is true for writing. On the GED® test, you will NOT be asked about the terms for parts of a sentence. However, learning about parts of a sentence will help you to prepare for the GED writing test by providing the terminology to talk about sentence errors and giving a review of sentence construction.

IN THIS CHAPTER

After completing this chapter, you will be able to

→ **IDENTIFY NOUNS IN A SENTENCE**

→ **IDENTIFY PRONOUNS IN A SENTENCE**

→ **IDENTIFY VERBS IN A SENTENCE**

→ **IDENTIFY PHRASES**

→ **IDENTIFY CLAUSES**

→ **IDENTIFY INDEPENDENT CLAUSES**

→ **IDENTIFY SIMPLE SUBJECTS**

→ **IDENTIFY SIMPLE PREDICATES**

NOUNS

A **noun** names or labels a person, place, thing, or abstraction.

EXAMPLES

Person	soldier	Corporal Victor Smith
Place	city	Thunder Bay
Thing	table	
Abstraction	love	

Nouns may refer to a generic person (i.e. soldier, woman, teacher, child) or name a specific person (such as Corporal Victor Smith, Chandra Abrams, Naomi Ward). A noun can refer to a type of place (for example, city, store, or office) or name a specific place (Thunder Bay, Canada, or Moore's Drug Mart). It can refer to a physical thing (a table, fish, or elbow) or an abstract thing (for example, love, freedom, peace).

TIP

A noun names or labels a person, place, thing, or abstraction.

PRACTICE

Which of the following words are nouns?

a. Mrs. Deerborn
b. walking
c. blue
d. carpet
e. living room
f. information
g. she
h. although

i. satellite
j. testify
k. flag
l. Vancouver
m. Olympic Stadium
n. announcement
o. quickly
p. professionalism

ANSWERS

a, d, e, f, i, k, l, m, n, p

PRACTICE

Underline the nouns in each of the following sentences.

1. The officer was waiting beside the road to catch any speeders who came by.
2. Although Jacob was hungry, he couldn't eat the meatloaf in the cafeteria.
3. The constitution of Canada describes rights and freedoms of all citizens.
4. Good listening skills are one key to effective communication.
5. Shari was late for her appointment with the dentist, Dr. Zanta.
6. The Bay of Fundy is one of the wonders of nature in Canada.
7. Although children like to receive presents, I think the part of Christmas that everyone remembers is spending time with family and friends.
8. If your computer is running slowly, it may have a virus.
9. Karen wants to continue her education at college so that she can work in counselling teenagers with addictions.
10. During the election, the local candidate advertised using television, radio, and billboards.
11. I really like to cook, but my kitchen is poorly designed.
12. For some reason, it seems that every show my wife and I like is cancelled after one season.

ANSWERS

1. The <u>officer</u> was waiting beside the <u>road</u> to catch any <u>speeders</u> who came by.
2. Although <u>Jacob</u> was hungry, he couldn't eat the <u>meatloaf</u> in the <u>cafeteria</u>.
3. The <u>constitution</u> of <u>Canada</u> describes <u>rights</u> and <u>freedoms</u> of all <u>citizens</u>.
4. Good listening <u>skills</u> are one <u>key</u> to effective <u>communication</u>.
5. <u>Shari</u> was late for her <u>appointment</u> with the <u>dentist</u>, <u>Dr. Zanta</u>.
6. The <u>Bay of Fundy</u> is one of the <u>wonders</u> of <u>nature</u> in <u>Canada</u>.

7. Although <u>children</u> like to receive <u>presents</u>, I think the part of <u>Christmas</u> that everyone remembers is spending <u>time</u> with <u>family</u> and <u>friends</u>.

8. If your <u>computer</u> is running slowly, it may have a <u>virus</u>.

9. <u>Karen</u> wants to continue her <u>education</u> at <u>college</u> so that she can work in counselling <u>teenagers</u> with <u>addictions</u>.

10. During the <u>election</u>, the local <u>candidate</u> advertised using <u>television</u>, <u>radio</u>, and <u>billboards</u>.

11. I really like to cook, but my <u>kitchen</u> is poorly designed.

12. For some <u>reason</u>, it seems that every <u>show</u> my <u>wife</u> and I like is cancelled after one <u>season</u>.

TIP

A noun that is a thing can be singular (one <u>season</u>) or plural (<u>freedoms</u>), or it can be possessed, (my <u>kitchen</u>).

PRACTICE

Underline the nouns in each of the following sentences.

1. This poor weather has lasted for three weeks.

2. Phillip printed several resumes to take to his interview.

3. Her truck has an extended cab and a two-ton towing capacity.

4. In the movie, a gang of thieves held a group of people captive at a bank.

5. Outdoor adventures can help young people build self-confidence and teamwork skills.

6. When their plane landed, the passengers made their way to the terminal.

7. The Smiths have a dog named Spot, but he doesn't have any spots.

8. Homemade TV dinners are a good way to save money and have a healthy lunch.

9. Javid volunteers his time at the library for their early reading program.

10. Victoria loves to shop for shoes, although she already owns forty-seven pairs.

11. High in a tree, the young birds called softly for their mother.

12. The thing about hockey is that in the playoffs any team can win.

ANSWERS

1. This poor <u>weather</u> has lasted for three <u>weeks</u>.

2. <u>Phillip</u> printed several <u>resumes</u> to take to his <u>interview</u>.

3. Her <u>truck</u> has an extended <u>cab</u> and a two-<u>ton</u> towing <u>capacity</u>.

4. In the <u>movie</u>, a <u>gang</u> of <u>thieves</u> held a <u>group</u> of <u>people</u> captive at a <u>bank</u>.

5. Outdoor <u>adventures</u> can help young <u>people</u> build <u>self-confidence</u> and teamwork <u>skills</u>.

6. When their <u>plane</u> landed, the <u>passengers</u> made their <u>way</u> to the <u>terminal</u>.

7. The <u>Smiths</u> have a <u>dog</u> named Spot, but he doesn't have any <u>spots</u>.

8. Homemade TV <u>dinners</u> are a good <u>way</u> to save <u>money</u> and have a healthy <u>lunch</u>.

9. <u>Javid</u> volunteers his <u>time</u> at the <u>library</u> for their early reading <u>program</u>.

10. <u>Victoria</u> loves to shop for <u>shoes</u> although she already owns forty-seven <u>pairs</u>.

11. High in a <u>tree</u>, the young <u>birds</u> called softly for their <u>mother</u>.

12. The <u>thing</u> about <u>hockey</u> is that in the <u>playoffs</u> any <u>team</u> can win.

Select one or two paragraphs in a newspaper, book, or magazine. Underline the nouns. Discuss your answers with a teacher, friend, or another student.

PRONOUNS

A **pronoun** substitutes for a noun.

EXAMPLE

Mariah sold the book to Alphonse. (The nouns are: Mariah, book, and Alphonse.)
She sold it to him.

Pronouns are used in place of a noun that is already known. Without pronouns, we might have to say something like this: "Kyle got up. Kyle ate breakfast. Kyle brushed Kyle's teeth." Instead, we use pronouns to say, "Kyle got up. *He* ate breakfast. *He* brushed *his* teeth." We know that all of these pronouns mean Kyle.

There are different kinds of pronouns in English, but all do the same job.

PERSONAL PRONOUNS—take the place of a person or thing (I, you, he, she, it, we, they)

POSSESSIVE PRONOUNS—take the place of a person or thing to show ownership (mine, yours, his, hers, its, ours, theirs)

OBJECTIVE PRONOUNS—take the place of a person or thing (me, you, him, her, it, us, them)

REFLEXIVE PRONOUNS—take the place of a person or thing that acts on itself (myself, yourself, himself, herself, itself, ourselves, themselves) i.e. Kyle hurt Kyle—Kyle hurt *himself.*

RELATIVE PRONOUNS—refer back to a person or thing already mentioned (who, that, which)

DEMONSTRATIVE PRONOUNS—refer to specific things (this, that, these, those)

INDEFINITE PRONOUNS—refer to people or things in general (everyone, everybody, no one, anyone, anything)

INTERROGATIVE PRONOUNS—ask questions by referring to things we don't know yet (how, what, which, who, whom, whose)

TIP

A pronoun substitutes for a noun.

The GED tests will not ask you to identify or define nouns or pronouns; however, learning about them is a good introduction to sentences, which make up 30% of the questions on the GED Language Arts, Writing Test, Part 1.

PRACTICE

Write pronouns to fill in the blanks in these sentences.

1. David knew about the birthday party _____ parents had planned.

2. My wife and I are celebrating _____ sixteenth anniversary.

3. Katelyn is not a person _____ likes to dance.

4. Juan and Maria asked _____ friends to wait for _____.

5. The coat _____ Dominique bought is _____ favourite colour.

6. The cat was purring as _____ cleaned _____ fur.

7. Children love soccer because _____ like to run.

8. I want to get a GED so that _____ can achieve _____ personal goals.

9. Alexa loves Halifax; _____ says _____ is _____ favourite city.

10. Although _____ was snowing, Jameela was wearing _____ spring jacket.

11. When Hannah and Darrah were young, _____ spent summers at _____ grandparents' cottage.

12. Joseph enjoyed _____ at the harbour as _____ navigated the sailboat towards open water.

ANSWERS

1. David knew about the birthday party his parents had planned.

2. My wife and I are celebrating our sixteenth anniversary.

3. Katelyn is not a person who likes to dance.

4. Juan and Maria asked their friends to wait for them.

5. The coat that Dominique bought is her favourite colour.

6. The cat was purring as it cleaned its fur. (could also use he, his or she, her if the gender is known)

7. Children love soccer because they like to run.

8. I want to get a GED so that I can achieve my personal goals.

9. Alexa loves Halifax; she says it is her favourite city.

10. Although it was snowing, Jameela was wearing her spring jacket.

11. When Hannah and Darrah were young, they spent summers at their grandparents' cottage.

12. Joseph enjoyed himself at the harbour as he navigated the sailboat towards open water.

PRACTICE

Underline the pronouns in the following sentences.

1. To whom it may concern:

2. Please accept this resume as my application for the sales position you advertised.

3. You will see from my resume that I have an extensive sales background and experience working with others.

4. I pride myself on my strong work ethic and I am results-oriented.

5. Yours truly, Jane Doe.

6. Those end tables and that chair will go well in this corner of the room.

7. Cooking with fresh ingredients is one of the keys to great flavour.

8. Everyone at the party agreed that Christmas was their favourite family holiday.

9. Talking with him about his vacation to Africa, she realized that he had made everything up.

10. A lot of Canada's tourism is based around its four largest cities, known for **their** culture and diversity.

11. In 1870, what province became the fifth to enter confederation?

12. This discovery led researchers to the hypothesis that a significant correlation existed between free-radicals and aging, which they have still not been able to prove.

ANSWERS

1. To <u>whom</u> <u>it</u> may concern:

2. Please accept <u>this</u> resume as <u>my</u> application for the sales position <u>you</u> advertised.

3. <u>You</u> will see from <u>my</u> resume that <u>I</u> have an extensive sales background and experience working with <u>others</u>.

4. <u>I</u> pride <u>myself</u> on <u>my</u> strong work ethic and <u>I</u> am results-oriented.

5. <u>Yours</u> truly, Jane Doe.

6. <u>Those</u> end tables and <u>that</u> chair will go well in <u>this</u> corner of the room.

7. Cooking with fresh ingredients is one of the keys to great flavour. (none)

8. <u>Everyone</u> at the party agreed <u>that</u> Christmas was <u>their</u> favourite family holiday.

9. Talking with <u>him</u> about <u>his</u> vacation to Africa, <u>she</u> realized that <u>he</u> had made <u>everything</u> up.

10. A lot of Canada's tourism is based around <u>its</u> four largest cities, known for <u>their</u> culture and diversity.

11. In 1870, <u>what</u> province became the fifth to enter confederation?

12. <u>This</u> discovery led researchers to the hypothesis <u>that</u> a significant correlation existed between free-radicals and aging, <u>which</u> <u>they</u> have still not been able to prove.

CHALLENGE EXERCISE

Select one or two paragraphs in a newspaper, book, or magazine. Underline the pronouns. Identify what nouns the pronouns refer to. Discuss your answers with a teacher, friend, or another student.

Practice with Nouns and Pronouns

In each sentence below, circle the noun that the underlined pronoun refers to.

EXAMPLE

The (soldiers) cast <u>their</u> advance ballots for the federal election.

---

1. A large storm is making <u>its</u> way up the Bay of Fundy.

2. Before <u>their</u> guests arrived, Pierre and Francis hastily cleaned up the dishes.

3. The sulky drivers gave the horses <u>their</u> heads as they came into the final stretch.

4. Every year, the town of Windsor, Nova Scotia hosts <u>its</u> annual pumpkin boat race.

5. Michelle told Estella that she had hurt <u>herself</u>, slipping on Patricia's stairs.

6. For many residents of the Prairies, spring flood watch is an annual occurrence as rivers rise and threaten to flood <u>their</u> banks.

7. Giving <u>them</u> a final hug before boarding the plane, the parents realized how much they would miss their children.

8. Canada's Dr. Frederick Banting and Charles Best discovered insulin, <u>which</u> has saved millions of lives.

9. The committee prepared the results of their study and released <u>them</u> to the media.

10. Most Thai food contains peanuts, so my friend Anne is allergic to <u>it</u>.

11. The English system of measurement, <u>which</u> involves miles and gallons, is no longer used in England.

12. With growing social awareness of environmental issues, many businesses believe that <u>they</u> should be an important part of an effective marketing strategy.

ANSWERS

1. storm
2. Pierre and Francis
3. horses
4. town
5. Michelle
6. rivers
7. children
8. insulin
9. results
10. food
11. system
12. issues

ACTION VERBS

A **verb** names an action or indicates a condition or state of being.

One type of verb is an action verb. It describes dynamic movement or activity. Examples include things such as run, dance, produce, identify, or deliver. As with nouns, there can be more than one verb in a sentence.

PRACTICE

Identify the action verbs in the sentences that follow.

1. Anchor Ranch in Alberta raises bison, which they sell to specialty grocery stores.

2. The children ran and danced when they saw the presents.

3. On the motorcycle test, Demar drove slowly in a figure eight.

4. Most days, Marcel arrives home before his wife, so he cooks supper.

5. When she heard about the sale, Amy went straight to the shoe store and bought several new pairs.

6. Personally, I think that Jessica loves her puppy more than the puppy likes her.

7. The helicopter hovered for a moment and then came in for a landing.

8. The crowd cheered when the celebrity waved.

9. Susan stood beside the desk while Yan confessed that he cheated on the test.

10. Sasha lost ten pounds during her vacation.

11. I get up early each morning and eat breakfast and read the paper before I go to work.

12. The fans celebrated when their team won the super bowl.

ANSWERS

1. Anchor Ranch in Alberta <u>raises</u> bison, which they <u>sell</u> to specialty grocery <u>stores</u>.

2. The children <u>ran</u> and <u>danced</u> when they <u>saw</u> the presents.

3. On the motorcycle test, Demar <u>drove</u> slowly in a figure eight.

4. Most days, Marcel <u>arrives</u> home before his wife, so he <u>cooks</u> supper.

5. When she <u>heard</u> about the sale, Amy <u>went</u> straight to the shoe store and <u>bought</u> several new pairs.

6. Personally, I <u>think</u> that Jessica <u>loves</u> her puppy more than the puppy <u>likes</u> her.

7. The helicopter <u>hovered</u> for a moment and then <u>came</u> in for a landing.

8. The crowd <u>cheered</u> when the celebrity <u>waved</u>.

9. Susan <u>stood</u> beside the desk while Yan <u>confessed</u> that he <u>cheated</u> on the test.

10. Sasha <u>lost</u> ten pounds during her vacation.

11. I <u>get up</u> early each morning and <u>eat</u> breakfast and <u>read</u> the paper before I <u>go</u> to work.

12. The fans <u>celebrated</u> when their team <u>won</u> the super bowl.

To identify action verbs, ask yourself, "What do the people or things in this sentence *do*?" For example, look at the previous exercise. What does Anchor Ranch do? They *raise* and they *sell* bison. What did the children do? They *ran*, *danced*, and *saw*. In question 6, what do I do? I *think*. What does Jessica do? She *loves*. What does the puppy do? The puppy *likes*.

PRACTICE

Underline the action verbs in the following sentences.

1. The brakes failed and the car rolled slowly into the ditch.
2. Lydia practices the cello for an hour every day.
3. The drug store offers free clinics for people who worry about their cholesterol.
4. The skater slid to a stop, his blades showering the spectators with snow.
5. Bethany missed the lecture by the speakers who visited from Uganda.
6. Matt never worries about money because he spends it so well.
7. Walking the streets of Old Quebec, I admired the many fine restaurants I saw.
8. The hardware store carries one line of tools that they guarantee for life.

ANSWERS

1. The brakes <u>failed</u> and the car <u>rolled</u> slowly into the ditch.
2. Lydia <u>practices</u> the cello for an hour every day.
3. The drug store <u>offers</u> free clinics for people who <u>worry</u> about their cholesterol.
4. The skater <u>slid</u> to a stop, his blades <u>showering</u> the spectators with snow.
5. Bethany <u>missed</u> the lecture by the speakers who <u>visited</u> from Uganda.
6. Matt never <u>worries</u> about money because he <u>spends</u> it so well.
7. <u>Walking</u> the streets of Old Quebec, I <u>admired</u> the many fine restaurants I <u>saw</u>.
8. The hardware store <u>carries</u> one line of tools that they <u>guarantee</u> for life.

TIP

Some words can be different parts of speech depending on how they are used in a sentence. For example, *run* is an action verb, but if you go for a *run*, it is a thing, a noun.

CHALLENGE EXERCISE

Make your own practice sheet. Write ten sentences that contain action verbs. Make an answer sheet that shows the action words in each sentence. Discuss your practice sheet with a teacher, friend, or another student.

NON-ACTION VERBS

A verb can be an action, but there are also non-action verbs that indicate a condition or state of being.

Here is a list of some non-action verbs:

is	be	have	could
are	been	had	should
was	do	may	would
were	did	might	
will	does	ought	
shall	has	can	

PRACTICE

Underline the action and non-action verbs in the sentences that follow.

1. It was a dark and stormy night, and lightning lit the sky.
2. There is nothing to fear but fear itself.
3. One of my children wants the toy fire truck because the other one has it.
4. Why did the chicken cross the road?
5. The taxi driver was slow, so we were late for work.
6. She asked if I was going to the mall, and I said I might.
7. You should take your time when you are buying a car.
8. The frog was really a prince who was under a magic spell.
9. Shani has a headache; she will take some pain killers.
10. The reason the dog may have a sore ear is that he has ear mites.
11. The con man wore sun glasses so he could hide his identity.
12. Under the wide branches of the maple tree, there was a cool patch of shade.

ANSWERS

1. It <u>was</u> a dark and stormy night, and lightning <u>lit</u> the sky.
2. There <u>is</u> nothing to fear but fear itself.
3. One of my children <u>wants</u> the toy fire truck because the other one <u>has</u> it.
4. Why <u>did</u> the chicken <u>cross</u> the road?
5. The taxi driver <u>was</u> slow, so we <u>were</u> late for work.
6. She <u>asked</u> if I <u>was</u> <u>going</u> to the mall, and I <u>said</u> I <u>might</u>.
7. You <u>should</u> <u>take</u> your time when you <u>are</u> <u>buying</u> a car.
8. The frog <u>was</u> really a prince who <u>was</u> under a magic spell.

9. Shani <u>has</u> a headache; she <u>will take</u> some pain killers.

10. The reason the dog <u>may have</u> a sore ear <u>is</u> that he <u>has</u> ear mites.

11. The con man <u>wore</u> sun glasses so he <u>could hide</u> his identity.

12. Under the wide branches of the maple tree, there <u>was</u> a cool patch of shade.

CHALLENGE EXERCISE

Look at the ten sentences that contain action verbs that you wrote in the previous challenge exercise. Check to see if they also contain non-action verbs and underline them. Share your practice sheet with a teacher, friend, or another student.

Verb Phrases

Non-action verbs can stand alone. They can also function as helping (auxiliary) verbs to form a **verb phrase**. A verb phrase has two or more verbs that work together.

> **EXAMPLES**
>
> She <u>has been having</u> a bad day.
> They <u>are</u> not <u>singing</u> very loudly.
> I <u>will</u> never <u>understand</u> how they get the caramel inside the chocolate bar.
>
> When you are identifying verb phrases, remember this:
>
> - <u>Not</u> is not a verb
> - <u>Never</u> is never a verb

PRACTICE

Underline the verbs and verb phrases in the sentences that follow.

1. We had been waiting for the bus for over an hour before it finally arrived.

2. After the business had closed for the night, Shannon locked up and put the key in her pocket.

3. The waiter brought a clean fork because Brianna had dropped hers on the floor.

4. I have not done as much work this morning as I usually accomplish before lunch.

5. My favourite singer is giving a concert in the park on Sunday.

6. Although they have taken more shots on goal, my team is losing.

7. A parachutist once survived a fourteen-thousand foot fall, and when she had recovered from her injuries, returned to sky diving.

8. One of the reasons I will always enjoy a good book is that you cannot take a computer into the bathtub.

9. In the movie, a group of aliens invaded the Earth and were driven back by a group of high-school science students.

10. I will be leaving for the airport at noon.

11. When doing business overseas, it is important that Canadians learn about the local customs.

12. When you are lifting or carrying a load, maintain a good posture and use your legs.

ANSWERS

1. We <u>had been waiting</u> for the bus for over an hour before it finally <u>arrived</u>.
2. After the business <u>had closed</u> for the night, Shannon <u>locked up</u> and <u>put</u> the key in her pocket.
3. The waiter <u>brought</u> a clean fork because Brianna <u>had dropped</u> hers on the floor.
4. I <u>have</u> not <u>done</u> as much work this morning as I usually <u>accomplish</u> before lunch.
5. My favourite singer <u>is giving</u> a concert in the park on Sunday.
6. Although they <u>have taken</u> more shots on goal, my team <u>is losing</u>.
7. A parachutist once <u>survived</u> a fourteen-thousand foot fall, and when she <u>had recovered</u> from her injuries, <u>returned</u> to sky diving.
8. One of the reasons I <u>will</u> always <u>enjoy</u> a good book <u>is</u> that you <u>cannot take</u> a computer into the bathtub.
9. In the movie, a group of aliens <u>invaded</u> the Earth and <u>were driven</u> back by a group of high-school science students.
10. I <u>will be leaving</u> for the airport at noon.
11. When <u>doing</u> business overseas, it <u>is</u> important that Canadians <u>learn</u> about the local customs.
12. When you <u>are lifting</u> or <u>carrying</u> a load, <u>maintain</u> a good posture and <u>use</u> your legs.

PRACTICE

How much do you remember? Identify the part of speech of the underlined words.

1. Brendan claimed that he did not <u>remember</u> where he put his keys.
   a. noun
   b. pronoun
   c. verb

2. The store is closed for business because of the <u>holiday</u>.
   a. noun
   b. pronoun
   c. verb

3. Mr. Corelis dropped his <u>car</u> off at the garage for an oil change.
   a. noun
   b. pronoun
   c. verb

4. Cooking is one of my passions, but I am not great with spices, so I cook by <u>smell</u>.
   a. noun
   b. pronoun
   c. verb

5. The gambler told <u>me</u> that taking chances is one of the secrets to success in poker.
   a. noun
   b. pronoun
   c. verb

6. These days a lot of people <u>seem</u> to be very interested in mixed martial arts fighting.
   a. noun
   b. pronoun
   c. verb

7. Amber told herself that this skirt was worth the price because it looked so much better than <u>that</u> one.
   a. noun
   b. pronoun
   c. verb

8. Before the discovery of <u>penicillin</u>, many people died of simple infections.
   a. noun
   b. pronoun
   c. verb

9. For Easter dinner, Marta made her secret recipe of candied ham that <u>has been basted</u> with pineapple and brown sugar.
   a. noun
   b. pronoun
   c. verb

10. <u>Head-Smashed-In Buffalo Jump</u>, located in Alberta, is a UNESCO World Heritage Site.
    a. noun
    b. pronoun
    c. verb

ANSWERS

1. c	4. a	7. b	10. a
2. a	5. b	8. a	
3. a	6. c	9. c	

CHALLENGE EXERCISE

Pick one or two paragraphs in a newspaper, book, or magazine. Underline the nouns, double underline the pronouns, and circle the verbs. Discuss your answers with a teacher, friend, or another student.

PREPOSITIONAL PHRASES

A **phrase** is a group of words that go together as a single unit within a sentence. A phrase usually has a noun OR a verb, but not both. There are many types of phrases.

Prepositional phrases begin with words such as in, on, under, at, about, for, of, to, around, beside, etc. and end with a noun.

Examples of prepositional phrases:

- in a haystack
- under the bed
- after the wedding
- to the store

PRACTICE

Underline the nouns in the phrases below.

1. after the party
2. in the morning
3. beside the still brook
4. to the city
5. at the bus station
6. for a moment

7. until tomorrow
8. about a boy
9. with my grandparents
10. from the first
11. of the people
12. into the sunset

ANSWERS

1. after the <u>party</u>
2. in the <u>morning</u>
3. beside the still <u>brook</u>
4. to the <u>city</u>
5. at the bus <u>station</u>
6. for a <u>moment</u>

7. until <u>tomorrow</u>
8. about a <u>boy</u>
9. with my <u>grandparents</u>
10. from the <u>first</u>
11. of the <u>people</u>
12. into the <u>sunset</u>

PRACTICE

Underline the prepositional phrases in the sentences below.

1. The dog was in the car.
2. In her childhood, she was a dancer.
3. Jensen took English classes at the college.
4. The horse raced around the track.
5. With great strides, he ran across the beach.
6. She was late for her meeting at the bank.
7. Before the workout, Fakid put his bag in the locker.
8. Underline the phrases in the sentences.
9. At the restaurant, the couple ordered a platter that came with a free beverage.
10. Until Monday, the stores in the downtown area have a no GST sale.

ANSWERS

1. The dog was <u>in the car</u>.

2. <u>In her childhood</u>, she was a dancer.

3. Jensen took English classes <u>at the college</u>.

4. The horse raced <u>around the track</u>.

5. <u>With great strides</u>, he ran <u>across the beach</u>.

6. She was late <u>for her meeting</u> <u>at the bank</u>.

7. <u>Before the workout</u>, Fakid put his bag <u>in the locker</u>.

8. Underline the phrases <u>in the sentences</u>.

9. <u>At the restaurant</u>, the couple ordered a platter that came <u>with a free beverage</u>.

10. <u>Until Monday</u>, the stores <u>in the downtown area</u> have a no GST sale.

CHALLENGE EXERCISE

Write phrases containing each of the following words:

in	under	to	at	with
beside	about	for	of	around
by	from	on	through	

Next, write sentences for each phrase.

CLAUSES

A **clause** is a group of words that go together. It has both a noun (or pronoun) AND a verb.

EXAMPLES

- because Jason (noun) went (verb) to Quebec City for a vacation
- that she (pronoun) was standing (verb) in the rain

PRACTICE

Underline the nouns in the clauses that follow.

1. when she went to the cottage last summer

2. Nancy enjoyed the forest by the lake

3. because life in the city seems so far from nature

4. Aldea was in a crowd scene in the movie

5. although she had never been an actress before

6. after her brief moment of fame had ended

7. she decided

8. that acting lessons would be a good idea

9. my first car was a 1967 Mustang

10. which I customized with chrome wheels and mag tires

11. despite what many people think

12. black is not my favourite colour

ANSWERS

1. when she went to the <u>cottage</u> last <u>summer</u>

2. <u>Nancy</u> enjoyed the <u>forest</u> by the <u>lake</u>

3. because <u>life</u> in the <u>city</u> seems so far from <u>nature</u>

4. <u>Aldea</u> was in a crowd <u>scene</u> in the <u>movie</u>

5. although she had never been an <u>actress</u> before

6. after her brief <u>moment</u> of <u>fame</u> had ended

7. she decided

8. that acting <u>lessons</u> would be a good <u>idea</u>

9. my first <u>car</u> was a 1967 <u>Mustang</u>

10. which I customized with chrome <u>wheels</u> and mag <u>tires</u>

11. despite what many <u>people</u> think

12. black is not my favourite <u>colour</u>

TIP

A clause contains both a noun or pronoun and a verb.

PRACTICE

Underline the verbs in the clauses.

1. when she went to the cottage last summer

2. Nancy enjoyed the forest by the lake

3. because life in the city seems so far from nature

4. Aldea was in a crowd scene in the movie

5. although she had never been an actress before

6. after her brief moment of fame had ended

7. she decided

8. that acting lessons would be a good idea

9. my first car was a 1967 Mustang

10. which I customized with chrome wheels and mag tires

11. despite what many people think

12. black is not my favourite colour

ANSWERS

1. when she <u>went</u> to the cottage last summer

2. Nancy <u>enjoyed</u> the forest by the lake

3. because life in the city <u>seems</u> so far from nature

4. Aldea <u>was</u> in a crowd scene in the movie

5. although she <u>had</u> never <u>been</u> an actress before

6. after her brief moment of fame <u>had ended</u>

PARTS OF A SENTENCE 149

7. she <u>decided</u>

8. that acting lessons <u>would be</u> a good idea

9. my first car <u>was</u> a 1967 Mustang

10. which I <u>customized</u> with chrome wheels and mag tires

11. despite what many people <u>think</u>

12. black <u>is</u> not my favourite colour

Types of Clauses

There are two types of clauses:

- Independent clauses
- Dependent / subordinate clauses

An **independent clause** could stand alone as a sentence.

EXAMPLES

- The guitar needed new strings
- The former model started a talent agency
- My grandfather and his brothers were all boxers in college

A **dependent / subordinate clause** cannot stand alone. It needs to be combined with an independent clause to make a complete sentence.

EXAMPLES

- because the old strings were broken
- after her own modeling career had ended
- although they all went on to other careers

TIP

An independent clause can stand alone as a sentence.

PRACTICE

Identify the independent clauses. Which of the following clauses could stand alone as a sentence?

1. when she went to the cottage last summer

2. Nancy enjoyed the forest by the lake

3. because life in the city was so busy and stressful

4. Aldea was in a crowd scene in the movie

5. although she had never been an actress before

6. after her brief moment of fame had ended

7. she decided

8. that acting lessons would be a good idea

9. my first car was a 1967 Mustang

10. which I customized with chrome wheels and mag tires

11. despite what many people think

12. black is not my favourite colour

ANSWERS

2, 4, 7, 9, 12

CHALLENGE EXERCISE

Combine the clauses in the previous exercise to make complete sentences. Try to use all of the clauses. Discuss your answers with a teacher, friend, or another student.

SIMPLE SUBJECTS

The **simple subject** of a sentence is the person, place, or thing that the sentence is about. It can be a

- Noun
- Pronoun
- Noun phrase

The simple subject is usually, but not always, found near the beginning of the sentence. It is the one who is doing the action or is being described. It is the one the sentence is about.

EXAMPLES

- The <u>dog</u> wanted to go for a walk.
- <u>They</u> arrived early for dinner.
- <u>That you can hold your breath for so long</u> is amazing.

The first sentence is about the dog. It is the dog who wants to go for a walk. The subject of the second sentence is "they," the pronoun doing the action. In the final example, what is it that is amazing? It is not simply one word. It is the whole thing, "that you can hold your breath for so long," that is being discussed.

TIP

Simple subject—the person, place, or thing that the sentence is about.

PRACTICE

Underline the simple subject in the following sentences.

1. They say you should never cook with a wine you wouldn't drink.

2. The competition has launched the careers of several star singers.

3. The hair stylist took too much off last time I got a cut.

4. She bought her sister some leopard pattern sneakers for her birthday.

5. Our granddaughter will be four years old in September.

6. Prom is apparently all about the dress.

7. She had a hard time deciding whom to vote for in the election.

8. Playing the trombone is a lot of fun.

9. I am not sure what this book is about.

10. Have you ever ridden a horse?

11. The key to my car is broken off in the lock.

12. Having a true friend is one of the most important things in life.

ANSWERS

1. <u>They</u> say you should never cook with a wine you wouldn't drink.

2. The <u>competition</u> has launched the careers of several star singers.

3. The hair <u>stylist</u> took too much off last time I got a cut.

4. <u>She</u> bought her sister some leopard pattern sneakers for her birthday.

5. Our <u>granddaughter</u> will be four years old in September.

6. <u>Prom</u> is apparently all about the dress.

7. <u>She</u> had a hard time deciding whom to vote for in the election.

8. <u>Playing the trombone</u> is a lot of fun.

9. <u>I</u> am not sure what this book is about.

10. Have <u>you</u> ever ridden a horse?

11. The <u>key</u> to my car is broken off in the lock.

12. <u>Having a true friend</u> is one of the most important things in life.

A simple subject is usually near the beginning of a sentence, but not always. Sometimes, a phrase or dependent clause at the beginning gives information about when, where, or in what way. The subject is not in this part. The subject is always in the independent clause of the sentence.

TIP

The subject is always in the independent clause of the sentence.

EXAMPLES

- After the movie, <u>we</u> went for dinner.
- With a loud bang, the <u>car</u> finally started.
- Although she likes country music, the <u>radio</u> was blasting rock and roll.

PRACTICE

Underline the simple subjects in the following sentences.

1. If you like to download music, you should always do it legally.

2. Because he wasn't feeling well, Tim didn't go to school today.

3. Even though Carol doesn't really like children, she works in a daycare.

4. Andrea likes working out in the morning because it helps her wake up.

5. On their first album, the band did a remake of an old classic.

6. Before Manuel went to see the dentist, he brushed.

7. While the judges watched carefully, the cheerleading squad went through their routine.

8. In the first act of the play, the lead actress tripped on her dress.

9. Although they have not taken ballroom dance lessons, they are very good at the foxtrot.

10. Chylynn resisted buying anything at the sale although she loves to shop.

152 HOW TO PREPARE FOR THE GED® TEST, CANADIAN EDITION

11. After spending thirty minutes on the treadmill in his basement, Tristan rested.

12. The flight was about to board when Jules realized that he had forgotten his passport.

ANSWERS

1. If you like to download music, <u>you</u> should always do it legally.

2. Because he wasn't feeling well, <u>Tim</u> didn't go to school today.

3. Even though Carol doesn't really like children, <u>she</u> works in a daycare.

4. <u>Andrea</u> likes working out in the morning because it helps her wake up.

5. On their first album, the <u>band</u> did a remake of an old classic.

6. Before Manuel went to see the dentist, <u>he</u> brushed.

7. While the judges watched carefully, the cheerleading <u>squad</u> went through their routine.

8. In the first act of the play, the lead <u>actress</u> tripped on her dress.

9. Although they have not taken ballroom dance lessons, <u>they</u> are very good at the foxtrot.

10. <u>Chylynn</u> resisted buying anything at the sale although she loves to shop.

11. After spending thirty minutes on the treadmill in his basement, <u>Tristan</u> rested.

12. The <u>flight</u> was about to board when Jules realized that he had forgotten his passport.

Compound Subjects

A **compound subject** is a list of two or more simple subjects joined with the words *and, or, nor.*

> **EXAMPLES**
>
> - <u>Gina</u> and <u>Steve</u> enjoyed the movie.
> - <u>Raul</u>, <u>Kassandra</u>, and <u>Walter</u> took a trip to Cuba.
> - Either the <u>wallpaper</u> or the <u>carpet</u> has to go.
> - Neither <u>Arturo</u> nor <u>Miguel</u> plays football.

PRACTICE

Combine each group of sentences to make one sentence with a compound subject.

Example:
Kris has a new job. Lynda has a new job.
Kris and Lynda have new jobs.

1. Salmon was on sale at the fish market. Scallops were also on sale.

2. My mother gossiped for hours. She gossiped with her friends.

3. Marcus was not at the meeting. Jessica was not at the meeting either.

4. Sherri will drive me to the airport. Justine might drive me to the airport instead.

5. Michael Ondaatje is a famous Canadian writer. Alice Munro is another famous Canadian writer.

6. Amanda has not done her homework. Olamide has not done hers either.

7. The band April Wine was inducted into the Canadian Music Hall of Fame. Rush was also inducted into the Canadian Music Hall of Fame.

8. Credit cards are accepted forms of payment. Debit cards can be used in the alternative.

ANSWERS

1. Salmon and scallops were on sale at the fish market.

2. My mother and her friends gossiped for hours.

3. Neither Marcus nor Jessica was at the meeting.

4. Either Sherri or Justine will drive me to the airport.

5. Michael Ondaatje and Alice Munro are famous Canadian writers.

6. Neither Amanda nor Olamide has done her homework.

7. The bands April Wine and Rush were inducted into the Canadian Music Hall of Fame.

8. Either credit cards or debit cards are accepted forms of payment. (Credit cards and debit cards are accepted forms of payment.)

CHALLENGE EXERCISE

Select one or two paragraphs in a newspaper, book, or magazine. Underline the simple subject in each sentence. Discuss your answers with a teacher, friend, or another student.

SIMPLE PREDICATES

The **simple predicate** of a sentence is the main verb that describes the subject. It describes the action or condition of the subject. The simple predicate can be a(n):

- Action verb
- Non-action verb
- Main verb with its auxiliary / helping verbs

> ### EXAMPLES
>
> - *Devon* plays the piano.
> - *Maria* has three children.
> - *Mariah* has been baking all day.

To identify the simple predicate of a sentence, it is helpful to first identify the subject.

PRACTICE

Underline the simple subject and make bold-italic the simple predicate in the following sentences.

1. Nathan wants to be a reporter.

2. She went to the grocery store.

3. Alexa loves sailing.

4. Joachim was early for the meeting.

5. Chantal has always loved figure skating.

6.   Vancouver is beautiful in the summer.

7.   Nathan will arrive on the evening train.

8.   Winnipeg is known as a multicultural city.

9.   Evangeline was the name of my grandmother.

10.   Mary has travelled widely in Canada.

11.   Derrick has not been having a good day.

12.   Half of British Columbia is comprised of a vast wilderness.

ANSWERS

1.   <u>Nathan</u> ***wants*** to be a reporter.

2.   <u>She</u> ***went*** to the grocery store.

3.   <u>Alexa</u> ***loves*** sailing.

4.   <u>Joachim</u> ***was*** early for the meeting.

5.   <u>Chantal</u> ***has*** always ***loved*** figure skating.

6.   <u>Vancouver</u> ***is*** beautiful in the summer.

7.   <u>Nathan</u> ***will arrive*** on the evening train.

8.   <u>Winnipeg</u> ***is known*** as a multicultural city.

9.   <u>Evangeline</u> ***was*** the name of my grandmother.

10.   <u>Mary</u> ***has travelled*** widely in Canada.

11.   <u>Derrick</u> ***has*** not ***been having*** a good day.

12.   <u>Half</u> of British Columbia ***is comprised*** of a vast wilderness.

Remember that the simple subject and simple predicate are always in the main part of the sentence.

TIP

Remember—
not is not a verb
and *never* is
never a verb.

PRACTICE

Underline the simple subject and make bold-italic the simple predicate in the following sentences.

1.   When we arrived, we discovered that the airline had lost our luggage.

2.   Although we were concerned, we did not make a big fuss.

3.   On Thanksgiving Day, the whole family were gathered for dinner.

4.   Soon after her eighteenth birthday, Samantha was standing first in line to vote in her first election.

5.   If Simon wants to be a fire fighter, he will need to be in better condition.

6.   To help protect peace at home, Canadian troops serve as peace keepers abroad.

7.   Although she says she doesn't like oysters, she has never eaten one.

8.   Canada's first television stations began broadcasting in Toronto and Montreal in 1952.

9.   When many politicians give speeches, they use teleprompters.

10.   One of the biggest board games ever, Trivial Pursuit was invented by two Canadians.

11. In the Yukon Territory, summer days have almost twenty-four hours of daylight.

12. Despite the sunny weather, a cold wind is blowing off the ocean.

ANSWERS

1. When we arrived, <u>we</u> ***discovered*** that the airline had lost our luggage.

2. Although we were concerned, <u>we</u> ***did*** not ***make*** a big fuss.

3. On Thanksgiving Day, the whole <u>family</u> ***were gathered*** for dinner.

4. Soon after her eighteenth birthday, <u>Samantha</u> ***was standing*** first in line to vote in her first election.

5. If Simon wants to be a fire fighter, <u>he</u> ***will need*** to be in better condition.

6. To help protect peace at home, Canadian <u>troops</u> ***serve*** as peace keepers abroad.

7. Although she says she doesn't like oysters, <u>she</u> ***has*** never ***eaten*** one.

8. Canada's first television <u>stations</u> ***began broadcasting*** in Toronto and Montreal in 1952.

9. When many politicians give speeches, <u>they</u> ***use*** teleprompters.

10. One of the biggest board games ever, <u>Trivial Pursuit</u> ***was invented*** by two Canadians.

11. In the Yukon Territory, summer <u>days</u> ***have*** almost twenty-four hours of daylight.

12. Despite the sunny weather, a cold <u>wind</u> ***is blowing*** off the ocean.

Compound Predicates

A **compound predicate** is a list of two or more simple predicates joined by *and, or, nor*.

EXAMPLES

- The motorcycle engine <u>sputtered</u>, <u>coughed</u>, and <u>died</u>.
- The poker player either <u>will call</u> or <u>will fold</u>.
- She neither <u>heard</u> nor <u>saw</u> anything

PRACTICE

Combine each group of sentences to make one sentence with a compound predicate.

Example:
   James swept the floor. James also washed the floor.
   James swept and washed the floor.

1. The apple tree was flowering. It was beginning to bear fruit.

2. Caroline did not study for the exam. She did not prepare for the exam.

3. The soccer team ran at practice. They also did core exercises at practice.

4. Although Marcus was treated unfairly, he did not complain. He did not protest.

5. Robert writes children's books. He illustrates children's books.

6. The clouds were gathering. The clouds were threatening rain.

ANSWERS

1. The apple tree <u>was</u> <u>flowering</u> and <u>beginning</u> to bear fruit.
   or The apple tree <u>was</u> <u>flowering</u> and <u>was beginning</u> to bear fruit.

2. Caroline <u>did</u> not <u>study</u> or <u>prepare</u> for the exam.
   or Caroline neither <u>studied</u> nor <u>prepared</u> for the exam.

3. The soccer team <u>ran</u> and <u>did</u> core exercises at practice.

4. Although Marcus was treated unfairly, he <u>did</u> not <u>complain</u> or <u>protest</u>.
   or Although Marcus was treated unfairly, he neither <u>complained</u> nor <u>protested</u>.

5. Robert <u>writes</u> and <u>illustrates</u> children's books.

6. The clouds <u>were</u> <u>gathering</u> and <u>threatening</u> rain.
   or The clouds <u>were gathering</u> and <u>were threatening</u> rain.

CHALLENGE EXERCISE

Look at the exercises on previous pages in which you underlined simple subjects. Circle the simple predicates. Discuss your answers with a teacher, friend, or another student.

CHAPTER CHECK-UP

Complete these practice exercises, and check the answers and analysis that follow (on page 163). After you mark your work, review any topic in the chapter that you had trouble with or did not understand.

1. Write definitions in your own words for each of the terms.

Noun   _____

Pronoun   _____

Verb   _____

Simple Subject   _____

Simple Predicate _____

Phrase   _____

Clause   _____

Independent Clause _____

Questions 2–10 are based on the following article.

(A)

(1) When preparing for a job interview, candidates should dress for success. (2) Appearance plays a vital role and creates the first impression. (3) The clothes you wear say a lot about who you are and your suitability for the job.

(B)

(4) Depending on the type of job you are applying for, different clothing may be appropriate, which means that you should choose clothes that match the job. (5) For example, when applying for a business position, you should wear business attire. (6) For men, this means dress pants and shirt, together with a tie and jacket. (7) For women, business attire might include a business suit with pants or skirt, a coordinated blouse, and conservative shoes. (8) In short, dress professionally for a professional position.

(C)

(9) Other types of positions require different apparel. (10) For example, no one will hire a person in a business suit to work in a warehouse or do landscaping. (11) However, you should always be clean and neat, and avoid excessive jewellery and makeup and strong scents. (12) Depending on the job, tattoos and piercings should also be minimized to make them less visible. (13) Your appearance tells the employer that you are serious about the job and that you will be a dependable employee.

2. Sentence 1: When preparing for a job interview, candidates should dress for success.

    Which of these words is a noun?

    (1) when
    (2) preparing
    (3) should
    (4) dress
    (5) success

3. Sentence 2: Appearance plays a vital role and creates the first impression.

    What is the simple predicate of this sentence?

    (1) plays and creates
    (2) appearance
    (3) plays
    (4) creates
    (5) impression

4. Sentence 4: <u>Depending on the type of job you are applying for</u>, different clothing may be appropriate, which means that you should choose clothes that match the job.

    The underlined portion of this sentence is a
    (1) prepositional phrase
    (2) clause
    (3) independent clause
    (4) simple subject
    (5) simple predicate

5. Sentence 5: For example, when applying for a business position, you should wear business attire.

   Which of these words is a pronoun?

   (1) example
   (2) applying
   (3) position
   (4) you
   (5) should

6. Sentence 6: For men, this means dress pants and shirt, together with a tie and jacket.

   What is the simple subject of the sentence?

   (1) men
   (2) this
   (3) dress pants
   (4) together
   (5) tie and jacket

7. Sentence 8: In short, dress professionally <u>for a professional position</u>.

   The underlined portion of this sentence is a

   (1) prepositional phrase
   (2) clause
   (3) independent clause
   (4) simple subject
   (5) simple predicate

8. Sentence 9: Other types of positions require different apparel.

   What is the simple predicate of this sentence?

   (1) types
   (2) positions
   (3) require
   (4) different
   (5) types of positions

9. Sentence 10: For example, no one will hire a person in a business suit to work in a warehouse or do landscaping.

   Which of the words in this sentence is a pronoun?

   (1) no one
   (2) person
   (3) suit
   (4) warehouse
   (5) do

10. Sentence 12: Depending on the job, <u>tattoos and piercings</u> should also be minimized to make them less visible.

   The underlined portion of this sentence could best be described as a

   (1) simple subject
   (2) phrase
   (3) simple predicate
   (4) clause
   (5) independent clause

Questions 11–20 are based on the following paragraph.

(1) Parents are a problem in youth sports. (2) Many focus on winning instead of fun. (3) Good coaches see the big picture. (4) They know that not all winning is done on the scoreboard. (5) They may require their parents to sign a contract that states that they will only say positive things to everyone involved in a competition.

11. Sentence 1: Parents are a problem in youth sports.

   What are the nouns in this sentence?

   (1) parents, sports
   (2) parents, problem, sports
   (3) problem, youth
   (4) are, problem, youth
   (5) parents, are, problem, youth

12. Sentence 1: Parents are a problem in youth sports.

   What is the simple subject of the sentence?

   (1) parents
   (2) are
   (3) problem
   (4) youth
   (5) sports

13. Sentence 3: Good coaches see the big picture.

   What is the simple predicate of the sentence?

   (1) coaches
   (2) see
   (3) big
   (4) picture
   (5) the big picture

14. Sentence 3: Good coaches see the big picture.

    What is the simple subject of the sentence?

    (1) coaches
    (2) see
    (3) big
    (4) picture
    (5) the big picture

15. Sentence 4: They know that not all winning is done on the scoreboard.

    What prepositional phrase is contained in this sentence?

    (1) they know
    (2) that
    (3) all winning
    (4) is done
    (5) on the scoreboard

16. Sentence 5: They may require their parents to sign a contract that states that they will only say positive things to everyone involved in a competition.

    What are the pronouns in the sentence?

    (1) they
    (2) they, their, contract
    (3) they, their, that, that, they, everyone
    (4) require, sign, states, say
    (5) parents, contract, things, competition

17. Sentence 5: They may require their parents to sign a contract that states that they will only say positive things to everyone involved in a competition.

    What are the nouns in the sentence?

    (1) they
    (2) they, their, contract
    (3) they, their, that, that, they, everyone
    (4) require, sign, states, say
    (5) parents, contract, things, competition

18. Sentence 5: They may require their parents to sign a contract that states that they will only say positive things to everyone involved in a competition.

    What are the verbs in the sentence?

    (1) they
    (2) they, their, contract
    (3) they, their, that, that, they, everyone
    (4) require, sign, states, say
    (5) parents, contract, things, competition

19. Sentence 5: They may require their parents to sign a contract that states that they will only say positive things to everyone involved in a competition.

What is the simple subject of the sentence?

(1) they
(2) parents
(3) contract
(4) things
(5) competition

20. Sentence 5: They may require their parents to sign a contract that states that they will only say positive things to everyone involved in a competition.

What is the simple predicate of the sentence?

(1) may require
(2) states
(3) say
(4) will say
(5) parents

21. Which of the following are independent clauses? Choose all that apply.

(1) Although he was late
(2) He arrived
(3) Before the meeting started
(4) If you don't put on sunscreen
(5) You may get a burn
(6) Shimerra worked on a large dairy farm
(7) That her uncle bought in Alberta
(8) Although she doesn't like cows or getting dirty
(9) The flowers in the vase on the centre of the table died
(10) Because they had been there for a very long time

22. Combine each group of clauses to make one sentence. Then underline the simple subject and put the simple predicate in bold-italic.

Example:
    When it started to rain
    Because the bus was late
    The children got very wet
    When it started to rain, the <u>children</u> **got** *very wet because the bus was late.*

(1) Although he was late
    He arrived
    Before the meeting started

(2) If you don't put on sunscreen
    You may get a burn

(3)   Shimerra worked on a large dairy farm

That her uncle bought in Alberta

Although she doesn't like cows or getting dirty

(4)   The flowers in the vase on the centre of the table died

Because they had been there for a very long time

ANSWERS AND ANALYSIS

1. Your answers will be similar to those below.

   - Noun: names or labels a person, place, thing, or abstraction
   - Pronoun: substitutes for a noun
   - Verb: names an action or indicates a condition or state of being
   - Simple Subject: the person, place, or thing that the sentence is about
   - Simple Predicate: the main verb that describes the action or condition of the subject
   - Phrase: a group of words that go together
   - Clause: a group of words that go together and contain both a noun and a verb
   - Independent Clause: a clause that could stand alone as a sentence

2. **(5)** success—success is an abstract thing, therefore a noun

3. **(1)** plays and creates—the simple subject, appearance, does two things. It plays and creates. This is a compound predicate.

4. **(2)** clause—this group of words contains both nouns and verbs, but cannot stand alone as a sentence. It is a subordinate or dependent clause.

5. **(4)** you—a pronoun that takes the place of the noun, which is the name of the person addressed

6. **(2)** this—remember that the simple subject is found in the main part of the sentence, which in this case is, *this means dress pants and shirt*. The subject is the pronoun *this*. The simple predicate is the verb *means*.

7. **(1)** prepositional phrase—a group of words that goes together and begins with a preposition, such as for, in, at, or, to, etc.

8. **(3)** require—this verb describes the simple subject *types*

9. **(1)** no one—an indefinite pronoun

10. **(1)** tattoos and piercings—a list of two or more simple subjects joined with the words *and, or, nor*

11. **(2)** parents, problem, sports—each of these words labels a thing

12. **(1)** parents—the sentence is about the noun *parents*

13. **(2)** see—the verb modifies the simple subject *coaches*

14. **(1)** coaches—the sentence is about the noun *coaches*

15. **(5)** on the scoreboard—a phrase beginning with the preposition *on*

16. **(3)** they, their, that, that, they, everyone—each of these is a personal, possessive, relative, or indefinite pronoun

17. **(5)** parents, contract, things, competition—each of the other choices given includes either a pronoun or verb

18. **(4)** require, sign, states, say—each is an action verb. All other responses contain either nouns or pronouns.

19. **(1)** they—it is *they*, meaning the coaches, who may require their parents to sign a contract

20. **(1)** may require—the verb phrase that describes the simple subject

21. The following are independent clauses:

     (2) He arrived
     (5) You may get a burn
     (6) Shimerra worked on a large dairy farm
     (9) The flowers in the vase on the centre of the table died

22. Your answers may be similar to those below.

     (1) Although he was late, <u>he</u> ***arrived*** before the meeting started.
     (2) If you don't put on sunscreen, <u>you</u> ***may get*** a burn.
     (3) Although she doesn't like cows or getting dirty, <u>Shimerra</u> ***worked*** on a large dairy farm that her uncle bought in Alberta.
     (4) The <u>flowers</u> in the vase on the centre of the table ***died*** because they had been there for a very long time.

Types of Sentences

2

SIMPLE SENTENCES

A **simple sentence** consists of a single independent clause:

- It has a subject and a predicate.
- It expresses a complete thought.

A **simple sentence** has only one subject and one predicate.

<u>Amir</u> <u>sings</u> in a local choir.
(This simple sentence is an independent clause with one subject "Amir" and one predicate "sings.")

TIP

A simple sentence has one subject and one predicate.

Sometimes the subject could be understood, such as the command "Go brush your teeth." The subject is the word "you," which is understood although not written. "You go brush your teeth."

Also, the subject or predicate could be compound. That is, there could be two or more elements joined with a word such as "and," "but," or "or."

Myra and Connor entered a contest and won a trip to Florida.
(This is also a simple sentence. It is a single independent clause with a compound subject "Myra and Connor" and a compound predicate "entered and won."

PRACTICE

Which of the following could stand alone as an independent clause or simple sentence?

1. Every simple sentence is an example of an independent clause
2. If Sherry wants to sell her house
3. Do not look at me that way
4. Although we have not been introduced
5. Lynda and Scott went to the coffee shop
6. Jenna and Lawrence went to dinner and went dancing
7. The police car that was hidden near the construction zone
8. Stop
9. Some of the recipes on the cooking channel
10. The woman with the red dress, the high heeled black boots, and the silver wig
11. Mary arrived
12. The red car with the shiny wheels swerved and avoided the oncoming truck.

ANSWERS

1, 3, 5, 6, 8, 11, 12

The cat	ate	the food
Subject →	**Verb** →	**Object**

Simple sentences can be different lengths. They can be short, as the single word command "Stop!" (with the understood subject, "you"). Simple sentences can also be long, with additional descriptive words or phrases.

EXAMPLES

The cat ate the food.
The scruffy grey cat from the white house across the street ate the entire bowl of delicious food.

PRACTICE

Combine each of the following groups of sentences to create one sentence.

> **Example:**
>
> I bought a new car.
> The car was red.
> The car was a sports car.
>
> **Answer:** I bought a new red sports car.

1. Nicole wants to study at the university.
   She wants to study mechanical engineering.

2. Mercy went to Victoria.
   Her sister Faith went to Victoria too.
   They went so that they could go shopping.

3. Marcie wrote a new song.
   The song is a country song.
   The song is beautiful.

4. Jordon has a dog.
   The dog is a beagle.
   The dog is friendly.
   The dog's name is Waldo.

5. Lynda has a granddaughter.
   The granddaughter is four years old.
   Her name is Madison.

6. The store has a sale on computers.
   The computers are laptops.
   The sale price is 25% off.

7. Tyler will arrive on the bus.
   This will take place in the morning.
   The bus will come from Hamilton.

8. There is a printer in the office.
   It is a colour printer.
   The printer is broken.

9. Karen works as counsellor.
   She is a counsellor for teenagers.
   The teenagers have addiction problems.

10. There was a racoon.
    The racoon got into our garbage.
    This happened at the campground.

11. Alexis went to the flea market.
    Stephen went to the flea market too.
    They went to buy some children's clothes.
    They went to buy some toys.

12. Myra is a nurse.
    She works at the hospital.
    She works in the emergency department.

ANSWERS

Your answers may differ slightly but will be similar to those below.

1. Nicole wants to study mechanical engineering at the university.
2. Mercy and her sister Faith went to Victoria to shop.
3. Marcie wrote a beautiful new country song.
4. Jordon has a friendly beagle named Waldo.
5. Lynda has a four-year-old granddaughter named Madison.
6. The store has a 25% off sale on laptop computers.
7. In the morning, Tyler will arrive on the bus from Hamilton.
8. The colour printer in the office is broken.
9. Karen works as counsellor for teenagers with addiction problems.
10. At the campground, a racoon got into our garbage.
11. Alexis and Stephen went to the flea market to buy some children's clothes and toys.
12. Myra works as a nurse in the hospital emergency department.

CHALLENGE EXERCISE

Headlines or titles of newspaper or magazine articles are often abbreviated short sentences. Look at a newspaper or magazine or find one on the Internet. Find five headlines and rewrite them as simple sentences. Discuss your answers with a teacher, friend, or another student.

Example: Local Boat Wins Race
               A local sailboat won a race.

COMPOUND SENTENCES

A **compound sentence** occurs when two sentences are joined together using:

- A comma and a joining word
- A semi-colon
- A semi-colon and a connecting adverb

Since both parts of a compound sentence could stand alone as independent clauses, they are equally important. This also means that there is a subject and a predicate in each part.

EXAMPLES

Sonya likes smoked salmon. (simple sentence)
Erin does not. (simple sentence)
Sonya likes smoked salmon, but Erin does not. (compound sentence)

Compound Sentence

Sentence   +   , but   +   Sentence
                , and

One way to make a compound sentence is to use a comma and a joining word (coordinating conjunction). These are the most common joining words used to make a compound sentence:

and   but   so   or   nor

Other possible joining words are *for* (meaning "because") and *yet* (meaning "but").

EXAMPLES

We went to the market, and we bought some corn.
She likes contemporary dance, but she doesn't like tap.
The dog was afraid of the storm, so she hid under the bed.

PRACTICE

Use a comma and a joining word to make a compound sentence.

Example: Maria and Ted went on a cruise. They left their kids at home.
Maria and Ted went on a cruise, but they left their kids at home.

1. She went to Banff. She did not go to Lake Louise.
2. Kareem's watch had stopped. He was late for the meeting.
3. The sun set. The moon shone over the water.
4. Will Zane take piano lessons? Will he study guitar instead?
5. *Heart* is not a Canadian band. They began their career in Canada.
6. The truck was driving slowly. Katelyn pulled out to pass it.
7. Ben does not like green beans. He does not like yellow beans.
8. Paco worked at the youth centre. He has retired now.
9. The clouds are coming in. The rain will soon follow.
10. Carla and Holly drove from Toronto to Thunder Bay. Then they continued on to Winnipeg.
11. In the winter, Naomi likes to ski. She has difficulty getting time off work to go.
12. Some children are allergic to nuts. Nuts are banned in many schools.

> **TIP**
>
> This is a compound sentence: "She likes ham, and she likes eggs."
>
> This is NOT a compound sentence: "She likes ham and eggs."

ANSWERS

Your answers may differ slightly but will be similar to those below.

1. She went to Banff, but she did not go to Lake Louise.
2. Kareem's watch had stopped, so he was late for the meeting.
3. The sun set, and the moon shone over the water.
4. Will Zane take piano lessons, or will he study guitar instead?
5. *Heart* is not a Canadian band, but they began their career in Canada.
6. The truck was driving slowly, so Katelyn pulled out to pass it.
7. Ben does not like green beans, nor does he like yellow beans.
8. Paco worked at the youth centre, but he has retired now.
9. The clouds are coming in, and the rain will soon follow.
10. Carla and Holly drove from Toronto to Thunder Bay, and then they continued on to Winnipeg.
11. In the winter, Naomi likes to ski, but she has difficulty getting time off work to go.
12. Some children are allergic to nuts, so nuts are banned in many schools.

Another way to make a compound sentence is to join the sentences with a semi-colon. This is usually done only if the ideas are closely related.

EXAMPLES

Cathy enjoys buying shoes. (simple sentence)
She owns more than thirty pair. (simple sentence)
Cathy enjoys buying shoes; she owns more than thirty pair. (compound sentence)

PRACTICE

Use a semi-colon to combine each of the following into a compound sentence.

1. The branch gave way. The kitten tumbled to the ground.
2. The party next door was very loud. It kept Tobias awake all night.
3. Kevin loves motorcycles. He has driven them for years.
4. The children's shoes were soaked. They had been jumping in mud puddles.

ANSWERS

1. The branch gave way; the kitten tumbled to the ground.
2. The party next door was very loud; it kept Tobias awake all night.
3. Kevin loves motorcycles; he has driven them for years.
4. The children's shoes were soaked; they had been jumping in mud puddles.

Another way to make a compound sentence is to use a semi-colon, a connecting adverb, and a comma. A connecting adverb is not a joining word, but it shows the close relationship between the sentences. It includes words such as the following:

however	therefore	nevertheless
consequently	obviously	fortunately
unfortunately	otherwise	moreover

EXAMPLES

The kitten tumbled from the tree; fortunately, it landed safely
The party next door was very loud; consequently, Tobias did not get much sleep.
Kevin loves motorcycles; however, he does not own one.
The children had been jumping in mud puddles; therefore, their shoes were soaked.

Compound Sentence
Sentence + ; however, + Sentence

PRACTICE

Make a compound sentence using the connecting adverb given.

Example: She is a popular American singer. She was born in Canada.
however
She is a popular American singer; however, she was born in Canada.

1. The car ran out of gas. It stopped right in front of a gas station.
fortunately

2. The credit card offered many rewards. It also had a high interest rate.
however

3. The dog is eleven years old. He thinks he is a puppy.
nevertheless

4. Cars are more complicated than they used to be. They are harder to fix yourself.
consequently

5. We thought she had left. We were wrong.
obviously

6. The children surprised us by cleaning the house. They did all the dishes.
moreover

7. Mark and Peter arrived late for the barbeque. The food was all gone.
unfortunately

8. It rained the last day we were in Florida. The weather was beautiful.
otherwise

9. We are supposed to have a lightning storm today. The soccer game is cancelled.
therefore

ANSWERS

1. The car ran out of gas; <u>fortunately,</u> it stopped right in front of a gas station.

2. The credit card offered many rewards; <u>however,</u> it also had a high interest rate.

3. The dog is eleven years old; <u>nevertheless,</u> he thinks he is a puppy.

4. Cars are more complicated than they used to be; <u>consequently,</u> they are harder to fix yourself.

5. We thought she had left; <u>obviously,</u> we were wrong.

6. The children surprised us by cleaning the house; <u>moreover,</u> they did all the dishes.

7. Mark and Peter arrived late for the barbeque; <u>unfortunately,</u> the food was all gone.

8. It rained the last day we were in Florida; <u>otherwise,</u> the weather was beautiful.

9. We are supposed to have a lightning storm today; <u>therefore,</u> the soccer game is cancelled.

PRACTICE

Choose the best answer to each of the following questions:

1. Our hockey team went to Medicine <u>Hat and they</u> had a great time.

   What is the best way to write the underlined part of this sentence? If you think the original is the best way, choose option (1).

   (1) Hat and they
   (2) Hat, and they
   (3) Hat. And they
   (4) Hat; and they
   (5) Hat and. They

2. Petrov and Bernice work in a restaurant. But they are planning to start a business of their own.

   Which correction should be made to the passage above?

   (1) insert a comma before <u>and Bernice</u>
   (2) replace the period after <u>restaurant</u> with a comma and remove the capitalization
   (3) insert a comma after <u>But</u>
   (4) insert a period after <u>planning</u>
   (5) No correction necessary

3. Samuel Champlain discovered a new river on Saint John the Baptist Day. He called it the Saint John River.

   A compound sentence based on these sentences could include which of the following?

   (1) Saint John the Baptist Day, but he called it
   (2) Saint John the Baptist Day, he called it
   (3) Saint John the Baptist Day; he called it
   (4) Saint John the Baptist Day; otherwise, he called it
   (5) Saint John the Baptist Day and he called it

4. Michel's car has broken down <u>several times, consequently he</u> carries an emergency kit in the trunk.

    What is the best way to write the underlined part of this sentence? If you think the original is the best way, choose option (1).

    (1) several times, consequently he
    (2) several times, consequently, he
    (3) several times; consequently he
    (4) several times; consequently, he
    (5) several times consequently he

5. Both a chipmunk and a squirrel visited our campsite and I concluded that chipmunks are much cuter and less high strung.

    What correction should be made to this sentence?

    (1) insert a comma after <u>chipmunk</u>
    (2) insert a comma after <u>campsite</u>
    (3) insert a comma after <u>cuter</u>
    (4) insert a semi-colon after <u>campsite</u>
    (5) insert a period after <u>concluded</u>

6. Carmel was not feeling well. She went to cheerleading practice.

    A compound sentence based on these sentences could include which of the following?

    (1) feeling well and she went
    (2) feeling well; but she went
    (3) feeling well; and, she went
    (4) feeling well, but she went
    (5) feeling well, she went

7. Fakid is a long distance <u>runner and an excellent</u> tennis player.

    What is the best way to write the underlined part of this sentence?

    (1) runner, and an excellent
    (2) runner. An excellent
    (3) runner; an excellent
    (4) runner; and, an excellent
    (5) No correction necessary

8. Good nutrition is an important part of a healthy lifestyle. It is important to follow Canada's Food Guide.

    A compound sentence based on these sentences could include which of the following?

    (1) lifestyle, but it is important
    (2) lifestyle; consequently, it is important
    (3) lifestyle, however, it is important
    (4) lifestyle and it is important
    (5) lifestyle; and it is important

TIP

A complex sentence has one main idea and one or more ideas that are less important (subordinate).

COMPLEX SENTENCES

A **complex sentence** is an independent clause joined with one or more dependent clauses using:

- A subordinate conjunction
- A relative pronoun

A complex sentence has one independent clause (a part that could stand alone as a sentence). It also has one or more dependent (or subordinate) clauses that cannot stand alone because they do not form a complete sentence.

Here are some examples of dependent clauses:

> Because she loves him
> Who we met last year
> Until the final song is played

Dependent clauses cannot stand alone, so they are not as important as the independent clause. Dependent clauses can be found at the beginning, end, or middle of the sentence.

There are many subordinate conjunctions that can be used to begin a dependent clause and make a complex sentence. Here are some of the most common:

because	despite	where	even though
although	since	as	while
until	before	after	as long as
when	if	unless	

A dependent clause can also begin with a relative pronoun, such as

who	whom	whose
which	that	what
whomever	whichever	whatever

PRACTICE

In the complex sentences that follow, underline the independent clause. Make bold-italic the subordinate conjunctions and relative pronouns.

Examples:

> ***If*** Janice goes to the store, she will pick up a dozen eggs.
> Harold is always tired at work ***because*** he stays up too late at night.
> Squirrels, ***although*** they are very cute, can be quite destructive to property.
> ***Although*** the car is old, it runs well ***unless*** it is raining.

1. While his mother was sleeping, Baby Eric climbed out of his crib.

2. The girl with the golden hair sat at the table alone until her date finally arrived.

3. Whatever our country's faults may be, I am proud to be a Canadian.

4. If you think you can do better, you are welcome to try although I don't think you will succeed.

5. When Mary and Bob returned from their trip, they discovered that they had left the front door unlocked the whole time.

6. My wife has a new red cell phone, which she got to match the colour of her car.

7. Where the forest was touched by fire, more wildflowers are now growing than you can imagine.

8. Someone told her that iceberg lettuce has no nutritional value.

9. Although the weather is cold, we will meet at Lookout Point where we are going star gazing.

10. Wherever you may wander in your life, I will be there.

11. Coyotes, which are not native to Eastern Canada, are now starting to become a problem.

12. The International Monetary Fund is important to world peace because it helps to stabilize national economies and prevent social unrest.

ANSWERS

1. *While* his mother was sleeping, Baby Eric climbed out of his crib.

2. The girl with the golden hair sat at the table alone *until* her date finally arrived.

3. *Whatever* our country's faults may be, I am proud to be a Canadian.

4. *If* you think you can do better, you are welcome to try *although* I don't think you will succeed.

5. *When* Mary and Bob returned from their trip, they discovered *that* they had left the front door unlocked the whole time.

6. My wife has a new red cell phone, *which* she got to match the colour of her car.

7. *Where* the forest was touched by fire, more wildflowers are now growing *than* you can imagine.

8. Someone told her *that* iceberg lettuce has no nutritional value.

9. *Although* the weather is cold, we will meet at Lookout Point *where* we are going star gazing.

10. *Wherever* you may wander in your life, I will be there.

11. Coyotes, *which* are not native to Eastern Canada, are now starting to become a problem.

12. The International Monetary Fund is important to world peace *because* it helps to stabilize national economies and prevent social unrest.

TIP

Which adds extra information and is always preceded by a comma.

That adds necessary information and is not preceded by a comma.

Examples:

She has a new car, which is red.

The house that she bought is lovely.

You would think that the main idea would always come first in a sentence, followed by the subordinate clause. That is not always the case. If the main idea does come first, then a comma is not needed.

```
╭─────────── EXAMPLE ───────────╮

  The children went swimming because it was a hot day.

╰───────────────────────────────╯
```

A complex sentence can also be written with the subordinate clause coming first. In this case, a comma is required after the subordinate clause and before the independent clause.

```
╭─────────── EXAMPLE ───────────╮

  Because it was a hot day, the children went swimming.

╰───────────────────────────────╯
```

PRACTICE

Reorganize the sentences so that the subordinate clause comes first. (Don't forget the comma.)

Example:

Nancy has been studying hard since she began the course.
Since she began the course, Nancy has been studying hard.

1. The insurance company offers a discount if customers insure both their home and auto.
2. Fakid drove slowly as he approached the construction zone.
3. Danielle joined the military because she had always wanted to become a pilot.
4. Brady is a talented basketball player even though he is not very tall.
5. Our neighbours picked up our mail while we were away.
6. Mercedes did not get the job although she is fluently bilingual.
7. Your request will be denied unless you return this form within ten days.
8. You should continue to take the antibiotic until the entire bottle is gone.
9. Many diet foods contain more salt although they are lower in fat.
10. Will you pick up some toothpaste since you are going to the store anyway?

ANSWERS

1. If customers insure both their home and auto, the insurance company offers a discount.
2. As he approached the construction zone, Fakid drove slowly.
3. Because she had always wanted to become a pilot, Danielle joined the military.
4. Even though he is not very tall, Brady is a talented basketball player.
5. While we were away, our neighbours picked up our mail.
6. Although she is fluently bilingual, Mercedes did not get the job.

7. Unless you return this form within ten days, your request will be denied.

8. Until the entire bottle is gone, you should continue to take the antibiotic.

9. Although they are lower in fat, many diet foods contain more salt.

10. Since you are going to the store anyway, will you pick up some toothpaste?

PRACTICE

Reorganize the following sentences so that the subordinate clause comes at the end.

Example:

As soon as everyone was seated, Ken began to carve the Thanksgiving turkey.
Ken began to carve the Thanksgiving turkey as soon as everyone was seated.

1. Because the company offered low-interest financing, Shelly bought a new car.

2. After the children had gone home, the daycare workers could finally clean up.

3. Whenever he is in Quebec city, Jorge visits his favourite restaurant.

4. Although many people enjoy them, Cynthia does not like horror movies.

5. Since no one else came to the reception, Karla and Brian left early.

6. Unless you want to quit, it is difficult to stop smoking.

7. Before the wedding party arrived, the photographer arranged the lights in his studio.

8. As long as we have known her, she has had that cat.

9. Ever since he was a little boy, Julian has been interested in sharks.

10. Unless you have a better idea, we will stick with the plan.

ANSWERS

1. Shelly bought a new car because the company offered low-interest financing.

2. The daycare workers could finally clean up after the children had gone home.

3. Jorge visits his favourite restaurant whenever he is in Quebec city.

4. Cynthia does not like horror movies although many people enjoy them.

5. Karla and Brian left early since no one else came to the reception.

6. It is difficult to stop smoking unless you want to quit.

7. The photographer arranged the lights in his studio before the wedding party arrived.

8. She has had that cat as long as we have known her.

9. Julian has been interested in sharks ever since he was a little boy.

10. We will stick with the plan unless you have a better idea.

IMPROPER COORDINATION AND SUBORDINATION

Some questions on the GED Language Arts, Writing Skills Test, Part 1 will be about improper coordination and subordination. That is, some questions will be about making compound sentences and complex sentences. To answer these questions, you need to be able to:

- Recognize when there are errors in compound or complex sentences
- Recognize how errors can be corrected
- Recognize how sentences could be combined or reorganized to create compound or complex sentences

Things to Remember

1. A compound sentence is two or more complete sentences combined to make one sentence. Each part of the compound sentence could stand alone as a sentence.
2. When parts of a compound sentence are joined by a coordinating conjunction (and, but, or, nor, so), there is a comma before the conjunction.
3. A compound sentence can be made by using a semi-colon instead of a period when there is a close relationship between the sentences.
4. A semi-colon and connecting adverb (for example, however, therefore, consequently) can make a compound sentence. Use a comma after the adverb.
5. In a complex sentence, there is a main part (independent clause) that is more important and other parts that are less important (subordinate).
6. A clause that begins with a subordinate conjunction (because, although, since, until, and so forth) cannot stand alone as a sentence.
7. If a sentence begins with a subordinate clause, there is a comma before the main part of the sentence.

CHALLENGE EXERCISE

Make your own "Types of Sentences" quiz that tests identifying simple, compound, and complex sentences. Write ten sentences for identification. Make an answer key on a separate sheet of paper. Remember, with challenge exercises, it is okay to make mistakes. It is part of the learning process.

CHAPTER CHECK-UP

Complete these practice exercises, and then check the answers and analysis that follow. After you mark your work, review any topic in the chapter that you had trouble with or did not understand.

1. Write definitions in your own words for each of the terms.

   Simple Sentence   _____

   Compound Sentence   _____

   Coordinating Conjunction   _____

Connecting Adverb _____

Complex Sentence _____

Subordinate Conjunction _____

Questions 2–8 are based on the following paragraphs.

(A)

(1) Records management is a field that has become increasingly valued in recent years. (2) As many large organizations have come to recognize the importance of managing information to effective operation and reducing costs. (3) In today's economy, information is a vital asset. (4) Most large organizations now have some kind of records-management policy in place.

(B)

(5) Think of all the records an organization possesses and the people and equipment required to process and maintain them. (6) Records could include invoices, contracts, employee records, email messages, orientation videos, and much more, however not all records are worth keeping. (7) Consider the number of email messages and electronic records in a large organization or government agency and the number of servers and computer technicians required to maintain them. (8) Consider the number of paper records and the file rooms and cabinets required to store them. (9) If organizations introduce records-management strategies they can reduce the costs of employees, equipment, and space required to maintain records.

(C)

(10) A number of factors must be considered in managing records. (11) Most provinces and the federal government have privacy legislation. (12) Organizations must consider this legislation to ensure records are protected. (13) Some records must be kept for a certain length of time as required by law. (14) Still other records are important to ongoing operations but other records have no value at all. (15) An effective records-management program determines which records should be kept, by whom, for how long, and how they should be disposed of.

2. Sentences 1 and 2: Records management is a field that has become increasingly valued in recent years. As many large organizations have come to recognize the importance of managing information to effective operation and reducing costs.

   What is the best way to write the underlined part of this sentence? If you think the original is the best way, choose option (1).

   (1) recent years. As many
   (2) recent years as many
   (3) recent years; as many
   (4) recent years, as many
   (5) recent years; as many,

3. Sentences 3 and 4: In today's economy, information is a vital asset. Most large organizations now have some kind of records-management policy in place.

    The most effective way to combine sentences 3 and 4 includes which of the following?

    (1) vital asset, and most
    (2) vital asset; nevertheless, most
    (3) vital asset and most
    (4) vital asset, but most
    (5) vital asset so most

4. Sentence 5: Think of all the records an organization possesses and the people and equipment required to process and maintain them.

    What correction should be made to this sentence?

    (1) insert a comma after possesses
    (2) insert a comma after people
    (3) insert a semi-colon after possesses
    (4) insert a comma after process
    (5) no correction necessary

5. Sentence 6: Records could include invoices, contracts, employee records, email messages, orientation videos, and much more, however not all records are worth keeping.

    What correction should be made to this sentence?

    (1) remove the comma after videos
    (2) insert a period after all records
    (3) change more, however not to more; however, not
    (4) change include invoices, contracts to include invoices. Contracts
    (5) change much to many

6. Sentence 9: If organizations introduce records-management strategies they can reduce the costs of employees, equipment, and space required to maintain records.

    What correction should be made to this sentence?

    (1) remove the comma after equipment
    (2) insert a period after employees
    (3) insert a comma after strategies
    (4) change equipment, and space to equipment; and, space
    (5) insert a comma after organizations

7. Sentences 11 and 12: Most provinces and the federal government have privacy legislation. Organizations must consider this legislation to ensure records are protected.

    An effective combination of sentences 11 and 12, beginning with "Most provinces and the federal government have privacy legislation," would continue with what words?
    (1) and must be considered
    (2) organizations must
    (3) because these must be considered
    (4) however, these must be considered
    (5) which must be considered

8. Sentence 14: Still other records are important to ongoing <u>operations but other records</u> have no value at all.

    What is the best way to write the underlined part of this sentence? If you think the original is the best way, choose option (1).

    (1) operations but other records
    (2) operations, but other records
    (3) operations. But other records
    (4) operations; but, other records
    (5) operations, but, other records

<u>Questions 9–15</u> are based on the following paragraphs.

(A)

(1) Differences in culture can sometimes lead to misunderstandings. (2) In Canada, we greet others by shaking hands, call our bosses by their first names, and look people in the eye when speaking with them. (3) Customs are not the same in all cultures. (4) You should research cultural differences; if you are planning to do business or visit another country. (5) Canada is known as a cultural melting pot. (6) Learning about cultural differences can also help us understand one another better.

(B)

(7) Here are some examples of cultural differences. (8) The Chinese, for example, do not talk with their hands, so large hand movements while speaking may distract your listeners. (9) Business situations are formal, so you should use titles rather than first names and be prepared to present and receive business cards. (10) Business cards should be presented and received with both hands and must be treated with respect.

(C)

(11) In Indonesia, it is rude to have your hands in your pockets when speaking with someone and it is an insult to beckon someone with your finger. (12) Men and women do not touch in public, except sometimes a handshake. (13) It is also rude not to eat everything on your plate and giving someone an umbrella can mean you don't want to see that person again. (14) These are just some examples. (15) When you travel for any reason. (16) Learn and respect the cultures of the countries you visit.

9. Sentences 2 and 3: In Canada, we greet others by shaking hands, call our bosses by their first names, and look people in the eye when speaking with them. Customs are not the same in all cultures.

    A combination of sentences 2 and 3 that includes the word "however" would include which of the following?

    (1) them; however, customs
    (2) them. However customs
    (3) them, however, customs
    (4) them however customs
    (5) them; however customs

10. Sentence 4: You should research cultural <u>differences; if you</u> are planning to do business or visit another country.

What is the best way to write the underlined part of this sentence? If you think the original is the best way, choose option (1).

(1) differences; if you
(2) differences. If you
(3) differences; if, you
(4) differences, if you
(5) differences if you

11. Sentences 5 and 6: Canada is known as a cultural melting pot. Learning about cultural differences can also help us understand one another better.

An effective combination of these sentences could include which of the following?

(1) melting pot, however
(2) melting pot. But
(3) melting pot, and
(4) melting pot but
(5) melting pot; although

12. Sentence 8: The Chinese, for example, do not talk with their hands, so large hand movements while speaking may distract your listeners.

What correction should be made to this sentence?

(1) replace the comma after <u>hands</u> with a semi-colon
(2) insert a comma after <u>movements</u>
(3) remove the comma after <u>Chinese</u>
(4) insert a period before <u>movements</u>
(5) no correction necessary

13. Sentence 9: Business situations are formal, so you should use titles rather than first names and be prepared to present and receive business cards.

An effective revision of sentence 9, beginning with "You should use titles rather than first names" would include which of the following?

(1) although prepared to present
(2) however situations in business
(3) and preparation to present
(4) because business situations
(5) until first names

14. Sentence 11: In Indonesia, it is rude to have your hands in your pockets when speaking with someone and it is an insult to beckon someone with your finger.

What correction should be made to this sentence?

(1) remove the comma after <u>Indonesia</u>
(2) insert a comma after <u>hands</u>
(3) insert a period after <u>pockets</u>
(4) insert a comma after <u>someone</u>
(5) no correction necessary

15. Sentences 15 and 16: When you travel for <u>any reason. Learn</u> and respect the cultures of the countries you visit.

What is the best way to write the underlined part of this sentence? If you think the original is the best way, choose option (1).

(1) any reason. Learn
(2) any reason, learn
(3) any reason; learn
(4) any reason, and learn
(5) any reason but learn

<u>Questions 16–20</u> are based on the following article.

Centre to Receive New Funding

(A)

(1) The Provincial Minister of Social Development today announced increased funding for a local women's advocacy centre. (2) Although the centre recently announced that it was closing its doors, the funding will enable continued operation, at least in the short term. (3) "The government is committed to support for women. (4) We feel it is vital to community development," said the minister.

(B)

(5) The women's advocacy centre provides a variety of development and support programs for women? (6) Programs include addictions counselling, anger management, self-esteem classes, and adult basic education, all offered free of charge. (7) The centre is not out of the woods. (8) The announcement grants a temporary reprieve. (9) "This funding gives us some breathing room; nevertheless we need to renew our community fundraising efforts," commented the centre director.

16. Sentence 2: Although the centre recently announced that it was closing its <u>doors, the funding</u> will enable continued operation, at least in the short term.

What is the best way to write the underlined part of this sentence? If you think the original is the best way, choose option (1).

(1) doors, the funding
(2) doors. The funding
(3) doors the funding
(4) doors; the funding
(5) doors, and the funding

17. Sentences 3 and 4: "The government is committed to support for women. We feel it is vital to community development," said the minister.

An effective combination of these sentences could include which of the following?

(1) women, therefore we feel
(2) women but we feel
(3) women, we feel
(4) women we feel
(5) women, and we feel

18. Sentence 5: The women's advocacy centre provides a variety of development and support programs for women?

What correction should be made to this sentence?

(1) insert a period after centre
(2) insert a period after development
(3) insert a comma before and
(4) replace the question mark with a period
(5) no correction necessary

19. Sentences 7 and 8: The centre is not out of the woods. The announcement grants a temporary reprieve.

In a combination of these sentences beginning with the word "although," the next words would be which of the following?

(1) there is a centre
(2) the announcement
(3) the woods
(4) the grants are not
(5) a temporary reprieve

20. Sentence 9: "This funding gives us some breathing room; nevertheless we need to renew our community fundraising efforts," commented the centre director.

What is the best way to write the underlined part of this sentence? If you think the original is the best way, choose option (1).

(1) room; nevertheless we
(2) room, nevertheless we
(3) room; nevertheless, we
(4) room, nevertheless, we
(5) room nevertheless we

ANSWERS AND ANALYSIS

1. Your answers will be slightly different, but they should be similar to those below.

    - Simple Sentence: a single independent clause, containing a subject and predicate and forming a complete thought.
    - Compound Sentence: a sentence made of two or more independent clauses joined together.
    - Coordinating Conjunction: a joining word that connects things of equal importance, such as items in a list or parts of a compound sentence; for example, *and, but, or, so, nor, yet, for.*
    - Connecting Adverb: an adverb that shows a close connection between two sentences; for instance, *however, consequently, nevertheless, therefore, fortunately.*
    - Complex Sentence: a sentence formed by combining an independent clause and one or more dependent clauses, connected by a subordinate conjunction or relative pronoun.
    - Subordinate Conjunction: a joining word that introduces a dependent clause; words such as *because, although, since, until, if, unless, when.*

2. **(2)** recent years as many—Sentence 2 is a dependent clause beginning with the subordinate conjunction *as.* It cannot stand by itself as a sentence and should be combined with sentence 1. No punctuation is needed because the independent clause comes first.

3. **(1)** vital asset, and most—A compound sentence requires a comma and coordinating conjunction, such as *and.* Answers (3) and (5) cannot be correct because there is no comma. In addition, *and* is the only joining word given with the correct meaning for this situation.

4. **(5)** no correction necessary—This is not a compound sentence and no comma is required.

5. **(3)** change more, however not to more; however, not—A connecting adverb (however, therefore, consequently, and so on) can sometimes be used to make a compound sentence. Use a semi-colon before the adverb and a comma after.

6. **(3)** insert a comma after organizations—If a sentence begins with a subordinate clause, there is a comma before the main part of the sentence.

7. **(5)** which must be considered—Make a complex sentence by using a subordinate conjunction.

8. **(2)** operations, but other records—A compound sentence combines two independent clauses using a comma and a joining word.

9. **(1)** them; however, customs—To form a compound sentence with a connecting adverb, use a semi-colon and a comma.

10. **(5)** differences if you—A comma is not usually required in a complex sentence when a subordinate clause comes after the independent clause.

11. **(3)** melting pot, and—A compound sentence can be formed using a comma and a joining word.

12. **(5)** no correction necessary—This compound sentence uses a comma and the conjunction *so.*

13. **(4)** because business situations—This complex sentence preserves the original meaning of the compound sentence with the conjunction "so."

14. **(4)** insert a comma after <u>someone</u>—To form a compound sentence, use a comma and a conjunction.

15. **(2)** any reason, learn—This complex sentence begins with a dependent clause, which should be followed by a comma before the main part of the sentence begins.

16. **(1)** doors, the funding—This complex sentence is properly subordinated, beginning with a dependent clause that is followed by a comma.

17. **(5)** women, and we feel—This response is the only option that is correctly written with a comma and conjunction to create a compound sentence.

18. **(4)** replace the question mark with a period—This simple sentence is not a question and should not end with a question mark.

19. **(2)** the announcement—The sentence would read, "Although the announcement grants a temporary reprieve, the centre is not out of the woods."

20. **(3)** room; nevertheless, we—To form a compound sentence with a connecting adverb, use a semi-colon and a comma.

Sentence Structure

THINK ABOUT IT

Have you ever tried to make a jigsaw puzzle and found that some of the pieces don't fit? Creating a written composition is similar, in some ways, to assembling a jigsaw puzzle. The puzzle pieces are sentences. If some of the sentences are incomplete or are not constructed correctly, the pieces do not fit and the picture does not emerge.

IN THIS CHAPTER

The ability to write good sentences is a key to success on the GED Language Arts, Writing Test, Parts 1 and 2. Not only are 30% of the questions on Part 1 of the test about sentences, understanding good sentences forms a base for recognizing other writing errors and will be a vital component to constructing a well-written essay on Part 2.

After completing this chapter, you will be able to

→ **IDENTIFY AND CORRECT SENTENCE FRAGMENTS**

→ **IDENTIFY AND CORRECT RUN-ON SENTENCES**

→ **IDENTIFYAND CORRECT ERRORS IN PARALLELISM**

→ **IDENTIFY AND CORRECT IMPROPER MODIFICATION**

SENTENCE FRAGMENTS

A **sentence fragment** is not a complete sentence. It is a group of words that is written as a sentence, but which is missing one or more required elements:

- Subject
- Predicate
- Complete thought

EXAMPLES

Watching a movie or playing a video game.
(missing subject—who is watching a movie or playing a video game?)

The big yellow dog who was wagging his tail.
(missing predicate—wagging his tail describes the dog. What did the big yellow dog who was wagging his tail do?)

Although it is a beautiful day outside.
(incomplete thought—this is a dependent clause, not a complete thought.)

Some ways **to fix a sentence fragment** are

1. Add a subject
2. Add a predicate
3. Complete the thought
4. Combine the fragment with the independent clause before or after it

---

Sentence fragments are common in everyday speech. We understand the meaning because of context, gestures, tone of voice, body language, and many other clues.

> Greg: Going out tonight?
> Tabi: No, got to work.

In writing, these clues are not available and sentence fragments are not acceptable.

> Greg: Are you going out tonight?
> Tabi: No, I have to work.

PRACTICE

Rewrite and correct each sentence fragment by adding a subject as needed.

Example:
    While the Hendersons were visiting Charlottetown, attending the drama festival.
    While the Hendersons were visiting Charlottetown, they *attended* the drama festival.

1. Leaving by train in the morning.
2. Before the frost, were gathered into the storehouse.
3. Chasing the cat around the yard.
4. Because Sarah's friend telephoned, arriving late to the meeting.
5. Standing under the oak tree in the gentle light of the moon.
6. Taking her grandchildren to the beach to play in the sand.
7. Until the evening was over, dancing together to the sounds of the jazz band.
8. Although some health foods are lower in fat, often having much more salt than regular products.

ANSWERS

There are many ways to correct the sentence fragments. Your answers may be different, but some sample answers are given below.

1. They were leaving by train in the morning.
2. Before the frost, the crops were gathered into the storehouse.
3. The dog *was* chasing the cat around the yard.
4. Because Sarah's friend telephoned, she *arrived* late to the meeting.
5. The horse *stood* under the oak tree in the gentle light of the moon.
6. She *took* her grandchildren to the beach to play in the sand.

7. Until the evening was over, <u>the couple</u> *danced* together to the sounds of the jazz band.

8. Although some health foods are lower in fat, <u>they</u> often *have* much more salt than regular products.

PRACTICE

Rewrite and correct each sentence fragment by adding a predicate as needed.

Example:

The deck that I built last summer.

The deck that I built last summer <u>is nice to sit on</u>.

1. The new grey truck with four-wheel drive and a five-ton towing capacity.

2. Although they train extensively, the Canadian peacekeepers who are often faced with very difficult situations.

3. Canada, the second largest country in the world.

4. Spanning from the sands of Africa to the shores of England, the ancient Roman Empire.

5. The new advertising campaign which was launched in television commercials during the Super Bowl.

6. The new Chinese buffet restaurant with over one hundred items at the mall.

7. After the concert, the buses that would take the fans home.

8. Ingredients for your custom ice cream sundae from the wide selection available.

ANSWERS

There are many ways to correct the sentence fragments. Your answers may be different, but some sample answers are given below.

1. The new grey truck <u>has</u> four-wheel drive and a five-ton towing capacity.

2. ~~Although~~ they train extensively, the Canadian peacekeepers <u>are often faced</u> with very difficult situations.

3. Canada <u>is</u> the second largest country in the world.

4. The ancient Roman Empire <u>spanned</u> from the sands of Africa to the shores of England.

5. The new advertising campaign <u>was launched</u> in television commercials during the Super Bowl.

6. The new Chinese buffet restaurant at the mall <u>has</u> over one hundred items.

7. After the concert, the buses that would take the fans home <u>waited outside</u>.

8. <u>Choose</u> ingredients for your custom ice cream sundae from the wide selection available.

PRACTICE

Rewrite and correct each sentence fragment by adding a complete thought as needed.

Example:

Because he had studied hard for the GED.

Because he had studied hard for the GED, he passed the tests.

1. Although Jenson is a vegetarian and has been for years.
2. As a result of natural disasters, such as earthquakes, drought, and floods.
3. If the finance company offered a more competitive interest rate.
4. As long as you are willing to do the dishes.
5. Even though there was a sale on winter tires.
6. When the movie critics saw the film for the first time.
7. Despite the fact that the garden was full of weeds.
8. Before he began the steep climb up the mountain.

ANSWERS

There are many ways to correct the sentence fragments. Your answers may be different, but some sample answers are given below.

1. ~~Although~~ Jenson is a vegetarian and has been for years.
2. There is hunger throughout the world as a result of natural disasters, such as earthquakes, drought, and floods.
3. If the finance company offered a more competitive interest rate, they would receive more business.
4. As long as you are willing to do the dishes, I will cook the meal.
5. Even though there was a sale on winter tires, they were very expensive.
6. When the movie critics saw the film for the first time, they enjoyed it.
7. Despite the fact that the garden was full of weeds, it was very beautiful.
8. Before he began the steep climb up the mountain, he made sure his equipment was in good condition.

There are many possible answers to the preceding sentence fragment practice exercises. Compare and discuss your answers with another student or discuss your answers with a teacher or friend. How are your answers different or the same?

CHALLENGE EXERCISE

Sentence fragments are common in everyday speaking. Write down a conversation you have overheard or create an imaginary dialogue. Identify and correct any sentence fragments.

TIP

A sentence fragment is not a complete sentence.

PRACTICE

Homemade Baby Food

(A)

(1) Making your own baby food, a healthy alternative. (2) Start with fresh ingredients, good quality food. (3) After washing fruits and vegetables and removing the fat from meat. (4) Cook the food in a little bit of water. (5) Puree it in the blender until smooth.

(B)

(6) It's easy to do. (7) Homemade baby food can be made in as little as an hour a week. (8) Food can be stored in the fridge for up to three days. (9) In the freezer for up to a month.

1. Sentence 1: Making your own baby <u>food, a healthy</u> alternative.

   What is the best way to write the underlined part of this sentence? If you think the original is the best way, choose option (1).

   (1) food, a healthy
   (2) food. A healthy
   (3) food is a healthy
   (4) food, and a healthy
   (5) food; a healthy

2. Sentence 2: Start with fresh ingredients, good quality food.

   What correction should be made to this sentence?

   (1) insert a period after <u>ingredients</u>
   (2) change <u>fresh ingredients</u> to <u>fresh-ingredients</u>
   (3) insert a comma after <u>quality</u>
   (4) remove the comma after <u>ingredients</u>
   (5) no correction necessary

3. Sentences 3 and 4: After washing fruits and vegetables and removing the fat from meat. Cook the food in a little bit of water.

   What correction should be made to these sentences?

   (1) insert a comma after <u>fruits</u>
   (2) change <u>meat. Cook</u> to <u>meat, cook</u>
   (3) insert a period after <u>vegetables</u>
   (4) insert a semi-colon after <u>vegetables</u>
   (5) change <u>meat. Cook</u> to <u>meat, and cook</u>

4. Sentences 6 and 7: It's easy to <u>do. Homemade</u> baby food can be made in as little as an hour a week.

   What is the best way to write the underlined part of this sentence? If you think the original is the best way, choose option (1).

   (1) do. Homemade
   (2) do, homemade
   (3) do homemade
   (4) do; but homemade
   (5) do, because homemade

5. Sentences 8 and 9: Food can be stored in the fridge for up to <u>three days. In the freezer</u> for up to a month.

What is the best way to write the underlined part of the above? If you think the original is the best way, choose option (1).

(1) three days. In the freezer
(2) three days or in the freezer
(3) three days; in the freezer
(4) three days in the freezer,
(5) three days after the freezer

Debt-settlement Warning

(A)

(1) Canadians the latest victims of a U.S. scam. (2) Consumer protection agencies are warning the public to be wary of companies. (3) That identify themselves as debt-settlement experts or credit counsellors. (4) Television advertisements claim that those who are struggling to make ends meet can reduce their debt by hiring them to negotiate lower payments with their creditors. (5) Too good to be true?

(B)

(6) Some such companies demand the majority of their fees up front. (7) In addition, some consumers claim that they made regular payments to the company. (8) But none of it went to their creditors, who were never contacted. (9) The Better Business Bureau advises that there are established non-profit organizations in many jurisdictions. (10) To negotiate with your creditors is to call them yourself.

6. Sentence 1: Canadians the latest victims of a U.S. scam.

What is the best way to revise this sentence?

(1) Canadians, the latest victims of a U.S. scam.
(2) Canadians with debt problems the latest victims of a U.S. scam.
(3) Canadian victims of U.S. scam.
(4) U.S. scams that victimize Canadians.
(5) Canadians may be the latest victims of a U.S. scam.

7. Sentences 2 and 3: Consumer protection agencies are warning the public to be wary of <u>companies. That identify</u> themselves as debt-settlement experts or credit counsellors.

What is the best way to write the underlined part of this sentence? If you think the original is the best way, choose option (1).

(1) companies. That identify
(2) companies, that identify
(3) companies that identify
(4) companies; that identify
(5) companies, and that identify

8. Sentence 5: Too good to be true?

    What is the best way to revise this sentence?

    (1) Does this sound too good to be true?
    (2) Too good to be true.
    (3) And it is too good to be true.
    (4) Too good, to be true?
    (5) Too good and not true.

9. Sentences 7 and 8: In addition, some consumers claim that they made regular payments to the company. But none of it went to their creditors, who were never contacted.

    What correction should be made to this sentence?

    (1) remove the comma after <u>addition</u>
    (2) insert a period after <u>consumers</u>
    (3) replace the period after <u>company</u> with a comma and change <u>But</u> to <u>but</u>
    (4) change <u>creditors, who</u> to <u>creditors. Who</u>
    (5) no correction necessary

10. Sentence 10: To negotiate with your creditors is to call them yourself.

    What is the best way to revise this sentence?

    (1) Negotiate with your creditors is to call them yourself.
    (2) To negotiate is to call them yourself.
    (3) The best way to negotiate with your creditors is to call them yourself.
    (4) Negotiate with your creditors is to call them.
    (5) If you negotiate with your creditors, is to call them yourself.

ANSWERS

1. **(3)** This sentence fragment requires a verb.
2. **(5)** This is not a sentence fragment. The last phrase *good quality food* restates what is meant by *fresh ingredients.*
3. **(2)** Sentence 3 is a dependent clause and cannot stand alone.
4. **(1)** These are two complete sentences, and no correction is required.
5. **(2)** Sentence 9 is a sentence fragment, a phrase that should be combined with the previous sentence.
6. **(5)** Add a predicate verb to correct this sentence fragment.
7. **(3)** Sentence 3 is a dependent clause that cannot stand alone.
8. **(1)** Add a predicate verb to correct this sentence fragment.
9. **(3)** A comma before the conjunction *but* joins two sentences as a compound sentence.
10. **(3)** Provide a subject to complete the sentence.

RUN-ON SENTENCES

A **run-on sentence** occurs when two or more separate sentences are incorrectly written together as one.

EXAMPLES

Scott has a new car. Haley has an old one. (These are two separate sentences)

Scott has a new car Haley has an old one. (Run-on sentence)

Scott has a new car, Haley has an old one. (A form of run-on sentence called a comma splice, in which two sentences are incorrectly joined using a comma.)

PRACTICE

Write *C* beside each correct sentence and *RO* beside each run-on sentence or comma splice.

1. During rush hour, the 401 highway is wall-to-wall traffic.

2. Genevieve and Antonio were high-school sweethearts, they have been married now for twenty years.

3. The basement was damp there was a musty smell in the air.

4. Several people are out sick this week, consequently the office is very busy.

5. I have two roommates both of them are very messy.

6. Some people thought the computer age would mean the end of paper, however there is more paper used now than ever before.

7. Salina can't cook it's a good thing her husband can.

8. Having a driver's license is important for rural Canadians because the distances between places are so great.

9. Canada is one of the wealthiest economies in the world with the world's ninth-largest economy.

10. The Yukon International Storytelling Festival was started in 1988, it enables native peoples and others from various countries and backgrounds to tell stories in their native languages.

11. The roses in the garden were crushed there were tire tracks across the lawn.

12. Although the lake was frozen over, the ice was not thick enough for skating.

13. You may not always like the people you work with, you still have to get along.

14. The rain poured down thunder boomed.

15. The child jumped out from hiding Mona was startled.

16. In the cold water of the fast-moving stream, the fishermen stood for hours, casting their flies in hopes of catching a salmon.

17. The doctor came into the room she examined the little boy.

18. Many Canadians do not know about the Canadian Space Agency, which was established in 1989.

19. Most people have never seen the Northern Lights, they are one of nature's most splendid shows.

20. It seems that in the past, manufactured goods were made to last longer than they do today.

ANSWERS

1.	(C)	6.	(RO)	11.	(RO)	16.	(C)
2.	(RO)	7.	(RO)	12.	(C)	17.	(RO)
3.	(RO)	8.	(C)	13.	(RO)	18.	(C)
4.	(RO)	9.	(C)	14.	(RO)	19.	(RO)
5.	(RO)	10.	(RO)	15.	(RO)	20.	(C)

Some ways **to fix run-on sentences** are

1. Put a period (or other end punctuation mark) between the independent clauses that make up the run-on sentence.
2. Use a comma and coordinating conjunction (and, but, or, so, nor, for, yet) to make a compound sentence.
3. Put a semi-colon between the independent clauses to make a compound sentence if the sentences are closely related.
4. Use a semi-colon, connecting adverb (however, consequently, therefore, and so on), and comma to make a compound sentence.
5. Add a subordinate conjunction or relative pronoun to make one of the independent clauses into a dependent clause.

EXAMPLES

Scott has a new car Haley has an old one. (Run-on sentence)
Scott has a new car. Haley has an old one.
Scott has a new car, but Haley has an old one.
Scott has a new car; Haley has an old one.
Scott has a new car; however, Haley has an old one.
Although Scott has a new car, Haley has an old one.

PRACTICE

1. The Internet has changed the news <u>business, newspapers</u> are struggling to adapt.

   What is the best way to write the underlined part of this sentence? If you think the original is the best way, choose option (1).

   (1) business, newspapers
   (2) business newspapers
   (3) business. But newspapers
   (4) business; although newspapers
   (5) business, and newspapers

2. Dante watched the movie with Monica football was on another channel.

    What is the best way to write the underlined part of this sentence? If you think the original is the best way, choose option (1).

    (1)   Monica football was
    (2)   Monica, football was
    (3)   Monica although football was
    (4)   Monica. And football was
    (5)   Monica, because, football was

3. Cell phones today have more processing power than my first computer had back in the 1980s.

    What is the best way to write the underlined part of this sentence? If you think the original is the best way, choose option (1).

    (1)   processing power than
    (2)   processing power. Than
    (3)   processing power; than
    (4)   processing power, but than
    (5)   processing power although

4. Graduates of college or university earn a higher income, many are loaded with debt by the time they graduate.

    What is the best way to write the underlined part of this sentence? If you think the original is the best way, choose option (1).

    (1)   income, many
    (2)   income; however, many
    (3)   income. But many
    (4)   income many
    (5)   income. Although many

5. She was frightened; and the sound was coming closer.

    What is the best way to write the underlined part of this sentence? If you think the original is the best way, choose option (1).

    (1)   frightened; and the sound
    (2)   frightened. And the sound
    (3)   frightened, the sound
    (4)   frightened. The sound
    (5)   frightened, however, the sound

6. Some health problems that plague the elderly result from lack of <u>exercise, it is</u> important to exercise at least three times each week.

What is the best way to write the underlined part of this sentence? If you think the original is the best way, choose option (1).

(1) exercise, it is
(2) exercise it is
(3) exercise; consequently, it is
(4) exercise and it is
(5) exercise because it is

7. Michelle reads a lot of <u>books she downloads</u> and reads them on her cell phone.

What is the best way to write the underlined part of this sentence? If you think the original is the best way, choose option (1).

(1) books she downloads
(2) books; she downloads
(3) books. Because she downloads
(4) books. Although she downloads
(5) books; and she downloads

8. The sun is the most renewable energy <u>source; it is</u> also the most powerful.

What is the best way to write the underlined part of this sentence? If you think the original is the best way, choose option (1).

(1) source; it is
(2) source; and it is
(3) source; however it is
(4) source. However it is
(5) source it is

9. Estheticians are trained in giving beauty <u>treatments, such as</u> facials, manicures, and pedicures.

What is the best way to write the underlined part of this sentence? If you think the original is the best way, choose option (1).

(1) treatments, such as
(2) treatments. Such as
(3) treatments; such as
(4) treatments; however,
(5) treatments. Like

10. Destiny is going to the eye doctor <u>next week, Norman</u> went yesterday.

What is the best way to write the underlined part of this sentence? If you think the original is the best way, choose option (1).

   (1) next week, Norman
   (2) next week; Although, Norman
   (3) next week but Norman
   (4) next week. Norman
   (5) next week, however, Norman

11. I glanced at the speedometer when I saw the flashing lights, I knew I was caught.

Which of the following is the best way to rewrite the sentence?

   (1) When I saw the flashing lights, I glanced at the speedometer, I knew I was caught.
   (2) When I saw the flashing lights, I glanced at the speedometer. I knew I was caught.
   (3) I knew I was caught when I glanced at the speedometer, I saw the flashing lights.
   (4) I saw the flashing lights, I glanced at the speedometer, I knew I was caught.
   (5) When I saw the flashing lights. I glanced at the speedometer. I knew I was caught.

12. It was a perfect day in Halifax, the weatherman was calling for rain.

Which of the following is the best way to rewrite the sentence?

   (1) It was a perfect day in Halifax although the weatherman was calling for rain.
   (2) It was a perfect day in Halifax. The weatherman, was calling for rain.
   (3) Although the weatherman was calling for rain; it was a perfect day in Halifax.
   (4) Although the weatherman had called for rain. It was a perfect day in Halifax.
   (5) The day in Halifax was perfect. But the weatherman had called for rain.

13. Mohamed enjoys the local diner, Roberta prefers fine food.

Which of the following is the best way to rewrite the sentence?

   (1) Mohamed enjoys the local diner; Roberta prefers fine food.
   (2) Although Mohamed enjoys the local diner. Roberta prefers fine food.
   (3) Roberta prefers fine food, Mohamed enjoys the local diner.
   (4) Roberta prefers fine food; although Mohamed enjoys the local diner.
   (5) Mohamed enjoys the local diner; but Roberta prefers fine food.

14. Carlos got a new job as a result he had to get some new clothes.

Which of the following is the best way to rewrite the sentence?

   (1) Carlos got a new job, he had to get some new clothes as a result.
   (2) Carlos got a new job, so he had to get some new clothes.
   (3) Carlos had to get some new clothes. For his new job.
   (4) Carlos got a new job, therefore he got some new clothes.
   (5) As a result of his new job. Carlos had to get some new clothes.

15. The car drove slowly up the road it stopped in front of the house.

    Which of the following is the best way to rewrite the sentence?

    (1) The car drove slowly up the road and stopped in front of the house.
    (2) The car drove slowly up the road. And stopped in front of the house.
    (3) The car drove slowly up the road, it stopped in front of the house.
    (4) The car drove slowly. Up the road. It stopped in front of the house.
    (5) No correction necessary

16. The group of young people went to New York where they handed out blankets to the homeless, visited an AIDS hospital, and helped out at a soup kitchen.

    Which of the following is the best way to rewrite the sentence?

    (1) The group of young people went to New York. Where they handed out blankets to the homeless, visited an AIDS hospital, and helped out at a soup kitchen.
    (2) The group of young people went to New York in which they handed out blankets to the homeless, visited an AIDS hospital, and helped out at a soup kitchen.
    (3) The group of young people went to New York; where they handed out blankets to the homeless, visited an AIDS hospital, and helped out at a soup kitchen.
    (4) The group of young people went to New York, but they handed out blankets to the homeless, visited an AIDS hospital, and helped out at a soup kitchen.
    (5) No correction necessary

17. She was very thirsty, all she could think about was getting a cool drink.

    Which of the following is the best way to rewrite the sentence?

    (1) She was very thirsty all she could think about was getting a cool drink.
    (2) All she could think about was a cool drink, she was very thirsty.
    (3) She was so thirsty that all she could think about was getting a cool drink.
    (4) Although she was so thirsty. All she could think about was getting a cool drink.
    (5) No correction necessary

18. French and English are Canada's official languages, Chinese is now the third most-spoken language in the country.

    Which of the following is the best way to rewrite the sentence?

    (1) French and English are Canada's official languages. But Chinese is now the third most-spoken language in the country.
    (2) Although French and English are Canada's official languages, Chinese is now the third most-spoken language in the country.
    (3) French and English are Canada's official languages. Although Chinese is now the third most-spoken language in the country.
    (4) French and English are Canada's official languages Chinese is now the third most-spoken language in the country.
    (5) French and English are Canada's official languages, now the third most-spoken language in the country is Chinese.

IMPROPER PARALLELISM

Parallelism is using the same pattern of words, phrases, or clauses to express a sequence of ideas in a sentence.

TIP

Parallel words, phrases, or clauses have to be written in the same form.

EXAMPLES

Julia enjoys swimming, reading, and to go dancing. (Improper parallelism)
Julia enjoys swimming, reading, and dancing. (Correct)

Every weekday morning, Andre gets up at six, lacing up his sneakers, and goes for a run. (Improper parallelism)
Every weekday morning, Andre gets up at six, laces up his sneakers, and goes for a run. (Correct)

She had neither the knowledge of how to make a soufflé, nor did she want to learn. (Improper parallelism)
She had neither the knowledge of how to make a soufflé, nor the desire to learn. (Correct)

To be parallel, items in a list must be similar kinds of things. For example, you wouldn't have several animals and a sport in the same list, as in: She likes cats, dogs, and playing soccer. Parallel words, phrases, or clauses in a sentence are also usually joined by a coordinating conjunction, such as *and* or *or*.

To fix improper parallelism, revise the items in the sequence so that they follow the same pattern or express consistent ideas.

PRACTICE

In each sequence, identify and replace the item that is not parallel.

Example:
to be happy
to be wealthy
~~being wise~~ *to be wise*

1. sight
sound
touching
smell

2. tells good jokes
beautiful
intelligent

3. ran her fingers through her hair
   was sighing for a moment at the reflection in the mirror
   smiled at a long forgotten memory

4. under the trees
   beside the brook
   after breakfast

5. fluttering in the breeze
   danced lightly on currents of air
   soaring high above the grey canyon

6. doe, a deer a female deer
   ray, a drop of golden sun
   me is the name I call myself

ANSWERS

1. ~~touching~~ *touch*
2. ~~tells good jokes~~ *funny*
3. ~~was sighing~~ *sighed* for a moment at the reflection in the mirror
4. ~~after breakfast~~ (Answers will vary. For example: *on the rock*)
5. ~~danced~~ *dancing* lightly on currents of air
6. me, ~~is~~ the name I call myself

CHALLENGE EXERCISE

Many poems and songs contain parallelism. Some use it extensively; for example, *Cover of the Rolling Stone* by Dr. Hook, and *Rock Star* by Nickleback. Look up or write out the lyrics to one of these songs, or another song or poem that uses parallelism. Underline the examples of parallelism. Discuss your answers with a teacher, friend, or another student.

Parallel structures can also use certain pairs of words that go together. They include:

- Either… or…
- Neither… nor…
- Both… and…
- Not only… but also…
- Whether… or…

PRACTICE

Rewrite each sentence and correct errors in parallel structure. If the sentence is already correct, write *Correct*.

1. Omar enjoys camping, hiking, and to fish.
2. Muriel is very good at subjects related to math, such as chemistry, physics, and calculus.
3. The old sofa either needs to be thrown out or I could reupholster it.
4. We couldn't decide whether to stay another night or if we should go home.

5. Jasper did not realize the height or how steep the mountain was.

6. Samantha was interested in neither going to school nor going to work.

7. Both the boy's bicycle and his wagon were fire engine red.

8. In the afternoon, we went for a drive, saw some sights, having a relaxing time.

9. Annette's friend needed her understanding and being guided.

10. She was not only a good friend but also they were cousins.

11. The male loon dove under the canoe, surfaced nearby, and called out noisily to distract the intruders from his young family.

12. In college, Mark neither went to class regularly nor was his homework done on time.

ANSWERS

1. Omar enjoys camping, hiking, and *fishing*.

2. Correct

3. The old sofa either needs to be thrown out or *to be reupholstered*.

4. We couldn't decide whether to stay another night or *to go home*.

5. Jasper did not realize *how high* or how steep the mountain was.

6. Correct

7. Correct

8. In the afternoon, we went for a drive, saw some sights, *and had* a relaxing time.

9. Annette's friend needed her understanding and *her guidance*.

10. She was not only a good friend but also *her cousin*.

11. Correct

12. In college, Mark neither went to class regularly nor *did* his homework on time.

PRACTICE

Choose the best way to write the underlined part of each sentence. If you think the original is the best way, choose option (1).

1. Serving your community and to put others before yourself are ideas that seem not to be common any more.
   (1) Serving your community and to put others before yourself
   (2) Serving your community nor to put others before yourself
   (3) Serving your community and putting others before yourself
   (4) Serving your community and to be putting others before yourself
   (5) To be serving your community and to put others before yourself

2. Lia Maria, who recently arrived from El Salvador and not a good English speaker, is taking language classes at the church.
   (1) not a good English speaker
   (2) who doesn't speak English very well
   (3) a poor English speaker
   (4) and poorly at speaking English
   (5) speaking English poorly

3. Shaylee is very smart, <u>with kindness, and has consideration for</u> others.
    (1) with kindness, and has consideration for
    (2) kindness, and consideration for
    (3) kind, and with consideration for
    (4) kind, and considerate of
    (5) with kindness, and consideration for

4. The baseball coach told him to hold the bat firmly, keep his eye on the ball, and <u>step into the pitch</u>.
    (1) step into the pitch
    (2) to step into the pitch
    (3) stepping into the pitch
    (4) to take a step into the pitch
    (5) have a step into the pitch

5. I need some kind of evidence either <u>scientific or from personal experience</u> before I can believe in UFOs.
    (1) scientific or from personal experience
    (2) from science or from personal experience
    (3) science or from personal experience
    (4) to be scientific or from personal experience
    (5) from scientific or from personal experience

6. Many years ago, Carolyn started what would eventually become a soup kitchen when she and some other housewives began <u>making soup at home and took it</u> to homeless people on the street.
    (1) making soup at home and took it
    (2) to make soup at home and took it
    (3) to make soup at home and taking it
    (4) making soup at home and to take it
    (5) making soup at home and taking it

7. Paul, a member of the student council and <u>who is also captain of the football team</u>, will speak at the awards banquet.
    (1) who is also captain of the football team
    (2) captain of the football team
    (3) who is also too captain of the football team
    (4) besides is captain of the football team
    (5) also who is captain of the football team

8. Bethany is a lovely girl, but she is also rough, tough, and <u>always wants to be the best at everything</u>.
    (1) always wants to be the best at everything
    (2) wants to win
    (3) competitive
    (4) doesn't like to not be the best at everything
    (5) likes to be the best at everything

ANSWERS

1. (3)		3. (4)		5. (2)		7. (2)	
2. (2)		4. (1)		6. (5)		8. (3)	

IMPROPER MODIFICATION

A **modifier** is a word or group of words that describes or changes something in the sentence.

> **EXAMPLES**
>
> She drives a *red* car. (red describes the car)
> The replay showed the accident *in slow motion*. (describes how it was shown)
> *After the sun goes down*, the mosquitoes come out. (describes when they come out)

A modifier is right beside the thing it describes. However, sometimes a modifier is misplaced in the sentence, so the meaning is incorrect.

> **EXAMPLES**
>
> Blowing fiercely through the trees, Ruth wrote a poem about the wind.
> Mercedes wrote a story about aliens in her bedroom.

In the first example, the **misplaced modifier** says that Ruth was blowing fiercely through the trees. The second example says that aliens were in Mercedes' bedroom. **To fix a misplaced modifier**, move the modifier beside the thing it should describe.

> Ruth wrote a poem about the wind blowing fiercely through the trees.
> In her bedroom, Mercedes wrote a story about aliens.

Sometimes, the thing being described is not clear or is not in the sentence at all, making the meaning unclear. This is called a dangling modifier.

> **EXAMPLES**
>
> Looking at my baby granddaughter, she seems to be perfect.
> Doing the sentence structure practice exercises, they did not seem too hard.

In the first example, it is unclear who is looking. This **dangling modifier** probably refers to "I," but "I" is not in this sentence. Similarly, in the second example, it is not clear who was doing the practice exercises. **To fix a dangling modifier**, requires more than moving the modifier. You need to rewrite the sentence to make the sentence clear.

> When I look at my baby granddaughter, she seems to be perfect.
> When Joan was doing the sentence structure practice exercises, they did not seem too hard.

TIP

A *misplaced modifier* describes the wrong thing. With *dangling modifiers*, readers do not know what the modifier is describing.

PRACTICE

Rewrite the following sentences to correct dangling or misplaced modifiers. Rearrange the sentences and add or take out words as necessary.

1. After leaving the party, the music was turned up full volume.
2. Waiting for the waitress to return with the order, the lunch hour seemed to drag by.
3. Thrown behind the dryer, Jack found his missing sock.
4. John sped around the track in a 1978 Vega with a 450 engine wearing a crash helmet.
5. I discovered an unusual animal at the zoo with a duck-like face and a beaver tail.
6. Arnold should not be working on scaffolding with a heart problem.
7. When I demanded my money, my tenants left town on the first bus owing two months rent.
8. Dressed in her best clothes, the dog got its muddy paws all over her.
9. Buried under all of the junk in her handbag, Fran could not find her glasses.
10. Bubbling and sputtering cheerfully on the stove, Mary stirred the spaghetti sauce.
11. While still on probation for auto theft, the judge found Jimmy guilty of shoplifting.
12. As a youth, the cabin in the woods seemed much larger to me.
13. Waiting for over an hour, her date did not arrive.
14. She takes the bus often to the city.
15. The old man next door, a good friend of the family, has lived since I was a child.
16. The young girl wears shoes so her mother can always tell where she is that squeak with each step.
17. Dana almost won all the top awards in the music festival.
18. Her shoulder was injured while playing football.

ANSWERS

Your responses may differ somewhat, but will be similar to these sentences.

1. After <u>we left</u> the party, the music was turned up full volume. (Insert a person or people who left.)
2. <u>The lunch hour seemed to drag by as I waited for the</u> waitress to return with the order. (Insert a person or people who waited.)
3. Jack found his missing sock thrown behind the dryer.
4. Wearing a crash helmet, John sped around the track in a 1978 Vega with a 450 engine.
5. At the zoo, I discovered an unusual animal with a duck-like face and a beaver tail.
6. Arnold <u>has a heart problem</u> and should not be working on scaffolding. (This sentence must be rewritten to make it clear that it is Arnold, not the scaffolding, who has the heart problem.)
7. When I demanded my money, my tenants, <u>who owed two months rent</u>, left town on the first bus.
8. The dog got its muddy paws all over <u>her best clothes</u>.
9. Fran could not find her glasses buried under all of the junk in her handbag.

10. Mary stirred the spaghetti sauce, which bubbled and sputtered cheerfully on the stove.

11. <u>While Jimmy was still on probation</u> for auto theft, the judge found him guilty of shoplifting.

12. The cabin in the woods seemed much larger to me <u>when I was a youth</u>.

13. <u>Although she waited</u> for over an hour, her date did not arrive. (Rewrite to make it clear that she was the one who waited.)

14. She <u>often takes</u> the bus to the city. (*Often* is an adverb that modifies the verb *takes*. Otherwise the sentence could mean that she takes the bus, often to the city and sometimes other places.)

15. A good friend of the family, <u>the old man next door has lived there</u> since I was a child. (Revise to clarify that the old man has lived next door since I was a child, not that he has lived.)

16. The young girl wears <u>shoes that squeak with each step</u>, so her mother can always tell where she is.

17. Dana won <u>almost all the top awards</u> in the music festival. (To say Dana "almost won" would mean that he didn't win any of the awards, he only almost won. This revision clarifies that he did win almost all of the top awards.)

18. Her shoulder was injured <u>while she was playing football</u>. (All of her was playing football, not just her shoulder.)

CHALLENGE EXERCISE

Misplaced and dangling modifiers can be funny; for instance: Cheeks stuffed with peanuts, Elsie saw the chipmunk scurry away from the picnic basket. This misplaced modifier says that Elsie's cheeks were stuffed with peanuts. Make up five sentences of your own with misplaced or dangling modifiers. See if another person can spot the mistakes.

CHAPTER CHECK-UP

Complete these practice exercises, and then check the answers and analysis that follow. After you mark your work, review any topic in the chapter that you had trouble with or did not understand.

1. Write definitions in your own words for each of the terms.

Sentence Fragment _____

Run-on Sentence _____

Comma Splice _____

Parallelism _____

Misplaced Modifier _____

Dangling Modifier _____

Questions 2–11 are based on the following article.

(A)

(1) Several thousand Canadians embark every year on new careers as real estate salespeople. (2) Real estate plays a vital role in our economy, not only is a home purchase the largest single expenditure in most people's lives, real estate sales are an important indicator of economic health. (3) In addition to other figures, such as unemployment and inflation. (4)Economists consider the number of new home starts and of home sales when evaluating the state of the economy.

(B)

(5) Many people fail to realize that in starting a career as a real estate salesperson, they are really going into business for themselves. (6) Although they will work for a real estate company, they are responsible for most of their own expenses, such as cell phone, laptop, connecting to Internet service, and transportation. (7) In addition, real estate companies charge their salespeople for things such as desk usage, clerical support, business cards, office phone, and advertising. (8) It may also take several months or more for a new salesperson to sell a house and earn any kind of income, and it is common to take several years to establish a reputation and client base.

(C)

(9) One critical step when starting out in real estate, as with beginning any new business, is making a business plan. (10) A business plan should clearly project expenses, it should also identify sources of funding that will cover start-up, operating, and living expenses for at least a year. (11) The business plan should also include a marketing strategy that outlines the steps to establish a client base. (12) With hard work and careful planning, a career as a real estate salesperson can be not only financially beneficial but also a personal reward. (13) You earn a good income and help families find a home, you also play an important role in the health of the economy.

2. Sentence 1: Several thousand Canadians embark every year on new careers as real estate salespeople.

   Which of the following is the best way to write this sentence? If you think the original is the best way, choose option (1).

   (1)   Several thousand Canadians embark every year on new careers as real estate salespeople.
   (2)   Several thousand Canadians embark every year on careers as new real estate salespeople.
   (3)   Every year, several thousand new Canadians embark on careers as real estate salespeople.
   (4)   Every year, several thousand Canadians embark on new careers as real estate salespeople.
   (5)   Several thousand new Canadians every year embark on careers as real estate salespeople.

3. Sentence 2: Real estate plays a vital role in our economy, not only is a home purchase the largest single expenditure in most people's lives, real estate sales are an important indicator of economic health.

    What correction should be made to this sentence?

    (1) insert a period after economy
    (2) insert a period after lives
    (3) insert a comma after purchase
    (4) change lives, real estate to lives, and real estate
    (5) no correction necessary

4. Sentences 3 and 4: In addition to other figures, such as unemployment and inflation. Economists consider the number of new home starts and of home sales when evaluating the state of the economy.

    What is the best way to write the underlined part? If you think the original is the best way, choose option (1).

    (1) inflation. Economists
    (2) inflation; economists
    (3) inflation, economists
    (4) inflation, and economists
    (5) inflation economists

5. Sentence 5: Many people fail to realize that in starting a career as a real estate salesperson, they are really going into business for themselves.

    What is the best way to write the underlined part of the sentence? If you think the original is the best way, choose option (1).

    (1) salesperson, they
    (2) salesperson. They
    (3) salesperson, and they
    (4) salesperson; they
    (5) salesperson, but they

6. Sentence 6: Although they will work for a real estate company, they are responsible for most of their own expenses, such as cell phone, laptop, connecting to Internet service, and transportation.

    What correction should be made to this sentence?

    (1) insert a period after company
    (2) change connecting to Internet service to Internet service
    (3) insert a period after laptop
    (4) insert a comma after responsible
    (5) change expenses, such to expenses, and such

7. Sentence 8: It may also take several months or more for a new salesperson to sell a house and earn any kind of income, and it is common to take several years to establish a reputation and client base.

What correction should be made to this sentence?

(1) change is common to take to commonly takes
(2) change income, and to income. And
(3) insert a period after salesperson
(4) insert a comma after years
(5) no correction necessary

8. Sentence 10: A business plan should clearly project expenses, it should also identify sources of funding that will cover start-up, operating, and living expenses for at least a year.

What correction should be made to this sentence?

(1) change expenses, it to expenses. It
(2) insert a period after funding
(3) remove the comma after expenses
(4) change living expenses to money to live
(5) Move for at least a year to the start of the sentence

9. Sentence 11: The business plan should also include a marketing strategy that outlines the steps to establish a client base.

What is the best way to write the underlined part of the sentence? If you think the original is the best way, choose option (1).

(1) strategy that outlines
(2) strategy, and that outlines
(3) strategy. That outlines
(4) strategy; that outlines
(5) strategy. Outlines

10. Sentence 12: With hard work and careful planning, a career as a real estate salesperson can be not only financially beneficial but also a personal reward.

What correction should be made to this sentence?

(1) insert a period after planning
(2) insert a period after salesperson
(3) change a personal reward to personally rewarding
(4) change careful planning to a careful plan
(5) no correction necessary

11. Sentence 13: You earn a good income and help families find a home, you also play an important role in the health of the economy.

What correction should be made to this sentence?

(1) change home, you to home. You
(2) insert a comma after role
(3) insert a comma after income
(4) change you also play to you also are playing
(5) no correction necessary

Questions 12–20 are based on the following article.

(A)

(1) Planning is the key to designing an effective website for a small business or community organization. (2) First, identify the intended audience and what the purpose is of the site. (3) Who is the website for? (4) A site for professional auto mechanics will be very different from one for do-it-yourself car enthusiasts. (5) Think about it a site that attempts to appeal to both of these groups will end up appealing to neither. (6) Next, define the purpose of the site. (7) Here is a hint. (8) Purposes usually include verbs, such as "Inform," "Motivate," "Train," and "Sell."

(B)

(9) Second, identification of responsibilities and resources. (10) How much will be invested in the site? (11) Who will build it, who will maintain it? (12) As well as being visually appealing, visitors want websites to contain current information. (13) Someone must be responsible to update the site to keep visitors coming back.

(C)

(14) Third, identify a means to determine the success of the site. (15) For example, set a target number for visitors to the site, how many brochures are downloaded, or email inquiries. (16) Measurable outcomes related to the purpose. (17) Check to see periodically if the goals are being met.

12. Sentence 2: First, identify the intended audience and what the purpose is of the site.

What is the best way to revise this sentence? If you think the original is the best, choose option (1)

(1) First, identify the intended audience and what the purpose is of the site.
(2) First, identify what is the intended audience and what the purpose is of the site.
(3) Identify first the intended audience and what the purpose is of the site.
(4) First, identify the intended audience and purpose of the site.
(5) Identify the intended audience first. And what the purpose is of the site.

13. Sentence 5: Think about it a site that attempts to appeal to both of these groups will end up appealing to neither.

What is the best way to write the underlined part of the sentence? If you think the original is the best way, choose option (1).

(1) about it a site
(2) about it; a site
(3) about it, and a site
(4) about it, a site
(5) about it, when a site

14. Sentences 7 and 8: Here is a hint. Purposes usually include verbs, such as "Inform," "Motivate," "Train," and "Sell."

What is the best way to write the underlined part of the sentence? If you think the original is the best way, choose option (1).

(1) hint. Purposes usually
(2) hint, purposes usually
(3) hint. Purposes, usually
(4) hint purposes usually
(5) hint, but purposes usually

15. Sentence 9: Second, identification of responsibilities and resources.

What is the best way to revise this sentence? If you think the original is the best way, choose option (1)

(1) Second, identification of responsibilities and resources.
(2) Second, identification of responsibilities and of resources.
(3) Second is identification of responsibilities and resources.
(4) Second, identify responsibilities and resources.
(5) Second is the identification of responsibilities and of resources.

16. Sentence 11: Who will build it, who will maintain it?

What correction should be made to this sentence?

(1) replace build it, who with built it, and who
(2) delete the comma after build it
(3) change build it to be building it
(4) change build it, who to build it and who
(5) no correction necessary

17. Sentence 12: As well as being visually appealing, visitors want websites to contain current information.

What is the best way to revise this sentence? If you think the original is the best way, choose option (1)

(1) As well as being visually appealing, visitors want websites to contain current information.
(2) Visitors, as well as being visually appealing, want websites to contain current information.
(3) In addition to being visually appealing, visitors want websites to contain current information.
(4) As well as being visually appealing, websites should contain current information.
(5) As well as being visually appealing. Visitors want websites to contain current information.

18. Sentence 15: For example, set a target number for visitors to the site, <u>how many brochures are downloaded</u>, or email inquiries.

What is the best way to write the underlined part of the sentence? If you think the original is the best way, choose option (1).

(1) how many brochures are downloaded
(2) brochure downloads
(3) the number of brochures downloaded
(4) downloading of brochures
(5) brochures to be downloaded

19. Sentence 16: Measurable outcomes related to the purpose.

What is the best way to revise this sentence? If you think the original is the best way, choose option (1)

(1) Measurable outcomes related to the purpose.
(2) Choose measurable outcomes related to the purpose.
(3) Measurable business outcomes related to the purpose.
(4) Realistic and measurable outcomes related to the purpose.
(5) Measurable outcomes that are related to the purpose.

20. Sentence 17: Check to see periodically if the goals are being met.

What correction should be made to this sentence?

(1) move <u>periodically</u> to the beginning of the sentence
(2) insert a comma before <u>if</u>
(3) insert a period before <u>if</u>
(4) insert a comma after <u>check</u>
(5) no correction necessary

ANSWERS AND ANALYSIS

1. Your answers may be slightly different, but they should be similar to those below.

   - Sentence Fragment—an incomplete sentence, missing a subject or predicate or not forming a complete thought
   - Run-on Sentence—two or more sentences, incorrectly written together as one sentence
   - Comma Splice—a type of run-on sentence in which a comma is used in place of a period
   - Parallelism—grammatical pattern of words, phrases, or clauses in a sequence
   - Misplaced Modifier—a modifying word or phrase that is incorrectly placed so that it describes the wrong thing in the sentence
   - Dangling Modifier—a modifying word or phrase that is incorrectly placed so that readers are unsure what the modifier is describing

2. **(4)** This is the only alternative that does not contain a dangling modifier. Options (1) and (2) both suggest that the same people start new careers every year in real estate. Options (3) and (5) incorrectly refer to "new Canadians" rather than new careers.

3. **(1)** This is an instance of the comma splice type of run-on sentence. A period is needed to clearly define the two separate sentences.

4. **(3)** The introductory part is not a complete thought and cannot stand alone as a sentence.

5. **(1)** Correct as written.

6. **(2)** Fix parallel structure by listing all items in the same way.

7. **(1)** Parallel structure, "it may also take" and "it commonly takes."

8. **(1)** This is an instance of the comma splice type of run-on sentence.

9. **(1)** Correct as written.

10. **(3)** Parallel structure, "financially beneficial" and "personally rewarding."

11. **(1)** This is an instance of the comma splice type of run-on sentence.

12. **(4)** Parallel structure, "intended audience and purpose."

13. **(2)** Fix this run-on sentence by using a semi-colon to join the two independent clauses and create a compound sentence.

14. **(1)** Correct as written.

15. **(4)** This sentence fragment requires a predicate. Although options 3 and 5 would also make a complete sentence, they lack parallelism with sentences 2 and 15, which give the first and third steps. On the GED writing test, you must consider not only the individual sentence, but the passage as a whole when identifying the correct answer.

16. **(1)** This is an instance of a comma splice. One way to correct the run-on sentence is to use a comma and coordinating conjunction to make a compound sentence.

17. **(4)** This is the only option that corrects the misplaced modifier, which otherwise says that the visitors are visually appealing rather than the website.

18. **(2)** Fix parallel structure by listing all items in the same way.

19. **(2)** Fix this sentence fragment by adding a predicate, the verb *choose*. The subject of the sentence is understood although not written. *You choose measurable outcomes related to the purpose.*

20. **(1)** Move the misplaced modifier to make the meaning clear, *periodically check* not *periodically see.*

Paragraphs

4

THINK ABOUT IT

Have you ever heard someone talking who just never seems to stop? We all know someone like this. The person hardly seems to pause, and you wonder how the person gets a breath because there is never a break. Conversation like that is overwhelming and hard to pay attention to, just like a piece of writing without paragraphs.

IN THIS CHAPTER

The word *paragraph* comes from two Greek words that mean *mark beside.* Originally, that's what a paragraph was. It was a mark beside the text that broke up the page and gave readers a chance to rest their eyes and keep their place. This is still one purpose of paragraphs; however, they also serve other purposes. They allow writers to organize their work by separating ideas into smaller units.

Writing and correcting paragraphs is part of organized writing. Organization accounts for 15% of the questions on the GED Language Arts, Writing Test, Part 1 and will be an important skill in creating a well-written essay on Part 2.

After completing this chapter, you will be able to

- → **DEFINE PARAGRAPHS**
- → **IDENTIFY TOPIC SENTENCES IN PARAGRAPHS**
- → **IDENTIFY SUPPORTING SENTENCES IN PARAGRAPHS**
- → **EDIT PARAGRAPHS FOR UNITY**
- → **EDIT PARAGRAPHS FOR COHESION**
- → **SUB-DIVIDE PARAGRAPHS**
- → **WRITE WELL-ORGANIZED PARAGRAPHS**

WHAT IS A PARAGRAPH?

A **paragraph** is an organized group of related sentences. It has a **topic sentence**, which gives the main idea of the paragraph. It also has supporting sentences that give details, reasons, explanations, or examples to support the topic sentence. The sentences flow naturally and logically from one to the next, so that the paragraph is a coherent unit or sub-unit of a larger piece of writing.

One common mistake of inexperienced writers is making paragraphs that are too short and do not contain enough supporting sentences or supporting information. Paragraphs that are too short are not effective because they do not give enough detail to make the meaning clear and to hold the reader's interest. All paragraphs should be at least three sentences long.

Paragraphs that are a full page are too long and should be broken into smaller pieces. There are two ways to indicate paragraphs. You can skip a line between paragraphs or indent the first line of each paragraph; however, use one method or the other, not both.

EXAMPLE

There is no better place to visit than Nunavut for those who are looking for ecotourism adventures in Canada's north. Visitors can go polar bear watching or caribou hunting. They can go canoeing, hiking, sea kayaking, or dog sledding. They can learn about the habitat of narwhals or go fishing for Arctic char. Most importantly, perhaps, visitors can learn about Inuit culture and traditions, which have bonded the people with their land of ice for thousands of years.

In the example paragraph, the underlined sentence is the topic sentence. The paragraph is about ecotourism in Nunavut. The remaining sentences are supporting sentences that give explanation and details. They give examples of some of the ecotourism opportunities that visitors might find there.

TOPIC SENTENCES

All writing needs to have structure. A paragraph is not just a group of sentences. It has structure, with a **topic sentence** that gives the main idea of the paragraph and supporting sentences that provide additional depth of detail.

A topic sentence is

- Usually found at the beginning of a paragraph
- Broad enough that more can be said about it
- Specific enough to restrict the topic

Paragraphs can be organized in different ways, but most commonly the topic sentence is the first sentence. The topic sentence is broad enough that it can be supported by detail sentences, but it is specific enough that it clearly identifies the main idea of the paragraph.

EXAMPLES

Martine's home town is best known for its unique winter festival.
The television show was cancelled for two reasons.

One of the most common mistakes of inexperienced writers is writing paragraphs that are too short.

PRACTICE

In each group, indicate which sentence would make the best topic sentence for a paragraph.

Example:

   a) <u>Fibre is one of the most important parts of a healthy diet.</u>
   b) This cereal contains 30% of the daily recommended intake of fibre.
   c) Fibre is a good thing to eat.

Sentence a) is the best topic sentence. You can imagine the reader thinking "why," which is probably what will be answered in the supporting sentences. Sentence b) would not be a good topic sentence because it only gives a detail. Sentence c) is not as strong a statement as sentence a).

1. a) The network started a new reality cooking show.
   b) Reality television cooking shows receive higher ratings than traditional cooking programs.
   c) The network's new reality cooking show will capture higher ratings for several reasons.

2. a) Gang violence has become an increasing problem in Canadian cities.
   b) There has been gang violence in many Canadian cities.
   c) Gang-related violent crimes increased .04% in Canada last year.

3. a) Soft-tissue injuries resulting from improper lifting techniques are one of the greatest dangers in the workplace.
   b) It is important to learn how to lift correctly.
   c) Soft-tissue injuries can result from improper lifting.

4. a) There is a mommy and baby movie club that meets at the local cinema on Tuesday mornings every week.
   b) Movies are very popular.
   c) The mommy and baby movie club at the local cinema is a great way for new mothers to meet and make friends.

5. a) Our family has a reunion every year.
   b) Every year, our family looks forward eagerly to our annual family reunion.
   c) Although not a lot of families do it on a regular basis, our family has a reunion every year.

6. a) School cafeteria food is not the best.
   b) School cafeteria food does not have nutritional components to support learning.
   c) The school cafeteria serves a variety of foods.

7. a) Mount Logan in Yukon is Canada's highest mountain.
   b) Mount Logan is 5959 metres tall.
   c) Mount Logan is located in Yukon and is 5959 metres tall.

8. a) Spring storms are known for producing a wide range of dangerous weather conditions.
    b) Dangerous thunderstorms can occur, causing flooding.
    c) Weather conditions can range from rainstorms to hail to snow.

ANSWERS

1.	c	3.	a	5.	b	7.	a
2.	a	4.	c	6.	b	8.	a

TIP

A topic sentence states the main idea of the paragraph.

Good paragraphs have **unity**, which means that the paragraph is about only one main topic. The topic sentence is the one that gives the main idea and unifies the paragraph. It ties everything together.

PRACTICE

Write a topic sentence for each group of supporting sentences.

Example:

The increasing cost of living is a problem for many families.

a) Prices for food, clothing, and other necessities are always on the rise.
b) Housing-related expenses, such as rent, energy, and utilities, also continue to climb.
c) Meanwhile, wages are not increasing at the same rate.
d) The average family simply can't keep up.

1. _____

    _____

a) Nurses earn a good income.
b) They are in great demand throughout Canada and the United States.
c) With North America's aging population, there is little chance that the demand for nurses will decrease.

2. _____

    _____

a) Many options are available for those who have had a few drinks to find their way home.
b) They can take a cab or call a friend or family member.
c) If they are going out with friends, they can appoint a designated driver.
d) The simple fact is, driving drunk just isn't worth the risk.

3. _____

   _____

   a) One reason is that cats are easy to take care of.
   b) The fact that they can use a litter box instead of going on the carpet is a big plus.
   c) Another reason is that they are very affectionate although people who aren't cat lovers don't seem to think so.
   d) Finally, cats are independent.
   e) They can amuse themselves when their owners don't feel like paying attention to them and cats aren't always underfoot.

4. _____

   _____

   a) French fries are high in fat and often coated with salt.
   b) Hamburgers are also high in fat and in cholesterol.
   c) Even the salads at fast food restaurants may not be nutritious.
   d) Dressing is high in fat and iceberg lettuce has little food value.

5. _____

   _____

   a) First, check the odometer and compare the reading with your perception of the overall condition of the used vehicle.
   b) Second, inspect the body carefully, looking for signs of rust or a previous accident.
   c) Third, look at the overall appearance of the car to see if it appears to be well maintained.

6. _____

   _____

   a) Game show host Alex Trebek was born in Sudbury, Ontario.
   b) Actor Donald Sutherland was born in Saint John, New Brunswick.
   c) Singer and poet Leonard Cohen was born in Montreal, Quebec.
   d) For a country with a small population, we have produced our share of famous entertainers.

7. _____

   _____

   a) Make sure you arrive for the interview on time and that your appearance is clean and neat.
   b) Make eye contact as you introduce yourself and shake hands with a firm grip.
   c) Speak in a friendly, but professional manner.
   d) You never get a second chance to make a first impression.

8. _____

_____

    a) Children do not spend as much time reading as before.

    b) They do not spend as much time outside exercising.

    c) Instead, they pass their time with their smart phones, video games, televisions, and computers.

    d) Studies indicate that Canadian children spend almost eight hours per day using some kind of electronic device.

ANSWERS

Your answers will be different, but see the sample answers below.

1. Nursing is a good choice for a career.

2. There is no excuse for people to drink and drive.

3. Cats make the best pets.

4. Eating too often at fast food restaurants is not a healthy diet.

5. When considering the purchase of a used car, there are three things you should do.

6. Many world-famous entertainers were born in Canada.

7. When interviewing for a new job, it is important to make a good first impression.

8. Young people today spend too much time using electronic devices.

The topic sentence is found in one of four places in a paragraph:

1. **AT THE BEGINNING**—The topic sentence is most often the first sentence and is followed by supporting sentences. This is especially true within the body of a piece of writing.

2. **AT THE END**—Supporting sentences can lead up to the main idea. This is especially common in introductory paragraphs.

3. **IN THE MIDDLE**—A paragraph may begin by stating a problem or asking a question and be followed by a topic sentence.

4. **NOWHERE**—The topic may sometimes be understood if it is clear that the supporting sentences refer to an idea that was introduced in a previous paragraph.

PRACTICE

Underline the topic sentence in each of the following paragraphs.

1. Victoria has something for everyone! There's so much to do and see —it's just a matter of choosing. Whether you're strolling along the causeway in the Inner Harbour, enjoying a whale-watching adventure, indulging in the distinct West Coast cuisine, or taking in a local theatre production, Victoria's attractions add up to a trip that's nothing short of breathtaking.

2. This is where the sun rises first. This is where Vikings landed over 1,000 years ago. This place is home to the oldest settlement and the oldest city in North America, but is the youngest province of Canada. This is a land of rich history and natural wonders: stunning coastlines, breaching whales, icebergs, and some of the most incredible skyscapes you'll ever see. From vibrant cities to quaint, historical outports, mountain ranges, rivers, waterfalls, and winding coastlines, there are always fascinating places to see and countless things to do in Newfoundland.

3. Earthworms can help your garden in many ways. They do a good job of incorporating organic material into the soil. Worms also produce fertilizer. Castings are the mixed mass of soil and nutrients cast off by earthworms as they pass through the soil. Castings have a much higher nutrient level than surrounding soil, including higher levels of nitrogen, phosphorous, potassium and beneficial bacteria and enzymes. Worms are very efficient in their production and it does not take many to maintain healthy plants in a small garden.

4. This gets to the crux of how to pick people to manage your money. How can you tell if someone is lucky, good or both? If someone shoots the moon for ten years, can they just be on a really, really good hot streak? How can you know? If a hedge fund manager is down, maybe they are just unlucky, right? How can you tell the truly good from the merely lucky?[1]

5. Picture a magnificent row of fragrant blossoms gracing your walkway each spring. Imagine the delight of plucking fresh fruit right off your own trees and carrying a heaping basket into the kitchen. Think about a bubbling pan of pear crisp or a peach pie fresh from the oven made with the fruits of your labours. These are all reasons to plant your own fruit trees.[2]

6. In 1935, during the Great Depression, Newfoundland was largely bankrupt. Normal government operations were suspended and it was ruled by a commission and a British governor. It was against this backdrop that the Newfoundland Rangers were formed. For fifteen years, this group provided many government services. They functioned as police, fisheries officers, truant officers, customs agents, and more. In 1950, a year after confederation with Canada, the rangers were replaced by the RCMP.

TIP

The topic sentence can be found at the beginning, middle, or end of a paragraph or it may simply be understood.

ANSWERS

1. <u>Victoria has something for everyone!</u> There's so much to do and see—it's just a matter of choosing. Whether you're strolling along the causeway in the Inner Harbour, enjoying a whale-watching adventure, indulging in the distinct West Coast cuisine, or taking in a local theatre production, Victoria's attractions add up to a trip that's nothing short of breathtaking.

[1]Extracted From: "Luck vs. Talent vs. Skill." *Forbes.* 13 July 2009. Downloaded from *http://www.forbes.com/2009/07/13/trading-money-manager-intelligent-investing-strategy.html 8 Nov 2013.*

[2]Adapted from Fitts, Maribeth. "Juicy Fruits: Pick Fresh Peaches and Pears." Canadian Gardening Magazine (online). *http://www.canadiangardening.com/gardens/fruit-and-vegetable-gardening/juicy-fruits-pick-fresh-peaches-and-pears/a/1219* Downloaded 8 Nov 2013.

2. This is where the sun rises first. This is where Vikings landed over 1,000 years ago. This place is home to the oldest settlement and the oldest city in North America, but is the youngest province of Canada. This is a land of rich history and natural wonders: stunning coastlines, breaching whales, icebergs, and some of the most incredible skyscapes you'll ever see. From vibrant cities to quaint, historical outports, mountain ranges, rivers, waterfalls, and winding coastlines, there are always fascinating places to see and countless things to do in Newfoundland.

3. Earthworms can help your garden in many ways. They do a good job of incorporating organic material into the soil. Worms also produce fertilizer. Castings are the mixed mass of soil and nutrients cast off by earthworms as they pass through the soil. Castings have a much higher nutrient level than surrounding soil, including higher levels of nitrogen, phosphorous, potassium and beneficial bacteria and enzymes. Worms are very efficient in their production and it does not take many to maintain healthy plants in a small garden.

4. This gets to the crux of how to pick people to manage your money. How can you tell if someone is lucky, good or both? If someone shoots the moon for ten years, can they just be on a really, really good hot streak? How can you know? If a hedge fund manager is down, maybe they are just unlucky, right? How can you tell the truly good from the merely lucky?

5. Picture a magnificent row of fragrant blossoms gracing your walkway each spring. Imagine the delight of plucking fresh fruit right off your own trees and carrying a heaping basket into the kitchen. Think about a bubbling pan of pear crisp or a peach pie fresh from the oven made with the fruits of your labours. These are all reasons to plant your own fruit trees.

6. In 1935, during the Great Depression, Newfoundland was largely bankrupt. Normal government operations were suspended and it was ruled by a commission and a British governor. It was against this backdrop that the Newfoundland Rangers were formed. For fifteen years, this group provided many government services. They functioned as police, fisheries officers, truant officers, customs agents, and more. In 1950, a year after confederation with Canada, the rangers were replaced by the RCMP.

CHALLENGE EXERCISE

Select one or two paragraphs in a newspaper, book, or magazine. Try to find and underline the topic sentence in each paragraph.

SUPPORTING SENTENCES

The topic sentence gives the main idea of a paragraph. The **supporting sentences** say more about it. They may give:

- Explanations
- Reasons
- Details
- Information
- Examples

The evening was perfect. Although the air outside was chilly and felt like rain, it was warm and snug at Melvin's Bar. Everyone was looking forward to the reunion of the local jazz band. The small crowd chatted quietly, and there was expectancy in the air. The musicians quickly went about the business of setting up, and even Dave, the drummer, seemed in a good mood. Then Dutch sat down to the piano, Julia picked up her saxophone, and they began to play.

The paragraph begins with the topic sentence, "The evening was perfect." The first supporting sentence explains what the topic sentence means by perfect. The next sentence gives the reason. The sentences that follow give more details and information. All of the sentences are directly related to the main idea.

PRACTICE

For each of the topic sentences below, write three or more supporting sentences to make a complete paragraph.

1. Before heading south for a vacation this winter, there are some things you should consider.
2. Showers are better than baths.
3. When tourists come to my home town, they go to see these attractions.
4. Many people enjoy winter sports.
5. Canada is the best country in which to live.
6. Freshly fallen snow is very beautiful.
7. The cost of buying groceries is going up.
8. Regular pop is better than diet pop.

ANSWERS

Answers will vary; however, your supporting sentences should give:

1. Examples of things to consider.
2. Reasons that showers are better than baths.
3. Examples of attractions and, perhaps, some information about them.
4. Examples of and information about winter sports.
5. Reasons why Canada is the best country in which to live.
6. Details that describe the beauty of snow.
7. Examples and information about increasing costs.
8. Explanations and reasons why regular pop is better.

TIP

Each paragraph has supporting sentences that say more about the topic sentence.

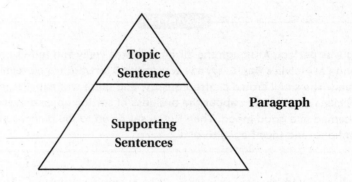

PRACTICE

Write a paragraph about each of the following topics. Each paragraph should include a topic sentence and several supporting sentences.

My favourite memory

The best thing I ever ate

The province I live in

Canada's military

Why family is important

ANSWERS

Answers will vary. Make sure each paragraph has a topic sentence and supporting sentences.

UNITY

Unity refers to harmony or agreement among the parts of a paragraph. To ensure unity, a paragraph must

- Be about a single idea (contained in the topic sentence)
- Have supporting sentences that are all related to the topic

To edit paragraphs for unity, you sometimes remove sentences that are not related to the topic sentence.

PRACTICE

In each paragraph, which sentence does not belong?

1. Fridays are now dress-down days for the children's hospital. Employees may pay three dollars to dress in casual clothes instead of regular work clothes. Acceptable casual wear must be clean and neat and does not include jeans. There are lots of good charities out there. Money collected will go to the local children's hospital.

2. City Laundry announced today that they are going out of business. The company was established in 1918 and has served the community with laundry and dry cleaning services for nearly a hundred years. Several other businesses in the city have been around even longer. Declining business and high cost of new equipment are cited as reasons for the closure. Twenty people will lose their jobs.

3. New students are invited to attend orientation activities at the university on Wednesday, September 7, at 2 pm. There will be a campus tour, refreshments, and a casino with a chance to win some great prizes. Students who have not yet chosen their courses can meet with a counsellor. The bookstore will be open. The university reminds you not to drink and drive.

4. The First Nation will be conducting ceremonies at the harbour from August 26 through August 29. The Lake Road and Harbour may be difficult to access on these dates because of traffic going to the ceremony. The lake is very beautiful this time of year. The Provincial Parks Association is asking that the public respect this ceremony and be patient with any inconvenience. Campsites in and around the area will be closed to camping for the period. If possible, please make plans to visit other areas of the lakeshore during this time.

ANSWERS

1. Fridays are now dress down days for the children's hospital. Employees may pay three dollars to dress in casual clothes instead of regular work clothes. Acceptable casual wear must be clean and neat and does not include jeans. ~~There are lots of good charities out there.~~ Money collected will go to the local children's hospital.

2. City Laundry announced today that they are going out of business. The company was established in 1918 and has served the community with laundry and dry cleaning services for nearly a hundred years. ~~Several other businesses in the city have been around even longer.~~ Declining business and high cost of new equipment are cited as reasons for the closure. Twenty people will lose their jobs.

3. New students are invited to attend orientation activities at the university on Wednesday, September 7, at 2 pm. There will be a campus tour, refreshments, and a casino with a chance to win some great prizes. Students who have not yet chosen their courses can meet with a counsellor. The bookstore will be open. ~~The university reminds you not to drink and drive.~~

4. The First Nation will be conducting ceremonies at the harbour from August 26 through August 29. The Lake Road and Harbour may be difficult to access on these dates because of traffic going to the ceremony. ~~The lake is very beautiful this time of year.~~ The Provincial Parks Association is asking that the public respect this ceremony and be patient with any inconvenience. Campsites in and around the area will be closed to camping for the period. If possible, please make plans to visit other areas of the lakeshore during this time.

COHESION

Cohesion means sticking pieces or parts together. In paragraphs, cohesion refers to positioning the sentences together so that they are connected and flow from one to the next. There are many techniques that can be used to connect sentences with one another.

- Repetition—reusing a key word from a previous sentence
- Synonym—using a word that has the same meaning as a key word from the previous sentence
- Antonym—using a word that has the opposite meaning of a key word from the previous sentence
- Enumeration—using words that suggest an order to the sentences, such as first, second, third, next, or finally
- Parallelism—using similar grammatical structures in the sentences
- Linking words—Using words such as *however*, *therefore*, *consequently*, and *as a result*, which guide the readers from one sentence to the next throughout the paragraph
- Pronoun references—using pronouns, such as *this*, to refer back to ideas that were mentioned in previous sentences

EXAMPLE

Ottawa Limits Caffeine in Energy Drinks
Many people are concerned about the caffeine contained in energy drinks. In 2011, Ottawa decided to do something about it by starting to limit the amount. The changes (1) introduced by Health Canada would also include warnings to be placed on the beverages. However, (2) the medical community had hoped for stricter regulations, including restricting purchases to those over eighteen years of age. Health Canada (3) will instead restrict the amount of caffeine to a maximum of 180 milligrams in one single-serving container.

1. **SYNONYM**—"The changes" repeats the idea of "starting" in the previous sentence.
2. **LINKING WORD**—"However" shows a change in the argument.
3. **REPETITION**—Repeats an idea from a previous sentence

PRACTICE

In each paragraph, underline the words or phrases that connect the sentences and provide cohesion.

1. Replacing the windows in your home can help to improve energy efficiency; however, you need to choose the right windows. First, make sure you buy energy-efficient windows. Just because windows are new, doesn't mean they are energy-efficient. Second, buy windows with low-E glass. Third, get windows with frames that do not require regular maintenance, such as vinyl windows. Keeping these considerations in mind will help you choose the best value for your home.

2. Thursday night's performance by the high school drama club was a highlight of the school year. Like a silent movie, the show includes no dialogue or lyrics, but relies on action and instrumental music to tell the story. The original production is an interesting take on the Dracula story and was composed by music teacher Matt Dublin.

3. New Canadians face many challenges when arriving in Canada. They are faced with a new culture. They may need to learn a new language. They experience new ways of working and conducting business. As a result, many employers are reaching out to new Canadians, helping to reduce barriers and ease the transition to the Canadian work-place.

ANSWERS

1. Replacing the windows in your home can help to improve energy efficiency; <u>however</u>, you need to choose the right windows. <u>First</u>, make sure you buy energy-efficient windows. Just because windows are new, doesn't mean they are energy-efficient. <u>Second</u>, buy windows with low-E glass. <u>Third</u>, get windows with frames that do not require regular maintenance, such as vinyl windows. Keeping <u>these considerations</u> in mind will help you choose the best value for your home. (linking, enumeration, pronoun reference)

2. Thursday night's <u>performance</u> by the high school drama club was a highlight of the school year. Like a silent movie, the <u>show</u> includes no dialogue or lyrics, but relies on action and instrumental music to tell the story. The original <u>production</u> is an interesting take on the Dracula story and was composed by music teacher Matt Dublin. (synonym)

3. New Canadians face many challenges when arriving in Canada. <u>They are faced with a new culture</u>. <u>They may need to learn a new language</u>. <u>They experience new ways</u> of working and conducting business. <u>As a result</u>, many employers are reaching out to new Canadians, helping to reduce barriers and ease the transition to the Canadian work-place. (parallelism, linking)

Problems with Cohesion

- When paragraphs lack cohesion, the sentences do not seem connected. This can occur when Linking Words do not lead readers logically through the sentences
- Techniques such as enumeration are not applied consistently

PRACTICE

1. (1) A fjord is a long narrow inlet from the ocean with steep mountain sides. (2) They are usually found where deep coastal valleys have been formed by glacial action. (3) They are in Norway. (4) However, they are also common along the coast of Newfoundland.

   What change would improve the cohesion of this paragraph?

   (1) Change <u>A fjord is a long narrow inlet</u> to <u>Although a fjord is a long narrow inlet</u>
   (2) Replace sentence (3) with <u>Fjords are most commonly identified with Norway</u>.
   (3) Delete <u>However</u>
   (4) Replace <u>However</u> with <u>Although</u>

2. (1) I have heard it said that there are three keys to a happy life. (2) First, marry someone you are compatible with and with whom you can have fun. (3) Second, choose a career you like. (4) Thirdly, don't sweat the small stuff.

What change would improve the cohesion of this paragraph?

(1) In sentence 2, change First to Consequently
(2) Start a new sentence after compatible with
(3) Delete second
(4) Change Thirdly to Third

3. (1) Nothing is more nutritious than homemade soup. (2) It is low in fat and rich in vitamins and minerals. (3) For instance, a cup of homemade beef broth has only about 35 calories, with little salt and fat. (4) In contrast, a cup of canned beef vegetable soup can have more than 70 calories. (5) Therefore, homemade soup is richer in vitamins and antioxidants.

What change would improve the cohesion of this paragraph?

(1) Replace Nothing with Although
(2) Change For instance to However
(3) Delete In contrast
(4) Change Therefore to In addition

ANSWERS

1. **(2)** repetition
2. **(4)** be consistent with enumeration—first, second, third
3. **(4)** guide the reader logically

CHALLENGE EXERCISE

Select a paragraph of four or more sentences in a book, newspaper, or magazine (or write one of your own).

1. Underline the topic sentence.
2. Number the supporting sentences.
3. Cross out any sentences that do not relate to the main idea (if any).
4. Circle words or phrases that connect the sentences together and provide cohesion.
5. Discuss your answers with a teacher, friend, or another student.

SUB-DIVIDING PARAGRAPHS

Paragraphs serve two purposes:

1. To organize writing with one topic sentence and several supporting sentences
2. To make writing easier to read by breaking it into smaller units

On the GED® test, some questions may ask you to improve organization by sub-dividing paragraphs that are too long or that include more than one topic. Divide the paragraph where a new topic begins.

(1) Health-conscious Canadians are turning increasingly to bottled water. (2) In fact, bottled water has become one of the best-selling beverages in the country. (3) Concerns about pollutants in drinking water and the taste of chlorinated tap water have led many people to purchase their water in bottles. (4) Now, more than 60% of Canadians drink bottled water every day. (5) With the increase in consumption comes the question of what to do with all the bottles. (6) Some environmentalists now claim that one of the biggest things Canadians can do to protect the environment is to stop drinking bottled water. (7) They say that the empty water bottles are becoming a serious problem. (8) The water companies, however, say that bottles make up less than 1% of the content of landfills.

This paragraph has two main ideas. The first is contained in sentence 1, which is a topic sentence about bottled water. The second main idea begins in sentence 5, which is a topic sentence about the problem of disposing of empty bottles. The organization of the passage would be improved by beginning a new paragraph in sentence 5.

PRACTICE

1. (1) Order great pizza-meal deals for your family and get money-saving coupons. (2) This week, when you order two large, three-topping pizzas, you will receive coupons for over $30 in future savings. (3) This offer is good until the end of the month. (4) It applies to take-out orders only. (5) Also, be sure to join our pizza rewards club. (6) Ask for your pizza-club points every time you buy. (7) Cash in your points for free rewards, such as pizzas, drinks, or pasta.

    The organization of this passage would be improved by beginning a new paragraph starting with

    (1) Sentence 3
    (2) Sentence 4
    (3) Sentence 5
    (4) Sentence 6
    (5) No revision necessary

2. (1) From 1949 to 1978, the Canadian Film Awards were the forum for annual recognition of Canadian film artists. (2) As there were few Canadian films produced each year, it was a relatively small affair. (3) During some years, there were so few films that none was found worthy to be film of the year. (4) Since that time, Canadian film has changed and grown. (5) The Canadian Film Awards became the Genies in 1980, a prestigious award indeed.

    The organization of this passage would be improved by beginning a new paragraph starting with

    (1) Sentence 2
    (2) Sentence 3
    (3) Sentence 4
    (4) Sentence 5
    (5) No revision necessary

3. (1) The quinzee is a kind of shelter made from snow, which probably originated in Canada. (2) Unlike an igloo, a quinzee is not intended as a long-term shelter. (3) It is a temporary shelter that can be made in a few hours and can serve in a variety of situations, including as an emergency shelter. (4) To build a quinzee, start by making a pile of snow. (5) Wait for several hours for the snow to settle and become firm. (6) Next, begin to hollow out the mound. (7) Start with an entrance tunnel and then hollow out a sleeping chamber. (8) How big the chamber can be will depend on the snow conditions. (9) Finally, use your arm or several long sticks to make several air holes in the dome.

The organization of this passage would be improved by beginning a new paragraph starting with

   (1) Sentence 3
   (2) Sentence 4
   (3) Sentence 5
   (4) Sentence 6
   (5) No revision necessary

ANSWERS

1. **(3)** A new topic sentence is given about pizza-club points.

2. **(5)** There is one main idea introduced in the first sentence, the Canadian Film Awards, with other supporting sentences.

3. **(2)** Start a new paragraph with sentence 4, which introduces the topic of how to build a quinzee.

CHAPTER CHECK-UP

Complete these practice exercises, and then check the answers and analysis that follow. After you mark your work, review any topic in the chapter that you had trouble with or did not understand.

Questions 1–4 are based on the following.

(A)

(1) Anyone who has ever asked for directions or tried to follow the instructions for an "easy to assemble" children's toy knows how difficult such things can be to follow. (2) There are many children's toys out there. (3) However, writing instructions is a very important part of technical writing in our society. (4) Imagine if you bought a new software package and there was no manual or if your office got a new high-tech photocopier and there were no directions. (5) Such documents are an essential part of the age in which we live.

(B)

(6) If instructions are often difficult to follow, they are even harder to write. (7) They require a thorough analysis of the task at hand and an acute awareness of the audience for whom they are written. (8) Your purpose in writing instructions will always be the same—to enable readers to perform a particular task. (9) The success of your writing will be judged by the success of the reader in safely and correctly completing the task. (10) In most cases, unless you are writing for a particular group of people, your audience will vary greatly. (11) You should

generally assume that your reader knows little or nothing about the task. (12) You must make sure that your instructions are complete, well organized, easy to follow, and clear. (13) The challenge for the reader should be to perform the task, not to figure out your instructions.

1. Which sentence states the topic for paragraph A?
   (1) Sentence 1
   (2) Sentence 2
   (3) Sentence 3
   (4) Sentence 4
   (5) No topic sentence

2. The unity of paragraph A could be improved by deleting
   (1) Sentence 1
   (2) Sentence 2
   (3) Sentence 3
   (4) Sentence 4
   (5) Sentence 5

3. The organization of paragraph B would be improved by beginning a new paragraph starting with
   (1) Sentence 8
   (2) Sentence 9
   (3) Sentence 10
   (4) Sentence 11
   (5) No revision necessary

4. Sentence 11: You should generally assume that your reader knows little or nothing about the task.

   What linking word would most improve the cohesion of this paragraph?
   (1) Therefore
   (2) However
   (3) Unless
   (4) Because
   (5) Although

Questions 5–8 are based on the following memorandum.

To: Mary Stuart, Human Resources Officer
From: Henry Tudor, Shipping and Receiving
Date: February 12
Subject: Report of Personal Injury Accident, Shipping and Receiving Area, February 10

(A)

(1) The incident occurred about 10:15 a.m., when several boxes fell from a palate that was being unloaded. (2) A Majestic Transport truck had arrived with a shipment of paper products. (3) George Windsor was operating the forklift and was removing the palates from the

truck. (4) Richard was, apparently, standing in the loading bay near the back of the truck. (5) On February 10, Richard Plantagenet was injured in an accident in the shipping and receiving area.

(B)

(6) The events of the day occurred as follows: (7) As George backed the forklift off the truck, two boxes from the top of the load fell, one of them landing on Richard Plantagenet's foot. (8) Next, George stopped the forklift and, on discovering that Richard was injured, called me to the scene. (9) Then, I drove Richard to the hospital emergency room where it was determined he had suffered two broken toes on his right foot. (10) Fourth, I completed an incident report.

(C)

(11) In my opinion, George Windsor, the operator of the forklift, was not at fault in any way. (12) I would like to take a course in accident investigation for professional development in the future. (13) I inspected the palate from which the boxes fell and found it to be properly loaded, but not properly secured with either straps or plastic. (14) In addition, Richard Plantagenet was wearing sneakers and not work boots, which are required in the shipping and receiving area.

5. The organization of paragraph A would be improved by moving which sentence to the beginning?
   (1) Sentence 2
   (2) Sentence 3
   (3) Sentence 4
   (4) Sentence 5
   (5) No change necessary

6. The organization of paragraph B would be improved by beginning a new paragraph starting with
   (1) Sentence 7
   (2) Sentence 8
   (3) Sentence 9
   (4) Sentence 10
   (5) No revision necessary

7. Sentence 10: Fourth, I completed an incident report.

   What change should be made to this sentence?

   (1) Delete the comma after Fourth
   (2) Change completed to had completed
   (3) Change completed to will complete
   (4) Insert a comma after incident
   (5) Replace Fourth with Finally

8. The unity of paragraph C could be improved by deleting
   (1) Sentence 11
   (2) Sentence 12
   (3) Sentence 13
   (4) Sentence 14
   (5) No revision necessary

Questions 9–10 are based on the following letter.

Dear Mr. Whitman:

(A)

(1) For the past three years, I have been self-employed doing landscape and outdoor maintenance work in the Thompson area. (2) I find the work challenging but rewarding, and I enjoy the feeling of satisfaction that comes from making someone's property look nice. (3) I feel, however, that I would be of more benefit to my customers if I were a part of an experienced team. (4) In addition, I believe that my base of established clients would benefit a potential employer. (5) This letter and accompanying résumé are my application for the position of Landscaper, which you recently advertised in the Leaf and Stump Journal. (6) I have earned a GED diploma and meet your educational requirements. (7) In addition, I am licensed to operate a tractor and backhoe. (8) Furthermore, my experience in landscaping and my real enjoyment of this type of work would make me a valuable addition to your company.

I look forward to meeting you for a personal interview. Please, contact me at 453-2385.

Sincerely,
Franklin Hood

9. The unity of the paragraph could be improved by deleting
   (1) Sentence 2
   (2) Sentence 4
   (3) Sentence 5
   (4) Sentence 8
   (5) No revision necessary

10. The organization of the paragraph would be improved by beginning a new paragraph starting with
    (1) Sentence 4
    (2) Sentence 5
    (3) Sentence 6
    (4) Sentence 7
    (5) No revision necessary

ANSWERS AND ANALYSIS

1. **(3)** The topic of the paragraph is the importance of writing instructions. All of the other sentences in the paragraph should support this sentence.

2. **(2)** The paragraph is about writing instructions. This sentence is about children's toys, which is not the topic of the paragraph.

3. **(3)** The first part of this paragraph talks about how difficult it is to write instructions. The second part of the paragraph, beginning with sentence 10, talks about understanding your audience.

4. **(1)** The word "therefore" is the only option with an appropriate meaning. It connects sentence 11 with the sentence that came before. The reason that you would assume your audience knows nothing is that the audience could vary greatly.

5. **(4)** In this paragraph, the topic sentence needs to be clearly identified at the beginning to make sense of the supporting sentences.

6. **(5)** This is one paragraph with supporting sentences that are all related to the topic of the events of the day.

7. **(5)** Other sentences in the paragraph are not numbered. Improve the coherence and the logic of the paragraph.

8. **(2)** This sentence is not related to the topic of the paragraph, which is determining fault.

9. **(5)** No sentences need to be deleted. All are related to the topic sentences.

10. **(2)** A new paragraph should begin with sentence 5, which introduces the topic of applying for a job.

Organization

5

THINK ABOUT IT

Put these words and phrases in the order you think they would appear in an essay.

Because	1.	_____
We can conclude	2.	_____
For example	3.	_____
I think	4.	_____
This shows	5.	_____

Compare your answers with someone else. You probably have similar responses. Why did you choose the order you did?

IN THIS CHAPTER

Just as a paragraph has a structure—with a topic sentence, supporting sentences, unity, and coherence—a longer piece of writing also needs to be organized. Whether it is an article, letter, essay, or story, every piece of writing should have the following:

- A topic/thesis sentence that gives the main idea
- Supporting paragraphs that give reasons, details, examples, or explanations
- Unity and coherence techniques that give a flow and connection among the paragraphs
- An ending that wraps up what has been said

In this *Think About It* exercise, you put words and phrases in the order they might appear in an essay. Near the beginning of an essay is a topic or thesis sentence that gives the main idea. It might include the words "I think." The next paragraphs could give reasons, examples, or explanations of the main idea, using words such as "because," "for example," and "this shows." Finally, the writing would have an ending paragraph that wraps up what has been said. It might include words such as "we can conclude." In this chapter, you will learn how to revise the organization of a document and make it more effective.

After completing this chapter, you will be able to

→ **IDENTIFY THE TOPIC OR THESIS SENTENCE**
→ **MOVE PARAGRAPHS**
→ **COMBINE PARAGRAPHS**
→ **APPLY TECHNIQUES FOR COHESION BETWEEN PARAGRAPHS**

THESIS STATEMENT

A paragraph has a topic sentence that gives the main idea of the paragraph. An essay has a **thesis statement**, which gives the main idea of the essay or article. It tells what the essay is all about. Everything else revolves around it. Every good essay or article has a thesis statement.

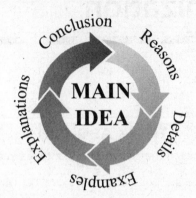

A thesis statement comes near the beginning. In an essay, it is often the last sentence of the first paragraph. In something like a newspaper article, it might be the very first sentence. To identify the thesis or topic sentence of a written passage ask yourself these questions:

1. What is the main idea of the essay or article?
2. Does the passage take a position about the main idea?
3. What sentence near the beginning states the position about the main idea?

EXAMPLE

You may have heard the expression that all work and no play is not a good thing. It seems that many employers agree. Companies today do want employees who work hard and are committed to the firm, but they do not want employees who do nothing but work. <u>One characteristic that many companies look for in employees is a healthy work-and-life balance.</u>

Work-and-life balance means being able to set priorities to balance career and ambition on one hand with things like family and personal interests on the other. For example, employees should have the commitment to show up on time for work and to do their best work while they are there. They should be willing to put in a little extra time when necessary to get the job done. They should take personal pride in the quality of their work and care about the success of their employer. At the same time, they should know when to go home and be able to put work aside. They should have interests and friends outside of work and a healthy spiritual and emotional life.

Those who have too little work ethic are obviously not good employees, but those who have too much can also be a problem. Employees who do not have a healthy work-and-life balance are more likely to experience stress at work and to miss time because of stress-related illnesses. In fact, in recent years, stress-related absences from work have doubled, costing companies hundreds of millions of dollars. In addition, employees who work too much often do not make good team players and create a poor work environment.

A healthy work-and-life balance is important for today's employees. Maintaining a balance between career and personal concerns helps reduce stress and create a better work experience for employees. It also saves companies money and creates a more productive workplace.

What is the main idea of this passage? It is about a healthy work-and-life balance. The passage takes the position that this is important to a productive workplace. The sentence near the beginning that states the main idea or thesis is found at the end of the first paragraph. This idea is the subject of the whole passage.

> **THESIS STATEMENT**
> 1. What is the main idea?
> 2. Does the passage give an opinion about the main idea?
> 3. What sentence states the opinion of the main idea?

PRACTICE

Underline the thesis statement in each of the following passages.

1. What We Can Learn from our Grandparents

To the editor:

(A)

(1) I think that our grandparents and great-grandparents had the right idea when they saved their money and avoided debt. (2) Many of them had lived through hard financial times when money and jobs were hard to come by. (3) They knew the value of a dollar and did not like to borrow money for unnecessary things. (4) They saved their money to buy what they wanted instead of buying on credit.

(B)

(5) Most people in our society live under a mountain of debt. (6) Want a new car? (7) Buy it on credit. (8) Need a new couch? (9) Make monthly payments. (10) Take a cash advance from one credit card to pay another. (11) Then there are the sneaky debts. (12) You can have a free cell phone if you pay a monthly cell phone bill for three years. (13) The result is that many people live on credit and the majority of their paycheck goes to pay debt.

(C)

(14) Our grandparents had it right. (15) Save your money; pay cash for what you want. (16) If you don't have enough, wait and keep saving until you do. (17) If you can't afford it, you don't need it. (18) Imagine how much it would reduce the stress of everyday life if you didn't have credit cards, loans, or other debt payment.

2. Hockey Must Change

(A)

(1) Medical experts agree that fundamental changes are required to many facets of the game of minor hockey if concussions are to be prevented. (2) Coaches, trainers, parents, and medical professionals have held ongoing discussions about steps that should be taken to stop these serious and often life-threatening injuries. (3) It is clear, however, that the solution is not simply the design of a better helmet. (4) What is required is a culture shift in the way that Canadians traditionally think about the game.

(B)

(5) For example, coaches and officials must take a more serious attitude to incidents of hitting players while their heads are down. (6) This was something that was once encouraged, even though it could lead to concussion. (7) According to Hockey Canada, more than rule changes are required. (8) It also requires respect for other players and holding up if you see somebody with their head down.

(C)

(9) Concussions have received much attention as a result of head injuries to high-profile players in the National Hockey League. (10) A number of great players have seen their careers cut short because of repeated concussions, and even Canadian great Sidney Crosby was out of action with a concussion for ten months several years ago. (11) This is not just an issue for professional sports. (12) Children playing in recreational or various levels of competitive hockey are the most commonly injured.

(D)

(13) Hockey Canada, the governing body for the sport in our country, agrees that changes are required. (14) To date, some rule changes have been implemented and the culture is changing. (15) The work of keeping our players safe, however, is not yet done.

3. Angler's Paradise—Sooke, B.C.
(A)

(1) Sooke: The name is synonymous with trophy salmon fishing at its finest. (2) Anglers from far and wide travel annually to sample its riches. (3) Situated on the southwest coast of Vancouver Island and just a thirty-minute drive from scenic Victoria, Sooke offers myriad angling opportunities. (4) One of the oldest settlements on the West Coast of Vancouver Island, it is as though Sooke is situated with recreational fishing in mind.

(B)

(5) Otter Point, west of the Sooke basin entrance, is an excellent spot to look for larger Chinook salmon, as the plentiful baitfish schools get tossed around the point into a naturally forming rip and back-eddy. (6) Here, larger salmon tend to hold within the back-eddy, anticipating the emergence of baitfish. (7) The underwater landscape consists of a 60- to 120-foot shoal stretching out a few hundred yards before dropping to depths of up to 400 feet. (8) This shoal, coupled with the tidal rips and back-eddies, provides suitable holding water for passing, migrant salmon.

(C)

(9) Eastward from Church Point before reaching Race Rocks, is Christopher Point. (10) Midland between Becher and Pedder Bay, it is capable of producing back-eddies on either side, which will collect intermittent pockets of baitfish, and subsequently produce occasional results of migrating salmon.

(D)

(11) All in all, Sooke and the surrounding areas add up to an angler's paradise, with world class angling opportunities to be had. (12) Everything needed to complete any angling vacation is here. (13) Accommodations, marinas, tackle shops, and best of all, world class fishing. (14) Come visit Sooke—you'll love it![1]

[1]Ray Bone. Source *http://www.sportfishingbc.com/articles/index.html?Angler-s-Paradise---Sooke-B.C.-128.*

ANSWERS

1. Sentence 1   2. Sentence 4   3. Sentence 4

CHALLENGE EXERCISE

The articles above came from newspapers and websites. Sometimes thesis statements are the first sentence. Sometimes they are at the end of the first paragraph or in the middle. In a longer piece of writing, the thesis statement could be further in. Find the thesis statements in three essays or articles on the Internet or in a magazine or newspaper. Show the passages to another student or friend to see if that person can find the thesis statement.

To find the thesis sentence, don't forget to ask yourself these questions:

1. What is the main idea of the essay or article?
2. Does the passage take a position about the main idea?
3. What sentence near the beginning states the position about the main idea?

MOVE PARAGRAPHS

Paragraphs must be in a logical sequence. On the multiple-choice section of the GED writing tests, there are questions about the order of paragraphs. For example, "Can the organization of this passage be improved by moving paragraph B?"

The first paragraph in a written passage is the introduction. It contains the thesis statement and introduces the main idea. The last paragraph is the conclusion.

The paragraphs in the middle can be organized in several ways:

- Chronological
- Process
- Comparison and contrast
- Cause and effect
- Description
- Increasing importance

A + B + C + D = E
The paragraphs of an essay must add up.

CHRONOLOGICAL—Follows the order of time in which things happened from first to last

PROCESS—Provides a sequence of steps; step one, step two, step three, and so on.

COMPARISON AND CONTRAST—Comparison shows how two things are the same, and contrast shows how two things are different.

CAUSE AND EFFECT—Explains the cause and then the resulting effect

DESCRIPTION—Describes a logical sequence of physical features

INCREASING IMPORTANCE—When stating reasons to prove a statement, gives the most important reason last. This is the common format for argumentative or persuasive essays.

On the GED® test, you will be asked to recognize if paragraphs should be moved to improve the organization.

EXAMPLE

Are Professional Athletes Paid Too Much?

(A)

(1) Today's professional athletes deserve the money they are paid because everyone else makes even more. (2) How much is a big-name basketball player worth if he can fill a 50,000-seat arena? (3) Then there are the millions of dollars in television revenues and merchandizing. (4) Athletes also make extra money advertising products, but how does that compare to the millions that the companies get in sales?

(B)

(5) Many people argue that today's professional athletes are overpaid. (6) The elite in every sport earn millions of dollars a year and then get even more in endorsements. (7) Yet we all admire their amazing skills. (8) We wear their names on our jerseys and have their posters on our walls. (9) We talk about them with our friends and watch them on TV. (10) Today's athletes are not overpaid.

(C)

(11) Athletes deserve to be well paid because they have worked hard to get where they are. (12) They have spent thousands of hours practicing alone in addition to organized team play to perfect their skills. (13) For years, they have sacrificed their time with family and friends, watched their diet, and exercised regularly. (14) Then there are the sacrifices of parents in time and money and the thousands of hours of work from coaches and community organizations to develop their skills.

(D)

(15) Athletes deserve to be paid well because they are among a select few. (16) In baseball, for example, millions of children play the sport. (17) Hundreds of thousands play at the high-school level. (18) Over ten thousand athletes in North America play baseball at the university or college level. (19) Several thousand play at the professional or semi-pro level, but only seven hundred and fifty of the best players in the world make the major leagues. (20) They have earned the right to be well paid.

(E)

(21) Yes, it is true. (22) Today's top athletes make an amazing amount of money. (23) However, they have sacrificed for years to rise among millions of players to get where they are. (24) The simple fact is, they get paid a lot because they earned it.

1. To improve organization of this passage:
   (1) Move paragraph A after paragraph B
   (2) Move paragraph A after paragraph C
   (3) Move paragraph A after paragraph D
   (4) Move paragraph B after paragraph E
   (5) Move paragraph D to the beginning

Take some time to read and think about this passage. If you are given a question about the organization of paragraphs, start by finding the introduction paragraph. You will quickly see that paragraph B is the introduction. It introduces the topic and contains the thesis statement. Paragraph A must be moved so that B can be at the beginning. The question is where to place paragraph A. You can see that this is an argumentative essay. It gives three reasons to prove that athletes are not overpaid.

1. They have worked hard
2. They are a select few
3. They make even more money for other people

In this type of organization, reasons are given by increasing importance. Paragraph A gives the most important reason, so it should be moved to the end, just before the conclusion.

The answer is: 3) Move paragraph A after paragraph D

PRACTICE

Respond to questions about the organization of paragraphs in the following passages.

How to Quit Smoking

(A)

(1) More than 19%—or almost six million—of all Canadians smoke. (2) The health effects of smoking are well known and most people would like to experience the improved quality of life that comes from quitting. (3) Quitting is hard, but it can be done if you are determined. (4) You can improve your chance of quitting by following a process.

(B)

(5) When the day comes, implement your plan and quit completely. (6) Do not smoke even a little bit. (7) The fact is that you are addicted, and continuing to smoke just prolongs the agony. (8) Throw away all your cigarettes, lighters, and ashtrays and avoid situations where you usually smoke. (9) It will be difficult, but remember your reasons for wanting to quit and stick with it.

(C)

(10) The first step is to pick a specific day when you intend to quit and stick to it. (11) Mark it on your calendar and count down the days. (12) Tell family and friends the day that you plan to quit so that your commitment will be increased. (13) Start making changes to your daily routine in preparation for quitting, such as changing where you go on your coffee break or not smoking in the car.

(D)

(14) The next step is to plan an approach to quitting smoking. (15) You need to have a plan. (16) Make a list of activities that you will do instead of smoking, such as a new exercise program or hobby. (17) Also, choose a quit-smoking method. (18) Will you join a support group or use a nicotine replacement like nicotine gum or patch? (19) Will you ask your doctor for a prescription to help you combat withdrawal? (20) Will you adopt a strategy such as chewing sunflower seeds? (21) Some people choose to quit cold turkey, which is a difficult strategy, but can be successful if you really want to stop.

(E)

(22) The chances of success at quitting smoking improve if you follow a process. (23) Pick a day to quit, pick a strategy, and implement your plan. (24) If you do have a relapse, don't give up. (25) Persistence is the key to success.

TIP

If you are given a question about the organization of paragraphs, start by finding the introduction paragraph.

1. What sentence is the thesis statement that states the main idea of the passage?
   - (1) Sentence 1: More than 19%—or almost six million—of all Canadians smoke.
   - (2) Sentence 4: You can improve your chance of quitting by following a process.
   - (3) Sentence 5: When the day comes, implement your plan and quit completely.
   - (4) Sentence 9: It will be difficult, but remember your reasons for wanting to quit and stick with it.
   - (5) Sentence 15: You need to have a plan.

2. Does paragraph E provide an effective conclusion to the passage?

3. What is the organization of paragraphs in the body of the passage?
   - (1) Chronological
   - (2) Process
   - (3) Comparison and contrast
   - (4) Cause and effect
   - (5) Increasing importance

4. To improve the organization of the passage
   - (1) Move paragraph B after paragraph D
   - (2) Move paragraph C before paragraph B
   - (3) Move paragraph D before paragraph B
   - (4) Move paragraph E to the beginning
   - (5) Move paragraph A after paragraph B

Which Is More Painful?

(A)

(1) There are many difficult things we have to do in our lives and many things people do not like. (2) One thing that ranks high for many is going to the dentist. (3) However, for people who do not like to write, creating an essay is even more painful. (4) Some people would even prefer to go to the dentist than write an essay.

(B)

(5) Writing an essay and going to the dentist are the same in many ways. (6) Most people don't like either one. (7) You spend a lot of time before getting started, worrying about the pain to come. (8) The dentist looking in your mouth often has the same facial expression as the teacher who marks your essay. (9) They both frown and say things like, "Oh, my. That isn't good." (10) Then you find yourself sitting and waiting for the bad news.

(C)

(11) There are many differences as well. (12) You only have to go to the dentist twice a year, but for students in school, essays are a common occurrence. (13) In addition, you can do things like brushing your teeth and flossing to make visits to the dentist less scary. (14) However, what can you do to lessen the pain of writing an essay?

(D)

(15) Another similarity between writing an essay and going to the dentist is the power of anticipation. (16) Everybody expects them both to hurt. (17) When you are done, however, often it isn't as bad as you feared.

(E)

(18) People who have naturally good teeth or are instinctively good writers cannot understand the fear of dentists or of writing essays. (19) For the rest of us, however, they both inspire dread. (20) Which one is more painful to you?

5. What sentence is the thesis statement that states the main idea of the passage?
   (1) Sentence 1: There are many difficult things we have to do in our lives and many things people do not like.
   (2) Sentence 3: However, for people who do not like to write, creating an essay is even more painful.
   (3) Sentence 4: Some people would even prefer to go to the dentist than write an essay.
   (4) Sentence 11: There are many differences as well.
   (5) Sentence 15: Another similarity between writing an essay and going to the dentist is the power of anticipation.

6. Does paragraph E provide an effective conclusion to the passage?

7. What is the organization of paragraphs in the body of the passage?
   (1) Chronological
   (2) Process
   (3) Comparison and contrast
   (4) Cause and effect
   (5) Increasing importance

8. To improve the organization of the passage
   (1) Move paragraph B after paragraph D
   (2) Move paragraph C before paragraph B
   (3) Move paragraph D after paragraph B
   (4) Move paragraph E to the beginning
   (5) Move paragraph A after paragraph B

ANSWERS

1. **(2)** Sentence 4. This essay describes the process for quitting smoking.

2. Yes. Paragraph E restates the main idea and summarizes the points from the essay.

3. **(2)** The essay describes the steps of the process to quit smoking.

4. **(1)** Put the steps of the process in order. According to the passage, the steps are to pick a day, pick a strategy, and implement your plan. The paragraphs should be in the same order as the steps.

5. **(3)** Sentence 4. This introduces the position on the topic that many people prefer going to the dentist to writing an essay.

6. Yes. Paragraph E summarizes the main idea of the essay.

7. **(3)** The essay compares writing essays and going to the dentist and talks about the differences.

8. **(3)** In this essay, all the points about the similarities should go together. Paragraph D should be moved right after paragraph B.

COMBINING PARAGRAPHS

Each paragraph in a passage of writing needs to have enough information to explain its topic clearly. In addition to a topic sentence, each paragraph has supporting sentences that give explanation, examples, and details. Paragraphs have three or more sentences to give enough information about the topic. Often paragraphs have five or six sentences, or even more.

Sometimes, organization can be improved by joining paragraphs together. A paragraph might have been divided by mistake with the topic sentence and some supporting details in one paragraph and the other supporting sentences in another. These paragraphs need to be combined.

EXAMPLE

(A)
(1) When the cruise ship sank off the coast of a small island in the Mediterranean, people wondered how such an accident could happen.

(B)
(2) The ship was larger than three football fields long. It was the height of luxury, a floating palace. (3) It had all of the modern navigation equipment and an experienced captain and crew. (4) It was sailing in an area that had been well-charted for hundreds of years. (5) Yet it struck rocks not a kilometre from shore, ripping open the hull and sinking in thirty metres of water.

In this example, paragraph (A) has only one sentence. This should be the topic sentence for the paragraph. Paragraph (B) contains the supporting details for the paragraph. To improve organization, they should be combined to make one paragraph.

PRACTICE

Popularity of Texas Hold'Em

(A)

(1) There are many different types of poker: five-card draw, seven-card stud, Omaha, razz, horse, pineapple, and more. (2) Poker was invented in the United States in the early 1800s and went through a slow evolution with the addition of the flush and wildcards and different types of the game emerging over the next century. (3) Tournament play became popular in the 1970s. (4) In the twenty-first century, however, poker has become extremely popular. (5) The most popular type of poker is Texas hold'em.

(B)

(6) Texas hold'em is a type of community poker in which players receive several individual cards, but other cards are shared by all players. (7) Each individual player receives two cards face down, which are not seen by the other players.

(C)

(8) The dealer then places three other cards, called "the flop," face up. (9) These are community cards that are part of everyone's hand. (10) A fourth and fifth card, called "the turn" and "the river," are also placed face up. (11) The player with the highest five-card hand, based on the individual and community cards, is the winner.

(D)

(12) Awareness of Texas hold'em poker grew rapidly when the game was popularized in several films, including the remake of *Casino Royale*, in the early 2000s. (13) At the same time, the game was spread through local poker games and the rise of online gaming. (14) When the World Series of Poker was first televised in 2003, the game reached a whole new audience. (15) Popularity of the game shot through the roof when an Internet amateur won the tournament.

(E)

(16) Texas hold'em is by far the most popular form of poker in North America. (17) Its popularity will only continue to grow. (18) Games continue to be televised with increasing regularity. (19) In addition, the Internet offers many ways for people to learn the game online and to play online in a wide variety of free or for-profit tournaments.

1. The organization of this passage could be improved by
   (1) Combining paragraphs A and B
   (2) Combining paragraphs B and C
   (3) Combining paragraphs C and D
   (4) Move paragraph B after paragraph C
   (5) Move paragraph C before paragraph B

Tourist Destination Cancun

(A)

(1) There are lots of places where Canadians go to get away from the cold. (2) Many families travel to Florida to enjoy the warmer weather and attractions such as theme parks and aquariums, as well as other attractions that are fun for the kids and parents too. (3) Others take the long flight to Hawaii. (4) Other tourist activities for cold Canadians include sipping mojitos on the beaches of Cuba or relaxing on a Caribbean Cruise.

(B)

(5) However, the most popular destination for Canadian sun worshipers is Cancun, Mexico.

(C)

(6) Going to the island of Cancun is almost a religious experience. (7) Located on the tip of Mexico, it has gone from being a fisherman's island to being one of the top tourist destinations in the world. (8) Long beaches of white sand stretch out along turquoise water. (9) Visit ancient Mayan ruins or be entertained by traditional native dancers. (10) Swim, dive, sail, jet-ski, or relax in the sun. (11) There are tons of ways to relax in Cancun.

(D)

(12) Why is Cancun the number one sun destination for Canadians? (13) It may have to do with the natural beauty or the consistently warm temperatures, although other areas are

equally beautiful. (14) More likely, it is because the resort area has reached a critical mass with over one hundred and twenty hotels and thirty-five thousand rooms and millions of visitors each year. (15) As a result, there are many cheap flights, cheap rooms, and cheap all-inclusive packages, making it one of the least-expensive alternatives as well.

2. The organization of this passage could be improved by
   (1) Combining paragraphs A and B
   (2) Combining paragraphs B and C
   (3) Combining paragraphs C and D
   (4) Move paragraph D before paragraph C
   (5) Move paragraph C to the end

ANSWERS

1. **(2)** Paragraphs B and C should be one paragraph. Sentence 6 is the topic sentence, which introduces the topic of how Texas hold'em is played. Sentences 7 to 11 give supporting information.

2. **(1)** Paragraphs A and B must be combined. Paragraph B is only one sentence and cannot be a paragraph by itself. Sentence 5 is the thesis statement for the passage and should be combined with the introductory paragraph A.

CHALLENGE EXERCISE

Newspaper articles are often written in short paragraphs of only one or two sentences. This is because newspapers are written in columns and normal paragraphs would look too long. Choose an article from a newspaper and rewrite it. Combine short paragraphs where necessary so topic sentences and supporting details are together. Remember that every paragraph should have at least three sentences.

TRANSITIONS BETWEEN PARAGRAPHS

You know that it is important to have cohesion inside a paragraph and to have a connection or flow between sentences. It is equally important to have a connection or flow between paragraphs. Each paragraph should seem like it is connected to the one before.

Good organization helps to connect paragraphs. The writing passage should follow a logical sequence: introduction, body, and conclusion. In addition, there are techniques that can be used to **transition**, or move smoothly, between paragraphs:

1. **REPEAT A WORD**—Use a key word from the last sentence of one paragraph in the first sentence of the next paragraph
2. **RESTATE AN IDEA**—Talk about an idea that was used in the previous paragraph
3. **USE A TRANSITION WORD**—Put in linking words that connect the first sentence of a paragraph with the paragraph that came before. Some transition words are:

- Nevertheless
- However
- Consequently
- Unfortunately
- Therefore

- Despite this
- In addition
- As well as

4. **USE A TRANSITION SENTENCE**—Remember that the first sentence of the paragraph is a linking sentence.

EXAMPLE

(A)
(1) There is no rush quite like the feeling of weightlessness, unbound by gravity, the wind in your face. (2) You dangle on air and feel every gust and billow as the earth streams bellow. (3) The smell of pine creeps under your helmet as you rise above a wooded hill. (4) It's like driving a motorcycle through the air. (5) Ultralight pilots truly know the freedom of flight.

(B)
(6) At its most basic, an ultralight aircraft is little more than a wing with a seat and engine beneath. (7) Under Canadian regulations, a basic ultralight weighs no more than 165 kg, it has only one seat, and it is built by the owner. (8) There are many places where you can get kits to make your own. (9) You can also buy more advanced ultralights. (10) Some are two-seater small planes with an enclosed seat, but the funnest kind have an open seat on a frame with a wing above and wheels, skis, or floats below.

(C)
(11) In addition to the fixed-wing type of ultralight, there are related craft that fall into the same category. (12) These include powered paragliders and powered parachutes. (13) Imagine yourself sitting in a seat on a metal frame, three wheels below, and the parachute spread out on the field behind waiting for takeoff.

(D)
(14) Why are ultralights increasing in popularity? (15) They are inexpensive and they are easy to fly. (16) A single-seat powered parachute can cost as little as $5,000. (17) The requirements for a license include being sixteen years old, some classroom instruction, and ten hours of flight time, including thirty takeoffs and landings. (18) That is all it takes. (19) Then you can find yourself flying low and slow, experiencing a freedom you have never known.

In this example, sentence (6) repeats the word "ultralight" from the previous sentence and "aircraft" repeats the idea of "pilots" and "flight." Sentence (11) uses linking words. Sentence (14) is a transition sentence and also repeats the word "ultralights."

In addition to checking transitions, you may sometimes need to add a sentence to make the transition between paragraphs. This could be necessary, for example, if the paragraph does not have a topic sentence. Such questions are worded something like this:

What sentence below would be most effective if added to the beginning of paragraph B?

CHALLENGE EXERCISE

Look at a passage in a book or magazine or previous exercises in this book. Note techniques that are used for transitions between paragraphs. See if you can identify ways the transitions could be improved. Discuss the passage and transitions with a family member, friend, or another student. Remember, you may not always agree. Discussion is one of the main purposes of the challenge exercises.

CHAPTER CHECK-UP

Complete these practice exercises, and then check the answers and analysis that follow. After you mark your work, review any topic in the chapter you had trouble with or did not understand.

Questions 1–4 are based on the following letter.

June 24, 20__

Principal Sharon Taylor
Whilton Public School
1212 Market Street
Cumberfield, ON K4C 1L8

Dear Principal Taylor:

(A)

(1) My son Patrick just finished kindergarten at your school. (2) You probably know Patrick and know that he has autism, but he loves going to school. (3) He has had a very good year and I want to thank you and your staff for your professionalism. (4) I especially want to thank his aide Sarah and to let you know what a good job she has done.

(B)

(5) On the first day of school, I was nervous for Patrick. (6) I didn't know if he would adjust to school and to meeting new people.

(C)

(7) I was afraid that he would be scared and that the other kids wouldn't know how to relate to him. (8) Sarah was there to greet him the first day and helped him to fit right in.

(D)

(9) Now that the year is over, Patrick will have to get used to not waiting for the bus every day. (10) He will miss Sarah over the summer, but he will hope to see her again in the fall. (11) I just wanted to tell you what a good job she did. (12) I hope Patrick can have her again next year.

(E)

(13) By Christmastime, Sarah had already become a very important person to Patrick. (14) She was always very patient and kind with him, but she also treated him with respect like any other child. (15) The Christmas card she gave him meant a lot to him.

Yours truly,
Anne R.

1. What sentence best states the main idea of the passage?
   (1) Sentence 1: My son Patrick just finished kindergarten at your school.
   (2) Sentence 2: You probably know Patrick and know that he has autism, but he loves going to school.
   (3) Sentence 4: I especially want to thank his aide Sarah and to let you know what a good job she has done.
   (4) Sentence 5: On the first day of school, I was nervous for Patrick.
   (5) Sentence 8: Sarah was there to greet him the first day and helped him to fit right in.

2. What is the organization of paragraphs in the body of the passage?
   (1) Chronological
   (2) Process
   (3) Comparison and contrast
   (4) Cause and effect
   (5) Increasing importance

3. The organization of this passage could be improved by
   (1) Combining paragraphs A and B
   (2) Combining paragraphs B and C
   (3) Combining paragraphs C and D
   (4) Combining paragraphs D and E
   (5) No change necessary

4. To improve the organization of this passage:
   (1) Move paragraph A after paragraph B
   (2) Move paragraph B after paragraph C
   (3) Move paragraph A after paragraph D
   (4) Move paragraph B after paragraph D
   (5) Move paragraph E before paragraph D

Questions 5–8 are based on the following passage.

(A)

(1) So you want to market your small business, but you don't know where to start. (2) Just comparing prices of different advertising media isn't the best way to come up with ideas. (3) Your business needs to have a strategy that reaches your customers.

(B)

(4) Who are they? (5) Where do they get their information? (6) How do they communicate with each other? (7) What is the best way for you to get a message to them?

(C)

(8) These days, there are many tools available for small businesses to reach their clients in addition to traditional media, such as newspaper, television, radio, and direct mail.

(D)

(9) The Internet especially offers many options in addition to a company website. (10) You can use email distribution lists to send electronic flyers to your clients or even to send text

messages to their cell phones. (11) You can create a social media page for your customers. (12) You can make videos about your products and services and make them available online. (13) There are many other tools as well.

(E)

(14) Many online resources are free or low cost, but it takes time to continually update your information and stay in touch with customers. (15) In addition, you have to learn what all the online tools are and how to use them. (16) As you know, time is also money. (17) If you don't have the time to implement these strategies yourself, we can help. (18) Our company will work with you to develop and maintain a custom marketing strategy for your small business.

5. What sentence best states the main idea, or thesis, of the passage?
   (1) Sentence 1: So you want to market your small business, but you don't know where to start.
   (2) Sentence 3: Your business needs to have a strategy that reaches your customers.
   (3) Sentence 8: These days, there are many tools available for small businesses to reach their clients in addition to traditional media such as newspaper, television, ratio, and direct mail.
   (4) Sentence 9: The Internet especially offers many options in addition to a company website.
   (5) Sentence 18: Our company will work with you to develop and maintain a custom marketing strategy for your small business.

6. What sentence below would be most effective if added to the beginning of paragraph B?
   (1) The way to get started with your strategy is to think about your customers.
   (2) What are the best methods to reach them?
   (3) Marketing should be based on information.
   (4) Examine what you know.
   (5) Begin at the beginning by identifying necessary information.

7. The organization of this passage could be improved by
   (1) Combining paragraphs A and B
   (2) Combining paragraphs B and C
   (3) Combining paragraphs C and D
   (4) Combining paragraphs D and E
   (5) No change necessary

8. To improve the organization of this passage:
   (1) Move paragraph A after paragraph B
   (2) Move paragraph B after paragraph C
   (3) Move paragraph C after paragraph D
   (4) Move paragraph E before paragraph A
   (5) No change necessary

ANSWERS AND ANALYSIS

1. **(3)** Sentence 4: This passage is a letter of thanks for the good job done by the aide Sarah.

2. **(1)** The passage is in chronological order. It talks about what happened at the beginning of the year, at Christmas, and at the end of the year.

3. **(2)** Paragraphs B and C should be combined. Paragraph C contains detail sentences that support the topic of paragraph B.

4. **(5)** If the passage is in chronological order, it should start at the beginning of the year, then Christmas, and then the end of the year.

5. **(3)** This passage is about marketing strategies that meet the needs of customers.

6. **(1)** This transition sentence repeats the words "strategy" and "customers" to connect with the final sentence of the previous paragraph.

7. **(3)** Although paragraphs B and C are both short, they do not contain related ideas. However, sentence 8 could easily be a topic sentence for paragraph D.

8. **(5)** The paragraphs of the passage are in a logical order.

Punctuation

6

IN THIS CHAPTER

Good writers know that punctuation is an important part of writing. On the GED® test, they want to know that you can recognize and correct punctuation problems that cause confusion or make the meaning unclear.

After completing this chapter, you will be able to

→ **IDENTIFY AND CORRECT ERRORS IN END PUNCTUATION**

→ **IDENTIFY AND CORRECT COMMA ERRORS IN A SERIES**

→ **IDENTIFY AND CORRECT COMMA ERRORS AFTER INTRODUCTORY ELEMENTS**

→ **IDENTIFY AND CORRECT COMMA ERRORS WITH APPOSITIVES**

→ **IDENTIFY AND CORRECT COMMA ERRORS IN COMPOUND SENTENCES**

→ **IDENTIFY AND CORRECT OVERUSE OF COMMAS**

→ **IDENTIFY AND CORRECT ERRORS WITH SEMI-COLONS**

END PUNCTUATION

You have learned that a sentence has a subject. It also contains an action or description, and it expresses a complete thought. At the end of every sentence is a punctuation mark to show that the sentence has ended.

.—a period is used at the end of a statement

?—a question mark is used at the end of a sentence that asks a question

!—an exclamation mark is used at the end of a sentence (or after an interjection) that shows strong emotion

---

EXAMPLES

Bad company corrupts good character.
Who put him in charge?
Get yourself ready!

TIP

End punctuation shows that the sentence is ended and what kind of sentence it is.

PRACTICE

Write a period, exclamation mark, or question mark in each blank or write "NA" if the words do not make a sentence.

1. Although you know Adam, my sister Carrissa _____

2. Remember that you promised to arrive early _____

3. Solomon was reputed to be the wisest man of his age and, perhaps, ever _____

4. Should I be nervous _____

5. I strongly disagree _____

6. The visitors were standing on the south side of the building when the man _____

7. Why do people make promises they know they can't keep _____

8. When Austin had finished speaking _____

9. Hide the chocolate _____

10. Then Nathan and all his friends went back to the mall _____

11. The ending was very sad, wasn't it _____

12. That was a huge mistake _____

13. The earth in the garden smelled rich and alive _____

14. She asked me if I could give her a drive _____

ANSWERS

1. NA	5. !	9. !	13. .
2. .	6. NA	10. .	14. . .
3. .	7. ?	11. ?	
4. ?	8. NA	12. !	

Be careful of indirect questions, like *She asked me if I could give her a drive.* This sentence does not ask a question. It just tells you a question was asked. Look at the difference:

> She asked me if I could give her a drive. (Statement)
> Could you give me a drive? (Question)

Something else that sometimes causes confusion with end punctuation is quotation marks. In North America, quotations are preceded by a comma or sometimes a colon and end punctuation almost always comes before the closing quotation marks.

> Martin said, "The garage is filled with clutter."
> Celia exclaimed, "Be careful!"
> Marcie asked, "Would you pass that plate?"

Other Uses for Periods

In addition to ending sentences, periods have several other uses:

- Periods are used after initials
- Periods are used after most abbreviations

EXAMPLES

W.B. Yeats is my favourite poet.
Dr. Mobray received his M.D. in 1973.

PRACTICE

Insert periods, question marks, and exclamation marks where necessary in the following sentences.

1. Mr Arnold was born in St John's on Jan 30, 1987 at 4:13 pm

2. Marta asked, "Did you hear that Dr Joe left his cigar where Mrs Jones's appendix used to be "

3. Miss A T Saunders of 13 Russell St fell into the Bow River

4. She asked the witness where he had been on Aug 4, 1993, at 10 pm

5. Dr Arthur L Cogswell is teaching the first year chem course

6. You took Psych 1000 from Prof Karl A Hume, didn't you

7. Pres Anne Hooper of Novelty Computers, Co hired Ms Jesse James of Creative Accounting, Inc to prepare her tax return

8. Do you work for the Dept of Education

9. Hey You take your hands off that duck

10. Did you study the poems of Charles G D Roberts in school

ANSWERS

1. Mr. Arnold was born in St. John's on Jan. 30, 1987, at 4:13 p.m.

2. Marta asked, "Did you hear that Dr. Joe left his cigar where Mrs. Jones's appendix used to be?"

3. Miss A.T. Saunders of 13 Russell St. fell into the Bow River.

4. She asked the witness where he had been on Aug. 4, 1993, at 10 p.m.

5. Dr. Arthur L. Cogswell is teaching the first year chem. course.

6. You took Psych. 1000 from Prof. Karl A. Hume, didn't you?

7. Pres. Anne Hooper of Novelty Computers, Co. hired Ms. Jesse James of Creative Accounting, Inc. to prepare her tax return.

8. Do you work for the Dept. of Education?

9. Hey! You take your hands off that duck!

10. Did you study the poems of Charles G. D. Roberts in school?

COMMAS

The GED® test does not test all rules for commas. It only tests ways that comma errors could lead to confusion. These include:

- Commas in a list
- Commas in a compound sentence
- Commas after introductory elements
- Commas around appositives
- Commas in direct address
- Overuse of commas
- Misuse of commas, creating a comma splice (run-on sentence)

TIP

Commas are always used for a reason, not just for a pause.

Comma Rule 1: Use commas to separate items in a list.

EXAMPLE

The puppy is my friend, my companion, my entertainment and my family

---

You may ask if a comma should be used before the final "and" at the end of a list. This comma is optional. It is really not needed, but a comma may be used before "and" at the end of a list.

In a similar rule, when you list the items of a date or address, they are separated using commas.

EXAMPLES

Mother Teresa was born in Macedonia on Saturday, August 27, 1910.
The hotel is located near St. Paul's Cathedral at 36 Carter Lane, London, England.

PRACTICE

Rewrite each of the following sentences and put commas between items in a list where necessary. If the commas are already used correctly, write "correct."

1. The cottage floor was five metres wide and six metres long.
2. Brandon Susan and Russell went to their friend's wedding in Oakville Ontario.
3. Start the snow blower by priming the motor putting on the choke and pulling the cord.
4. The town of Neepawa Manitoba was incorporated in September 1883.
5. The process to become a plumber includes formal education several years of apprenticeship and certification exams.
6. The website gives information about the history of the city places to stay places to eat and upcoming events.
7. Martha sold her old washing machine and her old dryer.
8. Take a right at the next intersection go through two sets of lights and the store will be on your left.

ANSWERS

1. Correct. No comma is needed in a list of only two things.
2. Brandon, Susan, (optional) and Russell went to their friend's wedding in Oakville, Ontario.
3. Start the snow blower by priming the motor, putting on the choke, (optional) and pulling the cord.
4. The town of Neepawa, Manitoba was incorporated in September, 1883.
5. The process to become a plumber includes formal education, several years of apprenticeship, (optional) and certification exams.
6. The website gives information about the history of the city, places to stay, places to eat, (optional) and upcoming events.
7. Correct. No comma is needed in a list of only two things.
8. Take a right at the next intersection, go through two sets of lights, (optional) and the store will be on your left.

Comma Rule 2: Use a comma and a joining word to combine two or more sentences and make one compound sentence.

Use a comma and a joining word, or *coordinating conjunction*, to join two sentences together and make a compound sentence. The most common joining words are *and, but, or, so,* and *nor.*

Commas show construction in a sentence, separating
items or showing a change in structure.

The weather report gave a storm warning. The sky looked dark and gloomy.
(Two sentences)
The weather report gave a storm warning, <u>and</u> the sky looked dark and gloomy.
(Compound sentence)

The Toronto Maple Leafs won their game on Monday. They lost on Tuesday.
(Two sentences)
The Toronto Maple Leafs won their game on Monday, <u>but</u> they lost on Tuesday.
(Compound sentence)

You can have toast for breakfast. I can make you an omelette.
(Two sentences)
You can have toast for breakfast, <u>or</u> I can make you an omelette.
(Compound sentence)

Comma Rule 3: Use a comma after an introductory element at the beginning of a sentence.

Instead, the men did their best to row the boat to land.
When you make a promise, do not delay in fulfilling it.
Because of her years of service, they gave her an award.

Introductory words, such as *yes, no, please,* or *suddenly* are followed by a comma. In this case, the introductory word is *instead.*

Sometimes, a sentence begins with an introductory phrase or clause, which often says where, when, or how. In this example, the introductory clause tells when.

Another type of introductory clause begins with a word such as *because, although, until,* or *since.* In all of the examples, the main part of the sentence begins after the comma.

PRACTICE

1. After a fire at the saw mill the RCMP, WorkSafe BC, and the Fire Marshal came to investigate the cause.

    What correction should be made to this sentence?

    (1) Insert a comma following <u>After</u>
    (2) Insert a comma following <u>mill</u>
    (3) Remove the comma after <u>RCMP</u>
    (4) Remove the comma after <u>BC</u>
    (5) No change necessary

2. Look, your complaint is right but there is no manager or supervisor here to help you.

What correction should be made to this sentence?

(1) Remove the comma after Look
(2) Insert a comma before but
(3) Insert a comma after manager
(4) Insert a comma after supervisor
(5) No change necessary

3. Yes, Miranda brought pop, chips and treat bags for the birthday party, but she forgot to bring the cake.

What correction should be made to this sentence?

(1) Remove the comma after Yes
(2) Remove the comma after pop
(3) Insert a comma after chips
(4) Remove the comma after party
(5) No change necessary

4. Under, the cover of darkness, the thief made off with jewels, other valuables, and cash.

What correction should be made to this sentence?

(1) Remove the comma after Under
(2) Remove the comma after darkness
(3) Insert a comma after thief
(4) Remove the comma after valuables
(5) No change necessary

5. Please take off your boots, hang up your coat, and stay for a while.

What correction should be made to this sentence?

(1) Insert a comma after Please
(2) Remove the comma after boots
(3) Remove the comma after coat
(4) Insert a comma after stay
(5) No change necessary

ANSWERS

1. **(2)** *After a fire at the saw mill* is an introductory phrase.

2. **(2)** Use a comma before the joining word to make a compound sentence.

3. **(5)** Commas are used correctly in the sentence. A comma before and at the end of a list is optional and is not required.

4. **(1)** The introductory phrase is *Under the cover of darkness*.

5. **(1)** Insert a comma after the introductory word *Please*.

Comma Rule 4: Use commas to separate words in apposition from the rest of the sentence.

Appositives, or words in apposition, are words that restate or add more definition to the noun right before them, such as *Mr. Brown, my neighbour*.

EXAMPLES

There was a messenger, someone I had never seen before, coming down the road.
Ms. Jones and Mr. Douglas, two teachers at the school, ran in the marathon.

TIP

Appositive means words that say the same thing twice, such as Mr. Brown, my neighbour.

The first example refers to a messenger. The next words are separated from the rest of the sentence. *Someone I had never seen before* also refers to the messenger. These words are in apposition because they refer specifically to the noun that was just said.

Look at the second example. *Two teachers at the school* better defines *Ms. Jones and Mr. Douglas*. They are separated from the rest of the sentence using a comma before and after.

PRACTICE

Insert commas where needed to set off appositives in each of the following sentences. If the commas are already used correctly, write "correct."

1. Iris and Jennifer two friends from high school are now working together at the mall.
2. On Princess Street is the Old Italian Pizzeria my favourite restaurant.
3. The movie *X-Men* one of the best superhero films was shot in Toronto.
4. Although they never met, Jason and Maria were employees of the same company for more than seven years.
5. According to the news, the last people to leave the crime scene two RCMP officers discovered a crucial piece of evidence.
6. Head-Smashed-In Buffalo Jump is a World Heritage Site located in Alberta.
7. The company's latest product a tablet computer was unveiled at the computer show in plenty of time for Christmas sales.
8. Warnings about an epidemic of the dengue virus in more than 100 countries was issued by the World Health Organization the public health arm of the United Nations.
9. Mr. Charles Brown my neighbour has lived in the area for more than sixty years.
10. Tommy Leech a daredevil who in 1911 survived a plunge over Niagara Falls in a steel barrel eventually died in New Zealand because of complications when he slipped on an orange peel.

ANSWERS

The appositives are indicated by being underlined and commas are inserted in the answer key.

1. Iris and Jennifer, two friends from high school, are now working together at the mall.
2. On Princess Street is the Old Italian Pizzeria, my favourite restaurant.
3. The movie *X-Men,* one of the best superhero films, was shot in Toronto.

4. Correct

5. According to the news, <u>the last people to leave the crime scene,</u> two RCMP officers, discovered a crucial piece of evidence.

6. Correct.

7. <u>The company's latest product, a tablet computer,</u> was unveiled at the computer show in plenty of time for Christmas sales.

8. Warnings about an epidemic of the dengue virus in more than 100 countries were issued by <u>the World Health Organization, the public health arm of the United Nations.</u>

9. <u>Mr. Charles Brown, my neighbour,</u> has lived in the area for more than sixty years.

10. <u>Tommy Leech, a daredevil who in 1911 survived a plunge over Niagara Falls in a steel barrel,</u> eventually died in New Zealand because of complications when he slipped on an orange peel.

Comma Rule 5: Use commas to separate the name of a person directly addressed in a sentence.

If you write to someone and use the person's name to address the person directly, separate the name from the rest of the sentence using commas. Look at the following examples. In the first example, the writer speaks to *John* directly and uses his name. In the second, the writer uses the words *my friends* like a name to speak directly to them. The names are separated from the rest of the sentence using commas.

EXAMPLES

Thank you, John, for your help yesterday.
You know, my friends, that we enjoyed our visit with you.

CHALLENGE EXERCISE

Make two example sentences of your own for each of the first five comma rules.

Comma Rule 6: Do not overuse commas. Use commas only to follow the rules of punctuation, not to indicate a pause in reading.

You may have heard that commas should be used to show a pause. This is NOT true. Commas are always used for a reason, such as separating items in a list or creating a compound sentence. Some writers have the problem of using too many commas. On the GED® test, you will recognize and correct the overuse of commas in writing.

EXAMPLES

Moses, plans to be a carpenter, because he likes to work with his hands. (Incorrect)
Moses plans to be a carpenter because he likes to work with his hands. (Correct)

One of my favourite movies, is *The African Queen*, but my wife doesn't like it. (Incorrect)
One of my favourite movies is *The African Queen*, but my wife doesn't like it. (Correct)

Commas are overused in two of the examples above. Look at the first sentence. The sentence is about Moses. The action that he does is *plans*. Do not use a comma to separate the subject and predicate. There is also usually no need for a comma before *because* near the end of a sentence.

Look at the second sentence. Subject: *One of my favourite movies*; Predicate: *is*. Do not use a comma to separate the subject and predicate of a sentence. However, the comma before *but* is needed to make the compound sentence. Only use commas if there is a reason.

---

7 RULES FOR COMMAS

Use commas to separate

1. Items in a list
2. Parts of a compound sentence
3. Introductory elements
4. Appositives
5. Name of a person directly addressed

Do not

6. Overuse commas
7. Use a comma in place of a period

PRACTICE

In the following sentences, choose the number of the underlined part that has a comma error. If the sentence is correct as written, choose (5) no error.

1. The two brothers, Michael and Bruce, took over their father's garage and continued to
    (1)   (2)   (3)
   operate it, as a family business. (No error)
        (4)   (5)

2. I want you to know Bruce Taylor, that the office will be closed today, so you can stay in
                       (1)   (2)   (3)
   bed, your favourite thing to do. (No error)
    (4)   (5)

3. The Bricklin, was a car built and financed in Saint John, New Brunswick, but it was only
       (1)   (2)   (3)   (4)
   available for purchase in the United States. (No error)
                                               (5)

4. The only one who was not impressed with the performance of the cast, was the
              (1)   (2)   (3)
   director, a perfectionist in every way. (No error)
      (4)   (5)

5. As the <u>bride, Denise,</u> it is common to arrive <u>late, for</u> the <u>ceremony, so</u> do not worry that
              (1)   (2)   (3)

   the <u>groom will</u> be nervous. (No error)
        (4)   (5)

6. The woman at the front of the <u>line was</u> very <u>upset because</u> she <u>thought that</u> the cans of
                               (1)   (2)   (3)

   chicken <u>soup were</u> on sale. (No error)
           (4)   (5)

7. The path wound between the <u>trees and</u> led down to the <u>stream where</u> my <u>sister, and</u> I
                            (1)   (2)   (3)

   used to go <u>fishing in</u> the shadows of a broad oak tree. (No error)
           (4)   (5)

8. The Canada <u>Games, the</u> country's highest-level amateur sporting <u>event, were</u> first
             (1)   (2)

   <u>held in</u> Quebec City in <u>1967, as</u> part of centennial celebrations. (No error)
    (3)   (4)   (5)

ANSWERS

1. **(4)** There is no reason for a comma here.
2. **(1)** A comma should come before and after the name of a person who is directly spoken to.
3. **(1)** There is no reason for a comma. Never use a comma to separate a subject and verb.
4. **(3)** The subject is *the only one who was not impressed with the performance of the cast.* Do not use a comma to separate the subject and verb.
5. **(2)** There is no reason for a comma before this prepositional phrase.
6. **(5)** No commas are needed in the sentence.
7. **(3)** No commas are needed in the sentence
8. **(4)** There is no reason for a comma here.

Comma Rule 7: Do not use a comma in place of a period.

One common overuse of commas is a type of run-on sentence called a comma splice. This occurs when two sentences are incorrectly joined using a comma instead of a period. To correct a comma splice, replace the comma with a period. A semi-colon can also be used if the sentences are closely related.

EXAMPLES

Everyone at the party was starving, the caterers had not arrived. (Incorrect)
Everyone at the party was starving. The caterers had not arrived. (Correct)

Scott has a new car, Haley has an old one. (Incorrect)
Scott has a new car; Haley has an old one. (Correct)

Several other uses of the comma include:

- Separating information that adds extra information from the rest of the sentence

  There are four national statutory holidays in Canada, including Christmas.
  The pacific dogwood, which flowers in April and May, is the provincial flower of British
  Columbia.

- Separating interjections that interrupt the normal flow of the sentence

  Lacrosse, of course, is Canada's national sport.

- Following the salutation and complimentary close of a friendly letter

  Dear Sally,
  Yours truly,

PRACTICE

1. Lucy Maud Montgomery was born in Clifton Prince Edward Island on November 30,
   1874.

   What correction should be made to this sentence?

   (1) Insert a comma after <u>Montgomery</u>
   (2) Insert a comma after <u>Clifton</u>
   (3) Insert a comma after <u>Island</u>
   (4) Remove the comma after <u>30</u>
   (5) No correction necessary

2. The car was very <u>expensive a red</u> convertible with leather seats and shiny rims.

   Which is the best way to write the underlined part of the sentence? (If you think the
   original is the best way, choose option 1.)

   (1) expensive a red
   (2) expensive. A red
   (3) expensive; a red
   (4) expensive, a red
   (5) expensive, and a red

3. As an artist, Marty works with a variety of different media, including watercolours char-
   coal and oil pastels.

   What correction should be made to the sentence?

   (1) Remove the comma after <u>artist</u>
   (2) Remove the comma after <u>media</u>
   (3) Insert a comma after <u>watercolours</u>
   (4) Insert a comma after <u>charcoal</u>
   (5) No correction necessary

4. The store had a sale on <u>electronics, many</u> products were priced below cost.

Which is the best way to write the underlined part of the sentence? (If you think the original is the best way, choose option 1.)

(1) electronics, many
(2) electronics many
(3) electronics but many
(4) electronics. Many
(5) electronics. And many

5. Tyler always wears a life jacket when he goes canoeing.

Which is the best way to rewrite the sentence, beginning with "When."

(1) When Tyler goes canoeing, he always wears a life jacket.
(2) When Tyler goes canoeing he always wears a life jacket.
(3) When he goes canoeing. Tyler always wears a life jacket.
(4) When he goes canoeing Tyler always wears a life jacket.
(5) When Tyler goes canoeing. He always wears a life jacket.

6. Joan you can get financing to buy a used car from the dealership on Main Street.

What correction should be made to this sentence?
(1) Insert a comma after <u>Joan</u>
(2) Insert a comma after <u>financing</u>
(3) Insert a comma after <u>car</u>
(4) Insert a comma after <u>dealership</u>
(5) No correction necessary

7. Jacob, spent a long time searching, for just the right Christmas present, to get his mother.

What correction should be made to this sentence?

(1) Remove the comma after <u>Jacob</u>
(2) Remove the comma after <u>searching</u>
(3) Insert a comma before <u>Christmas</u>
(4) Remove the comma after <u>present</u>
(5) Remove all commas in the sentence

8. Marcie did well in the local singing competition. She did not win.

Which of the following is the best way to combine the sentences?

(1) Marcie did well in the local singing competition, she did not win.
(2) Marcie did well in the local singing competition, but she did not win.
(3) Marcie did well in the local singing competition but she did not win.
(4) Marcie did well in the local singing competition, and she did not win.
(5) Marcie did well in the local singing competition and she did not win.

ANSWERS

1. **(2)** Separate items in a date or address using commas.

2. **(4)** The red convertible refers to and further defines the noun *the car*. Use commas to separate appositives from the sentence.

3. **(3)** Use commas to separate items in a list.

4. **(4)** Do not use a comma in place of a period.

5. **(1)** Use a comma after introductory elements.

6. **(1)** Use commas to set off the name of a person directly addressed.

7. **(5)** Do not overuse commas.

8. **(2)** Use a comma and conjunction to make a compound sentence. The conjunction *but* has the right meaning for this context.

SEMI-COLONS

Semi-colons can be used in two ways:

1. In place of a period to show a close relationship between sentences
2. To separate items in a complicated list

A semi-colon is a yield sign at an intersection between sentences.

EXAMPLES

One clown stumbled over another; both fell down together.

Taylor always worked hard at her job and always arrived on time; therefore, she received a promotion to assistant manager.

In these sentences, the semi-colon is used instead of a period. In the first example, the ideas in the independent clauses are closely connected. In the second example, the connecting adverb "therefore" shows the close relationship between the clauses. Connecting adverbs include such words as:

Therefore	However	Similarly
Furthermore	Nevertheless	Moreover
Likewise	Indeed	
Afterward	Consequently	

TIP

Use a semi-colon where you could also use a period.

Note that a comma follows the connecting adverb at the beginning of the second independent clause. You should also not overuse semi-colons. They should be used sparingly. Some people hardly ever use them at all.

PRACTICE

Insert or correct semi-colons where necessary in each of the following sentences.

1. Albert went to Baltimore on vacation; but Jill stayed home and went camping with the girls.

2. When I first got my dog, I enrolled him in an obedience course, consequently, he is extremely well behaved.

3. The Philistines were a fairly advanced people, involved in trade with many nations nevertheless; their name is now synonymous with ignorance and a lack of appreciation of the arts.

4. Nobody knows the troubles I've seen nobody knows my sorrow.

5. Many Canadian children know that George Washington was the first president of the United States—How many know the name of the first prime minister of their own nation?

6. The strawberry shortcake is almost ready; however, I forgot to buy whipped cream.

ANSWERS

1. Albert went to Baltimore on vacation, but Jill stayed home and went camping with the girls.

2. When I first got my dog, I enrolled him in an obedience course; consequently, he is extremely well behaved.

3. The Philistines were a fairly advanced people, involved in trade with many nations; nevertheless, their name is now synonymous with ignorance and a lack of appreciation of the arts.

4. Nobody knows the troubles I've seen; nobody knows my sorrow.

5. Many Canadian children know that George Washington was the first president of the United States; how many know the name of the first prime minister of their own nation?

6. Correct

The second way to use semi-colons is to separate items in a complicated list. Do this if the items already have commas. In the first example below, it would look like there were six people at the meeting if you only used commas. Use semi-colons to show that *Mike, the president,* is one person and *June, the treasurer,* is another. The second example also requires semi-colons for clarity.

EXAMPLES

The board meeting was attended by Mike, the president; June, the treasurer; and Bill, the secretary.

My flight reaches Toronto by way of Fredericton, New Brunswick; Halifax, Nova Scotia; and Montreal, Quebec.

CHALLENGE EXERCISE

Write a paragraph or two of your own or copy from a book, newspaper, or magazine. Make sure the passage contains periods, question marks, commas, and semi-colons. Then, remove all the punctuation. If you have someone else to work with, exchange passages and try to put the punctuation back in. If you are working alone, put the passage aside for two days, and then try to put the punctuation back. Compare your answers with the original. Remember, there could be different ways to punctuate correctly. Think about or discuss any differences.

CHAPTER CHECK-UP

Complete these practice exercises, and then check the answers and analysis that follow. After you mark your work, review any topic in the chapter that you had trouble with or did not understand.

Questions 1–8 are based on the following letter of application.

May 2, 2014

Gabrielle Roy
City of Hamilton
Public Works Department
71 Main Street
Hamilton, ON L8E 2T6

(A)

(1) This letter is to apply for the position of Gardner II, which was advertised in the Monday April 30, 2014 edition of the newspaper. (2) My combination of education and work experience, make me an ideal candidate for the job. (3) I have worked as a landscaper and as a greenhouse attendant. (4) I have taken a number of training courses. (5) In addition, I have a class D driver's license and already possess pesticide licenses.

(B)

(6) You will see in my resume Ms. Roy, that I have worked at MultiCare Lawn Services for the past two years. (7) Before that, I worked for Marigolds Nursery. (8) At the nursery, I learned a great deal about plant care, including how to assess and diagnose annual, perennial, shrub soil and turf problems. (9) At Lawn Services, I learned to operate various tools and equipment, I also received training and licenses in pesticide use. (10) I truly enjoy my work with Lawn Services, however, I am looking for full-time hours.

(C)

(11) Thank you for considering my application. (12) I look forward to meeting you for a personal interview.

Yours truly,
Ray Butlerwaite

1. Sentence 1: This letter is to apply for the position of Gardner II, which was advertised in the Monday April 30, 2014 edition of the newspaper.

   Which correction should be made to this sentence?

   (1) Insert a comma after <u>letter</u>
   (2) Remove the comma after <u>Gardner II</u>
   (3) Insert a comma after <u>advertised</u>
   (4) Insert a comma after <u>Monday</u>
   (5) Remove the comma after <u>April 30</u>

2. Sentence 2: My combination of education and <u>work experience, make</u> me an ideal candidate for the job.

   What is the best way to write the underlined portion of the sentence? (If you think the original is the best way, choose option 1.)

   (1) work experience, make
   (2) work experience make
   (3) work experience. Make
   (4) work experience; make
   (5) work experience, and make

3. Sentences 3 and 4: I have worked as a landscaper and as a greenhouse attendant. I have taken a number of training courses.

   The best way to combine these sentences would include which of the following?

   (1) attendant, and I
   (2) attendant and I
   (3) attendant; and I
   (4) attendant. And I
   (5) attendant I have

4. Sentence 5: In addition, I have a class D driver's license and already possess pesticide licenses.

   Which correction should be made to this sentence?

   (1) Remove the comma after <u>addition</u>
   (2) Insert a comma after <u>license</u>
   (3) Insert a period and start a new sentence after <u>license</u>
   (4) Change the period at the end of the sentence to a question mark
   (5) No change necessary

5. Sentence 6: You will see in my resume Ms. Roy, that I have worked for MultiCare Lawn Services for the past two years.

   What correction should be made to this sentence?

   (1) Insert a comma after <u>resume</u>
   (2) Remove the comma after <u>Roy</u>
   (3) Insert a comma after <u>worked</u>
   (4) Insert a comma after <u>services</u>
   (5) No correction necessary

6. Sentence 8: At the nursery, I learned a great deal about plant care, including how to assess and diagnose annual, perennial, shrub soil and turf problems.

What correction should be made to this sentence?

   (1) Remove the comma after <u>nursery</u>
   (2) Insert a comma after <u>deal</u>
   (3) Remove the comma after <u>care</u>
   (4) Insert a comma after <u>shrub</u>
   (5) Insert a comma after <u>soil</u>

7. Sentence 9: At Lawn Services, I learned to operate various tools and <u>equipment, I also</u> received training and licenses in pesticide use.

Which is the best way to write the underlined portion of the sentence? (If you think the original is the best way, choose option 1.)

   (1) equipment, I also
   (2) equipment. I also
   (3) equipment I also
   (4) equipment; and I also
   (5) equipment also I

8. Sentence 10: I truly enjoy my work with Lawn <u>Services, however, I</u> am looking for full-time hours.

Which is the best way to write the underlined portion of the sentence? (If you think the original is the best way, choose option 1.)

   (1) services, however, I
   (2) services, however I
   (3) services; however, I
   (4) services; however I
   (5) services. However I

Questions 9–12 are based on the following advertisement.

(1) Are you looking for something different to do this evening. (2) Visit the Broken Cue at 98 Kenmount Street, St. John's Newfoundland. (3) We have nine tables. (4) You will always find an open table. (5) On Tuesday evenings we have league night, and Wednesday is ladies night. (6) The Broken Cue offers something for everyone.

9. Sentence 1: Are you looking for something different to do this evening.

Which correction should be made to this sentence?

   (1) Insert a comma after <u>looking</u>
   (2) Insert a comma after <u>different</u>
   (3) Insert a comma after <u>to do</u>
   (4) Insert a question mark instead of a period after <u>evening</u>
   (5) Insert a semi-colon after <u>something</u>

10. Sentence 2: Visit the Broken Cue at 98 Kenmount Street, St. John's Newfoundland.

Which correction should be made to this sentence?

(1) Insert a comma after Cue
(2) Remove the comma after Street
(3) Insert a comma after St. John's
(4) Change the period at the end of the sentence to a question mark
(5) No correction necessary

11. Sentences 3 and 4: We have nine tables. You will always find an open table.

The most effective combination of these sentences would include which of the following?

(1) nine tables, so you will
(2) nine tables, you will
(3) nine tables you will
(4) nine tables, but you will
(5) nine tables. And you will

12. Sentence 5: On Tuesday evenings we have league night, and Wednesday is ladies night.

Which correction should be made to the sentence?

(1) Change the comma after night to a semi-colon
(2) Remove the comma after night
(3) Insert a comma after Wednesday
(4) Insert a comma after evenings
(5) No correction necessary

Questions 13–18 are based on the following obituary notice.

Martinson, John James—(1) After a brief battle with cancer, John died peacefully in his home at the age of 85 on Saturday, October 28, 2012, at 7:43 pm. (2) He is survived by Gladys, his wife, Maria, his daughter, and Carter, his son. (3) He also leaves seven grandchildren and three great grandchildren. (4) John worked for thirty-seven years for Canada Post but he was also well known for his volunteer work with church groups and local non-profit organizations. (5) For expressions of sympathy, the family would appreciate donations to the Canadian Cancer Society, the family also wishes to express their thanks to the palliative care staff at the local hospital. (6) The family will receive visitors at Albert G Philmore Funeral home on Wednesday from 7:00–9:00 p.m. (7) However, the service will be a small ceremony a private gathering of family and friends.

13. Sentence 1: After a brief battle with cancer, John died peacefully in his home at the age of 85 on Saturday, October 28, 2012, at 7:43 pm.

What correction should be made to this sentence?

(1) Remove the comma after cancer
(2) Remove the comma after Saturday
(3) Remove the comma after 28
(4) Remove the comma after 2012
(5) Change pm to p.m.

14. Sentence 2: He is survived by Gladys, his wife, Maria, his daughter, and Carter, his son.

    What is the best way to write this sentence? (If you think the original is the best way, choose option 1.)

    (1)   He is survived by Gladys, his wife, Maria, his daughter, and Carter, his son.
    (2)   He is survived by Gladys, his wife; Maria, his daughter; and Carter, his son.
    (3)   He is survived by Gladys, his wife. Maria, his daughter. And Carter, his son.
    (4)   He is survived by Gladys; his wife; Maria; his daughter; and Carter; his son.
    (5)   He is survived by Gladys his wife, Maria his daughter, and Carter, his son.

15. Sentence 4: John worked for thirty-seven years for Canada Post but he was also well known for his volunteer work with church groups and local non-profit organizations.

    Which correction should be made to this sentence?

    (1)   Insert a comma after <u>thirty-seven years</u>
    (2)   Insert a comma after <u>Canada Post</u>
    (3)   Insert a comma after <u>well known</u>
    (4)   Insert a comma after <u>work</u>
    (5)   Insert a comma after <u>and</u>

16. Sentence 5: For expressions of sympathy, the family would appreciate donations to the Canadian Cancer <u>Society, the family also</u> wishes to express their thanks to the palliative care staff at the local hospital.

    Which is the best way to write the underlined part of the sentence? (If you think the original is the best way, choose option 1.)

    (1)   Society, the family also
    (2)   Society the family also
    (3)   Society; the family, also
    (4)   Society. The family also
    (5)   Society, the family, also

17. Sentence 6: The family will receive visitors at Albert G Philmore Funeral home on Wednesday from 7:00–9:00 p.m.

    Which is the best way to correct this sentence?

    (1)   Insert a comma after <u>family</u>
    (2)   Insert a comma after <u>home</u>
    (3)   Insert a period in <u>Albert G. Philmore</u>
    (4)   Insert a comma after <u>Wednesday</u>
    (5)   No correction necessary

18. Sentence 7: However, the service will be a small ceremony a private gathering of family and friends.

Which correction should be made to this sentence?

(1) Remove the comma after <u>however</u>
(2) Insert a comma after <u>ceremony</u>
(3) Insert a comma after <u>family</u>
(4) Insert a period and start a new sentence after <u>ceremony</u>
(5) No correction necessary

ANSWERS AND ANALYSIS

1. **(4)** Use a comma to separate items in a date or address.

2. **(2)** Do not overuse commas by separating the subject and predicate.

3. **(1)** Use a comma and joining word to make a compound sentence

4. **(5)** No correction is needed. Keep the comma after the introductory element.

5. **(1)** When speaking to a person and using her name, separate her name from the rest of the sentence using commas.

6. **(4)** Use commas to separate items in a list. A comma before *and* at the end of the list is optional.

7. **(2)** This is a comma splice. Do not use a comma in place of a period.

8. **(3)** Form a compound sentence with a semi-colon and connecting adverb, followed by a comma.

9. **(4)** The sentence asks a question and should end with a question mark.

10. **(3)** Separate elements of a date or address with commas.

11. **(1)** Use a comma and a joining word to make a compound sentence.

12. **(4)** Use a comma after an introductory element, such as *On Tuesday evenings.*

13. **(5)** Use periods after abbreviations.

14. **(2)** Use semi-colons to separate items in a complicated list that already has commas.

15. **(2)** Use a comma and a joining word to make a compound sentence.

16. **(4)** This is a comma splice. Do not use a comma in place of a period.

17. **(3)** Use a period after initials.

18. **(2)** *A small ceremony* and *a private gathering of family and friends* are both referring to the same thing. Use commas to set off appositives.

Mechanics

THINK ABOUT IT

Mechanics refers to the standard conventions that make writing work, such as punctuation, capitalization, and spelling.

IN THIS CHAPTER

On the GED Language Arts, Writing Test, Part 1, questions about mechanics make up 25% of the questions. They include identifying and correcting errors in punctuation, capitalization, and spelling. In the area of spelling, the GED® tests do not examine all the possible types of errors. They only examine mistakes that involve contractions, possessives, and homonyms.

   After completing this chapter, you will be able to

→ **APPLY RULES OF CAPITALIZATION**

→ **IDENTIFY AND CORRECT ERRORS IN SPELLING CONTRACTIONS**

→ **IDENTIFY AND CORRECT ERRORS IN SPELLING POSSESSIVES**

→ **IDENTIFY AND CORRECT ERRORS IN SPELLING HOMONYMS**

CAPITALIZATION

Using capital letters correctly is a part of good mechanics.

   The most important rule to remember about capitalization is this: Names begin with a capital letter.

1. The <u>name</u> of a specific person, place, or thing always begins with a capital letter.

TIP

Names begin with a capital letter.

EXAMPLES	
dog	Rover
woman	Mary
city	Winnepeg
lake	Lake Utopia
church	Saint James Church

The word *dog* is not capitalized because it could refer to any dog. *Rover* is capitalized because it is the name of a specific dog. The word *woman* is not capitalized because it could mean any woman, but *Mary* is capitalized because it names a specific woman. The same is true for the other examples. Notice that when a name has more than one word, all the words are capitalized, as in *Lake Utopia* and *Saint James Church*.

PRACTICE

Underline the words below that should have a capital letter:

1. son	7. country	13. angel
2. president	8. prince william	14. library
3. george	9. justice	15. teacher
4. alberta	10. canada	16. north america
5. friends	11. centre square mall	17. city
6. premier charest	12. lake superior	18. mother

ANSWERS

3, 4, 6, 8, 10, 11, 12, 16

You already know that you should capitalize the name of a person, place, or thing. Following are some more rules about capitalizing names.

2. Capitalize the names of nationalities and languages.

> **EXAMPLE**
>
> *Canadians* are a multicultural group as you can tell from our bank machines, which often offer services in *English*, *French*, and *Chinese*.

Also capitalize descriptive words based on the names of people or countries, as in *Mexican* food or *Edwardian* furniture.

3. Capitalize the names of all bodies of water: for example, streams, lakes, rivers, oceans.

> **EXAMPLE**
>
> The *St. Lawrence Seaway* is a system of rivers, canals, and lakes that goes from the *Atlantic Ocean* all the way to *Lake Superior*.

4. Capitalize the names of days, months, and holidays, but not the words for seasons.

> **EXAMPLE**
>
> Youth bowling is *Saturday* mornings in *May* and *June*, but there is no league in the *summer*.

5. Capitalize a person's title <u>only</u> if it is used as part of a name or if it is used like a name.

EXAMPLE

Yesterday, *Captain* <u>*Elliot*</u> went to see the *doctor*. After doing some tests, *Doctor* <u>*Jones*</u> told the *captain* that he was fine.

You are in perfect health, <u>*Captain*</u>.

6. Capitalize family titles only when they are used as part of a name or in place of a name.

EXAMPLES

Although <u>*Uncle*</u> <u>*Joe*</u> is not really my *uncle*, he is a good friend of the family.
Naomi, Ashley, and <u>*Mom*</u> spent the day at a spa.

When a family title follows a possessive word, such as *my, your, his*, etc., it is not being used as a name, so it is not capitalized.

7. Capitalize all the words in the name of an organization or company.

EXAMPLE

Anita got a job with the <u>*North American Motor Company*</u>.

---

8. Capitalize the first word, last word, and all important words in a title.

EXAMPLE

One of my favourite novels is <u>*The Book of Negroes*</u> by Lawrence Hill.

Don't capitalize unimportant words like *a, the, and, of, in*, etc. unless they are the first or last word in the title.

9. Capitalize the names of religions, religious books, and words referring to the main deity or deities in an organized religion.

EXAMPLE

Many people believe the *Holy* <u>*Bible*</u> is the word of <u>*God*</u>, while others follow the <u>*Quran*</u> or other sacred books.

Often you will find the pronouns *he, him*, and *his* are capitalized when they refer to the Christian Almighty God, Yahweh, Krishna, etc., but this is not as common in more modern writing.

PRACTICE

In each sentence, underline the words that should be capitalized.

1. I took mother to saint joseph's hospital to see the doctor.

2. My aunt and uncle live in thunder bay on lake superior.

3. My favourite italian restaurant is mother mary's pizzeria.

4. The bible study group at main street baptist church meets on tuesday evenings during the fall and switches to wednesdays in the winter.

5. Have you heard the story of king canute who commanded the tide of the atlantic ocean not to rise?

6. The president of telextec corporation speaks english, french, german, and spanish.

7. The writer george eliot wrote *the mill on the floss* and *silas marner.*

8. In march, basketball teams from many american universities compete in the ncaa national championships.

ANSWERS

1. I took <u>Mother</u> to <u>Saint Joseph's Hospital</u> to see the doctor.

2. My aunt and uncle live in <u>Thunder Bay</u> on <u>Lake Superior</u>.

3. My favourite <u>Italian</u> restaurant is <u>Mother Mary's Pizzeria</u>.

4. The <u>Bible</u> study group at <u>Main Street Baptist Church</u> meets on <u>Tuesday</u> evenings during the fall and switches to <u>Wednesdays</u> in the winter.

5. Have you heard the story of <u>King Canute</u> who commanded the tide of the <u>Atlantic Ocean</u> not to rise?

6. The president of <u>Telextec Corporation</u> speaks <u>English</u>, <u>French</u>, <u>German</u>, and <u>Spanish</u>.

7. The writer <u>George Eliot</u> wrote *The Mill on the Floss* and *Silas Marner.*

8. In <u>March</u>, basketball teams from many <u>American</u> universities compete in the NCAA national championships.

More Rules About Capitalization

In addition to rules about names, here are some more rules involving capitalization:

- Capitalize the first word of every sentence.
- Always capitalize the word *I.*
- Capitalize the first word in every quotation.

EXAMPLE

She said to the boy, "<u>You</u> are my son."

- Capitalize all letters in an acronym or similar abbreviation (words made from the first letters of other words).

> ┤ **EXAMPLE** ├
>
> NATO—North Atlantic Treaty Organization
> IMF—International Monetary Fund

- Do not capitalize directions unless they are part of a specific name.

> ┤ **EXAMPLE** ├
>
> In 1492, Christopher Columbus sailed east from Spain across the Atlantic Ocean and discovered North America.

PRACTICE

Revise the underlined part of each sentence to correct capitalization. If the capitalization is already correct, write "Correct."

1. And <u>god said, "let</u> there be light."
2. Leave here, turn <u>east and follow martell street</u> to the second set of lights.
3. Joanie and <u>i applied for a grant from cybf</u>—the Canadian Youth Business Foundation.
4. Mindy replied, <u>"is that captain smith</u>, who was an officer in the Royal Canadian Mounted Police?"
5. At the <u>library, May's aunt</u> signed out the book *Life of Pi*.
6. The <u>hudson's bay company</u> is the oldest company in Canada.
7. If you are looking for a <u>new Doctor, I recommend Doctor Miller</u>.
8. On <u>tuesday, march 3 we arrived for spring break</u> in Florida.
9. The <u>longest street in the country, yonge street in Toronto</u>, was once officially the longest street in the world.
10. Marcie wants to go <u>south to Phoenix for the winter</u>.

ANSWERS

1. God said, "Let
2. <u>east and follow Martell Street</u>
3. <u>I applied for a grant from CYBF</u>
4. <u>"Is that Captain Smith</u>
5. Correct
6. <u>Hudson's Bay Company</u>
7. <u>new doctor, I recommend Doctor Miller.</u>
8. <u>Tuesday, March 3 we arrived for spring break</u>
9. <u>longest street in the country, Yonge Street in Toronto</u>
10. Correct

SUMMARY

Here is a summary of the rules of capitalization.

1. The <u>name</u> of a specific person, place, or thing always begins with a capital letter.
2. Capitalize the names of nationalities and languages.
3. Capitalize the names of all bodies of water, such as streams, lakes, rivers, oceans.
4. Capitalize the names of days, months, and holidays, but not the words for seasons.
5. Capitalize a person's title <u>only</u> if it is used as part of a name or in place of a name.
6. Capitalize family titles only when they are used as part of a name or in place of a name.
7. Capitalize all the words in the name of an organization or company.
8. Capitalize the first, last, and all important words in a title.
9. Capitalize the names of religions, religious books, and words referring to a major deity or deities.
10. Capitalize the first word of every sentence.
11. Always capitalize the word *I*.
12. Capitalize the first word in every quotation.
13. Capitalize all letters in an acronym or similar abbreviation.

CHALLENGE EXERCISE

Make up one example sentence of your own for each of the capitalization rules.

SPELLING CONTRACTIONS

Contractions occur when words are combined in a shortened form, such as *is not* to *isn't* or *will not* to *won't*. An apostrophe is used in a contraction to show that a letter or letters have been left out.

he is	→	he's
did not	→	didn't
there is	→	there's

Generally, the biggest problem with spelling contractions is careless errors. We may know how to spell contractions, but we make mistakes or fail to notice errors because contractions are so commonly used. The most frequent errors involve:

1. Mispronunciation
2. Confusion with possessives

Sometimes people mispronounce words and spell them out incorrectly. With contractions, often people mispronounce the words *would've* (would have), *could've* (could have) and *should've* (should have). This can lead to incorrect spellings such as *would of* or *could of*.

Another common spelling problem with contractions is confusing them with possessives that also sound the same. For example, *they're* (they are) can be confused with *their*; *it's* (it is) can be confused with *its* (possessive); and *who's* (who is) is confused with *whose*.

TIP

Avoid misspelling commonly mispronounced words:

would've—would have

should've—should have

could've—could have

PRACTICE

Write contractions for each group of words below.

I am	I will	do not	who is
you are	you will	did not	there is
he is	he will	does not	cannot
she is	she will	has not	could not
it is	we will	have not	would not
we are	they will	had not	should not
they are	will not		

ANSWERS

I'm	I'll	don't	who's
you're	you'll	didn't	there's
he's	he'll	doesn't	can't
she's	she'll	hasn't	couldn't
it's	we'll	haven't	wouldn't
we're	they'll	hadn't	shouldn't
they're	won't		

SPELLING POSSESSIVES

Possessives are words that show ownership, such as *theirs* or *Anne's*. Mistakes in spelling possessives usually involve:

1. Confusing contractions and possessives
2. Misplaced apostrophes

Remember this: *it's* **always means** *it is*. The possessive *its* does not take an apostrophe. For example, the dog wagged *its* tail. In fact, no possessive pronoun takes an apostrophe (my, his, hers, its, ours, yours, theirs).

TIP

Do not add an apostrophe to any possessive pronoun. *It's* **always means** *it is.*

PRACTICE

Choose the right word to complete each sentence.

1. (It's, Its) my party and I'll cry if I want to.

2. The car honked (it's, its) horn and revved (it's, its) engine.

3. (It's, Its) a good idea to leave the bike on (it's, its) stand.

4. Once the sale starts (it's, its) going to be crazy in here.

5. (It's, Its) colour was blue and gold.

6. Whatever you want to do, (it's, its) okay with me.

7. Although (it's, its) early, (it's, its) never too early to start.

8. (It's, Its) the early bird that gets (it's, its) worm.

ANSWERS

1. It's my party
2. its horn and its engine
3. It's a good idea, its stand
4. it's going to be crazy
5. Its colour
6. it's okay
7. it's early, it's never too early
8. It's the early bird, its worm

Misplaced Apostrophes

To spell possessives correctly, you must know how and when to use apostrophes correctly.

1. Add an apostrophe and *s* to singular nouns (even those that end in *s*) to show possession.

> **EXAMPLES**
>
> The dog belongs to the boy → The boy's dog
> The car belongs to Chris → Chris's car

2. Add an apostrophe and *s* to plural nouns that DO NOT end in *s* to show possession.

> **EXAMPLES**
>
> The coats belong to the women → The women's coats
> The wool of several sheep → Sheep's wool

3. Add only an apostrophe to plural nouns ending in "s" to show possession.

> **EXAMPLES**
>
> The dog belongs to two boys → The two boys' dog
> The cars belong to the teachers → The teachers' cars

PRACTICE

Choose the best word to complete each sentence.

1. James says that (Jane's, Janes) mother does not like him.
2. The (flowers', flowers) bloomed by the bank of the winding river.
3. Of all of the (sheep's, sheeps) fleeces, the black one was the most impressive.
4. The (women's, women) on the committee have very different ideas on this issue.
5. The letters YMCA stand for Young (Men's, Mens) Christian Association.
6. I find the (song's, songs) beat a little too fast.
7. The four (jets', jet's, jets) engines were cooling down.
8. The two (heroes, heroe's, heroes') were given an award.

ANSWERS

1. Jane's
2. flowers
3. sheep's
4. women
5. Men's
6. song's
7. jets'
8. heroes

PRACTICE

Insert apostrophes as needed in each sentence.

1. The dog chased its tail for hours but couldnt catch it.
2. Theres nothing like Grandmothers apple pie.
3. They bought their new car the same day we bought ours.
4. The *Peoples Court* is one of Chris favourite shows.
5. Sallys three cats have had their claws removed.
6. Although its true that Janice doesnt like animals, shes decided to become a vet.
7. The hands of the cowboys moved at lightning speeds as they drew their guns and fired.
8. Its often said that dogs are mans best friends.
9. Mrs. Johnsons son, Stan, has sixteen dollars and seventeen cents in the bank.
10. If its wagging its tail and growling, too, which end do you believe?

ANSWERS

1. The dog chased its tail for hours but <u>couldn't</u> catch it.
2. <u>There's</u> nothing like <u>Grandmother's</u> apple pie.
3. They bought their new car the same day we bought ours.
4. The *<u>People's</u> Court* is one of <u>Chris's</u> favourite shows.
5. <u>Sally's</u> three cats have had their claws removed.
6. Although <u>it's</u> true that Janice <u>doesn't</u> like animals, <u>she's</u> decided to become a vet.
7. The hands of the cowboys moved at lightning speeds as they drew their guns and fired.
8. <u>It's</u> often said that dogs are <u>man's</u> best friends.
9. Mrs. <u>Johnson's</u> son, Stan, has sixteen dollars and seventeen cents in the bank.
10. If <u>it's</u> wagging its tail and growling, too, which end do you believe?

SPELLING HOMONYMS

Homonyms, or more correctly homophones, are words that sound the same but have different meanings and spellings. Some homonym spelling mistakes are often simply a result of careless errors. It is easy to write the wrong *there, their,* or *they're* and everyone has done it. Other times, people might get confused about the meaning or the correct spelling. Here are a few homonyms:

there	their	they're	
to	two	too	
your	you're	new	knew
hear	here	desert	dessert

There are many homonyms in the English language. You do not need to memorize them all. You should practice any homonyms that you commonly misspell in your writing. You should also be familiar with correcting common homonym errors to prepare for the multiple-choice questions on Part 1 of the GED writing test.

Study this list of some common homonyms.

Accept	Receive something	Principal	Administrator of a school
Except	Excluding	Principle	Value or theory
Ad	Advertisement	Rain	Precipitation, weather
Add	Mathematical addition	Reign	Rule of a king or queen
Affect	Influence, most often used as a verb	Rein	Straps to control a horse
Effect	The result of a cause, most often used as a noun	Raise	Lift up
		Rays	Beam of light
Bare	Naked or uncovered	Right	Correct; or, a direction
Bear	Hold or support; or, an animal	Write	To form letters and language
		Road	Street
For	Preposition (as in for me)	Rode	The past of ride
Four	Number four	Rowed	Propel a boat with oars
		Role	Character, position
Heal	Make healthy	Roll	Tumble like a ball; round or rolled up, as in a roll of paper or bread roll
Heel	Part of the foot		
He'll	He will		
Higher	Above	Sight	Ability to see
Hire	Employ a person	Site	Location of something
Hole	Pit	Stationary	Not moving
Whole	Entire thing	Stationery	Paper and writing material
Morning	Early part of the day	Steal	Take something that doesn't belong to you
Mourning	Sorrow for one who died		
		Steel	Type of metal
One	The number one	Threw	Past of throw
Won	Succeeded in a contest	Through	Finished; or, from side to side
Pain	Physical hurt	Way	Path or direction
Pane	Plate of glass in a window	Weigh	Heaviness
Pair	Two of something	Weak	Not strong
Pare	Cut away the outer skin	Week	Seven days
Pear	A kind of fruit		
		Wear	Put on clothing
Peace	Calm, opposite of war	Where	Question to determine place
Piece	A part of something		
		Weather	Climate conditions
Picture	Image, photo, painting	Whether	If; or, introduces alternatives
Pitcher	Container for liquid; or, a position in baseball.	Whine	Complain
		Wine	Alcoholic drink

PRACTICE

Choose the (right, write) word to complete each sentence.

1. Can you tell us (weather, whether) you will be coming for dinner?
2. Parents all want to (raise, rays) their children well.
3. Please (accept, except) me for who I am.
4. Joan said (there, their, they're) having second thoughts about moving to Florida.
5. Please remain (stationary, stationery) behind the yellow line until the bus comes to a complete stop.
6. I can't believe I ate the (hole, whole) thing.
7. The (principal, principle) of catch and release is employed by environmentally conscious sports fishermen.
8. The new restaurant will be constructed on a (sight, site) just around the corner.
9. Sometimes cold medicines have a strange (affect, effect) on me.
10. Martine wore an old coat and down-at-the- (heal, heel) shoes.
11. The girls talked (threw, through) the entire class.
12. The cost of a newspaper (ad, add) has increased a lot in the past few years.
13. On the mound, the (picture, pitcher) calmly eyed the approaching batter.
14. The family is still in (morning, mourning) after the death of their mother.
15. I don't know (wear, where) we are on the map.

ANSWERS

1. Can you tell us (weather, <u>whether</u>) you will be coming for dinner?
2. Parents all want to (<u>raise</u>, rays) their children well.
3. Please (<u>accept</u>, except) me for who I am.
4. Joan said (there, their, <u>they're</u>) having second thoughts about moving to Florida.
5. Please remain (<u>stationary</u>, stationery) behind the yellow line until the bus comes to a complete stop.
6. I can't believe I ate the (hole, <u>whole</u>) thing.
7. The (principal, <u>principle</u>) of catch and release is employed by environmentally conscious sports fishermen.
8. The new restaurant will be constructed on a (sight, <u>site</u>) just around the corner.
9. Sometimes cold medicines have a strange (affect, <u>effect</u>) on me.
10. Martine wore an old coat and down-at-the- (heal, <u>heel</u>) shoes.
11. The girls talked (threw, <u>through</u>) the entire class.
12. The cost of a newspaper (<u>ad</u>, add) has increased a lot in the past few years.
13. On the mound, the (picture, <u>pitcher</u>) calmly eyed the approaching batter.
14. The family is still in (morning, <u>mourning</u>) after the death of their mother.
15. I don't know (wear, <u>where</u>) we are on the map.

CHALLENGE EXERCISE

Most people misspell a limited number of words that they use often when they write. The best way to improve your spelling is to practice words you often misspell. Start a personal spelling list. Think of five or six words that you commonly use in writing and have trouble with. Keep the list and add to it while you continue studying for the GED® test. Practice the words to improve your spelling.

CHAPTER CHECK-UP

Complete these practice exercises, and then check the answers and analysis that follow. After you mark your work, review any topic in the chapter that you had trouble with or did not understand.

Questions 1–13 are based on the following passage.

Canadian Vacation Ideas

(A)

(1) When you consider an exotic vacation, you may imagine the site of the Empire State Building in New York or think of sipping cocktails on a beach in Cuba. (2) However, Canadas natural wonders and diverse culture offer many exotic vacation options right here at home. (3) Here are some option's for Canadians to consider.

(B)

(4) With a view of the St. Lawrence river is beautiful Old Quebec. (5) Their is almost too much beauty to see as you walk the cobblestone roads of this historic city. (6) Visit the Plains of Abraham and other historic locations, but you really have to eat here to get the hole experience. (7) Many of the cities' restaurants have been well reviewed by *The Quebec Chronicle-Telegraph* and are some of the finest anywhere.

(C)

(8) Make your way to Cape Breton Island, at the tip of Nova Scotia, to hear celtic music and enjoy Maritime culture. (9) Tour Prince Edward Island's Anne of Green Gables Homestead, based on the novel by Lucy Maude Montgomery. (10) Go to Calgary, Alberta, wear you can experience the Calgary Stampede, experience a local jazz bar, or visit nearby Banff or other mountain resorts.

(D)

(11) There are so many more things to choose from. (12) The Italian, Cuban, Polish, Chinese, and other communities in many Canadian cities offer food and cultural events. (13) There are also regional events and festivals for you're enjoyment. (14) The affect of Canadians vacationing in Canada is that it helps us to know a new pride in our country.

1. Sentence 1: When you consider an exotic vacation, you may imagine the site of the Empire State Building in New York or think of sipping cocktails on a beach in Cuba.

    Which correction should be made to this sentence?

    (1) Change site to sight
    (2) Remove the capital letters from Empire State Building
    (3) Change New York to New york
    (4) Capitalize Cocktails
    (5) Capitalize Beach

2. Sentence 2: However, Canadas natural wonders and diverse culture offer many exotic vacation options right here at home.

    What is the best way to write the underlined portion of the sentence? (If you think the original is the best way, choose option 1.)

    (1) However, Canadas natural wonders and diverse culture offer
    (2) However, Canadas natural wonders, and diverse culture offer
    (3) However Canadas natural wonder's and diverse culture offer
    (4) However, Canada's natural wonders and diverse culture offer
    (5) However, Canadas natural wonders. And diverse culture offer

3. Sentence 3: Here are some option's for Canadians to consider.

    Which correction should be made to this sentence?

    (1) Insert a comma after Here
    (2) Change option's to options
    (3) Change Canadians to canadians
    (4) Change Canadians to Canadian's
    (5) Insert a comma after option's

4. Sentence 4: With a view of the St. Lawrence river is beautiful Old Quebec.

    What correction should be made to this sentence?

    (1) Change view to views
    (2) Change St. Lawrence to St. lawrence
    (3) Change river to River
    (4) Insert a comma after beautiful
    (5) Remove the capitalization from Old Quebec

5. Sentence 5: Their is almost too much beauty to see as you walk the cobblestone roads of this historic city.

    What is the best way to write the underlined portion of the sentence? (If you think the original is the best way, choose option 1.)

    (1) Their is almost too much beauty to see
    (2) There is almost to much beauty to see
    (3) Their is almost too much beauty to sea
    (4) Their is almost too much beauty too see
    (5) There is almost too much beauty to see

6. Sentence 6: Visit the Plains of Abraham and other historic locations, but you really have to eat here to get the hole experience.

What correction should be made to this sentence?

(1) Change Plains to Plain's
(2) Capitalize Historic Locations
(3) Change hole to whole
(4) Change experience to experiences
(5) Remove the comma after locations

7. Sentence 7: Many of the cities' restaurants have been well reviewed by *The Quebec Chronicle-Telegraph* and are some of the finest anywhere.

Which of the following is the best revision of the underlined portion of the sentence?

(1) Many of the cities' restaurants
(2) Many of the city's restaurants
(3) Many of the citys' restaurants
(4) Many of the Cities restaurants
(5) Many of the Restuarants found in the city

8. Sentence 8: Make your way to Cape Breton Island, at the tip of Nova Scotia, to hear celtic music and enjoy Maritime culture.

What correction should be made to this sentence?

(1) Change way to weigh
(2) Change Cape Breton Island to Cape Breton's Island
(3) Replace hear with here
(4) Capitalize Celtic
(5) Capitalize Culture

9. Sentence 9: Tour Prince Edward Island's Anne of Green Gables Homestead, based on the novel by Lucy Maude Montgomery.

What correction should be made to this sentence?

(1) Change Island's to Islands
(2) Remove capitalization from Green Gables
(3) Change novel to Novel
(4) Change Maude to Maude's
(5) No correction necessary

10. Sentence 10: Go to <u>Calgary, Alberta, wear you can experience</u> the Calgary Stampede, experience a local jazz bar, or visit nearby Banff or other mountain resorts.

What correction should be made to this sentence?

(1) Calgary, Alberta, where you can experience
(2) Calgary, Alberta wear you can experience
(3) Calgary's Alberta, wear you can experience
(4) Calgary, Alberta, the place wear you can experience
(5) No correction necessary

11. Sentence 12: The Italian, Cuban, Polish, Chinese, and other communities in many Canadian cities offer food and cultural events.

What correction should be made to this sentence?

(1) Remove the comma after <u>Chinese</u>
(2) Capitalize <u>Communities</u>
(3) Change cities to citys
(4) Remove the capitalization from <u>Canadian</u>
(5) No correction necessary

12. Sentence 13: There are also regional events and festivals for your enjoyment.

Which of the following is the best revision of this sentence?

(1) There are also regional events and festivals for you're enjoyment.
(2) There are also regional event's and festival's for you're enjoyment.
(3) There are also regional events and festivals for your enjoyment.
(4) There are also. Regional events and festivals for you're enjoyment.
(5) Regional events and festivals for your enjoyment.

13. Sentence 14: <u>The affect of Canadians vacationing in Canada</u> is that it helps us to know a new pride in our country.

What is the best way to write the underlined portion of the sentence? (If you think the original is the best way, choose option 1.)

(1) The affect of Canadians vacationing in Canada
(2) The effect of Canadians vacationing in Canada
(3) The affect of Canadians' vacationing in Canada
(4) The affect of Canadian's vacationing in Canada
(5) The effect of Canadians' vacationing in Canada

Questions 14–21 are based on the following passage.

9 March 20__

Top Notch Discount Store
45 Iola Avenue
Regina, SK SBS 4R6

Re: Refund Request

To whom it may concern:

(A)

(1) One Tuesday evening this Winter, I stopped by your store with my aunt to browse. (2) At first, aunt Mary and I did not know you had a 25% off shoe sale. (3) When we found out about the sale, we bought several pear and went out to our car. (4) In the car, we saw that the shoes buckles were made of cheap plastic, not metal. (5) We went right back in and tried to return the shoes, but were told that all sales were final. (6) I asked to speak to a Manager, but there was no manager in.

(B)

(7) I right to you now to demand a refund. (8) We were'nt told there were no returns and we didn't even leave the parking lot. (9) I shop at Top Notch discount store a lot and I expect better treatment.

Yours truly,
Don R. Adams

14. Sentence 1: One Tuesday evening this Winter, I stopped by your store with my aunt to browse.

What correction should be made to this sentence?

(1) Change Tuesday to tuesday
(2) Change Winter to winter
(3) Change by to buy
(4) Change to browse to too browse
(5) Remove the comma after Winter

15. Sentence 2: At first, aunt Mary and I did not know you had a 25% off shoe sale.

What correction should be made to this sentence?

(1) Capitalize Aunt Mary
(2) Change I to i
(3) Change know to no
(4) Change shoe to shoe's
(5) No correction necessary

16. Sentence 3: When we found out about the sale, we bought several pear and went out to our car.

What correction should be made to this sentence?

(1) Insert a comma after <u>out</u>
(2) Change <u>sale</u> to <u>sail</u>
(3) Change <u>pear</u> to <u>pears</u>
(4) Inset a comma before <u>and</u>
(5) Change <u>pear</u> to <u>pair</u>

17. Sentence 4: In the car, we saw that <u>the shoes buckles</u> were made of cheap plastic, not metal.

What is the best way to write the underlined portion of the sentence? (If you feel the original is the best way, choose option 1.)

(1) the shoes buckles
(2) the shoe's buckles
(3) the shoes' buckles
(4) the shoes buckle's
(5) the shoes buckles'

18. Sentence 6: I asked to speak to a Manager, but there was no manager in.

What correction should be made to this sentence?

(1) Change <u>Manager</u> to <u>manager</u>
(2) Remove the comma before <u>but</u>
(3) Change <u>there</u> to <u>their</u>
(4) Change <u>manager</u> to <u>Manager</u>
(5) No correction necessary

19. Sentence 7: I right to you now to demand a refund.

What correction should be made to this sentence?

(1) Change <u>right</u> to <u>write</u>
(2) Change <u>now</u> to <u>know</u>
(3) Insert a comma after <u>now</u>
(4) Insert a period after <u>now</u>
(5) No correction necessary

20. Sentence 8: We were'nt told there were no returns and we didn't even leave the parking lot.

What correction should be made to this sentence?

(1) Change <u>were'nt</u> to <u>weren't</u>
(2) Change <u>there</u> to <u>they're</u>
(3) Change <u>didn't</u> to <u>don't</u>
(4) Change <u>didn't</u> to <u>did'nt</u>
(5) Insert a comma after <u>leave</u>

21. Sentence 9: <u>I shop at Top Notch discount store</u> a lot and I expect better treatment.

What is the best way to write the underlined portion of the sentence? (If you think the original is the best way, choose option 1.)

(1) I shop at Top Notch discount store

(2) I shop, at Top Notch discount store

(3) I Shop at the Top Notch discount store

(4) I shop at Top Notch Discount store

(5) I shop at Top Notch Discount Store

ANSWERS AND ANALYSIS

1. **(1)** Change <u>site</u> to <u>sight</u>—see the Empire State Building.

2. **(4)** Canada's—The sentence refers to natural wonders and diverse culture that belong to Canada.

3. **(2)** Options should be plural, not possessive.

4. **(3)** The entire name of the body of water should be capitalized, St. Lawrence River.

5. **(5)** *There* is not possessive.

6. **(3)** Whole or entire thing.

7. **(2)** city's—To make the singular word *city* possessive, add an apostrophe and an *s.*

8. **(4)** Celtic—Capitalize the name of nationalities and people groups.

9. **(5)** Capitalization and spelling are correct.

10. **(1)** Use the correct spelling of the homonym *where* to refer to a place.

11. **(5)** Spelling and capitalization are correct.

12. **(3)** Use the correct homonym *your* to indicate possession.

13. **(2)** Use the correct homonym *effect* to indicate the result of Canadians vacationing in Canada.

14. **(2)** Do not capitalize seasons.

15. **(1)** Capitalize family titles if they are part of a name.

16. **(5)** Use *pair* meaning two, not *pear* the fruit.

17. **(3)** When a possessive word already ends in *s,* such as *shoes,* add an apostrophe after the *s* to form the possessive.

18. **(1)** There is no reason to capitalize a title unless it is part of a name, such as Doctor Ross.

19. **(1)** Use the correct homonym.

20. **(1)** Correctly spell the contraction.

21. **(5)** All words in the company name should be capitalized.

Usage

8

THINK ABOUT IT

A blacksmith is a person who hammers out shapes in metal. Sometimes a writer is called a wordsmith, like someone who hammers out meaning with words. As a writer, words are your tools. You need to use the correct tools and use them the right way to get the job done.

IN THIS CHAPTER

Usage is saying and writing the right words in the normal and correct way. It includes using the correct form of a word, such as saying *I saw* and not *I seen*. It also includes making sure that the different parts of a sentence fit together. For example, if the subject of a sentence is one person, you use a verb form that fits with one person, such as *he runs*. If the subject is more than one person, you use a form of the verb that fits, such as *they run*. On the GED Language Arts, Writing Test, Part 1, 30% of the questions involve usage.

   After completing this chapter, you will be able to

→ **CORRECT ERRORS IN SUBJECT-VERB AGREEMENT**

→ **CORRECT ERRORS IN VERB TENSE**

→ **IDENTIFY AND CORRECT COMMON PROBLEMS WITH VERBS**

→ **CORRECT UNCLEAR PRONOUN REFERENCES**

→ **CORRECT PRONOUN SHIFTS**

→ **CORRECT ERRORS WITH RELATIVE PRONOUNS**

SUBJECT-VERB AGREEMENT

Nouns (or pronouns) and the verbs that go with them must agree (or fit together). Mistakes in agreement between subjects and their verbs are one of the most common mistakes in writing. Here are some rules to help you identify and correct errors.

1. **SUBJECTS AND THEIR VERBS MUST AGREE IN NUMBER.** If a noun is singular, then the verb must be singular too. If a noun is plural, then a verb that goes with it must be plural too.

EXAMPLES

John <u>enjoys</u> walking in the rain.
She <u>wants</u> to go home.

Martin and Harry <u>like</u> to play softball.
The radios <u>play</u> loudly in the store.

These subjects and verbs agree in number. You can see that the singular *John enjoys* and the two people *Martin and Harry like*. Nouns and verbs work differently. With nouns, a plural usually ends in "s," such as *radios*. However, with verbs it is singular verbs that often end with "s," such as *one radio plays*.

PRACTICE

Choose the correct option so that the subject and verb will agree in number.

1. The Hawks (hopes, hope) for an easy win over the Bulls.
2. The officers (disagrees, disagree) about the best route to the base.
3. The idea to raise chickens (appeals, appeal) to the children.
4. The salesmen's boss (wants, want) them to sell the old stock first.
5. The streets of the city (is, are) in need of repair.
6. Jenny and Oscar's dog, covered with fleas, (is, are) running around the house.
7. The banks' interest rates (rises, rise) and (falls, fall) with the Bank of Canada rate.
8. One of the province's most popular attractions (is, are) closed for the season.
9. The child's toys (was, were) on the floor.
10. One of the many sports memorabilia items (has, have) sold for ten thousand dollars.

ANSWERS

1. The *Hawks* hope
2. *officers* disagree
3. The *idea* appeals
4. The *boss* wants
5. The streets are

6. The *dog* is
7. The *rates* rise and fall
8. *One* is
9. The *toys* were
10. *One* has sold

2. A COLLECTIVE NOUN TAKES A SINGULAR VERB. A collective noun is a word that refers to a group. For example, *committee* is a collective noun. It is one committee even if it has a number of people.

> **EXAMPLES**
>
> The class was [singular] on its best behaviour.
> The committee meets [singular] every second Tuesday.

The exception is if you use a collective noun, but you mean all the individuals in the group, not the group itself. For example, "The hockey team put on their skates." In this exception, use the plural *put* not the singular *puts* because you mean all the individual members of the team put on their skates.

3. **A COMPOUND SUBJECT THAT CONTAINS *AND* TAKES A PLURAL VERB.** A compound subject is a list of two or more nouns or pronouns. A compound subject connected by *and* is always plural because it is more than one thing.

EXAMPLES

John and Bertha [compound subject] meet [plural] for cocktails every Thursday.

French watercolours, Victorian poetry, and fine wine [compound subject] are [plural] among my favourite topics of conversation.

---

4. **A COMPOUND SUBJECT THAT CONTAINS *OR* OR *NOR* TAKES A SINGULAR VERB IF THE PART CLOSEST TO THE VERB IS SINGULAR.** *Or* and *nor* do not join things together. If I have this OR that, it means I only have one. If I have neither this NOR that, then I don't have any. The subjects are not plural, unless the subject closest to the verb is plural.

EXAMPLES

Either Matthew or Mark [compound subject] is [singular] coming to visit.
Neither John nor Luke [compound subject] likes [singular] to travel by air.
Either the teachers or the principal [compound subject] is [singular] responsible.
Neither Jane nor the other students [note the part of this compound subject that is closest to the verb is the plural *students*] like [plural] studying grammar.

PRACTICE

Choose the correct option so that the subject and verb will agree in number.

1. Both the chicken and the duck (likes, like) the bird seed.
2. Neither the chicken nor the duck (is, are) going to be dinner tonight.
3. Either the chicken or the duck (has, have) escaped from the coop.
4. The tour group (has, have) arrived at the airport.
5. Either the manager or the employees (is, are) responsible to clean up this mess.
6. Giovanni Malloy and Sheri Zinc (work, works) for the post office.
7. The director who is filming the movie or the actress who is playing the lead role (was, were) staying at the hotel by the bay.
8. The chess club (meet, meets) every Thursday evening.
9. The boxer and his manager (jog, jogs) five kilometres every morning.
10. Does the old car or the new one (get, gets) better gas mileage?
11. The track team all (wear, wears) new uniforms.
12. Neither Lili Kristakov nor Serge Morenski (has, have) a passport.

ANSWERS

1. The chicken and the duck like
2. Neither the chicken nor the duck is
3. Either the chicken or the duck has

4. The tour group <u>has</u>

5. Either the manager or the employees <u>are</u> (the verb is plural because the subject closest to the verb—*employees*—is plural)

6. Giovanni Malloy and Sheri Zinc <u>work</u>

7. The director or the actress <u>was</u>

8. The chess club <u>meets</u> (one club is singular even though it has a number of people)

9. The boxer and his manager <u>jog</u>

10. Does the old car or the new one <u>get</u>

11. The track team all <u>wear</u> (the verb is plural because each person on the team wears a new uniform)

12. Neither Lili Kristakov nor Serge Morenski <u>has</u>

5. **USE A SINGULAR VERB IF THE SUBJECT IS AN INDEFINITE PRONOUN.** Indefinite pronouns include such words as *any, some, none, each, few, anyone, no one, somebody, everything,* and *everyone.* They are called indefinite pronouns because you do not know, with the exception of *none,* how many people or things they refer to. They are usually treated as singular.

> **EXAMPLES**
>
> <u>None</u> [subject] of these letters <u>has</u> [singular] been properly addressed.
> <u>Everything</u> [subject] <u>has</u> [singular] gone wrong today.

PRACTICE

Correct faulty subject-verb agreement in each of the following sentences. Some sentences may be correct.

1. My book club, which meets at seven on Tuesday evenings, have been reading *St. Urbain's Horseman.*

2. Although there's several people who have visited the house, no one have made an offer.

3. Of all the people I have met since moving into the neighbourhood, Peter, George, and Mary is the only ones I would consider friends.

4. The squirrels living in the attic of my barn is becoming a problem.

5. The discussion in our family about Canadian artists, especially those known as the Group of Seven, have gone on for several hours now.

6. Melissa's family have decided not to exchange gifts with one another this Christmas.

7. Although most of the oil was cleaned up before it could cause much damage to marine life, some lying nearer the oyster flats were not discovered until it was too late.

8. On appeal, the board, which has reviewed your petition, have decided to grant your request.

9. Neither the cat nor the dog have the required immunizations or licenses.

10. The candidates running for council in the municipal election were speaking at a public meeting last night.

11. The pilots' association have professional-development training to help pilots learn about recent changes in their field.

12. The freshly falling flakes of snow blanket the field in a pure coat of white.

TIP

A collective noun refers to a group as one thing.

ANSWERS

1. *My book club*, which meets at seven on Tuesday evenings, <u>has</u> been reading *St. Urbain's Horseman*.

2. Although *there* <u>are</u> several people who have visited the house, *no one* <u>has</u> made an offer.

3. Of all the people I have met since moving into the neighbourhood, *Peter, George, and Mary* <u>are</u> the only ones I would consider friends.

4. *The squirrels* living in the attic of my barn <u>are</u> becoming a problem.

5. *The discussion* in our family about Canadian artists, especially those known as the Group of Seven, <u>has</u> gone on for several hours now.

6. Correct. All the members of the family have decided not to exchange gifts.

7. Although most of the oil was cleaned up before it could cause much damage to marine life, *some* lying nearer the oyster flats <u>was</u> not discovered until it was too late.

8. On appeal, *the board*, which has reviewed your petition, <u>has</u> decided to grant your request.

9. *Neither the cat nor the dog* <u>has</u> the required immunizations or licenses.

10. Correct.

11. *The* pilots' *association* <u>has</u> professional-development training to help pilots learn about recent changes in their field.

12. Correct.

VERB TENSE

Verbs are the only kinds of words that change to indicate when actions occur. These different forms are called **verb tenses**.

EXAMPLES

I run	habit, regular action
I am running	now
I ran	past
I have run	started in the past and may continue
I had run	occurred before something else in the past
I will run	future

On the GED Writing Test, Part 1, you will identify and correct mistakes in verb tense. There can be several kinds of errors.

1. **VERB SHIFT**—A passage begins in one time period and shifts to another.

> **EXAMPLE**
>
> Once upon a time there was a horse named Chester. He is the fastest horse alive.

In this example, the story begins in the past (there <u>was</u> a horse), and then suddenly shifts to the present (he <u>is</u> the fastest). When writing, or identifying errors, ensure that the time of the story or passage is consistent.

2. **VERB SENSE**—The tenses of verbs do not fit together.

> **EXAMPLE**
>
> Before the plane takes off, the wings had been cleared of ice.

The tenses of verbs in this example do not make sense. They are not logical. *Before the plane takes off* is something that will happen in the future. *The wings had been cleared* is something in the past. When editing any writing, ensure that the verb tenses are logical. There are several ways to correct this sentence. You should choose the way that best fits the whole passage:

- Before the plane takes off, the wings will be cleared of ice.
- Before the plane took off, the wings were cleared of ice.

PRACTICE

Correct the tense of the underlined verbs as needed. Make no change if the verbs are already correct.

1. Last night, the dog <u>had barked</u> when the racoons got into the garbage.
2. When the fog comes in at the end of the day, it always <u>headed</u> straight to the ball field.
3. Since the kids were young, we <u>vacationed</u> at the Blue Pine Campground.
4. After the singers <u>have performed</u>, the judges made their remarks.
5. While the athletes <u>were preparing</u> for the competition, their parents will raise money to pay for the trip.
6. The flowers in the garden will blossom again in the spring after they <u>slept</u> for the winter.
7. The soldiers <u>stood</u> stiffly at attention while the trumpeter is playing.
8. Bats are very useful creates because they <u>ate</u> insects, including mosquitos.
9. The famous board game Trivial Pursuit <u>had been invented</u> by two Canadians in 1979 while they were playing a game of Scrabble.
10. The passengers <u>have been waiting</u> in the rain for three hours before their bus arrived.

Verbs can change to indicate different times. The times of verbs in a sentence must be logical.

ANSWERS

1. barked	6. sleep
2. heads	7. are standing *or* stand
3. have vacationed	8. eat
4. performed	9. was invented
5. are preparing *or* prepare	10. had been waiting *or* waited

PROBLEMS WITH VERBS

Verbs have different forms. For example, sometimes you add *ing* to a verb to use it with a helping verb. Sometimes you add *ed* to a verb to put it in the past or with *has, have,* or *had.* Other verbs are irregular, and you do not add *ed.* Some common errors involve irregular verbs.

These verbs require a helping verb: seen, done, begun, driven, taken.

Common Error	Correct	
I been	I was	I have been
They begun	They began	They had begun
She has boughten	She bought	She has bought
He come	He came	He has come
We done	We did	We have done
You driven	You drove	You have driven
She drunk	She drank	She has drunk
He forgotten	He forgot	He has forgotten
They give me	They gave	They have given
They grown	They grew	They have grown
They all run home	They ran	They have run
I seen	I saw	I have seen
You shaken	You shook	You have shaken
They sung	They sang	They have sung
The ship sunk	The ship sank	The ship has sunk
She swum	She swam	She has swum
We taken	We took	We have taken
She has went	She went	She has gone
He has wrote	He wrote	He has written

Here are some other common verb errors:

Incorrect	Correct
Loan me (loan is a noun)	Lend me
She learned him (wrong word)	She taught him
Suppose to	Supposed to
Use to	Used to

PRACTICE

Choose the right word or phrase to complete each sentence.

1. The bartender (shook, shaken) the martini, but did not stir it.

2. They (took, taken) their time getting here.

3. Justin was sick and had not (went, gone) to work for three days.

4. Shelby got a good mark on the test because she (did, done) her homework.

5. Every day last summer, the kids had (swam, swum) in the lake by their cottage.

6. For the last three days, we have (saw, seen) Amy at the restaurant in the morning.

7. The children's choir (sang, sung) in the festival.

8. Alain had worked there for five years before they (give, gave) him a raise.

9. Burton told me that he would (loan, lend) me a book.

10. The house that we have just (bought, boughten) is the largest purchase we will ever make.

11. Gina has (forgot, forgotten) more about cooking than I will ever know.

12. Before the guests arrived, the staff (began, begun) to get ready.

ANSWERS

1.	shook	5.	swum	9.	lend
2.	took	6.	seen	10.	bought
3.	gone	7.	sang	11.	forgotten
4.	did	8.	gave	12.	began

CHALLENGE EXERCISE

Write sentences containing each of the following verbs: begun, come, done, driven, forgotten, given, grown, seen, sunk, taken, gone, written. Discuss your sentences with a teacher, friend, or another student.

PRONOUN AND ANTECEDENT

By themselves, pronouns don't mean anything. They must refer back to a noun—called an *antecedent*—that was given before.

EXAMPLES

<u>She</u> has a new toy.   <u>They</u> don't work.

What do the pronouns *she* and *they* mean? They each need an antecedent, a specific noun coming before the pronoun.

EXAMPLES

The cat is happy. She has a new toy.
The cold pills have expired. They don't work.

Every pronoun must have a clear antecedent. On the GED Writing Test, Part 1, you will identify and correct mistakes when the antecedent is not clear.

Paul took his son for a drive. <u>He</u> was very tired. **Incorrect**
(To whom does *he* refer, Paul or his son?)

Jennifer and Mary work together, but *she* doesn't like *her* very much. **Incorrect**
(To whom do *she* and *her* refer?)

Ann arrrived. She was late.

Pronouns must agree with their antecedents in number and gender. Singular pronouns go with singular antecedents and plural pronouns with plural antecedents. Also, if the antecedent is male or female, then the pronoun should match.

the boy	he
the girl	she
Alex and Brad	they

In business writing, it has become common to refer to one person as "they" to avoid sexist language. Although it is common, it is not the best way and can cause confusion. When you are writing, a better approach is to use a plural antecedent or no pronoun at all in such situations. On the GED Writing Test, Part 1, you will identify and correct errors in pronoun agreement.

TIP

Every pronoun refers to something else. The pronoun and antecedent have to match.

An <u>office manager</u> [antecedent] should interview candidates carefully before <u>they</u> (pronoun) hire them. **Incorrect**

See how confusion can occur. *They* is a plural pronoun, but the only plural antecedent is *candidates*. Does *they* mean the singular office manager or the plural candidates?

Here are some better ways to write the sentence:

An <u>office manager</u> should interview candidates carefully before hiring them.
(no pronoun)

<u>Office managers</u> should interview candidates carefully before <u>they</u> hire them.
(plural antecedent)

On the GED Language Arts, Writing Test, Part 1, you will have to identify and correct errors with pronouns and antecedents. Sometimes the antecedent may not be clear. Sometimes the pronoun and antecedent may not agree in number or gender.

PRACTICE

1. Hannah's father doesn't like her dating Otto. Last week she went out with Otto anyway. She says <u>he doesn't care</u> about her feelings.

    What is the best way to write the underlined part above? (If you think the original is the best way, choose option 1.)

    (1) he doesn't care
    (2) John doesn't care
    (3) Jane doesn't care
    (4) they don't care
    (5) her father doesn't care

2. When people own puppies, they should be spayed or neutered.

    Which is the best way to write the sentence above? (If you think the original is the best way, choose option 1.)

    (1) When people own puppies, they should be spayed or neutered.
    (2) When a person owns a puppy, it should be spayed or neutered.
    (3) When people own a puppy, they should be spayed or neutered.
    (4) When a person owns puppies, it should be spayed or neutered.
    (5) When a person owns a puppy, they should be spayed or neutered.

3. When the audience and the critics saw the movie, the critics praised it but they didn't enjoy it.

    What correction should be made to this sentence?

    (1) Change <u>it</u> to <u>them</u>
    (2) Change <u>they</u> to <u>the audience</u>
    (3) Change <u>the critics praised</u> to <u>they praised</u>
    (4) Delete <u>enjoy it</u>
    (5) No correction necessary

4. Not all the students have handed in their homework.

    What correction should be made to this sentence?

    (1) Change <u>all the students</u> to <u>every student</u>
    (2) Change <u>their</u> to <u>his</u>
    (3) Change <u>have</u> to <u>has</u>
    (4) Insert a comma after <u>students</u>
    (5) No correction necessary

5. In case of a medical emergency, they dial 911 and calmly provide information to the operator.

    What correction should be made to this sentence?

    (1) Change <u>medical emergency</u> to <u>medical emergencies</u>
    (2) Delete <u>they</u>
    (3) Remove the comma after <u>emergency</u>
    (4) Change <u>information</u> to <u>their information</u>
    (5) No correction necessary

6. The granite counter and new sink were installed in the kitchen, but it needed to be cleaned.

   What correction should be made to this sentence?

   (1) Change it to they
   (2) Delete it
   (3) Remove the comma after kitchen
   (4) Insert a comma after counter
   (5) No correction necessary

7. Not every customer was satisfied with the quality of service they received.

   Which is the best way to write the sentence above? (If you think the original is the best way, choose option 1.)

   (1) Not every customer was satisfied with the quality of service they received.
   (2) Not all the customers were satisfied with the quality of service it received.
   (3) Not all the customers were satisfied with the quality of service they received.
   (4) Not every customer was satisfied with the quality of their service.
   (5) Not all the customers were satisfied with their service.

8. Either one of the boys may have their license revoked because of the accident.

   What is the best way to write the underlined part above? (If you think the original is the best way, choose option 1.)

   (1) have their license revoked
   (2) have their licenses revoked
   (3) have his license revoked
   (4) has their license revoked
   (5) has his license revoked

9. The rock climber and the guide had his equipment packed for the climb.

   What correction should be made to this sentence?

   (1) Change his to their
   (2) Change rock climber to rock climbers
   (3) Change guide to guides
   (4) Change equipment to equipments
   (5) No correction necessary

ANSWERS

1. **(5)** Does *he* mean the father or Otto? Clarify the unclear pronoun reference.

2. **(2)** This is the only option with agreement between the subject *puppy* and the pronoun *it*, and that also makes it clear that it is the puppy that should be spayed or neutered.

3. **(2)** It is unclear who *they* refers to. Clarify the unclear pronoun reference.

4. **(5)** The subject *students* and pronoun *their* agree in number.

5. **(2)** The sentence has no antecedent for *they*. In this case, delete *they* to make a command.

6. **(1)** What does *it* refer to? Change *it* to *they*, which clearly refers to the counter and sink.

7. **(3)** The singular *every customer* would require a singular pronoun. The plural *all the customers* agrees with the plural pronoun *they*.

8. **(3)** A compound subject with *either* (like or) is singular. Either boy, but not both, may have his license revoked.

9. **(1)** A compound subject with *and* is plural and requires a plural pronoun.

CHALLENGE EXERCISE

Choose several paragraphs from a book, newspaper, or magazine. Make sure the paragraphs contain pronouns. Draw lines to connect each pronoun to its antecedent.

PRONOUN SHIFT

TIP

Avoid pronoun shift. Use one pronoun to refer to the same person or people in a passage.

Another error in the use of pronouns occurs when writers change the pronoun they are using. For example, a writer might begin using the pronoun *one* and then switch to *they* and then to *you*.

EXAMPLE

Later in the week I was speaking with a friend of mine and told him that I wanted to start a new direction in my life. My friend suggested I begin by buying a new home. I thought to myself, "A new home? What more could you ask for? When one buys a house it gives them a whole new start in life."

In the example, see how the pronouns switch from *I* to *you* to *one* to *them*. Good writing is consistent and stays with the same pronoun to avoid confusion and make the meaning clear. Sometimes, correcting a pronoun shift only involves changing a pronoun. Other times it may involve some rewriting.

EXAMPLE

Later in the week I was speaking with a friend of mine and told him that I wanted to start a new direction in my life. My friend suggested I begin by buying a new home. I thought to myself, "A new home? What more could I ask for? Buying a house would give me a whole new start in life."

RELATIVE PRONOUNS

Another kind of usage error with pronoun references involves relative pronouns. Relative pronouns (who, that, which) refer back to a person or thing already mentioned.

Here are some guidelines for using relative pronouns:

- Use *who* to refer to people
- Use *that* to add required information about a thing
- Use *which* to add additional information about a thing

The relative pronouns *who* and *whom* are used for people. *That* can sometimes be used for people too. Do not worry about the difference between *who* and *whom* as this distinction is not often made in today's writing. *Who* is used without a comma to add information that is required in the sentence. *Who* is also used with a comma to add extra information that is not required.

EXAMPLES

The person *who* I marry will be someone kind and thoughtful.
My friend Sue, *who* has worked with me for years, is retiring next year.

Some people use the relative pronouns *that* and *which* like they were the same. They are a little bit different. *That* is used to add information that is required in the sentence. *Which* is supposed to be used with a comma to add extra information that is not required.

EXAMPLES

The couch that I bought last year has a tear in the cushion.
The couch, which I bought last year, has a tear in the cushion.

Think about the difference between these two sentences. The first sentence is about the couch that I bought last year. It isn't about just any couch or the one I bought five years ago. *That I bought last year* is required information in the sentence. The second sentence is just about the couch. The fact that I bought it last year is just some extra information.

PRACTICE

Choose the correct relative pronoun to complete each sentence.

1. The homemade bread (who, that, which) I made yesterday is the best I have ever made.
2. Sarah, (who, that, which) once skated in the winter Olympics, is now a spokesperson for a children's charity.
3. Before studying at university, Taylor, (who, that, which) wanted to study respiratory therapy, had to upgrade her biology mark.
4. For dinner tonight we are going to have the same chicken stir fry (who, that, which) I made last week.
5. The cost of medical care, (who, that, which) is one of the province's biggest expenses, continues to rise.
6. The bowling alley, (who, that, which) is down the street from my house, is where I work.
7. The desk, (who, that, which) once belonged to my great grandfather, has been in the family for over one hundred years.
8. The sports car (who, that, which) I had when I was a teenager was one sweet ride.
9. One legacy (who, that, which) my grandmother left our family was a love of music.
10. You have to admit that the photographer (who, that, which) took your wedding pictures did a good job.

TIP

who—used for people

that—for required information about things

which—for extra information about things (usually preceded by a comma)

ANSWERS

1. that	5. which	9. that
2. who	6. which	10. who (alternatively that)
3. who	7. which	
4. that	8. that	

CHAPTER CHECK-UP

Complete these practice exercises, and then check the answers and analysis that follow. After you mark your work, review any topic in the chapter that you had trouble with or did not understand.

Questions 1–12 are based on the following passage.

Canada's Ballerina

(A)

(1) Evelyn Hart, which became a world-famous ballerina and principal dancer of the Royal Winnipeg Ballet, was born in Toronto in 1956. (2) She seen a televised performance of Romeo and Juliet, when she was ten, performed by Veronica Tennant and the National Ballet of Canada. (3) The beautiful performance of the dancers were inspiring to her. (4) She determined to become a ballerina and convinced her parents to enroll her in classes.

(B)

(5) When she was thirteen years old, Evelyn had been accepted into a summer program at the National Ballet School in Toronto. (6) In 1970, her parents enrolled her in a dance school operated by Dorothy and Victoria Carter in London, Ontario. (7) Evelyn credits them for inspiring her and says, "Without them, I wouldn't be where I am."

(C)

(8) Evelyn was suppose to attend the National Ballet School in 1971 as a full-time student, but she had to withdraw after a short time. (9) She suffered from anorexia and needed time to recover. (10) In 1973, after battling the physical and psychological effects of it, she was accepted into the Royal Winnipeg Ballet School. (11) By 1976, she had been accepted as a member of the Royal Winnipeg Ballet Company, and she become the principal dancer in 1979, only three years later.

(D)

(12) Recognition of Evelyn Hart's talents have resulted in numerous awards during her career. (13) In 1980, she is the first Canadian to be awarded a gold medal at the International Ballet Competition in Varna, Bulgaria. (14) The government of Canada have made her a Companion of the Order of Canada, and she has been inducted into Canada's Walk of Fame. (15) She has been recognized with many other awards and honorary degrees and was Manitoba Woman of the Year. (16) Her fans, which have been mesmerized by her performances, will always appreciate her ability to connect with them on an emotional level.

1. Sentence 1: Evelyn Hart, which became a world-famous ballerina and principal dancer of the Royal Winnipeg Ballet, was born in Toronto in 1956.

   What correction should be made to this sentence?

   (1) Change which to who
   (2) Change which to that
   (3) Change became to become
   (4) Change was born to were born
   (5) No correction necessary

2. Sentence 2: She seen a televised performance of Romeo and Juliet, when she was ten, performed by Veronica Tennant and the National Ballet of Canada.

   If you were to rewrite the sentence beginning with the words "When she was ten," the next words should be

   (1) she seen a televised performance
   (2) a televised performance was seen
   (3) she had saw
   (4) Victoria Tennant was seen
   (5) she saw a televised performance

3. Sentence 3: The beautiful performance of the dancers were inspiring to her.

   What correction should be made to this sentence?

   (1) Change performance to performances
   (2) Change dancers to dancer
   (3) Replace were with are
   (4) Change were inspiring to has been inspiring
   (5) Replace were with is

4. Sentence 5: When she was thirteen years old, Evelyn had been accepted into a summer program at the National Ballet School in Toronto.

   What is the best way to write the underlined portion of the sentence? (If you think the original is the best way, choose option 1.)

   (1) Evelyn had been accepted
   (2) Evelyn has been accepted
   (3) Evelyn was accepted
   (4) Evelyn is accepted
   (5) She had been accepted

5. Sentence 7: Evelyn credits them for inspiring her and says, "Without them, I wouldn't be where I am."

   What correction should be made to this sentence?

   (1) Change credits them to credits the Carters
   (2) Change inspiring her to inspiration
   (3) Insert a comma after her
   (4) Delete the comma after says
   (5) No correction necessary

6. Sentence 8: Evelyn was suppose to attend the National Ballet School in 1971 as a full-time student, but she had to withdraw after a short time.

   If you were to rewrite the sentence beginning with the words "In 1971," the next words should be

   (1) Evelyn has been attending
   (2) the National Ballet School was
   (3) as a full-time student
   (4) Evelyn had been
   (5) Evelyn was supposed to

7. Sentence 10: In 1973, after battling the <u>physical and psychological effects of it</u>, she was accepted into the Royal Winnipeg Ballet School.

   What is the best way to write the underlined portion of the sentence? (If you think the original is the best way, choose option 1.)

   (1) physical and psychological effects of it
   (2) physical and psychological effects of this
   (3) physical and psychological effects of them
   (4) physical and psychological effects of this disorder
   (5) physical and psychological effects it had

8. Sentence 11: By 1976, she had been accepted as a member of the Royal Winnipeg Ballet <u>Company, and she become the principal dancer</u> in 1979, only three years later.

   What is the best way to write the underlined portion of the sentence? (If you think the original is the best way, choose option 1.)

   (1) Company, and she become the principal dancer
   (2) Company. And she become the principal dancer
   (3) Company, and she became the principal dancer
   (4) Company, and she become the principle dancer
   (5) Company; and she had been the principal dancer

9. Sentence 12: Recognition of Evelyn Hart's talents have resulted in numerous awards during her career.

   What correction should be made to this sentence?

   (1) Change <u>Hart's</u> to <u>Harts</u>
   (2) Change <u>talents</u> to <u>talent</u>
   (3) Change <u>have</u> to <u>has</u>
   (4) Replace <u>numerous</u> with <u>many</u>
   (5) Insert a comma after <u>awards</u>

10. Sentence 13: In 1980, <u>she is the first Canadian</u> to be awarded a gold medal at the International Ballet Competition in Varna, Bulgaria.

What is the best way to write the underlined portion of the sentence? (If you think the original is the best way, choose option 1.)

(1) she is the first Canadian
(2) she has been the first Canadian
(3) she will be the first Canadian
(4) she became the first Canadian
(5) she had become the first Canadian

11. Sentence 14: The government of Canada have made her a Companion of the Order of Canada, and she has been inducted into Canada's Walk of Fame.

What correction should be made to this sentence?

(1) Change <u>have</u> to <u>has</u>
(2) Remove the comma before <u>and she</u>
(3) Change <u>has been</u> to <u>was</u>
(4) Change <u>Canada's</u> to <u>Canadas</u>
(5) No correction necessary

12. Sentence 16: Her fans, which have been mesmerized by her performances, will always appreciate her ability to connect with them on an emotional level.

What correction should be made to this sentence?

(1) Change <u>Her fans</u> to <u>She has fans</u>
(2) Change <u>which</u> to <u>who</u>
(3) Change <u>have been</u> to <u>were</u>
(4) Change <u>will</u> to <u>have</u>
(5) Change <u>them</u> to <u>us</u>

Questions 13–18 are based on the following letter.

Re: Guest Speaker

Dear Community Centre Member:

(A)

(1) This year, your community centre have been pleased to offer a series of public speakers about health and nutrition topics. (2) Next week, we feature *Nutrition 101* presented by lifestyle coach Lorraine Current, and one is sure you will enjoy it. (3) Lorraine is a certified nurse and dietician who had worked for the past twelve years as a personal trainer and lifestyle consultant. (4) She is also a body builder and helped them with conditioning for members of Canada's National Women's Football Team.

(B)

(5) In the Nutrition 101 workshop, you will learn about how to eat healthy in the 21st century. (6) You will discover how shopping and the products which are available in your grocery store have changed. (7) You will also explore how the busy lifestyles of today impact cooking and dining habits. (8) Finally, the workshop will learn you strategies for making healthy choices, selecting natural alternatives, and eating right in today's world.

(C)

(9) To register, contact the centre and speak to Sue. (10) Cost for the workshop is $40.

13. Sentence 1: This year, your community centre have been pleased to offer a series of public speakers about health and nutrition topics.

    What is the best way to write the underlined portion of the sentence? (If you think the original is the best way, choose option 1.)

    (1) your community centre have been pleased
    (2) your community centre are pleased
    (3) your community centre were pleased
    (4) your community centre has been pleased
    (5) your community centre pleased

14. Sentence 2: Next week, we feature *Nutrition 101* presented by lifestyle coach Lorraine Current, and one is sure you will enjoy it.

    What correction should be made to this sentence?

    (1) Change we feature to we will feature
    (2) Change presented by to presented with
    (3) Replace one with they
    (4) Replace one is with we are
    (5) Replace it with them

15. Sentence 3: Lorraine is a certified nurse and dietician who had worked for the past twelve years as a personal trainer and lifestyle consultant.

    If you were to rewrite the sentence beginning with the words "A certified nurse and dietician," the next words should be

    (1) Lorraine has worked
    (2) Lorraine for the past twelve months
    (3) Lorraine had worked
    (4) for the past twelve months
    (5) a personal trainer and lifestyle consultant

16. Sentence 4: She is also a body builder and helped them with conditioning for members of Canada's National Women's Football Team.

    What correction should be made to this sentence?

    (1) Change is to was
    (2) Delete them
    (3) Insert a comma after Canada's
    (4) Replace with conditioning with to condition
    (5) No correction necessary

17. Sentence 6: You will discover how shopping and the products which are available in your grocery store have changed.

    What is the best way to write the underlined portion of the sentence? (If you think the original is the best way, choose option 1.)

    (1) the products which are available
    (2) the products, which are available
    (3) the products that are available
    (4) the products and that are available
    (5) the products which were available

18. Sentence 8: Finally, the workshop will learn you strategies for making healthy choices, selecting natural alternatives, and eating right in today's world.

    What correction should be made to this sentence?

    (1) Remove the comma after Finally
    (2) Change learn to teach
    (3) Replace making with to make
    (4) Replace selecting with to select
    (5) No change necessary

ANSWERS AND ANALYSIS

1. **(1)** Use the relative pronoun *who* to add extra information about a person.

2. **(5)** This is a common verb error. The past of the verb is *saw*. *Seen* requires a helping verb, such as *had*.

3. **(1)** This is the only option that will create agreement between a plural subject, *performances*, and plural verb, *were*.

4. **(3)** Avoid shifts in verb tense and remain in the simple past.

5. **(1)** It is unclear whether the pronoun refers to the Carters or her parents.

6. **(5)** This is a common verb error and should be *supposed to.*

7. **(4)** It is unclear what antecedent *it* refers to.

8. **(3)** This is a common verb error. The past of the verb is *became. Become* requires a helping verb, such as *had.*

9. **(3)** The subject and verb must agree, *recognition has.*

10. **(4)** Avoid shifts in verb tense.

11. **(1)** The collective noun *government* is singular.

12. **(2)** Use the relative pronoun *who* to add extra information about a person.

13. **(4)** The collective noun takes a singular verb.

14. **(4)** Avoid pronoun shift—we feature and we are sure

15. **(1)** Ensure verb tenses are consistent. She is a nurse who has worked.

16. **(2)** The pronoun *them* has no antecedent. In this case, the error can be corrected by just deleting the pronoun.

17. **(3)** The relative pronoun *that* is needed because the information is required. It is *the products that are available* that have changed.

18. **(2)** This is a common verb error. You teach other people, and they learn.

Language Arts

WRITING, PART 2

Overview of the Essay

Part 2 of the Language Arts, Writing Test includes:

- one essay on a given topic
- 45-minute time limit

On this test, you will write an expository essay. An expository essay is one in which you explain or inform people about a topic. Usually, the essay should state your opinion and support it with personal experiences and observations.

ORGANIZATION IS THE KEY

The purpose of writing is communication. Your essay does not have to be perfect. The people who mark the essay will not use a red pen to circle all the punctuation errors and other mistakes. The markers are looking to see that you are able to communicate your ideas effectively in writing.

Writing correctly is important; however, effective organization is the key to a good essay. Take a moment to organize your thoughts before you begin to write. Then organize your writing so that your essay will have this structure:

- Introduction
- Body
- Conclusion

TIP

Organization is a key to good communication.

In total, your essay for the GED should probably be about five paragraphs or 200–300 words. The first paragraph will be the introduction. The middle three paragraphs will be the body. The last paragraph will be the conclusion.

HOW THE ESSAY IS SCORED

Each essay is given a score between 1 and 4. It is marked by two different people, and the marks are averaged together. You must get a score of 2 or higher to pass, and you must pass the essay to pass the Language Arts, Writing Test. When you get the results of your test, if your score is shown as 0 or no mark for Language Arts, Writing, you did not pass the essay.

Here is what the scores mean:

4—Effective: Reader can easily understand and follow your ideas.

3—Adequate: Reader can understand and follow your ideas.

2—Marginal: Reader sometimes has trouble understanding and following your ideas.

1—Inadequate: Reader has difficulty understanding and following your ideas.

The essay is marked holistically, which means the markers do not write on the paper. Instead, they choose a mark based on an overall impression of your essay, considering the following things.

- Response to the prompt—How well does the essay address the topic? The essay should clearly explain the topic. Essays that do not stay on topic receive a low score.
- Organization—Does the essay follow a clear plan with an introduction, body, and conclusion?
- Development of details—Does the essay support ideas by giving details, examples, and explanations based on personal experience?
- Standard written English—Does the essay have correct sentence structure, mechanics, and usage, following the standards of academic writing?
- Word choice—Does the writer choose the right words to express ideas?

HOW THE TEST WORKS

When you finish answering questions on the Language Arts, Writing Test, Part 1, if your time is not up, you can immediately start working on the essay. This can give you more time than the allotted 45 minutes.

You will be given one topic to write about. It will be a general topic about which most adults will have some knowledge or experience.

You can organize notes or make an outline on scrap paper, but the essay itself is written on the lined sections of the answer sheet. You have about two pages to write your essay, so it also cannot be too long.

Essay

9

THINK ABOUT IT

Building an essay is like carpentry. To do the job well, you need to have the right

- Building materials
- Blueprint
- Tools of the trade

In essay writing, the building materials are the ideas and information that you use to come up with the content. The blueprint is the outline. The tools are the paragraphs, sentences, and punctuation that you use to put it all together.

Think back to the first time you tried to do some simple carpentry. Do you remember how difficult it was to hammer the nails, to cut the boards to the right size, and to assemble all the pieces the right way? Like carpentry, essay writing is a skill. Having all the necessary materials and equipment is not enough. It also takes practice to learn how to build a good essay.

IN THIS CHAPTER

Writing is a skill. It takes practice. In this chapter, you will learn about writing essays. You will also need to practice writing essays to improve your skills. Writing one essay is not enough practice. You will need to write a number of practice essays to improve your skills. You must also review your essays after you write them to identify areas for improvement. In addition to practice, you will find it easier to write essays if you have a process to follow.

After completing this chapter, you will be able to

→ **NARROW THE TOPIC**

→ **GENERATE IDEAS**

→ **MAKE AN OUTLINE**

→ **WRITE A WELL-ORGANIZED ESSAY**

→ **PROOFREAD AN ESSAY**

NARROW THE TOPIC

The type of essay that you will write on the GED® test is called an *expository* essay. In an expository essay, you

- Explain your point of view on a given topic
- Give details and examples to support your position.

TIP

The first step in writing is to narrow the topic.

One reason many people have trouble writing essays is that they cannot think of how to begin. This is often because the topic is very broad. If you think of everything you know about the topic, there are so many things you could say that it is hard to decide where to begin. The first step in writing an essay is to narrow the topic to the aspect that you want to talk about.

Narrowing the topic involves writing a sentence that states your point of view. This sentence, often called a thesis statement, will eventually come near the beginning of your essay.

The thesis statement is the single most important sentence in any essay. Although it is basically a statement of your opinion, it is not as easy to write as it may seem. When writing a thesis statement, remember the following points:

1. The statement must clearly and directly address the topic
2. The statement must be something you can say more about
3. The statement should give an opinion or position
4. The statement should be limited to one aspect of the topic

EXAMPLE

You are asked to write an essay about the following topic:

From various types of ethnic music to rock, jazz, country, and classical, the music of North America is as varied as its people. In an essay, identify your favourite type of music. Use your personal observations, experience, and knowledge to support your point of view.

Thesis statements:

- In my opinion, music is a very important part of any culture. **Poor**
- In my opinion, country music originated in the American west. **Poor**
- I enjoy listening to classical music, but jazz and funk are more fun to play, and I like folk lyrics the best. **Poor**
- Although I like many types of music, my favourite is contemporary folk because of its creativity, acoustic sound, and meaningful lyrics. **Good**

Can you see what is wrong with the first three thesis statements? The first does not clearly address the topic, which asks writers to identify their favourite type of music and explain why they like it. This statement is about the importance of music in culture, which is not the topic at all.

The second statement is not something that the writer can say more about. It is not an opinion or position; it is a fact. Country music did originate in the American west—end of story.

The third statement addresses too many aspects of the topic. This writer has picked too many things to write about effectively.

The fourth statement is effective. This statement clearly addresses the topic of the writer's favourite type of music. It is also a statement that the writer can say more about. In this case, the writer has even outlined reasons that will be discussed in the rest of the essay, although this is not necessary.

The thesis statement is the most important sentence in an essay because it tells what the essay will be about. As you will see when we begin brainstorming and webbing, all the ideas in the essay are related to the thesis statement. Although a good thesis statement is no guarantee of success, a poor thesis statement almost always results in a poor essay.

How To Write a Thesis Statement

One way to write an effective thesis statement is to read the topic carefully, and then answer with a sentence that begins with the words, "In my opinion…" Once you are satisfied with the wording of the sentence, delete the opening words.

EXAMPLE

~~In my opinion~~ Dogs make the best pets because they offer security, love, and loyalty.

PRACTICE

Choose the best thesis statement for each of the topics given below.

1. What is one traditional holiday that you feel is still important in today's society?

   In an essay, identify that holiday. Explain how you feel it is important. Use personal observations, experiences, and knowledge to support your essay.

   (1) Mother's Day is a holiday.
   (2) In our family, we always gather together at my parents' house to celebrate traditional holidays.
   (3) Most traditional holidays are not as important in today's society as they used to be, and I think that Easter and Christmas have especially become too commercial.
   (4) Christmas is one traditional holiday that is still important in today's society.
   (5) In my opinion it is still important to celebrate holidays in today's society.

2. Suppose you had the opportunity to lead an activity at a children's summer camp.

   In an essay, identify what activity you would lead and explain how you would lead it. Use personal observations, experiences, and knowledge to support your essay.

   (1) I have not had the opportunity to lead an activity at a children's summer camp, but I enjoy singing in the local choir.
   (2) Making crafts is an activity I would enjoy leading at a children's summer camp.
   (3) Many children go to both summer camps every year.
   (4) Leading group activities at summer camp is a lot of fun.
   (5) I would enjoy leading either basketball or canoeing at a children's summer camp, which provides a good opportunity to counsel kids about their problems.

3. Throughout history, what invention do you think has had the greatest impact on humanity?

In an essay, identify the invention. Explain how it has impacted on humanity. Use personal observations, experiences, and knowledge to support your essay.

(1) The cordless curling iron is the invention with the greatest impact on humanity because it is portable and economical and helps build self-esteem.

(2) In my opinion, the telephone was invented by Alexander Graham Bell.

(3) The wheel has had the greatest impact on humanity of any invention and has led to other inventions, such as the car, which is also a very important invention.

(4) Children today are not fit or healthy enough because they spend too much time watching television.

(5) There have been many great inventions that have impacted humanity throughout history.

4. *Canadians can be radical, but they must be radical in their own peculiar way, and that way must be in harmony with our national traditions and ideals.*—Agnes MacPhail

In an essay, explain what this quotation means to you. Use personal observations, experiences, and knowledge to support your essay.

(1) There are many famous quotations about Canadians.

(2) This quotation means that even when Canadians do not succeed at first, they find strength in their national traditions to try again.

(3) Although MacPhail claims Canadians are radical in their own way, the real truth is that we do not like to rock the boat.

(4) Canadians are radicals, they are radicals in a way that is consistent with their national ideals.

(5) This quotation is from Agnes MacPhail, the first woman elected to the Canadian House of Commons.

5. What is one strategy that community organizations can use to attract involvement from young people?

In an essay, identify a strategy. Explain how the strategy will help. Use personal observations, experience, and knowledge to support your essay.

(1) Most community volunteers today are older people.

(2) Having upbeat music in the offices, fun social activities, and hiring young directors are one way that organizations can involve more young people.

(3) Community organizations need to have a strategy to attract more young people because there are not enough young people becoming involved in helping the community.

(4) Community groups offer many services, such as feeding the hungry and helping the homeless.

(5) One strategy that community groups can use to attract young people is to show them how community service is relevant to them.

ANSWERS

1. What is one traditional holiday that you feel is still important in today's society?
    (1) This is a fact. **Poor** thesis statement.
    (2) This is a fact and does not address the topic. **Poor** thesis statement.
    (3) This statement deals with too many topics. **Poor** thesis statement.
    (4) Christmas is one traditional holiday that is still important in today's society. **Good.**
    (5) Not on topic. **Poor** thesis statement.

2. Suppose you had the opportunity to lead an activity at a children's summer camp.
    (1) Not on topic. **Poor** thesis statement.
    (2) Making crafts is an activity I would enjoy leading at a children's summer camp. **Good.**
    (3) This is a fact and doesn't identify an activity. **Poor** thesis statement.
    (4) This is a fact and doesn't identify an activity. **Poor** thesis statement.
    (5) Deals with too many activities. The person wants to talk about counselling, which is not on topic. **Poor** thesis statement.

3. Throughout history, what invention do you think has had the greatest impact on humanity?
    (1) The cordless curling iron is the invention with the greatest impact on humanity because it is portable and economical and helps build self-esteem. **Good.**
    (2) This is a fact. **Poor** thesis statement.
    (3) Too complicated and gives two inventions, not one as the topic requested. **Poor** thesis statement.
    (4) Not on topic. **Poor** thesis statement.
    (5) Does not choose an invention, so not on topic. **Poor** thesis statement.

4. *Canadians can be radical, but they must be radical in their own peculiar way, and that way must be in harmony with our national traditions and ideals.*—Agnes MacPhail
    (1) A fact. **Poor** thesis statement.
    (2) Incorrect interpretation of the quote. **Poor** thesis statement.
    (3) Although MacPhail claims Canadians are radical in their own way, the real truth is that we do not like to rock the boat. **Good**. It is okay to disagree with the topic.
    (4) Run-on sentence. A thesis statement must be a good sentence. **Poor.**
    (5) A fact. **Poor** thesis statement.

5. What is one strategy that community organizations can use to attract involvement from young people?
    (1) Fact (whether true or not). **Poor** thesis statement.
    (2) Topic calls for one strategy and this contains three. **Poor** thesis statement.
    (3) Does not give a strategy. Not on topic. **Poor** thesis statement.
    (4) Fact and not on topic. **Poor** thesis statement.
    (5) One strategy that community groups can use to attract young people is to show them how community service is relevant to them. **Good.**

PRACTICE

Write thesis statements for each of the topics given. Follow this process:

- Read the topic carefully.
- Respond with ONE sentence that begins with the words, *In my opinion.*
- Delete the words, *In my opinion.*

1. Imagine you could take a dream vacation anywhere in the world. In an essay, identify where you would like to go and why. Use personal observations, experiences, and knowledge to support your essay.

2. Although most stores have traditionally been closed on Sundays, in many places Sunday shopping is now the norm. In an essay, indicate whether you think Sunday shopping is a good thing or a bad thing and why. Use personal observations, experiences, and knowledge to support your essay.

3. What do you think is the most important component in building a strong, healthy romance? In an essay, identify that component. Explain how it helps to strengthen a romance. Use personal observations, experiences, and knowledge to support your essay.

4. What do you think is the greatest need in our society today? In an essay, identify that need. Explain why you think it is society's greatest need today. Use personal observations, experiences, and knowledge to support your essay.

5. An old saying says, "Cleanliness is next to godliness." If you could rewrite this saying, what would you say is next to godliness? In an essay, identify what you would say is next to godliness. Explain your reasons. Use personal observations, experiences, and knowledge to support your essay.

6. Suppose a teenager you know decided to drop out of school. In an essay, describe the advice that you would give this teenager. Use your personal observations, experiences, and knowledge to support your essay.

ANSWERS

Answers will vary. Evaluate your thesis statements in light of the following points.

1. The statement must clearly and directly address the topic
2. The statement must be something you can say more about
3. The statement should give an opinion or position
4. The statement should be limited to one aspect of the topic

GENERATE IDEAS

Another reason many people have trouble writing essays is that they can't think of enough to say. Their essays are too short. They do not have enough building materials. After narrowing the topic by writing a thesis statement, the next step is to find the right building materials by generating ideas.

Generating ideas is also called *brainstorming*. One method is called *webbing*. Following this approach, we will make a web that shows ideas about the topic and how the ideas relate to one another. Then, we will use the web to make an outline or blueprint of the essay.

Imagine you are asked to write an essay about the following topic:

Topic: What is one important thing that you think government should do to improve quality of life in our country? In an essay, identify one thing that government can do. Explain how you feel it will improve quality of life. Use personal observations, experiences, and knowledge to support your essay.

You begin by narrowing your topic and writing a thesis statement:

~~In my opinion,~~ *Spending more money on health care is one important thing government can do to improve quality of life for Canadians.*

The next step is to generate ideas by building a web. On a piece of scrap paper, write your thesis statement in the middle of the page. You do not have to write the whole sentence. Just write one or two words to remind you of the thesis.

Next, write three or four key points that support the thesis statement. Again, you do not have to write a whole sentence. You can write just one or two words to remind you of the points. In this case, your points might be that

- Health care is one of the basic services that government provides.
- People feel insecure because there is insufficient health care.
- More health care spending is important to quality of life because our population is aging.

So far, your web might look something like this:

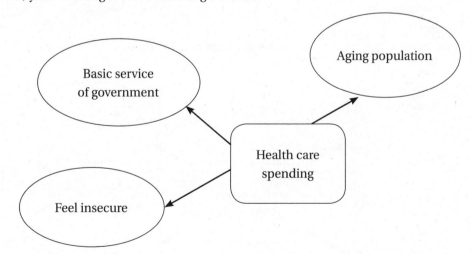

Each of the key points in the web will be the topic sentence for a paragraph in your essay. You can have three to five points. Any more than this and your essay will be too long for the GED®.

TIP

One way to identify key points is to say your thesis statement and *because*. In this case, you might say:

Spending more money on health care improves quality of life because . . .

If you cannot think of any reasons or other points, you may not have a good thesis statement. Make sure your thesis is something you can say more about.

PRACTICE

Write three or four key points for each thesis statement to complete the webs below.

1. Thesis: The Internet is one invention that has changed the way we live.

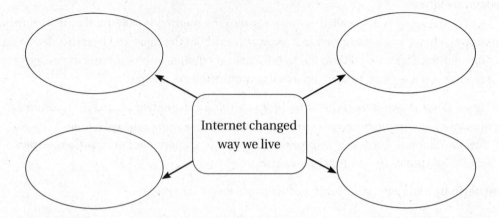

2. Thesis: Team sports are an important component of a child's social and physical development.

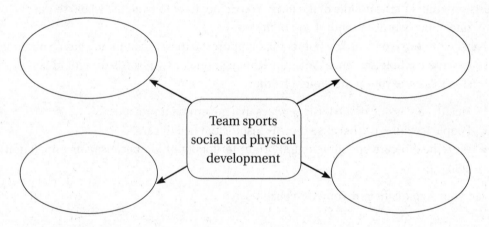

3. Thesis: Being a good citizen means doing things to help others.

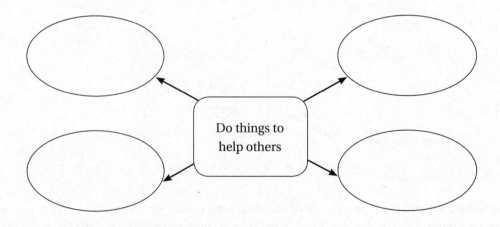

ANSWERS

Answers will vary; however, they may be similar to the following.

1. Answers might include three or four ways that the Internet has changed the way we live, such as access to information, shopping, and online dating.

2. Answers might include three or four areas of social and physical development that can be improved by participation in team sports, such as physical coordination and fitness, friendship, and responsibility. Another approach to an essay like this might be to talk about a particular child and how sports helped, such as *baseball helped my son with self-esteem, with setting goals, and with making friends.*

3. Answers might include three or four different types of things one could do to help others. Another approach would be to give three or four reasons that helping others makes one a good citizen.

Building the Web

After you have identified the key points, build the web by adding details and examples for each point, such as:

- A fuller explanation of the key point
- Reasons to support the key point
- Details and facts from your personal knowledge and experience
- Examples from your general knowledge or personal experience

For example, in the essay about spending on health care to improve quality of life, one key point was that people feel insecure. You might give an explanation of this point, saying that *with scarce health care resources, people worry about their own health and that of their families.* A reason to support the point might be that people feel concerned because there are often *long waits for tests or to see a specialist.* A fact or detail that supports the point might be that *many people do not have a family doctor.* An example of feeling insecure might be to ask readers to imagine that they have a *child with asthma.* How would they feel if they did not have a regular family doctor?

Here is an example of a completed web:

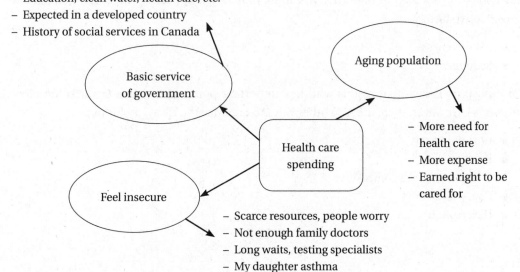

– Education, clean water, health care, etc.
– Expected in a developed country
– History of social services in Canada

Basic service of government

Aging population

Health care spending

– More need for health care
– More expense
– Earned right to be cared for

Feel insecure

– Scarce resources, people worry
– Not enough family doctors
– Long waits, testing specialists
– My daughter asthma

PRACTICE

Write a thesis statement and make a web for <u>one</u> of the following topics.

1. Imagine that you became a well-known athlete or entertainer. How do you think fame would change you? In an essay, describe how you think you would change and whether for better or worse. Use personal observations, experiences, and knowledge to support your essay.

2. Winter, spring, summer, or fall—which is your favourite season? In an essay, identify which is your favourite and explain why or why not. Use personal observations, experiences, and knowledge to support your essay.

3. There are many jobs that are important in our society, but not all of them receive the appreciation they deserve. In an essay, identify one job and explain why it is important. Use personal observations, experiences, and knowledge to support your essay.

ANSWERS

Answers will differ, but should include the following components:

1. Thesis statement
    a. The statement must clearly and directly address the topic.
    b. The statement must be something you can say more about.
    c. The statement should give an opinion or position.
    d. The statement should be limited to one aspect of the topic.

2. Three or four key points that support the thesis statement

3. For each key point, give three or four details or examples, such as:
    a. A fuller explanation of the key point.
    b. Reasons to support the key point.
    c. Details and facts from your personal knowledge and experience.
    d. Examples from your general knowledge or personal experience.

MAKE AN OUTLINE

The next step is to make a blueprint or plan of your essay: an outline. To begin, number the key points of your web in the order you think they might appear in the essay. You should consider two factors:

- Effectiveness
- Sequence

An expository essay often begins with less important points and builds towards the most important. However, there are also other ways to organize the essay, including:

- Chronological
- Process
- Comparison and contrast
- Cause and effect
- Description

In the example essay, the fact that health care is a basic service may not be less important, but it is an obvious point and so is less effective. This point should, therefore, come first.

Another factor is sequence; that is, sometimes one point may logically come before or after another. In this essay, it might be logical to go from people feeling insecure to talking about caring for our aging population.

After you have numbered the main points, begin to write the outline. Write the thesis statement at the top. List the key points in the order you have numbered them. Beneath each point, order and list the related supporting points, details, and examples from your web.

When putting the supporting points, details, and examples in order, consider effectiveness and sequence. At this point, you may also find that some of the supporting points you identified in your web don't belong. They may be interesting points, but if they do not fit with your other points, they do not belong.

Outline

Thesis: *Spending more money on health care is one important thing government can do to improve quality of life for Canadians.*

1. Basic service of government
   - Education, clean water, health care, for instance
   - Expected in a developed country
   - History of social services in Canada
     - Universal education
     - Social assistance and unemployment insurance
     - Universal health care
     - Proud tradition
2. Feel insecure
   - Scarce resources, people worry
   - Not enough family doctors
   - Long waits, testing specialists
   - My daughter asthma
     - No family doctor
     - Regional health centers, clinics closing
     - Worry about emergency services and ongoing treatment
3. Aging population
   - More need for health care
   - More expense
   - Earned right to be cared for
     - My parents
     - Worked hard
     - I want to know they will be okay

PRACTICE

Write an outline based on the web you made in the previous exercise. Your completed outline will look a lot like the one above.

ANSWERS

Compare your outline with the one above. Did you number your key points in the order you want them to appear? Did you list your other points in the order you want? You can add additional points if you wish.

WRITE A WELL-ORGANIZED ESSAY

When you first start to write essays, it will take some time to make a thesis statement and generate a web and outline. With practice, you will get much faster.

On the GED®, you will have 45 minutes to write your essay. Spend a maximum of five to ten minutes at the beginning to write your thesis and make a quick web and outline. This leaves plenty of time to write the essay. It will also be much easier to write the essay with an outline to follow.

A good essay must be divided into paragraphs. Each paragraph should be a minimum of three sentences in length. The essay must also be well organized, containing the following:

- Introduction
- Body
- Conclusion

Introduction

An introductory paragraph is different from other kinds of paragraphs. It is usually pictured like a funnel. It begins with a general statement about the topic and ends with the thesis statement.

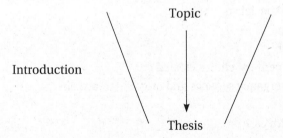

Consider the topic that was given above: *What is one important thing that you think government should do to improve quality of life in our country?* The topic is how government can improve quality of life. The introductory paragraph might begin with a general statement about the topic and then narrow to the thesis statement. Narrowing the topic can include summarizing the key points you will use later in the essay, but this is not required.

Example Introduction

Quality of life refers to the well-being of a society and the people who live in it. It includes things such as physical well-being, happiness, freedom from hunger and poverty, and human rights. There are many things that government can do to improve quality of life. Spending more money on health care is one important thing government can do to improve quality of life for Canadians.

PRACTICE

Write an introductory paragraph for <u>three</u> of the topics below. You can use the thesis statements you wrote for the same topics in "Narrow the Topic."

1. Imagine you could take a dream vacation anywhere in the world. In an essay, identify where you would like to go and why. Use personal observations, experiences, and knowledge to support your essay.

2. Although most stores have traditionally been closed on Sundays, in many places Sunday shopping is now the norm. In an essay, indicate whether you think Sunday shopping is a good thing or a bad thing and why. Use personal observations, experiences, and knowledge to support your essay.

3. What do you think is the most important component in building a strong, healthy romance? In an essay, identify that component. Explain how it helps to strengthen a romance. Use personal observations, experiences, and knowledge to support your essay.

4. What do you think is the greatest need in our society today? In an essay, identify that need. Explain why you think it is society's greatest need today. Use personal observations, experiences, and knowledge to support your essay.

5. An old saying says, "Cleanliness is next to godliness." If you could rewrite this saying, what would you say is next to godliness? In an essay, identify what you would say is next to godliness. Explain your reasons. Use personal observations, experiences, and knowledge to support your essay.

6. Suppose a teenager you know decided to drop out of school. In an essay, describe the advice that you would give this teenager. Use your personal observations, experiences, and knowledge to support your essay.

ANSWERS

When you review your paragraphs, ask yourself the following questions:

1. Does the paragraph contain at least three sentences?

2. Does the paragraph end with the thesis statement?

3. When you read the paragraph, does it sound natural and flow smoothly?

Body

The body is the largest part of the essay, but it may also be the easiest. You already did most of the work in brainstorming and making the outline.

In the GED® essay, the body should probably be three or four paragraphs. Begin the first paragraph of the body with a sentence that contains the first key point from your outline. Use the supporting points, details, and examples from your outline to make the other sentences of the paragraph. The second paragraph will begin with the second key point from your outline, and so on.

The outline shows the organization for the body of the essay, so you can concentrate on good writing. Write complete sentences. Choose the right words to state your meaning clearly and to give your essay the flow and style you want. You may discover as you write that some points in your outline don't quite fit or that there are other points you want to add. It is okay to make changes. The outline is only a guide.

Conclusion

The final paragraph of the essay is the conclusion. A concluding paragraph is like an introductory paragraph's funnel shape, but upside down.

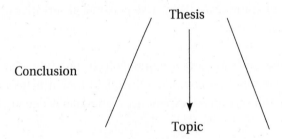

Begin the conclusion by restating your thesis statement, but using different wording. Next, summarize the important points you made in the essay. The last sentence is a statement about the topic. This is your final word on the subject. It should contain the concluding point, idea, moral, or lesson that you want to leave the reader thinking about.

You will find an example of a conclusion in the last paragraph of the sample essay that follows.

Title

Finally, you may wish to give your essay a title. This is not required; however, it can add polish. Titles should be catchy and should reflect the theme of the essay. A title for the sample essay might be something like "A Healthy Quality of Life."

PROOFREADING

The final step in writing the essay should be proofreading. Take the time to read over your essay and make corrections. Try not to make too many corrections by crossing out or inserting words or phrases. This will make your essay messy and hard to read.

When proofreading, watch for obvious writing mistakes. Do not worry too much about every little spelling or punctuation mistake. You should try to catch spelling and punctuation mistakes, but you should be more concerned about the overall effectiveness and quality of the writing.

When proofreading your essay for the GED®, you should look at three principle areas.

1. **ORGANIZATION**—Does your essay have a clearly focused main idea? Does it have a logical organization with an introduction, body, and conclusion? Is it all about the topic you were given? Are there specific and relevant details and examples to support your main points?

2. **MECHANICS**—Is the essay correctly written in complete sentences without sentence fragments or run-ons? Are the sentences effectively organized into paragraphs? Is the essay written using correct Standard English, with correct spelling, punctuation, grammar, and capitalization?

3. **EFFECTIVENESS**—Will readers find the essay easy to read and the ideas easy to follow? Is the writing effective with a variety of sentence types and precise word choice? Is the essay convincing?

Sample Essay

Look at this sample essay to see how the steps of narrowing the topic, brainstorming, making an outline, and proofreading go together to make an essay.

Topic: What is one important thing that you think government should do to improve quality of life in our country? In an essay, identify one thing that government can do. Explain how you feel it will improve quality of life. Use personal observations, experiences, and knowledge to support your essay.

Healthy Quality of Life

Quality of life refers to the well-being of a society and the people who live in it. It includes things such as physical well-being, happiness, freedom from hunger and poverty, and human rights. There are many things that government can do to improve quality of life. Spending more money on health care is one important thing government can do to improve quality of life for Canadians.

Government provides many services that are important to quality of life, such as education, access to clean water, health care, and more. These services have come to be expected in a developed and industrialized country. In Canada especially, we have a proud tradition of social services, including universal education, financial assistance for the poor and unemployed, and universal health care.

Health care is one area in which many Canadians now feel insecure. Health care resources are scarce and people worry about their own health and that of their loved ones. In many parts of the country, there are not enough family doctors and many Canadians go without. Regional health centers in smaller communities and suburbs are being closed and people must travel farther to access health care. There are long waiting periods for people to have testing or to see specialists. I know that I personally worry about access to emergency services and ongoing treatment for my daughter who has asthma.

Health care is especially important to quality of life for Canadians because our population is aging. As we age, there will be an increased need for health care and for more spending to maintain the same level of service. Some people in government talk about the "health care crisis" and say that spending should be cut. However, when I think about my own parents and other older Canadians, I feel that they have worked hard and have earned the right to good health care. We all want to know that we will be okay as we get older.

One way government can improve quality of life for Canadians is to spend more money on health care. Canadians have a proud history of social services and have come to expect the security of universal health care. Reduction in services, however, is causing many Canadians to worry, especially as the population ages. Government should make health care a priority to maintain our quality of life.

CHAPTER CHECK-UP

Choose ONE of the topics below and write an essay. Follow the five steps: narrow the topic; generate ideas; make an outline; write a well-organized essay; and proofread your work. When you have finished, put the essay aside for a day, and then review it using the self-scoring guide in the suggested answers.

1. Imagine you were asked to identify one person or event that best demonstrates to you the true meaning of love. In an essay, identify a person or event from your own experience and explain how you feel it demonstrates the meaning of love. Use personal observations, experience, and knowledge to support your essay.

2. Many people dream of owning a business. If you could start a business of your own, what would it be? In an essay, identify the business you would like to own and why and how you would make it successful. Use personal observations, experience, and knowledge to support your essay.

3. Do you think that television plays a role in shaping how our society thinks and feels? In an essay, identify whether or not you think television plays a role and explain the reasons for your opinion. Use personal observations, experience, and knowledge to support your essay.

4. Cheerleading is now recognized by many people as a sport. In an essay, identify whether or not you think cheerleading is a sport and explain why or why not. Use personal observations, experience, and knowledge to support your essay.

ANSWERS AND ANALYSIS

Put your essay aside for a day, and then review it using the self-scoring guide.

ESSAY SELF-SCORING GUIDE

Read your essay, and then answer each question about the essay with "Yes," "Fair," or "No."

	Yes	Fair	No
1. Is the essay all about the topic that was given and only about the topic that was given?			
2. Is the essay appropriate length (200–300 words)?			
3. Does the essay have an introduction, body, and conclusion?			
4. Does the introduction contain a clear thesis statement of your position on the topic?			
5. Is the essay divided into paragraphs of about 3–6 sentences, each paragraph being about only one main point in the essay?			
6. Does the essay give details and examples from your personal experience that support your points?			
7. Is the essay written in complete sentences with no sentence fragments or run-ons?			
8. Does the essay use correct spelling and capitalization?			
9. Does the essay use punctuation correctly, including apostrophes, commas, question marks, periods, semicolons, exclamation marks, and quotation marks?			
10. Does the essay use an effective word choice to communicate your meaning clearly?			
11. Is the essay easy to read, flowing smoothly from sentence to sentence and paragraph to paragraph?			
12. Is your essay convincing; would it persuade a reader that your position on the topic is reasonable?			

Scoring: Give yourself 2 points for every "Yes," 1 point for every "Fair," and 0 for every "No" to get a total mark out of 24. Divide the total by 6 to find your GED essay score out of 4.

Total = ___/24 ÷ 6 = ___/4

INTERPRETING RESULTS

Less than 2	Continue to write a practice essay at least once every two weeks as you prepare for the GED® tests. Focus on writing an introduction, body, and conclusion, staying on topic, and using complete sentences.
2–3	Continue to write a practice essay at least once every two weeks as you prepare for the GED® tests. Focus on the areas to which you responded "Fair" or "No."
3–4	Continue to write practice essays as you prepare for the GED®. Focus on areas to which you responded "Fair" or "No."

Language Arts, Writing—Practice Test

Directions: The Language Arts, Writing Test contains two parts. **The first part includes 50 multiple-choice questions. Do not spend more than 75 minutes on Part 1.** When you finish the multiple-choice questions, you can immediately begin working on Part 2, the essay, even if your time is not over. You can use any time you have left over plus an additional 45 minutes to work on the essay.

The Language Arts, Writing Test evaluates your knowledge of writing in Standard English. Remember that accepted standards for writing are different than for speaking. This practice test reviews topics in the Language Arts, Writing chapters and enables you to practice and prepare for the GED Language Arts, Writing Test, Part 1 and Part 2.

The practice test includes written passages in which paragraphs are identified by letters and sentences are numbered. The passages include errors in sentence structure, organization, mechanics, and usage. After reading a passage, answer the multiple-choice questions that follow. Questions will ask you to identify and correct errors in writing. Some questions may refer to sentences that are already correct as written. In every case, the correct answer will be one that is correct within the sentence and in the context of the passage as a whole.

Record your responses on the answer sheet that follows. For each question, mark the numbered space that corresponds with your answer choice.

EXAMPLE

Sentence 1: A new physician at the hospital is doctor Charles.

What correction should be made to this sentence?
(1)   Insert a comma after <u>physician</u>
(2)   Change the spelling of <u>new</u> to <u>knew</u>
(3)   Change <u>doctor</u> to <u>Doctor</u>
(4)   Replace <u>is</u> with <u>were</u>
(5)   No correction is necessary

In this example the word "Doctor" should be capitalized as part of the name Doctor Charles. Fill in answer space 3 on the answer sheet.

 ① ② ● ④ ⑤

ANSWER SHEET
Language Arts, Writing
Practice Test, Part 1

1. ① ② ③ ④ ⑤
2. ① ② ③ ④ ⑤
3. ① ② ③ ④ ⑤
4. ① ② ③ ④ ⑤
5. ① ② ③ ④ ⑤
6. ① ② ③ ④ ⑤
7. ① ② ③ ④ ⑤
8. ① ② ③ ④ ⑤
9. ① ② ③ ④ ⑤
10. ① ② ③ ④ ⑤
11. ① ② ③ ④ ⑤
12. ① ② ③ ④ ⑤
13. ① ② ③ ④ ⑤
14. ① ② ③ ④ ⑤
15. ① ② ③ ④ ⑤
16. ① ② ③ ④ ⑤
17. ① ② ③ ④ ⑤
18. ① ② ③ ④ ⑤
19. ① ② ③ ④ ⑤
20. ① ② ③ ④ ⑤

21. ① ② ③ ④ ⑤
22. ① ② ③ ④ ⑤
23. ① ② ③ ④ ⑤
24. ① ② ③ ④ ⑤
25. ① ② ③ ④ ⑤
26. ① ② ③ ④ ⑤
27. ① ② ③ ④ ⑤
28. ① ② ③ ④ ⑤
29. ① ② ③ ④ ⑤
30. ① ② ③ ④ ⑤
31. ① ② ③ ④ ⑤
32. ① ② ③ ④ ⑤
33. ① ② ③ ④ ⑤
34. ① ② ③ ④ ⑤
35. ① ② ③ ④ ⑤
36. ① ② ③ ④ ⑤
37. ① ② ③ ④ ⑤
38. ① ② ③ ④ ⑤
39. ① ② ③ ④ ⑤
40. ① ② ③ ④ ⑤

41. ① ② ③ ④ ⑤
42. ① ② ③ ④ ⑤
43. ① ② ③ ④ ⑤
44. ① ② ③ ④ ⑤
45. ① ② ③ ④ ⑤
46. ① ② ③ ④ ⑤
47. ① ② ③ ④ ⑤
48. ① ② ③ ④ ⑤
49. ① ② ③ ④ ⑤
50. ① ② ③ ④ ⑤

ANSWER SHEET
Language Arts, Writing
Practice Test, Part 2

Directions: Please record your answer for the GED Language Arts, Writing Test, Part 2 here in the space provided. You may organize your thoughts and make notes on scrap paper. The scrap paper must be turned in with this answer sheet at the end of the test; however, the scrap paper will not be marked. Only the essay written on the official answer sheet will be marked.

_____

_____

_____

_____

_____

_____

_____

_____

_____

_____

_____

_____

_____

LANGUAGE ARTS, WRITING TEST, PART 1

> **Directions:** Complete the practice test, and then check the answers and analysis that follow. After you mark your work, review any topics you had trouble with or did not understand.

Questions 1—12 are based on the following passage.

Are You a Fashion Diva?

(A)

(1) A strange animal you may have seen in todays society is the fashion diva. (2) She conducts herself like a queen which is displaying her finery. (3) She likes to have things her own way and always expects the best. (4) Especially when it comes to fashion. (5) Her clothes makes a statement about who she is, and that statement is stylish elegant and chic. (6) Many of these women are not aware of there diva status.

(B)

(7) What is a fashion diva? (8) Perhaps, you have heard about a famous singer who wore a Pucci designer dress that was so tight she had to be carried upstairs to the event she had attended. (9) There are many up and coming designers in Toronto. (10) Then there are the fashionistas who are assisted from their cars at red-carpet events because they need help to get up on their heels. (11) There are many famous fashion divas. (12) There are everyday divas as well. (13) Are you a fashion diva? (14) Do you have a separate closet just for your shoes in your house? (15) If you had a job at a clothing store, would you have to quit or end up owing more than you earn? (16) Have you ever met someone for the first time and the first thing you said was, "I love your hair?" (17) If one answered in the affirmative to any of these questions, they are a fashion diva.

1. Sentence 1: A strange animal you may have seen in todays society is the fashion diva.

   What correction should be made to this sentence?

   (1) Insert a comma after <u>animal</u>
   (2) Replace <u>may</u> with <u>might</u>
   (3) Change <u>seen</u> to <u>saw</u>
   (4) Change <u>todays</u> to <u>today's</u>
   (5) Replace <u>is</u> with <u>which is</u>

2. Sentence 2: She conducts herself like a queen which is displaying her finery.

   What correction should be made to this sentence?

   (1) Insert a period after <u>queen</u>
   (2) Insert a comma after <u>queen</u>
   (3) Change <u>is displaying</u> to <u>displays</u>
   (4) Replace <u>which</u> with <u>who</u>
   (5) No correction necessary

3. Sentences 3 and 4: She likes to have things her own way and always <u>expects the best. Especially</u> when it comes to fashion.

What is the best way to write the underlined portion? (If you think the original is the best way, choose option 1.)

(1) expects the best. Especially
(2) expects the best, especially
(3) expects the best; especially
(4) expects the best: especially
(5) expects the best; and especially

4. Sentence 5: Her clothes make a statement about who she is, and that statement is stylish elegant and chic.

What correction should be made to this sentence?

(1) Change <u>clothes</u> to <u>cloths</u>
(2) Replace <u>make</u> with <u>makes</u>
(3) Insert a period between <u>statement</u> and <u>about</u>
(4) Delete the comma after <u>she is</u>
(5) Insert a comma after <u>stylish</u>

5. Sentence 6: Many of these women are not aware of there diva status.

What correction should be made to this sentence?

(1) Change <u>there</u> to <u>their</u>
(2) Replace <u>these</u> with <u>those</u>
(3) Insert a comma after <u>women</u>
(4) Change <u>are</u> to <u>is</u>
(5) No correction necessary

6. Sentence 8: Perhaps, you have heard about a famous singer who wore a Pucci designer dress that was so tight she had to be carried up stairs to the event she had attended.

What correction should be made to this sentence?

(1) Remove the comma after <u>Perhaps</u>
(2) Insert a comma after <u>dress</u>
(3) Insert a period after <u>tight</u>
(4) Change <u>be</u> to <u>been</u>
(5) Change <u>had attended</u> to <u>was attending</u>

7. Sentence 10: Then there are the fashionistas who are assisted from their cars at red-carpet events because they need help to get up on their heels.

What correction should be made to this sentence?

(1) Change <u>there</u> to <u>they're</u>
(2) Replace <u>who</u> with <u>that</u>
(3) Insert a comma after <u>cars</u>
(4) Insert a comma after <u>events</u>
(5) No correction necessary

8. Sentences 11 and 12: There are many famous fashion divas. There are everyday divas as well.

The most effective combination of these sentences would include which of the following?

(1) divas, however, there are
(2) divas; however, there are
(3) divas, there are
(4) divas, also there are
(5) divas there are

9. The unity of paragraph B could be improved by deleting

(1) Sentence 7
(2) Sentence 8
(3) Sentence 9
(4) Sentence 10
(5) Sentence 11

10. Sentence 14: Do you have a separate closet just for your shoes in your house?

Which of the following is the best way to write this sentence? If you think the original is the best way, choose option (1).

(1) Do you have a separate closet just for your shoes in your house?
(2) Do you have a separate closet, for your shoes in your house?
(3) Do you have just for your shoes in your house a separate closet?
(4) Do you have a separate closet in your house just for your shoes?
(5) Just for your shoes, do you have a separate closet in your house?

11. Sentence 17: If one answered in the affirmative to any of these questions, they are a fashion diva.

What correction should be made to this sentence?

(1) Insert a comma after answered
(2) Replace one and they with you
(3) Remove the comma after questions
(4) Start a new sentence after questions
(5) No correction necessary

12. The organization of paragraph B would be improved by beginning a new paragraph starting with

(1) Sentence 9
(2) Sentence 10
(3) Sentence 11
(4) Sentence 13
(5) No revision necessary

Questions 13—20 are based on the following letter.

City Tax Letter

Dear Sir or Madam:

(A)

(1) According to our records the balance of the water and sewerage account for your property is $241.49. (2) Payment in full of the past-due amount must be received immediately. (3) Service may be suspended. (4) This is the last notice which will be sent prior to a shut-off order being issued. (5) If you wish to discuss this matter, we may be reached at 342-1937 from 8:30 a.m. to 4:30 p.m. each business day. (6) If payment has been forwarded prior to receipt of this letter, please except our thanks. (7) Please note that all City payments can be made in one of the following ways. (8) First, payment is available at the payment counter on the second floor of city hall. (9) Second, payments can be made by telephone with a credit card. (10) Lastly, payment by cheque or money order can be sent by mail to the address below.

Collections office
The City of Saint John

13. Sentence 1: According to <u>our records the balance</u> of the water and sewerage account for your property is $241.49.

    What is the best way to write the underlined portion of the sentence? (If you think the original is the best way, choose option 1.)

    (1) our records the balance
    (2) our records, the balance
    (3) our records; the balance
    (4) our records. The balance
    (5) our records, and the balance

14. Sentences 2 and 3: Payment in full of the past-due amount must be received immediately. Service may be suspended.

    The most effective combination of sentences 2 and 3 would include which of the following?

    (1) immediately, service may be suspended
    (2) immediately service may be suspended
    (3) immediately and service may be suspended
    (4) immediately, or service may be suspended
    (5) immediately, however service may be suspended

15. Sentence 4: This is the last notice which will be sent prior to a shut-off order being issued.

What correction should be made to this sentence?

(1) Change which to that
(2) Insert a comma before which
(3) Start a new sentence after sent
(4) Insert a comma after order
(5) No correction necessary

16. Sentence 5: If you wish to discuss this matter, we may be reached at 342-1937 from 8:30 a.m. to 4:30 p.m. each business day.

If you were to revise the sentence beginning with the words "Each business day," the next words should be:

(1) if you wish
(2) this matter
(3) we may be reached
(4) from 8:30 a.m. to 4:30 p.m.
(5) you may wish

17. Sentence 6: If payment has been forwarded prior to receipt of this letter, please except our thanks.

What correction should be made to this sentence?

(1) Change has been to had been
(2) Insert a comma after forwarded
(3) Change this to that
(4) Remove the comma after letter
(5) Change except to accept

18. Sentence 7: Please note that all City payments can be made in one of the following ways.

What correction should be made to this sentence?

(1) Insert a comma after note
(2) Change that to which
(3) Change City to city
(4) Insert a comma after payments
(5) Change can be to could be

19. Which change would most improve the organization of the passage?
(1) Delete sentence 4
(2) Change Lastly in sentence 10 to Third
(3) Delete sentence 8
(4) Start a new paragraph with sentence 3
(5) Delete sentence 7

20. The organization of this passage would be improved by beginning a new paragraph starting with

    (1)   Sentence 3

    (2)   Sentence 6

    (3)   Sentence 7

    (4)   Sentence 8

    (5)   Sentence 9

Questions 21—32 are based on the following passage.

Dental Floss

(A)

(1) Although awareness of flossing is high, compliance is low. (2) Studies indicate that the vast majority of patients did not floss as often as they should. (3) The reasons are many. (4) One reason is that people find putting fingers wrapped in string into their mouths unpleasant. (5) There are products they can buy to make flossing easier. (6) The real reason for most people is that they are tired and just want to get to bed so they don't want to take the time.

(B)

(7) Dentists and hygienists agree; that flossing is one of the most important things you can do for your teeth. (8) Flossing removes debris and plaque a bacterial biofilm, between the teeth. (9) Plaque between the teeth is the cause of most cavities. (10) It is also a cause of the gum disease gingivitis.

(C)

(11) Maintaining healthy teeth is part of a healthy lifestyle and good personal hygiene. (12) Some people seem to be born with strong, healthy teeth; while others have to work harder to maintain them. (13) However, there are steps that everyone can take to maintain your teeth and gums. (14) One important step is regular flossing.

(D)

(15) Regular brushing and use of floss are both necessary components for good oral care. (16) Canadian Dentists state that flossing only takes a few minutes, but it cleans away plaque that a toothbrush cannot reach. (17) Make flossing part of your twice-daily routine to help your teeth last your hole lifetime.

21. Sentence 2: Studies indicate that the vast majority of patients did not floss as often as they should.

    What correction should be made to this sentence?

    (1)   Change indicate to indicated

    (2)   Replace patients with patient's

    (3)   Insert a comma after patients

    (4)   Change did to do

    (5)   Insert a comma after often

22. Sentences 4 and 5: One reason is that people find putting fingers wrapped in string into their mouths unpleasant. There are products they can buy to make flossing easier.

The best way to combine the sentences would include which of the following?

(1) unpleasant; however, there
(2) unpleasant. However there
(3) unpleasant, however, there
(4) unpleasant, however there
(5) unpleasant. However; there

23. Sentence 6: The real reason for most people is that they are tired and just want to get to bed so they don't want to take the time.

What correction should be made to this sentence?

(1) Insert a comma after people
(2) Insert a comma after tired
(3) Insert a comma after bed
(4) Change don't to didn't
(5) Change to take to to have taken

24. Sentence 7: Dentists and hygienists agree; that flossing is one of the most important things you can do for your teeth.

What is the best way to write the underlined portion of the sentence? (If you think the original is the best way, choose option 1.)

(1) agree; that flossing
(2) agree. Flossing
(3) agree, that flossing
(4) agree. That flossing
(5) agree: that flossing

25. Sentence 8: Flossing removes debris and plaque a bacterial biofilm, between the teeth.

What correction should be made to this sentence?

(1) Insert a comma after Flossing
(2) Change removes to had removed
(3) Insert a comma after plaque
(4) Remove the comma after biofilm
(5) Change between to among

26. Sentences 9 and 10: Plaque between the teeth is the cause of most cavities. It is also a cause of the gum disease gingivitis.

If you were to combine the sentences beginning with the words "The cause of most cavities" it should be followed by:

(1) , plaque is also
(2) , and it is also
(3) ; gum disease is also
(4) . It is also
(5) and gingivitis is also

27. Sentence 12: Some people seem to be born with strong, healthy teeth; while others have to work harder to maintain them.

What correction should be made to this sentence?

(1) Change seem to seems
(2) Insert a comma after born
(3) Replace the semicolon after teeth with a comma
(4) Change others to other's
(5) Delete the semicolon after teeth

28. Sentence 13: However, there are steps that everyone can take to maintain your teeth and gums.

What correction should be made to this sentence?

(1) Insert a comma after steps
(2) Change your to their
(3) Change everyone to anyone
(4) Insert your before gums
(5) Insert a comma after teeth

29. Sentence 15: Regular brushing and use of floss are both necessary components for good oral care.

What is the best way to write the underlined portion of the sentence? (If you think the original is the best way, choose option 1.)

(1) Regular brushing and use of floss
(2) Regular brushing and to use floss
(3) Regularly brushing and use of floss
(4) Regular brushing and flossing
(5) Regularly to brush and to use

30. Sentence 16: Canadian Dentists state that flossing only takes a few minutes, but it cleans away plaque that a toothbrush cannot reach.

What correction should be made to this sentence?

(1) Change Dentists to dentists
(2) Remove the comma after minutes
(3) Insert a comma after plaque
(4) Change it to they
(5) No correction necessary

31. Sentence 17: Make flossing part of your twice-daily routine to help your teeth last your hole lifetime.

What correction should be made to this sentence?

(1) Insert a comma after twice
(2) Insert a comma after routine
(3) Change your teeth to you're teeth
(4) Start a new sentence after routine
(5) Change hole to whole

32. To improve organization of this passage:
    (1) Move paragraph A after paragraph B
    (2) Move paragraph A after paragraph C
    (3) Move paragraph B after paragraph C
    (4) Move paragraph C after paragraph D
    (5) Move paragraph C to the beginning

Questions 33—43 are based on the following passage.

(A)

(1) Weather young or old, audiences are loving the local high-school production of a musical entitled "Offically Blonde." (2) From the opening number to the closing scene, the show is fast paced. (3) It is also quirky and totally entertaining. (4) There are several musicals like this that have been made from movies. (5) This production, as you will hear from any who have attended, is the hit of the High School season.

(B)

(6) The production is directed by Dr D. Ellis Andrews of the school's drama department. (7) Andrews came to the school five years ago she has earned a reputation as an innovative director since then. (8) One of the things she is best known for are her sets, which are elaborate and always beautifully painted. (9) However, she is best known to her students and cast members as an inspiration. (10) The most recent production may be her best. (11) It is funny at unpredictable moments and thoroughly entertaining throughout. (12) The productions lead role is played by Moira Erkhart, who charms the audience with her engaging personality. (13) The production runs for three more nights at the school theatre, and, if you have a chance, they should see it.

33. Sentence 1: (1) Weather young or old, audiences are loving the local high-school production of a musical entitled "Officially Blonde."

    What correction should be made to this sentence?

    (1) Remove the comma after old
    (2) Change Weather to Whether
    (3) Replace the comma after old with a period
    (4) Change are loving to loved
    (5) No correction necessary

34. Sentences 2 and 3: From the opening number to the closing scene, the show is fast paced. It is also quirky and totally entertaining.

    The most effective combination of these sentences would include which of the following?

    (1) and is also quirky and is totally entertaining
    (2) also quirky and totally entertaining
    (3) ; however, it is also
    (4) fast paced, quirky, and totally entertaining
    (5) or quirky and entertaining

35. Sentence 5: This production, as you will hear from any who have attended, is the hit of the High School season.

What correction should be made to this sentence?

(1) Remove the comma after production
(2) Change hear to here
(3) Remove the comma after attended
(4) Replace is with was
(5) Remove capitalization in high school

36. The organization of paragraph A would be improved by
(1) Deleting sentence 4
(2) Moving sentence 5 to the beginning
(3) Beginning a paragraph at sentence 3
(4) Moving sentence 1 to the end
(5) No correction necessary

37. Sentence 6: The production is directed by Dr D. Ellis Andrews of the school's drama department.

What correction should be made to this sentence?

(1) Insert a comma after directed
(2) Insert a period after Dr
(3) Insert a comma after Andrews
(4) Change school's to schools
(5) Capitalize Drama

38. Sentence 7: Andrews came to the school five years ago she has earned a reputation as an innovative director ever since.

What correction should be made to this sentence?

(1) Change came to had come
(2) Change years to year's
(3) Start a new sentence after ago
(4) Insert a comma after reputation
(5) Replace as with to be

39. Sentence 8: One of the things she is best known for are her sets, which are elaborate and always beautifully painted.

What correction should be made to this sentence?

(1) Insert a comma after things
(2) Change is to was
(3) Change are her sets to is her sets
(4) Change which to that
(5) Delete the comma after sets

40. Sentence 11: It is funny at unpredictable <u>moments and thoroughly entertaining</u> throughout.

What is the best way to write the underlined portion of the sentence? (If you think the original is the best way, choose option 1.)

(1) moments and thoroughly entertaining
(2) moments, and thoroughly entertaining
(3) moments; and thoroughly entertaining
(4) moments. Thoroughly entertaining
(5) moments; thoroughly entertaining

41. Sentence 12: The productions lead role is played by Moira Erkhart, who charms the audience with her engaging personality.

What correction should be made to this sentence?

(1) Change <u>productions</u> to <u>production's</u>
(2) Insert a comma after <u>role</u>
(3) Delete the comma before <u>who</u>
(4) Insert a comma after <u>audience</u>
(5) Change <u>charms</u> to <u>charmed</u>

42. Sentence 13: The production runs for three more nights at the school theatre, and, if you have a chance, they should see it.

What correction should be made to this sentence?

(1) Change <u>runs</u> to <u>has run</u>
(2) Change <u>nights</u> to <u>night's</u>
(3) Remove the comma after <u>theatre</u>
(4) Change the comma to a semicolon
(5) Change <u>they</u> to <u>you</u>

43. The organization of this passage would be improved by beginning a new paragraph starting with

(1) Sentence 3
(2) Sentence 4
(3) Sentence 8
(4) Sentence 9
(5) Sentence 10

Questions 44–50 are based on the following passage.

Due Diligence

(A)

(1) Government acts provide no-fault insurance to protect employees from injuries in Canadian provinces and territories at work. (2) However, if an accident does occur. (3) An employer can be charged with an offense if considered negligent. (3) The employer's best legal defence is to show due diligence. (4) Both employees and employers are expected to show due diligence with respect to workplace safety.

(B)

(5) Due diligence is a legal term that means taking reasonable care to protect the well-being of employees or co-workers. (6) How much care is reasonable depends on several factors, such as the seriousness of the possible injury and the risk of an incident occurring. (7) Is the potential danger high. (8) Then a high level of care is expected. (9) Similarly, if there is a high likelihood of an incident occurring, extreme care should be took. (10) You may know someone who was injured at work.

(C)

(11) To show due diligence, employers must follow government acts and regulations. (12) As well, employers must have written safety policies, practices, and follow procedures. (13) Employers must also provide education to their workers to learn them to work safely. (14) For their part, employees should follow the policies and procedures that are put in place for their protection.

44.   Sentence 1: Government acts provide no-fault insurance to protect employees from injuries in Canadian provinces and territories at work.

      What is the best way to write this sentence? (If you think the original is the best way, choose option 1.)

      (1)   Government acts provide no-fault insurance to protect employees from injuries in Canadian provinces and territories at work.
      (2)   Government acts provide no-fault insurance to protect employees from injuries at work in Canadian provinces and territories.
      (3)   Government acts provide in Canadian provinces and territories no-fault insurance to protect employees from injuries at work.
      (4)   In Canadian provinces and territories, government acts provide no-fault insurance to protect employees from injuries at work.
      (5)   Government acts provide no-fault insurance to protect in Canadian provinces and territories employees from injuries at work.

45. Sentences 2 and 3: However, if an accident does <u>occur. An employer</u> can be charged with an offense if considered negligent.

What is the best way to write the underlined portion of the sentences? (If you think the original is the best way, choose option 1.)

(1) occur. An employer
(2) occur, an employer
(3) occur, and an employer
(4) occur; an employer
(5) occur, but an employer

46. Sentence 7: Is the potential danger high.

What is the best way to write this sentence? (If you think the original is the best way, choose option 1.)

(1) Is the potential danger high.
(2) If the potential danger is high.
(3) Is the potential danger high?
(4) Potentially, if the danger is high.
(5) How high is the potential danger.

47. Sentence 9: Similarly, if there is a high likelihood of an incident occurring, extreme care should be took.

What correction should be made to this sentence?

(1) Remove the comma after <u>Similarly</u>
(2) Remove the comma after <u>occurring</u>
(3) Change the comma after <u>occurring</u> to a period
(4) Replace <u>is</u> with <u>are</u>
(5) Change <u>took</u> to <u>taken</u>

48. Sentence 12: As well, employers must have written <u>safety policies, practices, and follow procedures</u>.

What is the best way to write the underlined portion of the sentence? (If you think the original is the best way, choose option 1.)

(1) safety policies, practices, and follow procedures
(2) safety policies, practices, and procedures
(3) safety policies, practices, and to follow procedures
(4) safety policies, practices, and following procedures
(5) safety policies, practices, and should follow procedures

49. Sentence 13: Employers must also provide education to their workers to learn them to work safely.

What correction should be made to this sentence?

(1) Change learn to teach
(2) Change Employers to Employer's
(3) Change their to they're
(4) Change their to there
(5) No correction necessary

50. The organization of this passage would be improved by which of the following:
(1) Move paragraph A to the end
(2) Start a new paragraph at sentence 8
(3) Move paragraph C before paragraph B
(4) Delete sentence 10
(5) No revision necessary

LANGUAGE ARTS, WRITING TEST, PART 2

This part of the Language Arts, Writing Test includes an essay on the prompt and topic below to be completed in 45 minutes. When you finish the multiple-choice questions on Part 1, you can immediately begin working on the essay, which will give you additional time. Do not spend a total of more than 75 minutes for Part 1 plus 45 minutes for Part 2.

PROMPT

On International Stand Up to Bullying Day people wear pink shirts to show their stand against bullying. The trend was started by two Nova Scotia high school boys who wore pink shirts when another student was bullied for wearing one. Soon, hundreds of students were doing the same to show their support.

In an essay, identify whether you think bullying in schools is a problem and what kinds of things should be done in response. Use personal observations, experience, and knowledge to support your essay.

> **Directions:** Please record your answer for the GED Language Arts, Writing Test, Part 2 on the answer sheet provided. You may organize your thoughts and make notes on scrap paper. The scrap paper must be turned in with the answer sheet at the end of the test; however, the scrap paper will not be marked. Only the essay written on the official answer sheet will be marked.

LANGUAGE ARTS, WRITING TEST, PART 1
ANSWERS AND ANALYSIS

ANSWERS

1. **(4)**	16. **(3)**	31. **(5)**	46. **(3)**
2. **(4)**	17. **(5)**	32. **(5)**	47. **(5)**
3. **(2)**	18. **(3)**	33. **(2)**	48. **(2)**
4. **(5)**	19. **(2)**	34. **(4)**	49. **(1)**
5. **(1)**	20. **(3)**	35. **(5)**	50. **(4)**
6. **(5)**	21. **(4)**	36. **(1)**	
7. **(5)**	22. **(1)**	37. **(2)**	
8. **(2)**	23. **(3)**	38. **(3)**	
9. **(3)**	24. **(2)**	39. **(3)**	
10. **(4)**	25. **(3)**	40. **(1)**	
11. **(2)**	26. **(1)**	41. **(1)**	
12. **(4)**	27. **(5)**	42. **(5)**	
13. **(2)**	28. **(2)**	43. **(5)**	
14. **(4)**	29. **(4)**	44. **(4)**	
15. **(1)**	30. **(1)**	45. **(2)**	

Interpret Your Results

Test Area	Questions	Recommended Minimum Score	Your Score
Sentences	3, 4, 8, 14, 16, 22, 24, 27, 29, 34, 38, 40, 44, 45, 48	11	
Organization	9, 12, 19, 20, 32, 36, 43, 50	5	
Mechanics	1, 5, 13, 17, 18, 23, 25, 30, 35, 37, 41, 46	9	
Usage	2, 6, 7, 10, 11, 15, 21, 26, 28, 31, 33, 39, 42, 47, 49	11	
Total		36	

Check your answers and calculate how you scored in each test area. If you scored less than the recommended minimum score in any test area, you should review topics in the relevant chapters.

ANSWER ANALYSIS

1. **(4)** Use an apostrophe and an *s* to show possession.

2. **(4)** The relative pronoun *which* is not used for people. It often adds extra information about a thing and is preceded by a comma.

3. **(2)** Correct the sentence fragment by joining the independent and adverbial clause,

4. **(5)** Use commas to separate items in a list. A comma before *and* at the end of the list would be an optional addition.

5. **(1)** Use the correct spelling for the possessive pronoun.

6. **(5)** Verb tenses need to fit with one another. *Had attended* would be used before an event in the past. In this sentence, she *was attending* the event at the same time the pictures were taken and she was carried up the stairs.

7. **(5)** The sentence is correct as written.

8. **(2)** One way to form a compound sentence is with a semicolon and a conjunctive adverb, followed by a comma.

9. **(3)** Although the sentence may be true, it is not related to the topic of the paragraph, which is *Are you a fashion diva?*

10. **(4)** The modifier *in your house* should be next to the thing it describes, the closet.

11. **(2)** The pronoun *you* has been used throughout the passage. Avoid pronoun shift.

12. **(4)** Sentence 13 introduces a new topic and is followed by supporting sentences.

13. **(2)** Insert a comma after an introductory word or phrase.

14. **(4)** Make a compound sentence using a comma and coordinate conjunction.

15. **(1)** The relative pronoun *that* is used for necessary information about a thing.

16. **(3)** The independent clause would follow an introductory phrase.

17. **(5)** Spell the homonyms *accept* and *except* correctly. *Accept* means to receive.

18. **(3)** Only capitalize a word such as *city* if it is part of a name, such as Labrador City.

19. **(2)** To preserve parallel structure and consistent organization of the passage, the word should be *third* to go with the previous *first* and *second*.

20. **(3)** The end part of the passage is about methods of payment, which is introduced in topic sentence 7.

21. **(4)** When editing writing, consider the entire passage. The verb *do* must be in the present tense to be consistent with the sentences that come before and after.

22. **(1)** To combine sentences with a conjunctive adverb such as *however*, use a semicolon to join the sentences, and a comma after the adverb.

23. **(3)** *They don't want to take the time* is an independent clause. Use a comma before the coordinating conjunction *so* to form a compound.

24. **(2)** No punctuation would be needed before the relative pronoun *that*; however, this is not one of the options given. The other option is to remove the relative pronoun and start a new sentence.

25. **(3)** *Plaque* and *a bacterial biofilm* are the same thing. Use commas to separate appositives.

26. **(1)** Use the antecedent to take the place of the pronoun after the introductory phrase.

27. **(5)** Using a semicolon would create a sentence fragment. No punctuation is needed to separate the independent clause from the dependent clause that follows it.

28. **(2)** Everyone refers to more than one person and requires a plural pronoun.

29. **(4)** List items in parallel form.

30. **(1)** *Dentists* is not part of a name and should not be capitalized.

31. **(5)** *Hole* is a pit, while *whole* refers to the entire thing.

32. **(5)** Paragraph C should clearly be the introduction. It introduces the connection between dental hygiene and a healthy lifestyle and ends with a thesis statement.

33. **(2)** *Whether* refers to choices, but the homonym *weather* refers to climate.

34. **(4)** The ideas in these sentences could easily be combined in a list.

35. **(5)** The words *high school* are not part of a name.

36. **(1)** Sentence 4 is not related to the rest of the passage.

37. **(2)** Use a period after a title if it is part of a name.

38. **(3)** Insert a period to correct the run-on sentence.

39. **(3)** The singular subject *one* requires a singular verb *is*.

40. **(1)** This is one complete sentence and no additional punctuation is required. The sentence is not a compound; it is a list of two things, funny and entertaining. A comma is not used in a list of two.

41. **(1)** Use an apostrophe and an *s* to spell a singular possessive.

42. **(5)** Correct the pronoun shift from *you* to *they*.

43. **(5)** This topic sentence is followed by supporting sentences that explain why the production may be her best.

44. **(4)** Correct the misplaced modifier to show that it is in Canadian provinces and territories that government acts provide this protection.

45. **(2)** Correct the sentence fragment by placing a comma after <u>occur</u> at the end of the sentence fragment to connect it to the independent clause.

46. **(3)** Use a question mark at the end of a question.

47. **(5)** Use *taken* not *took* with a helping verb, such as *be* <u>taken</u>.

48. **(2)** For parallel structure, all items in the list should be in the same form.

49. **(1)** One person teaches another. The student learns.

50. **(4)** Sentence 10 is not related to the topic of the paragraph, which is the meaning of due diligence.

LANGUAGE ARTS, WRITING TEST, PART 2 ANSWERS AND ANALYSIS

If self-evaluating your essay, put the essay aside for at least one day before reviewing it. Use the Essay Self-Scoring Guide on page 333 to assess your writing.

Language Arts

READING

Overview of the Reading Test

The Language Arts, Reading Test includes:

- 40 multiple-choice questions
- 65-minute time limit

To answer questions on the GED Reading Test, you must be able to understand and analyze various types of written passages. The questions will test your ability to comprehend, apply, analyze, and synthesize written information.

READING IN EVERYDAY LIFE

Reading is something we all do every day. We can't help it; we are surrounded by writing everywhere we go. We read signs, labels, emails, text messages, instructions, reports, letters, newspapers, books, and much more. In our computerized society, there is more reading and writing than ever before in the history of the world. Some people are better readers than others, but reading is a skill that can be improved with practice.

Reading is more than just reading the words. You need to learn to read between the lines to understand how information fits together, to draw conclusions, and to apply information to other situations. You must also learn to analyze and evaluate what you read and to synthesize or combine it with other information. These are reading skills that a high-school graduate is expected to bring to the workplace or to further training and education.

TIP

Reading is more than just reading the words.

WHAT'S ON THE TEST?

On the Canadian GED Language Arts, Reading Test, there might not be any Canadian literature selections. The literature passages will be from works by well-known international writers who might appear on a highschool exam. At the beginning of each passage is a **purpose question** to help candidates know what the passage is about.

The Language Arts, Reading Test includes written passages of 200–400 words, followed by multiple-choice questions.

- 75% of questions are based on literature texts, including:

  - Poetry
  - Drama
  - Prose fiction written before 1920
  - Prose fiction 1920–1960
  - Prose fiction after 1960

- 25% of questions are based on nonfiction texts, including:

  - ☐ Nonfiction prose
  - ☐ Critical reviews of visual and performing arts
  - ☐ Workplace and community documents

Questions on the GED Language Arts, Reading Test evaluate the following skills:

- Comprehension (20%)—Restate, summarize, or explain a passage.
- Application (15%)—Use information in a different context.
- Analysis (30–35%)—Analyze consequences, style, structure, character, figurative language, conclusions, supporting details, cause and effect, inferences and assumptions.
- Synthesis (30–35%)—integrate and interpret information from different sources, style, tone, purpose, and comparison and contrast.

Introduction to Reading

10

READING FOR COMPREHENSION

There are different levels of reading skill. Comprehension is the most basic level. 20% of the questions on the GED Reading Test evaluate comprehension. Comprehension refers to your ability to

- Understand what a passage says
- Restate a passage
- Identify the main idea
- Explain the clear meaning of the passage

What It Says

At the most basic level, comprehension is recognizing the information that is stated in the passage.

Restate a Passage

Show comprehension by stating ideas from the passage using different words or by recognizing different ways to say the same thing.

Identify the Main Idea

Show comprehension by recognizing statements that summarize the main idea of a passage.

Explain the Clear Meaning

Show comprehension by identifying statements that explain what the passage clearly means and the clear implications of the passage.

PRACTICE

What are the workplace policies?

All employees of our corporation have the right to a positive workplace that promotes mutual respect and recognizes individual differences in a team environment. A respectful workplace is more than a legal requirement; it is a culture of productivity that values all individuals and that is free of sexual or personal harassment of any kind.

Harassment is any conduct of a sexual or personal nature that is unwelcome or persistent or that may reasonably be considered offensive, disrespectful, or hostile. Harassment may be spoken, written, or physical. It may include words, sounds, images, media, or gestures. All employees of the corporation are expected to conduct themselves in a professional manner and to promote productivity and teamwork, and they have the right to expect such treatment from others. Note that harassment does not include performance feedback given in a professional manner by managers and supervisors.

1. Based on the information in this excerpt, the corporation believes that a respectful workplace is
   (1) a right
   (2) a privilege
   (3) a legal requirement
   (4) a difference
   (5) unwelcome

2. What is the meaning of the clause *it is a culture of productivity that values all individuals* (line 3)?
   (1) a respectful workplace is not a legal requirement
   (2) a respectful workplace is valuable
   (3) a respectful workplace yields greater production
   (4) a respectful workplace is more individualistic
   (5) a respectful workplace promotes the arts

3. This passage is primarily about
   (1) corporate policy
   (2) employee rights and responsibilities
   (3) the role of managers and supervisors
   (4) what constitutes harassment
   (5) benefits of a respectful workplace

4. Based on the information in this excerpt, when is harassing or offensive conduct acceptable?
   (1) It is never acceptable
   (2) It is acceptable if communicated by email
   (3) It is acceptable if included in feedback by managers or supervisors
   (4) It is acceptable only if delivered towards specific individuals
   (5) It is acceptable if not of a sexual nature

TIP

Comprehend
- **Understand**
- **Restate**
- **Main idea**
- **Clear meaning**

ANSWERS

1. **(1)** Recognize what the passage says, that a respectful workplace is a right of all employees.

2. **(3)** Restate the meaning of the passage by saying that a respectful workplace creates a *culture of productivity*, which indicates that there is greater production.

3. **(2)** The passage is primarily about the rights and responsibilities of employees with regard to a respectful workplace. While the other topics are included, they are elements that support the main idea.

4. **(1)** It is the clear implication of this passage that such conduct is never acceptable in any form or directed at any individual. Performance feedback given in a professional manner by managers and supervisors is not harassment.

CHALLENGE EXERCISE

Often, titles and subheadings (if any) give a clue about important information. For example, a newspaper headline might say, *Earthquake in Asia*. Change the headline to a question, such as *What were the effects of the earthquake in Asia?* Find the answer to identify important information in the passage. Choose an article from a newspaper or choose an excerpt from a magazine article or book. Change the headings and any subheadings into questions. Find the answers to practice reading for comprehension.

PRACTICE WITH FICTION

Many of the reading passages are based on excerpts from fiction. These are passages from short stories or novels. The excerpts will have a beginning, middle, and end, although they will not be the whole story. Many of the fiction passages will be from American writers and others will be well-known writers of the world, possibly including some Canadians. All the passages will be from well-known writers, whose work could appear on a high school exam.

The passages will be from different time periods to test your ability to understand different styles of writing and uses of language in literature. Some passages will be from older works, written before 1920. Others will be from the mid-twentieth century. Other passages will be from more modern works,

PRACTICE

Read each passage and respond to the questions to test your comprehension skills.

Questions 1–5 are based on the following extract.

Why Was the Painter Evil?

She was a maiden of rarest beauty, and not more lovely than full of glee. And evil was the hour when she saw, and loved, and wedded the painter. He, passionate, studious, austere, and having already a bride in his Art; she a maiden of rarest beauty, and not more lovely than full of glee; all light and smiles, and frolicsome as the young fawn; loving and cherishing all things; hating only the Art which was her rival; dreading only the pallet and brushes and other untowards instruments which deprived her of the countenance of her lover. It was thus a terrible thing for this lady to hear the painter speak of his desire to portray even his young bride. But she was humble and obedient, and sat meekly for many weeks in the dark, high turret-chamber where the light dripped upon the pale canvas only from overhead. But he, the painter, took glory in his work, which went on from hour to hour, and from day to day. And he was a passionate, and wild, and moody man, who became lost in reveries; so that he would not see that the light which fell so ghastly in that lone turret withered the health and the spirits of his bride, who pined visibly to all but him.

—from "The Oval Portrait" by Edgar Allan Poe

TIP

Comprehension is understanding what a passage says.

1. What was the woman like at the beginning of the story?
   - (1) Sad
   - (2) Happy
   - (3) Depressed
   - (4) Lonely
   - (5) Jealous

2. Why was it an evil hour when she married the painter?
   - (1) He was passionate
   - (2) She did not love him
   - (3) He did not love her
   - (4) He was already married to his art
   - (5) He was wild and moody

3. What is the meaning of the line, *dreading only the pallet and brushes and other untowards instruments which deprived her of the countenance of her lover* (lines 5–6)?
   - (1) She did not like art
   - (2) She was afraid of her husband's appearance
   - (3) Paint supplies were a cause of her fear
   - (4) There was no explanation for the behaviour of her husband
   - (5) She feared the art that took her husband's attention from her

4. This passage is primarily about
   (1) A woman neglected by her husband
   (2) Art
   (3) A woman's dreams
   (4) The passion of a painter for his art
   (5) Fear of the supernatural

5. By the end of the passage, the woman in the story had changed because she had
   (1) Adopted her husband's love of art
   (2) Fallen out of love
   (3) Lost her beauty
   (4) Become sick and unhappy
   (5) Become tired

Questions 6–10 are based on the following extract.

What Was the Summer Place Like?

The place I speak of—write of—where Mrs. Lewis died, is an old hotel that sits above the sand in Maine. Every summer, since the summer I was born, we have gone down to this hotel from Toronto, just as all the summers since the summer *he* was born, my father went down before us. That is the sort of hotel—of place—it is.

In front of the hotel, between the hotel and the sea, there is a stretch of sand precisely one-and-one-eighth miles long, on which the children play and the athletes run all summer. This sand is also walked by a variety of older people; some, like my father, life-time summer residents: and there is one old man who, every summer, stops each person in turn to remark that, if he had the eyes of several hundred eagles and was facing out to sea, nothing should hinder his view of South America. But, of course, the distance does and there is nothing to be seen but the endless curve of the horizon. And there are the ships: an occasional tanker or steamer, or Boston-bound freighter puffs away, always losing its balance and disappearing over the edge and there are sailboats on the weekends and lobster-boats whenever the traps are ripe or need resetting.

At either end of the beach there is a promontory, each with descending stretches of sea-rocks that are prone to the tides. In the olden days, these were the scene of much shipwreck and disaster. Now, there is still the occasional fool, trapped out walking on the rocks, who will be drowned at high tide: but this is rare and there has been no death by drowning for the last three years.

—from "The People on the Shore" by Timothy Findley

6. The hotel is the sort of place that
   (1) People die
   (2) People go to from Toronto
   (3) Is for older people
   (4) Is a nice place to visit
   (5) Families return to every year

7. What hinders the old man's view of South America?
    (1) Eagles
    (2) The endless curve of the horizon
    (3) The distance
    (4) Ships
    (5) A Boston-bound freighter

8. The main purpose of the passage is to describe
    (1) The narrator's childhood
    (2) The narrator's family
    (3) The place the narrator spent summers
    (4) The coast of Maine
    (5) A hotel in Maine

9. The passage describes ships losing their *balance and disappearing over the edge* of what?
    (1) The horizon
    (2) The ocean
    (3) The rocks
    (4) The world
    (5) South America

10. What is the meaning of the phrase, *that are prone to the tides* (line 16)?
    (1) Above the high tide line
    (2) Covered at high tide and revealed at low tide
    (3) Below the water
    (4) Dangerous to shipping
    (5) Exposed to the elements

Questions 11–15 are based on the following extract.

What Was the Man Looking For?

Upon his arrival from England Mr. Willy had surveyed the various prospects of living in the quickly growing city of Vancouver with the selective and discarding characteristics which had enabled him to make a fortune and retire all of a sudden from business and his country in his advanced middle age. He settled immediately upon the very house. It was a small old house overlooking the sea between Spanish Banks and English Bay. He knocked out the north wall and made the window. There was nothing particular to commend the house except that it faced immediately on the seashore and the view. Mr. Willy had left his wife and her three sisters to play bridge together until death should overtake them in England. He now paced from end to end of his living-room, that is to say from east to west, with his hands in his pockets, admiring the northern view. Sometimes he stood with his hands behind him looking through the great glass window, seeing the wrinkled or placid sea and the ships almost at his feet and beyond the sea the mountains, and seeing sometimes his emancipation. His emancipation drove him into a dream, and sea sky mountain swam before him, vanished, and he saw with immense release his wife in still another more repulsive hat. He did not know, nor would he have cared, that much discussion went on in her world, chiefly in the afternoons, and that he was there alleged to have deserted her. So he had, after providing well for her physical needs which were all the needs of which she was capable. Mrs. Willy went on saying "…and he would come home my dear and never speak a word I can't tell you my dear how frightful it was night after night I might say for years I simply can't tell you…" No, she could not tell but she did, by day and night. Here he was at peace, seeing out the window the crimped and wrinkled sea and the ships which passed and passed each other, the seabirds and the dream-inducing sky.

—from "The Window" by Ethel Wilson

11. Where did Mr. Willy come from originally?
    (1) England
    (2) Vancouver
    (3) Spanish Banks
    (4) English Bay
    (5) The mountains

12. Which of the following best describes Mr. Willy?
    (1) Lonely
    (2) Depressed
    (3) Old
    (4) Rich
    (5) Annoyed

13. What was the topic of discussion that went on in his wife's world?
    (1) Playing bridge
    (2) Complaints about her husband
    (3) Her physical needs
    (4) Hats
    (5) The beauty of the sky and sea

14. What was Mr. Willy looking for out the window of his new house in Vancouver?
    (1) Money
    (2) Friends
    (3) A new love
    (4) Freedom
    (5) Nature

ANSWERS

1. **(2)** She is described as full of glee.
2. **(4)** The story describes him as "already having a bride in his art."
3. **(5)** She was afraid because his art consumed him and denied her his attention.
4. **(1)** He is so completely absorbed by his art that he doesn't really see her and does not even notice her health declining as he paints her portrait.
5. **(4)** She has become withered in health and spirit.

6. **(5)** The narrator had visited every summer since he was born, as had his father before him. Later, the passage refers to "life-time summer residents."

7. **(3)** The passage states that "the distance does."

8. **(3)** Although the passage does describe a hotel, which is located on the coast of Maine, it is significant because it is the place the narrator and his family spent their summers.

9. **(1)** The endless curve of the horizon.

10. **(2)** The rocks below the cliffs are exposed at high tide and underwater at low tide, which is why people sometimes drown.

11. **(1)** The passage begins with his arrival from England.

12. **(4)** Mr. Willy has deliberately left his wife and business behind to start a new life. He is described as late middle aged, which might be old, but he is definitely rich. He has made "a fortune," which enabled him to retire and come to Canada. He also provided money for his wife.

13. **(2)** Although he doesn't know or care, she continues to complain about him to her friends.

14. **(4)** Looking out the window, he sometimes sees emancipation—freedom. He is also glad to feel the freedom of release from his wife and her repulsive hats and complaints.

CHALLENGE EXERCISE

Look on the Internet, in the library, or in a book of Canadian literature for a copy of the short story "The Painted Door" by Sinclair Ross. Read the story and, if possible, discuss what happened in the story with another person. On a piece of paper, make a list of the events in the story in the order they happened.

PRACTICE WITH NONFICTION

Nonfiction is a type of prose literature that gives representation, interpretations, or opinions about real world issues, situations, or events. Nonfiction includes things such as biographies or autobiographies, essays, articles, commentaries, or editorials. On the GED Reading Test, there will be questions about two nonfiction documents. These questions will make up 25% of the questions on the reading test. The documents will be examples of:

■ Nonfiction prose, such as essays, commentaries, travelogues, nature writing, and the like
■ Critical reviews of visual or performing arts
■ Business and community documents, such as letters, manuals, reports, legal documents, business policies, mission or goal statements

Applying reading skills to nonfiction is the same as with other types of literature. Comprehension of nonfiction includes understanding what the passage says, being able to restate part of a passage, being able to identify the main idea, and being able to explain the clear meaning of the passage.

PRACTICE

Read each passage and respond to the questions to test your comprehension skills.

Why Did the Theatre Close?

For a financially troubled city landmark, once the centre of a vibrant theatre community, tonight was the final curtain. Following ninety-nine years and thousands of performances by professional and amateur companies, divas, and rising stars, the theatre's board came to the conclusion that it could not last. Saddled by debt too great to delay even to its centennial anniversary only a few months away, it was finally time to close the doors.

On Friday afternoon, the dismal announcement was made that the theatre would close after the following night's performance. While the closure itself caught few by surprise—the local theatre's financial woes being generally well known—the abruptness with which it would cease operations came as a shock. The final show was only one day away, more than eight weeks before the end of the current season.

On Saturday night, the atmosphere at the theatre (a facility owned and run by a non-profit organization that had raised funds to purchase and save it from oblivion not a decade before) was electric. Long after the house lights went up and the small but enthusiastic crowd departed, the managing director and the board chair remained, watching the sets being struck for the final time.

"It still seems unreal to me," said the director. "I spent half the night watching the crowd and feeling the energy in the room. I think they enjoyed the show, but they also felt the loss." Outside the theatre, a crowd of well-wishers gathered together. "It's a shame to see it go," said one, "but it has been a good run."

1. Who decided that the theatre should close?
   (1) the city
   (2) the board
   (3) the theatre performers
   (4) the artistic managing director
   (5) theatre-goers

2. What was a surprise about the closure?
   (1) The decision to close
   (2) The financial challenges
   (3) The choice of final production
   (4) The support of the crowd
   (5) The suddenness of the closure

3. What is the meaning of the clause, *Saddled by debt too great to delay even to its centennial anniversary only a few months away* (lines 4–5)?
   (1) The theatre closed before its one-hundredth year
   (2) The theatre closed on its anniversary
   (3) The theatre would not close
   (4) The final show would not take place
   (5) The board made the decision without consulting the public

4. How did people feel about the closure?

(1) Angry

(2) Surprised

(3) Sad

(4) Betrayed

(5) Happy

DECLINE OF BICYCLE
New York Paper Thinks Its Day Nearly Over
New York Times, October 1900

Even the most popular of toys must have its day and pass. Not even golf, that now absorbs the interest of old and young as few outdoor sports have done, can be assured of a permanent hold upon its present devotees or an equal number of followers. It will never be as "popular" as the bicycle still is. Four years ago, the whole country, the whole world, for that matter, was so fascinated by the improved bicycle, that afforded an easily acquired, rapid, cheap, and exhilarating method of travel that the demand for wheels could scarcely be met by the manufacturers, notwithstanding that the old plants for their production were being greatly enlarged and new plants were going up all over the land.

Possibly no town in the United States is so fully adapted to the use of the bicycle as Washington, D.C. Practically all its streets are paved with asphaltum, there are few heavy grades, most streets are shaded so completely that drivers of wheels may ride for miles at noonday with little absolute necessity for exposure to the sun, and the suburban roads are good. Yet the *Washington Post* has observed a marked decline in the use of the wheel. Society seems to have given it up altogether, and now it is chiefly used as an article of utility to get clerks and workmen to and from their business, and occasionally to carry former bicycle devotees to the golf grounds.

In New York, it has been evident for some time that the "craze" was over. The bicycle is still seen, and upon the boulevard in considerable numbers though not in the interminable lines that formerly made the wheel parade a Sunday wonder. As Washington, and in some rural localities recently observed, shopboys, newspaper carriers, carpenters, and other tradesmen use the bicycle in business, and find it a cheap and valuable conveyance. But it is not a toy with them....

The bicycle will not wholly disappear. The misfortune of those who suffer from bicycle accidents will not deter many others from experiments with a method of locomotion that has its charms and advantages. But it will probably find a place along with other such relics of former crazes as the game of croquet.

5. According to the passage, what will never be as popular as the bicycle was at the time of writing?

(1) An outdoor sport

(2) Golf

(3) The "wheel"

(4) Travel

(5) Sunday parades

6. What is the meaning of the clause "old plants for their production were being greatly enlarged" (lines 7–8)?
   (1) Demand for bicycles has grown
   (2) There are new manufacturing plants to build bicycles
   (3) Older style bicycles were no longer being produced
   (4) Existing manufacturing facilities are being expanded
   (5) Increased production facilities are no longer needed

7. Based on the passage, what is another word that was used to mean "bicycle?"
   (1) Wheel
   (2) Ashphaltum
   (3) Locomotion
   (4) Croquet
   (5) Method of travel

8. It is clear from this passage that the writer regards the bicycle as
   (1) A necessary form of transportation
   (2) A fun family activity
   (3) Dangerous
   (4) A fad
   (5) An experiment

9. What was one of the best places to ride bicycles?
   (1) New York
   (2) Suburban roads
   (3) Washington
   (4) Rural localities
   (5) The golf course

10. The writer feels that bicycles will continue to be used primarily as
    (1) A Sunday wonder
    (2) An inexpensive means of transportation
    (3) A craze
    (4) A toy
    (5) A relic of former crazes

ANSWERS

1. **(2)** The board came to the conclusion that it was necessary to close.

2. **(5)** The speed at which the company would cease operations was a shocker.

3. **(1)** The passage states the company had existed for ninety-nine seasons. The golden anniversary must refer to the fiftieth.

4. **(3)** Although people rallied, they celebrated the accomplishments of the theatre and felt the loss.

5. **(2)** The passage states that golf will never be as popular as the bicycle still is.

6. **(4)** *Old plants* refers to existing manufacturing plants that were being expanded, *enlarged.*

7. **(1)** The passage frequently refers to bicycles as *wheels.*

8. **(4)** The writer frequently refers to the bicycle as a toy, craze, and relic.

9. **(3)** Washington is described as a town that is most fully adapted to use of the bicycle because of paved streets, few hills, and many shade trees.

10. **(2)** It is described as a cheap and valuable conveyance.

PRACTICE WITH POETRY

The Language Arts, Reading Test will contain at least one poem. Poetry often uses figurative language, so many of the questions may involve higher-level reading skills. At the comprehension level, questions may examine your ability to understand what the poem says and to understand imagery, similes, and metaphors.

IMAGERY: Descriptive language that creates pictures in the mind of the reader.

> *Soft green waves crested with sparkles of sunlight swelled gracefully to the shore.*

SIMILE: A comparison, using *like* or *as*, between things that are very different except in one way.

> *The lake was calm and bleak like the surface of a mirror reflecting darkly.*

METAPHOR: A comparison, not using *like* or *as*, between things that are very different except in one way.

> *The road was a ribbon of silver draped over the hills.*

On the GED Reading Test, you do not need to identify or define imagery, simile, or metaphor. You do need to be able to read and comprehend figurative language so that you understand what the passage says. As with any other type of passage, comprehension questions about poetry require you to

- Understand what a poem says
- Restate parts of a poem
- Identify the main idea
- Explain the clear meaning of the poem

Comprehend the meaning of figurative language.

PRACTICE

Read each passage and respond to the questions to test your comprehension skills.

What Happened in the House Across the Street?

There's been a Death, in the Opposite
    House,
As lately as Today–
I know it, by the numb look
Such Houses have—alway–

The Neighbours rustle in and out–
The Doctor–drives away–
A Window opens like a Pod–
Abrupt–mechanically–

Somebody flings a Mattress out–
The Children hurry by–
They wonder if it died–on that–
I used to–when a Boy–

The Minister–goes stiffly in–
As if the House were His–
And He owned all the Mourners–now–
And little Boys–besides

And then the Milliner–and the Man
Of the Appalling Trade–
To take the measure of the House–
There'll be that Dark Parade–

Of Tassels–and of Coaches–soon–
It's easy as a Sign–
The Intuition of the News–
In just a Country Town–

—by Emily Dickinson

1. This poem is primarily about
    (1)   What happens when a neighbour dies
    (2)   The sadness of death
    (3)   Fear of the unknown when someone dies
    (4)   The number of people who profit from a death
    (5)   Mourning for a person who has died

2. What is referred to by the lines, *There'll be that Dark Parade–Of Tassels–and of Coaches–
    soon* (lines 21–22)?
    (1)   A funeral procession
    (2)   The parade of people going in and out
    (3)   Death coming for us all
    (4)   The decorations at the funeral
    (5)   The embalmer's art

3. What do the children wonder about?
    (1)   How the person died
    (2)   Whether they will have to go to the parade
    (3)   What the minister is doing
    (4)   If the person died on that mattress
    (5)   If the person who died was a boy

4. How can the speaker tell that someone has died?
   - (1) The blank expression of the house
   - (2) The window opens
   - (3) The doctor leaves
   - (4) The minister arrives
   - (5) News in a town

What Was Their Sacrifice?

In Flanders fields the poppies blow
Between the crosses, row on row,
That mark our place; and in the sky
The larks, still bravely singing, fly
Scarce heard amid the guns below.

We are the Dead. Short days ago
We lived, felt dawn, saw sunset glow,
Loved and were loved, and now we lie,
In Flanders fields.

Take up our quarrel with the foe:
To you from failing hands we throw
The torch; be yours to hold it high.
If ye break faith with us who die
We shall not sleep, though poppies grow
In Flanders fields.

—by John McCrae

TIP

Comprehension includes understanding the main idea.

5. What is being described in the first stanza of the poem?
   - (1) Fields of flowers
   - (2) A nature scene with singing birds
   - (3) A graveyard
   - (4) A battlefield
   - (5) An imaginary scene from the speaker's mind

6. The poem is told from the point of view of
   - (1) Someone unknown
   - (2) A naturalist
   - (3) Someone who has lost a loved one
   - (4) Someone who has lost a friend
   - (5) A dead soldier

7. What is meant by the lines,

   To you from failing hands we throw
   The torch (lines 11–12)?

   (1) Readers of the poem should remember the sacrifices of others
   (2) Dying soldiers give responsibility to continue the fight to the reader of the poem
   (3) Readers should take on the struggle to protect nature's beauty
   (4) It is becoming dark and you should light a torch
   (5) Live for today because we cannot know what tomorrow will bring

8. This poem is primarily about
   (1) The horrors of war
   (2) The pointless nature of war
   (3) Soldiers dying for an important cause
   (4) The beauty of nature even during human conflict
   (5) Preserving democracy

What Is so Great About Birthdays?

Let us have birthdays every day,
(I had the thought while I was shaving)
Because a birthday should be gay,
And full of grace and good behaving.
We can't have cakes and candles bright,
And presents are beyond our giving,
But let it us cherish with delight
The birthday way of lovely living.

For I have passed three-score and ten
And I can count upon my fingers
The years I hope to bide with men,
(Though by God's grace one often lingers.)
So in the summers left to me,
Because I'm blest beyond my merit,
I hope with gratitude and glee
To sparkle with the birthday spirit.

Let me inform myself each day
Who's proudmost on the natal roster;
If Washington or Henry Clay,
Or Eugene Field or Stephen Foster.
oh lots of famous folks I'll find
Who more than measure to my rating,
And so thanksgivingly inclined
Their birthdays I'll be celebrating.

For Oh I know the cheery glow
Of Anniversary rejoicing;
Let me reflect its radiance so
My daily gladness I'll be voicing.
And though I'm stooped and silver-haired,
Let me with laughter make the hearth gay,
So by the gods I may be spared
Each year to hear: "Pop, Happy Birthday."

—Robert William Service

9. Based on this poem, why would it be good to have a birthday every day?
   (1) To get presents
   (2) To have cake
   (3) To not get any older
   (4) To make every day special
   (5) To always be childlike

10. How old is the person speaking in this poem?
    (1) A young child, about 7
    (2) A young man
    (3) A middle aged man, about 40
    (4) More than seventy
    (5) Not given

11. What is meant by lines 10 and 11?

    And I can count upon my fingers
    The years I hope to bide with men,

    (1) He can count the birthdays he has spent with male friends
    (2) He expects to live only about ten or fewer more years
    (3) He counts down the days to his birthday
    (4) He hopes to show a birthday spirit each day in his remaining years
    (5) He cannot count on how much time he has left

12. This poem is clearly about
    (1) Enjoying life
    (2) Thanksgiving
    (3) Family
    (4) Aging
    (5) Birthdays

ANSWERS

1. **(1)** The poem is primarily about what happens when a neighbour dies.

2. **(1)** These lines describe a funeral procession behind the coach or hearse.

3. **(4)** Children wonder if the mattress is from the bed where the person died.

4. **(1)** The speaker claims to tell from the numb look of the house, like a facial expression.

5. **(3)** The stanza describes rows of crosses that mark graves, flowers growing between them.

6. **(5)** The speaker says *we are the dead*, including himself in that number. *The foe* clearly indicates that he is a soldier.

7. **(2)** The soldier instructs readers to *take up our quarrel*, continue the fight.

8. **(3)** Although the poem describes a graveyard and dead soldiers, the speaker encourages readers to continue the fight, which shows the importance of what they fought for.

9. **(4)** He wants to celebrate the *birthday way of living every day* so that he can always be filled with glee, but also so he can be spared the happy birthday wishes once a year.

10. **(4)** He is more than three-score and ten ($3 \times 20 + 10$) or seventy years old.

11. **(2)** He expects not to live more than the number of years he can count on his fingers.

12. **(1)** The poem says that we should be filled with birthday glee every day.

CHALLENGE EXERCISE

One way to test your comprehension of poetry, and to practice and improve your reading skills, is to write a paraphrase. A paraphrase is when you rewrite something in your own words. For example, here is a paraphrase of another famous poem.

> With rue my heart is laden
> For golden friends I had,
> For many a rose-lipt maiden
> And many a lightfoot lad.
>
> By brooks too broad for leaping
> The lightfoot boys are laid;
> The rose-lipt girls are sleeping
> In fields where roses fade.
>
> —by A.E. Houseman

Paraphrase: My heart is filled with sadness for the friends of my youth, the young women with their red lips and the young men who loved to run and jump. Now the young men jump no more as they are dead and buried. The young women also lie beneath fields where flowers fade and die.

Practice your comprehension skills. Choose one of the poems in this section. Write a paraphrase to explain the poem in detail in your own words. You may wish to discuss the poem and your paraphrase with a family member, friend, or another student. Remember that you will probably disagree about some details. It is by discussing and explaining our different ideas that we learn to read with more insight.

PRACTICE WITH DRAMA

On the GED Language Arts, Reading Test you may be asked questions about one or more excerpts from a play. Reading drama is different from reading other types of literature because it is written to be performed. All you have is the dialogue that people say and a few stage instructions. Unlike stories and novels, drama does not say what the characters look like or what they are thinking about or what their tone of voice is like. This is all interpreted by the actors on the stage. When you read drama, you have to imagine these things in your head.

PRACTICE

Read each passage and respond to the questions to test your comprehension skills.

Why Might They Leave the Farm?

BRUCE *(turning to the portrait of his father)*: My father came out here and took a homestead. He broke the prairie with one plough and a team of horses. He built a house to live in out of sod. You didn't know that, did you? He and mother lived here in a sod shanty and struggled to make things grow. They built a one-roomed shack; and when the good years came, they built this house. The finest in the country! I thought my son would have it.

RUTH [his wife] *(moving to him)*: What is here left to give a son? A house that stirs with ghosts. A piece of worn-out land where the rain never comes.

BRUCE: That's not all. I don't suppose you can understand.

RUTH *(turning away from him, deeply hurt)*: No, I don't suppose I can. You give me little chance to know how you feel about things.

BRUCE *(his anger gone)*: Ruth, I didn't mean that. But you've always lived in town. (He goes to the window and stands looking out for a moment, then turns.) Those rocks along the fence out there, I picked up every one of them with my own hands and carried them with my own hands across the field and piled them there. I've ploughed that southern slope along the coulee every year since I was twelve. *(His voice is torn with a kind of shame for his emotion.)* I feel about land like Hester does about the house, I guess. I don't want to leave it. I don't want to give it up.

RUTH *(gently)*: But it's poor land, Bruce.

(Bruce sits down, gazing gloomily at the fire. Hester [his sister] comes in from the kitchen with the small lamp and places it on the sideboard. Then she sits at the table, taking up her knitting. As Bruce speaks, she watches him intently.)

BRUCE: Yes, it's strange that in a soil that won't grow trees a man can put roots down, but he can.

RUTH *(at his side)*: You'd feel the same about another place, after a little while.

BRUCE: I don't know. When I saw the wind last spring blowing the dirt away, the dirt I ploughed and harrowed and sowed to grain, I felt as though part of myself was blowing away in the dust. Even now, with the land three feet under snow, I can look out and feel it waiting for the seed I've saved for it.

RUTH: But if we go, we'll become nearer other people, not cut off from everything that lives.

BRUCE: You need people, don't you?

HESTER: Yes. She needs them. I've seen her at the window looking towards the town. Day after day she stands there.

(Bruce and Ruth, absorbed in the conflict between them, had forgotten Hester's presence. At Hester's words, Ruth turns on them both, flaming with anger.)

—Extract from "Still Stands the House" by Gwen Pharis Ringwood
Samuel French Publishers, 1939

1. Based on this passage, what is the farmer's house like?
   (1) A luxurious mansion
   (2) A one-room shack
   (3) A sod shanty
   (4) A nice house
   (5) Very old

2. What is the problem on the farm?
   (1) Crops won't grow
   (2) The wife doesn't like it there
   (3) The sister does not like the wife
   (4) The couple don't get along
   (5) The house is haunted

3. What is the meaning of the sentence *Yes, it's strange that in a soil that won't grow trees a man can put roots down, but he can.* (lines 19–20)?
   (1) Bruce feels lonely out on the farm
   (2) It is odd that the soil can't grow trees, but people still live there
   (3) Although the earth is no longer fertile, he feels it is home
   (4) A man can't put down roots on a farm
   (5) It is strange that the soil will not grow trees although a man can plant them

4. In this passage, it is clear that Bruce is
   (1) Unhappy about the possibility of leaving the farm
   (2) No longer in love with his wife
   (3) Having a conflict with his sister
   (4) Longing for a son
   (5) Interested in moving into town

5. What time of year is it?
   (1) Winter
   (2) Spring
   (3) Summer
   (4) Autumn
   (5) Unknown

TIP

When reading drama, interpret character, mood, and theme based only on dialogue and stage directions.

What Do They Dream Of?

Exterior of the Farmhouse. It is sunset of a day at the beginning of summer in the year 1850. There is no wind and everything is still. The sky above the roof is suffused with deep colors, the green of the elms glows, but the house is in shadow, seeming pale and washed out by contrast.

EBEN: God! Purty! (*His eyes fall and he stares about him frowningly. He is twenty-five, tall and sinewy. His face is well-formed, good-looking, but its expression is resentful and defensive....*)

SIMEON (*grudgingly*): Purty.

PETER: Ay-eh.

SIMEON (*suddenly*): Eighteen years ago.

PETER: What?

SIMEON: Jenn. My woman. She died.

PETER: I'd fergot.

SIMEON: I rec'lect—now an' agin. Makes it lonesome. She'd hair long's a hoss' tail—an' yaller like gold!

PETER: Waal—she's gone. (*this with indifferent finality—then after a pause*) They's gold in the West, Sim.

SIMEON (*still under the influence of sunset—vaguely*): In the sky?

PETER: Waal—in a manner o' speakin'—thar's the promise. (*growing excited*) Gold in the sky—in the West—Golden Gate—Californi-a!—Goldest West!—fields o' gold!

SIMEON (*excited in his turn*): Fortunes layin' just atop o' the ground waitin' t' be picked! Solomon's mines, they says! (*For a moment they continue looking up at the sky—then their eyes drop.*)

PETER: (*with sardonic bitterness*) Here—it's stones atop o' the ground—stones atop o' stones—makin' stone walls—year atop o' year—him 'n' yew 'n' me 'n' then Eben—makin' stone walls fur him to fence us in!

SIMEON: We've wuked. Give our strength. Give our years. Plowed 'em under in the ground—(*he stamps rebelliously*)—rottin'—makin' soil for his crops! (*a pause*) Waal—the farm pays good for hereabouts.

PETER: If we plowed in Californi-a, they'd be lumps o' gold in the furrow!

SIMEON: Californi-a's t'other side o' earth, a'most. We got t' calc'late—

—From *Desire Under the Elms* by Eugene O'Neill

6. What do Peter and Simeon think is "purty"?
    (1) Gold
    (2) Jenn
    (3) Rocks
    (4) Sunset
    (5) California

7. What is it that sometimes makes Simeon lonesome?
   (1) Sunsets
   (2) Remembering the death of his woman
   (3) Yellow hair
   (4) Stones on the ground
   (5) Gold in the west

8. What is the meaning of the line, *Fortunes layin' just atop o' the ground waitin' t' be picked!* (line 15)?
   (1) In California, people can become rich picking up gold nuggets lying on the ground
   (2) They would have a fortune if they had money for every rock they have picked up
   (3) They have no strength left to earn their fortune
   (4) They should go out west to make their fortune
   (5) They pile stones upon stones to build a wall

9. It is clear from the excerpt that Simeon and Peter are
   (1) Hobos
   (2) Miners
   (3) Farmers
   (4) Travellers
   (5) Builders

ANSWERS

1. **(4)** Although his parents started with nothing, they eventually built the nicest house around.

2. **(1)** There are many things that tell you crops won't grow. Ruth calls the land *worn-out*. Bruce describes it as unable to grow even trees. He also describes the dirt blowing away as he ploughed.

3. **(3)** Although the land will not grow things, he still feels his roots are there.

4. **(1)** We see throughout that Bruce is clearly unhappy about any thought of leaving. He had hoped to leave the farm to a son. It is a family farm that his parents started from nothing. He can feel it waiting for him under the snow.

5. **(1)** He says he can now feel the land waiting for him under the snow.

6. **(4)** They are looking at the sunset.

7. **(2)** He says that when he *recollects* the death of his woman, he feels lonesome sometimes.

8. **(1)** They are talking about gold in California and how gold nuggets can apparently be found lying on the ground.

9. **(3)** It is clear they work on a farm. Simeon says that they have worked for years ploughing rocks under and comments that the farm pays pretty well.

READING FOR APPLICATION

Application is another level of reading that accounts for 15% of the questions on the GED Reading Test. Application refers to your ability to comprehend what you read and

- Follow instructions
- Use information in a different context
- Recognize how an argument in one situation relates to another situation

Application is using the information you read. For example, in real life you might read and follow instructions to complete a form. You might read about how one person wrote a cover letter and use the information to format your own. You might read an opinion about a topic and conclude what the writer's opinion might be about another similar situation.

PRACTICE

Read each passage and respond to the questions to test your application skills.

How Is Technology To Be Used?

Company information technology systems, including computers, networks, mobile devices, and all forms of Internet access, are used for company business and authorized purposes only. Technology and network resources are provided for the pursuance of business, and all communications, files, and documents created thereby are the property of the company.

Occasional personal use of information technology systems is acceptable, only if it is not excessive or inappropriate and does not interfere with performance of duties or violate company policies. Inappropriate use of computers includes, but is not limited to, activities such as:

- Email communication of jokes, chain letters, or spam
- Personal or other business activities other than company business
- Slander, harassment, derogatory, profane, or racist communication
- Viewing or communication of pornography
- Recreational activities, games, and social media
- Installation of unauthorized software
- Any act that is illegal or threatens the security and integrity of company systems or information

Managers and supervisors must report violations of the computer policy to Human Resources. Employees who abuse technology systems may be subject to corrective action, up to and including dismissal.

1. According to the policy, an employee is permitted to
    (1) Send a joke a day to a group of co-workers
    (2) Make brochures for a personal business
    (3) Play online games
    (4) Copy company software
    (5) Send an email to a friend accepting a dinner invitation

2. Based on the information in this passage, which of the following would also not be permitted?
   (1) Using work email to contact a customer
   (2) Taking a laptop home to work after hours
   (3) Sending a personal fax
   (4) Having a password
   (5) Placing a business-related long-distance call

3. Based on the information in this passage, an employee who uses company technology a lot for personal reasons could reasonably expect to
   (1) Receive a new computer
   (2) Be disciplined
   (3) Have computer privileges revoked
   (4) Be fired
   (5) Receive a written warning

4. Based on this policy, if a supervisor discovered an employee was receiving harassing email messages from a co-worker, the supervisor should
   (1) Speak to the employee
   (2) Have a talk with the employee who sent the email
   (3) Take corrective action against the employee
   (4) Inform the Human Resources department
   (5) Let the employees work the matter out themselves

Does She Fear Death?

When I am dead, my dearest,
 Sing no sad songs for me;
Plant thou no roses at my head,
 Nor shady cypress tree.
Be the green grass above me
 With Showers and dewdrops wet;
And if thou wilt, remember,
 And if thou wilt, forget.

I shall not see the shadows,
 I shall not feel the rain;
I shall not hear the nightingale
 Sing on as if in pain.
And dreaming through the twilight
 That doth not rise nor set,
Haply I may remember,
 And haply may forget.

—*Song* by Christina Rossetti (1848)

5. A funeral for the speaker in this poem should include:
   (1) A simple burial
   (2) Happy music
   (3) Flowers
   (4) Planting of an oak tree
   (5) A beautiful eulogy

6. The author of this poem is likely to agree with which of the following?
   (1) Life is pain
   (2) Death is a new beginning
   (3) It doesn't matter what happens after we die
   (4) Death is a dream world
   (5) Death is happy experience

A Famous Poet Dies

Henry Wadsworth Longfellow, the sweet poet, the gentle scholar, the genial gentleman and admirable citizen, whose pure thoughts, embodied in verse, have carried joy and peace to the hearts of millions of many nations, yesterday yielded up his life peacefully and calmly in the midst of his family. His gentle heart had scarcely ceased its pulsations when the sorrowful fact was made known to the denizens of Cambridge by seventy-five strikes upon the telegraph alarm bells, that number being the sum of his earthly years.

For many months his failing health has compelled an almost complete withdrawal from society, and during that period he has remained at his historic home declining all invitations, his thoughts centred upon his own immediate friends and neighbours. His last appearance in public was on the occasion of the 250th anniversary of the settlement of Cambridge, in December, 1880, when, at the morning exercises at the Sanders Theatre, he made a brief address to the children of the public schools, who, at the conclusion of the programme, clustered about him, eager to grasp his honoured hand.

The news of his death was entirely unexpected by the public, as his dangerous symptoms were not generally known until Wednesday, but long before sunset yesterday there were numerous tokens of mourning displayed from private houses, and it is probable that on the day of the funeral, which has not been definitely settled upon, the whole city will assume a funeral aspect.

—From Longfellow's Obituary published in 1885

7. Based on the information in this obituary, information about the death should be printed in newspapers in
   (1) Cambridge
   (2) Boston
   (3) The United States
   (4) Canada
   (5) Many countries

8. People who were welcome to visit Longfellow during the last few months included
   (1) Children
   (2) Town officials
   (3) Family members
   (4) School teachers
   (5) No one

9. Based on the information in the obituary, it is likely that many people:
   (1) Will settle in Cambridge
   (2) Are concerned about cause of death
   (3) Will attend the funeral
   (4) Go to morning exercises at the Sanders theatre
   (5) Visited his historic home

10. Based on this obituary, if church bells were rung during the service, how many times should they ring?
    (1) 25
    (2) 50
    (3) 75
    (4) 250
    (5) Unknown

ANSWERS

1. **(5)** Occasional personal use is acceptable.

2. **(3)** All other examples are work-related use.

3. **(2)** The policy does not state the specific consequences, only that corrective action may be taken. Dismissal is a possibility that is mentioned, but only indicated as a last resort.

4. **(4)** Supervisors must report violations to Human Resources.

5. **(1)** The speaker does not want music, roses, or trees, only to be buried under green grass and open skies.

6. **(3)** She says she will be happy whether she remembers or forgets her life.

7. **(5)** The obituary says he was loved by millions of people in many nations.

8. **(5)** Although it is unclear who may have visited, it states that he withdrew almost completely from society and declined all invitations because of illness. His friends and neighbours remained in his thoughts.

9. **(3)** It states that the whole town will assume a funereal aspect and that many homes show signs of mourning.

10. **(3)** He was 75 years old and this is the number of times the telegraph alarm bells rang on his death.

CHAPTER CHECK-UP

Complete these practice exercises, and check the answers and analysis that follow. After you mark your work, review any topic in the chapter that you had trouble with or did not understand.

<u>Questions 1–4</u> are based on the following excerpt.

Who Is the Man in the Bed?

She stands up in the garden where she has been working and looks into the distance. She has sensed a shift in the weather. There is another gust of wind, a buckle of noise in the air, and the tall cypresses sway. She turns and moves uphill towards the house, climbing over a low wall, feeling the first drops of rain on her bare arms. She crosses the loggia and quickly enters the house.

In the kitchen she doesn't pause but goes through it and climbs the stairs which are in darkness and then continues along the long hall, at the end of which is a wedge of light from an open door.

She turns into the room which is another garden—this one made up of trees and bowers painted over its walls and ceiling. The man lies on the bed, his body exposed to the breeze, and he turns his head slowly towards her as she enters.

Every four days she washes his black body, beginning at the destroyed feet. She wets a washcloth and holding it above his ankles squeezes the water onto him, looking up as he murmurs, seeing his smile. Above the shins the burns are worst. Beyond purple. Bone.

1. Why does the woman stand up at the beginning of the excerpt?
    (1) To look around
    (2) She knows it will rain
    (3) To go climbing
    (4) She wants to go to bed
    (5) To go to the kitchen

2. What was the room like where the man lay?
    (1) A garden
    (2) Filled with plants
    (3) Dark
    (4) Cold
    (5) Painted with trees

3. It is clear from this passage that the woman is the man's
    (1) Nurse
    (2) Lover
    (3) Sister
    (4) Mother
    (5) Patient

4. Based on the information in this passage, the woman washes his body every four days by
   (1) Rubbing him with damp clothes
   (2) Taking him out to the rain
   (3) Pouring water over him
   (4) Giving him a bath
   (5) Squeezing water from a washcloth

Questions 5–9 are based on the following soliloquy from Shakespeare's *Hamlet*.

How Does the Speaker Feel?

Tis now the very witching time of night,
When churchyards yawn and hell itself breathes out
Contagion to this world: now could I drink hot blood,
And do such bitter business as the day
Would quake to look on. Soft! now to my mother.
O heart, lose not thy nature; let not ever
The soul of Nero enter this firm bosom:
Let me be cruel, not unnatural:
I will speak daggers to her, but use none;
My tongue and soul in this be hypocrites;
How in my words soever she be shent,
To give them seals never, my soul, consent!

5. Based on the information in this passage, what time is it when the soliloquy is spoken?
   (1) Midnight
   (2) Day
   (3) Morning
   (4) Evening
   (5) Not stated

6. What is the meaning of the lines,

   And do such bitter business as the day
   Would quake to look on (lines 4–5)?

   (1) Be so unhappy the day seems like night
   (2) Become so depressed during the day that the speaker becomes afraid
   (3) And be so ill and contagious he shakes during the day
   (4) Commit acts so evil the daylight would be afraid to see them
   (5) Be so bitterly unhappy it causes the speaker to shake

7. What is the meaning of the line, *I will speak daggers to her, but use none* (line 9).
   (1) My words will be like daggers
   (2) There is no reason to use a dagger against her
   (3) I will use sharp words, but not harm her
   (4) My tongue will be like a dagger
   (5) I will take my time and not act rashly

8. In this passage, it is clear that the speaker is feeling
   (1) Vengeful
   (2) Sick
   (3) Depressed
   (4) Afraid
   (5) Loving

9. The speaker of this soliloquy is likely to agree with which of the following statements?
   (1) All wicked deeds should be done at night
   (2) Wickedness cannot be hidden because it is like a sickness in the world
   (3) The tongue is one of the most dangerous weapons
   (4) Even when angry, you must control your temper with your mother
   (5) The human soul is not cruel by nature

Questions 10–13 are based on the following passage.

Who Is Responsible for Workplace Safety?

This policy is intended to ensure maximum compliance by employees and managers with safe work practices and the safe handling of hazardous materials in the workplace. Adherence to procedures regarding the Workplace Hazardous Materials Information System (WHMIS) is a priority for our company.

Safety is the responsibility of everyone in the workplace. The company has an obligation to provide information about hazardous workplace products and to train employees in their handling. The company is also responsible to provide appropriate safety equipment and to enforce procedures. For their part, employees have the right to know about hazardous materials in the workplace and to receive training in safe handling. They also have a responsibility to follow company policies and safe work practices.

All employees are required to participate in WHMIS training. They should be aware of the location of Material Safety Data Sheets (MSDS) and should be proficient in reading them. They must not remove supplier labels from packaging and must properly apply workplace labels to products that are transferred to other containers. Most important, they should take steps to acquaint themselves with potentially hazardous products in their work area, as well as safe handling and storage, personal protective equipment, and first-aid procedures.

10. Based on the information in this passage, who is responsible for safe handling of workplace hazardous materials?
    (1) The company
    (2) The employees
    (3) Company and employees
    (4) Government
    (5) Workplace Safety Committee

11. The main idea of this passage is
    (1) Workplace safety
    (2) Company WHMIS policy
    (3) Safety is everyone's responsibility
    (4) Importance of following workplace procedures
    (5) Material Safety Data Sheets

12. Based on the information in this passage, which of the following is the responsibility of the employer?
    (1) Safe handling of hazardous materials in the workplace
    (2) Following company policies and safe work practices
    (3) Providing WHMIS training
    (4) Removing supplier labels
    (5) Acquainting themselves with first aid procedures

13. Based on the information in this passage, what should employees do if they transfer a hazardous product to a new container?
    (1) Apply a supplier label
    (2) Become familiar with personal protective equipment
    (3) Learn the location of the MSDS
    (4) Take steps to acquaint themselves with potential hazards
    (5) Apply a workplace label

Questions 14–16 are based on the following excerpt from a poem.

What Is the Sound of the Ocean?

The sea is calm to-night.
The tide is full, the moon lies fair
Upon the straits;—on the French coast the light
Gleams and is gone; the cliffs of England stand,
Glimmering and vast, out in the tranquil bay.
Come to the window, sweet is the night-air!
Only, from the long line of spray
Where the sea meets the moon-blanched land,
Listen! You hear the grating roar
Of pebbles which the waves draw back, and fling,
At their return, up the high strand,
Begin, and cease, and then again begin,
With tremulous cadence slow, and bring
The eternal note of sadness in....
—from *Dover Beach* by Matthew Arnold

14. What time of day is it at the beginning of the poem?
    (1) Midnight
    (2) Dawn
    (3) Night
    (4) Sunset
    (5) Noon

15. What is the meaning of, *…the long line of spray / Where the sea meets the moon-blanched land* (lines 7–8)?
    (1) The shoreline
    (2) The surf
    (3) The rocks on shore
    (4) The coast of France
    (5) A storm

16. What is the sound that the poem describes?
    (1) Waves crashing on the shore
    (2) Ships at night
    (3) Pebbles moving as waves lap the shore
    (4) Rain against the window
    (5) A sad breeze against the window

ANSWERS AND ANALYSIS

1. **(2)** She senses the change and stands to look in the distance. By the time she crosses the wall, she feels the first drops of rain.

2. **(5)** There were trees and bowers painted over its walls and ceiling.

3. **(1)** She cares for him by washing his burned body.

4. **(5)** It says that she squeezes the water onto him.

5. **(1)** The *witching time of night* would be midnight.

6. **(4)** He feels capable of committing such bloody acts that the day would *quake*.

7. **(3)** This is the only option that explains the whole meaning of the line.

8. **(1)** This is the only option that is consistent with the violence of his words.

9. **(4)** Although he is in a violent mood, he cautions himself several times not to harm his mother.

10. **(3)** The passage says that safety is everyone's responsibility.

11. **(2)** Although the passage is about safety, it is specifically about the WHMIS policy.

12. **(3)** The passage specifically states that the company has an obligation to train employees.

13. **(5)** The passage states that employees should properly apply workplace labels to products that are transferred to other containers.

14. **(3)** The specific time is not stated, but the references to *tonight* and the *moon* indicate that it is night.

15. **(1)** The lines describe where the line of water meets the shore.

16. **(3)** The poem describes the sound of pebbles dragged back by the receding waves and then tossed forward as they come in.

Reading and Analysis

> ## THINK ABOUT IT
>
> Some people do not like to analyze writing. They say it interferes with their enjoyment of what they read. Analysis is to break the elements of a passage down. You take the passage apart and look at the pieces, so you can see how it works and understand it better. Analysis can help you enjoy reading more, just like understanding how a car works can increase your appreciation and enjoyment of driving.
>
> ## IN THIS CHAPTER
>
> After completing this chapter, you will be able to
>
> → **DRAW CONCLUSIONS AND INFERENCES FROM WRITTEN PASSAGES**
> → **IDENTIFY CAUSES AND THEIR EFFECTS**
> → **INTERPRET ELEMENTS OF CHARACTERIZATION IN WRITING**
> → **IDENTIFY SUPPORTING DETAILS FOR TOPIC SENTENCES**
> → **INTERPRET ELEMENTS OF TONE AND MOOD**
> → **RECOGNIZE A WRITER'S BIAS AND ASSUMPTIONS**

WHAT IS ANALYSIS?

There are different levels of reading skill. The most basic are *comprehension* and *application.* Another level of reading is *analysis.* 30%–35% of the questions on the GED Reading Test evaluate analysis.

Analysis is the ability to break down what you read. You look at elements or components of the passage to gain a more complete understanding. Analysis refers to your ability to

- Apply reasoning skills to facts or information
- Identify relationships among elements and their effects
- Interpret elements of structure and writing

Apply Reasoning Skills

Analysis is applying your reasoning skills to make deductions about facts or information in the passage. You see how the facts or information add up, what conclusions can be reached, or what the consequences will be.

Identify Relationships

Analysis is seeing the relationship between elements in the passage and the outcomes or results. This includes things such as recognizing causes and effects, supporting details and topic statements, as well as elements of characterization and what they say about the character.

Analysis— Break down what you read to gain better understanding.

Interpret Elements

Analysis is looking at the impact of elements of writing, such as word usage, that create tone or mood or show the writer's bias. In addition, it may include looking at the structure of the passage and the way information is organized.

CONCLUSIONS AND INFERENCES

One type of analysis is drawing conclusions and inferences. Both are ways you apply reasoning skills to interpret evidence in a reading passage. When you draw conclusions, you make deductions based on the facts and information given. Identifying inferences means recognizing what is suggested, but not directly stated in the passage.

Drawing conclusions is something you do often in everyday life. For example, your mail always comes before noon. At one o'clock you have received no mail. You conclude that there is no mail for you today. Inferences are like small conclusions. You recognize what is suggested, but not stated, by information. For example, you see a teenager get on the bus with a backpack and assume he is on his way to school.

PRACTICE

Read each passage and respond to the questions to test your analysis skills.

How Does the Church Make Her Feel?

We often had our dinner at Kettner's in Soho. Naturally there were plenty of continental or Oriental restaurants in Soho, but there was something over and around and beneath good food and pleasant wine at the unspectacular Kettner's so we went there for choice without quite knowing why.

It must have been in 1947, because that was the first year that I had been in London following the bombing. In a weak-kneed way I had been afraid to see bombed England and especially bombed London. My husband had been there during the war, but I had had only my desperate imaginings. One night we came out of Kettner's after dinner and stood for a few minutes at the entrance. The sky was blue-black over London with many stars. We looked to left and right, very comfortable, very easy, ready for anything. X Street stopped a little distance to our right and in the not-much-lighted night we saw at the end of the street the façade of a bombed and gutted church. Very theatrical it looked against the blue-black and the stars, as though the characters would soon come out and sing, or do their murder. The doorman said something to us that struck me as poetic and unlike a doorman. But what are doormen like? What is anybody like? One never knows, and I have never been able to remember what the doorman said; only that it was truly poetic. We walked along the pavement—which was narrow—to the bombed church, and increasingly the feeling of the night and the past and the theatre of the gutted church combined. No doubt in the daylight the church would be mere stone and dingy at that, inhabited by cats.

1. When does the story take place?
   (1) Shortly after World War II
   (2) During a time of war
   (3) In the Great Depression
   (4) After the Great London Fire
   (5) In a time of prosperity

2. Why did they go to dinner at Kettner's restaurant?
   (1) Because of the good food
   (2) Because of the pleasant wine
   (3) Because of the atmosphere
   (4) Because it is a fancy restaurant
   (5) It is the only restaurant in Soho

3. Which of the following statements do you think the speaker would agree with?
   (1) You can tell a lot about people by their job
   (2) Doormen are unpredictable
   (3) Empty churches have a desolate feeling
   (4) You can't tell what people are like based on their profession
   (5) Everything looks different at night

4. Based on the information in this passage, you can conclude that
   (1) They come to the restaurant often
   (2) They often went to different restaurants in Soho
   (3) They were out for a romantic evening
   (4) They did not pay much attention to their surroundings
   (5) They were new to the area and had not been there before

How Has Technology Changed Live Performance?

Modern technology is changing live performances in theatre and in music. Some people say that it is changing things too much. They argue that the arts are becoming too dependent on technology and that technology is often taking centre stage rather than the performance itself.

However, the use of technology in live stage performances is nothing new. In Shakespeare's time, theatre companies made abundant use of the technology of the day to thrill their audiences. Although there were no modern lights or sound systems, there were elaborate stages and costumes, fireworks, and smoke effects. Shakespeare's Globe Theatre had three trap doors, one of which was located in an area known as *The Heavens* from which actors could be lowered on ropes. Shakespeare even used real cannons for sound effects, which ultimately caught the theatre on fire and burned it to the ground during a performance.

Modern live performances also often use technology both to enhance the spectacle for audiences and as a part of the art. A live performance in Banff, Alberta, by the Canadian band Hedley, for example, was the quietest concert ever. There was no public address system. All one thousand people in the audience were provided with wireless headphones, giving them a unique experience of live music.

Internet technology was also used in Toronto in a performance based on ancient Greek tragedies by Sophocles. Although the plays were written over 2400 years ago, the use of

TIP

Conclusions are deductions based on facts and information you read.

technology helped to make them relevant to events today. In the performance, which ran for five nights in a small makeshift theatre, the main character has a Skype conversation with a friend who is about to be deployed with Canadian forces to Afghanistan. The conversation is displayed as an Internet conversation on a screen and the audience listens in on headphones attached to their seats. The use of technology shows the physical and psychological distance between Canadian soldiers and those who remain at home, as well as between them and the decision-makers who command them.

Does the use of technology detract from live performances of today? Perhaps, but only if live performance is measured just by the words and gestures of the actors and does not include the overall experience of the audience.

5. Based on information in this passage, the attitude of the writer to the use of technology in live performances is
   (1) negative
   (2) supportive
   (3) enthusiastic
   (4) positive if used to enhance the art
   (5) that it detracts from the art

6. Which character in a Shakespearean play would be most likely to appear from a trap door in *The Heavens*?
   (1) Fairy
   (2) Canadian soldier
   (3) King
   (4) General
   (5) Musician

7. Based on the information in this excerpt, why does the audience hear the conversation in the play using headphones attached to their seats?
   (1) Because the company can't afford a sound system
   (2) To simulate battle experience
   (3) To make the conversations more intimate
   (4) Because one character is supposed to be in Afghanistan
   (5) To simulate the way people communicate over the Internet

8. Based on the information in this passage, you can conclude that the theatre artists who produced the Sophocles play think that Canadian civilians
   (1) Do not understand Canadian soldiers
   (2) Learn about war through the media
   (3) Have been lied to by politicians
   (4) Should communicate with soldiers using the Internet
   (5) Are proficient in the use of technology

9. Based on the information in this extract, you can conclude that the Toronto performance of Sophocles' plays was
   (1) A major Broadway production
   (2) Funded by the Canadian military
   (3) A small private production
   (4) Broadcast on the Internet
   (5) A production by visiting Greek artists

What Does the Writer Think of Shakespeare?

What needs my Shakespeare for his honored bones
The labour of an age in piled stones?
Or that his hallowed relics should be hid
Under a star-y pointing pyramid?
Dear son of memory, great heir of fame,
What need'st thou such weak witness of thy name?
Thou in our wonder and astonishment
Hast built thyself a livelong monument.
For whilst, to the shame of slow-endeavoring art,
Thy easy numbers flow, and that each heart
Hath from the leaves of thy unvalued book
Those Delphic lines with deep impression took,
Then thou, our fancy of itself bereaving,
Dost make us marble with too much conceiving,
And so sepulchred in such pomp dost lie
That kings for such a tomb would wish to die.

10. Based on this poem, you can conclude that some people at the time of writing thought Shakespeare
    (1) Wrote too slowly
    (2) Should have a memorial built for him
    (3) Should be hidden away
    (4) Would produce many more great plays
    (5) Was not properly appreciated

11. In the lines, *Thou in our wonder and astonishment*

    Hast built thyself a livelong monument (lines 7–8), the poet infers that Shakespeare

    (1) Will be remembered through his writing
    (2) Has no need for a monument for himself
    (3) Has a weak name that will not be remembered
    (4) Surprised people with his success
    (5) Will not be properly appreciated by future generations

12. This poem is primarily about how Shakespeare will be remembered, and the writer clearly feels that physical memorials are not important. Which line best expresses this sentiment?
    (1) Under a star-y pointing pyramid?
    (2) Dear son of memory, great heir of fame
    (3) What need'st thou such weak witness of thy name?
    (4) Dost make us marble with too much conceiving,
    (5) Kings for such a tomb would wish to die.

ANSWERS

1. **(1)** The year, 1947, was shortly after World War II. Other clues include the references to bombed England and the fact that the church still has bomb damage.

2. **(3)** The passage refers to something beneath the food and pleasant wine, which suggests the atmosphere. The restaurant itself is described as *unspectacular*, but it has some indefinable quality they like.

3. **(4)** She says that one never knows what a doorman or anybody else is really like.

4. **(1)** When the speaker says that they went to Kettner's for choice, and then later says *one night we came out of Kettner's*, it suggests that this is a place they go to regularly.

5. **(2)** The writer clearly sees no problem with the use of technology in live performances and points out that it has been done since Shakespeare's time. The closing line shows that the writer thinks technology is important to the overall experience of the audience.

6. **(1)** Actors could be lowered by ropes from the heavens, suggesting they played characters who could fly.

7. **(5)** The excerpt tells us that the video is like a flickering Internet image. You can conclude that the audio is also to simulate the Internet.

8. **(1)** The excerpt speaks of the physical and psychological distance between Canadian citizens and soldiers.

9. **(3)** You can conclude that it was a small private production because it only ran for 5 days in a small theatre.

10. **(2)** The reference to Shakespeare's bones being in a pile of stones or starry pyramid refers to a monument, which the writer says is not needed.

11. **(1)** The lines clearly state that Shakespeare has clearly built a lasting monument of his own, and you can conclude it is from his writing, which is described as in the references to slow-endeavoring art, Delphic lines, and leaves (pages) of thy unvalued book.

12. **(3)** This line describes monuments as a weak witness, so you can conclude that the writer feels they are not a good way to remember people.

CAUSE AND EFFECT

Part of analysis is breaking down a passage to see the relationship between its parts, including causes and their effects. A *cause* is the reason something happens, the source of an end result; it is something that produces an effect. An *effect* is a result or consequence, something that occurs because of some other action.

Cause and effect can be seen at various levels. Within a single sentence, you can find cause and effect, indicated by words such as *so, because, since,* or *consequently.* For example, "She was late for the concert, so she did not get a seat." The cause is that she was late. The effect or result is that she did not get a seat.

Cause and effect can also be seen in paragraphs or in information found in different parts of a passage. Sometimes, the cause and effect may be indicated by words or phrases such as *therefore, as a result, consequently, and so,* or *for that reason.* At other times, you may have to recognize the cause-and-effect relationship based on your reasoning skills and comprehension of the text. For example, "I did not weed the garden regularly this year. The crop of vegetables was not as good as usual." The cause was that I did not weed the garden regularly. The effect was that the crop of vegetables was not as good. Cause and effect can also be a way that a passage is organized. The passage could be about the causes that lead to a particular outcome.

PRACTICE

In each sentence, underline the cause.

1. Since there had been no rain for over a month, the city water reservoir was dangerously low.

2. Takeoff of the flight was delayed because ice needed to be removed from the wings.

3. Young people are more susceptible to advertising. There are a lot of commercials on children's television channels.

4. Some people say that as life is short, you should relax and enjoy it.

5. Miriam was expecting a visit from her friend Trina, so she cleaned her best china and got out the good silverware.

6. The teenagers did not talk on their date because they were too busy sending text messages to each other.

7. Stephen loves music and plays several instruments; consequently, he has decided to go to college and study recording engineering.

8. The warranty on the car expired last month; therefore, Sue had to pay for the repairs.

9. My dog actually likes cats, but my cat doesn't like dogs, so they fight anyway.

10. The heat bill was lower this winter because the weather was milder than usual.

ANSWERS

1. <u>Since there had been no rain for over a month</u>, the city water reservoir was dangerously low.

2. Takeoff of the flight was delayed <u>because ice needed to be removed from the wings</u>.

3. <u>Young people are more susceptible to advertising</u>. There are a lot of commercials on children's television channels.

4. Some people say that <u>as life is short</u>, you should relax and enjoy it.

5. <u>Miriam was expecting a visit from her friend Trina</u>, so she cleaned her best china and got out the good silverware.

6. The teenagers did not talk on their date <u>because they were too busy sending text messages to each other.</u>

7. <u>Stephen loves music and plays several instruments</u>; consequently, he has decided to go to college and study recording engineering.

8. <u>The warranty on the car expired last month</u>; therefore, Sue had to pay for the repairs.

9. My dog actually likes cats, but <u>my cat doesn't like dogs</u>, so they fight anyway.

10. The heat bill was lower this winter <u>because the weather was milder than usual.</u>

PRACTICE

Read each passage and respond to the questions to test your analysis skills.

What Was Life Like for Early Pioneers?

But it is time that I should give you some account of our log-house, into which we moved a few days before Christmas. Many unlooked for delays having hindered its completion before that time, I began to think it would never be habitable.

The first misfortune that happened was the loss of a fine yoke of oxen that were purchased to draw in the house logs, that is, the logs for raising the walls of the house. Not regarding the bush as pleasant as their former master's cleared pastures, or perhaps foreseeing some hard work to come, early one morning they took into their heads to ford the lake at the head of the rapids, and march off leaving no trace of their route excepting their footing at the water's edge. After many days spent in vain search for them, the work was at a stand, and for one month they were gone, and we began to give up all expectation of hearing any news of them. At last we learned they were some twenty miles off, in a distant township, having made their way through bush and swamp, creek and lake, back to their former owner, with an instinct that supplied to them the want of roads and compass.

—From *The Backwoods of Canada* by Catharine Parr Traill (1836)

1. What was the effect of the unlooked for delays in completing the house?
   (1) The writer began to think they would never be able to live in it
   (2) They moved in to the house
   (3) It is time to give account of the log-house
   (4) There were delays in completing the house
   (5) They lost a yoke of fine oxen

2. According to the passage, what was one reason the oxen decided to leave?
   (1) They left no trace
   (2) They were purchased to move logs
   (3) They forded the lake
   (4) The work was at a standstill
   (5) They didn't like hard work

What Was Life Like for Animals During Pioneer Times?

At the same time the calf, having nursed sufficiently, and feeling his baby legs tired of the weight they had not yet learned to carry, laid himself down. On this the cow shifted her position. She turned half round, and lifted her head high. As she did so a scent of peril was borne in upon her fine nostrils. She recognised it instantly. With a snort of anger she sniffed again; then stamped a challenge with her fore hoofs, and levelled the lance points of her horns towards the menace. The next moment her eyes, made keen by the fear of love, detected the black outline of the bear's head through the coarse screen of the juniper. Without a second's hesitation, she flung up her tail, gave a short bellow, and charged.

The moment she saw herself detected, the bear rose upon her hindquarters; nevertheless she was in a measure surprised by the sudden blind fury of the attack. Nimbly she swerved to avoid it, aiming at the same time a stroke with her mighty forearm, which, if it had found its mark, would have smashed her adversary's neck. But as she struck out, in the act of shifting her position, a depression of the ground threw her off her balance. The next instant one sharp horn caught her slantingly in the flank, ripping its way upward and inward, while the mad impact threw her upon her back.

—From "When Twilight Falls on the Stump Lots" by Sir Charles G. D. Roberts, 1902.

3. Why did the cow charge at the bear?
   (1) She was angry
   (2) She was afraid
   (3) To protect her calf
   (4) Because she saw the bear behind the juniper bush
   (5) Because she smelled the bear

4. Why did the bear's blow not break the cow's neck?
   (1) She lost her balance and missed
   (2) The cow struck her with a horn
   (3) The cow's charge threw her on her back
   (4) She swerved to avoid the cow's attack
   (5) She struck with her mighty forearm

Who Was Jack?

In the village of So-and-so lived an old woman, Rebecca Cracknell, who had a dog with an odd eye and the name of Jack, a kitten with an odd tail and the name of Jack, and a green drake with odd ambitions that was called Jack. The old woman's only son was young Jack, and her husband, long since dead, had been known as old Jack. They began by having different names, every one of them, but the forces of habit were so strong in the good old woman that she always called everything and everybody by that one name. The drake was a middle-aged duck, cooped up in a yard as dry as the deserts of Egypt. Sometimes it tried to go sporting out into the great wet world of gutters and puddles and pools, but Rebecca could not bear to see it behaving so untidily so she confined it, and there in the dry yard it pined and lived.

—From *The Green Drake* by A. E. Coppard

5. Why was the drake called Jack?
   (1) That was his name
   (2) He liked the name Jack
   (3) The old woman called everyone Jack
   (4) It was the old woman's favourite name
   (5) It was a common name in the village

6. Why was the drake not allowed out of the yard?
   (1) Because it was unhappy
   (2) The woman didn't want it to get dirty
   (3) The woman didn't like the drake to have fun
   (4) The woman liked to keep her pets close
   (5) It might get chased by the dog

ANSWERS

1. **(1)** The other responses are all true, but are not results of the delays.

2. **(5)** The other responses are all true; however, they are not reasons. One reason given is that they foresaw some hard work to come.

3. **(3)** All the answers are true, but the reason she was angry and afraid is that she wanted to protect her calf.

4. **(1)** The story says that she stepped in a depression in the ground. This caused the bear to lose her balance and miss.

5. **(3)** The drake's name was not Jack, but the old woman called everyone and everything Jack out of force of habit.

6. **(2)** The drake wanted to play in puddles and pools. The reason given for keeping him in the yard is that the woman did not like to see him behaving untidily.

CHARACTERIZATION

One aspect of analysis in reading is analyzing character. Literature such as stories, novels, dramas, and even some poems contains people, and part of understanding what you read is to identify what those people, or characters, are like. Analyzing character when reading is just like analyzing the character of people you meet in real life. For example, if someone asks you what your friend Bobby is like, you name his qualities. Then you give reasons or examples to support these qualities.

When analyzing character, you look for clues in the story that tell you what the character is like, just as you do when analyzing the character of real people. What does the person look like? What are the things the person says? What does the person do? What do other people say about the character?

There are two methods of characterization that writers use: explicit and implicit. Explicit characterization is when the narrator or another character in the story says things about the character. Just like real life, this can be valuable information, but you have to decide whether or not to believe what is said. Implicit characterization is when you make judgments about a character based on what the character says or does. For example, if a person in real life gives money to charity, you might describe that person as kind. Do the same thing when you read about characters.

EXAMPLE

In the story, "A White Heron" by Sarah Orne Jewett, a girl is walking in the woods when she meets a young hunter.

> She did not dare to look boldly at the tall young man, who carried a gun over his shoulder, but she came out of her bush and again followed the cow, while he walked alongside.
>
> "I have been hunting for some birds," the stranger said kindly, "and I have lost my way, and need a friend very much. Don't be afraid," he added gallantly. "Speak up and tell me what your name is, and whether you think I can spend the night at your house, and go out gunning early in the morning."
>
> Sylvia was more alarmed than before. Would not her grandmother consider her much to blame? But who could have foreseen such an accident as this? It did not appear to be her fault, and she hung her head as if the stem of it were broken, but managed to answer "Sylvy," with much effort when her companion again asked her name.

One characteristic of the girl is that she is shy. What are the clues that tell us? She does not dare to look boldly at the young man. She is alarmed when he suggests coming to her house. She hangs her head before answering. One characteristic of the young man is that he is gentle. We know this because the story says he speaks "kindly" and answers "gallantly."

PRACTICE

Read each passage and respond to the questions to test your analysis skills.

What Does the Young Hunter Want?

The guest waked from a dream, and remembering his day's pleasure hurried to dress himself that it might sooner begin. He was sure from the way the shy little girl looked once or twice yesterday that she had at least seen the white heron, and now she must really be persuaded to tell. Here she comes now, paler than ever, and her worn old frock is torn and tattered, and smeared with pine pitch. The grandmother and the sportsman stand in the door together and question her, and the splendid moment has come to speak of the dead hemlock-tree by the green marsh. But Sylvia does not speak after all, though the old grandmother fretfully rebukes her, and the young man's kind appealing eyes are looking straight in her own. He can make them rich with money; he has promised it, and they are poor now. He is so well worth making happy, and he waits to hear the story she can tell.

No, she must keep silence! What is it that suddenly forbids her and makes her dumb? Has she been nine years growing, and now, when the great world for the first time puts out a hand to her, must she thrust it aside for a bird's sake? The murmur of the pine's green branches in her ears, she remembers how the white heron came flying through the golden air and how they watched the sea and the morning together, and Sylvia cannot speak; she cannot tell the heron's secret and give its life away.

—From "A White Heron" by Sarah Orne Jewett

1. What line in the passage might suggest that the girl likes the young man?
    (1) Here she comes now, paler than ever
    (2) But Sylvia does not speak after all
    (3) He is so well worth making happy
    (4) She must keep silence
    (5) She has been nine years growing

TIP

Characterization—
Look for detail
and clues to
interpret what a
character is like,
just as in real life.

2. How could you describe the girl's character based on the following line? *She cannot tell the heron's secret and give its life away.*
    (1) Gentle
    (2) Angry
    (3) Shy
    (4) Loving
    (5) Loyal

3. Which of the following is the best way to describe the young man?
    (1) A nice, considerate young man
    (2) A spoiled rich boy
    (3) A demanding, impatient hunter
    (4) An inconsiderate, pushy tattle-tale
    (5) A weak, but excitable youngster

What Did the Woman Dream of?

She suffered ceaselessly, feeling herself born for all the delicacies and all the luxuries. She suffered from the poverty of her dwelling, from the wretched look of the walls, from the worn-out chairs, from the ugliness of the curtains. All those things, of which another woman of her rank would never even have been conscious, tortured her and made her angry. The sight of the little Bretton peasant who did her humble housework aroused in her regrets which were despairing, and distracted dreams. She thought of the silent antechambers hung with Oriental tapestry, lit by tall bronze candelabra, and of the two great footmen in knee breeches who sleep in the big armchairs, made drowsy by the heavy warmth of the hot-air stove. She thought of the long salons fitted up with ancient silk, of the delicate furniture carrying priceless curiosities, and of the coquettish perfumed boudoirs made for talks at five o'clock with intimate friends, with men famous and sought after, whom all women envy and whose attention they all desire.

When she sat down for dinner at the round table covered with a three-days-old cloth, opposite her husband, who took the cover off the soup-tureen, exclaiming delightedly: "Aha! Scotch broth! What could be better?" she imagined delicate meals, gleaming silver, tapestries peopling the walls with folk of a past age and strange birds in faery forests; she imagined delicate food served in marvellous dishes, murmured gallantries, listened to with an inscrutable smile as one trifled with the rosy flesh of trout or wings of asparagus chicken.

—From "The Necklace" by Guy de Maupassant, 1884

4. Which of the following is the best way to describe the woman in this passage?
   (1) Rich
   (2) Lonely
   (3) Humble
   (4) Entitled
   (5) Graceful

5. What do these words tell us about the husband's character? "Aha! Scotch broth! What could be better?"
   (1) He shared his wife's ambitions
   (2) He was content with simple things
   (3) He was foolish
   (4) He did not love his wife
   (5) He was honest

What Does the Man in the Nursing Home Dream of?

"So what's on the menu tonight?" I grumble as I'm steered into the dining room. "Porridge? Mushy peas? Pablum? Oh, let me guess, it's tapioca isn't it? Is it tapioca? Or are we calling it rice pudding tonight?"

"O, Mr. Jankowski, you are a card," the nurse says flatly. She doesn't need to answer, and she knows it. This being Friday, we're having the usual nutritious but uninteresting combination of meat loaf, creamed corn, reconstituted mashed potatoes, and gravy that may have been waved over a piece of beef at some point in its life. And they wonder why I lost weight.

I know some of us don't have teeth, but I do, and I want pot roast. My wife's, complete with leathery bay leaves. I want carrots. I want potatoes boiled in their skins. And I want a deep, rich cabernet sauvignon to wash it all down, not apple juice from a tin. But above all, I want corn on the cob.

Sometimes I think that if I had to choose between an ear of corn or making love to a woman, I'd choose the corn. Not that I wouldn't love to have a final roll in the hay—I am a man yet, and some things never die—but the thought of those sweet kernels bursting between my teeth sure sets my mouth to watering.

—From *Water for Elephants* by Sara Gruen, Harper Collins, 2006.

6. The man's complaints at the beginning of the passage show him to be
   (1) Curious
   (2) Disinterested
   (3) Cheerful
   (4) Good natured
   (5) Sarcastic

7. How could you describe the nurse's character based on the following line? *"O, Mr. Jankowski, you are a card," the nurse says flatly.*
   (1) Curious
   (2) Disinterested
   (3) Cheerful
   (4) Good humoured
   (5) Sarcastic

8. What does the old man's craving for corn on the cob tell us about his character?
   (1) He misses his wife
   (2) He wishes he was younger
   (3) He is a vegetarian
   (4) He is discontented
   (5) He loves life

ANSWERS

1. **(3)** In addition to having promised them money, the girl wants to make him happy.
2. **(5)** The girl is loyal to the heron and cannot tell the hunter where to find it.
3. **(1)** The young man looks at the girl kindly. He is anxious to know what she can tell him, but he only looks at her with kind, appealing eyes.
4. **(4)** The woman is not poor. She has everything she needs and even a Bretton servant. However, she feels entitled to be rich. There are many clues in the passage, such as her feeling tortured and that she felt she was born for all the delicacies.
5. **(2)** Scotch broth, as the name implies, is a simple meal. His genuine pleasure shows that he is content with the simple, good things.
6. **(5)** The old man is sarcastic as he indirectly comments on the bland food.
7. **(2)** She answers flatly, clearly not really interested in the old man or his complaints.
8. **(5)** The man still craves the rich sensuous taste of potatoes, corn, and wine.

SUPPORTING DETAILS

Many types of reading passages—especially things such as articles, essays, and commentaries—are organized into paragraphs that contain topic sentences and supporting details. The topic sentences give the main ideas in the passage. The supporting details give reasons, explanations, examples, and other information to show the truth of the topic sentences.

When analyzing reading passages, you should be able to identify the supporting details and the main ideas that they prove.

PRACTICE

Read each passage and respond to the questions to test your analysis skills.

How Did the Huron People Govern Themselves?

The sex we have so unjustly excluded from power in Europe have a great share in the Huron government; the chief is chose by the matrons from amongst the nearest male relations, by the female line, of him he is to succeed; and is generally an aunt's or sister's son; a custom which, if we examine strictly into the principle on which it is founded, seems a little to contradict what we are told of the extreme chastity of the married ladies.

The power of the chief is extremely limited; he seems rather to advise his people as a father than command them as a master; yet, as his commands are always reasonable, and for the general good, no prince in the world is so well obeyed. They have a supreme council of ancients, into which every man enters of course at an age fixed, and another of assistants to the chief on common occasions, the members of which are like him elected by the matrons. I am pleased with the last regulation, as women are, beyond all doubt, the best judges of the merit of men.

—From *The History of Emily Montague* by Frances Brooke, 1769.

1. Which detail supports the point that Huron women played an important role in their government?
   (1) Older women select the chief
   (2) Women are excluded from power in Europe
   (3) The chief is a man
   (4) Exclusion from power in Europe is unjust
   (5) Many of the women were married

2. Which detail supports the statement that the power of the chief is extremely limited?
   (1) He seems to advise rather than command
   (2) His commands are always reasonable
   (3) No prince in the world is so well obeyed
   (4) There is a council of ancients
   (5) Women are the best judges of men

Did the Reviewer Enjoy the Book?

The Incomparable Atuk was Richler's follow-up to his best known work, *Duddy Kravitz*. The story starts with Atuk gaining fame as a gifted Eskimo poet and falling into a crowd of memorable characters. Although it is a short book, the NCL edition comes in at 178 pages with big print, it is very dense in the amount of story that is packed between the covers. It would be hard to summarize the novel because the book is basically just a bunch of random stuff that happens to Atuk and his inner circle; some of these include game show appearances with deadly punishments, cannibalism, swimming Lake Ontario, Eskimos being locked in a basement being forced to create "authentic" pieces of art, and of course Richler's trademark witticisms on the state of post-WWII Judaism.

Something that always impresses me with Richler's work from the 50s and 60s is his ability to seamlessly shift point-of-view with almost every chapter while still keeping the book as a whole very cohesive. I think part of the reason Richler is able to pull this off is because of how unique and memorable his characters are. All of his novels have a lot of characters and almost all of these characters are very well developed. Within two pages you have a sense of what this character is all about.

You can never go wrong with a Mordecai Richler book. *The Incomparable Atuk* is a great representation of his approach to writing and the themes that are explored throughout his writing career as a whole. Richler was a master at holding a mirror up to Canadian society and exposing our foibles with hilarious and biting satire. If you liked *Cocksure* you would definitely enjoy *Atuk*.

3. *Game show appearances with deadly punishments, cannibalism, swimming Lake Ontario* are details that support what point?
   (1) The book was Richler's follow-up to *Duddy Kravitz*
   (2) Atuk gains fame as an Eskimo poet
   (3) The story is very dense
   (4) The book is a bunch of random stuff that happens to Atuk
   (5) Richler's trademark is witticisms on post-WWII Judaism

4. *Almost all of these characters are very well developed* is a point that supports what position?
   (1) Richler can seamlessly shift point-of-view
   (2) The book as a whole is very cohesive
   (3) Richler's characters are unique and memorable
   (4) All his novels have a lot of characters
   (5) Within two pages you have a sense of what this character is all about

5. What is a reason the writer thinks you can never go wrong with a Mordecai Richler book?
   (1) *Atuk* is a great representation of his approach
   (2) *Atuk* contains common Richler themes
   (3) Richler was a master at holding a mirror to Canadian society
   (4) Richler is funny
   (5) If you liked *Cocksure* you would enjoy *Atuk*

 TIP

What details, examples, and information support the main ideas?

What Are the Requirements of a Sonnet?

The sonnet is a fairly restrictive form of poetry in that it has rigid and established conventions. It, therefore, offers a great challenge to the writer. Not only must poets confine their ideas to fourteen lines, but the lines must contain a certain rhythm and a certain number of syllables and must follow a certain rhyme pattern. In addition, the ideas are expected to develop in a particular manner.

The sonnet has been with us for hundreds of years. It was developed in Italy in the thirteenth century. It was refined by a poet named Petrarch in the fourteenth century, and was brought to England by Thomas Wyatt—who translated Petrarch's sonnets and composed a number of his own. The sonnet form was gradually modified in England, and Shakespeare is generally credited with writing the greatest of the modified—now called Shakespearean—sonnets. Sonnets are generally published in a sonnet sequence—a series of interrelated poems revolving around a single theme.

6. What is meant by *a fairly restrictive form of poetry*?
    (1) It has rigid and established conventions
    (2) It offers a great challenge to the writer
    (3) Poets must confine their ideas to fourteen lines
    (4) The lines must contain a certain rhythm
    (5) The ideas must be developed in a particular manner

7. *It was refined by a poet named Petrarch in the fourteenth century* is a detail that supports what point?
    (1) The sonnet has been with us for hundreds of years
    (2) It was developed in Italy in the thirteenth century
    (3) Petrarch's sonnets were translated by Thomas Wyatt
    (4) Shakespeare wrote the greatest modified sonnets
    (5) Sonnets are generally published in a series

ANSWERS

1. **(1)** The fact that the chief is chosen by the matrons shows that Huron women have an important share in government, unlike women in Europe.

2. **(1)** Although the other details are also given in the passage, that he seems to advise is the only detail that shows his power is limited.

3. **(4)** The details give examples of some of the "random stuff" that happens.

4. **(3)** According to the passage, the fact that most of the characters are well developed contributes to making them unique and memorable, which in turn contributes to Richler's ability to shift point-of-view while keeping the book cohesive.

5. **(3)** All the details show that readers might enjoy *Atuk*. The only reason given that you can never go wrong with a Richler book is that he held up a mirror to Canadian society to expose us to ourselves in a humorous way.

6. **(1)** This is an explanation of what is meant. The other points give details to support the statement.

7. **(1)** This detail is one that shows the history of sonnets and that they have been with us for hundreds of years.

FACT AND OPINION

Not everything we read is a fact. Indeed, many arguments that are most convincing are not facts at all, but opinions. For example, which of the following statements is an opinion?

- The Smiths have the nicest apartment in the building.
- Their apartment has three bedrooms.
- The apartment is a corner unit.
- The apartment has a recently updated kitchen.

Facts are things that can be measured or confirmed. They do not include value judgments. They are just true. The apartment does have three bedrooms. It is a fact. The apartment is a corner unit. Facts can be checked and confirmed. Opinions are equally or even more important, but they make a value judgment. That the Smiths have the nicest apartment is an opinion. Opinions must be supported by facts. As readers, we must recognize which are facts and which are opinions and be prepared to evaluate opinions and make judgments of our own.

PRACTICE

Indicate which of the following statements is a fact (F) or an opinion (O).

___ 1. There are more people alive today than have lived and died in the history of the world.

___ 2. Home and garden furniture is now on sale at prices you cannot afford to pass up.

___ 3. Canada is the second-largest peat moss producer in the world and harvests 22% of the world's supply.

___ 4. The new album is a landmark in Canadian country music.

___ 5. The majority of people interviewed said that they preferred coffee over tea as a breakfast beverage.

___ 6. The colour and pattern of the new couch do not go with the wallpaper in the living room.

___ 7. The woman wore a long coat, a scarf was over her head, obscuring her face, and she stooped as she looked about her.

___ 8. She seemed furtive, looking about her, as though she was afraid.

___ 9. If there were life on other planets, we would have definitive evidence by now.

___ 10. The Hubble telescope has floated above the Earth's atmosphere since 1990.

___ 11. It is one of the most important tools ever developed for advancing our knowledge of the universe.

___ 12. Thousands of articles have been published based on observations of the Hubble telescope.

ANSWERS

1. F	5. F	9. O
2. O	6. O	10. F
3. F	7. F	11. O
4. O	8. O	12. F

MOOD AND TONE

Mood and tone are both aspects of writing that require you to analyze the writer's style. All writers develop their own unique styles of writing, which may vary somewhat from work to work, but that express their individuality. When analysing an author's style, consider the way the author writes, and the effect of the style on the reader.

Mood is the feeling that the writer tries to give the reader. A lot of things contribute to mood, such as the images the writer uses and word choice. For example, the mood of a passage might be described as light or dark or suspenseful. Mood is created by the way the author writes, by the imagery and descriptions and choice of words. For example, a passage might contain a description of a car driving rapidly through the streets. It might contain words and images such as *suddenly, screeching tires, blaring horns*, or *danger*. These are ways that the writer creates a mood or feeling of excitement.

Tone is another aspect of style. It refers to how the writing in a passage sounds, so to speak. Is the vocabulary formal or informal? Is it characteristic of a particular class, profession, or region? Would you describe the tone as distinguished? Scientific? Journalistic? Angry? Does the writer use a lot of imagery or description? Does the writer use short, simple sentences or long, complex sentences? Is the tone positive or negative, harsh or peaceful, and what impact does it have on the meaning?

PRACTICE

Read each passage and respond to the questions to test your analysis skills.

What Was the Chateau Like?

The chateau into which my valet had ventured to make forcible entrance rather than permit me, in my desperately wounded condition, to pass a night in the open air, was one of those piles of commingled gloom and grandeur which have so long frowned among the Apennines, no less in fact than in the fancy of Mrs Radcliffe. To all appearance it had been temporarily and very lately abandoned. We established ourselves in one of the smallest and least sumptuously furnished apartments. It lay in a remote turret of the building. Its decorations were rich, yet tattered and antique. Its walls were hung with tapestry and bedecked with ninefold and multiform armorial trophies, together with an unusually great number of very spirited modern paintings in frames of rich golden arabesque. In these paintings, which depended from the walls not only in their main surfaces but in very many nooks which the bizarre architecture of the chateau rendered necessary—in these paintings my incipient delirium, perhaps, had caused me to take deep interest…

—From "The Oval Portrait" by Edgar Allan Poe

1. The mood of the excerpt could be described as
    (1) Light
    (2) Eerie
    (3) Romantic
    (4) Desperate
    (5) Artistic

2. The tone of the writing could best be described as
   (1) Informal
   (2) Direct
   (3) Ornate
   (4) Reflective
   (5) Journalistic

What Impact Would the Snowstorm Have?

The blizzard started on Wednesday morning. It was that rather common, truly western combination of a heavy snowstorm with a blinding northern gale—such as piles the snow in hills and mountains and makes walking next to impossible.

   I cannot exactly say that I viewed it with unmingled joy. There were special reasons for that. It was the second week in January; when I had left 'home' the Sunday before, I had been feeling rather bad; so my wife would worry a good deal, especially if I did not come at all. I knew there was such a thing as its becoming quite impossible to make the drive. I had been lost in a blizzard once or twice before in my lifetime. And yet, so long as there was the least chance that horse-power and human will-power combined might pull me through at all, I was determined to make or anyway try it.

   —From "Snow" in *Over Prairie Trails*
   by Frederick Philip Grove

3. The mood of the excerpt could be described as
   (1) Unemotional
   (2) Dark
   (3) Tense
   (4) Stark
   (5) Sad

4. The tone of writing in the excerpt is
   (1) Descriptive
   (2) Elaborate
   (3) Direct
   (4) Reflective
   (5) Angry

5. The tone of the line *I cannot exactly say that I viewed it with unmingled joy* could be described as
   (1) Understated
   (2) Anxious
   (3) Worried
   (4) Joyous
   (5) Journalistic

TIP

Mood—The feeling that the writer tries to give the reader.

Tone—vocabulary, sentence structure, style.

Did the Woman Have a Weak Heart?

He was a soldier and an ambitious one, but he resigned his commission. Louise's health forced her to spend the winter at Monte Carlo and the summer at Deauville. He hesitated a little at throwing up his career, and Louise at first would not hear of it; but at last she yielded as she always yielded, and he prepared to make his wife's last few years as happy as might be.

"It can't be very long now," she said. "I'll try not to be troublesome."

For the next two or three years Louise managed, notwithstanding her weak heart, to go beautifully dressed to all the most lively parties, to gamble very heavily, to dance and even to flirt with tall, slim young men. But George Hobhouse had not the stamina of Louise's first husband and he had to brace himself now and then with a stiff drink for his day's work as Louise's second husband. It is possible that the habit would have grown on him, which Louise would not have liked at all, but very fortunately (for her) the war broke out. He rejoined his regiment and three months later was killed.

—From "Louise" in *Cosmopolitans* by W. Somerset Maugham
(London: Heinemann, 1936).

6. The mood of this excerpt could be described as
   (1) Dark
   (2) Humorous
   (3) Sad
   (4) Pathetic
   (5) Resigned

7. The tone of writing could be described as
   (1) Journalistic
   (2) Depressing
   (3) Critical
   (4) Tongue in cheek
   (5) Reflective

8. The tone of the line, *For the next two or three years Louise managed, notwithstanding her weak heart, to go beautifully dressed to all the most lively parties...* could be described as
   (1) Sad
   (2) Happy
   (3) Sarcastic
   (4) Angry
   (5) Judgmental

ANSWERS

1. **(2)** The excerpt is set at night, and the main character is wounded. The atmosphere of the chateau is gloomy. It is abandoned, rich, and tattered—an eerie setting.

2. **(3)** The writing is formal and filled with detail and ornate description.

3. **(1)** The excerpt describes a blizzard and states that the speaker feels bad that he has been lost in blizzards before, but there is little description or emotion.

4. **(3)** The tone of writing is direct and plain, almost expressionless.

5. **(1)** The writer understates his feeling of the situation there is a blizzard and he may not be able to get home.

6. **(2)** The excerpt takes a light and humorous approach to describing Louise's poor health, which somehow requires her to spend the winter in vacation spots and go to lively parties.

7. **(4)** The manner of writing is ironic and insincere.

8. **(3)** The line has a tone of contemptuous irony.

ASSUMPTIONS AND BIAS

Don't believe everything you read. Many people accept anything they read in a newspaper, magazine, or report as fact. However, everyone has opinions, even writers, and assumptions and biases can be found in their works. Sometimes, biases are cultural or social. For example, in Canada we assume that government-sponsored healthcare is a right, but in the United States it is not seen that way at all. Other biases may reflect company priorities. For example, in a business report a company presents its own products in a positive way. Other biases reflect personal values.

Assumptions and bias are not bad. Writers need to interpret facts and information to help readers understand the message. However, as readers we should also be able to recognize bias and assumptions so we can make judgments of our own. Some clues in the manner of writing include:

1. **DESCRIPTION**—Are there positive or negative describing words or phrases? For example, a business report might say, "We have a proud thirty-year history" instead of "We have been in business for thirty years."

2. **WORD CHOICE**—Writers show bias by the words they choose. For example, a writer could describe someone as "thrifty" or "cheap." The dictionary meanings are similar, but one is positive and one negative.

3. **COMPARISONS**—Comparisons are sometimes used in description. We might say that someone "slept like a baby" or "yelled like a banshee." Positive comparisons in the passage show a positive bias towards the subject.

4. **DETAILS AND BALANCE**—Bias can be seen in supporting details that are included or left out. Is there an equal balance of details on both sides of an issue? Are both sides equally represented?

PRACTICE

Words have different kinds of meanings: denotations (dictionary definitions) and connotations (positive or negative feelings associated with the words). Identify whether the following words have positive or negative connotations.

a) prattle	d) cunning	g) skinny
b) share	e) thoroughbred	h) slender
c) clever	f) mongrel	i) puppy

ANSWER

a) negative	d) negative	g) negative
b) positive	e) positive	h) positive
c) positive	f) negative	i) positive

PRACTICE

Read each passage and respond to the questions to test your analysis skills.

What Does the Writer Think of Politicians?

The Canadian Charter of Rights and Freedoms continues to speak for disenfranchised Canadians. Our new constitution is now more than 30 years old, but despite criticisms from those who claim the Supreme Court is weak and ineffective, they continue to apply the charter to champion the rights of the powerless. In particular, the court has limited the efforts of conservative politicians in their war on drugs and prostitution. Guided by their own narrow minded agendas, such political hacks have experienced first-hand that the charter has lost none of its vitality.

1. Which descriptive word shows that the writer sees those involved with drugs and prostitution as victims?
   (1) Disenfranchised
   (2) Weak
   (3) Ineffective
   (4) Champion
   (5) Conservative

2. The writer's bias in this passage could be described as
   (1) Opposed to conservative political approaches
   (2) Supportive of drug abuse
   (3) Opposed to the Supreme Court
   (4) Supportive of politicians
   (5) Opposed to the Charter of Rights and Freedoms

3. How do you think this writer would think of a needle exchange program for drug users?
   (1) Opposed
   (2) It is unethical
   (3) Supportive
   (4) It is illegal
   (5) It is narrow minded

TIP

Readers should recognize the writer's viewpoint and bias.

Do Car Ads Contain Bias?

If you are looking for value in a new car, we have a deal for you. Our new hybrids are sleek and sporty, and you'll save a bundle as you blast past the pumps in your new ride. We invite you to test drive our competitors' cheap models before trying our inexpensive alternatives. We'll make you feel like you are driving an expensive sports car, while equipping you with a practical family vehicle that won't break the bank. Our car offers the best fuel efficiency and resale value in its class. Drive theirs first, you'll drive ours last.

4. Which statement best describes the writer's bias in this passage?
   (1) Their cars are less expensive than the competitors'
   (2) Their cars are more fun to drive than the competitors'
   (3) Their cars are better for families than the competitors'
   (4) Their cars are more sporty than the competitors'
   (5) Their cars are a better value than the competitors'

5. What word choice is used to suggest that the competitors' cars are poorer quality.
   (1) Sleek
   (2) Cheap
   (3) Inexpensive
   (4) Expensive
   (5) First

6. What comparison is used to create a positive impression of the writer's car?
   (1) Our new hybrids are sleek
   (2) Blast past the pumps
   (3) Like driving an expensive sports car
   (4) A practical family vehicle
   (5) Best fuel efficiency and resale value

What Is the Best Vacation Spot?

By mid-February, many Canadians have begun to find that the days are short and the winter is long, and they are ready for some fun and sunshine. March break vacations to sun-and-sand destinations are common. Some popular escapes include Florida and Jamaica. Many people enjoy the beaches of Cuba and Mexico, while others prefer Hawaii, California, or a Mediterranean cruise.

Not everyone goes south. Canadians are a hardy lot and, like the early pioneers, some continue to thrive on the challenges of our climate. Many find their sun on the slopes, enjoying clean air and the pristine beauty of nature under a blanket of white snow. While their countrymen laze on white sand in foreign climes, they slice firmly down mountain trails, only the sound of their skis breaking the stillness. While many sip dainty umbrella drinks by the pool in southern tourist traps, others adventure in the wonders of our nation.

7. In this passage, the writer's bias is in favour of what type of vacation during March break?
   (1) Fun and sunshine
   (2) Florida and Jamaica
   (3) Beaches of Cuba and Mexico
   (4) Mediterranean cruises
   (5) Canadian ski vacations

8. What is the writer's attitude towards people who vacation in warm climates? He sees them as
   (1) Idle
   (2) Energetic
   (3) Smart
   (4) Indecisive
   (5) Adventurous

9. What word choice is used to give a positive connotation to the weather of Canadian winter?
   (1) Hardy
   (2) Challenges
   (3) Blanket
   (4) Firmly
   (5) Adventure

ANSWERS

1. **(1)** The passage speaks of *disenfranchised Canadians* who are later referred to as *powerless* and associated with the war on drugs and prostitution.

2. **(1)** The writer describes conservative politicians and their viewpoint as *narrow-minded* and *political hacks*.

3. **(3)** The writer clearly opposes conservative views and supports more liberal approaches.

4. **(5)** Advertising is intended to be biased. In this ad, the writer attempts to show that their cars are a better value.

5. **(2)** The competitors' cars are described as *cheap*, which has a negative connotation, and the writer's car is described as *inexpensive*, which has a positive connotation.

6. **(3)** This is the only comparison given in the passage.

7. **(5)** The first paragraph describes sunshine vacations in a matter of fact way. The second paragraph uses positive descriptions, such as *clean air* and *pristine beauty* to describe winter ski vacations in a positive way.

8. **(1)** They are described as lazing on white sand, sipping dainty umbrella drinks by the pool.

9. **(2)** The writer speaks of the *challenges* of our climate. A writer with a different bias might speak of the *problems* or *harsh realities*.

CHALLENGE EXERCISE

Choose a newspaper or magazine article or an editorial. Does the writer have a bias about the subject? What is the bias? Describe how the following factors (and/or others) created bias: descriptions, word choice, comparisons, details / balance.

CHAPTER CHECK-UP

Complete these practice exercises, and check the answers and analysis that follow. After you mark your work, review any topic in the chapter that you had trouble with or did not understand.

Questions 1–7 are based on the following excerpt.

Does Your Family Have a Plan?

All levels of government in Canada recommend that families be prepared for emergencies. Many of us have been stranded in our homes or experienced power outages for hours or days because of ice storms, blizzards, or lightning storms. Others have fled their homes and neighbourhoods when ice jams or annual thaws cause rivers to overflow their banks. Forest fires are also a risk in many parts of Canada. In addition to natural disasters, industrial accidents or acts of terrorism can result in emergency situations.

Emergencies happen unexpectedly and sometimes occur when family members are not all together. What do you do if you are at work and the children at school when an emergency occurs? How will you communicate to make sure everyone is okay and to give instructions? Every family should have an emergency plan and an emergency kit prepared in advance.

An emergency plan includes information such as safe exists from the home, family meeting place, and safe route out of the neighbourhood. It could include where the children should go if you are not home, as well as the location of the fire extinguisher, water shutoff, electrical panel, and gas valve. You should also have a basic emergency kit to provide for the family for up to one or two days. It should include a flashlight, battery-operated radio, canned food, several litres of water, blankets, some cash in small bills, and other emergency supplies. If you are prepared, you will respond to emergencies with confidence.

1. Based on the information in this passage, you could conclude that
   (1) Canada is a dangerous place to live
   (2) Natural crises occur in many parts of Canada
   (3) Everyone has experienced a flood
   (4) Industrial accidents commonly cause emergencies
   (5) Cell phones do not work in an emergency

2. Which of the following sayings do you think the speaker would agree with?
   (1) A penny saved is a penny earned
   (2) A bird in the hand is worth two in the bush
   (3) A leopard can't change its spots
   (4) A stitch in time saves nine
   (5) Add fuel to the fire

3. What main idea is supported by the line, *What do you do if you are at work and the children at school when an emergency occurs?*
   (1) Many of us have been stranded by natural disasters
   (2) Industrial accidents or acts of terrorism can result in emergency situations
   (3) Emergencies happen unexpectedly
   (4) Every family should have an emergency kit
   (5) An emergency plan includes a family meeting place

4. During a power outage, debit machines might not be working in local stores. As a result, your emergency kit should contain
   (1) Small bills
   (2) Water
   (3) Food
   (4) Flashlight
   (5) Other emergency supplies

5. Which of the following is a statement of opinion?
   (1) Emergencies happen unexpectedly
   (2) Forest fires are also a risk
   (3) Many of us have been stranded
   (4) Terrorism can result in emergency situations
   (5) Every family should an emergency plan

6. Why does the government suggest families should have an emergency plan and kit?
   (1) To respond to natural disasters
   (2) To respond to industrial accidents
   (3) To remain in communication with family members
   (4) To provide for your family for several days
   (5) To respond to emergencies with confidence

7. The tone of the writing could best be described as
   (1) Informal
   (2) Poetic
   (3) Ornate
   (4) Reflective
   (5) Journalistic

Questions 8–11 are based on the following excerpt.

Who Is He Waiting For?

On the seventh day, Lucien returns to their spot. The very chill and silence of the place—a toy meadow lying soft between a rock outcrop and three stout oaks—is so complete that he knows in his body, somehow, that she will not come today.

The ground is damp so he sits on a fallen tree. Its angle of repose and the spikes of its many broken branches make it hard to find a patient seat. Again and again he closes his Horace and stands and tries another place on the tree. In the end, he climbs and sits up on the rock outcrop, which also gives him a better perch from which to penetrate, with unceasing gaze, every direction of the forest. *Ars Poetica* he keeps closed on his lap. He had wanted to show her letters, words. It would make her understand him better perhaps, though it also carried the danger of showing her their impossible distance, and driving her away. He is wary of his desire to impress her. There is something troubling in how confident she is with him. She is not in awe of the French, or of him. Though neither is Membertou, who is possibly her uncle. None of them seem to be. Though they love—love—their bread, and would indeed trade meat for it in equal size.

—From the novel *The Order of Good Cheer* by Bill Gaston, House of Anansi Press Inc. (distributed by Harper Collins Canada), 2009.

8. What is the effect of the silence of the meadow?
    (1) It caused him to return
    (2) It caused him to wait
    (3) It made the meadow seem soft
    (4) It caused him to sense that she would not come
    (5) It caused the meadow to seem unreal

9. How could Lucien's feelings in this passage be described, based on the line *Again and again he closes his Horace and stands and tries another place on the tree* (lines 5–6)?
    (1) Restless
    (2) In love
    (3) Lonely
    (4) Longing
    (5) Afraid

10. You can conclude that *Ars Poetica* is probably a
    (1) Poem
    (2) Song
    (3) Painting
    (4) Gift
    (5) Book

11. What can we conclude about the woman based on the line, *She is not in awe of the French, or of him* (lines 11–12)?
    (1) They have just met
    (2) She isn't sure how she feels
    (3) She is from a different culture
    (4) She does not like him
    (5) She is just a child

Questions 12–15 are based on the following excerpt.

> That's my last Duchess painted on the wall,
> Looking as if she were alive. I call
> That piece a wonder, now; Frà Pandolf's hands
> Worked busily a day, and there she stands.
> Will't please you sit and look at her? I said
> "Frà Pandolf" by design, for never read
> Strangers like you that pictured countenance,
> The depth and passion of its earnest glance,
> But to myself they turned (since none puts by
> The curtain I have drawn for you, but I)
> And seemed as they would ask me, if they durst,
> How such a glance came there; so, not the first
> Are you to turn and ask thus. Sir, 'twas not
> Her husband's presence only, called that spot
> Of joy into the Duchess' cheek; perhaps
> Frà Pandolf chanced to say "Her mantle laps
> Over my lady's wrist too much," or "Paint
> Must never hope to reproduce the faint
> Half-flush that dies along her throat": such stuff
> Was courtesy, she thought, and cause enough
> For calling up that spot of joy. She had
> A heart—how shall I say?—too soon made glad,
> Too easily impressed; she like whate'er
> She looked on, and her looks went everywhere.
>   —From "My Last Duchess" by Robert Browning

12. Based on the information in this passage, what can you conclude about the Duchess?
    (1) She is dead
    (2) Her husband misses her
    (3) She was an artist
    (4) She was unfaithful
    (5) She was the Duke's mother

13. How could you describe the speaker's character based on the line, *Since none puts by the curtain I have drawn for you, but I* (lines 9–10)?
    (1) He likes to be in control
    (2) The picture makes him sad
    (3) He is embarrassed by the painting
    (4) He is proud of the painting
    (5) He is a very private person

14. What detail supports the idea that the speaker was jealous of the Duchess?
    (1) Her picture was painted by Frà Pandolf
    (2) She had a depth of passion and earnest glance
    (3) It was not only her husband who made a spot of joy appear on her cheek
    (4) She was easily impressed
    (5) He keeps the picture behind a curtain

15. Based on the information in this passage, how could the Duchess's character be described?
    (1) Sad
    (2) Joyful
    (3) Withdrawn
    (4) Flirtatious
    (5) Aggressive

ANSWERS

1. **(2)** You can conclude that natural crises occur in many parts of Canada based on the information that many of us have been stranded, experienced power outages, or floods.

2. **(4)** This saying reflects the sentiment that it is best to be prepared.

3. **(3)** This detail supports the idea that emergencies can happen unexpectedly, including when family members are not together.

4. **(1)** All these items should be in the kit, including small bills that could be used to make purchases if debit machines are down.

5. **(5)** The word *should* indicates an opinion.

6. **(5)** Being prepared means having a plan and kit to respond to emergencies with confidence.

7. **(5)** The tone of writing is similar to a newspaper style.

8. **(4)** The silence gave him a sense in his body that she would not come today.

9. **(1)** There are many clues in this passage that show his restlessness as he waits for her to come, including his being up and down and then sitting on the rock outcrop and looking with an unceasing gaze.

10. **(5)** As it sits closed in his lap, it is probably a book.

11. **(3)** This line and other clues show that she is not French and suggests she is from a very different culture.

12. **(1)** He comments that she looks as if alive, so she is clearly dead.

13. **(1)** No one else is permitted to draw the curtain.

14. **(3)** Later he also complains that her looks went everywhere.

15. **(2)** He states that she was easily impressed and liked everything, including her husband, but also took joy in everything else.

CHALLENGE EXERCISE

Look on the Internet or in a book for the poem "My Last Duchess" by Robert Browning. Read the poem and determine how she died and why? How does the Duke feel about possessions? How does he feel about the Duchess? If you were the guest, what kind of person would you think the Duke is?

Reading and Synthesis

12

THINK ABOUT IT

You have probably heard the line from the Greek philosopher Aristotle, "The whole is more than the sum of its parts." There are many examples of this saying in everyday life, in which simple elements combine to form something greater. For example, consider homemade bread. The elements are simple—flour, water, sugar, and yeast—yet when combined they make something more than just ingredients. What are some other everyday examples you can think of? Consider the buildings and streets that make up the skyline of your home town. Separately they are just buildings, but together they are the familiar view of home.

How does this apply to writing? How does a writer combine elements of a passage together to make something more, and how can we train ourselves to recognize this when reading?

IN THIS CHAPTER

After completing this chapter, you will be able to

→ **RECOGNIZE ORGANIZATIONAL STRUCTURE**

→ **COORDINATE INFORMATION FROM DIFFERENT PARTS OF A TEXT**

→ **INTERPRET POINT OF VIEW, PURPOSE, AND STYLE**

→ **COMPARE AND CONTRAST ELEMENTS WITHIN A WORK**

→ **INTEGRATE ADDITIONAL INFORMATION ABOUT THE AUTHOR OR WORK**

WHAT IS SYNTHESIS?

There are different levels of reading skill. To completely understand a reading passage, you must first comprehend and apply what it says. You must also be able to break down elements of the passage to analyze them and draw conclusions. Finally, you must be able to put elements together, or synthesise them, to see the big picture, which is more than the sum of the parts.

Synthesis questions make up 30–35% of the questions on the GED Reading Test. Synthesis refers to your ability to recognize:

- Overall pattern of organization in a work
- Relationships between information in different parts of the passage
- Perspective and purpose
- Relevance of external information

 TIP

Synthesis is your ability to see the big picture.

Pattern of Organization

How does the writer organize the information presented in the text? Is the passage descriptive, narrative, expository? Does the passage present reasons with supporting details, opinions with related personal experience, causes, and their effects?

Relationships Between Information

Recognize the relationships between information found in different parts of a passage and draw conclusions.

Perspective and Purpose

Interpret the viewpoint of characters in a work or the writer's purpose in writing about a topic.

External Information

Synthesis can also mean integrating what you read with personal experience or other information you already know. On the GED Reading Test, questions of this type give additional information about the author or the work and ask you to interpret elements of the passage.

PRACTICE

How Did Modernist Poetry Come to Canada?

To Canada modernism has come more slowly and less violently than elsewhere. This applies more particularly to poetry, and indeed to literature in general. The older generation of Canadian poets, Carman and Scott—and Lampman in a lesser degree because his career was so ultimately cut short—had already initiated a departure, a partial departure, from the Victorian tradition of poetry, years before the movement began in England. They had been profoundly influenced by the transcendentalism of Emerson and the New England school of thought. They were more immediately in contact with nature, and they looked upon her with less sophisticated eyes. And in the deep but more or less unconscious optimism of a new country whose vision is fixed upon the future, they had no time for the pessimism and disillusionment of the old world. Therefore there was no violence of reaction. They kept one hand, as it were, on the Victorian tradition while they quietly stepped aside and in advance of it. Carman had long ago developed the seeds of change which he found in his master, Browning, and had harked far back to Blake for his further inspiration. Lampman, in his great sonnets, had not carried it on beyond the point where for his part, had found in Meredith; and had kept in the forefront of his time. He remains always, by a process of imperceptible gradations, a contemporary of the youngest generation.

And so it has come about that since there was no repression, there has been no revolt. Eager young spirits who thirsted to imitate Miss Sitwell or E.E. Cummings, have disgustedly felt themselves patted on the back instead of pasted in the breeches. Modernism has come softly into the poetry of Canada, by peaceful penetration rather than by rude assault.

—From "A Note on Modernism" by Sir Charles G.D. Roberts (1931)

1. How is this excerpt organized?
   (1) Physical description integrated with interpretation
   (2) Narrative where one person tells a story to another
   (3) Specific arguments followed by examples
   (4) Topic sentences with supporting details
   (5) Statements of fact with detailed descriptions

2. The beginning of the excerpt states that modernism came more slowly to Canada, but then it says that the older generation of Canadian poets had partly departed from Victorian poetry before the movement began in England. Based on this information, you can conclude that
   (1) Modernism came to Canada before England
   (2) Something came between Victorian and Modernist poetry in Canada
   (3) Victorian poetry came to Canada before Britain
   (4) Modernism began in New England
   (5) Canadian poets come from an older school of thought

3. The writer believes that one contrast between Canada as a young country and England as an older one is that
   (1) Canadian poets are more optimistic
   (2) Canadians are less sophisticated
   (3) They are not part of the Victorian tradition
   (4) They are not as influenced by American writers
   (5) Canadian poets are not part of the modernist movement

4. Edith Sitwell and E.E. Cummings were British and American modernist poets who faced early criticism of their work. Based on this information, what is meant by *since there was no repression, there has been no revolt*?
   (1) Canadian writers should be criticised more thoroughly like American and British poets
   (2) Sitwell and Cummings would have been better off writing in Canada
   (3) Canadian poets still wrote in a Victorian style as they are not criticised
   (4) Canadian poetry has changed, but not as much as in other places
   (5) Modernism was not a rebellion in Canada as poets were not criticised like American and British poets

5. The author's purpose in writing this excerpt is to
   (1) Show that Canadian poetry is more sophisticated than English poetry
   (2) Show American influences on Canadian poetry
   (3) Explain the evolution of poetry in Canada
   (4) Contrast the optimism of Canadian poetry with pessimism of old-world poetry
   (5) Describe the influences of several Canadian poets

ANSWERS

1. **(4)** The first paragraph begins with a topic sentence, followed by sentences that give explanation and details. The second paragraph also begins with a topic sentence, which is supported by those that follow.

2. **(2)** Modernism came more slowly in Canada, but something else came between. The excerpt explains that Canadians followed Victorianism in some ways, but in others had moved to something different through their appreciation of nature.

3. **(1)** The excerpt contrasts Canadian and English writers, stating that Canadians are more optimistic, partly because of their vision of nature and partly because they were a new country, looking towards the future.

4. **(5)** In fact, the passage says that some young Canadian writers were a little disappointed at being praised rather than criticised, but that modernism came in gently because there was no criticism for them to rebel against.

5. **(3)** The purpose of the excerpt is to explain the progress of Canadian poetry from Victorian to Modernist.

ORGANIZATIONAL STRUCTURE

Organization is a key to good writing. As a writer, you follow a pattern of organization that effectively communicates your message. As a reader, you should be able to recognize how a passage is organized, so you can better understand the message. For example, you should recognize what the pattern is of a passage that presents arguments for and against a proposition. You should recognize when a passage shows the similarities and then the differences between two things.

A passage of writing could be organized in many different ways. Those listed below are just a few examples:

- Order of importance (persuasive order)—to persuade readers of your opinion, present and explain a series of arguments in order of increasing importance
- Reverse order of importance—common in newspaper articles, information is given with the most important facts or arguments first
- Cause/effect—an explanation of reasons or contributing factors, followed by results
- Problem to solution—describe a problem and then one or more solutions
- Comparison/contrast—explain similarities between two things and then show differences.
- Chronological order—sequence of events in the order they occurred from first to last
- Process order—explain the steps of a method in sequence
- Classification order—the topic is divided into categories, each described individually, such as a passage about cooking techniques organized based on frying, baking, simmering, and grilling
- Spatial order—describe objects in order based on where they are located, such as the furniture and other parts of a room

On the GED Reading Test, questions about organization will not use terms such as *classification order*. Instead, they will ask about the specific organization of that passage, such as:

- General policy statements followed by specific examples
- Reasons supported by details and examples
- Debate of foreign vacations versus Canadian vacations
- Sequence of events in order they happened

PRACTICE

Read each passage and respond to the questions to test your synthesis skills.

What Does It Take To Be a Writer?

Writing is an arduous process that relies more on determination and self-discipline than it does on a personal muse. First, discipline yourself by setting a specific time each day, or on established days, when you will write. Second, begin writing. It is not uncommon to find yourself staring at a blank page or screen waiting for inspiration. Write something, your name if you have to, but begin. Third, set goals and deadlines for yourself so that you can measure your progress and avoid endless rewriting. Finally, share your work. Don't be afraid to submit your work to publishers or show it to friends or writers' circles. Art is meant to be shared.

1. How is this passage organized?
   (1) A main idea with supporting details
   (2) Similarities and then differences between writing and other forms of art
   (3) Statements and explanations in order of increasing importance
   (4) A process with a sequence of steps
   (5) Classification of types of writing with explanations

Was It Love at First Sight?

Most of the Mulliners have fallen in love at first sight, but few with so good an excuse as Mordred. She was a singularly beautiful girl, and for a while it was this beauty of hers that enchained my nephew's attention to the exclusion of all else. It was only after he had sat gulping for some minutes like a dog with a chicken bone in its throat that he detected the sadness in her face. He could see now that her eyes, as she listlessly perused her four-months-old copy of *Punch*, were heavy with pain.

His heart ached for her, and as there is something about the atmosphere of a dentist's waiting-room which breaks down the barriers of conventional etiquette he was emboldened to speak.

"Courage!" he said. "It may not be so bad, after all. He may just fool about with that little mirror thing of his, and decide that there is nothing that needs to be done."
For the first time she smiled—faintly, but with sufficient breadth to give Mordred another powerful jolt.

—From "The Fiery Wooing of Mordred"
from *Young Men in Spats* by P.G. Wodehouse

2. How is this excerpt organized?
   (1) Description of events in the order that Mordred experienced them
   (2) List of the reasons with examples that Mordred fell in love
   (3) Definition of "Love at first sight" with explanation
   (4) Description of a cause, which leads to a result
   (5) General statement followed by specific details

How Should a Company Protect Its Rights?

Conflict of interest occurs whenever the personal or private business of an employee interferes with the employer's conduct of business, rights of intellectual property, or allocation of resources. Sale of any product or service that competes with the company's products and services is a conflict of interest. Compromising or utilizing intellectual property that is rightfully owned by the company is a conflict of interest. Use of company technology, equipment, client lists, or other resources for personal gain is also a conflict of interest. Employees who have private businesses or also work for other employers are required to complete a conflict-of-interest form to declare any potential conflict.

3. How is this passage organized?
   (1) A process with a sequence of steps
   (2) Cause of conflict of interest followed by effects
   (3) Reasons in order of increasing importance
   (4) Description of a problem and possible solutions
   (5) Definition followed by specific examples

How Do We Mourn a Loved One?

As virtuous men pass mildly away,
 And whisper to their souls, to go,
Whilst some of their sad friends do say,
 "The breath goes now," and some say, "No."

So let us melt, and make no noise,
 No tear-floods, nor sigh-tempests move;
'Twere profanation of our joys
To tell the laity our love,
                    —From "A Valediction: Forbidding
                       Mourning" by John Donne

4. How is this excerpt from the poem organized?
   (1) List of qualities of virtuous men
   (2) List of events in the order they happened
   (3) Description of the mourning process
   (4) Comparing the way virtuous men die and how we should mourn
   (5) A main idea with supporting details

What Are the Woods Like in Winter?

I enjoy a walk in the woods of a bright winter-day, when not a cloud, or the faint shadow of a cloud, obscures the soft azure of the heavens above; when but for the silver covering of the earth I might look upwards to the cloudless sky and say, "It is June, sweet June." The evergreens, as the pines, cedars, hemlock, and balsam firs, are bending their pendent branches, loaded with snow, which the least motion scatters in a mimic shower around, but so light and dry is it that it is shaken off without the slightest inconvenience.

The tops of the stumps look quite pretty, with their turbans of snow; a blackened pine-stump, with its white cap and mantle, will often startle you into the belief that someone is approaching you thus fancifully attired. As to ghosts or spirits they appear totally banished from Canada. This is too matter-of-fact country for such supernaturals to visit.

—From *The Backwoods of Canada* by Catharine Parr Traill (1836)

5. How is this excerpt organized?
   (1) List of events in the order they occurred
   (2) General statement followed by specific examples
   (3) Description of a problem, followed by a solution
   (4) Cause of an event, followed by a description of the outcome
   (5) Opinion with supporting detail in order of increasing importance

ANSWERS

1. **(4)** The passage describes and enumerates the steps to follow: first, second, third, finally.

2. **(1)** The excerpt tells the story of the events in the order they happened.

3. **(5)** The passage begins by stating what conflict of interest is and then gives specific examples.

4. **(4)** The first stanza describes how virtuous men die quietly and friends mark their death with understated sadness. The second goes on to say *So let us* do similarly with our loved ones.

5. **(2)** The writer states that she likes to walk in the woods, and then gives specific examples of the things she sees there.

COORDINATE INFORMATION

One aspect of synthesis is the ability to coordinate information from different parts of the reading passage and put elements together to see a bigger picture. For example, there can be pieces of information in different parts of the passage that have one meaning, but have a larger meaning or implications when taken together.

For example, coordinating information can mean taking clues from different parts of a passage and putting them together to interpret a character. The story "The Fly" by New Zealand writer Katherine Mansfield is about a man known only as "The Boss." At the beginning of the story, he meets with a retired employee and becomes upset when the old man talks about their sons, who had both died in World War I. In the middle of the story, the boss sees a fly on his desk and watches it struggle in a blot of ink. At the end, he cannot remember what he was upset about. In this story, readers must take their observations from all three parts of the story to interpret the character of the Boss.

Basing an interpretation on just one part would not give the whole picture.

Another way you sometimes coordinate information is when there is surprise information at the end of a passage. The new information requires you to look back at what you previously read and see it in a different way.

PRACTICE

Read the excerpt and answer the question that follows to practice coordinating information. (Remember that on the actual GED Language Arts, Reading Test, all questions will be multiple-choice.)

What Is the Identity of the Ghost?

He killed me quite easily by crashing my head on the cobbles. *Bang!* Lord, what a fool I was! All my hate went out with that first bang; a fool to have kicked up that fuss just because I had found him with another woman. And now he was doing this to me—*bang!* That was the second one, and with it *everything* went out.

My sleek young soul must have glistened somewhat in the moonlight: for I saw him look up from the body in a fixed sort of way. That gave me an idea: I would haunt him. All my life I had been scared of ghosts: now I was one myself, I would get a bit of my own back. *He* never was: he said there weren't such things as ghosts. Oh, weren't there! I'd soon teach him. John stood up, still stared in front of him: I could see him plainly: gradually all my hate came back. I thrust my face close up against his: but he didn't seem to see it, he just stared. Then he began to walk forward, as if to walk through me: and I was afeared.

—From "The Ghost" in *A Moment of Time* by Richard Hughes

1. The story is about a murdered young woman who becomes a ghost and haunts the man who killed her. At the end of the story, we learn that she is not dead. In fact, she is the one who killed him. List at least three things in the excerpt that you now see differently.

_____

_____

_____

_____

Synthesis—Combine information from different parts of the passage.

ANSWERS

Your answers may vary, but here are some examples:

- She is not a ghost; he is.
- It says, "I saw him look up from the body," because he is dead on the ground.
- She says she was always afraid of ghosts, and she is "afeared" when he comes towards her because he is a ghost.
- John stood up because he was the one dead on the ground.
- He stares in front of him because he is dead and can't see her.
- He was going to walk through her because he is a ghost.

PRACTICE

Read each passage and respond to the questions to test your synthesis skills.

What Makes a Story Interesting?

A story, then, must not only tell something; it must also be about something. In your individual story Herbert, let us say, is to be shown falling in love with Sylvia and finally winning her. Well, Herberts have fallen in love with Sylvias, have won them and lost them, since time began. Why should a reader be interested this time?...

One of the most frequent of presentations is that of Herbert struggling against obstacles seemingly insuperable. From the time of David and Goliath, and long before, the story of the weak conquering the strong, the strong destroyed by a pebble, has been assured of readers' interest. It has been, because the reader's habit of mind in reading is identical with his habit of mind in daily experience. If he pass a man walking along the sidewalk, one of a thousand on his way home from work, he barely sees him or sees him not at all. If he pass the same man struggling to street level from a suddenly opened crevice, clinging to a window ledge high above the street, he not only sees him, he stops to stare, cannot go on till the crisis has resolved itself—man proved stronger than obstacle, obstacle stronger than man. Those stories in which Herbert is a bank clerk and Sylvia the bank president's daughter, Herbert a divinity student and Sylvia a night club singer, draw their essential interest not from Herbert's love, which is more or less taken for granted, but from the question of whether, through the impulse of that love, he can get free of what impedes him....

But if your story is to hold a reader's interest, there has to be in it an implied generalization as well as a special case. The reader has to see in Herbert's success or failure an exemplification of some part of his own philosophy or to find in Herbert some vague identification with himself or his neighbor. Otherwise this strangely absorbed Herbert is merely dull to read of.

—From "The Substance of the Story" by Edith Ronald Mirrielees (died 1962)

1. What makes the story of a man falling in love about something?
   (1) Romance
   (2) He faces an obstacle
   (3) He is a bank clerk or divinity student
   (4) He wins her and loses her
   (5) It is something special

2. What similarly attracts attention in stories and real life?
   (1) A special case
   (2) A high ledge
   (3) A deep pit
   (4) An impulse of love
   (5) A crisis

3. What is required to hold the reader's interest in the story?
   (1) Identification with the struggle
   (2) Success
   (3) A strange absorption
   (4) Similar philosophy
   (5) Interest in Herbert's love

What Happened to Sam McGee?

There are strange things done in the midnight sun,
  By the men who moil for gold;
The Arctic trails have their secret tales
  That would make your blood run cold;
The Northern Lights have seen queer sights,
  But the queerest they ever did see
Was that night on the marge of Lake Lebarge
  I cremated Sam McGee.

Now Sam McGee was from Tennessee,
where the cotton blooms and blows.
Why he left his home in the South to roam
'round the Pole, God only knows.
He was always cold, but the land of gold
seemed to hold him like a spell;
Though he'd often say in his homely way
  that "he'd sooner live in hell."

On a Christmas Day we were mushing our way
over the Dawson trail.
Talk of your cold! Through the parka's fold
it stabbed like a driven nail.
If our eyes we'd close, then the lashes froze
till sometimes we couldn't see;
It wasn't much fun, but the only one
to whimper was Sam McGee.

And that very night, as we lay packed tight
in our robes beneath the snow,
And the dogs were fed, and the stars o'erhead
were dancing heel and toe,
He turned to me, and "Cap," says he,
"I'll cash in this trip, I guess;
And if I do, I'm asking you that you
won't refuse my last request."

Well, he seemed so low that I couldn't say no;
then he says with a sort of moan:
"It's the cursed cold, and it's got right hold
till I'm chilled clean through to the bone.
Yet 'tain't being dead—it's my awful dread
of the icy grave that pains;
So I want you to swear that, foul or fair,
you'll cremate my last remains."

—Excerpt from "The Cremation of Sam McGee"
by Robert W. Service

4. Why was Sam McGee travelling the Dawson trail?
   (1) Search for cotton
   (2) Because it was Christmas
   (3) Search for gold
   (4) Look for secrets
   (5) See the Northern lights in the Arctic

5. Why was Sam the only one to complain?
   (1) He was not brave
   (2) He was from a warm climate
   (3) He was afraid to die
   (4) It was dark
   (5) The others were from hell

ANSWERS

1. **(2)** The passage states that a story must be about something and goes on to discuss struggling with obstacles.

2. **(5)** According to the excerpt, in real life or in stories we can pass people every day without seeing them unless a crisis attracts our attention, at which point we cannot turn away.

3. **(1)** The struggle is not enough to hold the reader's interest. The passage states that there must be a generalization of some kind that enables readers to identify in some way.

4. **(3)** The excerpt speaks of men who moil, or search, for gold and says the land of gold held him in its spell.

5. **(2)** The excerpt says he was from Tennessee and left his home in the south.

CHALLENGE EXERCISE

Look on the Internet or in your local library for a copy of the short story "The Fly" by Katherine Mansfield. Read the story. Consider the Boss at the beginning of the story, his reaction to the mention of his son, the scene with the fly, and the ending. When you consider all the parts, what is the character of the Boss like? Write a paragraph in which you describe the character of the Boss or discuss it with another person who has read the story. Use examples from different parts of the story to support your opinion.

PERSPECTIVE AND PURPOSE

How something looks depends on where you are standing. For example, imagine looking at the CN Tower in Toronto. Would it look different from the bottom, from the top, from a distance away? In reading, the position from which the author writes can influence the meaning. For example, how would an article about the Halifax theatre district be different from the perspective of a tourist, a local theatre goer, a theatre critic, or a business person?

Perspective is the manner or starting point from which a subject is viewed. Perspective is not bad, but it does influence the meaning. In nonfiction, recognizing the writer's perspective can help us to recognize bias and assumptions, and to understand the author's purpose in writing.

In fiction and other types of literature, perspective also has an influence. For example, consider the narrator in a story. What is the narrator's perspective (the person telling the story)? Is it a first-person narrator, telling his or her own story? Is it a third-person narrator, telling someone else's story? If it is a third-person narrator, what is the relationship to the story? If the narrator is a character in the story, what do you know about the character, and are the narrator's judgments reliable?

PRACTICE

Read each passage and respond to the questions to test your synthesis skills.

What Is Fracking?

Fracking is a process by which previously inaccessible reserves of natural gas can be freed from shale rock beneath the surface. Millions of gallons of water, combined with sand and other additives are forced far underground. The force of the water causes small cracks, or fissures, in the rock, which allows the gas to escape. The cracks are kept open by the sand. The pipes used to drill the well are then surrounded and capped by cement to prevent contaminated water from returning to the surface.

Critics argue that fracking poses environmental risks. However, supporters point out that it provides access to a clean-burning, inexpensive fuel that is abundantly available all across North America. Many of the claims of environmental activists are exaggerated or untrue. Properly regulated, exploitation of natural gas resources provides jobs and is good for the environment.

1. This passage reflects which of the following perspectives?
   (1) Environmentalists
   (2) Ordinary concerned citizens
   (3) Government regulators
   (4) Human rights groups
   (5) Natural gas industry supporters

2. What is the writer's purpose in this passage?
   (1) Give information about fracking
   (2) Raise concerns about fracking
   (3) Argue for legislation about fracking
   (4) Gain support for fracking
   (5) Increase awareness of industry safety practices

TIP

Purpose—
What is the
passage trying
to accomplish?
What is
the writer's
viewpoint on
the topic?

Are There Environmental Concerns?

Fracking is a technique for extracting natural gas from shale rock formations below the earth's surface. The process involves pumping millions of litres of water, mixed with chemicals, into the ground under high pressure, which causes the shale to crack and releases the gas. The unconventional process is now being used in almost every province and territory.

Our group is opposed to fracking. The process consumes large quantities of water that cannot be reclaimed. In addition, it results in high carbon emissions and disruption of wildlife, as well as threatening groundwater and drinking water, which endangers human health and the environment. We call on all provincial governments to put an end to fracking in their jurisdictions.

3. This passage reflects which of the following perspectives?
   (1) Environmentalists
   (2) Most Canadian citizens
   (3) Government regulators
   (4) Human rights groups
   (5) Natural gas industry supporters

4. What is the writer's purpose in this passage?
   (1) Give information about fracking
   (2) Raise concerns about fracking
   (3) Argue for legislation about fracking
   (4) Gain support for fracking
   (5) Increase awareness of industry safety practices

What Was the Woman Like?

There was a woman who was beautiful, who started with all the advantages, yet she had no luck. She married for love, and the love turned to dust. She had bonny children, yet she felt they had been thrust upon her, and she could not love them. They looked at her coldly, as if they were finding fault with her. And hurriedly she felt she must cover up some fault in herself. Yet what it was that she must cover up she never knew. Nevertheless, when her children were present, she always felt the centre of her heart go hard. This troubled her, and in her manner she was all the more gentle and anxious for her children, as if she loved them very much. Only she herself knew that at the centre of her heart was a hard little place that could not feel love, no, not for anybody. Everybody else said of her: "She is such a good mother. She adores her children." Only she herself, and her children themselves, knew it was not so. They read it in each other's eyes.

—From "The Rocking Horse Winner" by D. H. Lawrence

5. What is the perspective of the narrator in this passage?
   (1) Emotionally detached observer
   (2) Character in the story
   (3) Critical commentator
   (4) Enthusiastic proponent
   (5) Personal reflection

6. What is the writer's purpose in this passage?
   (1) Show positive qualities of the character
   (2) Describe the life of the rich
   (3) Create unsympathetic feeling towards the character
   (4) Explain the difficulties of wealth
   (5) Create empathy for the character

ANSWERS

1. **(5)** Coordinating clues from different parts of the passage you can see that it represents an industry perspective. The passage explains fracking in a positive manner, dismisses conflicting concerns, and provides arguments for why it is beneficial.

2. **(4)** The purpose of the passage is clearly to gain support for fracking.

3. **(1)** The passage contains information and perspectives that would be known only by those with environmental knowledge.

4. **(2)** The passage presents information in a manner that raises concerns. It also calls for a ban on fracking.

5. **(1)** The third-person narrator describes the woman in a factual manner, without judgment.

6. **(3)** The casual description of the unfeeling woman creates an unsympathetic feeling for the reader.

COMPARE AND CONTRAST

TIP

Compare—
Show how two
things are the
same.

Contrast—
Show how
two things are
different.

As part of your synthesis reading skills, you should be able to compare and contrast elements within the passage. For example, how does the author's treatment of one topic compare with the treatment of another? What are the differences? In addition, you should be able to recognize and comprehend comparisons and contrasts that the author makes in the passage.

PRACTICE

Read each passage and respond to the questions to test your synthesis skills.

Which Is More Beautiful?

Shall I compare thee to a summer's day?
Thou art more lovely and more temperate;
Rough winds do shake the darling buds of May,
And summer's lease hath all too short a date;
Sometime too hot the eye of heaven shines,
And often is his gold complexion dimm'd;
And every fair from fair sometime declines,
By chance or nature's changing course untrimm'd;
But thy eternal summer shall not fade,
Nor lose possession of that fair thou ow'st;
Nor shall Death brag thou wander'st in his shade,
When in eternal lines to time thou grow'st:
So long as men can breathe or eyes can see,
So long lives this, and this gives life to thee.

—*Sonnet 18* by William Shakespeare

1. In this poem, Shakespeare describes a beautiful young friend by speaking of a summer day. The poem primarily focuses on:
   (1) Similarities
   (2) Differences
   (3) Similarities and differences
   (4) Best qualities
   (5) Weather

2. According to the poem, the primary contrast between the young friend and a summer day is:
   (1) He will not change
   (2) Nature is more lovely
   (3) Summer is too short
   (4) Heaven shines on them both
   (5) Both are very pleasant

What Is it Like To Write?

They thought that writing was always wonderful, but most of the time it was the loneliest job in the world. That crippling stillness when you sat down to try the first few lines. As if everything you looked at was tensed for you to make a sound and you were tongue-tied, like someone in a nightmare. If that lasted long enough you would sit there then and hear the sound of your own life going by. A lifetime is not forever, and yours was already half gone. You would think of all the other times you'd sat here alone, while the rest were building something tangible. Together. Really together with the real thing, not this shadow of it. The laughing and the touching and the joining with the same thoughts.... It wasn't wonderful then....

But it could be wonderful. Like now. The day when there would be a single thing to fasten on. A thing that had been cloudy and coreless inside you, like an ache; but you hadn't given up, and now you read the words, there it was, almost exactly in the shape you could see it must have, and outside you.

3. Based on the excerpt, what is the most important difference between building something physical and writing that is not going well?
   (1) Inspiration
   (2) Stillness
   (3) Relaxation
   (4) Companionship
   (5) Time

4. What makes the difference when writing goes well and when it doesn't?
   (1) Cloudiness
   (2) Being tongue tied
   (3) Focus
   (4) Loneliness
   (5) Nightmare

5. Based on this excerpt what comparison can be made between writing and making something physical? They both involve
   (1) Loneliness
   (2) Togetherness
   (3) Building
   (4) Standards
   (5) Wonder

ANSWERS

1. **(2)** The poem contrasts the friend and a summer's day, showing the differences.

2. **(1)** The biggest difference between the summer's day and the young friend is that the friend's beauty will remain unchanged because he has been made immortal in this poem.

3. **(4)** The excerpt describes the loneliness of writing, which seems like wasting life when it is not going well, compared with the togetherness and camaraderie of those who build physical things.

4. **(3)** Two possible answers are 3 and 4, but it never implies that writing is not lonely when it goes well. It does have focus, a single thing to fasten on, that makes words take shape.

5. **(3)** The similarity is that they both involve building although one builds tangible things and the other shadows.

INTEGRATE INFORMATION

When reading, one thing we try to avoid is the *intentional fallacy*. That is, we try to keep the writer and the work separate. We cannot try to deduce what the writer intended to say or make conclusions about the writer. For example, if we know a writer grew up poor, it does not mean the writer necessarily intends to comment on poverty in a work. In a story about a teenager who has a difficult relationship with her mother, we cannot conclude that the writer had a difficult relationship with her mother. The writer and the work are separate. Our interpretations should be based on, and limited to, the work.

At the same time, authors are influenced by the world around them. Knowing about the writer and his or her work can give us perspective on what we read if we are careful not to make the intentional fallacy. For example, Canadian writer Mordecai Richler grew up on St. Urbain Street in a predominately Jewish area of Montreal in the 1930s and 1940s. His novels and stories are all set in this area. Having an understanding of the buildings and culture in this area and what it was like to grow up there can help us gain a better understanding of the stories.

On the GED Reading Test, questions about integration will give additional information about the author or the author's work. You will then integrate this information with what you read in the text to gain a better understanding.

PRACTICE

Read each passage and respond to the questions to test your synthesis skills.

How Does the Sled Dog Learn His Job?

Dave was wheeler or sled dog, pulling in front of him was Buck, then came Sol-leks; the rest of the team was strung out ahead, single file, to the leader, which position was filled by Spitz.

Buck had been purposely placed between Dave and Sol-leks so that he might receive instruction. Apt scholar that he was, they were equally apt teachers, never allowing him to linger long in error, and enforcing their teaching with their sharp teeth. Dave was fair and very wise. He never nipped Buck without cause, and he never failed to nip him when he stood in need of it. As Francois' whip backed him up, Buck found it to be cheaper to mend his ways than to retaliate. Once, during a brief halt, when he got tangled in the traces and delayed the start, both Dave and Sol-leks flew at him and administered a sound trouncing. The resulting tangle was even worse, but Buck took good care to keep the traces clear thereafter; and ere the day was done, so well had he mastered his work, his mates about ceased nagging him. Francois' whip snapped less frequently, and Perrault even honored Buck by lifting up his feet and carefully examining them.

—From *Call of the Wild* by Jack London

1. This excerpt tells of a house dog, Buck, who finds himself in the Arctic as part of a sled team. Many critics say that Buck represents the struggle of everyday working people. If this is true, what does Dave represent?
   (1) A bully
   (2) An employer
   (3) A defensive person protecting his territory
   (4) A competing co-worker
   (5) An experienced older worker

2. If Buck's struggle is symbolic, what lesson from this excerpt can working people apply to their own struggle?
   (1) Adapt and learn
   (2) Be careful of people you work with
   (3) Hard work is not rewarded
   (4) Employers should treat workers more kindly
   (5) Do not worry about mistakes

3. The author of this excerpt, Jack London, spent a lot of time in the North. Based on this excerpt, how might we conclude the writer views the North?
   (1) Relaxing
   (2) Pleasant
   (3) Harsh
   (4) Frightening
   (5) Sorrowful

What Is the Poet's Lament?

So we'll go no more a-roving
  So late into the night,
Though the heart be still as loving,
  And the moon be still as bright.

For the sword outwears its sheath,
  And the soul wears out the breast,
And the heart must pause to breathe,
  And Love itself have rest.

Though the night was made for loving,
  And the day returns too soon,
Yet we'll go no more a-roving
  By the light of the moon.
                —"So we'll go no more a-roving"
                          by Lord Byron

4. The Romantic period poet George Gordon Lord Byron was a well-known adventurer and womanizer, who had many romantic affairs. Based on this information, you can conclude that this poem is about
   (1) Death
   (2) Being tired of romance
   (3) Giving up war-like adventures
   (4) Resolving not to travel
   (5) The shortness of life

ANSWERS

1. **(5)** Dave is like an experienced older worker who is stern, but fair and wise in helping Buck learn his role.

2. **(1)** Buck finds himself in a difficult situation, but works hard to adapt and learn, earning the respect of the other dogs (co-workers) and masters.

3. **(3)** The author presents the environment as harsh, but not frightening or sorrowful.

4. **(2)** This says that although the lovers' moon is still as bright, love must have a rest, and he will go no more a-roving.

CHAPTER CHECK-UP

Complete these practice exercises, and check the answers and analysis that follow. After you mark your work, review any topic in the chapter that you had trouble with or did not understand.

Questions 1–3 are based on the following excerpt.

Why Were They in the Boat?

Many a man ought to have a bath-tub larger than the boat which here rode upon the sea. These waves were most wrongfully and barbarously abrupt and tall, and each froth-top was a problem in small boat navigation.

The cook squatted in the bottom and looked with both eyes at the six inches of gunwale which separated him from the ocean. His sleeves were rolled over his fat forearms, and the two flaps of his unbuttoned vest, dangled as he bent to bail out the boat....

The oiler, steering with one of the two oars in the boat, sometimes raised himself suddenly to keep clear of water that swirled in over the stern. It was a thin little oar and it seemed often ready to snap.

The correspondent, pulling at the other oar, watched the waves and wondered why he was there.

The injured captain, lying in the bow, was at this time buried in that profound dejection and indifference which comes, temporarily at least, to even the bravest and most enduring when, willy nilly, the firm fails, the army loses, the ship goes down.

—From "The Open Boat" by Stephen Crane

1. How is this passage organized?
   (1) Thesis followed by supporting ideas in increasing performance
   (2) Description of boat passengers individually
   (3) Events in chronological order
   (4) A process with a sequence of steps
   (5) Topic statements with supporting sentences

2. What is the situation described in this excerpt?
   (1) Fishermen lost at sea in an open boat
   (2) A group of men share life experiences
   (3) Men on an ocean adventure
   (4) Crewmembers help an injured captain
   (5) Men in a lifeboat after their ship sank

3. What is the point of view of the narrator in this passage?
   (1) A character telling a personal story as it happens
   (2) A character telling a story of his past
   (3) A detached observer telling the story of others
   (4) A character telling the story of loved ones
   (5) A critic giving an editorial

Questions 4–7 are based on the following sonnet.

What Does He Fear?

When I have fears that I may cease to be
  Before my pen has glean'd my teeming brain,
Before high-piled books, in charact'ry,
  Hold like rich garners the full ripen'd grain;
When I behold, upon the night's starr'd face,
  Huge cloudy symbols of a high romance,
And think that I may never live to trace
  Their shadows, with the magic hand of chance;
And when I feel, fair creature of an hour,
  That I shall never look upon thee more,
Never have relish in the faery power
  Of unreflecting love;—then on the shore
Of the wide world I stand alone, and think
Till love and fame to nothingness do sink.

by John Keats

4. What is the perspective of the speaker in this poem?
   (1) Observer of relationships among others
   (2) Person commenting on personal friendships
   (3) Lover reflecting on love
   (4) Commentator on social issues
   (5) Person reflecting on own life

5. What quality do chance and love share in the poem?
   (1) Power
   (2) Magic
   (3) Fantasy
   (4) Emptiness
   (5) Beauty

6. The writer of this poem, John Keats, had tuberculosis, which eventually killed him. Based on this information, what might we conclude he is afraid of?
   (1) Dying unfulfilled
   (2) Falling in love
   (3) The pain of death
   (4) Mystery of the afterlife
   (5) Leaving loved ones behind

7. Based on information in other parts of the poem, why does the poem state that *love and fame to nothingness do sink*?
   (1) They are unimportant
   (2) They do not last
   (3) They are not real
   (4) They are magic
   (5) They are only for others

Questions 8–10 are based on the following extract from an employee manual.

What Does Professionalism Mean?

As dedicated employees of the company we hold ourselves at all times to the highest standards of professionalism. We are punctual and dress appropriately. We treat one another with respect and maintain a positive work environment.

Punctuality is an essential part of professionalism. We arrive for work in advance of our shift to review care plans and patient notes with departing staff. We take breaks at designated times as much as possible and return in a timely manner so that co-workers can take their breaks in turn. At the end of the shift, we communicate needed information to incoming staff before going home.

Appropriate dress is another component of professionalism. Our clothing is clean and allows freedom of movement. Our footwear is closed-toe with treads for good traction.

Maintaining a respectful workplace is essential to professionalism. We refrain from profanity and abusive or harassing communication when communicating with patients, families, and members of the care team. We always respect the feelings of others.

8. How is this passage organized?
   (1) Arguments in reverse order of importance
   (2) Events in chronological order
   (3) Topic sentences supported by explanation and details
   (4) Contrast descriptions of professionalism
   (5) Description of steps in a procedure

9. Based on the information in this passage, the employee manual is for what type of workplace?
   (1) Manufacturing company
   (2) Construction company
   (3) Retail store
   (4) Healthcare facility
   (5) Not enough information

10. The passage is written as if it is from the point of view of
    (1) Employees
    (2) Managers
    (3) Human resources
    (4) Customers
    (5) Government regulators

ANSWERS

1. **(2)** The passage names and describes each of the boat passengers in order.

2. **(5)** Combine clues from the passage. They are in a bath-tub sized boat. The cook is bailing. The correspondent wonders why he is there. Willy-nilly, the ship goes down.

3. **(3)** The passage has a third-person narrator, who dispassionately relates the story of others.

4. **(5)** The poem is written in the first person. The narrator is speaking of his own life.

5. **(2)** The poem speaks of the magic of chance and the faery power of love.

6. **(1)** The poet sometimes fears that he will die before he has written all the things in his brain, traced the shadows of romance, or experienced true love.

7. **(2)** Love and fame sink to nothingness if death comes before he has written or experienced true love.

8. **(3)** Each sentence begins with a topic sentence and is followed by explanation and details.

9. **(4)** Clues throughout the passage refer to care plans, patients, and care teams.

10. **(1)** The passage refers to employees as *we*.

Language Arts, Reading—Practice Test

Directions: The Language Arts, Reading Test **includes 40 multiple-choice questions. Do not spend more than 65 minutes on the test.**

The practice test includes multiple-choice questions based on reading passages that are excerpts from fiction, non-fiction, poems, and plays. Literature passages are drawn from significant works of world literature from pre-1920, 1920–1960, and post-1960. Non-fiction passages include articles about literature and the arts and at least one business document. Each reading section is preceded by a purpose question to help you focus your reading.

The Language Arts, Reading Test does not require specific knowledge of authors or literature. The questions test your ability to read and interpret information, including skills in comprehension, application, analysis, and synthesis.

Record your responses on the answer sheet that follows. For each question, mark the numbered space that corresponds with your answer choice.

EXAMPLE

Should We Be More Like a Stone?
How happy is the little Stone
That rambles in the Road alone,
And doesn't care about Careers
And Exigencies never fears.

by Emily Dickinson

Based on this excerpt from a poem, why is the stone happy?
(1) It is on the road
(2) It has places to go
(3) It has no worries
(4) It has no direction
(5) It is small

In this example, you need to apply reading comprehension skills to recognize that the stone has no worries about careers or exigencies. Fill in answer space 3 on the answer sheet.

ANSWER SHEET
Language Arts, Reading
Practice Test

1. ① ② ③ ④ ⑤
2. ① ② ③ ④ ⑤
3. ① ② ③ ④ ⑤
4. ① ② ③ ④ ⑤
5. ① ② ③ ④ ⑤
6. ① ② ③ ④ ⑤
7. ① ② ③ ④ ⑤
8. ① ② ③ ④ ⑤
9. ① ② ③ ④ ⑤
10. ① ② ③ ④ ⑤
11. ① ② ③ ④ ⑤
12. ① ② ③ ④ ⑤
13. ① ② ③ ④ ⑤
14. ① ② ③ ④ ⑤
15. ① ② ③ ④ ⑤

16. ① ② ③ ④ ⑤
17. ① ② ③ ④ ⑤
18. ① ② ③ ④ ⑤
19. ① ② ③ ④ ⑤
20. ① ② ③ ④ ⑤
21. ① ② ③ ④ ⑤
22. ① ② ③ ④ ⑤
23. ① ② ③ ④ ⑤
24. ① ② ③ ④ ⑤
25. ① ② ③ ④ ⑤
26. ① ② ③ ④ ⑤
27. ① ② ③ ④ ⑤
28. ① ② ③ ④ ⑤
29. ① ② ③ ④ ⑤
30. ① ② ③ ④ ⑤

31. ① ② ③ ④ ⑤
32. ① ② ③ ④ ⑤
33. ① ② ③ ④ ⑤
34. ① ② ③ ④ ⑤
35. ① ② ③ ④ ⑤
36. ① ② ③ ④ ⑤
37. ① ② ③ ④ ⑤
38. ① ② ③ ④ ⑤
39. ① ② ③ ④ ⑤
40. ① ② ③ ④ ⑤

LANGUAGE ARTS, READING

> **Directions:** Complete the practice test, and then check the answers and analysis that follow. After you mark your work, review any topics you had trouble with or did not understand.

Questions 1–5 are based on the following commentary.

Is the Character Believable?

The Stone Angel by Margaret Laurence is not a novel for the faint of heart nor is it one that will leave you feeling comfortably satisfied. In fact, it's profoundly disturbing but not in any overt way. As in life, it's the subtleties of each action or inaction that creates the final picture. Such is the case with Hagar Shipley, an elderly woman at the end of her life who, when looking back over more than ninety years, finds no joy. She is not sure if she has ever experienced love.

The Stone Angel is part of the reading curriculum in many high schools at the grade twelve level. Perhaps by reading it early in life, it can serve as a cautionary tale.

Laurence does not relent. The character's conviction carries Hagar from her rather forbidding Scottish father's home to a less than reasonable marriage where she repeats mistakes and favours one son over another. She has shared nothing of herself with anyone in her life, including her children. Her rigid sense of morality and what constitutes acceptable behaviour results in outward appearances that are at odds with the twisted and withered state of the soul and its ability to feel and to give. Add to this, Laurence's uncanny ability to cut to the heart of the matter with grace and grit and you have a novel that can't be ignored.

Don't expect a formula story wrapped up tidily at the end in ribbons of moral correctness. Nor will there be any predictable radiant outcomes involving forgiveness and group hugs. Instead, Laurence paints a vivid picture of characters true to their time and their convictions.

1. Based on the information in this commentary, how does the writer interpret the character of Hagar?
   - (1) Realistic
   - (2) Likeable
   - (3) Committed
   - (4) Kind
   - (5) Angry

2. What does the writer suggest might be a reason that readers might find the book disturbing?
   - (1) Writing style
   - (2) Character
   - (3) Old age
   - (4) Suffering
   - (5) Morality

3. Based on information in this commentary, the plot of *The Stone Angel* is about a(n)
   (1) Writer imagining old age
   (2) Relationship between mother and children
   (3) Actor
   (4) Old woman's life story
   (5) Heroic escape

4. Based on information in this commentary, a technique writers should apply to create realistic characters is to give them
   (1) A life of secrets
   (2) Memories
   (3) Positive and negative qualities
   (4) Strength and pride
   (5) Hardship

5. Which of the following best summarizes the commentator's opinion of *The Stone Angel*?
   (1) It was written by Margaret Lawrence.
   (2) It is required school reading.
   (3) The main character is elderly.
   (4) The main character is of Scottish origin.
   (5) It is a good book.

Questions 6–11 refer to the following excerpt from a play.

What Is So Important About Hockey?

The MOTHER of the FARMER'S SON enters. She is and is not the same woman that we saw on the Plains of Abraham. She addresses her SON.

MOTHER: So, this is it? The place you can't stay away from? So, you're never at home, you're never in school, you're never at church.

FARMER'S SON: Hi, M'man.

MOTHER: Alright, explain to me. What happens here? That's more important than helping your people, or your family, or yourself even? What is this place?

FARMER'S SON: It's a hockey rink.

MOTHER: Yes, I can see. Ice. And what happens here?

FARMER'S SON: Well, the people come. When they have the time. They get on the ice. There's the puck. The goals. They go from one end to the other. The idea is to get the puck in the goal.

He starts to demonstrate, in his own style, to the discomfiture of the stiff Anglo players of the REGIMENT.

But you can pass it, you see. Or, if the other side thinks you're going one way, you can go the other. Zip, zip, zip. Or flip it up over their sticks.

MOTHER: Games. That's right, isn't it? They play games!

FARMER'S SON: Yeah, it's a game.

MOTHER: I want to know, so what? So what, they play a game? So what?

FARMER'S SON: I dunno.

MOTHER: Is it important? Am I missing something? Is there something else here?

FARMER'S SON: I guess not.

MOTHER: You got no pride? You know what they're doing to our people in the West? You care? What's this got to do with us? Show me...so I'll understand...why a Canayen...a young, strong Canayen...in times like this...slides on ice! Come. Explain it to me. When you can.

She exits.

MACDONALD has been weighing things while observing this confrontation.

MACDONALD: Oh, it'll tear the country apart. So be it. It's the only way to keep us together. Riel must swing!

—Rick Salutin and Ken Dryden, *Les Canadiens*

6. You can deduce from the stage directions and the dialogue that this play is about
   (1) the Montreal Canadiens
   (2) the lack of respect of young people
   (3) a generation gap
   (4) French—English relations
   (5) hockey strategies

7. The Mother implies that
   (1) hockey is not important
   (2) her son is lazy
   (3) people do not understand hockey
   (4) games build good relationships
   (5) Anglo players are better

8. The word *Canayen* in this passage probably means
   (1) player
   (2) son
   (3) traitor
   (4) man
   (5) Canadian

9. MacDonald is probably a
   (1) hockey player
   (2) father
   (3) politician
   (4) referee
   (5) military officer

10. Based on this excerpt, the son is interested in hockey because
    (1) he has no pride
    (2) he does not care for his people
    (3) it is an escape
    (4) it annoys the English
    (5) it unifies the country

11. The play was written in 1977, one year after the *Parti Quebecois* (which wanted Quebec to separate from Canada) was elected to government. Based on this information, mother and son probably represent.
    (1) Ordinary Francophones
    (2) Aspiring athletes
    (3) English residents
    (4) Revolutionary separatists
    (5) Political commentators

Questions 12–18 refer to the following excerpt from a passage.

When my father removed all his clothes and leapt from the train, rushing into the Kadugannawa tunnel, the Navy finally refused to follow and my mother was sent for. He stayed in the darkness of that three-quarter-mile-long tunnel for three hours stopping rail traffic going both ways. My mother, clutching a suit of civilian clothing (the Army would not allow her to advertise his military connections), walked into that darkness, finding him and talking with him for over an hour and a half. A moment only Conrad could have interpreted. She went in there alone, his clothes in one arm—but no shoes, an oversight he later complained of—and a railway lantern that he shattered as soon as she reached him. They had been married for six years.

They survived that darkness. And my mother, the lover of Tennyson and early Yeats, began to realize that she had caught onto a different breed of dog. She was to become tough and valiant in a very different world from then on, determined, when they divorced, never to ask him for money, and to raise us all on her own earnings. They were both from gracious, genteel families, but my father went down a path unknown to his parents and wife. She followed him and coped with him for fourteen years, surrounding his behaviour like a tough and demure breeze. Talking him out of suicide in a three-quarter-mile-long tunnel, for god's sake! She walked in armed with clothes she had borrowed from another passenger, and a light, and her knowledgeable love of all the beautiful formal poetry that existed up to the 1930s, to meet her naked husband in the darkness, in the black slow breeze of the Kadugannawa tunnel, unable to find him until he rushed at her, grabbed that lantern and dashed it against the wall before he realized who it was, who had come for him.

"It's me!"

Then a pause. And, "How dare you follow me!"

"I followed you because no one else would follow you."

—From "Travels in Ceylon" by Michael Ondaatje

12. The best title for this selection is
    (1) "Tunnel of Fear"
    (2) "A Suit of Clothing"
    (3) "A Different World"
    (4) "Surviving the Darkness"
    (5) "The Shattered Lantern"

13. How long were the mother and father married?
    (1) three years
    (2) six years
    (3) fourteen years
    (4) twenty-four years
    (5) unknown

14. All of the following words could be used to describe the mother EXCEPT
    (1) determined
    (2) brave
    (3) hopeful
    (4) educated
    (5) strong

15. The mood of this passage could be described as
    (1) sad
    (2) angry
    (3) light
    (4) mournful
    (5) disapproving

16. In this passage, darkness represents
    (1) the tunnel
    (2) the relationship with the father
    (3) suicide
    (4) the parents' divorce
    (5) loneliness

17. This passage is written from the point of view of
    (1) A child telling his story
    (2) A third-person narrator
    (3) An adult reflecting on his past
    (4) A commentator on family relationships
    (5) A historian

18. The author of this excerpt was born in Ceylon, where the story is set. Based on this information, you might conclude that the author
    (1) was distant from his father
    (2) misses his homeland
    (3) dislikes tunnels
    (4) will bring his mother to Canada
    (5) is lonely

Questions 19–22 refer to the following excerpt from a business document.

The Government of Canada advises all Canadian citizens to carry a valid passport for every trip abroad, including to the United States. A passport is the only universally accepted secure document. It proves your identity and citizenship when travelling, and it shows that you have the right to re-enter Canada when you return.

Like a passport, a NEXUS card can also be used to establish identity and citizenship when travelling to the United States by land or water. The NEXUS card can also be used at self-serve, pre-clearance kiosks at designated airports when you fly to the United States. However, air travellers must still carry a passport and be able to present it when entering the U.S. or re-entering Canada.

Under U.S. Legislation called The Western Hemisphere Travel Initiative (WHTI), other types of approved secure documents can be used to enter the United States from within the western hemisphere. When entering by land or water, such documents include a Free and Secure Trade (FAST) card, an enhanced driver's licence, or a Secure Certificate of Indian Status (not yet available). However, the passport remains the best form of identification.

19. How is this passage organized?
    (1) Details followed by summarizing sentences
    (2) Reasons for passports with explanations
    (3) Identification described by decreasing importance
    (4) Chronological description of personal experience
    (5) Problem followed by a solution

20. Based on the information in this passage, what comparison can be made between a NEXUS card and passport? Both can be used
    (1) As universally accepted identification
    (2) To re-enter Canada by air
    (3) To enter the U.S. by land and water
    (4) To enter Europe by sea
    (5) To apply for Indian Status

21. Based on the information in this passage, an enhanced driver's license is an example of
    (1) A passport
    (2) A Free Trade Card
    (3) An approved secure document
    (4) A universally accepted proof of citizenship
    (5) A type of NEXUS card

22. Based on information in this passage, if you were to return to Canada on a flight from the United States without a passport, you could be
    (1) Asked for a NEXUS Card
    (2) Denied re-entry
    (3) Searched by customs
    (4) Asked for a driver's license
    (5) Required to show a birth certificate

Questions 23–27 are based on the following poem.

How Does Nature Affect Him?

A Summer Evening

The clouds grow clear, the pine-wood glooms and stills
With brown reflections in the silent bay,
And far beyond the pale blue-misted hills
The rose and purple evening dreams away.
The thrush, the veery, from mysterious dales
Rings his last round; and outward like a sea
The shining, shadowy heart of heaven unveils
The starry legend of eternity,
The day's long troubles lose their sting and pass,
Peaceful the world, and peaceful grows my heart.
The gossip cricket from the friendly grass
Talks of old joys and takes the dreamer's part.
Then night, the healer, with unnoticed breath,
And sleep, dark sleep, so near, so like death.

—Archibald Lampman

23. The main purpose of the poem is to
    (1) Represent the purity of nature
    (2) Tell of the troubles of today
    (3) Express the poet's depression
    (4) Describe a summer evening
    (5) Represent the peacefulness of death

24. The mood of the poem could best be described as
    (1) Peaceful
    (2) Sad
    (3) Mysterious
    (4) Dark
    (5) Uplifting

25. Shakespearean-style sonnets, such as this, are organized in three groups of four lines, followed by a closing couplet. Based on this information, you see the ideas in the poem are described in this order:
    (1) Birds, heaven, clouds, death
    (2) Water, birds, eternity, joy
    (3) Hill, reflections, legends, grass
    (4) Sunset, stars, dreams, sleep
    (5) Clouds, dreams, shadows, healing

26. Based on this poem, a good way to relax from the cares of the day is to
    (1) Plant a garden
    (2) Walk in the woods
    (3) Read a book
    (4) Listen to music
    (5) Watch a sunset

27. What does the poet mean by the line, *The shining, shadowy heart of heaven unveils \ the starry legend of eternity* (lines 7–8)?
    (1) There are stories told of heaven
    (2) The stars come out
    (3) He wishes he could live for eternity
    (4) Death is approaching
    (5) Nature is timeless

Questions 28–32 are based on the following extract from an essay.

It would be easier to talk sensibly about literature in a new country like Canada if more people understood that literature, unlike science, is an activity neither importable nor exportable. It must grow out of society itself. In reproof to Canadian writers it is constantly said that our literature has lagged behind our science, and though in a sense this statement is true, it has no significant implications whatever.

Certainly Canadian science compares favourably with the science of all but a very few countries in the world. Osler is generally regarded as the founder of modern medical practice. The work of Banting, Best, and Penfield has been seminal, and our nuclear physicists were able to play a part in the Manhattan Project. Marquis wheat was a Canadian development, and in every major university in the country there is at least one scientist internationally known.

But it confuses our picture of reality if we infer from this that the development of scientific techniques is any real indication of the collective spiritual growth of the Canadian people, or for that matter of any other people on earth. Osler learned his basic medical techniques in Germany, he developed them in Montreal, and later he took them with him to Baltimore and Oxford. His Canadian birth was quite incidental to his career, which would have been the same no matter where he had been born....

But literature is not an international activity in any sense, and though new visions and new techniques can flow across international borders, the substance of any living literature must come out of the society to which the writer belongs.

28. Based on the information in this passage, you can conclude that Canada is well known internationally for its achievement in
    (1) Science
    (2) Literature
    (3) Both science and literature
    (4) Neither science nor literature
    (5) Spiritual growth

29. According to this passage, the primary difference between Canada's scientific and literary development is that
    (1) Literature is not important
    (2) Science is not important
    (3) Science is not based on Canadian culture
    (4) Literature is international
    (5) Scientists were not born in Canada

30. Based on the information in this passage, Osler was probably a
    (1) Canadian doctor
    (2) Canadian writer
    (3) Immigrant to Canada
    (4) English politician
    (5) German developer

31. Based on the information in this passage, the work of an aspiring Canadian writer should reflect
    (1) Modern American themes
    (2) International influences
    (3) Canadian society
    (4) Individual values
    (5) New visions

32. The references to Osler, Banting, and Best—nuclear physicists—and Marquis wheat are details supporting the main idea that
    (1) Canadian universities have at least one famous scientist
    (2) Canadian science compares favourably with other countries
    (3) Science is not an international activity
    (4) International techniques influence scientific developments
    (5) Reality can be confusing

Questions 33–36 are based on the following poem.

Whose woods these are I think I know
His house is in the village, though;
He will not see me stopping here
To watch his woods fill up with snow.

My little horse must think it queer
To stop without a farmhouse near
Between the woods and frozen lake
The darkest evening of the year.

He gives his harness bells a shake
To ask if there is some mistake.
The only other sound's the sweep
Of easy wind and downy flake.

The woods are lovely, dark and deep.
But I have promises to keep,
And miles to go before I sleep,
And miles to go before I sleep.
                    —"Stopping by Woods on a Snowy Evening"
                                        by Robert Frost

33. This poem is primarily about
     (1) A horseman lost at night
     (2) The journey through life to death
     (3) The cold of winter
     (4) Longing for rest
     (5) A traveller who pauses at night

34. The tone of the writing could best be described as
     (1) Sarcastic
     (2) Matter-of-fact
     (3) Ornate
     (4) Elaborate
     (5) Suspenseful

35. The organization of this poem is based on a description of
     (1) The narrator's reflections in chronological order
     (2) A sequence of events in chronological order
     (3) Images of nature
     (4) The narrator's worries in order of increasing importance
     (5) The narrator's obligations in order of importance

36. Following the example of this poem, what lesson can you learn about coping with demanding schedules and responsibilities?
    (1) There is no time to delay
    (2) You must reluctantly continue on
    (3) Take time to appreciate small beauties
    (4) Nature is beautiful at night
    (5) Always respect private property

Questions 37–40 are based on the following extract.

No matter the time of life or the continent, the pungent, liberating smell of mint tea has always brought me back to my childhood in Bayo. From the hands of traders who walked for many moons with bundles on their heads, magical things appeared in our village just as often as people vanished. Entire villages and towns were walled, and sentries were posted with poison-tipped spears to prevent the theft of men, but when trusted traders arrived, villagers of all ages came to admire the goods.

Papa was a jeweller, and one day, he gave up a gold necklace for a metal teapot with bulging sides and a long, narrow, curving spout. The trader said that the teapot had crossed the desert and would bring luck and longevity to any who drank from it.

In the middle of the night, Papa stroked my shoulder while I lay in bed. He believed that a sleeping person has a vulnerable soul and deserves to be woken gently.

"Come have tea with your mama and me," Papa said.

I scrambled out of bed, ran outside and climbed into my mother's lap. Everybody else in the village was sleeping. The cocks were silent. The stars blinked like the eyes of a whole town of nervous men who knew of a terrible secret.

—From *The Book of Negroes* by Lawrence Hill,
Harper Collins, Canada, 2007.

37. Based on the information in this extract, where does the story take place?
    (1) England
    (2) France
    (3) Canada
    (4) Africa
    (5) Arctic

38. Which of the following terms could characterize the relationship between the child and her parents in this passage?
    (1) Fearful
    (2) Distant
    (3) Formal
    (4) Friendly
    (5) Intimate

39. Based on the information in this passage, how is a strange visitor likely to be greeted at the village?
    (1) Joyfully
    (2) Suspiciously
    (3) Violently
    (4) With gifts
    (5) Ceremonially

40. The narrator in the extract is an old black woman who has lived a life of slavery. Based on this information, why is the smell of mint tea important?
    (1) Hope for the future
    (2) Inspires magic
    (3) Indicates trust
    (4) Reminder of freedom
    (5) Reminder of the desert

ANSWERS

1	**(1)**	11	**(1)**	21	**(3)**	31	**(3)**
2	**(2)**	12	**(4)**	22	**(2)**	32	**(2)**
3	**(4)**	13	**(3)**	23	**(4)**	33	**(5)**
4	**(3)**	14	**(3)**	24	**(1)**	34	**(2)**
5	**(5)**	15	**(1)**	25	**(4)**	35	**(1)**
6	**(4)**	16	**(5)**	26	**(5)**	36	**(3)**
7	**(1)**	17	**(3)**	27	**(2)**	37	**(4)**
8	**(5)**	18	**(1)**	28	**(1)**	38	**(5)**
9	**(3)**	19	**(3)**	29	**(3)**	39	**(2)**
10	**(3)**	20	**(3)**	30	**(1)**	40	**(4)**

Interpret Your Results

Test Area	Questions	Recommended Minimum Score	Your Score
Comprehension 8	2, 3, 8, 12, 13, 23, 30, 33,	6	
Application 6	4, 22, 26, 31, 36, 39	4	
Analysis 12–14	5, 7, 9, 14, 15, 21, 24, 27, 28, 32, 34, 38	9	
Synthesis 12–14	1, 6, 10, 11, 16, 17, 18, 19, 20, 25, 29, 35, 37, 40	10	
Total		29	

Check your answers and calculate how you scored in each test area. If you scored less than the recommended minimum score in any test area, you should review topics in the relevant chapters.

ANSWER ANALYSIS

1. **(1)** She has both positive and negative qualities that give her the authenticity of life.

2. **(2)** The writer suggests that subtleties in the book may make readers uncomfortable, such as the character's lack of joy and love, treatment of her sons, and rigid sense of morality.

3. **(4)** According to the passage, the novel is about an old woman reliving memories of her life.

4. **(3)** According to the passage, Laurence draws a character who is true to her convictions, both good and bad.

5. **(5)** This is the only option that is an opinion.

6. **(4)** Much about the different levels of meaning in the play can be interpreted from the stage directions. The references to the Plains of Abraham, the Anglo regiment, and Louis Riel indicate that the play deals with French-English relations.

7. **(1)** The mother implies that hockey is not important. She refers to it as a game and then asks if her son has no pride and if he cares about his people.

8. **(5)** In this passage, *Canayen* is a mispronunciation of "Canadian."

9. **(3)** Sir John A. MacDonald was Canada's first prime minister. You can tell that he is a politician because of his concern that the country will be torn apart.

10. **(3)** You can see from the passage that the other answers are not correct. The son excels at hockey to the discomfiture of the Anglo players. It is a game he is good at, an escape from school, church, and the treatment of his people in the west and elsewhere.

11. **(1)** The characters may represent the concerns of ordinary Francophones and their sense of isolation.

12. **(4)** Surviving the darkness is a central theme of this passage. There is the darkness of the tunnel, the darkness of the father's depression, the darkness into which the mother enters in her encounter with the father, the darkness into which she descends from her love of poetry to cope with him, and the darkness of raising her family alone.

13. **(3)** She coped with him for a total of fourteen years.

14. **(3)** Despite her determination, bravery, and love of poetry, the mother never appears hopeful. She enters the tunnel out of duty, not hope.

15. **(1)** Although the narrator might have every reason to be angry, the mood here is more sad as he describes the darkness, his father's pitiful state, and his mother's hardship.

16. **(5)** The mother's love of poetry and demure toughness stand in contrast with the darkness of the father's behaviour and of their marriage, ultimately leaving everyone alone.

17. **(3)** The narrator in the passage is an adult telling of his childhood.

18. **(1)** The story may be somewhat autobiographical, in which case you might infer that the author also was distant in his relationship with his father and close to his mother.

19. **(3)** The passage begins talking about passports, which are clearly the most important documentation, based on the content. It then moves on to talk about NEXUS cards, which are also acceptable in some cases, followed by less-known forms of identification.

20. **(3)** The similarity in this list between passports and NEXUS cards is that both can be used to enter the U.S. by land or water.

21. **(3)** The enhanced driver's license is an example, given as a supporting detail, of an approved secure document.

22. **(2)** The passage states that a passport shows you have the right to re-enter the country. One can conclude that proper documentation would be required to re-enter Canada.

23. **(4)** This is a straightforward poem that describes the sights, sounds, and impressions of a summer evening.

24. **(1)** The poem is filled with calm and beautiful images, describing a peaceful evening.

25. **(4)** The poem flows with the passage of time, describing first the clouds growing clear, leading to the rose and purple of sunset. Then as the birds sing, the stars appear as if in a dark sea. Meanwhile the poet sits and listens and slips into a dreamy state. Then the night comes, suggesting sleep.

26. **(5)** The only choice described in the poem is watching a sunset, rose and purple evening.

27. **(2)** The line describes the stars in the night sky.

28. **(1)** The passage states that Canada compares favourably with other countries in science and lists Canadian scientific accomplishments.

29. **(3)** The passage says that literature, unlike science, must grow out of society itself.

30. **(1)** He is described as a founder of a medical practice and the passage states that he was born in Canada.

31. **(3)** The passage says that literature is not international, but grows out of the author's society.

32. **(2)** These examples support the contention that Canadian scientists are internationally known.

33. **(5)** The poem is a simple description of a horseman who pauses to admire some woods on a snowy evening, and then continues on his way.

34. **(2)** The manner of writing is very straightforward without flowery description or elaborate language.

35. **(1)** Nothing happens in the poem except that the horse shakes its harness. Everything else is the narrator's reflections. First, he thinks he knows who owns the woods. Then that the horse must think it strange they stopped. Finally, he realizes he still has a long way to go.

36. **(3)** The narrator takes time from his journey to appreciate the simple beauty of the woods.

37. **(4)** The reference to different continents, the name of the village Bayo, the walled village, and poisoned spears, and the reference to the desert suggest Africa.

38. **(5)** The relationship between the child and her parents is very close. The father strokes her shoulder gently to wake her and she goes to sit on her mother's lap.

39. **(2)** The people in the passage have an aura of fear as people are vanishing and men are being stolen. As a result, strangers are likely to be greeted with suspicion at the walled villages.

40. **(4)** The smell always reminds her of her childhood, a time when she was free.

Science

Overview of the Science Test

The GED Science Test includes:

- 50 multiple-choice questions
- 80-minute time limit

Science is not just for scientists. Everyday activities involve science too. Baking bread is chemistry. Planning a healthy diet and planting a garden are life science (often called biology). Star gazing is space science. Building a patio is engineering, a physical science. In addition, many careers require the ability to understand science concepts. Power engineering, nursing, interior design, and plumbing—all include science. The GED Science Test evaluates your ability to understand science as a process and to use scientific information to answer questions about our world, issues in society, and everyday life.

SCIENCE SKILLS

You do not need to remember everything about high-school science for the GED Science Test. You will not be asked questions that require specific knowledge of chemistry, biology, or physics. All the answers are found in the information that is given on the test. You do need a broad knowledge of basic science concepts. You need the ability to apply comprehension and reasoning skills to scientific information.

Questions on the science test reflect the United States National Science Education Standards. You will use your skills to think logically, to understand evidence and processes, and to analyze alternatives. The questions will test your ability to think about science as it applies to technology, personal and community health, the environment, and the challenges of our world.

TIP

You need a broad knowledge of basic science concepts.

WHAT'S ON THE TEST?

The Science Test has questions in three different areas:

1. Physical Science
2. Life Science
3. Earth and Space Science

PHYSICAL SCIENCE—Atoms, properties of matter, chemical reactions, force and motion, energy

LIFE SCIENCE—Cells, genetics, evolution, ecosystems, living systems, behaviour of organisms

EARTH AND SPACE SCIENCE—Energy in the Earth, geology, origin and evolution of the Earth and universe

HOW THE TEST WORKS

On the GED Science Test, you answer multiple-choice questions about science information that appears in written passages and in graphs, tables, charts, and diagrams. More than half the questions include a visual component. In most cases, there is a short passage of text or visual information, followed by only one question. Only 25% of the prompts have more than one question.

Physical Science

WHAT IS PHYSICAL SCIENCE?

There are three different areas of science examined on the GED® exam. Physical science questions account for 35% of the questions on the GED® Science Test. The questions will test your ability to comprehend, apply, and interpret science information in paragraphs, charts, tables, or diagrams. Physical science includes such areas of natural science as physics, chemistry, and astronomy.

Physical science concerns how the universe is constructed and how it operates (for example, what matter is made of), the physical laws (such as motion, gravity, and forces), forms of energy, electricity, and magnetism.

TIP

Physical science is about non-living things.

Questions on the GED Science Test reflect science skills expected of high-school graduates, including the ability to

- Comprehend unifying concepts and processes
- Apply skills of inquiry
- Analyze science and technology
- Evaluate and make decisions about personal and social issues

Unifying Concepts

In physical science, there are underlying concepts, such as the fact that matter is made up of atoms and that energy takes different forms but is never destroyed. You need to be able to understand underlying concepts and scientific processes that are described.

Inquiry

This refers to your ability to ask questions, seek answers, and think critically about physical-science topics.

Technology

Consider the relationship between technology and physical science.

Personal and Social Issues

Evaluate aspects of physical science that impact you or society, such as issues involving energy generation and food or product safety.

PRACTICE

Choose the best answer to each question.

1. Momentum is a "quality of motion," and at any given time the momentum of an object is its mass multiplied by its velocity. Since it involves motion, momentum has both a direction and a magnitude. The law of conservation of momentum states that momentum is never actually lost, but changes based on the forces that act on it.

   Which of the following statements describes what happens if a hockey stick strikes a stationary puck?
   (1) Momentum of the hockey stick is lost
   (2) Momentum of the hockey stick is transferred to the puck
   (3) Momentum of the puck is transferred to the hockey stick
   (4) Momentum of the puck is lost
   (5) Momentum of the puck changes the momentum of the stick

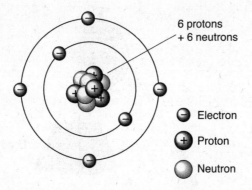

6 protons
+ 6 neutrons

− Electron

+ Proton

Neutron

2. An *ion* is an atom with additional electrons or protons. A *carbon anion* is called a carbide ion. It was a carbon atom, like the one in the diagram, but the atom gains additional electrons, which results in
   (1) Positive charge
   (2) More neutrons
   (3) Neutral charge
   (4) Negative charge
   (5) No charge

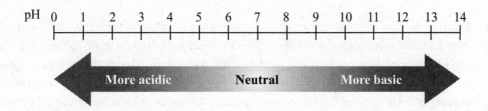

pH 0 1 2 3 4 5 6 7 8 9 10 11 12 13 14

More acidic   Neutral   More basic

3. The pH scale indicates the level of *acid* or *base* of a solution. A neutral solution, such as water, has a pH of 7. A low pH value indicates a high number of hydrogen ions and a high pH value indicates a lower number of hydrogen ions. Vinegar has a pH of about 3, which indicates that it
   (1) Has more hydrogen ions than water
   (2) Is a base
   (3) Has fewer hydrogen ions than water
   (4) Is neutral
   (5) Is not safe to drink

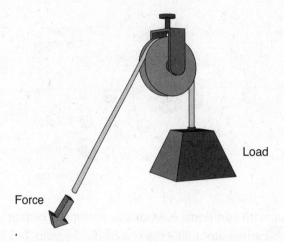

Force

Load

4. A fixed pulley is a simple machine that changes the direction of force. It has a mechanical advantage of 1, which means that the input force is equal to the output force. Using a fixed pulley, how much force would be required to move a box with a weight of 5kg?
   (1) 1kg
   (2) 2kg
   (3) 5kg
   (4) 6kg
   (5) 10kg

5. Relative density refers to the density (mass per unit) of a substance when compared with another substance. *Specific gravity* is a similar term that refers to the relative density of a substance (or solution) in comparison with water. Things that are more dense will sink in liquids, and things that are less dense will float. If a substance has a relative density of 1, then is has the same density as the reference substance. If a substance has a relative density of less than 1, then it has a lesser density than the reference substance.

   If an ice cube with a specific gravity of 0.91 is placed in a cup of water, which of the following will occur?
   (1) The water will freeze
   (2) The ice will sink
   (3) The water will boil
   (4) The ice will float
   (5) The ice will become more dense

ANSWERS

1. **(2)** The law of conservation of momentum states that momentum is not lost. The momentum of the stick is transferred to the puck to shoot it in the direction the stick was travelling.

2. **(4)** Electrons have a negative charge.

3. **(1)** A lower number is more acidic, which means it has a higher number of hydrogen atoms.

4. **(3)** The input force is equal to the output force.

5. **(4)** As the ice has a lower relative density (specific gravity), it is less dense and it will float.

ATOMS AND MOLECULES

The idea of atoms has been around since about 400 BC when it was first proposed by the Greek philosopher Democritus. Most people dismissed the idea, and it was not until the early 1800s that scientists again began to explore the fundamental building blocks of matter. In the early 1900s, scientists such as Ernest Rutherford and many others expanded our understanding of atoms.

> **ATOM**—A base unit of matter, the smallest unit of a chemical element that still has the properties of that element, having a nucleus of positively charged protons and neutrons (which have no charge), orbited by negatively charged electrons.

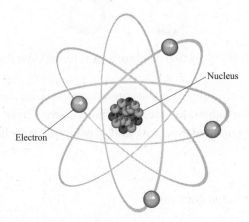

Atoms have a nucleus of neutrons and protons, surrounded by electrons.

Atoms are the smallest unit of an element. There are more than 100 known elements in the universe, which are shown on the periodic table of elements.

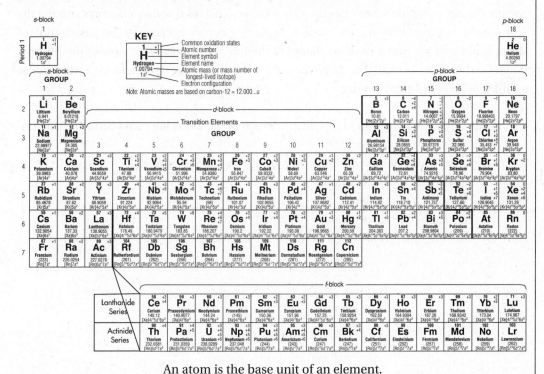

An atom is the base unit of an element.

MOLECULE—The smallest unit of a compound, formed by the chemical joining of two or more atoms.

A molecule is two or more atoms that have been joined together by a chemical process. For example, the chemical formula for water is **H₂O**. Each water molecule has two atoms of hydrogen and one atom of oxygen.

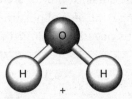

Molecules are two or more atoms joined together.

TIP

Atom—smallest unit of an element

Molecule— made of atoms, smallest unit of a compound

You do not have to know everything about atoms or molecules for the GED Science Test or to be able to read the periodic table. However, you should have a basic understanding of what atoms and molecules are and how they work and of what the periodic table is.

PRACTICE

Choose the best answer to each question.

Lightning, one of the most spectacular displays of nature, occurs as a result of ionization within storm clouds when atoms gain or lose electrons, creating an imbalance of positive and negative charges within the cloud or between the cloud and the air. Ions are atoms or molecules that have lost or gained electrons to become positively or negatively charged. They occur naturally in nature wherever energy is released, such as through solar rays striking the atmosphere or waves crashing on a beach. Lightning occurs because of the polarization of storm clouds, which gain a positive charge at the top and a negative charge at the bottom. When the difference in charge between the top and bottom of the cloud and the earth reaches a sufficient level, lightning occurs.

1. Based on the information in this article, which of the following could contribute to ionization within a storm cloud?
   (1) Striking together of whirling water droplets within the cloud
   (2) Grey colour of a storm cloud
   (3) The weight of the cloud
   (4) The mass of water droplets in the cloud
   (5) The difference in humidity between the air and ground

2. Based on the information in this article, which of the following is true of the ions at the top of a storm cloud?
   (1) They have a negative charge
   (2) They have gained electrons
   (3) They have lost electrons
   (4) They have the same number of electrons as protons
   (5) They have a greater negative charge than the ground

On the periodic table, the atomic number gives the number of protons in the nucleus of a single atom of an element. A neutral atom will always have a specific number of protons, and the number of electrons must equal the number of protons. The number of neutrons may vary.

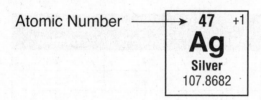

Atomic Number ⟶ 47 +1
Ag
Silver
107.8682

3. Based on this information, the number of electrons in one atom of silver is.
   (1) 23
   (2) 47
   (3) 94
   (4) 107.8682
   (5) Unknown

The temperature of an object or substance is related to the kinetic energy produced by the random motion of its atoms, moving about in all different directions. If all atoms in a substance were to stop moving, the substance would be at a temperature of absolute zero (–273°C). If two substances are at the same temperature, however, their atoms may not be moving at the same speed. For example, if water and an iron pan are at the same temperature, their atoms will be moving at different speeds to produce the same amount of kinetic energy.

4. Based on this information, you can conclude that factors influencing temperature are
   (1) speed of the random motion of atoms only
   (2) the number of protons in an atom only
   (3) weight of atoms in a substance only
   (4) both speed and weight of atoms in a substance
   (5) both weight of atoms and absolute zero

Atoms have valence energy levels of electrons that orbit the nucleus in an electron cloud. Valence electrons are simply the outermost electrons. The first valence energy level has up to 2 electrons. Subsequent levels have up to 8 electrons, called an *octet*. Atoms with a complete valence energy level of 8 electrons (such as in the elements argon or neon) are stable. Atoms that do not have a complete octet in the outer energy level are unstable and will attempt to bond with other atoms to achieve stability, either joining with atoms of the same element or with those of another element to create a new substance (compound). Atoms can bond in several ways: *covalent bonding* in which the nuclei of two or more non-metal atoms share electrons to achieve stability; *ionic bonding* involving the attraction of two oppositely charged ions (usually a metal and a non-metal); and *metallic bonding* that occurs only with metals and is really the formation of an alloy rather than a compound.

Element	# Valence Electrons	# Electrons needed
C	4	4
Fe	2	6
H	1	7
He	2	6
Ne	8	0
O	6	2

5. Which of the following compounds is most likely to be created in nature by ionic bonding?
   (1) CH_2
   (2) CO_3
   (3) He_2Ne
   (4) H_4Ne
   (5) FeO

ANSWERS

1. **(1)** According to the passage, ions are created when electrons become charged when energy is released, for example by the striking together of whirling water droplets.

2. **(3)** Positively charged ions would have lost negatively charged electrons.

3. **(2)** Since atoms have a neutral charge, the number of electrons and protons is equal.

4. **(4)** The iron atom will be heavier, so it will move at a slower speed than the lighter atoms of a water molecule to have the same kinetic energy.

5. **(5)** As 8 electrons in the outer valence energy level are needed for stability, the combination of 2 electrons from the outer energy level of iron and 6 from the outer energy level of oxygen creates a stable compound.

CHALLENGE EXERCISE

On the Internet or in a chemistry or physical science textbook, look up covalent, ionic, and metallic bonds. What are the differences between them?

COMPOSITION OF MATTER

The exact definition of matter is the subject of some debate when considering subatomic particles, such as neutrons, protons, or quarks, but the classic definition is that it is composed of atoms and has both mass and volume. Water, for example, is made of molecules, which are made of atoms. Mass is typically measured in grams or kilograms, but it is not the same as weight. Mass is the amount of matter that is in an object. Weight is the force by which the object is pulled towards the earth. Weight is equal to the mass of an object times the force of gravity and is measured in newtons (N). This means that the weight of an object would be different on the Earth and on the Moon, but the mass would be the same. Volume is the amount of space that an object takes up, or occupies.

MATTER—Anything composed of atoms and having both mass and volume.

Matter can exist in different states:

- Solid—Having fixed shape and volume
- Liquid—Having flexible shape and fixed volume
- Gas—Having flexible shape and flexible volume
- Plasma—Ionized gas with flexible shape and flexible volume

An ice cube is an example of a solid. If you put a square ice cube in a round container, the ice will still be square. The atoms in a solid are very attracted to one another; they vibrate but stay fixed. When the solid is heated, it increases the motion of the particles. The ice cube melts, and it becomes liquid. The amount (volume) of the water stays fixed, but the shape will change to fill the container. If the water is heated even more, it becomes a gas and will expand outside the container and have no definite shape.

Plasma is a less commonly known state of matter. It occurs when energy is transferred into a gas, often through heat, which excites the particles in the gas so that some of them lose electrons and become positively charged while others gain electrons and become negatively charged. The plasma itself has a neutral charge, but it is a good conductor of electricity and, as often happens when atoms become excited, it gives off light. Examples of plasma in nature are stars, lightning, and the tails of comets.

CHALLENGE EXERCISE

Make plasma at home with a grape and a microwave. Cut a grape almost all the way through, leaving a small connection between the two halves. Place the grape in the microwave and set it for 15 seconds. Watch for a burst of light. What do you think happened? You can also find videos of this experiment on the Internet.

> **Warning:** Do not leave the microwave unattended. Do not burn yourself on the hot grape. Turn the microwave off immediately when the light from the grape disappears. This experiment could make a mess in the microwave. Use reasonable care when operating the microwave.

TIP

Volume—The amount of space an object occupies

Mass—The amount of matter in an object

Weight—mass (m) × force of gravity (g)

PRACTICE

Choose the best answer to each question.

Density is a physical property of matter that is unique to each substance. Density can be calculated by dividing the mass of a substance by its volume. Density is used in comparing substances and in studying things such as buoyancy. Matter that is less dense will float in a liquid that has greater density. It seems intuitive that solids would have greater density than liquids, but this is not always the case. Water, for example, is at its greatest density at 4°C.

$$D = \frac{m}{v}$$

D—density

m—mass

v—volume

1. Based on this information, you know that:
   (1) An ice cube will sink in water
   (2) Ice cubes have greater density than water at 4°C
   (3) An ice cube will neither sink nor float in water
   (4) An ice cube will float in water
   (5) Ice cubes have the same density as water

2. Liquid mercury at room temperature has a density of 13.5 g/cm³. Which of the following substances will float in liquid mercury?
   (1) platinum 21.4 g/cm³
   (2) gold 19.3 g/cm³
   (3) uranium 18.7 g/cm³
   (4) californium 15.1 g/cm³
   (5) iron 7.8 g/cm³

3. A Canadian Halifax class naval frigate with a mass over 3500 tons will float, while a rock with a mass of 1 gram will sink. Which factor accounts for the difference?
   (1) volume
   (2) weight
   (3) length
   (4) movement
   (5) buoyancy

Matter has physical properties, such as density, shape, colour, volume, mass, and temperature, and can undergo physical changes, which are changes to these physical properties. Matter can also undergo changes to its chemical structure, producing one or more new substances, usually through interaction with another substance. While most physical changes are reversible, many chemical changes are not (though some are!).

4. Oxidization (rusting) of iron is an example of
   (1) Chemical property
   (2) Chemical change
   (3) Physical property
   (4) Physical change
   (5) Reversible change

The law of the conservation of mass is also known as the law of conservation of matter, and states that the mass of a closed system is constant and, therefore, matter is neither created nor destroyed, but may only change its properties or form. This is an important law in chemistry and is used to balance equations to show that the number of atoms in reactants is the same as the number of atoms in the resulting compound. For example, 4 hydrogen atoms and 2 oxygen atoms combine to create 2 water molecules, having the same number of atoms.

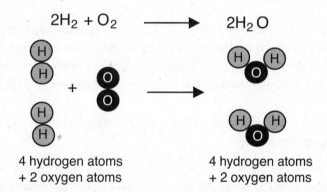

$$2H_2 + O_2 \longrightarrow 2H_2O$$

4 hydrogen atoms
+ 2 oxygen atoms

4 hydrogen atoms
+ 2 oxygen atoms

5. Based on these laws, if a quantity of vinegar and baking soda were combined in a closed container and the resulting chemical reaction were to cause the mixture to froth up and fill a larger volume of the container than before, which of the following would be true?
   (1) Mass within the container would be greater
   (2) Mass within the container would be less
   (3) Mass within the container would be unchanged
   (4) Mass of the vinegar and baking soda would increase
   (5) Mass of the vinegar and baking soda would decrease

ANSWERS

1. **(4)** Water has its greatest density at 4°C. Ice will, therefore, have a lower density and will float.

2. **(5)** Iron will float because it has a lower density than liquid mercury.

3. **(1)** A ship floats because the mass times its volume (length, width, and height) has a lower density than the water it displaces. A rock does not.

4. **(2)** Oxidization is a chemical change in which iron reacts with oxygen.

5. **(3)** Mass does not change in a closed system.

CHEMICAL REACTIONS

Matter can change in different ways. It can undergo physical change, which is a change to its physical properties, such as colour, volume, temperature, or state of matter, but the substance itself is still the same. Matter can also undergo chemical change, which is a change to its chemical properties—its molecular structure—to form a new substance.

> **CHEMICAL REACTION**—a change in one or more substances (reactants) to form a new substance (product)

Chemical reactions can occur in all phases of matter—solid, liquid, gas, or plasma. A chemical change involves electrons and the forming or breaking down of chemical bonds when atoms in molecules join together or break apart to make new molecules. Signs that a chemical reaction is taking place can include the production of things such as light, heat, odor, or gas.

There are different categories of chemical reactions. Although there are more than these, some common categories include:

SYNTHESIS—Two or more substances come together to form a new substance (for example, two hydrogen atoms and one oxygen atom share electrons to form water).

DECOMPOSITION—The opposite of synthesis, one substance breaks down into two or more substances. This may be caused by heat, radiation, acid, or other factors (such as adding acid to sugar can cause it to break down into carbon and water—don't try this at home).

SINGLE REPLACEMENT—One element of a compound is replaced by a different element to form a new compound (such as if zinc is mixed with hydrochloric acid, the chlorine leaves the acid and combines with the zinc, producing zinc chloride and hydrogen gas).

DOUBLE REPLACEMENT—Two compounds of a substance exchange elements to form new compounds (an example is when silver nitrate, $AgNO_3$, is mixed with potassium chloride, KCl, the two metals, silver and potassium, exchange their non-metal partners to form silver chloride, AgCl, and potassium nitrate, KNO_3).

Chemical reactions can be described in chemical equations, which show the reactants on the left side and the products on the right side. You do not have to remember types of chemical reactions, but you should understand what chemical reactions are and be able to read and understand passages about topics involving chemistry.

$$CH_4 + 2O_2 \rightarrow CO_2 + 2H_2O$$

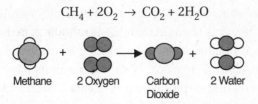

Methane   2 Oxygen   Carbon   2 Water
                       Dioxide

Equation for combustion of methane gas.

Read a chemical equation:

- Each element has a capital letter—CH_4 (methane) contains C (carbon) and H (hydrogen).
- Elements written together are molecules—CH_4 is a methane molecule, O_2 is an oxygen molecule.
- A small number after an element shows the number of atoms of an element in a molecule—CH_4 is one atom of carbon and four atoms of hydrogen.
- A large number before a molecule shows the number of molecules—$2H_2O$ is two water molecules.
- The number of atoms on each side of a chemical reaction equation is the same.

The preceding chemical equation describes what happens when methane gas is burned in the presence of oxygen, becoming carbon dioxide and water.

PRACTICE

Choose the best answer to each question.

Chemical reactions occur when particles collide with enough energy to initiate the reaction. In some cases, heat is a factor. Increase of temperature adds energy that can increase the rate of a chemical reaction by speeding up how fast the particles move, and by increasing how hard they collide. For some reactions that are impacted by temperature, an increase of approximately 10°C can double the rate of chemical change. By the same token, a decrease in temperature can slow a chemical reaction.

Some chemical reactions require extreme heat. For example, although silicon is one of the most common elements in the universe, and silicon dioxide is one of the most common compounds in the Earth's crust, pure silicon crystals are seldom found in nature, but most commonly in compounds such as sand and quartz. Pure silicon, used for a wide variety of purposes, is produced commercially when sand (SiO_2) and carbon (C) are heated to a temperature of 1400°C, forming silicon and carbon monoxide gas.

1. Based on the information in this passage, you might conclude that heat is used in the commercial production of silicon to
    (1) Accelerate the motion of atoms to create collisions and initiate the reaction
    (2) Melt the sand and carbon
    (3) Slow the rate of chemical reaction
    (4) Imitate conditions in the Earth's crust
    (5) Increase the rate of an existing chemical reaction

Chemical reactions can be characterised as either endothermic or exothermic. An *exothermic* reaction is one in which energy is released into the surroundings in the form of light or heat. An *endothermic* reaction is one in which energy from the surroundings is required to initiate the reaction. In an exothermic reaction, then, the reactants have more energy than the products of the reaction and that surplus energy is released. In an endothermic reaction, the reactants must absorb additional energy from the surroundings for the reaction to take place.

Literally translated, the word *endothermic* means "inside heat" and *exothermic* means "outside heat." An endothermic reaction is one that involves the breaking of stable molecular bonds, thus requiring energy. An exothermic reaction is one in which new, more stable bonds are formed.

2. One example of an endothermic reaction is
    (1) A burning campfire
    (2) A warm pile of decomposing vegetable matter
    (3) The interaction of iron and oxygen, creating rust and releasing small amounts of heat energy
    (4) A nuclear reactor
    (5) Plant use of sunlight to convert nutrients into glucose and oxygen

Acid is a term commonly used to describe chemical substances that, when combined with water, have a sour taste and a corrosive effect on metal. A *base* is a chemical substance that, when combined with water, has a bitter taste and soapy feel and when combined with an acid, interacts chemically to neutralize the acid (bring pH closer to 7) to form salt and water. Alkaline (base) substances can also be extremely corrosive, such as ammonia.

In chemistry, the symbol pH is used to indicate the level of acidity of a substance. The pH scale has 14 points, with 7 being neutral and lower numbers being acids and higher numbers indicating a base. The lower the number, the more acidic the substance. The higher the number, the more alkaline (also known as caustic).

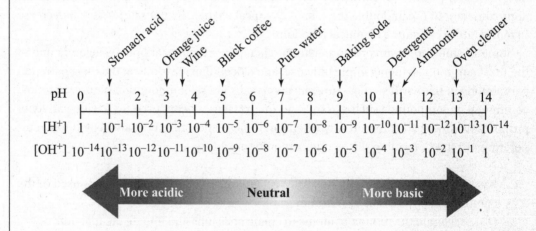

3. Which of the following is the most acidic?
    (1) Oven cleaner
    (2) Black coffee
    (3) Pure water
    (4) Baking soda
    (5) Ammonia

4. If baking soda is mixed with orange juice, a chemical reaction will occur in which
    (1) The orange juice becomes more acidic
    (2) An explosion occurs
    (3) The orange juice becomes less acidic
    (4) Natural sugars are formed
    (5) Nothing happens

Chemical reactions take place everywhere in nature, including within the human body. The digestive process, for example, is both a mechanical and chemical breakdown of food within the body, enabling the body to absorb nutrients. Digestion begins with the act of chewing (mastication), a physical process that breaks down solid food into smaller pieces. At the same time, the chemical processes have already begun in the mouth with the release of saliva, containing enzymes that begin to interact with starch. In the stomach, the food encounters gastric acid and digestive enzymes, such as pepsin. The function of the gastric acid is not so much to break down food as to provide digestive enzymes with the ideal pH and temperature in which to do the work of breaking down food molecules for better absorption by the body.

5. Which of the following is an enzyme that chemically reacts with food?
    (1) Mastication
    (2) Saliva
    (3) Gastric acid
    (4) Pepsin
    (5) pH

When a chemical reaction takes place within a liquid solution, a precipitate may be formed. A precipitate is a solid that is formed by the chemical reaction. Generally, the precipitate will sink to the bottom of the solution; however, sometimes the precipitate will consist of small particles, giving the solution a cloudy appearance as it slowly sinks. The remaining liquid is termed the supernatant. For example, lead nitrate and potassium iodide are both clear solutions. However, when the two are combined a chemical reaction takes place, forming a yellow coloured lead iodide, which seems to float in clear potassium nitrate as it slowly drifts downwards.

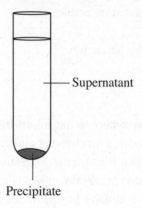

6. The precipitate produced in this experiment is
    (1) Supernatant
    (2) Clear
    (3) Lead nitrate
    (4) Potassium iodide
    (5) Lead iodide

ANSWERS

1. **(1)** Heat provides energy that increases the motion of the atoms.
2. **(5)** Plants absorb the external energy of sunlight for the endothermic reaction.
3. **(2)** Black coffee has the lowest pH of the substances listed and so is the most acidic.
4. **(3)** The more alkaline baking soda neutralizes the acids in the orange juice
5. **(4)** Pepsin is the only enzyme named. Saliva contains enzymes, but is not one.
6. **(5)** The yellow lead iodide is the precipitate, described as drifting downwards in clear fluid.

CHALLENGE EXERCISE

Fill a clean, small water bottle or pop bottle about 1/3 full with water. Add a little dish detergent so that you will be able to better see the reaction. Add about 2tsp of baking soda. Gently swirl the mixture to dissolve the baking soda. Add 2tsp of vinegar. What happens? What evidence of a chemical reaction do you observe? What happens to the level of water in the bottle? Why does the level change? How does this fit with the law of conservation of matter?

LAWS OF MOTION

In 1687, Sir Isaac Newton, an English mathematician and physicist, published a book that explained his three laws of motion. These laws explained forces acting on objects at rest or in motion in a closed system. That is, they explain how objects move in any environment, whether in space, on the Earth, or on the Moon. Newton's laws are still fundamental to physical science.

Newton's Laws:

1. **LAW OF INERTIA**—An object will remain at rest or in a constant state of motion at a constant speed unless acted on by a force.
2. **LAW OF ACCELERATION**—Acceleration of an object is in direct proportion to and in the same direction as the net force acting on the object and inversely proportional to its mass.
3. **LAW OF ACTION AND REACTION**—For every action, there is an equal and opposite reaction.

Isaac Newton also published the law of universal gravity in the same book, which explains how the forces of gravity work between any two objects. You do not need to memorize Newton's laws of motion for the GED® test, but you should understand the basic principles of how forces act on objects and be prepared to read passages and answer questions involving motion.

Newton's laws are fundamental principles that still help us understand how objects move.

PRACTICE

Choose the best answer to each question.

Newton's first law of motion, also known as the law of inertia, states that objects at rest or in motion will remain in that state unless acted upon by another force, called an unbalanced force. The law can also be expressed by stating that an object in motion stays in motion, and an object at rest stays at rest unless acted upon by an unbalanced force. The property of objects that resists change in its state of motion, including direction, is inertia.

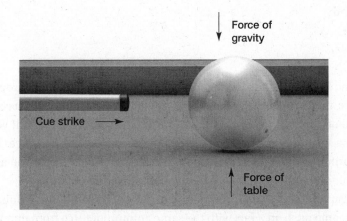

If a billiard ball is at rest on a pool table, it will remain in that state. Forces acting on the ball are the force of gravity that pulls the ball downward and the force of the table that holds the ball up. The forces are equal and move in opposite directions and are, therefore, balanced. A pool cue striking the ball from the side is an unbalanced force that changes the ball's state of motion. When the ball is rolling, how it started to roll does not matter. State of motion refers to the state of the object at any given moment. If no unbalanced force, such as friction, acts upon it, the ball will continue to roll in the same direction at the same speed indefinitely.

1. If a billiard ball is rolling on a table, an unbalanced force that would affect its state of motion is
   (1) inertia
   (2) gravity
   (3) upward force of table
   (4) friction
   (5) direction

2. According to Newton's first law, if a person were to swing upwards a glass filled with water and bring it to a sudden stop, the water would
   (1) stop suddenly
   (2) speed up
   (3) splash downward towards the bottom of the glass
   (4) continue moving in the same direction
   (5) change direction

3. How long will a rock sitting at the top of a hill remain at rest if no force acts on it?
   (1) forever
   (2) 1 day
   (3) 1 month
   (4) 1 year
   (5) 100 years

Newton's second law states that the acceleration of an object is directly proportional to the amount of force that acts on it. For example, if you pull a wagon, the acceleration of the wagon will depend directly on the amount of force with which you pull. If you pull harder, the wagon will accelerate more and go faster in the direction of the force. Acceleration is inversely proportional to the mass of the object. A wagon that is empty will accelerate more with the same amount of force than a wagon that holds a large man.

Force is measured in newtons. The forces that cause acceleration are unbalanced forces. That is, if two people push on a box with the same amount of force from opposite directions, the forces are balanced and the box will remain at rest. However, if one person pushes with a force of 5 newtons and the other with a force of 8 newtons, the net force will be 3 newtons, and the box will accelerate in the direction of the greater force.

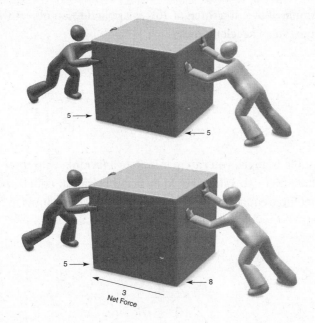

The formula for calculating acceleration is a mathematical expression of Newton's second law. It states that acceleration is equal to the net force on an object, divided by its mass. Acceleration itself is expressed in metres per second per second (m/s/s). This is because acceleration is not the same as velocity, which is an object's speed at any given time and is expressed in metres per second (m/s). Acceleration measures the change in velocity. For example, if an object were accelerating at a rate of 3m/s/s, this means that each second it is going 3m/s faster than the second before.

$$a = \frac{F\ net}{m}$$

Gravity is a factor that is problematic for some in understanding acceleration. It would seem intuitive that objects with a larger mass should fall faster or roll downhill faster than smaller objects. However, this is not true. Acceleration from gravity is constant as objects with a greater mass also require more force to move them. Barring any other factors, such as wind resistance, a billiard ball and a bowling ball dropped from a height will strike the ground at the same time.

4. Based on Newton's law, you can conclude that
   (1) Mass does not affect acceleration
   (2) Force does not affect acceleration
   (3) Balanced forces do NOT cause acceleration
   (4) Unbalanced forces do NOT cause an object to accelerate
   (5) Gravity does not cause a falling object to accelerate

5. A car is travelling at 80 km/h. This is a measure of the car's
   (1) velocity
   (2) acceleration
   (3) mass
   (4) gravity
   (5) net force

6. Using the formula above, if a force of 10N is applied to an object with a mass of 2kg, what will be the rate of acceleration?
    (1) 2 m/s^2
    (2) 5 m/s^2
    (3) 10 m/s^2
    (4) 20 m/s^2
    (5) 25 m/s^2

7. Using the formula triangle, you can manipulate a formula with three terms to find any unknown if the other two values are known. Acceleration equals *net force* divided by *mass*, while net force equals *acceleration* times *mass*. The formula to calculate the mass of an object is

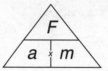

    (1) $a = mf$
    (2) $f = ma$
    (3) $m = fa$
    (4) $m = \dfrac{f}{a}$
    (5) $m = \dfrac{a}{f}$

8. Based on the information in this passage, all other factors being equal, if a bicycle and a large truck were to begin to roll down the same hill, which of the following would be true?
    (1) The truck would roll faster
    (2) The bicycle would roll faster
    (3) The bicycle and truck would accelerate at the same rate
    (4) The truck would reach the bottom first
    (5) The bicycle would reach the bottom first

Newton's third law is the well-known maxim that for every action, there is an equal and opposite reaction. This law is about how forces work when objects interact with one another. Forces come in pairs. Whenever there is an action force in one object, there is an equal reaction force in the opposite direction.

   This means that when your hand pushes against a wall, the wall pushes against your hand. When a butterfly's wings push down against the air, the air pushes up against the wings. When the ball of your foot pushes backwards against the ground, the ground pushes against your foot in the opposite direction, propelling your body forward and causing you to walk. These examples are called *action-reaction pairs*. Notice that in each example, there are forces from two bodies that are interacting with one another.

9. A hammer strikes a nail. The force of the hammer on the nail is _____ the force of the nail on the hammer.
   (1) greater than
   (2) less than
   (3) equal to
   (4) greater than or equal to
   (5) less than or equal to

10. In a rifle, the firing pin strikes a bullet and the forceful explosion of gases in the rifle causes the bullet to accelerate from the barrel. The equal and opposite reaction is that the
    (1) bullet strikes a target
    (2) rifle accelerates in the same direction as the bullet
    (3) the bullet slows because of wind resistance
    (4) the rifle recoils in the opposite direction
    (5) nothing

ANSWERS

1. **(4)** Friction has no balancing force and will eventually cause the ball to stop.
2. **(4)** The water is in motion and will remain in motion.
3. **(1)** An object at rest will stay at rest.
4. **(3)** The forces that cause acceleration are unbalanced forces.
5. **(1)** 80 km/h is a measure of the car's constant speed or velocity.
6. **(2)** A force of 10N divided by 2 kg = 5 m/s^2.
7. **(4)** If acceleration is equal to f over m, then mass must be equal to f over a.
8. **(3)** The acceleration of gravity is constant.
9. **(3)** Action–reaction pairs are equal.
10. **(4)** Acceleration of the bullet in one direction will cause the rifle to accelerate in the opposite direction (recoil).

CHALLENGE EXERCISE

Research terms on the Internet, dictionary, encyclopedia, or textbook. Write definitions in your own words of *inertia* and *momentum*. In a short paragraph, explain the difference between the two.

FORMS OF ENERGY

When we think of energy, we think of things such as solar power, oil, and wind. These are sources of energy, but what is energy itself? Energy is the capacity to do work. Typically, this is thought of as the ability to make something move. For example, moving a wheelbarrow from one place to another place requires energy. The energy can be the movement itself or the capacity to make it move. For example, a falling rock has energy. A rock sitting at the top of a cliff also has stored energy. Some other forms of energy can include:

- Sound—movement of waves
- Heat—increased movement of atoms and molecules
- Light—a form of radiant energy
- Electrical—movement of electrical charges
- Chemical—stored in chemical bonds

Energy can be potential or kinetic.

PRACTICE

Choose the best answer to each question.

There are many forms of energy, but all can be classified into two basic categories, kinetic energy or potential energy. *Kinetic* is the energy of movement. It includes the movement of objects, waves, or particles. For example, sound energy is the movement of energy through a substance in the form of waves.

Potential energy is energy that is stored. It results from the position or condition of an object. If a truck is parked at the top of a hill, it is not moving. However, the position of the truck means that it could roll down the hill. If the truck begins to move, the potential energy will be transformed into kinetic energy. In this case, the potential energy results from gravity and the position of the object. In other cases, potential energy could result from the condition of the object when force has been applied to it. If an archer applies force to draw back a bowstring and hold it, the bow is at rest but its condition of being bent has stored potential energy. When the archer releases the bowstring, the potential energy will be transformed into kinetic energy.

Kinetic	Potential
Mechanical (movement)	Gravitational
Sound	Stored mechanical
Electrical	Chemical
Radiant	Nuclear

1. Based on the table above, which of the following is a form of kinetic energy?
   (1) Potential
   (2) Gravitational
   (3) Sound
   (4) Stored mechanical
   (5) Chemical

2. Thermal energy is heat that results from the vibration or movement of atoms and molecules within a substance. Thermal energy would be categorized as
   (1) Kinetic
   (2) Potential
   (3) Electrical
   (4) Radiant
   (5) Nuclear

3. If a metal spring were compressed and held in place, this would be an example of which kind of energy?
   (1) Mechanical
   (2) Stored mechanical
   (3) Gravitational
   (4) Chemical
   (5) Radiant

The law of conservation of energy states that energy in a system is neither lost nor created. The energy is transformed from one type to another or from one object or substance to another, but the total amount of energy remains the same. For example, food energy in the body is transformed into mechanical energy to play a piano, which is transformed into mechanical energy as the piano keys move, and finally into sound energy.

One example of the law of conservation of energy is a swing, which is a basic pendulum. When the swing begins at point A, it is not moving and all of the energy is potential energy. Gravitational potential energy is calculated by multiplying the mass of the object by the acceleration of gravity and the height of the object. As the swing approaches point B, therefore, the amount of potential energy decreases and kinetic energy increases. As the swing begins upward progress, potential energy increases and kinetic energy decreases until it reaches zero at point C. Throughout, the amount of energy in the system remains constant. If there were no other factors, such as wind resistance or friction, the object would continue to swing indefinitely.

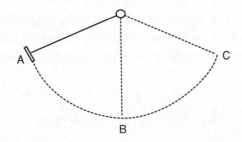

4. As the swing approaches point B, the potential energy of the swing
   (1) is transformed into kinetic energy
   (2) is lost
   (3) is lost while new kinetic energy is created
   (4) increases
   (5) is always equal to the kinetic energy

5. Based on the information in this passage, which of the following is true if no other factors, such as wind resistance or friction, act on the swing?

   (1) Potential energy of the swing is zero at point A
   (2) Kinetic energy of the swing is zero at point B
   (3) The height of the swing is greater at point B than point A
   (4) The speed of the swing at point B is zero
   (5) The height of the swing is the same at point A and point C

ANSWERS

1. **(3)** Sound is listed in the table under kinetic energy.

2. **(1)** Kinetic energy involves movement, including vibration of atoms and molecules.

3. **(2)** The spring is at rest, but its condition of being compressed has stored potential energy.

4. **(1)** Energy is never lost or created, only transformed.

5. **(5)** Since the amount of energy is always the same in a closed system, the height at both points would be the same.

CHALLENGE EXERCISE

The law of conservation of energy states that energy is neither created nor destroyed. At a playground swing, pull the swing back, holding it in front of you against your body. Let the swing go without pushing it. Stand still. What type of energy does the swing have when you are holding it? Why doesn't the swing hit you when it returns? What forces are acting on the swing?

MAGNETISM AND LIGHT

Magnetism is a flow of energy in an object that repels or attracts other objects. All magnets have two poles, north and south, at opposite ends. Lines of flux (flow) move in a circle through and around the object to create a magnetic field. Exactly what the field consists of is unclear, but objects that come within the magnetic field may be attracted or repelled. Some types of material, such as iron and other natural metals, are highly affected by a magnetic field and are called magnetic. Other types of material, such as the human body, cloth, or copper, do not respond strongly to magnetic fields and are called non-magnetic.

Magnetic Field of a Bar Magnet

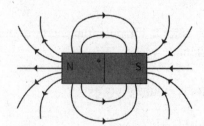

Magnets occur naturally, like pieces of the mineral magnetite called lodestones, and the Earth itself is a magnet. Magnets also occur when electricity moves in a circle. For example, if electrical current is passed through a coil of wire, it will form a magnet. Magnetic energy is similar and related to electrical energy, but different.

Another type of energy is electromagnetic radiation, which is electrical and magnetic energy moving together in waves. There are many types of electromagnetic energy, all with different wavelengths. A wavelength is simply the distance between two neighbouring waves. The spectrum of electromagnetic energy that we can see is visible light. Other kinds that we cannot see include radio waves, ultraviolet light, and gamma rays. Electromagnetic radiation is both particle and wave energy. Imagine a billiard ball—the way it moves is particle motion. Now imagine the ocean—the way it moves is wave motion. Electromagnetic radiation consists of a stream of small particles, or photons, that move in both a particle and wave-like way (called wave-particle duality).

PRACTICE

Choose the best answer to each question.

When we refer to the speed of light, we are generally referring to the speed of light in a vacuum, 299,792 kilometres per second, the famous c of Einstein's $E=mc^2$. Through other mediums, light travels more slowly. For example, in air it travels 299,704k/s, almost 88k/s slower. In water, the speed of light is approximately 224,900k/s, and through a diamond a mere 124,395k/s.

What happens when light passes from one medium to another? Snell's Law, or the law of refraction, tells us that when light passes from one medium to another, it will generally change direction. This change of direction is called refraction.

1. When light from the air strikes the surface of water at an angle, it will
    (1) speed up
    (2) stop
    (3) become brighter
    (4) change direction
    (5) gain energy

The speed of light through a substance can be calculated using its refraction index. Divide c (299,792k/s) by the refraction index to calculate the speed.

Substance	Index
Cubic Zirconia	2.15
Diamond	2.41
Silicon	3.96
Water	1.33
Zinc Oxide	2.4

2. The speed of light will be the lowest in which of the substances listed?
    (1) Cubic Zirconia
    (2) Diamond
    (3) Silicon
    (4) Water
    (5) Zinc Oxide

Reflection occurs when light bounces back from the surface of an object. The law of reflection states that the angle of incidence is equal to the angle of reflection.

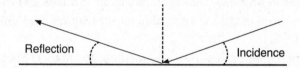

Reflection   Incidence

3. If light strikes a mirror at a 30°angle, at what angle will it reflect away from the surface?
    (1) 30°
    (2) 45°
    (3) 60°
    (4) 90°
    (5) 150°

Visible light appears to be white, but it is actually a combination of many colours representing a spectrum of wavelengths of electromagnetic energy. Using an optical prism, white light can be divided into its component colours of red, orange, yellow, green, blue, indigo, and violet (ROY G BIV for short).

4. The different colours that make up the spectrum of visible light all have different
    (1) magnetic energy
    (2) spectrums
    (3) prisms
    (4) speed
    (5) wavelengths

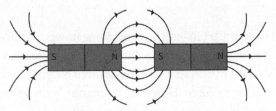

Attraction between opposite poles

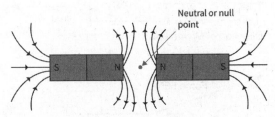

Neutral or null point

Repulsion between like poles

5. What principle of magnetism is illustrated by the graphics?
   (1) Like poles attract, opposites repel.
   (2) Like poles repel, opposites attract.
   (3) Magnets have no influence on one another.
   (4) The north pole of magnets face downward.
   (5) Magnets can produce electrical energy.

ANSWERS

1. **(4)** According to Snell's law, light will generally change direction, or refract, at the border of another medium.
2. **(3)** Silicon has the highest refraction index, therefore, the lowest speed of light of the substances listed.
3. **(1)** The angles of incidence and reflection are equal.
4. **(5)** The passage states that visible light is divided into colours of different wavelengths.
5. **(2)** In the first graphic, see how the lines join together. In the second graphic, the lines from the like poles push against one another and repel.

FORCE AND WORK

Force can be described as a push or a pull. It occurs between objects acting on one another: when a hammer strikes a nail; when gravity pulls on an object; when wheels push against a road. A force cannot occur by itself. It must act on something.

Force is a vector, which means it has two components, magnitude and direction, and is represented in diagrams as an arrow. Magnitude is the amount of the force and is measured in newtons (N). A force must also have a direction. Force also has the capacity to do work.

Work occurs when a force is applied to an object and it moves. If the object does not move, no work is done. The formula to calculate work is the amount of force multiplied by the distance moved. Work is measured in *joules*, with one joule being equal to a force of one Newton moving an object one metre.

TIP

If the object does not move, no work has been done.

PRACTICE

Forces may be applied to an object in various directions; however, the direction in which the force is applied might not be the same as the direction of movement. For example, a rope is applied to a box with a weight of 20N. If a horizontal force is applied to the rope, the box will accelerate in the direction of the force. However, if the rope is on a slight upwards angle, the box will not move upwards, but will still move horizontally.

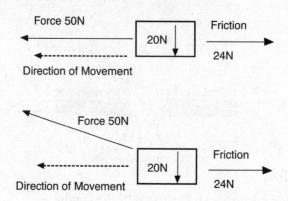

1. In diagram B, the box moves horizontally instead of upwards because of
   (1) the rope
   (2) friction
   (3) the direction of movement
   (4) gravity only
   (5) gravity and friction

2. If the force applied to the rope in diagram A were 24N, the box would
   (1) move in the direction of friction
   (2) move upward
   (3) move more slowly
   (4) move in the opposite direction
   (5) not move

3. In diagram B, how many forces are acting on the box?
   (1) 1
   (2) 2
   (3) 3
   (4) 4
   (5) 5

4. The basic formula to calculate the amount of work done is to multiply the force applied by distance the object is moved. How much work is done if a 20N box is lifted a height of 5 metres?
   (1) 4J
   (2) 5m
   (3) 20N
   (4) 100J
   (5) 125J

ANSWERS

1. **(5)** The box is affected by forces in several directions. The 20N force of gravity and 24 N force of friction act in different directions on the box. This causes the direction of movement to be somewhere between the forces applied. In diagram B, the box moves horizontally instead of upwards because of the direction of the forces.

2. **(5)** The force of the rope and friction would be balanced forces.

3. **(3)** The pull of the rope, gravity, and friction are forces that affect the box.

4. **(4)** 20N × 5m = 100J

CHAPTER CHECK-UP

Complete these practice exercises, and check the answers and analysis that follow. After you mark your work, review any topic in the chapter that you had trouble with or did not understand.

Most commonly, fog occurs as a result of warm air passing over a cooler surface, such as water or snow, causing the air temperature at ground level to cool nearly to the dew point. Water vapour in the air condenses into droplets because of the cooler temperature, combining with dust particles, to make what is essentially a cloud.

1. When water vapour condenses into droplets, it is an example of a
   (1) physical change
   (2) chemical change
   (3) vector
   (4) gravitational force
   (5) form of energy

The mass of an object is the amount of matter in the object. The weight of an object is the mass multiplied by the force of gravity. Thus, the weight of an object will be different on different planets, but the mass will remain the same. The following table shows the weight of a man with a mass of 80kg on different celestial bodies.

Earth	785N
Mercury	297N
Venus	712N
Moon	131N
Mars	296N
Jupiter	1856N
Uranus	697N
Neptune	883N
Sun	21252N

2. Based on the information in this table, on which celestial body would you weigh the most?
    (1) Earth
    (2) Moon
    (3) Jupiter
    (4) Neptune
    (5) Sun

3. Based on the information in this table, you might conclude that which of the celestial bodies has the lowest gravitational force?
    (1) Earth
    (2) Moon
    (3) Jupiter
    (4) Neptune
    (5) Sun

Inertia and momentum are two different, yet often confused, concepts. Inertia is a property of matter that finds its explanation in Newton's first law, which states that a body in motion will stay in motion and a body at rest will stay at rest unless influenced by a force. Inertia is the property of the object that resists change to its state of motion. Inertia is equal to the object's mass. If a baseball with a mass of 147g is at rest, the force that resists a change to its state of motion is its inertia of 147g. An object's inertia is always the same. Momentum is the force of an object in motion, measured by the mass of the object multiplied by its velocity.

4. A baseball with a mass of 147g is thrown at a speed of 144kmph (kilometres per hour), and then brought to a stop when it lands in the catcher's glove. At the moment the ball comes to a stop, its inertia is
    (1) 0
    (2) 3g
    (3) 144kmph
    (4) 147g
    (5) 21168g·kmph

Newton's law of universal gravitation states that every object in the universe attracts every other object in the universe. The force of gravity between any two objects is directly proportional to the mass of the objects and inversely proportional to their distance. In other words, the force is greater the larger the mass of the objects, and less the farther they are from each other.

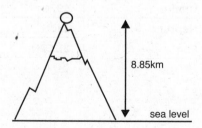

5. Weight is equal to the mass of an object multiplied by the force of gravity. A large rock is at the top of Mount Everest, over 8 kilometres above sea level. The weight of the rock at the top of the mountain will be _____ at sea level.

    (1) the same as
    (2) slightly greater than
    (3) slightly less than
    (4) equal to the mass
    (5) greater than the mass

Some acid-reducing tablets contain calcium hydroxide, $Ca(OH)_2$. When the tablets are ingested, a chemical reaction takes place with the hydrochloric acid in the stomach, $2HCl$. Chlorine atoms from the acid bond with the calcium atoms in the calcium hydroxide while the hydrogen and oxygen atoms from both compounds combine. The result is calcium chloride and water.

$$Ca(OH)_2 + 2\,HCl \rightarrow CaCl_2 + 2H_2O$$

6. As a result of this chemical reaction

    (1) two different compounds are created
    (2) two different elements are created
    (3) more atoms are created
    (4) chlorine gas is released
    (5) carbon dioxide gas is released

The law of conservation of energy states that energy in a system is neither created nor destroyed, Yet not all energy is converted into the use for which it is intended. The term *energy efficiency* refers to the amount of energy in a system that performs the desired work. For example, a car burns fuel so that it can move. However, not all of the energy that is released from this process is converted into motion. A portion of the energy is redirected because of inefficiencies in the system, producing engine heat, overcoming friction in the car's moving parts, and so on.

Electric generating stations may use a variety of fuel sources to produce electricity. All have one thing in common: they convert one type of energy into another. Hydroelectric stations convert mechanical energy of moving water into electrical energy. Nuclear generating stations convert the energy released by nuclear reactions into electrical energy. Fossil fuel power plants convert coal, oil, or natural gas into electrical energy. A comparison of each of these types of electric generating stations shows that some methods are more efficient than others in converting one type of energy to another. Note that these estimates do not include factors such as cost per unit of electricity generated nor impact on the environment.

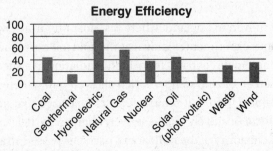

Efficiency values for converting fuel types into electric energy.

7. Based on this information, the most efficient method of generating electricity is
   (1) coal
   (2) hydroelectric
   (3) nuclear
   (4) solar
   (5) wind

8. Which of the following methods of generating electric power have approximately the same level of efficiency?
   (1) natural gas and wind
   (2) nuclear and waste
   (3) coal and oil
   (4) hydroelectric and solar
   (5) geothermal and wind

9. Hydroelectric generating stations use the mechanical energy of flowing water to turn a turbine that converts the energy using an electric generator. This is an example of which law?
   (1) Newton's first law of motion
   (2) Law of universal gravitation
   (3) Newton's second law
   (4) Law of conservation of energy
   (5) Law of energy efficiency

The father of modern nuclear physics was Ernest Rutherford, a New Zealand born physicist and chemist and the discoverer of the nuclear structure of the atom, who performed some of his early research in Canada. Working at McGill University in Montreal, Rutherford formulated the concept of nuclear decay and half-life, which is the time required for a radioactive substance to fall to half the level of radioactivity. Based on this discovery, he was able to show that radioactivity involved the chemical change of one substance into another. For this work, he was awarded the Nobel Prize for Chemistry in 1908.

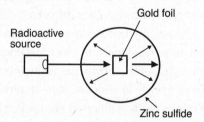

In 1907, Rutherford moved to England, where his most important work was still to come. Rutherford's most famous experiment is known as the gold foil experiment. He used a particle emitter containing radium to direct particles of alpha radiation at a sheet of gold foil. The foil was surrounded by a screen of zinc sulfide, which allowed him to detect where the particles struck using a microscope. Up to that time, scientists theorized that atoms were solid units that contained a mixture of positively and negatively charged particles. However, Rutherford discovered that the vast majority of the radioactive particles passed straight through the gold foil. This led him to conclude that atoms were mostly empty space and consisted of a nucleus orbited by electrons. While most of the alpha particles passed through the empty space, a few came close to, or collided with, the nucleus and were deflected. Rutherford's experiment and subsequent discovery of protons and neutrons are the basis for contemporary understanding of the structure of atoms.

10. Ernest Rutherford conducted his most important work in
    (1) New Zealand
    (2) Canada
    (3) The United States
    (4) Europe
    (5) England

11. The majority of alpha particles passed through the gold foil because of
    (1) empty space between electrons and the nucleus
    (2) positively charged protons
    (3) collision with the nucleus
    (4) space between atoms
    (5) radioactive decay

12. All colours are contained in white light. When light strikes an object, some colours are absorbed while others are reflected. The colours that are reflected are the ones we see.

    If we see an apple that is red, this means that
    (1) red colour is absorbed
    (2) red is reflected
    (3) red is absent from the light
    (4) more red is present in the light
    (5) red is a dominant colour

ANSWERS

1. **(1)** Condensing from vapour to droplets is a change in the physical characteristics but not the chemical structure of the water.
2. **(5)** According to the table, the man will have the greatest weight on the sun, which is the largest body and has the greatest gravitational force. Weight is equal to mass times gravity.
3. **(2)** We conclude that the moon has the lowest gravity because the man will weigh the least.
4. **(4)** Inertia is equal to the mass of the object and is constant.
5. **(3)** The rock will weigh slightly less (about 99.85% of the weight at sea level) because of its farther distance from the Earth.
6. **(1)** Following the chemical reaction, the calcium hydroxide and hydrochloric acid have changed to become calcium chloride and water.
7. **(2)** According to the chart, hydroelectric power converts about 90% of the energy to electricity.
8. **(3)** Coal 43% and oil 44% have the most similar levels of efficiency of the options given.
9. **(4)** Energy is neither created nor destroyed, but converted from one form to another.

10. **(5)** Although Rutherford won the Nobel Prize for his work done in Canada, the passage states that his most important work was done later in England.

11. **(1)** The passage of the alpha particles allowed Rutherford to deduce the empty space between electrons and the nucleus.

12. **(2)** The colour we see is reflected. Other colours are absorbed.

Life Science

14

THINK ABOUT IT

Which of the following things is alive?

a. Ice crystal
b. Sea sponge
c. Rose bush
d. Piece of wood
e. Elephant
f. Gold
g. Mold

If you said b, c, e, and g, you are correct; but how do you tell if something is alive? What are the characteristics of living things?

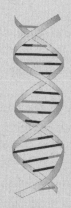

Do non-living things have DNA?

IN THIS CHAPTER

After completing this chapter, you will be able to

→ **DEFINE LIFE SCIENCE**

→ **DESCRIBE THE STRUCTURE OF A CELL**

→ **EXPLAIN PRINCIPLES OF GENETICS AND HEREDITY**

→ **DESCRIBE THE THEORY OF EVOLUTION**

→ **IDENTIFY THE LIFE CYCLE OF PLANTS**

→ **CLASSIFY ANIMALS ACCORDING TO THEIR CHARACTERISTICS**

→ **INVESTIGATE WAYS IN WHICH PLANTS AND ANIMALS DEPEND ON ONE ANOTHER**

→ **DESCRIBE THE FLOW OF ENERGY IN LIVING SYSTEMS**

→ **RESPOND TO QUESTIONS ABOUT SYSTEMS OF THE HUMAN BODY**

WHAT IS LIFE SCIENCE?

The second area of science examined on the GED Science Test is life science, which accounts for 45% of the questions on the test. The questions will test your ability to comprehend, apply, and interpret life-science information in paragraphs, charts, tables, or diagrams.

Life science is the study of things that are alive. It includes a wide range of scientific fields, such as biology, botany, microbiology, genetics, marine biology, health, environmental science, and ecology. There are many occupations that involve life science. Some of these include practical nurse, food inspector, biologist, environmental technician, athletic therapist, horticulturalist, medical laboratory technician, or conservation officer.

You do not need to remember specific information about life science to write the GED Science Test. You do need to be able to read and answer questions about life-science passages, diagrams, charts, and graphs.

TIP

Life science is about living things.

PRACTICE

Choose the best answer to each question.

Life science is the study of living things, but what makes something alive? Clearly, all plants and animals are living things, but for some things, it is not clear. Seven characteristics are commonly used to determine life:

1. **ORGANIZATION**—All living things are made of cells and have different levels of organization.
2. **MOVEMENT**—All living things move in some way. Even plants have the ability to turn and grow towards light.
3. **NUTRITION AND EXCRETION**—All living things take in and use energy for growth and maintenance and discard waste.
4. **RESPIRATION**—All living things breathe, exchanging gases with their environment.
5. **GROWTH**—All living things grow and develop.
6. **SENSITIVITY**—All living things respond to stimuli from their environment, such as light, sound, or temperature.
7. **REPRODUCTION**—All living things produce offspring and pass on genetic information to their offspring.

To be considered alive, something must exhibit all of these characteristics. Even non-living things may exhibit some characteristics. Ice crystals, for example, may grow, but they are not alive. A piece of wood has cells, but it is not alive. Non-living things can be of two types: things that were never alive, such as stones or water; and things that were once part of something alive, such as wood or bone. Another characteristic that is often attributed to living things is adaptation, the ability of an organism to adjust its behaviour—or, through mutation in genetic structure—to become better suited to changes in the environment.

1. Coal is formed from fossilized plant material that sank into swamps. Over time, it was buried in sediment and vegetation, which applied pressure and heat that caused a chemical reaction to occur, forming peat. Eventually, continued heat and pressure caused the peat to compact and harden into coal. Which of the following can you deduce from this passage?
   (1) Peat is alive
   (2) Coal is alive
   (3) Peat has adapted to its environment
   (4) Coal has adapted to its environment
   (5) Peat and coal are composed of things that were once alive

2. Which of the following things is alive?
   (1) Single-celled organism
   (2) Sand
   (3) Glass
   (4) Iceberg
   (5) Pimple

3. Every winter, grey whales migrate from the nutrient-rich cold waters of the Arctic Ocean to warmer waters near Mexico to give birth to their young, before returning in summer to their Arctic feeding ground. The round-trip journey of over 16,000 km is the farthest migration of any mammal and is an example of
   (1) Organization
   (2) Nutrition and excretion
   (3) Sensitivity
   (4) Behavioural adaptation
   (5) Physical adaptation

4. Earthworms are hermaphroditic, containing both sperm and eggs within their bodies, yet they cannot fertilize themselves. After mating with another worm, cocoons that contain fertilized eggs are left in the soil. This is an example of
   (1) Movement
   (2) Respiration
   (3) Reproduction
   (4) Growth
   (5) Organization

DNA (Deoxyribonucleic Acid) is a macromolecule with a double helix shape that is located in the nucleus of cells in human beings, and nearly every other organism. Virtually every cell in the human body contains the same DNA, which in turn contains all of the genetic information for the development and functioning of the organism. Your gender, hair colour, and height are all programmed in your DNA. Some believe that even elements of personality are embedded in DNA. Whenever a cell divides, the two child cells (which are always called daughter cells, regardless of gender) contain the same DNA as the parent.

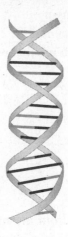

5. According to the information in this passage, every cell of an organism
    (1) shares one DNA
    (2) has identical DNA
    (3) has different DNA
    (4) has no DNA
    (5) has a double helix shape

6. Based on the information in this passage, you can conclude that
    (1) rocks do not have DNA
    (2) humans do not have DNA
    (3) fish do not have DNA
    (4) cells do not have DNA
    (5) plants do not have DNA

ANSWERS

1. **(5)** Both peat and coal are made of vegetation that was once alive but is no longer.
2. **(1)** Single-celled organisms contain all of the characteristics of life.
3. **(4)** The migration is a behaviour of whales to adapt to their environment.
4. **(3)** This is a description of how earthworms reproduce.
5. **(2)** Cells throughout the organism contain identical DNA.
6. **(1)** Rocks do not have cells, so they do not have DNA.

CHALLENGE EXERCISE

Are viruses alive? Viruses tread the grey area between living and non-living things. Use a book or the Internet to research the qualities of living and non-living things possessed by viruses. Do you think they are alive?

CELLS

All living things are made of cells, the smallest material that can contain all of the elements of life. Cells contain water, proteins, oxygen, carbon, hydrogen, and nitrogen. Some organisms are single-celled organisms, called protozoa, while others are made of many cells. The human body, for example, contains trillions of cells.

Cells come in different shapes and sizes, although most are too small to see with the naked eye. In complex organisms, such as people, there are hundreds of different types of cells that are specialized to perform different functions. They have different shapes because of their functions. For example, nerve cells are long and thin whereas blood cells are round. Where do cells come from? New cells are only made from existing cells.

In responding to questions about cells, you may encounter terms that name the parts and structures of a cell. You do not have to remember these terms for the GED Science Test, but you should know that cells have different parts that perform different functions.

TIP

All living things are made of cells.

- **CELL MEMBRANE**—The flexible outer container of a cell, like a balloon filled with jelly. The cell membrane is semi-permeable, which means that it lets some things pass through, such as nutrients, but does not allow other things to pass. All animal cells have a cell membrane.
- **CELL WALL**—The more rigid outer container of a plant cell, outside the cell membrane. A cell wall is also semi-permeable, allowing the passage of small molecules and proteins.
- **CYTOPLASM**—Everything inside the cell membrane except the nucleus. Sometimes you may see diagrams that refer only to the fluid as cytoplasm, but this is more properly cytosol. The cytoplasm includes both the organelles and the cytosol.
- **ORGANELLES**—Any of the structures within the cell, like "miniatures" of the organs in your body. Organelles may have their own membrane. The following are organelles:

    NUCLEUS—The part of the cell that contains DNA and RNA and is responsible for reproduction. It contains the genetic information.

    MITOCHONDRIA—These organelles take in and process nutrients to produce energy for the cell.

    VACUOLE—A fluid-filled space inside a cell, surrounded by a membrane. Often the vacuole contains waste or other undesirable substances, isolating them from the cell. A vacuole is formed when vesicles, which are the same thing but smaller, join together.

    LYSOSOME—Vesicles containing enzymes that break down or "digest" nutrients and wastes in the cell.

    RIBOSOMES—Found throughout the cell, these organelles manufacture proteins for use in the cell.

    ENDOPLASMIC RETICULUM—A network of membranes throughout the cell—some of which are connected to the nucleus—that aids in the creation, transportation, and storage of materials in the cell. There are two kinds in the cell: the smooth endoplasmic reticulum; and the rough endoplasmic reticulum, which is bonded with ribosomes, giving it a rough appearance.

    GOLGI APPARATUS—A stack-like structure of membranes containing enzymes, the Golgi apparatus (also called the Golgi body) makes, sorts, and transports complex proteins from materials delivered by the rough endoplasmic reticulum. It also plays a role in creating lysosomes, the digestive system of the cell.

    CENTRIOLES—Found near the nucleus, these organelles play a role in cell reproduction.

PRACTICE

Choose the best answer to each question.

Although there are many types of cells, all fall into one of two types: prokaryote and eukaryote. All plants, animals, and fungi, whether multicellular or singe-cellular, have eukaryotic cells. Bacteria and another group of single-celled organisms called *archaea* (similar in many ways to bacteria, generally living in extreme environmental conditions) are prokaryotes. Bacteria are prokaryotic and are the most numerous type of cell on earth.

The two types of cells have much in common. Like eukaryotic plant cells, prokaryotic cells have cell walls. Both prokaryotic and eukaryotic cells have cell membranes, cytoplasm, and ribosomes. Both have DNA. The primary difference between them is that prokaryotic cells do not have a nucleus.

Prokaryote cells are far less complex than eukaryote cells. Because they have no nucleus, they also have simpler DNA that is in circular strands, rather than the ladder-shaped double helix of the eukaryotic cells, and floats loosely in the cytoplasm. In addition, prokaryotic cells have fewer internal structures than eukaryotic cells. There are no mitochondria, and such organelles as there are do not have membranes. All prokaryote cells reproduce through cell division, so the daughter cells are identical to the parent.

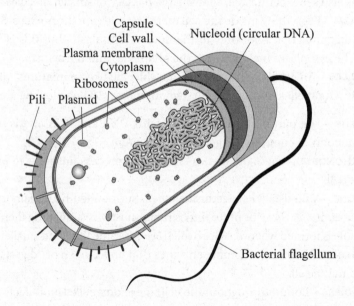

1. Although some bacteria are harmful and can cause illness or death, most are beneficial, even necessary. At all times, the human body is filled with millions of bacteria, which aid in digestion and other functions. Whether they are helpful or harmful, one thing all bacteria have in common is that they
   (1) are eukaryotic
   (2) have no DNA
   (3) have no nucleus
   (4) have no organelles
   (5) have no cell wall

2. A type of single-celled organism that might be found in hostile conditions such as a deep-sea hydrothermal vent is
   (1) bacteria
   (2) archaea
   (3) organelle
   (4) eukaryote
   (5) mitochondria

3. Based on the information in this passage, you can conclude that yeast, a type of single-celled organism
   (1) is a eukaryote
   (2) is a prokaryote
   (3) is a plant
   (4) is an archaea
   (5) is a molecule

Plant and animal cells have many similar structures, but some differences as well. Both have a nucleus, cytoplasm, and many similar organelles. Plants, however, have a cell wall made of cellulose, which allows them to maintain a fixed, generally rectangular shape. Animal cells have only a cell membrane, which gives them a more flexible, often rounded shape. In addition, plant and animal cells have some different organelles that aid the plant in photosynthesis and the animal cell in breaking down nutrients.

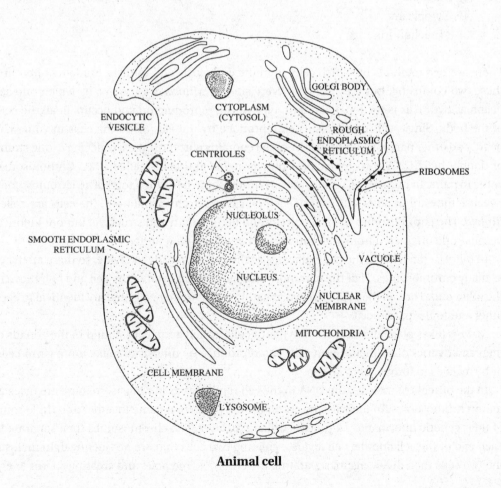

Animal cell

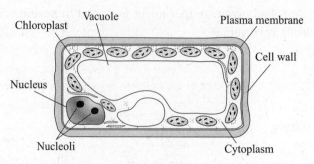

Vacuole

Chloroplast

Plasma membrane

Cell wall

Nucleus

Nucleoli

Cytoplasm

Plant cell

4. Based on the diagrams, which organelle is found in plant cells, but not in animal cells?
   (1) Cell membrane
   (2) Endoplasmic reticulum
   (3) Golgi apparatus
   (4) Mitochondria
   (5) Chloroplast

5. Based on the diagrams, which organelle is found in animal cells, but not usually in plant cells?
   (1) Nucleus
   (2) Lysosome
   (3) Vacuole
   (4) Cytoplasm
   (5) Mitochondria

There are two methods by which cells reproduce: meiosis and mitosis. Students often find these two confusing, but they are really very simple. *Mitosis* is a process by which one cell becomes two. This is the most common type of cell reproduction and occurs in all the cells of the body. Single-celled organisms all reproduce by mitosis, as do the cells in your skin, heart, and other parts of your body. Every cell contains chromosomes, which have one strand of double helix DNA (two molecules) plus proteins and acids called RNA. Chromosomes come in pairs. In human cells, there are 23 chromosome pairs for a total of 46 chromosomes. Because they are in pairs, and half of each pair came from each parent, the cells are called *diploid*. The chromosomes in each pair are similar in length and structure, but not identical because one originated from your mother and one from your father.

In mitosis, the DNA in the cell replicates as the cell gets ready to divide, so there are twice as many chromosomes. Half the chromosomes move to one end of the cell and half move to the other end. The cell then splits in two, creating two daughter cells that are identical to each other and to the parent cell.

Meiosis takes place only in certain types of cells, called germ cells, found in the gonads of men and ovaries of women. Germ cells can reproduce by mitosis to make more germ cells, or by meiosis to form eggs or sperm.

In the process of meiosis, the DNA in the cell replicates as in mitosis, so there are twice as many chromosomes. In meiosis, the chromosome pairs then come together and trade some of their genetic information, a process called *crossover*. The chromosomes then separate to each end of the cell and the cell divides, creating two cells that are not identical. In meiosis, the two cells then divide again, separating the chromosome pairs and creating sperm or egg cells that have only half the number of chromosomes of a normal cell. The cells are not identical, which is why the offspring of the same parents are not identical. Each cell of a gamete (sperm cell or egg cell) contains one complete set of chromosomes and is called a *haploid* cell. During sexual reproduction, the sperm cell fertilizes the egg to create a single cell with a normal number of paired chromosomes—the diploid cell—half from the father's sperm and half from the mother's egg.

6. Bacteria are single-celled organisms of the prokaryote type, meaning that they do not have a nucleus. Nevertheless, bacteria reproduce in the same manner as most other cells through
   (1) eukaryotes
   (2) meiosis
   (3) mitosis
   (4) chromosome pairs
   (5) sexual reproduction

7. The term *crossover* refers to
   (1) exchange of genetic information between chromosome pairs during meiosis
   (2) replication of DNA prior to cell division
   (3) the formation of haploid cells that all contain slightly different genetic information
   (4) the creation of chromosomes from DNA, RNA, and proteins
   (5) the most common type of reproduction, occurring in all cells of the body

8. A fertilized human egg is called a zygote. It has how many chromosomes?
   (1) 2
   (2) 8
   (3) 23
   (4) 46
   (5) 92

ANSWERS

1. **(3)** Bacteria are prokaryotes and have no nucleus.
2. **(2)** The passage states that archaea are a type of prokaryotes that generally live in extreme environmental conditions.
3. **(1)** Yeast is not a type of bacteria, so it is probably not prokaryotic.
4. **(5)** Chloroplast is unique to plant cells and aids in photosynthesis.
5. **(2)** Lysosomes are found in animal cells, but not in most plant cells.
6. **(3)** Only cells that will take part in sexual reproduction are formed through meiosis.
7. **(1)** In meiosis, chromosome pairs come together and crossover some genetic information.
8. **(4)** The zygote has 23 chromosomes from the sperm and 23 from the egg.

TIP

Genes contain
instructions for
observable and
unobservable
characteristics
of an organism.
A trait
(phenotype) is
an observable
inherited
characteristic.

GENETICS

Heredity is the passing on of traits from parents to offspring from generation to generation. Some traits are physical traits that can be observed, such as height or hair colour, while others cannot be seen. Mental and personal characteristics are also inheritable.

Genetics is the study of genes and the mechanics of heredity. Genes are strands of nucleotides (the elements that make up DNA) found within the chromosomes. A basic understanding of cell division through meiosis is helpful in understanding the basic concepts of genetics.

PRACTICE

Choose the best answer to each question.

Genes are the blueprint of the body. They design and control, through the manufacture of proteins, how the body grows, develops, and functions. Genes are located in the strands of DNA found in the chromosomes of cells. It is estimated that a human cell contains more than 25,000 genes, which control everything from hair colour to the shape of one's nose to height and unobservable things such as blood type.

Chromosome pairs are homologous, which means that they are approximately the same length and have DNA with genes about the same things, but they are not identical. This is because one chromosome originated with and contains genetic information from the mother and the other from the father. Information in each gene of the chromosome pair pertaining to a quality is called an *allele*. For example, information about hair colour is an allele. The resulting inherited feature, such as having brown hair, is a trait.

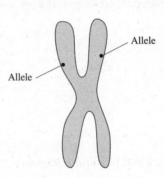

1. Based on the information in this passage, you can conclude that the alleles in a chromosome for any given feature are
   (1) identical
   (2) different
   (3) traits
   (4) homologous
   (5) DNA

2. If a person has inherited brown hair from his or her parents, this is called a
   (1) allele
   (2) chromosome
   (3) trait
   (4) gene
   (5) chromosome pair

For each genetic characteristic, chromosome pairs have two alleles, one in the chromosome originating from the father and one from the mother. For example, a person with brown hair may have one allele for brown hair and one for blond hair. Some alleles are dominant, which is to say that a person with alleles for both brown hair and blond hair will have brown hair as the brown hair gene is a dominant gene.

To explain how inheritance works and the likelihood of particular traits, an English geneticist, Richard Punnett, devised a technique that is known as the Punnett square. A grid is formed with the two alleles from one parent written across the top and those of the other at the side. The remaining areas of the grid are then filled in with the possible resulting combinations.

For example, a mother has alleles for both brown hair (abbreviated as B because it is dominant) and blond hair (abbreviated as b because it is recessive). The father also has alleles for both brown and blond hair. The possible combinations are revealed in the grid, showing that the child of these parents may have two alleles for brown hair, one each of brown and blond, or two alleles for blond hair. As brown is dominant, the child will have a trait of brown hair if either or both of the alleles is brown.

		Mother	
		B	b
Father	B	BB	Bb
	b	Bb	bb

3. Based on the information in the Punnett square, what is the percentage chance that a child of parents with alleles for both brown and blond hair will have blond hair?
   (1) 0%
   (2) 25%
   (3) 50%
   (4) 75%
   (5) 100%

4. If one of the parents had two alleles for brown hair (B) what is the percentage chance that the child would have blond hair?
   (1) 0%
   (2) 25%
   (3) 50%
   (4) 75%
   (5) 100%

ANSWERS

1. **(2)** The two alleles in a chromosome are different because they came from different parents.

2. **(3)** An observable inherited feature in a living organism is called a trait.

3. **(2)** Only one of the four possible combinations does not include the dominate brown hair allele.

4. **(1)** There would be no chance as every possible combination would have a dominant brown hair allele. However, there is a chance that this child could have offspring with brown hair as it could still carry the recessive blond hair gene.

EVOLUTION

TIP

Organisms change gradually over time through the process of natural selection.

Evolution is about change, and biological evolution is about how organisms change over time and new species come to exist. The modern understanding of biological evolution began with the publication of Charles Darwin's *On the Origin of Species* in 1859. In this work, Darwin outlined his observations and conclusions from five years as a naturalist on the HMS *Beagle*.

During his research, Darwin observed that individual organisms within a population differ from one another. For example, not all pigeons are the same. The differences can be inherited by their offspring, and offspring who have differences that better enable them to survive and prosper in their environment are more likely to reproduce and pass on their traits. Over time, small changes accumulate so that the organism of today is not the same as the organism of ten thousand years ago. Eventually, descendants of a population may have changed so much that they become another species.

Darwin theorized that all living things are related and that all species that are alive today are descended from only a few—or perhaps only one—common ancestors. In the manner of much like a family tree, each new branch from the base of the trunk splits off to many new branches that spread wide with their number. Evolution is a process that never stops. Organisms continue to slowly change over time, reproducing characteristics that are favourable in their given environment.

PRACTICE

Choose the best answer to each question.

No one truly knows how life on Earth began. *Biogenesis* is the hypothesis that life only comes from life. Living things can only be created by other living things through a process of reproduction and cannot spontaneously appear. Nonetheless, the assumption remains that 3.5 billion years ago *abiogenesis* occurred (life created from non-life), creating the first living thing on earth and the common ancestor of us all.

One theory about the origin of life is commonly known as the *primordial soup* theory. It is basically one of chemical evolution, which hypothesises that life began from chemical interactions in the volatile environment of the very early (primordial) Earth. At that time, the atmosphere was filled with gases, which were exposed to various forms of energy, such as lightning and heat. The conditions in the atmosphere resulted in the formation of simple organic compounds called *monomers* that gathered together in a mixture (soup) at shorelines and other areas, such as hot ocean vents. Through further transformation, the compounds continued to develop and become complex polymers, eventually becoming alive and forming the basis for further evolution. Although this theory has been widely accepted and taught in classrooms, there remain unanswered questions and little evidence to sustain its credibility.

1. The process of organic compounds becoming alive because of environmental conditions would be called
   (1) monomers
   (2) polymers
   (3) primordial soup
   (4) biogenesis
   (5) abiogenesis

2. Which of the following expresses the steps of the primordial soup theory in the correct order?
   (1) Gas-filled atmosphere, monomers, polymers, energy, life
   (2) Gas-filled atmosphere, energy, monomers, polymers, life
   (3) Monomers, gas-filled atmosphere, energy, polymers, life
   (4) Polymers, energy, monomers, gas-filled atmosphere, life
   (5) Energy, gas-filled atmosphere, monomers, life, polymers

Modern evolutionary biologists use numerous methods, such as fossil records, population genetics, and analysis of DNA sequences, as they continue to study the relationship among organisms. Much of the focus of research is to determine what changes occurred to which organisms and when. Through research, scientists have built a tree of life that shows the path of evolutionary change.

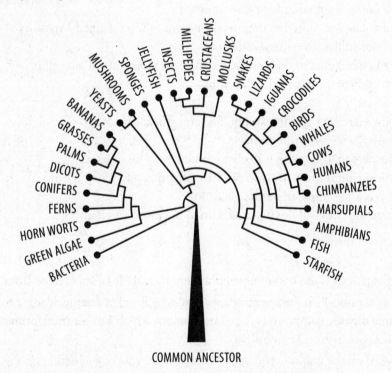

COMMON ANCESTOR

3. Based on the graphic, which of the following organisms is the oldest?
   (1) Sponges
   (2) Yeast
   (3) Insects
   (4) Mollusks
   (5) Crocodiles

4. Based on the graphic, which of the following is true?
   (1) Humans are descended from chimpanzees
   (2) Green algae is an ancestor of mushrooms
   (3) Birds and crocodiles have a common ancestor
   (4) There is a close evolutionary relationship between jellyfish and whales
   (5) There is a close evolutionary relationship between starfish and snakes

The term *survival of the fittest* did not originate with Darwin and does not, in fact, accurately reflect the much less dramatic process of evolution through the mechanism of mutation, leading to natural selection. The facts are that individuals in a population differ from one another, and that, as populations grow, the environment does not provide sufficient resources to support all individuals. As a result, those individuals that are best suited to prosper in their environment are most likely to produce offspring and pass on their traits. Mutation is not a dramatic process. It involves small changes that occur over generations when organisms reproduce. Furthermore, it is a genetic process and acquired characteristics are not passed on. Natural selection is not an intelligent process; there is no design and no plan. It is simply a question of chance mutations that better suit organisms for their environment.

5. Natural selection does not necessarily lead to more complex organisms. For example, fleas do not have wings, but it is believed they are descended from organisms with wings. We can conclude that fleas
   (1) are not well suited to their environment
   (2) are not as well suited to their environment as their winged ancestors
   (3) are not subject to natural selection
   (4) are better suited to their environment than their winged ancestors
   (5) are likely to mutate to develop wings

6. A person exercises regularly and builds large muscle mass.
   (1) The muscles are a mutation.
   (2) The person's offspring is likely to inherit large muscles.
   (3) The person is more likely to produce offspring and pass on traits
   (4) This is an example of natural selection
   (5) Large muscles will not be passed on to the person's offspring

ANSWERS

1. **(5)** Abiogenesis is the hypothetical phenomenon of life being created from non-life.

2. **(2)** The chemically reducing atmosphere was exposed to energy, leading to formation of simple organic compounds called monomers, which further transformed into more complex polymers and came alive.

3. **(2)** Based on the graphic, you can conclude that yeast began earlier on the evolutionary tree than other organisms listed.

4. **(3)** The graphic depicts birds and crocodiles as having a common ancestor. In fact, modern research shows that both are descendants of dinosaurs.

5. **(4)** Under natural selection, fleas without wings must be better suited to their environment.

6. **(5)** Muscles developed by exercise are acquired characteristics and are not inheritable.

PLANTS

Plants are living organisms, just like animals, insects, birds, and other living things. Plants have all of the same characteristics of life.

TIP

Plants are living things.

1. **ORGANIZATION**—Plants are made of cells.
2. **MOVEMENT**—Plants are able to move in rudimentary ways, such as turning towards sunlight, but movement also takes place within the plant in the transport of nutrients.
3. **NUTRITION AND EXCRETION**—Plants require nutrients, water, and energy.
4. **RESPIRATION**—Plants require air to breathe, consuming carbon dioxide and expelling oxygen.
5. **GROWTH**—Plants grow and eventually die.
6. **SENSITIVITY**—Plants respond to changes in the environment around them.
7. **REPRODUCTION**—Plants produce offspring.

Plants are also subject to evolution. In fact, at some distant point, we share common ancestors. As with other organisms, the mechanism of natural selection applies to plants. One of Charles Darwin's earliest books, *Fertilization of Orchids,* described how natural selection had equipped orchids to be attractive and hospitable to insects that are needed for pollination, leading to reproduction.

PRACTICE

Choose the best answer to each question.

Plants are among the few organisms categorized as *autotrophs*, meaning they are able to create their own food from their environment and, unlike animals, are not dependent on other organisms. The manner in which they do so is called *photosynthesis*, the process by which sunlight, water, carbon dioxide, and nutrients are converted into sugars that the plant uses to maintain itself and grow.

Plants are divided into two basic parts: the underground root structure; and the above ground shoot, including the stem, leaves, flowers, and fruits. The roots draw in water and nutrients from the soil. Carbon dioxide is drawn in through stomata, small pores in the leaves, and stems. Sunlight is captured by chlorophyll, a green pigment found in the chloroplast organelles within plant cells.

The first, light-dependent stage of photosynthesis takes place in the chloroplast and involves light and water. Chlorophyll captures energy from light. The chlorophyll molecules become excited, beginning a chemical reaction that splits the water molecules into hydrogen and oxygen and utilizes the hydrogen to form ATP, an energy-storing nucleotide that provides energy for cellular reactions, and a compound called NADPH. The oxygen from the water is then expelled through the stomata.

The second stage of photosynthesis takes place in the stoma and does not require light. It generally takes place during the day, but may continue into the night. During this stage, ATP and NADPH interact with carbon dioxide to convert it into sugars.

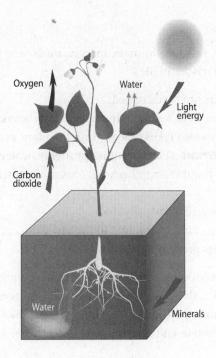

Oxygen

Water

Light energy

Carbon dioxide

Water

Minerals

1. Based on the information in this passage, you can conclude that
    (1) animals are dependent on other organisms for food
    (2) plants are dependent on other organisms for food
    (3) plants are the only autotrophs
    (4) plants are not alive
    (5) animals and plants synthesize food in similar ways

2. The first stage of photosynthesis takes place within the
    (1) stoma
    (2) leaves
    (3) plant cells
    (4) roots
    (5) water molecules

3. What is given off by the plant during photosynthesis?
    (1) Minerals
    (2) Carbon dioxide
    (3) Water
    (4) Oxygen
    (5) Light energy

4. Interaction of ATP and NADPH with carbon dioxide to form sugar could be described as a
    (1) chlorophyll
    (2) nutrient
    (3) chemical reaction
    (4) nucleotide
    (5) stoma

Are algae plants? Algae are single-celled and multi-celled members of the kingdom Protista that drift at or near the surface of water. They are autotrophs that generate food from the environment using photosynthesis. In fact, half of the world's oxygen is thought to result from photosynthesis in algae. Although algae are traditionally considered plants, technically they are not, as they lack roots, stems, leaves, flowers, and other vascular structures. In addition, all plants are multi-cellular, whereas many algae are single-celled, and plants are rooted in place, while algae are not.

5. What do plants and algae have in common?
   (1) Members of the kingdom Protista
   (2) Photosynthesis
   (3) Roots
   (4) Vascular structures
   (5) Leaves

ANSWERS

1. **(1)** The passage says that, unlike animals, plants do not depend on other organisms for food.
2. **(3)** The first stage takes place within the chloroplasts, which are organelles in the plant cells.
3. **(4)** The graphic illustrates oxygen given off and the other substances drawn in.
4. **(3)** The interaction between the molecules is a chemical reaction.
5. **(2)** Algae are not technically plants, but they do employ photosynthesis.

ANIMALS

All living organisms are traditionally classified into groups or *kingdoms*. The original classifications were made based on the form and structure of the organisms. Over time, the classifications have changed slightly. There are now considered to be six kingdoms under three domains of life.

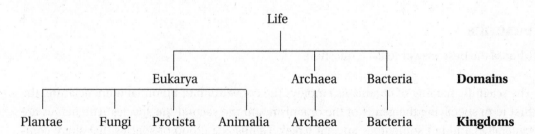

Animals are members of the kingdom *Animalia*. Animals are multicellular. They have the ability to move about voluntarily. They eat other organisms for their food. Organisms are further subdivided into additional classifications. At each level, there are more and more. For example, there are forty phyla of animals, more than eighty classes, and millions of species.

Animals include a wide range of organisms. The basic classes of animals that you read about could include: amphibians, birds, mammals, reptiles, fish, and invertebrates (including insects).

TIP

Animals can be classified as amphibians, birds, mammals, reptiles, fish, and invertebrates.

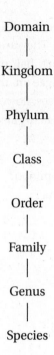

Domain

|

Kingdom

|

Phylum

|

Class

|

Order

|

Family

|

Genus

|

Species

On the GED® Science Test, you could be asked questions about a variety of animal topics, such as their biology, migratory patterns, endangered status, or interdependence with other organisms. Remember that on the GED® test, you do not need specific knowledge about animals. All of the information you need to answer the questions will be found in the passages, graphics, or diagrams on the test.

CHALLENGE EXERCISE

Using the Internet or library, research and name one species from each of the major categories of animals: amphibians, birds, mammals, reptiles, fish, and invertebrates. Identify one characteristic that is common to all of the species you named. Identify one characteristic about each that makes it unique from the others. Share and discuss your results with another student, family member, or friend.

PRACTICE

Choose the best answer to each question.

The scientific naming of organisms employs the convention of binomial nomenclature, the first term specifying the genus of the organism and the second the species. The names are generally Latin but sometimes ancient Greek. Genus is a group of species that share common characteristics and share a common ancestor more recently than with other organisms. For example, the genus *Equus* applies to the species of horse, donkey, and zebra, a closely related group of individuals capable of interbreeding. A wild horse is named *Equus ferus*, the second name denoting the species. Despite binomial nomenclature, species may also have subspecies, a distinction that remains above the level of a breed, and, therefore, have three names. The domestic horse is *Equus ferus caballus* and all breeds of domestic dog are *Canis lupis familiaris*.

Although organisms of the same species have the most genetic material in common, organisms within the same genus are often capable of interbreeding. However, the resulting offspring are usually sterile because of the differing number of chromosomes in its parents, which prevents the hybrid from producing functioning sex cells through meiosis.

1. The scientific name *Equus ferus przewalskii* denotes a
    (1) genus of horse
    (2) species of horse
    (3) subspecies of horse
    (4) hybrid
    (5) wild horse

2. A mule is the offspring of a female horse and male donkey that is likely to be
    (1) the same species as its mother
    (2) the same species as its father
    (3) a different genus than its mother
    (4) a different genus than its father
    (5) infertile

All animals are *heterotrophs*, meaning they derive their sustenance from other organisms. Within that scope, animals may be carnivore, herbivore, or omnivore. The carnivore is a predator who feeds on the flesh of other animals. An herbivore gains sustenance from plants. An omnivore will eat anything.

Animals have evolved distinct anatomical structures appropriate to the manner of their feeding. The dentition of mammals, in particular the number and type teeth and bite force, are often indicators of diet. There are four types of teeth that mammals may possess: incisors, canines, premolars, and molars, but not all animals have the same number of teeth or the same type, depending on their needs.

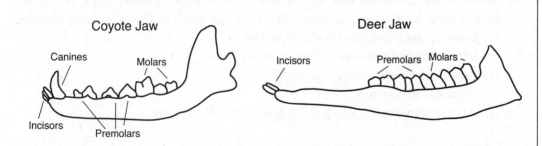

3. Based on the diagrams, you might conclude that canine teeth are not required by
    (1) herbivores
    (2) carnivores
    (3) omnivores
    (4) mammals
    (5) coyotes

Not all mammals live on land. The families of the order *Cetacea* are aquatic mammals that include the various species of whales, porpoises, and dolphins. They live their entire lives in the ocean, but they are mammals like the numerous species of land-living, warm-blooded animals that have hair and mammary glands and give birth to live young. Like other mammals, ocean inhabitants communicate using sound. For aquatic mammalian species, auditory communication is vital to survival because light is slowed and diffused in water, but sound travels four times faster in water than air.

Whales are well noted for their whale songs; however, not all whales communicate in the same manner. The well-known sound of whale songs, for example, is issued by the male humpbacked whale as it searches for a mate. They are also known to make other sounds to communicate, such as grunts, snorts, and groans. Other aquatic mammals make different sounds. Sperm whales, like dolphins, form a series of high-pitched clicks to communicate. Baleen whales communicate through drawn-out, low frequency sounds. Blue whales, a type of baleen whale and the largest animal on earth, make long moaning sounds, but have also been known to sing.

Scientists and environmentalists have been concerned about the survival of whale species. As recently as the 1970s, it seemed that numerous species were in danger of extinction. Although continued vigilance is needed, public awareness and legislation such as the international ban on the hunting of humpbacked whales has allowed populations to rebound from near extinction to a population of nearly 80,000 worldwide.

4. Based on the information in this passage, you can conclude that one of the major causes of the decline of whale populations was
    (1) other mammals
    (2) pollution
    (3) poor communication
    (4) hunting
    (5) lack of public awareness

5. Scientists are concerned that noise pollution from sonar, passing ships, and other human activities may be a continued threat to whale survival. This is probably because
    (1) auditory communication is vital to whales
    (2) light is diffused and moves more slowly in water
    (3) they are the largest animals on earth
    (4) sonar sounds like whale song
    (5) it is the humpbacked whale that is best known for its song

6. Which characteristic do whales share with dolphins and porpoises that distinguishes them from other ocean dwellers?
    (1) Gills
    (2) Dependence on auditory communication
    (3) Dependence on visual communication
    (4) Hair
    (5) Risk of extinction

ANSWERS

1. **(3)** According to the passage, three names indicate a subspecies.

2. **(5)** Hybrid organisms are likely to be infertile because of the differing number of chromosomes in the parents.

3. **(1)** Deer are herbivores and do not require canines for piercing and tearing, but they do require incisors for biting and stripping, and molars for grinding and chewing.

4. **(4)** As an international moratorium on the hunting of humpbacked whales was a factor in their recovery, you can conclude that hunting was a significant factor in their decline. Although lack of public awareness was also a factor, it did not directly threaten them.

5. **(1)** As sound travels faster and farther in water than air, you can conclude that noise pollution may interfere with whale communication, which is vital to their survival.

6. **(4)** The distinction mentioned in this passage is that they are mammals, which have certain characteristics in common, including hair.

INTERDEPENDENCE OF ORGANISMS

The GED Science Test will have questions about the interdependence of organisms in living systems. A living system is almost synonymous with an ecosystem, which can be defined as the interaction between a community of organisms and their non-living environment. The term *living system* focusses primarily on the living organisms within the environment. To quote the song from the movie *The Lion King*, it is the "circle of life." For example, grass grows, then it is eaten by rabbits, which, in turn, are eaten by a hawk. When the hawk dies, its body is broken down by bacteria, which contains nutrients that nourish the grass.

> **LIVING SYSTEM**—an open, self-organized interdependence of organisms that interact with their environment.

A living system can be big or small. For example, the whole earth is a living system of organisms that interact and depend on one another. A small pond in a field is also a living system of interacting organisms. Characteristics of a living system include that it is

- **OPEN**—living systems are not isolated and they interchange matter and energy with systems around them.
- **SELF-ORGANIZED**—the coordination of organisms arises spontaneously out of their interactions.
- **INTERDEPENDENT**—the organisms depend on one another to survive.
- **DYNAMIC**—constant change and movement occur to achieve and maintain a condition of stability called *homeostasis*.

Questions on the GED Science Test about interdependence of organisms in living systems could include a wide variety of topics, such as the relationship between two or more organisms, the food chain, the food pyramid, the carbon cycle, the role of bacteria, invasive species, and the impact of pollution.

TIP

Organisms in a living system depend on interaction with one another to survive and maintain stability of the system.

PRACTICE

Choose the best answer to each question.

Every living system is made up of *species*, groups of individuals that have the same structure and that breed together. A *population* is the number of organisms in a given group within the system. Together, the populations make up a *community*. Each species within the community plays a role in sustaining the system and the other populations in it.

Some species (generally plants) fulfill the role of producers, organisms that are capable of creating their own food from the environment. Next are consumers, organisms that are not capable of creating their own food, but who feed on other organisms. This is the beginning of the food chain. Consumers are described at different levels, depending on their distance from the producers. A primary consumer feeds on producers. Secondary consumers feed on primary consumers, and so on. The third category is decomposers, the organisms that break down consumers and producers that have died into simple substances that return to the environment.

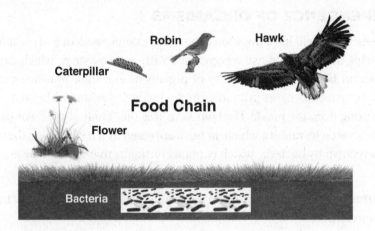

1. Which of the organisms below is a producer?
   (1) Bacteria
   (2) Flower
   (3) Caterpillar
   (4) Robin
   (5) Soil

2. What is the role of the hawk in the food chain?
   (1) Producer
   (2) Primary consumer
   (3) Secondary consumer
   (4) Tertiary consumer
   (5) Decomposer

A food chain shows the relationship between specific species of producers and consumers in a living system. A more complex diagram could be created to show the relationship among a greater number of species. Another diagram is the number pyramid, which gives different information about the relationship between the species in the food chain.

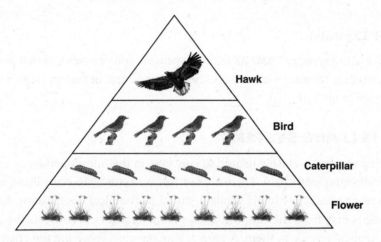

3. Based on the number pyramid, you can conclude that in this living system
   (1) there can never be as many birds as caterpillars
   (2) hawks do not eat birds
   (3) flowers are less important than other organisms
   (4) hawks are the most important population
   (5) it is unclear which species are producers and consumers

4. If the number of birds in the system were to suddenly increase, which of the following is likely to occur?
   (1) The number of hawks would decrease.
   (2) The number of caterpillars would decrease.
   (3) The number of flowers would increase.
   (4) The number of caterpillars would increase.
   (5) Hawks would no longer be able to hunt birds.

5. A sign on the highway at the Nova Scotia border warns that it is illegal to import honey bees into the province. The reason for the regulation could be that
   (1) flowers in Nova Scotia require less pollination
   (2) living systems in Nova Scotia do not include bees
   (3) honey bees are a major export of Nova Scotia
   (4) another species could disrupt the living system
   (5) hawks are not found in the same system as honey bees

ANSWERS

1. **(2)** The flowers are producers because they produce their own food from the environment and do not feed on other organisms.

2. **(4)** The hawk is the third level of consumer.

3. **(1)** As the birds eat caterpillars, there can never be as many. One principle of the number pyramid is that the population decreases the further from the base.

4. **(2)** More birds feeding would result in fewer caterpillars. As the population of caterpillars declines, however, there would not be enough food to sustain the birds, reducing their number and restoring balance.

5. **(4)** Introduction of a foreign species can disrupt a living system.

CHALLENGE EXERCISE

Your home is a living system. Name all of the organisms you can think of that are part of the system. How do they interact with one another? What matter or energy does it interchange with the systems around it?

ENERGY IN LIVING SYSTEMS

TIP

The two forms of energy in a living system are sunlight and chemical energy.

Energy in living systems is closely related to concepts in the interdependence of organisms and often parallels the food chain. There are two forms of energy in every living system: sunlight and chemical energy, which is sunlight stored in chemical compounds. For example, plants get their energy from the sun, which they store as sugars. A cow eats the plants, converting the chemical energy in them. A person eats the cow, receiving the chemical energy from the cow. At each stage, some of the energy seems to be lost, but is in fact transformed to another form (heat, biochemical, and so on). Each organism imperfectly metabolizes the energy from its source. In addition, energy is consumed by each organism through the process of life. Ultimately, all energy on earth in every living system comes directly or indirectly from the sun.

PRACTICE

Choose the best answer to each question.

Whether through photosynthesis or consumption of other organisms, all living things obtain and process nutrients that are transported to their cells. Within the cells, nutrients are then broken down through a process of oxidization to release energy and power the activities of the cell. *Cellular respiration* is the term for the reactions by which cells break down large nutrient molecules, creating smaller, more stable molecules and releasing energy. The process is similar to combustion, or burning of nutrients, except that it is broken down into stages. Glucose, carbohydrates, proteins, and fatty acids are all fuel sources used in cellular respiration. The mitochondria of the cell and the supply of oxygen play an important role in cellular respiration.

1. Cellular respiration could be described as a means of
   (1) breathing
   (2) photosynthesis
   (3) creating nutrients
   (4) cell formation
   (5) releasing biochemical energy

2. If a person is running or exercising strenuously, the person will breathe faster and more deeply in order to
    (1) obtain more oxygen for cellular respiration
    (2) obtain more nutrients for cellular respiration
    (3) suspend cellular respiration during the period of activity
    (4) create additional mitochondria
    (5) lower levels of oxygen

3. One fact stated by this passage is that
    (1) plants do not undergo cellular respiration
    (2) cellular respiration produces ATP, carbon dioxide, and water
    (3) only multicellular organisms undergo cellular respiration
    (4) all organisms undergo cellular respiration
    (5) mitochondria are known as the energy centres of the cell

Thermodynamics is the science of energy. The four laws of thermodynamics are unifying principles that apply to everything in the universe, including energy of living systems. The first law of thermodynamics, also known as the law of conservation of energy, states that energy is neither created nor destroyed, but can be transformed from one type to another. In a closed system, the amount of energy remains the same although energy can be converted to mechanical work or mass, or vice versa. In a plant, for example, some energy is stored while other energy is transformed into growth and cellular activity. Living systems require large amounts of energy for their activity and growth. Much of this energy comes from outside the system in the form of light and heat from the sun.

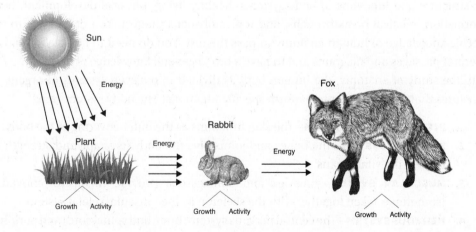

4. In a living system, the amount of energy decreases each time it is transferred. According to the first law of thermodynamics, this is because
    (1) some energy is lost
    (2) some energy is transformed
    (3) no new energy is created
    (4) new energy is created
    (5) the laws of thermodynamics do not apply

5. Energy in living systems comes from two sources, biochemical energy and the sun. This demonstrates that
   (1) living systems are closed systems
   (2) energy can be created
   (3) energy can be destroyed in living systems
   (4) living systems are open systems
   (5) the laws of thermodynamics do not apply

ANSWERS

1. **(5)** Cellular respiration is a biochemical process that releases energy from nutrients.

2. **(1)** Oxygen plays an important role in cellular respiration. Therefore, when cells are called upon for more energy, as during exercise, more oxygen is required.

3. **(3)** The passage states that all living organisms transport nutrients to the cells, where they are broken down to create energy. While mitochondria are known as energy centres and cellular respiration does involve ATP, these are not stated in the passage.

4. **(2)** According to the first law of thermodynamics, energy is neither created nor destroyed; however, at each level some energy is transformed into growth or cellular activity of the organism.

5. **(4)** All living systems are open systems and exchange energy and materials with their environment.

THE HUMAN BODY

TIP

Structures of the human body are divided into systems.

Some questions on the GED Science Test will be about the human body. Topics could include the structure and functions of body systems, healthy living, physical development, health information, medical breakthroughs, and topics of social interest. You don't have to have specific knowledge of human anatomy to pass the test. You do need to be able to read and interpret passages and diagrams and to have a broad general knowledge of the body.

In the study of anatomy, the human body is divided into eleven systems of organs and structures that work together to perform specific functions. The body systems are:

1. **INTEGUMENTARY SYSTEM**—the skin functions as the outer covering of the body.
2. **SKELETAL SYSTEM**—the bones and joints give the body its shape and strength and protect the vital organs.
3. **MUSCULAR SYSTEM**—muscles and soft tissues provide means of movement (sometimes taken together with the skeleton as the musculoskeletal system).
4. **NERVOUS SYSTEM**—the central nervous system (brain and spinal cord) and peripheral nervous system (nerves) send messages throughout the body.
5. **ENDOCRINE SYSTEM**—the system of glands secrete hormones.
6. **CARDIOVASCULAR (CIRCULATORY) STEM**—the heart, arteries, and veins move blood throughout the body.
7. **LYMPHATIC SYSTEM**—the spleen, lymph nodes, and networks throughout the body clean away cell debris and attack intruding or unfamiliar cells.
8. **RESPIRATORY SYSTEM**—the lungs and trachea control breathing and the oxygenation of blood.
9. **DIGESTIVE SYSTEM**—the stomach, intestines, liver, and other organs are all involved in the processing of food.

10. **URINARY SYSTEM**—the kidneys and bladder clean waste material from the blood and flush the waste products from the body.

11. **REPRODUCTIVE SYSTEM**—the ovaries and testes enable reproduction.

CHALLENGE EXERCISE

Using online, book, or library resources, identify the location within the body of the major human organs: the heart, lungs, stomach, liver, kidneys, pancreas, small intestine, and large intestine. Use your research to figure out exactly where on your own body each of the organs is located. Put your hands on the location of each organ. Work with a partner or friend to discuss and compare your research.

PRACTICE

Choose the best answer to each question.

The cardiovascular system is comprised of the heart, blood, and a network of vessels that carry the blood throughout the body to and from the heart to deliver nutrients and oxygen to the cells. Blood vessels are categorized by their function. *Arteries* carry oxygen and nutrients to the cells. *Veins* return oxygen-depleted blood to the heart. Networks of tiny blood vessels throughout the body, called *capillaries*, are attached to the arteries and have walls as thin as a single cell, allowing the transfer of oxygen and nutrient molecules to the cells.

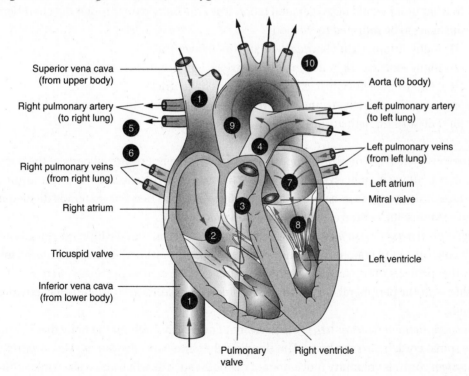

The powerhouse of the cardiovascular system is the heart, which has a system of chambers and valves that act like a pump to circulate the blood. The heart is divided into two very similar sides, each with a ventricle and an atrium. At the exit of each chamber is a valve that prevents the blood from flowing back. The two sides of the heart perform different roles. The right side of the heart gathers oxygen-poor blood as it returns from the body and pumps it to the lungs, where oxygen levels are replenished and carbon dioxide removed. The oxygen-rich blood then returns to the left side of the heart, from which it is sent to the rest of the body.

When the heart beats, it does so in two stages. In the first stage, the atria contract simultaneously, moving blood into the ventricles. In the second stage, the ventricles contract to send blood out to the lungs and body.

1. According to the diagram, which of the following structures brings blood back to the heart from the lungs?
   (1) Pulmonary veins
   (2) Pulmonary artery
   (3) Lower vena cava
   (4) Aorta
   (5) Upper vena cava

2. What prevents blood in the left ventricle from flowing back to the left atrium?
   (1) Aortic valve
   (2) Pulmonary valve
   (3) Tricuspid valve
   (4) Mitral valve
   (5) Inferior vena cava

3. In what order would deoxygenated blood from the body pass through the chambers of the heart to be returned to the body?
   (1) Right atrium, right ventricle, left atrium, left ventricle
   (2) Right ventricle, right atrium, left ventricle, left atrium
   (3) Left atrium, left ventricle, right atrium, right ventricle
   (4) Left ventricle, left atrium, right ventricle, right atrium
   (5) Left atrium, right atrium, left ventricle, right ventricle

The nervous system is a network of nerves that connect the brain with all parts of the body. It controls everything we perceive, think, and do; the movement of the body; and the automatic processes of the body, such as breathing and digestion. The nervous system is divided into two subsystems: the central and peripheral nervous systems.

The *central nervous system*, the brain and spinal cord, is contained within the dorsal cavity, which consists of the cranial cavity that protects the brain inside the skull and the vertebral cavity that protects the spinal cord with the vertebrae. The central nervous system functions together with the peripheral nervous system, which it controls, to coordinate all activities of the body.

The *peripheral nervous system* is the network of nerves throughout the body that connects to the spinal cord. It also can be broken down further into two subsystems. The *somatic nervous system* controls voluntary movement of the body, such as when you walk, wink, or move your arms. The *autonomic nervous system* controls automatic functions of the body, such as breathing or sweating.

The entire nervous system is made of neurons and glial cells. *Neurons* are nerve cells that send and receive messages throughout the body. *Glial cells* surround and support the neurons by insulating them, transporting nutrients, and clearing away dead neurons. Even the brain and spinal cord are made of neurons and glial cells.

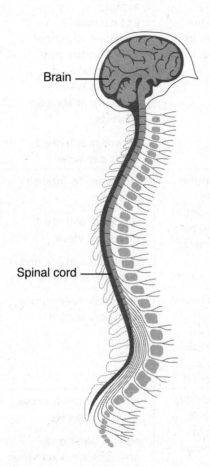

Brain

Spinal cord

4. The diagram above depicts the
   (1) brain
   (2) spinal cord
   (3) nerves
   (4) central and peripheral nervous system
   (5) central nervous system

5. Nodding one's head is a movement controlled by the
   (1) central nervous system
   (2) peripheral nervous system
   (3) somatic nervous system
   (4) autonomic nervous system
   (5) Glial cells

The following table shows physical activity guidelines recommended by the Government of Canada for all age groups.

Ages 5—12	60 minutes per day (Does not have to be all at once)	Moderate-to-intense activity For example - walking to school - walking the dog - skateboarding - riding a bike - playing at the park - Sports Vigorous activity 3 times per week	Moderate activities, including - a brisk walk - bike riding - skateboarding - walking the dog - yoga Vigorous activities, such as - Running - Cross-country skiing - Active sports such as basketball Muscle and bone strengthening, for instance, - push-ups - weight lifting - gardening - Swimming
Ages 12—17	60 minutes per day (Does not have to be all at once)	Moderate-to-intense activity Vigorous activity 3 times per week Combine aerobic and strength activities	
Ages 18—64	150 minutes per week (Done in 10-minute-or-more segments)	Moderate-to-vigorous aerobic exercise	
Ages 64+	150 minutes per week (Done in 10-minute-or-more segments)	Moderate-to-vigorous aerobic exercise Muscle and bone strengthening activities at least twice a week because muscle mass and bone density decrease with age.	

Maintaining health is a lifestyle of active living that includes physical activity every day in addition to a healthy diet.

6. Which of the following states a fact?
   (1) Children should exercise 60 minutes per day.
   (2) Muscle mass and bone density decrease with age.
   (3) The physical activity for the week should not be done all at once.
   (4) Older adults should get at least two-and-one-half hours of activity per week
   (5) Exercise is less important for adults than for youth

7. Based on the information in this passage, you could conclude that
   (1) Young people do not exercise enough
   (2) Older people do not exercise enough
   (3) People of different ages have different needs
   (4) Going to the gym regularly is needed for good health
   (5) Yoga is the best form of exercise for all age groups

ANSWERS

1. **(1)** *Pulmonary* means *lungs* and veins carry deoxygenated blood back to the heart.
2. **(4)** The mitral valve at the exit of the left atrium prevents blood from flowing back in.
3. **(2)** Deoxygenated blood from the body enters the right atrium through the superior and inferior vena cava and is pumped to the right ventricle, from which it is pumped to the lungs. Oxygenated blood returns to the left atrium and then the left ventricle to be sent to the body via the aorta.
4. **(5)** The graphic depicts the brain and spinal cord, which make up the central nervous system.
5. **(3)** Voluntary movements are controlled by the somatic nervous system, which is a subsystem of the peripheral nervous system.
6. **(2)** All other options are recommendations, or conclusions, not facts.
7. **(3)** The chart recommends different activities for different age groups. There is no information to support the other conclusions.

CHAPTER CHECK-UP

Complete these practice exercises, and check the answers and analysis that follow. After you mark your work, review any topic in the chapter that you had trouble with or did not understand.

Sexual reproduction in flowering plants utilizes stamen and pistils located within the flower. Anthers of the stamen produce pollen, which has grains that contain the male gametes. The pistil contains the ovary, which holds the ovules, each of which contains a female gamete. During pollination, pollen grains are transferred from the stamen to the stigma of the pistil by wind, water, or insects. The transfer may occur within the same flower, called self-pollination. Or the transfer may occur between different flowers in the same or different plants, called cross-pollination.

In fertilization, after pollination the male gamete makes its way down the inside of the style to fuse with the female gamete, forming a zygote. The zygote begins to divide within the ovule, while the ovule itself develops a tough outer coating to form a seed.

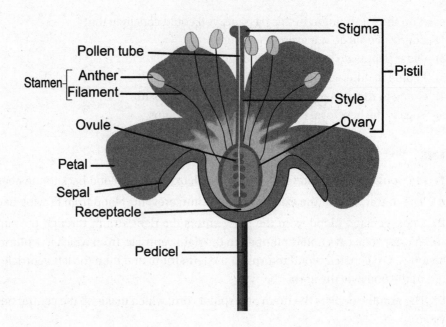

1. The female reproductive organ of the flower is the
    (1) stamen
    (2) ovule
    (3) pistil
    (4) style
    (5) ovary

2. Cross-pollination produces stronger, healthier offspring than self-pollination because
    (1) it involves more genetic material
    (2) it is easier to do
    (3) pollen is transported by insects
    (4) the transfer takes place within the same flower
    (5) the transfer takes place in a different flower

3. When the zygote begins to divide inside the ovule, it could be compared with a human
    (1) seed
    (2) zygote
    (3) embryo
    (4) reproductive organ
    (5) baby

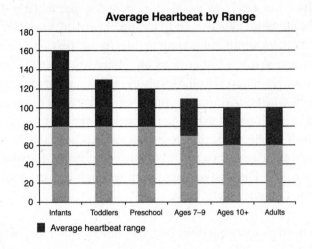

Average Heartbeat by Range

■ Average heartbeat range

4. The normal average heart rate varies by age. Which age group's average heartbeat has the widest range?
   (1) Infants
   (2) Toddlers
   (3) Preschoolers
   (4) Ages 7–9
   (5) Age 10+

5. Exercise and a healthy cardiovascular system lead to a stronger heart, able to beat more forcefully and circulate a greater volume of blood. Which of the following adult heart rates is most likely to be found in a high-performance athlete?
   (1) 45 bpm
   (2) 60 bpm
   (3) 80 bpm
   (4) 100 bpm
   (5) 120 bpm

Canadian researchers are active in the field of genetics, particularly in research centres located in British Columbia, Quebec, and Ontario. The field has even included a Nobel laureate, scientist Michael Smith, the founding director of the Genome Sequencing Centre in Vancouver, who received the Nobel Prize for Chemistry in 1993. Most of the research is conducted in universities and hospitals with the assistance of government funding; but increasingly, it is undertaken by private companies, particularly in the areas of agriculture and medicine, and by government departments, such as Agriculture and Agri-Food Canada. In the field of medical genetics, one pioneering project has been the BC Health Surveillance Registry, which since 1952 has kept a record of birth defects and handicapping disorders in newborns in the province. The data has permitted research into risk estimates and population trends for various genetic conditions.

6. According to the passage, what is the benefit of the Health Surveillance Registry of birth defects?
    (1) Prevent genetic disease
    (2) Warn potential carriers of genetic disease
    (3) Research into genetic markers
    (4) Historical perspective of genetic illness
    (5) Predict incidence of genetic conditions

Four species of Asian carp pose a potential threat to the Canadian Great Lakes system. They were initially imported to the Unites States to control unwanted vegetation in ponds and to be raised for food on fish farms. In the 1990s, flooding enabled some to escape into the Mississippi, and they have continued to thrive in the Mississippi-, Iowa-, and Illinois-River systems. The fish can grow up to 1.3 metres long and are voracious eaters, consuming vast quantities of zooplankton, phytoplankton, and underwater vegetation. The vigilance of both national governments and an electric fence in the canal that separates Lake Michigan from the Mississippi is all that prevents the carp's incursion into the Great Lakes.

7. Based on the information in this passage, what danger could Asian carp pose to the Great Lakes ecosystem?
    (1) Breaks in fishing nets
    (2) Disruption of the food chain
    (3) Consumption of needed oxygen
    (4) Introduction of foreign bacteria
    (5) Danger to shipping

Carbon is everywhere: in the earth, air, plants, and animals. Carbon dioxide in the air is consumed by plants during photosynthesis and becomes part of the organism. Some plants are eaten by animals and carbon becomes a part of their structure. When plants or animals die, they decay, aided by bacterial decomposers, and some of the carbon is released into the atmosphere. The movement of carbon, in its various forms, from the atmosphere through to plants, animals, the soil, and back again to the atmosphere is a process called the carbon cycle.

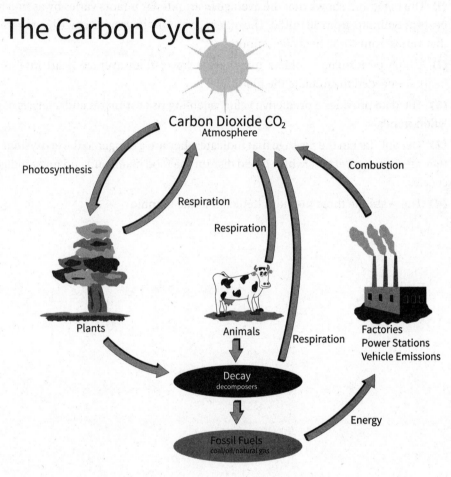

The Carbon Cycle

8. Based on the preceding passage and graphic, what are the methods by which carbon dioxide is released into the atmosphere.
   (1) plant respiration, animal respiration, evaporation
   (2) plant respiration, photosynthesis
   (3) animal respiration, photosynthesis, combustion
   (4) animal respiration, combustion, decay
   (5) photosynthesis, decay, factories

ANSWERS

1. **(3)** The pistil includes the ovary, style, and stigma, and is the female reproductive part as the stamen is the male.

2. **(1)** Cross-pollination combines genetic material from more than one flower and, often, more than one plant.

3. **(3)** The zygote divides to form an embryo.

4. **(1)** The bar graph shows that the average heart rate for infants varies by as much as 80 beats per minute, from 80 to 160. The other age groups have an average heart-rate range that varies from 40-50 beats per minute.

5. **(1)** A high-performance athlete may have a lower-than-average heart rate as fewer beats are needed to circulate the blood.

6. **(5)** The data provides a predictive value, enabling risk estimates and analysis of population trends.

7. **(2)** The only fact in the passage that indicates they are a danger to the ecosystem is that they are voracious eaters, which could disrupt the food chain and endanger indigenous species.

8. **(4)** These are the three methods depicted in the graphic.

Earth and Space Science

15

THINK ABOUT IT

How big is the universe?

The Earth is one planet that orbits one star in the Milky Way galaxy. Our tiny solar system is not the centre of the galaxy, but about 27,000 light years from the centre. The Milky Way is over 100,000 light years across and contains more than 350 billion stars. Outside of our galaxy are other galaxies. Scientists now estimate that there may be as many as 500 billion galaxies. All of the galaxies are moving rapidly away from each other so that the universe is continually expanding.

IN THIS CHAPTER

After completing this chapter, you will be able to

→ **DEFINE EARTH AND SPACE SCIENCE**

→ **DESCRIBE THE SOLAR SYSTEM**

→ **DESCRIBE THE GEOLOGICAL STRUCTURE OF THE EARTH**

→ **NAME THE LEVELS OF EARTH'S ATMOSPHERE**

→ **DESCRIBE THE WATER CYCLE**

→ **IDENTIFY TOPICS OF STUDY IN OCEANOGRAPHY**

WHAT IS EARTH AND SPACE SCIENCE?

The third area of science examined on the GED test is Earth and Space Science, which accounts for 20% of the questions on the test. Earth and Space Science is the study of the structure and origin of the Earth, solar system, and universe. It includes geology, oceanography, meteorology, and astronomy.

On the GED Science Test, there may be questions about the universe, where it came from and how it evolved. There may be questions about the origin and nature of the solar system and its influence on our world. There may also be questions about the Earth, its structure and the forces within it, the ocean, and the atmosphere. Finally, as with all science topics, there may be questions about the relationship between science and technology.

The questions will test your ability to understand concepts about the systems and organization of the Earth and universe. The test will examine your ability to understand form, structure, and function of the Earth's systems and how they affect our daily life.

PRACTICE

Choose the best answer to each question.

The surface of the Earth is predominantly water. More than seven-tenths of the globe is submerged in water, only 3% of which is fresh. The remaining 97% is the salt water of the oceans and seas. The oceans are not still. Prevailing currents travel in circular patterns, or gyres, transporting sea life and affecting climate by moving warm or cool waters along the coasts.

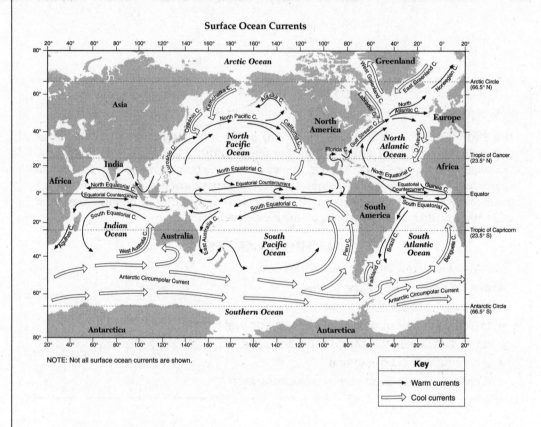

Surface Ocean Currents

NOTE: Not all surface ocean currents are shown.

Key

→ Warm currents

⇒ Cool currents

1. Based on the graphic, what is the difference between gyres in the northern and southern hemispheres?
   (1) Southern hemisphere currents are warmer.
   (2) They move in opposite directions.
   (3) Northern hemisphere currents are warmer.
   (4) Northern hemisphere currents move faster.
   (5) Southern hemisphere currents move faster.

2. What influence might currents in the South Atlantic have on climate?
   (1) Warm the coast of Australia
   (2) Warm the coasts of North America and Europe
   (3) Cool water to the Indian Ocean
   (4) Cool the east coast of South America
   (5) Cool the west coast of Africa and warm the east coast of South America

3. In the northern Pacific Ocean, the currents that flow past the west coast of North America next reach which coast?
   (1) Australia
   (2) Antarctica
   (3) South America
   (4) Asia
   (5) Europe

Although it cannot be detected with the naked eye, the surface of the Sun is very active. Sunspots, cooler areas of activity with strong concentrations of magnetic flux, move in pairs or groups of opposite polarity across its face. Occasionally, Sun spots flare out in a sudden brightness from such areas of activity, bursting forth to the outer limits of the Sun's atmosphere with the force of millions of atomic bombs. The frequency of Sun flares varies from several times a day to several per week.

Temperatures in the corona, or atmosphere, of the Sun are typically approximately 2 million degrees Kelvin. During a solar flare, the area of the atmosphere in which it occurs can reach temperatures of 20 million degrees Kelvin. Every type of electromagnetic energy is released, from radio waves to visible light to x-rays and gamma radiation. Despite the violent energy of a solar flare—about one-sixth as strong as the energy of the Sun—its energy does not penetrate the Earth's atmosphere.

4. The corona is
   (1) the Sun's atmosphere
   (2) a group of sunspots
   (3) a solar flare
   (4) an area of electromagnetic energy
   (5) an atomic reaction

5. During a solar flare, the Earth is
   (1) endangered by electromagnetic energy
   (2) threatened by heat and gamma radiation
   (3) protected by Earth's atmosphere
   (4) shielded by the corona
   (5) affected by violent energy

The structure of the Earth is made up of spherical layers, like the interior of an onion, one layer inside another. At the centre is the Earth's inner core, a dense ball of iron and nickel about 1200km across. Although it is estimated that the temperature of the inner core is over 5000°C, it is solid because of the extreme pressure. Around the inner core is the molten outer core of iron and nickel, 2200 km thick and almost 3000 km below the surface of the Earth. The temperature of the outer core is approximately 4500°C. Next is the mantle, with a thickness of 2900km, composed of solid silicate rock. The asthenosphere is the weaker upper part of the mantle that lies beneath lithosphere, the rigid layer at the base of the crust. The crust is the topmost layer of the Earth. It is the thinnest of the layers at approximately 10km.

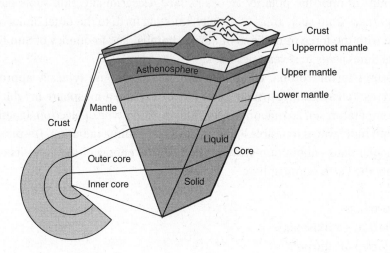

6. As temperature is higher in the solid inner core, why is the outer core liquid?
   (1) Different composition
   (2) Lower pressure
   (3) Higher temperature
   (4) Greater depth
   (5) More oxygen

7. In which layer of the Earth are coal and other fossil fuels found?
   (1) Crust
   (2) Asthenosphere
   (3) Mantle
   (4) Outer core
   (5) Inner core

ANSWERS

1. **(2)** The southern hemisphere is below the red line of the equator. Note that arrows marking currents move counterclockwise. Arrows in the northern hemisphere rotate clockwise.

2. **(5)** The different coloured arrows show the South Atlantic current bringing cold currents to the west coast of Africa and warm currents to the east coast of South America.

3. **(4)** Remember that the Earth is round. The two sides of a map connect. The current that passes the west coast of North America continues on the other side of the map to Asia.

4. **(1)** The passage states that the corona is the Sun's atmosphere.

5. **(3)** Energy of the solar flare does not penetrate Earth's atmosphere.

6. **(2)** The passage states the inner core is solid because of great pressure, which implies the outer core must have lower pressure as it has the same composition and lower temperature.

7. **(1)** The crust is 10km thick. Few fossil fuel mines would go so deep. Also, decayed vegetation and animal life that formed fossil fuels over years would not penetrate below it.

UNIVERSE AND SOLAR SYSTEM

Questions on the GED Science test may include questions about the universe and solar system. They could include a wide range of topics, such as where the universe came from and how it may end, the galaxy and stars. Other topics could include things like the planets of our solar system and their motions, comets, space exploration, the moon and its influence on the Earth, and more.

CHALLENGE EXERCISE

Constellation hunt—Using the Internet or the library, find a map, pictures, or video of constellations. Look at the sky at night and see if you can find at least three constellations, such as the Big Dipper (Ursa Major), Little Dipper (Ursa Minor), or Cassiopeia. (The constellations that are visible will vary depending on the time of year.) Are the stars you see part of our galaxy? How far away are they?

PRACTICE

Choose the best answer to each question.

What is the origin of the universe? The most popular scientific suggestion, known as the big bang theory, is that at one time, all matter and energy in the universe existed as a single, infinitely dense mass only a few millimetres in diameter. It was not a single point in an infinite emptiness because space and time themselves were contained within it. This state existed for only a fraction of a second before it exploded with unimaginable force, flinging all energy and mass outward.

The theory of the big bang was supported by the discovery by astronomer Edwin Hubble in 1929 of other galaxies, and the fact that the galaxies are moving away from one another at a rapid speed, as though emanating from a single point. By examining the speed of the galaxies and their trajectories, scientists estimate that the universe is approximately 13.7 billion years old.

The big bang theory does leave some questions unanswered. Where did the single tiny mass come from? What caused the big bang to occur?

1. Based on the information in this passage, you can conclude that the size of the universe is
   (1) infinite
   (2) the same size as our galaxy
   (3) continually expanding
   (4) infinitely small
   (5) 13.7 billion light years

2. The age of the universe is calculated based on
   (1) brightness of stars
   (2) energy of the big bang
   (3) age of the Earth
   (4) the direction and speed of galaxies
   (5) density of matter

3. The universe was created by
   (1) the big bang
   (2) divine action
   (3) Edwin Hubble
   (4) a black hole
   (5) scientifically unknown

The Sun is a star. How did it form? Stars are not as old as the universe. They are born and die and have a life cycle of their own. More than 4.6 billion years ago, there were massive molecular clouds of dust and hydrogen gas in the empty space (interstellar space) within our galaxy. Turbulence, caused perhaps by the shockwave of a distant supernova, caused the clouds to form together into clumps. Gravity between and within the clumps attracted more of the cloud, which continued to collapse on itself. The largest result of this process formed a *protostar* which increased in size and density until it reached a point where nuclear fusion began. For millions of years, the fiery ball, which would eventually form the heart of our young star, continued to pull the cloud into itself until it reached a critical point at which the outward pressure of the hydrogen reaction was greater than the inward pressure of gravity, and blasted the remaining gas and debris away. The process of formation lasted about 50 million years, but not all of the particles became part of the star, which is our Sun. Others gathered together to become planets, asteroids, and other bodies that make up the solar system. As long as our Sun has burned, it will not burn for eternity, but it is expected that it will live over 5 billion years more.

4. What is the expected life span of the Sun?
   (1) 4.6 billion years
   (2) About 10 billion years
   (3) 5 billion years
   (4) 50 million years
   (5) Infinite

5. The passage above describes the origin of the
   (1) solar system
   (2) sun
   (3) stars
   (4) protostars
   (5) hydrogen

There were once nine planets in our solar system, but a 2006 decision by the International Astronomical Union has decreased the number to eight. The change comes as a result of a new definition of the term *planet*" which has removed Pluto from that august rank. Under the new definition, a planet is a body that is large enough to be round because of the force of its own gravity, that orbits the sun, and that dominates its orbit. Pluto, which is only twice the size of its moon and whose orbit contains other debris, has, therefore, been demoted to the status of dwarf planet. As such, it joins four other dwarf planets, at least one of which is larger than Pluto, and it is estimated that there may be hundreds more in our solar system.

The New Solar System

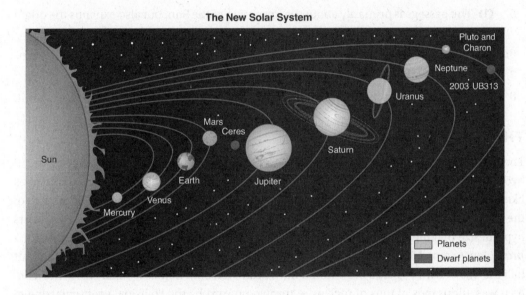

6. The moon is not considered a planet because it
   (1) is not round
   (2) is too close to the Sun
   (3) does not sustain life
   (4) orbits the Earth
   (5) has low gravity

7. Which is the 6th planet in the solar system?
   (1) Earth
   (2) Jupiter
   (3) Saturn
   (4) Uranus
   (5) Mars

8. Pluto is no longer considered to be a planet because
   (1) other bodies are bigger
   (2) it does not dominate its orbit
   (3) it is too far from the Sun
   (4) it has insufficient gravity
   (5) it is too small

ANSWERS

1. **(3)** The universe is continuing to expand as galaxies move away from each other.

2. **(4)** Looking at the speed and direction of the galaxies, scientists calculate backwards to estimate the age of the universe.

3. **(5)** The big bang is a widely regarded theory, but still a theory. The origin of the universe remains unknown and the subject of continued research.

4. **(2)** The passage states that the Sun is 4.6 billion years old and will live over 5 billion years more, a total life span of almost 10 billion years.

5. **(1)** The passage is primarily about the formation of the Sun, but also explains the origin of the planets and other bodies in the solar system.

6. **(4)** Planets orbit the Sun, but the moon orbits the Earth.

7. **(3)** Counting the orbits you can conclude Saturn is 6th from the Sun.

8. **(2)** Pluto is only twice the size of its moon and other objects are also found in its orbit.

THE EARTH

The early history of the Earth is one of violence. The coalescing cosmic cloud of dust and hydrogen gas that created our Sun and solar system created thousands of orbiting bodies like our own that raced around the Sun and often collided with terrible force. The surface of the young Earth, like all of the other planets, was scarred by countless collisions. Scientists hypothesize that the most tremendous impact took place more than four billion years ago. A *protoplanet* named Theia, about the size of Mars, struck the Earth a glancing blow. At about half the size of Earth, Theia's blow would have destroyed both bodies if it had struck head on. As it was, thousands of tons of rock were thrown upward by the collision, eventually drawn together by their own gravity to form our moon. In addition, energy from the blow, converted into heat, transformed the Earth into a molten ball. Heavier material sank towards the Earth's core, while lighter material, such as granite, rose towards the surface.

The massive-impact theory remains just that, but by whatever means the Earth was created, the series of events made it unique in our solar system as the only planet with the ability to support life. In addition to having water, Earth's distance from the Sun provides a moderate temperature in comparison to the 400 °C temperature of the surface of Mercury or the frigid temperatures of Mars. The size of Earth's moon is also vital to the ability of the planet to sustain life as its gravity keeps the Earth rotating on its axis, which enables a regular cycle of seasons. Many speculate that there may be life on other planets somewhere around the other billions of stars. Indeed, there may be. Yet, it is also possible that the evolution of our own life-giving planet occurred through a series of improbable events that will never recur.

In addition to the origins of the Earth, the GED Science Test may include questions about the four Earth systems:

1. **LITHOSPHERE**—crust and upper mantle of the Earth
2. **HYDROSPHERE**—water on the Earth's surface and in the atmosphere
3. **ATMOSPHERE**—the envelope of gases (air) that surrounds the Earth and is held in place by gravity
4. **BIOSPHERE**—the land, water, and air where there is life

It stands to reason that there could be questions about many topics, such as movement of the Earth's crust, earthquakes, volcanos, under-sea trenches, levels of the atmosphere, the water cycle, weather and climate.

PRACTICE

Choose the best answer to each question.

The Earth's crust is not one solid piece. The outer, hard surface of the Earth is called the *lithosphere* and consists of the crust and uppermost part of the mantle. The lithosphere is broken up into sections, called *plates*, which move on the *asthenosphere*, a weaker and hotter layer of mantle that lies below. At a temperature of approximately 1600°C, the asthenosphere is solid but malleable so that the plates are able to slide slowly across its surface.

The cracks between the plates are called *faults*, and the plates move against one another across the faults. Plates can move in three different directions. A divergent plate boundary occurs when plates move away from one another. This most often occurs in oceanic plates, which are thinner than continental plates. Lava from beneath the lithosphere is forced upward between the plates, filling the space between them and forming an oceanic ridge. This does not occur in all parts of the boundary at the same time, but over millions of years, the plates can move many hundreds of kilometres away from each other along the plate boundary.

Across a transform plate boundary, the plates move horizontally against one another. Transform plates are also most often found in the oceans, where they form deep valleys, often terminating at a divergent plate boundary. Transform plates form a zig-zag pattern across the ocean floor.

Convergent boundaries occur where plates move *towards* one another, resulting either in subduction or continental collision. In subduction, an oceanic plate moves under a continental plate or another oceanic plate into the mantle. It is always an oceanic plate that moves underneath because they are not only thinner (about 6km) but also denser, composed primarily of basalt (rock from volcanic eruptions). The continental crust averages 30km thick and is composed primarily of granite. Continental collision occurs when two continental crusts separated by an oceanic crust move towards one another. The oceanic crust is easily pulled downward under the continental plate, a process called subduction. When the continental crusts meet, the deep subduction continues of the much thicker continental crust, forcing rock upward where they meet.

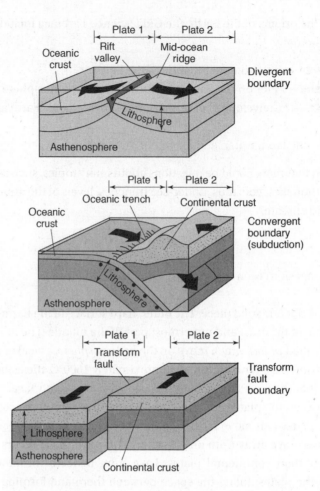

1. Which of the following might also be described as a constructive boundary?
   (1) Convergent plate boundary
   (2) Subduction
   (3) Transform plate boundary
   (4) Divergent plate boundary
   (5) Continental collision

2. At which of the following is rock likely to become older, the farther it is from the fault?
   (1) Convergent plate boundary
   (2) Subduction
   (3) Transform plate boundary
   (4) Divergent plate boundary
   (5) Continental collision

3. Why are oceanic plates always prone to subduction under continental plates at a convergent boundary?
   (1) They are heavier.
   (2) They are thinner.
   (3) They are younger.
   (4) They have more faults.
   (5) They are lighter.

4. Continental drift is the theory that Earth's continents are in a constant state of movement relative to one another. The theory posits that all of the present-day continents were originally together as one land mass dubbed Pangea. The motion of tectonic plates explains how continental drift occurs, especially the process of seafloor spreading at divergent plate boundaries. Which of the following best supports the theory of continental drift?

    (1) Kangaroos in Australia, but not other continents
    (2) Formation of mountain ranges
    (3) Earthquakes
    (4) Ocean currents
    (5) Identical plant fossils on different continents

Although serious earthquakes are a rare occurrence in Canada, dozens of small quakes occur every month, especially off the coast of British Columbia, Yukon, and Quebec along the St. Lawrence. In October 2012, a quake measuring 7.7 on the Richter scale occurred off the Haida Gwaii (Queen Charlotte Islands). No damage was reported, but the quake was felt across much of northern and central British Columbia and a tsunami warning was issued.

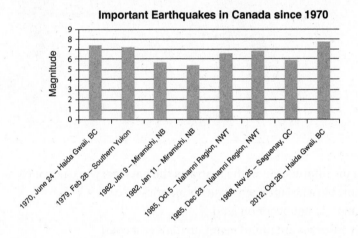

Important Earthquakes in Canada since 1970

5. The most powerful earthquake to occur in Canada since 1970 took place in

    (1) 1970, June 24
    (2) 1979, Feb 28
    (3) 1982, Jan 9
    (4) 1985, Dec 23
    (5) 2012, Oct 28

6. Based on the information in the chart, you might conclude that

    (1) earthquakes are increasing in frequency
    (2) strong earthquakes only occur in BC
    (3) earthquakes often recur in the same place
    (4) more serious earthquakes occur in summer
    (5) earthquakes are a serious danger in Canada

The name *ring of fire* describes a horseshoe shaped ring of volcanos that surround the Pacific Ocean. There are more than 450 live and dormant volcanos in the ring as a result of the subduction and collision of tectonic plates. More than 80% of serious earthquakes in the world take place around the ring of fire.

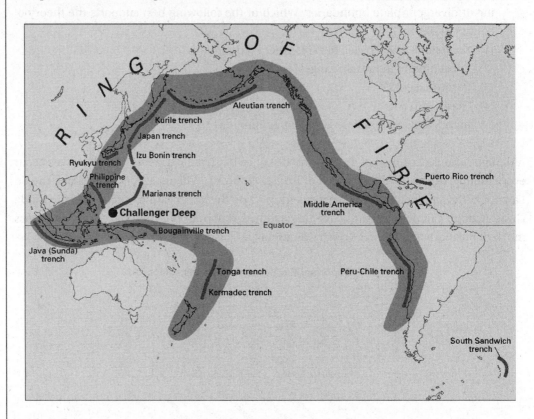

7. Based on the information in the map and the passage, you can conclude that
   (1) oceanic trenches indicate plate boundaries
   (2) volcanos do not occur on land
   (3) many volcanos are found near Canada's east coast
   (4) Asia experiences few earthquakes
   (5) the west coast of Africa has many volcanos

8. Not all plate boundaries result in an oceanic trench. For example, the numerous faults mark plate boundaries along the west coast of North America, but there is no oceanic trench. The Queen Charlotte fault extending from Vancouver Island to Haida Gwaii is part of the ring of fire, as is the Cascade Subduction Zone, extending from the western Vancouver Island to California. Based on this information you can conclude that
   (1) there are no volcanos in North America
   (2) there are no earthquakes in BC
   (3) tectonic plates do not move along the west coast of North America
   (4) BC is the most active earthquake region in Canada
   (5) Vancouver Island may someday sink into the sea

ANSWERS

1. **(4)** One can conclude that a divergent plate boundary could be called a constructive boundary because new crust is created from the material forced up through the fault from the asthenosphere.

2. **(4)** Again, one can conclude that rock gets progressively older as it moves away from a divergent boundary as new rock is formed when material is thrust up from the asthenosphere, causing the plates to move away from one another, and then more new rock is formed when the process repeats over time.

3. **(2)** The passage suggests that the reason is they are thinner.

4. **(5)** Fossils are extremely old. The fact that there are identical plant fossils on different continents suggests that the same plants once grew there and may indicate that they were once attached.

5. **(5)** This quake had a magnitude of 7.7.

6. **(3)** As the chart shows, earthquakes happen in the same places.

7. **(1)** Oceanic trenches occur as a result of subduction of oceanic plates.

8. **(4)** The passage says 80% of major earthquakes occur along the ring of fire. Because the BC faults are part of it, you conclude that the majority of Canadian earthquakes occur there.

CHALLENGE EXERCISE

Research the following things: What is seismology; what are seismic waves, and what causes them? Write your answers in your own words.

ATMOSPHERE

Atmosphere is the envelope of gases that surrounds the Earth and other planets. Gravity holds the atmosphere in place. Earth's atmosphere is composed primarily of nitrogen (78%) and oxygen (21%) with the remaining 1% made up of argon, carbon dioxide, and other trace gases. Earth's atmosphere is divided into layers based primarily on temperature, although density of the atmosphere also decreases with altitude.

Earth's atmosphere plays a vital role in the ability of the planet to maintain life. Upper reaches of the atmosphere absorb much of the sun's harmful radiation, protecting all living things. Greenhouse gases in the atmosphere also trap some of the sun's heat, providing sufficient warmth for life and preventing extreme differences in temperature between night and day. The atmosphere also contains water vapour and carries dust particles, enabling the cycle of evaporation and rain, and the winds of the atmosphere carry pollen to facilitate plant reproduction. Without the atmosphere, there would be no life on earth.

The GED® Science test may contain questions about the Earth's atmosphere or atmospheric issues, such as global warming, pollution, wind patterns, climate or weather.

PRACTICE

Choose the best answer to each question.

Earth's atmosphere has five layers. The top layer of the atmosphere is the *exosphere*, which extends from 600km to 10,000km above the Earth. This is an area that we would commonly think of as space because it is the area in which satellites orbit. It is composed primarily of lighter molecules of hydrogen and helium, as well as a smaller amount of heavier molecules of oxygen, nitrogen, and carbon dioxide. The exosphere is so dispersed that the substances do not behave like gases. It is possible that molecules could travel for hundreds of kilometres before colliding with another. Temperature of the exosphere varies with the extent of solar radiation, reaching as high as several thousand degrees on the day side of the Earth and plunging to near absolute zero at night.

The *thermosphere* extends from approximately 85km to 600km above the Earth. Like the exosphere, it is another layer with low density, which increases as it descends. A molecule can travel for as much as a kilometre before colliding with another. Temperature of the thermosphere increases as altitude increases and the layer approaches the exosphere. This is the layer at which the space shuttle docks with the orbiting International Space Station.

The *mesosphere* extends from 50km to 85km. In the mesosphere, temperature decreases as altitude increases. This is the layer in which meteorites usually burn up before reaching the lower atmosphere or the surface of the Earth. The upper reaches of the mesosphere can plunge to temperatures of –100°C, causing water vapour to freeze.

The *stratosphere* extends from approximately 12km to 50km and is extremely important because it also contains the ozone layer, which absorbs harmful radiation from the sun. As a result of absorption by the ozone, temperature increases in the stratosphere as altitude increases. However, the layer is still quite cold, reaching a high temperature just under 0°C at the upper limits.

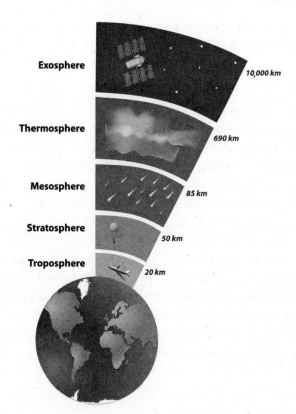

The lowest level of the atmosphere is the *troposphere*, which extends from the Earth to a height of approximately 12km. Temperature in the troposphere decreases with altitude. This is the layer in which planes fly and weather takes place. The jet stream, a high band of fast-moving, prevailing westerly air currents that encircle the globe, is found in the troposphere. Heat from the Earth is transferred to the troposphere from the surface, just as warmth from the Sun is reflected from the surface and held in the troposphere by greenhouse gases, giving the Earth an average temperature of 15°C, although temperature varies with geographic region and season.

In addition to the five main layers of the atmosphere, there are sub-layers, such as the *ozone layer, ionosphere,* and *tropopause.*

1. In which layer of the atmosphere are rain clouds found?
   (1) Troposphere
   (2) Stratosphere
   (3) Mesosphere
   (4) Thermosphere
   (5) Exosphere

2. In which layer does the International Space Station orbit?
   (1) Troposphere
   (2) Stratosphere
   (3) Mesosphere
   (4) Thermosphere
   (5) Exosphere

3. Which of the following can reach the highest temperature?
   (1) Lower stratosphere
   (2) Upper mesosphere
   (3) Lower thermosphere
   (4) Upper thermosphere
   (5) Upper exosphere

In weather reports, the meteorologist often speaks of high- and low-pressure areas and their movements. Most people know that a barometer measures high- and low-pressure systems and that they impact weather, but how are such pressure areas formed and what do they do?

As the Sun warms the Earth, molecules in the air near the warmed area become excited. The air expands, increasing in volume and decreasing in density. The lighter air rises, forming a low pressure area, and cool air from outside the system is drawn in underneath. Atmospheric pressure refers to the weight of the atmosphere on the Earth. Low pressure areas usually bring wind, clouds, and rain. Cool air drawn in underneath a low pressure system causes the air above it to cool, increase in density, and subside, creating a high pressure area that brings Sun and clear skies.

4. A low pressure system is one in which the weight of the atmosphere on the Earth is
   (1) higher
   (2) lower
   (3) warmer
   (4) cooler
   (5) blowing

5. Wind, the flow of air, probably occurs as a result of
   (1) sunlight
   (2) rain
   (3) unequal pressure in the atmosphere
   (4) high pressure areas
   (5) low pressure areas

ANSWERS

1. **(1)** The passage states that weather takes place in the troposphere.
2. **(4)** The passage states that the space shuttle docks with the International Space Station in the thermosphere
3. **(5)** The passage states that the temperature in the upper exosphere can reach several thousand degrees during the day.
4. **(2)** Atmospheric pressure refers to the weight of the atmosphere. A low pressure system has a lower weight because of the rising warm air.
5. **(3)** The passage describes cool air from outside the system being drawn in below a rising low pressure system. This unequal pressure is a cause of wind.

WATER CYCLE

One of the things that separates our planet from all others in the solar system is the existence of water, one of the essential ingredients of life. While there is some evidence of frozen or subterranean water on other moons and dwarf planets, none has been confirmed, and no other body is believed to have a cycle of water vapour in the air, ground water, and bodies of surface liquid water.

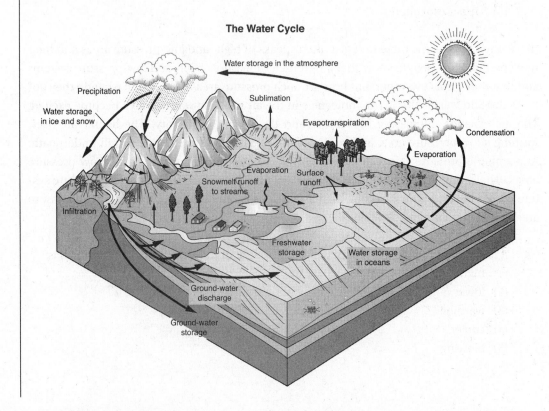

The Water Cycle

On the Earth, water moves in a cycle on, under, and above the surface, influencing climate and nourishing life. As with all things, the Sun provides the source of energy that initiates the cycle, and water molecules pass through the different states of liquid, gas, and sometimes solid in the process.

PRACTICE

Choose the best answer to each question.

1. Heat from the Sun converts liquid water on the surface to water vapour in the air through a process called
   (1) condensation
   (2) accumulation
   (3) evaporation
   (4) infiltration
   (5) transpiration

2. The process by which water is drawn in by plants and escapes as water vapour from the leaves is
   (1) condensation
   (2) accumulation
   (3) evaporation
   (4) infiltration
   (5) transpiration

3. Based on the graphic, water accumulates in standing bodies largely as a result of
   (1) precipitation
   (2) run off
   (3) ground water
   (4) ground water and runoff
   (5) ground water and infiltration

ANSWERS

1. **(3)** Evaporation is the process of water becoming vapour.
2. **(5)** In transpiration, water from plants evaporates from pores in the leaves.
3. **(4)** Groundwater and runoff flow into lakes, rivers, and oceans.

CHALLENGE EXERCISE

A number of factors—including wind, temperature, and geography—play an important part in creating weather. Research the average amount of rainfall in the city, province, or territory where you live. Research the average amount of rainfall in other parts of Canada. What causes some regions to get more rainfall than others?

OCEANOGRAPHY

More than 70% of the Earth is covered by oceans. In truth, there is only one ocean, as all of the bodies are connected; however, various regions have been given different names. The water covering the Earth is divided into three principle regions, the oceans, which include the Atlantic, Pacific, and Indian Oceans. Other smaller regions, which are parts of the oceans, are called seas, such as the Mediterranean and Caribbean Sea.

Oceans have wide dimensions. The Pacific, for example, is about 12,000km wide and stretches from Antarctica in the south to the Bering Strait in the north. The average depth of an ocean, however, is only 3–4 kilometres. The crust of the ocean is thinner than the continental crust, but heavier and denser and rides lower on the Earth's mantle.

Earth's oceans are like a world of their own. They have their own mountain ranges and prevailing currents. They have their own ecosystems and millions of species of life. Oceans and their currents also have a profound effect on temperatures and climate of the whole of the Earth. Oceanography is the study of the oceans—their geography, tectonic plate movement, ecosystems, species, currents, waves, and chemical composition.

PRACTICE

Choose the best answer to each question that follows:

There is more water in the oceans than the ocean basins can hold and so some of it spills over to cover low lying areas of the continental plates along the coasts of continents or around islands. These areas have an average depth of about 120 metres and then drop off to much greater depths to the ocean floor. They are typically areas of great biological activity and help to protect the land by dissipating tides. The Grand Banks off Canada's east coast are an example of a continental shelf.

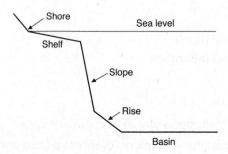

1. The slope of a continental shelf is the edge of
    (1) the oceanic crust
    (2) an oceanic ridge
    (3) sea level
    (4) the continental crust
    (5) the ocean floor

Waves are caused by wind blowing over the ocean. The height of the waves depends on the strength of wind, duration, and expanse of water over which it blows. Away from shore, water is too deep for waves to reach the bottom. Waves are called swells, rounded humps of water that move across the surface. As the swells approach shore, the troughs—the valleys between the water's crests—touch the bottom, causing the wave to slow and the wave height to increase, eventually breaking over receding water from the beach.

Waves can travel great distances. In an ocean swell, the water itself moves very little. Rather, the wave passes through the water, so very little energy is consumed.

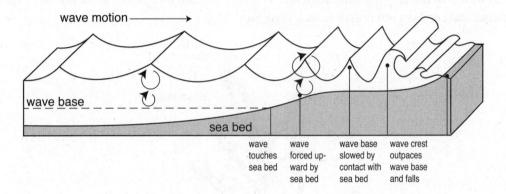

2. Based on the information in the graphic, the wave height could be defined as
    (1) elevation between bottom of trough and crest of swell
    (2) distance between crests
    (3) elevation of crest above the ocean floor
    (4) elevation of trough above ocean floor
    (5) elevation of crest above sea level

3. Wavelength can be described as
    (1) distance between crests
    (2) distance from crest to trough
    (3) width of a swell
    (4) distance from trough to crest
    (5) width of a trough

4. Waves near the shore when compared with waves that are farther out to sea
    (1) have less energy
    (2) have more energy
    (3) have a longer wavelength
    (4) have more force
    (5) have a shorter wavelength

Along the Pacific coast, in South America, South Africa, and Southern Australia, there lie beneath the waves vast forests of kelp. A type of seaweed, kelp comes in several varieties, some of which can reach heights of more than thirty metres. The plants have three primary parts: the holdfast (roots), stipe (stem), and blade (leaves). Unlike terrestrial plants that draw water and nutrients through the roots, the holdfast of kelp serves only to keep it in place while the ingredients for photosynthesis are drawn by the blades from the surrounding water.

As with terrestrial forests, life exists at all levels of the kelp forest. Sea urchin, sponges, crabs, and hundreds of other creatures live on the ocean floor. Fish swim among the stipes and blades of the kelp beneath the forest's canopy, hunted by sharks and larger fish. From above, seals and sea otters dive to seek their prey.

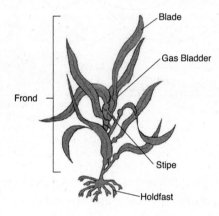

5. The difference between the holdfast of the kelp and the roots of a plant is that the holdfast
    (1) keeps the plant in place
    (2) is longer
    (3) does not gather nutrients
    (4) is not part of the main plant
    (5) is vital to photosynthesis

6. Which part of the kelp is most likely responsible for transporting nutrients to different parts of the organism?
    (1) Holdfast
    (2) Stipe
    (3) Blades
    (4) Frond
    (5) Gas bladder

ANSWERS

1. **(4)** The continental crust is thicker and some ocean water spills over to low lying areas along the coast, forming the continental shelf.

2. **(1)** Wave height is the height from the bottom of the trough to the crest.

3. **(1)** Wavelength is the distance between crests, although the distance between the bottom of each trough would be the same.

4. **(5)** Near the shore, waves have a shorter wavelength and greater magnitude because of contact with the bottom.

5. **(3)** The passage states that the holdfast, unlike roots, does not gather nutrients. Roots of a plant also hold it in place.

6. **(2)** The stipe, like the stem of a plant, connects its parts and transports nutrients.

CHAPTER CHECK-UP

Complete these practice exercises, and check the answers and analysis that follow. After you mark your work, review any topic in the chapter that you had trouble with or did not understand.

Comets are relatively small celestial bodies that travel in a highly elliptical orbit around the sun. The orbit is so long that they rarely pass close to the sun. The famous Halley's Comet, for example, only passes within sight of the Earth every 76 years. Other comets have even longer orbits.

At the centre of a comet is the nucleus, a small ball of ice, dust, and gas, usually ranging from 1 to 10 kilometres in diameter, but occasionally slightly larger. It is commonly referred to as the dirty snowball. Around it is the coma, a large envelope of gas, composed primarily of water vapour, dust, and carbon dioxide. A comet has two tails. The dust tail is composed of loose particles that emanate from the nucleus and coma. The ion tail, also called the plasma tail, is composed of gas ions and can be millions of kilometres long. This is the tail we can see. The ion tail always faces away from the Sun in the orbit of the comet, blown by streaming ions from the Sun, known as the solar wind. The tails are only present when the comet is in the vicinity of the Sun and vapourizing.

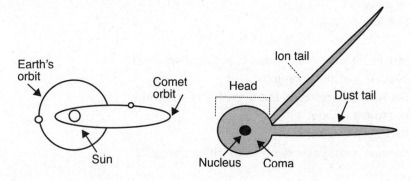

1. Why are comets seen so rarely?
    (1) They are very small.
    (2) They do not always have tails.
    (3) They have a long, elliptical orbit.
    (4) They are often behind the Sun.
    (5) They are obscured by their dust tail.

2. When a comet has circled the Sun and is streaming away with the Sun behind it, in which direction will the ion tail extend?
   (1) Behind the comet.
   (2) In front of the comet.
   (3) Beside the comet.
   (4) Inside the comet.
   (5) There will be no more ion tail.

Rocks are grouped into three main categories, based on the way in which they were formed. Within each category, there are different kinds of rock with different composition, acidity, and other characteristics. Igneous rocks are formed when the molten magma deep within the Earth seeps into cracks in the Earth's crust or erupts to the surface, where it is called magma, and cools. Examples of igneous rock are granite, basalt, and obsidian. Sedimentary rock is formed when particles of sand or pebbles accumulate in layers and are compressed over time to become rock. It is generally soft and may crumble easily. Fossils are most often found in this type of rock. Sandstone, limestone, and shale are examples of sedimentary rock. Metamorphic rock is formed under the surface of the Earth by heat and pressure, but not to the point of melting. The relative amounts of heat and pressure produce crystals within the rock. Marble is an example of metamorphic rock.

3. Which of the following is a type of sedimentary rock?
   (1) Marble
   (2) Granite
   (3) Obsidian
   (4) Shale
   (5) Basalt

4. Molten rock within the Earth is called
   (1) magma
   (2) lava
   (3) sedimentary
   (4) igneous
   (5) metamorphic

5. Why are fossils most often found in sedimentary rock?
   (1) Because it is more common
   (2) Because it is created in layers gradually, over time
   (3) Because it is softer
   (4) Because it is older
   (5) Because it erupts suddenly from within the earth

Heat is transferred in three ways: conduction (direct contact of solids), convection (movement of gases and liquids, including air and water), and radiation (without direct contact). Within the Earth, the molten outer core heats the bottom of the mantle, causing the mantle material to expand, become less dense, and rise. Reaching the bottom of the lithosphere, the current turns and flows under the crust, not quite liquid, but soft enough to flow very slowly. Eventually the flow cools and sinks. This cycle, called a convection cell, occurs throughout the Earth and is one of the forces that drives movement of tectonic plates.

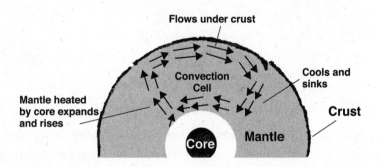

6. Heat is transferred from the outer core through the mantle towards the lithosphere through
   (1) conduction
   (2) convection
   (3) radiation
   (4) illumination
   (5) flow

7. Mantle material sinks back towards the core as it cools because it
   (1) is liquid
   (2) it flows more slowly
   (3) does not conduct heat
   (4) is less dense
   (5) is more dense

8. It is likely that convection cells within the Earth contribute to
   (1) continental drift
   (2) global warming
   (3) depletion of the ozone layer
   (4) warmth of the equator
   (5) earth's rotation

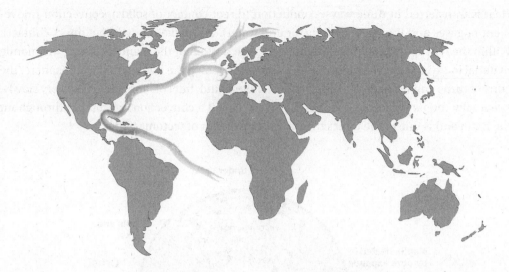

Ocean currents play an extremely important role in weather, able to carry large amounts of heat and moisture. The Gulf Stream is a warm-water current that commences at the tip of Florida, flows along the eastern coast of North America and then crosses the Atlantic Ocean. There the current separates, continuing northeast above northwestern Europe and south along the coast of Western Europe and Africa. In the winter, the Gulf Stream carries warm temperatures from southern climes along the North American coast and across the ocean to England and Europe. In summer, the current carries cooler temperatures from the north along the coast of Africa and back across the Atlantic.

9. The Gulf Stream brings warm air to
    (1) Florida
    (2) Africa
    (3) England
    (4) South America
    (5) British Columbia

10. One possible way that the Gulf Steam could be harnessed to produce renewable energy is
    (1) tidal power
    (2) thermal energy conversion
    (3) solar power
    (4) nuclear fusion
    (5) wind and tidal power

ANSWERS

1. **(3)** Orbits are long and elliptical, so they spend much time in space and only a short time near the Earth and Sun.

2. **(2)** The tail will be in front of the comet as the ion tail always extends away from the Sun.

3. **(4)** Shale is a type of sedimentary rock.

4. **(1)** Inside the Earth it is called magma. On the surface it is lava. When it hardens, it becomes igneous rock.

5. **(2)** Sedimentary rocks are formed from sediment, such as particles of sand or rock. When organisms die and are buried in the sediment, they may become part of the slowly forming rock.

6. **(2)** Convection is the transfer of heat through the movement of gases and liquids.

7. **(5)** Heat expands the volume of material, thus reducing density, making it lighter. Cooling reduces the volume of the material, increasing density.

8. **(1)** The passage states that convection cells are one of the forces that move tectonic plates, resulting in continental drift.

9. **(3)** The Gulf Steam is important to the climate of England and eastern North America. It brings cool air to Africa, South America, and Florida. BC is on the Pacific Ocean.

10. **(2)** Several methods are being studied; however, this passage was primarily about temperature and the Gulf Stream, suggesting thermal energy conversion.

Science—Practice Test

EXAMPLE

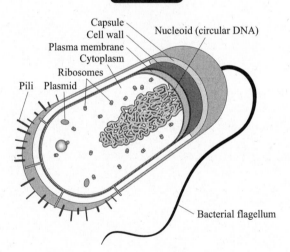

Bacteria cells are different from plant and animal cells because bacteria cells do not have

(1)   membranes
(2)   ribosomes
(3)   a nucleus
(4)   a cell wall
(5)   cytoplasm

In this example, almost all cells have a nucleus, but the diagram illustrates that bacteria cells do not. Fill in answer space 3 on the answer sheet.

ANSWER SHEET
Science Practice Test

1. ① ② ③ ④ ⑤
2. ① ② ③ ④ ⑤
3. ① ② ③ ④ ⑤
4. ① ② ③ ④ ⑤
5. ① ② ③ ④ ⑤
6. ① ② ③ ④ ⑤
7. ① ② ③ ④ ⑤
8. ① ② ③ ④ ⑤
9. ① ② ③ ④ ⑤
10. ① ② ③ ④ ⑤
11. ① ② ③ ④ ⑤
12. ① ② ③ ④ ⑤
13. ① ② ③ ④ ⑤
14. ① ② ③ ④ ⑤
15. ① ② ③ ④ ⑤
16. ① ② ③ ④ ⑤
17. ① ② ③ ④ ⑤
18. ① ② ③ ④ ⑤
19. ① ② ③ ④ ⑤
20. ① ② ③ ④ ⑤

21. ① ② ③ ④ ⑤
22. ① ② ③ ④ ⑤
23. ① ② ③ ④ ⑤
24. ① ② ③ ④ ⑤
25. ① ② ③ ④ ⑤
26. ① ② ③ ④ ⑤
27. ① ② ③ ④ ⑤
28. ① ② ③ ④ ⑤
29. ① ② ③ ④ ⑤
30. ① ② ③ ④ ⑤
31. ① ② ③ ④ ⑤
32. ① ② ③ ④ ⑤
33. ① ② ③ ④ ⑤
34. ① ② ③ ④ ⑤
35. ① ② ③ ④ ⑤
36. ① ② ③ ④ ⑤
37. ① ② ③ ④ ⑤
38. ① ② ③ ④ ⑤
39. ① ② ③ ④ ⑤
40. ① ② ③ ④ ⑤

41. ① ② ③ ④ ⑤
42. ① ② ③ ④ ⑤
43. ① ② ③ ④ ⑤
44. ① ② ③ ④ ⑤
45. ① ② ③ ④ ⑤
46. ① ② ③ ④ ⑤
47. ① ② ③ ④ ⑤
48. ① ② ③ ④ ⑤
49. ① ② ③ ④ ⑤
50. ① ② ③ ④ ⑤

SCIENCE

> Complete the practice test, and then check the answers and analysis that follow. After you mark your work, review any topics you had trouble with or did not understand.

Questions 1–3 are based on the following information.

Geothermal energy is produced from heat inside the earth. The intense heat of the earth's core radiates outward towards the surface. Close to the surface, below the frost line, the earth's crust remains at a constant temperature. A geothermal heat pump in your home and pipes reaching a depth of about three metres can use the constant temperatures to provide heat in winter and cooling during the summer.

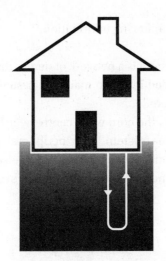

Geothermal energy can also be used to power large-scale power plants in geologically active areas near tectonic plate boundaries, and can involve wells more than a kilometre deep. These plants all use hot water and steam, deep within the earth, to move turbines to generate electricity. The water is then returned to the ground where it is heated again. The United States is the largest producer of geothermal electricity, especially in the geyser-rich area north of San Francisco. Many other countries also produce geothermal energy. In Iceland, which has 25 active volcanos, geothermal power heats more than 80% of the nation's homes.

Canada lags behind other countries in geothermal energy, but initiatives are underway. In Fort Laird, NT, a geothermal generator is expected to provide electricity for the small community and to use excess heat to warm greenhouses.

1. A geothermal pump warms a house in winter by
   (1) heat exchange
   (2) radiation
   (3) electricity
   (4) hot springs
   (5) volcanic energy

2. Electric plants are probably more common in geologically active regions because of
   (1) more groundwater
   (2) less groundwater
   (3) warmer atmosphere
   (4) radiation
   (5) higher underground temperature

3. Compared with fossil fuels, geothermal energy plants would produce
   (1) less electricity
   (2) more air pollution
   (3) higher cost
   (4) fewer greenhouse gas emissions
   (5) more environmental damage

Questions 4–5 are based on the following information.

Nerves are cells. The nervous system is a network of nerves that connect all parts of our bodies. The nervous system is divided into two main sub-systems: the central nervous system and the peripheral nervous system.

The central nervous system is the command centre, which sends and receives messages through the peripheral nervous system. The peripheral nervous system, which runs throughout the body, has two additional sub-systems: the somatic nervous system, which controls voluntary movement, and the autonomic nervous system, which controls automatic functions.

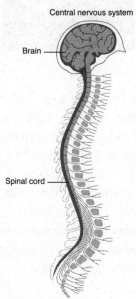

4. The sciatic nerve in the human leg is part of the
   (1) brain
   (2) spine
   (3) peripheral nervous system
   (4) central nervous system
   (5) command centre

5. Which of the following is a function of the autonomic nervous system?
    (1) walking
    (2) sweating
    (3) winking
    (4) chewing
    (5) sitting

Questions 6–8 are based on the following information.

Energy is the ability to do work. When a bicycle rolls down a hill, it is doing work and has kinetic energy. If the same bicycle is at rest at the top of the hill, it has the same amount of energy, but it is potential energy. The distinction between the potential energy in the bicycle at the top of the hill and the kinetic energy at the bottom is called the *potential difference*. In electricity, when electrons move through a wire and do work, such as illuminating a light bulb, they have kinetic energy. When the switch is off, electrons are not moving and no work is being done. The same amount of energy exists, but it is potential energy. The potential difference in electrical energy between two points is called voltage. In a battery, it is the difference between the negative and positive terminals.

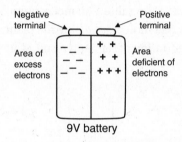

6. When a battery is not connected, the energy in the battery is
    (1) electrons
    (2) proton energy
    (3) mechanical energy
    (4) kinetic energy
    (5) potential energy

7. If the battery is connected to a light, electrons will flow from the
    (1) negative terminal to positive terminal
    (2) positive terminal to negative terminal
    (3) terminals to the light
    (4) light to the terminals
    (5) top to the bottom

8. Voltage of the battery is a measure of what between the terminals?
    (1) Kinetic energy
    (2) Electric charge
    (3) Potential difference
    (4) Work
    (5) Energy

9. Diffusion refers to the movement of particles within liquids and gases. In a cup of water, if a pinch of salt is added, the salt molecules move around in the water, moving from areas of higher concentration to areas of lower concentration, until the concentration of salt is equal throughout the cup of water. The same occurs in air. Based on diffusion, perfume sprayed in a closed room would
    (1) remain strongest where sprayed
    (2) remain weakest where sprayed
    (3) spread equally around the room
    (4) increase intensity over time
    (5) increase intensity as it spreads

Questions 10–12 are based on the following information.

Osmosis is a special kind of diffusion that occurs frequently in nature and is the process by which plants obtain water and nutrients through their roots. Osmosis is the diffusion of a liquid solution (such as water with salt and other particles) through a membrane.

Plants are made of cells that have a semi-permeable membrane, or cell wall. Semi-permeable means that the wall will let some things pass through, such as water, oxygen, nitrogen, and some salts, but it does not allow larger molecules to pass in or salt inside the cell to pass out. Inside plant cells the salinity (concentration of salt) is higher than in fresh groundwater around the roots. Salt molecules inside the plant cell cannot pass out, but diffusion tries to equalize the concentration of salt. As a result, water and other particles are drawn in through the cell wall.

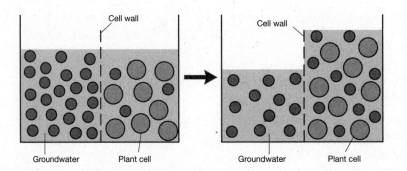

10. Osmosis draws water into the plant root because of
    (1) higher salinity in the cell
    (2) lower water pressure in the cell
    (3) lower salinity in the cell
    (4) lower water pressure in ground water
    (5) the cell nucleus

11. The wall and membrane of a plant cell are
    (1) permeable
    (2) flexible
    (3) semi-permeable
    (4) salty
    (5) nitrogen

12. Plant roots in salty seawater instead of fresh groundwater would
    (1) gain water
    (2) lose water
    (3) gain nitrogen
    (4) lose nitrogen
    (5) lose salt

Questions 13–15 are based on the following information.

Sound is energy that travels in waves through air, water, or another medium. It is perceived by the auditory organs of humans or other animals. Sound waves that are long have a lower frequency. Sound waves that are short have a higher frequency. Many comparisons have been made of the hearing ranges of animals. The results often vary because there can be differences among types of breeds of cats, dogs, and birds, for example, as well as differences between individuals and ages. Nonetheless, results help us to understand how animals hear differently.

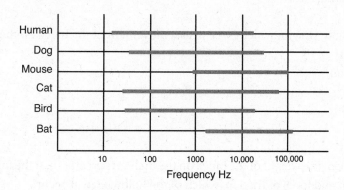

13. Which of the following hear sounds in the lowest frequencies?
    (1) Humans
    (2) Dogs
    (3) Cats
    (4) Birds
    (5) Bats

14. Which animal hears both lower and higher frequencies than dogs?
    (1) Humans
    (2) Mice
    (3) Cats
    (4) Birds
    (5) Bats

15. Which animal hears the highest frequencies?
    (1) Humans
    (2) Dogs
    (3) Cats
    (4) Birds
    (5) Bats

Questions 16–18 are based on the following information.

A block on an inclined plane is attached to a weight.

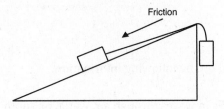

Friction

16. If the attached weight is equal to the weight of the block then the block will
    (1) move up at a constant speed
    (2) slide back at a constant speed
    (3) not move
    (4) accelerate up the incline
    (5) accelerate back

17. In addition to weight, which force resists movement of the block up the incline?
    (1) Gravity
    (2) Friction
    (3) Mass
    (4) Weight
    (5) Force

18. If the force of the weight of the block on the incline is greater than the force of the hanging weight and force of friction, which of the following will occur?
    (1) The block will accelerate up the incline.
    (2) The block will accelerate down the incline.
    (3) The block will not move.
    (4) The weight will accelerate downward.
    (5) The block will move upward at constant speed.

19. Homeostasis is the tendency in systems towards stability and balance. In biology, homeostasis refers to adjustments within an organism to maintain internal balance in spite of external conditions. In humans, an example of homeostasis to maintain an internal body temperature of 37°C is
    (1) fever
    (2) vomiting
    (3) increased heart rate
    (4) sweating
    (5) high blood pressure

When elements (atoms) join together to form molecules, it is called *bonding*. There are two types of bonding. Ionic bonds form when oppositely charged ions are attracted to one another. Covalent bonds occur when atoms join together to share electrons, making both atoms more stable.

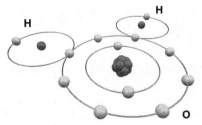

20. A water molecule is an example of
    (1) ionic bonding
    (2) elements
    (3) charged ions
    (4) attraction
    (5) covalent bonding

Questions 21–23 are based on the following information.

A volcano is a mountain formed by emergence of melted rock within the earth. There are different kinds of volcanoes: some that erupt violently and others quietly. Below the earth's crust is the mantle. The mantle is very hot, but mostly solid because of intense pressure. At boundaries where the plates of the earth's crust meet are spots where material from the mantle rises, forced upward through the more dense rock of the crust. As it rises, the material melts into a mixture of molten rock and gases called magma. The magma pools in its chamber beneath the volcano. When pressure within the magma chamber is greater than the containing force of rock, the chamber explodes, sending clouds of dust and ash out miles into the air while lava flows rapidly down the sides of the volcano.

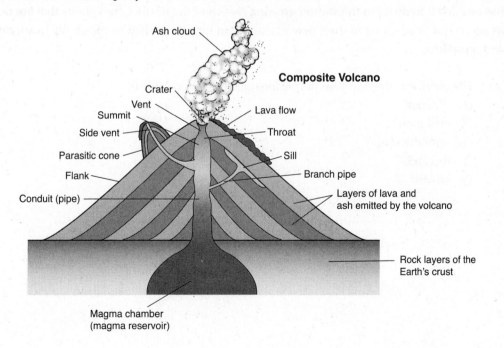

21. Melted rock beneath the surface of the Earth is
    (1) magma
    (2) lava
    (3) mantle
    (4) flow
    (5) crust

22. Material from the mantle rises through layers of rock because it is
    (1) liquid
    (2) hot
    (3) less dense
    (4) lava
    (5) erupting

23. The cone shaped opening through which a volcano erupts is the
    (1) chamber
    (2) pipe
    (3) lava flow
    (4) crater
    (5) rock layer

Questions 24–25 are based on the following passage.

Government agencies and scientists in Canada are concerned about the spread of invasive species, and research is underway to determine why some species thrive and become prevalent, while others do not. Recent research in Ontario about the invasive purple loosestrife plant may provide some answers. Researchers have discovered that purple loosestrife in northern Ontario are much smaller and flower earlier than those in southern Ontario, an adaptation that has occurred since the plant was first introduced from Europe and which has enabled it to thrive in the shorter growing season of the north. Other plants that are not as successful in adapting to their new environment may be limited in the ability to survive and reproduce.

24. The change in the northern purple loosestrife is an example of
    (1) invasion
    (2) evolution
    (3) reproduction
    (4) research
    (5) growth

25. If global warming leads to longer growing seasons in northern Canada, the rate of invasive species might
    (1) decrease
    (2) evolve
    (3) interfere with research
    (4) produce smaller plants
    (5) increase

Questions 26–27 are based on the following graphic.

26. In the graphic above, which of the following will occur?
    (1) The end with the lighter weight will go up.
    (2) The end with the heavier weight will go up.
    (3) The end with the lighter weight will go down.
    (4) The two ends will remain balanced
    (5) Both ends will go down.

27. Which of the following could enable the two ends of the seesaw to be balanced?
    (1) Move the heavier weight closer to the pivot
    (2) Move the lighter weight closer to the pivot
    (3) Move the heavier weight farther from the pivot
    (4) Move both weights farther from the pivot
    (5) Move both weights closer to the pivot

Questions 28–30 are based on the following information.

Stem cells are very important to medical research and offer the possibility of cures for conditions requiring generation of new tissue to repair damage from injury, disease, or aging. Stem cells are important because they are regenerative, undifferentiated cells. That is, they divide and reproduce themselves, but have not formed into a particular kind of cell. Eventually, they differentiate to form cells of all types, such as blood, nerves, organ and muscle tissue, and skin.

Stem cells are found in humans and animals. They are found in bone marrow, skin, umbilical cord blood, and embryos. Much debate has centred around use of embryonic stem cells. Opponents raise ethical issues; however, proponents argue that embryonic stem cells offer greater potential. Adult stem cells are specialized. For example, those formed in the skin will go on to form skin cells. Embryonic stem cells have greater potential to form any type of tissue.

Fortunately, new research may set concerns to rest. In 2007, a Japanese researcher discovered a way to create pluripotent (unspecialized) stem cells from skin cells by reprogramming some of the genes in the cells with a retrovirus. In 2009, a Canadian-Scottish team announced a method of creating pluripotent stem cells without a retrovirus.

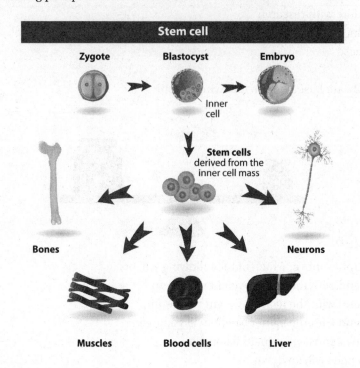

28. The diagram depicts
   (1) adult stem cells that form other cells
   (2) stem cells that form embryos
   (3) sources of stem cells
   (4) transformation of embryonic stem cells
   (5) destruction of embryonic stem cells

29. Proponents have supported use of embryonic stem cells in research because they are
   (1) younger
   (2) pluripotent
   (3) specialized
   (4) easily harvested
   (5) smaller

30. Which of the following could potentially be cured as result of stem cell research?
   (1) Common cold
   (2) Mental illness
   (3) Spinal injury
   (4) Bacterial infection
   (5) Food-borne illness

Questions 31–32 are based on the following information.

How does a hot air balloon fly? Density is a property of matter that is equal to its mass divided by volume. When the air in a balloon is heated, the heat energy is transferred to the air molecules, which increases their movement and makes them spread farther apart. The heated air inside a hot air balloon is, therefore, less dense than the air around it and the balloon rises.

31. Air that is heated has greater
    (1) density
    (2) mass
    (3) weight
    (4) matter
    (5) volume

32. *Buoyancy* is the term that describes the upward force that liquids and gases exert on substances that are less dense than themselves. This principle explains why a hot air balloon rises and
    (1) water flows
    (2) a boat floats
    (3) a rocket flies
    (4) birds fly
    (5) substances diffuse in water

Questions 33–34 are based on the following information.

A *terrarium* is an enclosed garden in a container, such as a large glass jar. Inside are placed soil, selected plants, and a small amount of water. The container is often closed, and observers are able to see the water cycle as moisture in the air of the container condenses on the walls and back down into the soil.

33. A terrarium is an example of a(n)
    (1) planet
    (2) food web
    (3) water cycle
    (4) ecosystem
    (5) chemical change

34. A terrarium would require which of the following from outside the system
    (1) water
    (2) food
    (3) oxygen
    (4) wind
    (5) sunlight

Questions 35–37 are based on the following information.

This food-web diagram shows the connection among producers, consumers, and decomposers in relation to the arctic hare. One can see how any disruption in the food web, such as a decline in population of the arctic hare, impacts all organisms in the ecosystem.

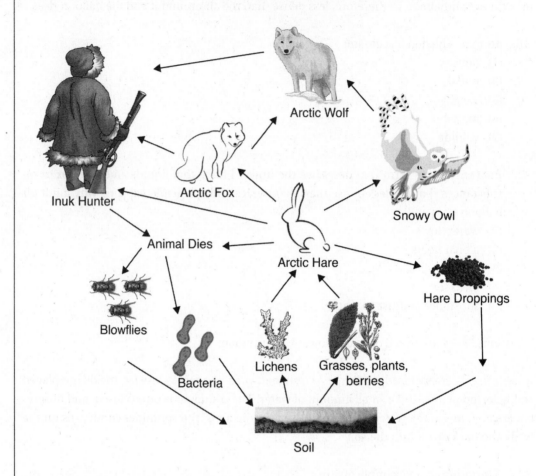

35. Which of the following organisms in the web is a producer, making its own food?
     (1) Lichens
     (2) Arctic hare
     (3) Arctic fox
     (4) Snowy owl
     (5) Inuk hunter

36. What is the role of blow flies in the food web?
     (1) Producer
     (2) Primary consumer
     (3) Decomposer
     (4) Hunter
     (5) Micro-organism

37. In this graphic, the arrows probably represent the flow of
    (1) water
    (2) energy
    (3) oxygen
    (4) air
    (5) temperature

Questions 38–40 are based on the following information.

When an object on a string is swung in a circular path, two forces are at work: centrifugal and centripetal force. Centrifugal force (A) is considered an artificial force. The law of inertia states that an object in motion will stay in motion at a constant speed and in a straight line unless acted on by another force. Centrifugal force is not really a force at all. It is created by the centripetal force and is simply the inertia of the object. Centripetal force (B) is a real force. It is the force on the string pulling inward that causes the object to travel in a circular motion.

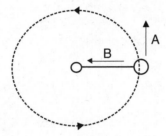

38. Centrifugal force could be described as an object's
    (1) velocity
    (2) inward motion
    (3) acceleration due to gravity
    (4) resistance to change in its state of motion
    (5) circular momentum

39. Which of the following statements about the diagram is true?
    (1) Force A is greater in magnitude than force B.
    (2) Force A and B are equal in magnitude.
    (3) Force B is greater in magnitude than force A.
    (4) Force A and force B are exerted in the same direction.
    (5) A has no force.

40. If the string is released while the object is spinning, which of the following occurs?
    (1) The object drops immediately to the floor.
    (2) Inertia ceases.
    (3) Centrifugal force remains.
    (4) Centripetal force remains.
    (5) Inertia remains.

Questions 41–44 are based on the following information.

The human ear is a complex structure that converts sound waves into signals that are perceived by the brain. The ear has three main parts: outer, middle, and inner ear. The ear flap (pinna) of the outer ear channels sound waves into the ear canal, causing the ear drum to vibrate. The vibration is transmitted to a series of three small bones in the middle ear, commonly called the hammer, anvil, and stirrup because of their distinctive shapes. The bones of the air-filled inner ear successively amplify the waves, which are then transmitted to the fluid of the inner ear, creating a compression wave that strikes cochlea. The cochlea converts the signal into nerve impulses that are transmitted to the brain by the cochlear (auditory) nerve.

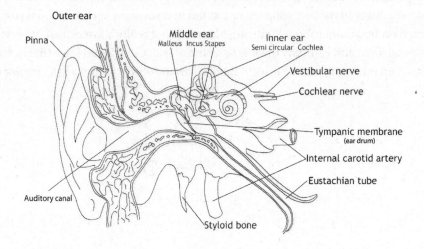

41. Which of the following is a bone of the middle ear?
    (1) Pinna
    (2) Outer ear
    (3) Incus
    (4) Styloid bone
    (5) Eustacian tube

42. The primary function of the cochlea is to
    (1) convert waves to nerve impulses
    (2) convert waves to particles
    (3) direct waves to the middle ear
    (4) amplify sound waves
    (5) create fluid

43. The middle ear is generally sterile, protected from bacteria by the
    (1) auditory canal
    (2) pinna
    (3) malleus
    (4) stapes
    (5) tympanic membrane

44. A profoundly deaf person may sometimes benefit from cochlear implants. The surgically implanted devices consist of two parts. The first, a microphone, speech analyzer, and transmitter, is connected to the outer ear. The second, an electrode array, transmits signals directly to the auditory nerve. It is most likely that cochlear implants
    (1) amplify sound waves
    (2) bypass damaged structures in the ear
    (3) are beneficial for mild hearing loss
    (4) transmits sound waves to the inner ear
    (5) transmits sound waves to the cochlea

Questions 45–47 are based on the following information.

The Canadian Shield, also known as the Precambrian Shield, covers more than half of Canada's land mass and is the oldest part of the North American continent. It is composed primarily of igneous (lava) rock, such as granite, that was formed during the Precambrian period that ranges from 4.5 billion to 540 million years ago. During the ice ages, the shield was covered and depressed by glaciers, which left only a thin layer of soil and dug out thousands of small lakes. Much of the soil is coarse and does not retain moisture well and is frozen by permafrost year round. The area is rich in minerals and several large diamond deposits have recently been found.

45. You can conclude from this passage that Precambrian rocks are among the
    (1) softest rocks in Canada
    (2) sedimentary rocks in Canada
    (3) rocks formed on the ocean floor
    (4) oldest rocks in Canada
    (5) youngest rocks in Canada

46. A reason that the Precambrian Shield region is thinly populated is probably that
    (1) it is not good for agriculture
    (2) it has few natural resources
    (3) it has few mineral deposits
    (4) it is very good for farming
    (5) there is a lack of water

47. The shield is composed primarily of igneous rock, which means that millions of years ago it was
    (1) covered by glaciers
    (2) at a higher elevation
    (3) home to many volcanos
    (4) under water
    (5) sedimentary rock

Questions 48–50 are based on the following information.

To split firewood, a person will often use a wedge and heavy hammer. The wedge is placed on top of the log and struck with the hammer, driving it into the wood.

48. The force with which the wedge strikes the wood will be
    (1) less than the force of the hammer on the wedge
    (2) insufficient to split the wood
    (3) less than the force of gravity
    (4) equal to the force of the hammer on the wedge
    (5) greater than the force of the hammer on the wedge

49. The wedge will be driven into the wood until the
    (1) resisting force of the wood is less than the force of the hammer
    (2) resisting force of the wood equals the force of the hammer
    (3) resisting force of the wood is greater than the force of the hammer
    (4) wood splits
    (5) momentum of the wedge exceeds momentum of the hammer

50. This example best illustrates which scientific law?
    (1) For every action, there is an equal and opposite reaction.
    (2) An object at rest stays at rest.
    (3) An object in motion stays in motion.
    (4) Every object in the universe attracts every other object.
    (5) Matter in a system is not created nor destroyed.

SCIENCE ANSWERS AND ANALYSIS

ANSWERS

1. **(1)**		16. **(3)**		31. **(5)**		46. **(1)**
2. **(5)**		17. **(2)**		32. **(2)**		47. **(3)**
3. **(4)**		18. **(2)**		33. **(4)**		48. **(4)**
4. **(3)**		19. **(4)**		34. **(5)**		49. **(2)**
5. **(2)**		20. **(5)**		35. **(1)**		50. **(1)**
6. **(5)**		21. **(1)**		36. **(3)**		
7. **(1)**		22. **(3)**		37. **(2)**		
8. **(3)**		23. **(4)**		38. **(4)**		
9. **(3)**		24. **(2)**		39. **(2)**		
10. **(1)**		25. **(5)**		40. **(5)**		
11. **(3)**		26. **(1)**		41. **(3)**		
12. **(2)**		27. **(1)**		42. **(1)**		
13. **(1)**		28. **(4)**		43. **(5)**		
14. **(3)**		29. **(2)**		44. **(2)**		
15. **(5)**		30. **(3)**		45. **(4)**		

Interpret Your Results

Test Area	Questions	Recommended Minimum Score	Your Score
Physical Science	6, 7, 8, 9, 16, 17, 18, 20, 26, 27, 31, 32, 38, 39, 40, 48, 49, 50	13	
Life Science	4, 5, 10, 11, 12, 13, 14, 15, 24, 25, 28, 29, 30, 33, 34, 35, 36, 37, 41, 42, 43, 44	16	
Earth and Space Science	1, 2, 3, 19, 21, 22, 23, 45, 46, 47	7	
Total		36	

Check your answers and calculate how you scored in each test area. If you scored less than the recommended minimum score in any test area, you should review topics in the relevant chapters.

ANSWER ANALYSIS

1. **(1)** In winter, cool temperatures in the house are exchanged with warmer temperatures from the ground. In summer, the opposite process provides helps keep the home cool.

2. **(5)** Geologically active areas are likely to have higher underground temperatures. For example these are areas where hot springs and geysers might be found.

3. **(4)** Fewer greenhouse gas emissions are produced because nothing is burned.

4. **(3)** The peripheral nervous system runs from the spinal cord throughout the body.

5. **(2)** Sweating is an autonomic function, not under our voluntary control.

6. **(5)** When no work is being done, it is potential energy.

7. **(1)** Electrons are negative. They will flow from the area of excess electrons to the positive terminal.

8. **(3)** Voltage is a measure of potential difference.

9. **(3)** Particles will move until the concentration is equal throughout the room.

10. **(1)** For concentration of salt particles to be equalized, more water will be drawn into the cell.

11. **(3)** They allow some particles to pass through, but not others.

12. **(2)** If salinity were higher in the seawater than the cell, water would flow out of the cell.

13. **(1)** According to the chart, humans can hear frequencies as low as 20Hz, lower than other animals listed.

14. **(3)** Although some hear lower and some higher frequencies, cats are the only animals listed who hear both lower and higher frequencies than dogs.

15. **(5)** Bats can hear frequencies over 100,000 Hz.

16. **(3)** If forces are balanced, neither object will move.

17. **(2)** Friction resists the movement of the object up the incline. The force of gravity is already included in its weight as weight is equal to mass times gravity.

18. **(2)** If the weight is greater, it will fall and pull the block up. However, objects do not fall at a constant rate. They accelerate because of the acceleration of gravity.

19. **(4)** Sweating is a way the body gets rid of excess heat.

20. **(5)** You can see in the diagram that the oxygen atom shares an electron with each of the hydrogen atoms.

21. **(1)** While still below the surface, molten rock is called magma.

22. **(3)** Magma rises through the more dense rock of the crust.

23. **(4)** In the diagram, you see that the opening is called the crater.

24. **(2)** The plant evolved quickly to adapt to a shorter growing season.

25. **(5)** A longer growing season would mean that species would not need to adapt to survive.

26. **(1)** The heavier weight will go down, causing the end with lighter weight to go up.

27. **(1)** Moving the heavier weight closer can equalize the load on either side of the pivot.

28. **(4)** The graphic depicts transformation from zygote to blastocyst, which is harvested for stem cells that reproduce and can differentiate to form various kinds of cells.

29. **(2)** They are not specialized and, therefore, have greater potential.

30. **(3)** Stem cells have potential for cures of damaged tissue.

31. **(5)** Mass, and even weight, remain the same, but heated air has greater volume and so less density.

32. **(2)** A boat floats for the same reason. It has lower density than the volume of water it displaces.

33. **(4)** A terrarium is an ecosystem, complete with soil, organisms, and water cycle.

34. **(5)** Although needs of specific types of plants will vary, every system needs energy, which comes from sunlight. This demonstrates than an ecosystem is not closed, but interacts with the systems around it.

35. **(1)** Plants are producers as they can create their own food through photosynthesis.

36. **(3)** In the graphic, you see that blow flies obtain energy from the dead hare, which suggests they aid in decomposition.

37. **(2)** In the diagram, arrows represent the flow of energy as it passes from producers to consumers.

38. **(4)** Centrifugal force is the object's inertia, which wants to go in a straight line and resists changes in its state of motion.

39. **(2)** For every action, there is an equal and opposite reaction, so the forces will be equal and in opposite directions.

40. **(5)** The centripetal force and, therefore, the centrifugal force will be gone, but the object's inertia will remain and it will continue on in a straight line until the force of gravity brings it to ground.

41. **(3)** The incus, also known as the stirrup, is a bone in the middle ear.

42. **(1)** The passage states that the cochlea converts the signal to nerve impulses.

43. **(5)** The tympanic membrane (ear drum) separates the outer and inner ear.

44. **(2)** As the cochlear implant transmits directly from the outer ear to the electrode array on the auditory nerve, it bypasses any damaged structures in the ear.

45. **(4)** As it is the oldest part of the North American crust, the rocks must be the oldest in North America.

46. **(1)** Early settlements usually arise in agricultural areas. The soil of the Canadian Shield is described as thin and course, not holding much moisture.

47. **(3)** Igneous rock comes from lava. Several billion years ago, when the shield was formed, there must have been volcanoes in the region it now covers.

48. **(4)** Every action has an equal and opposite reaction, so when the hammer strikes the wedge, the wedge will strike the wood with the same force.

49. **(2)** The equal and opposite reaction is the resisting force of the wood. As long as the resisting force is less, the wedge will continue to move. If the resisting force were more, the wedge would move in the opposite direction.

50. **(1)** The example clearly demonstrates Newton's third law.

Social Studies

Overview of the
Social Studies Test

The Social Studies Test includes:

- 50 multiple-choice questions
- 70-minute time limit

You do NOT need to know specific facts about social studies, such as dates of historical events or leaders of other countries, to prepare for the GED® test. You *do* need to be able to interpret social studies information. You also need a strong, general knowledge of world geography, history, and culture—especially of Canadian history, regions, and political structure.

READING IS A SKILL

The information you need to answer questions on the GED® Social Studies Test is in the reading passages and graphics provided on the test. Your success on the test will be based largely on your ability to read and interpret the information.

Reading is a skill. It is more than understanding what a passage says. There are different levels of reading:

COMPREHENSION—understand what is said; restate, summarize, or explain a passage

APPLICATION—recognize how information can be applied in different contexts

ANALYSIS—identify consequences, relationships, inferences, and implications; recognize main ideas, supporting details, fact and opinion, and bias

SYNTHESIS—integrate and interpret information based on different sources; recognize purpose; compare, contrast, and evaluate information.

Your ability to read and interpret social studies information will be based in part on your general knowledge about our country and the world. One of the best things you can do to prepare for the social studies test is to read the newspaper regularly and discuss what you read with family or friends.

WHAT'S ON THE TEST?

The GED Social Studies Test has questions in four different areas:

1. History
2. Geography
3. Civics and government
4. Economics

TIP

Read the newspaper and discuss what you read with others to prepare for the Social Studies Test.

HISTORY (40%)—Canadian History (25%) and World History (15%)—Questions could include a wide variety of topics from early civilizations to the middle ages, and on to the world wars. Canadian history could include such topics as aboriginal peoples, early explorers, and confederation.

GEOGRAPHY (15%)—Topics are about location and characteristics of countries, climates, and peoples and cultures in the world.

CIVICS AND GOVERNMENT (25%)—Questions and passages are about civics (rights and responsibilities of citizens) as well as government and political structure. Some Canadian topics could be included, such as questions about the Charter of Rights and Freedoms, Supreme Court, or Canadian Parliament.

ECONOMICS (20%)—Topics involve the Canadian or world economy, money, trade, and the production and distribution of resources.

When preparing for this test, it's important to remember that the GED is not a Canadian test. Although there is a Canadian edition, only 40% of questions on the GED Social Studies Test are about Canadian topics. The remaining questions will be about international topics, including the United States.

HOW THE TEST WORKS

On the GED Social Studies Test, you will answer questions based on different kinds of information, including:

- Reading passages (for example, information passages, newspaper articles, political speeches)
- Maps
- Tables
- Cartoons
- Photographs

Each test will also contain excerpts from at least one historical Canadian document, such as the Charter of Rights and Freedoms, and at least one practical document.

Foundations of Social Studies

16

MAPS AND ATLASES

Maps are diagrams of regions of the land or sea, showing its physical features. Maps are made to scale, which means that the distances between points on the map are proportionate to the actual distance. A map can depict the whole world or a small area. Because of the Internet, printed paper maps are not as common as they were, but we use maps more than ever. If you have ever used a GPS or got driving directions from an online service, you have used a map. Maps are also commonly a part of social studies information.

There are many different types of maps, which can be adapted to show just about anything from time zones to mineral deposits. The basic types of maps are as follows:

- **POLITICAL MAP**—shows the division between provinces. An example would be a typical map of Canada, showing the borders of the provinces and territories and borders with the United States, as well as the location of capitals and other large cities.
- **PHYSICAL MAP**—shows the physical features of the land, using different colours. Water is usually blue. Lower elevations are often green, higher elevations orange, and mountain ranges brown.
- **TOPOGRAPHICAL MAP**—similar to a physical map except that lines in a roughly circular pattern show changes in elevation. The closer the lines are together, the steeper the terrain, so a mountain would be indicated with a lot of circular lines close together.

- **CLIMATE MAP**—represents different climactic regions using colours. For example, a climate map of Canada might show the Arctic, Subarctic, Atlantic, Prairie, Pacific, Mountain, and Great Lakes regions.
- **ROAD MAP**—uses lines to show locations of minor and major roadways, as well as locations of cities, towns, and points of interest, such as airports, parks, and so on.
- **RESOURCE MAP**—shows the distribution of resources or economic activity using colours or symbols.

A physical map of Canada shows the division into provinces and territories.

PRACTICE

Choose the best answer for each of the following questions based on the map shown.

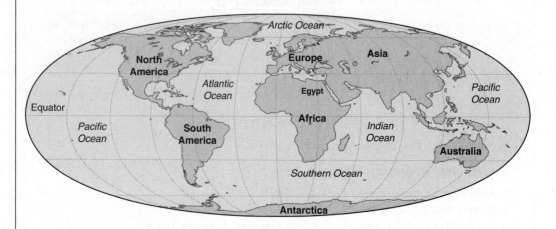

1. Which of the following continents is likely to have the lowest population?
    (1) Asia
    (2) North America
    (3) Europe
    (4) Australia
    (5) Antarctica

2. Based on the information on this map, Egypt is located on which continent?
    (1) Asia
    (2) Africa
    (3) Europe
    (4) South America
    (5) North America

3. A continent is defined as one of the large areas of continuous land mass that make up the Earth, usually divided—or somewhat divided—from others by an ocean. Based on this definition, which two continents might be considered one?

   (1) North America and South America
   (2) Europe and Africa
   (3) Europe and Asia
   (4) Asia and Africa
   (5) Asia and Australia

On a globe or map, you may find lines going around the Earth from side to side and from top to bottom. These are imaginary lines of latitude and longitude that help people to find where they are on the Earth. Lines of latitude, also called *parallels*, go from side to side. The lines are marked in degrees with the symbol °. Each line runs parallel to the equator. The part of the world above the equator is the Northern Hemisphere and below is the Southern Hemisphere. The lines from top to bottom are lines of longitude, also called *meridians*. The line at 0 longitude is known as the *prime meridian* and divides the world into the Western and Eastern Hemispheres.

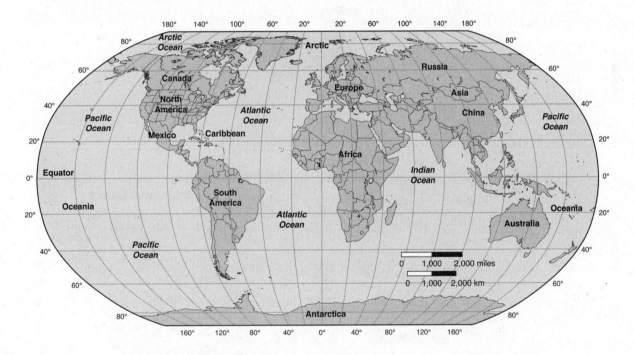

4. Canada is located in the

   (1) Western Hemisphere
   (2) Eastern Hemisphere
   (3) Southern Hemisphere
   (4) Equator
   (5) Prime meridian

5. The line of latitude at 30° south passes through which country?
    (1) Australia
    (2) Mexico
    (3) Canada
    (4) Russia
    (5) China

6. The location on the map at 60°N and 120°W is found in which country?
    (1) Australia
    (2) Mexico
    (3) Canada
    (4) Russia
    (5) China

7. The capital city of Nunavut is
    (1) Ottawa
    (2) Yellowknife
    (3) Apex
    (4) Iqaluit
    (5) Manitoba

8. The Great Lakes are found in which province?
    (1) Quebec
    (2) Ontario
    (3) Manitoba
    (4) Northwest Territories
    (5) Saskatchewan

9. Which of the following borders British Columbia?
    (1) Quebec
    (2) Ontario
    (3) Manitoba
    (4) Northwest Territories
    (5) Saskatchewan

ANSWERS

1. **(5)** Antarctica is the continent that includes the South Pole and is extremely cold with no permanent population.

2. **(2)** Egypt can be located on the map in Northern Africa.

3. **(3)** Europe and Asia are one continuous landmass and are traditionally separated more for political than geographic reasons. In some places, schools teach that there are six continents, with one being Eurasia. The area known as the Middle East, which sits on the border of Asia and Europe and is politically distinct from both, is not a continent, but part of the continent of Eurasia.

4. **(1)** Canada is located to the west (left) of the prime meridian and north of the equator, so it is in both the Western Hemisphere and the Northern Hemisphere.

5. **(1)** Following across the line of 30° latitude below the equator, it passes through Australia.

6. **(3)** Latitude is always listed first. Follow the line of 60°N to where it intersects 120°W.

7. **(4)** The larger dot within the area of Nunavut indicates the capital city.

8. **(2)** Although the name Great Lakes is not given on the map, the lakes south of Ontario are the largest enclosed bodies of water on the map.

9. **(4)** The Northwest Territories visibly share a small section of border with British Columbia.

CHALLENGE EXERCISE

An atlas is a book that has a collection of maps. A world atlas contains a map of the world and maps of different countries. A Canadian atlas contains maps of Canada and its regions. An atlas can still be found in a bookstore, but they can also be found online. Search online for an atlas of Canada or visit the Government of Canada website at *http://atlas.gc.ca/*. Explore the maps there to see what kinds of information can be listed on a map.

THE WORLD

Today the world seems like a very small place, and what happens in one part of the world has effects in others. One way our world is made smaller is by the global media, which gives us unprecedented knowledge of world events as they are happening. In part, it is made smaller by global trade and political connections, which mean that a war in the Middle East can increase the price of fuel in Canada, and unrest in a distant country can have political consequences at home.

The world is also a big place, in a number of ways, made up of many nations with different peoples, climates, governments, economic conditions, and cultures. In many cases, the misunderstandings between nations are a result of our lack of understanding of these differences.

You do not need to have specific knowledge of other nations or cultures to answer questions on the GED Social Studies Test, but you should have a strong general awareness of the world and be able to read and interpret information.

TIP

The world is made up of different peoples, climates, governments, economies, and cultures.

PRACTICE

Choose the best answer for each of the following questions.

Countries with Highest Birth Rate 2013			
Country	Births/ 1000 Population	Infant Deaths/ 1000 Live Births	GDP Capita
Niger	46.84	87.98	$800
Mali	46.06	106.49	$1100
Uganda	44.50	62.47	$1400
Burkina Faso	42.81	78.30	$1400
Zambia	42.79	68.58	$1700

Source: CIA *The World Factbook*

1. Which country has the highest birth rate?
   (1) Niger
   (2) Mali
   (3) Uganda
   (4) Burkina Faso
   (5) Zambia

2. In which country are children most likely to die in infancy?
   (1) Niger
   (2) Mali
   (3) Uganda
   (4) Burkina Faso
   (5) Zambia

3. Canada has a birth rate of 10.28 per 1,000 population and a GDP/Capita of $43,400. Based on this information, you can conclude that
   (1) Canada has a higher birth rate than other countries
   (2) Canada has a low standard of living
   (3) Canada's population is decreasing
   (4) birth rate may decrease with higher standard of living
   (5) birth rate may increase with higher standard of living

The nation of Peru is located in western South America between Chile and Ecuador. With an area over 1.2 million sq. km, it is the 20th-largest country in the world, slightly smaller than Quebec. The terrain varies from western coastal plains to the high altitudes of the Andes Mountains and eastern lowlands along the Amazon Basin. The climate varies from tropical in the east to dry desert in the west and frigid temperatures in the high Andes.

The seat of the former Incan Empire, which was conquered by the Spaniards in 1533, Peru gained independence in 1824. Throughout the years, it has experienced periods of military and democratic rule, periods of violence, and frequent economic turmoil. Since 1990, the country has experienced relative peace and economic growth.

Peru's economy reflects its varied geography. A wide range of important mineral resources are found in the mountainous and coastal areas, and Peru's coastal waters provide excellent fishing grounds. The Peruvian economy has been growing by an average of 6.4% per year since 2002 with low inflation. Despite Peru's strong economic performance, its dependence on minerals and metals exports and imported foodstuffs subjects the economy to fluctuations in world prices. Poor infrastructure also hinders the spread of growth to Peru's non-coastal areas. Peru's rapid expansion coupled with cash transfers and other programs have helped to reduce the national poverty rate, but more than 25% of the population remain below the poverty line.

4. The geography of Peru could best be described as
   (1) mountainous
   (2) tropical
   (3) plains
   (4) desert
   (5) varied

5. Which of the following contributes to Peru's high poverty rate?
   (1) Poor infrastructure
   (2) Low inflation
   (3) Mineral resources
   (4) Rapid expansion
   (5) Foreign aid

What is it like to grow up in Japan, a curious blend of modern western culture and traditional Japanese values? At first glance, modern Japanese families look very much like traditional Canadian families from several decades ago. There are typically two parents who raise one or more children. Families are small because raising children is expensive. In Japan, child-rearing is generally the role of mothers as fathers work long hours and are often not home until after the children are in bed. Although women make up 40% of the workforce, there are fewer career opportunities for women, and mothers with young children usually only work part-time.

For the Japanese, being part of a group is very important as it is seen as preparation for adulthood. Virtually all children attend pre-schools, for example, in which class sizes are much larger than in Canada to promote group interaction. Being part of a group is even more important for Japanese teenagers. Unlike Canadian parents who worry about peer pressure, Japanese parents encourage their teens to be part of a friendship group. These groups are very structured and members do not often change. The most common activity for friendship groups is to go shopping, so parents have to provide money for their children to take part.

Education is also a primary concern for Japanese families. Almost all children are placed in private pre-schools as young as age three. As children progress through school, they have tutors and extra lessons outside of school hours. Although education is important to Canadian families as well, Japanese strive for academic excellence in their children and to have them excel more than their peers. In fact, a woman's success as a mother is largely measured by the success of her children in school.

6. This passage is primarily about
   (1) differences between Canada and Japan
   (2) importance of education in Japan
   (3) Japanese values for child rearing
   (4) work ethic in Japan
   (5) the role of women in Japanese culture

7. Which value would be stressed less in raising children in Japan than in Canada?
   (1) Friendship
   (2) Education
   (3) Shopping
   (4) Individuality
   (5) Traditional values

8. Information in this passage presents Japanese culture in comparison with Canadian culture to be more
   (1) paternalistic
   (2) advanced
   (3) relaxed
   (4) moral
   (5) modern

ANSWERS

1. **(1)** Niger has the highest birth rate at 46.84 per thousand population.

2. **(2)** In Mali, 106.49 of every 1,000 children born die in infancy.

3. **(4)** Canada's birth rate is significantly lower and GDP/Capita higher, which indicates standard of living is much higher. In addition, the table shows that birth rate decreases slightly even with moderate changes in wealth.

4. **(5)** The terrain varies from coastal plains to the Andes Mountains, lowlands, and desert.

5. **(1)** Poor infrastructure hinders the spread of growth to non-coastal areas.

6. **(3)** Although the passage does talk about differences between Canada and Japan and the role of women, its primary focus is the values involved in child rearing.

7. **(4)** You can conclude that individuality is less stressed for Japanese children, except with respect to individual academic performance, because of the emphasis on groups.

8. **(1)** *Paternalistic* means rule by men. While the passage makes no value judgment, it states that there are fewer career opportunities for women, that they are the ones primarily responsible for the children and home, and that men focus on work.

CHALLENGE EXERCISE

One online source of information about countries of the world is the CIA's *The World Factbook*. Search the internet for CIA World Factbook (*https://www.cia.gov/library/publications/the-world-factbook/*). Click on a country or region, and then choose a country to learn about its geography, society, economy, and transnational issues.

Make a list of the top-five most interesting facts. Discuss what you have learned with a family member or friend or discuss with another student the similarities and differences with the country she or he researched.

EARLY CIVILIZATIONS

It is difficult to imagine that any civilization could be as advanced, influential, or wealthy as our modern one. Certainly, we have much more advanced technology than any previous society. Western civilization, particularly American, has wealth, military power, and cultural influence that extends around the world. Yet throughout the history of human beings, many civilizations have risen and fallen. Some of them, such as the ancient Greek and Roman civilizations, still have an influence on our thinking and government today.

PRACTICE

Choose the best answer for each of the questions that follow the next passages.

Homo sapiens have existed on earth for over 250,000 years, but the potential for larger societies did not come about until an agricultural way of life began about 12,000 years ago. Formation of civilizations, however, was still not possible until the beginning of some type of record keeping. Not only was there no way to keep histories, except through oral traditions, there was no way to record ownership of goods or property.

Mesopotamia (located in the area of modern Iraq) is the earliest known civilization, lasting from about 6000 to 4000 BC. Inventors of the oldest known form of written communication,

TIP

Some history writings use the terms BCE and CE instead of BC and AD to refer to time. BCE means *Before the Common Era* and refers to the same time period as BC. The abbreviation CE means *Common or Current Era* and refers to the same time period as AD.

they baked clay tokens with a + sign in them to represent ownership of sheep, grain, and other items. This was like an early form of money. As writing continued to evolve, it was carved into clay or stone tablets, in a type of writing called *cuneiform*, which was named for the wedge-shaped impressions that served as the earliest words.

Ancient Egyptian civilization (4000 to 1000 BC) thrived along the valley of the Nile River and was responsible for many accomplishments. Egyptians knew much about the movement of the stars and planets, knowledge that was not rediscovered until the past few centuries. Construction of the pyramids was an engineering feat that is still not duplicable today. One of the most important advances, however, was the development of papyrus, an early form of paper, about 3200 BC, which revolutionized the way people kept information. Other methods of making paper were later discovered in China and Arabia, but papermaking did not find its way to Europe until about 1100 AD.

There were many other ancient civilizations, such as Babylon and China (which has one of the longest histories of any civilization in the world), but two in particular had a great influence on modern western society. One was ancient Greece, whose government and philosophical writings still influence our thinking today. Another was ancient Rome, whose infrastructure, law, and art influenced much of the modern world.

1. Information in this passage suggests that it is difficult for civilizations to form among
   (1) agricultural societies
   (2) nomadic people
   (3) Mesopotamians
   (4) Egyptians
   (5) Babylonians

2. One of the first types of written communication was used for
   (1) recording histories
   (2) literature
   (3) philosophy
   (4) laws
   (5) money

3. Based on information in this passage, you can conclude that civilizations developed
   (1) first in the West
   (2) later in the West
   (3) because of war
   (4) because of trade
   (5) only in the past few centuries

4. According to the passage, which of the following played an essential role in the formation of early civilizations?
   (1) Science
   (2) Engineering
   (3) Writing
   (4) Law
   (5) Art

Ancient Greece was not one country, but was made up of many independent city-states. The largest and most stable of these was Athens, which was the birthplace of democracy. The word *democracy* comes from two Greek words: *demo*—meaning people, and *cracy*—meaning power. Literally, democracy means power of the people. Athens, unlike current societies, was not a representative democracy, but one in which all citizens were encouraged to take part.

The three branches of government in Athens were the Assembly, Boule, and Courts. Attendance at the Assembly was open to all male citizens over 20 years of age who had completed their military training. A quorum of 6,000 in attendance was required. The Assembly passed laws and held political trials. Voting was usually done by a show of hands. Most official positions were also elected by the Assembly and some positions of importance could only be held for a period of one year.

The courts had magistrates who did a very different job from judges today. Their job was to carry out administrative, rather than legal, functions. There were also no lawyers. A citizen could bring a suit if he or a family member had been wronged. A public suit could be brought by anybody as it involved an offense against everyone. For a private suit, there was a jury of 200 citizens. A trial for a public offense required a jury of 401 or more. The trial itself would last no more than a day. Jurors were often loud and would ask questions, make jokes, and express opinions about the testimony. If a person was found guilty of an offense, both the defense and the prosecutors would suggest a punishment and the jury would pick one.

The Boule, or council of 400, was the administrative arm of government. It had no power to pass legislation or hold trials, but administered the decisions of the Assembly and Courts. The head of the Boule changed every month and members served for only one year.

In Athens, not everyone was a citizen. There were three classes of residents: citizens, slaves, and foreign inhabitants. Women had few rights. Citizenship was reserved for those whose parents were both citizens. Nonetheless, Athens probably had over 100,000 citizens at its height. It is the largest example of participatory democracy that has ever occurred.

5. Based on information in this passage, a *representative democracy* refers to one in which
    (1) all citizens participate in the assembly
    (2) power is exercised by the people
    (3) government is not responsible to the people
    (4) only elected members participate in the assembly
    (5) administration is conducted by an appointed council

6. The Athenian Assembly is similar to the Canadian
    (1) Parliament
    (2) Senate
    (3) Judiciary
    (4) Cabinet
    (5) Military

7. Which of the following could not be members of the Boule?
    (1) Former elected officials
    (2) Former jurors
    (3) Citizens
    (4) Magistrates
    (5) Women

The Roman Empire, which reached the height of its power about 150 AD, was the largest European empire of its time. It included the Mediterranean region, Southern and Western Europe, Northern Africa, and much of the Middle East. Many of the countries that were conquered benefitted from Roman rule with ordered government, good roads, and water supplies.

The key to Roman expansion was the Roman army, one of the most efficient military machines in history. The army was divided into groups called *legions* of about 5,000 men. Each legion was led by a Legatus. A legion was generally composed of ten or more cohorts of 480 men. The *cohort* was composed of groups of 80 men, called *centuries*, which was led by a Centurion. The senior centurion would lead the cohort. Each legion was also accompanied by a small group of cavalry.

The common soldiers of the legion were the *legionnaires*, who were Roman citizens who went through extensive and arduous training. They were the best trained and most disciplined troops of their time. Legionnaires were expected to be able to march 30 km per day, carrying all of their food, weapons, and supplies. Discipline could be severe. The most brutal punishment that a military unit could face—for actions such as rebellion, cowardice, or failing to fight—was decimation, which was the ordered execution of every tenth man by his comrades.

Legionnaires fought in units, using three main weapons: the scutum, pilum, and gladius. The soldiers would advance in closely packed lines with their shields in front. For defense from things like arrows, the lines behind the front could place their shields above their heads in a formation called the turtle, so that the entire unit was protected from the front and top. Approaching the enemy, the legionnaires would throw the pilums, which were not a hand-to-hand weapon, but disrupted the front lines of the enemy. The main business of fighting was conducted with the gladius, while the unit maintained their formation and presented a wall of shields. At the height of the empire, there were none who could stand against the disciplined might of the legions.

8. Countries that were conquered by the Roman Empire often experienced
    (1) poverty
    (2) mass murder
    (3) improved government and infrastructure
    (4) forced recruitment into the army
    (5) imprisonment and forced labour

9. A legionnaire's main weapon was called a
    (1) pilum
    (2) gladius
    (3) turtle
    (4) scutum
    (5) shoulder plate

10. Brutal, tough training of Roman soldiers resulted in
    (1) poor morale
    (2) efficient troops
    (3) discipline problems
    (4) decimation
    (5) citizenship

ANSWERS

1. **(2)** The passage says the potential for larger societies did not come about until an agricultural way of life began. This would have enabled food production to support a larger number of people, and the construction of buildings—things not possible for nomadic, hunter-gatherer people.

2. **(5)** The Mesopotamians used baked tokens as an early form of money.

3. **(2)** All of the civilizations named are in the East. In addition, the late arrival of paper-making in the West shows that it was far behind.

4. **(3)** All of these are part of a civilization, but none would be possible without writing.

5. **(4)** In a representative democracy, such as Canada, members are elected to the assembly.

6. **(1)** The Assembly was the main decision-making part of government, similar to the Canadian Parliament.

7. **(5)** The passage states that women had few rights.

8. **(3)** Many nations benefitted from the improved government and infrastructure brought by the Roman conquest, although this may not have compensated for their loss of freedom.

9. **(2)** The gladius was the main weapon used in hand-to-hand combat.

10. **(2)** The passage implies that the brutally tough training made them the best trained fighting force in the world.

CHALLENGE EXERCISE

Choose one of the following ancient civilizations, or another of your own selection, to research. Where was it located? When did it hold dominance in its region? What were the political, economic, and social structures? Some civilizations to consider: Mayan, Ancient India, Ancient China, Ethiopia, Ottoman, Aztec.

AGE OF REVOLUTION

The Age of Revolution is an imprecise and unofficial term used to describe events of the late 18th and early 19th centuries. In this section, you will look at four major events that changed the shape of the Western world:

- Industrial Revolution 1760–1820
- American Revolution 1775–1783
- French Revolution 1789–1799
- Russian Revolution 1917

You do not need specific information about these events to pass the GED Social Studies Test; however, general knowledge may help you interpret some of the passages and information on the test. If you do know specific information about a topic on the test, a word of warning: Answer the questions based on the information *given on the test*, not your personal knowledge.

TIP

Answer questions based on the information given on the test.

PRACTICE

Choose the best answer for each of the questions that follow the passages.

The Industrial Revolution began in England about 1760 and soon spread to Europe and other parts of the world. It was the single greatest economic and social change in history and fundamentally changed everything about the way we live and work. The Industrial Revolution could be defined as a rapid change from individual production of goods to methods based on technology. Prior to the Industrial Revolution, goods were produced by individuals in their homes or small cottage industries.

Wool, for example, was spun by farmers' wives in their homes and then weavers wove it into cloth. In the Industrial Revolution, driven by changing technology and the invention of the steam engine, these home businesses were replaced by factories, which could produce thousands of times more cloth. Similar changes took place in other industries.

The Industrial Revolution had positive and negative effects on the population. The poor worked twelve hours a day or more, six days a week, for pay that barely enabled them to survive. Living conditions were sub-standard and working conditions unsafe. Child labour was common and many young children worked and died in factories and coal mines. Many argue, however, that this was not that much of a change from previous living conditions of the poor, and that the Industrial Revolution led to awareness and social activism that eventually resulted in labour laws.

1. The Industrial Revolution was a time of
   (1) war
   (2) extreme poverty
   (3) wealth for average people
   (4) rapid technological change
   (5) labour unrest

2. Based on the information in this passage, you can conclude that one consequence of the Industrial Revolution was
   (1) widespread hunger
   (2) movement of the population to cities
   (3) reduced production of goods
   (4) lower standard of living
   (5) longer work days

The American Revolution had no single, identifiable cause, but was a result of a series of events and legislation that increased tensions between Britain and some of her colonies in the New World. In 1764, the long war with France over North America ended, with the last French troops being defeated in the Ohio Valley. The long war had left Britain deeply in debt and a number of new taxes were introduced in the colonies to recover some of the costs and pay for continued protection. With the French threat gone, however, the colonists felt no need for British protection and resented the taxes.

Long before the Revolutionary War, the colonies had their own legislatures that could pass laws and levy taxes. Real power, however, still resided in the far-away British parliament. This was another sore point for the colonists because they were not allowed to elect their own representatives to British parliament, so they had no say in the laws that affected them. At first, most people did not want to separate from Britain. They wanted the British government to address their concerns, but the response from Britain was increasingly severe measures that made the situation worse.

The first problems began with the Proclamation Act, which was passed by the British Parliament and prohibited settlement beyond the Appalachian Mountains. The act was to appease Native Americans who had been allies with the French during the previous war, but colonists saw it as an infringement on their liberty. Other acts soon followed, including the Sugar Act and Stamp Act, which raised taxes and duties on sugar and related products, such as wine, as well as placing a tax on any type of document, from a newspaper to a marriage license. The Currency Act prohibited colonial legislatures from issuing their own money, and the Tea Act gave the British East India Company an advantage and virtual monopoly in the North American tea trade. The colonists became increasingly frustrated and some acts of civil disobedience and violence occurred, such as the Boston Tea Party. Instead of addressing the concerns, the British Parliament adopted a zero-tolerance policy and passed the Intolerable Act in 1774, which placed severe restrictions on the colonists, including banning town meetings and closing Boston Harbour.

As late as 1775, when twelve of the thirteen colonies that would later rebel met at the First Continental Congress, they hoped that Britain would listen to their concerns. British troops, however, marched on the cities of Lexington and Concord to seize colonial stores of gunpowder and arrest some leading supporters of independence. This sparked the first open warfare and, in 1776, thirteen colonies met in the Second Continental Congress to sign the Declaration of Independence, which began the Revolutionary War. Even at this time, not all Americans supported the revolution. Many were neutral and many remained loyal to Britain, eventually fleeing persecution from their neighbours and migrating to Canada as loyalists.

3. Based on information in the passage, you can conclude that the primary cause of the American Revolution was
   (1) money
   (2) a desire for freedom from tyranny
   (3) restrictive laws from British parliament
   (4) an end of war with France
   (5) aggressive acts of the British army

4. Which act was passed to assist the finances of the British East India Company?
   (1) Proclamation Act
   (2) Sugar Act
   (3) Stamp Act
   (4) Currency Act
   (5) Tea Act

5. The mid-late 1700s were also a time of new political thought. Philosophers in England, France, and America published pamphlets with new ideas about the role of government. One of the most influential was English philosopher John Locke, who argued that all people were born equal as a blank slate (tabula rasa) and that the responsibility of government was to protect the rights of the people to life, liberty, and property. Locke's arguments undermined which of the following ideas?

    (1) Divine right of kings
    (2) Declaration of independence
    (3) Freedom from tyranny
    (4) All people are created equal
    (5) Revolutionary war

Much inspired by the American Revolution and the works of Enlightenment philosophers, the French Revolution of 1789 began with lofty ideals. France, one of the richest countries in the world, was deeply in debt because of years of war and lavish spending by the king and nobles, who did not pay tax. Heavy taxes were placed on the poor and middle classes, but France was still virtually bankrupt.

The first stage of the French Revolution, known as the moderate phase, began in June 1789 when the third estate (non-noble) members of government were locked out of a meeting of the Estates-General. They moved to a nearby indoor tennis court where they swore an oath to continue meeting until France had a new constitution. They called themselves the National Assembly. France essentially became a constitutional monarchy. The king was kept under close watch and the National Assembly now made the laws. They outlawed slavery and the feudal system, confiscated and sold many lands belonging to the church, and passed a Declaration of the Rights of Man. At the same time, unrest and acts of rebellion continued to occur throughout the country.

During the radical phase of 1792–1794, more extreme elements gained influence. The idea of a constitutional monarchy gave way to a republic, and the National Assembly reformed as the National Convention. The king and his family were put on trial and executed in January 1793. This began a time known as the Reign of Terror, led by a man named Robespierre and his Committee for Public Safety. It resulted in the execution of more than 40,000 people, including nobles, peasants, and political opponents of Robespierre, who was executed himself in 1794.

By 1795, moderates were again in control. The National Assembly wrote a new constitution and formed a *Directoire* of five men to lead the government. This lasted until 1799, when the *Directoire* was replaced by a three-man *Consulate* that was headed by Napoleon Bonaparte, a popular general. Napoleon continued to gain power and fame through military success, controlling the government and declaring himself Emperor in 1804, bringing the revolution to an end.

Moderate Period 1789–1792	Radical Period 1792–1794	Directoire Period 1795–1799	Consulate Period 1799–1804
National Assembly	National Congress	Directoire	Consulate

June 20, 1789 Tennis Court Oath

July 14, 1789 Storming of Bastille

1790 Royals kept under watch

Jan 21, 1793 Execution of Louis XVI

Reign of Terror

June 28, 1794 French defeat Austria

July 26, 1794 Execution of Robespierre

Nov 2, 1795 First Directoire formed

Continued military Victories in Europe

Nov 9, 1799 Napoleon Abolishes Directoire

1804 Napoleonic Code of Law

Dec 2, 1804 Napoleon Emperor

6. Based on the information above, which of the following occurred first?
   (1) Reign of Terror
   (2) Napoleon becomes emperor
   (3) *Directoire* formed
   (4) Execution of the king
   (5) Military victories in Europe

7. Based on information in the passage, a *constitutional monarchy* refers to government by
   (1) an assembly and monarch
   (2) an elected assembly
   (3) a king or queen only
   (4) nobles and priests
   (5) terror squads

8. The passage is primarily about
   (1) causes of the French Revolution
   (2) consequences of the French Revolution
   (3) the rise of Napoleon
   (4) benefits of the French Revolution
   (5) stages of the French Revolution

The Russian Revolution took place in 1917, more than 100 years after the American and French revolutions, and is not generally considered part of the Age of Revolution. Nonetheless, it was an important event that changed the world and dictated the course of the 20th century. Heavy losses, high inflation, and food shortages had made the Russian people tired of World War 1. The Bolsheviks, led by Vladimir Lenin, rebelled against the Tsar, eventually gaining control of the country and signing a peace treaty with Germany. The Bolsheviks were followers of the communist teaching of Karl Marx, which stated that all people should be equal and share equally in the wealth and authority of the nation. This is an entirely different idea than expressed by the American and French revolutions, which were based on the rights of the individual, including ownership of property. In Marxism, the society owned everything together.

The Russian Revolution led to creation of the world's first communist government, which in practice was a tyrannical form of government in which the leader and members of the Communist party held absolute power, while common people had none. The stated goal of the Soviet Union (Russia and countries that came under its control) to spread communism throughout the world led to the Cold War and nuclear arms race with the United States and other democratic countries, which lasted for most of the 20th century.

9. The leader of the Bolsheviks in the Russian Revolution was
   (1) Karl Marx
   (2) Tsar Nicholas II
   (3) Vladimir Lenin
   (4) the United States
   (5) Germany

10. The communist ideals were
    (1) similar to principles of the American Revolution
    (2) based on collective ownership
    (3) formed around the rights of the individual
    (4) designed to support free enterprise
    (5) based on French philosophy

ANSWERS

1. **(4)** The Industrial Revolution was a time when rapid technological change altered methods of production.

2. **(2)** As most work was now found in factories, large numbers of people migrated to the cities.

3. **(3)** The British did not respond to the concerns of the colonies, but passed increasingly restrictive laws.

4. **(5)** The Tea Act gave the company a virtual monopoly in the tea trade.

5. **(1)** Locke's writings undermined the idea of divine right of kings because he said all people were born equal.

6. **(4)** According to the passage and timeline, the execution of Louis XVI occurred before the other events listed.

7. **(1)** France was a constitutional monarchy for the brief period that there was a National Assembly and king.

8. **(5)** The passage is primarily about stages or phases of the French Revolution

9. **(3)** Vladimir Lenin was the leader of the Bolsheviks and the first leader of communist Russia.

10. **(2)** Marxism was based on collective ownership of everything, with no individual property rights.

REGIONS IN CANADA

Canada is the second largest country in the world, with a total landmass of 9,984,670 km^2. The country is divided into ten provinces and three territories that are frequently grouped together as shown in the following chart.

Atlantic Provinces (Note: The Maritimes refers to the Atlantic Provinces minus Newfoundland.)	Newfoundland Nova Scotia New Brunswick Prince Edward Island
Central Canada	Quebec Ontario
Prairie Provinces	Manitoba Saskatchewan Alberta
West Coast	British Columbia
North	Nunavut Northwest Territories Yukon

PRACTICE

Choose the best answer for each of the questions that come after the following text and graphic.

Because of its size, Canada includes many distinct geographical regions. The Canadian Shield spans much of the country, carpeted in boreal forests, whereas the Arctic Lowlands are covered in snow.

Canadian Shield
Appalachian Region
St. Lawrence Lowlands
Interior Plains
Cordilleran Region
Arctic Lowlands
Innhitian Region

TIP

You should be able to recognize the areas of the provinces and territories on a map, even if no lines are given.

1. Which of the following is located in the Canadian Shield?
   (1) Manitoba
   (2) Nunavut
   (3) Alberta
   (4) Yukon
   (5) British Columbia

2. Nova Scotia is part of the
   (1) Interior Plains
   (2) St. Lawrence Lowlands
   (3) Cordilleran Region
   (4) Appalachian Region
   (5) Arctic Lowlands

3. The southern part of the three Prairie Provinces is part of the
   (1) Interior Plains
   (2) Canadian Shield
   (3) Cordilleran Region
   (4) St. Lawrence Lowlands
   (5) Arctic Lowlands

4. The fertile southern tip of Ontario is part of the
   (1) Cordilleran Region
   (2) Canadian Shield
   (3) St. Lawrence Lowlands
   (4) Interior Plains
   (5) Appalachian Region

ANSWERS

1. **(2)** Although much of northern Manitoba is also in the Canadian Shield, virtually the entire territory of Nunavut is located there.

2. **(4)** Nova Scotia, on the east coast, is part of the Appalachian Region.

3. **(1)** The Prairie Provinces are part of the Interior Plains.

4. **(3)** Southern Ontario is part of the St. Lawrence Lowlands.

CHAPTER CHECK-UP

Complete these practice exercises, and check the answers and analysis that follow. After you mark your work, review any topic in the chapter that you had trouble with or did not understand.

Questions 1–3 are based on the following map.

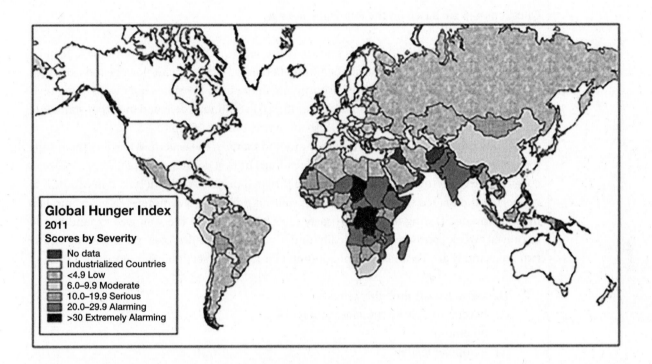

Source: von Grabmer et al., 2012. Reprinted with permission.

1. The greatest concentration of countries with serious-to-alarming hunger index rates is found in
   (1) Africa
   (2) Asia
   (3) Middle East
   (4) Europe
   (5) South America

2. The lowest rates of hunger are in
   (1) North America
   (2) Europe
   (3) Australia
   (4) Japan
   (5) Industrialized countries

3. The population of Asia in 2011 was 4.2 billion and Africa was 1.02 billion. This may mean that the largest total number of undernourished people is found in
   (1) Africa
   (2) Asia
   (3) Middle East
   (4) Russia
   (5) South Africa

Questions 4–6 are based on the following passage.

The period from 475 to 221 BCE is known as the *Warring States Period* of Chinese history. Seven of the region's nearly 150 city-states had emerged as dominant powers and existed in a state of near-constant war. As well as fortifying their cities, the states built walls along their borders to protect their territory. In 221 BCE King Qin Shihuang defeated the other states and unified China under the Qin Dynasty, also known as the First Empire.

To unify the country, the First Emperor ordered many of the walls and barriers separating the states to be torn down. However, the invading Huns, a nomadic people, were a cause of constant unrest in the north. To combat the threat, a project was undertaken in 215 BCE to connect and enhance some of the existing walls, a project that required ten years and two million workers. During the Han Dynasty (206 BCE—220 CE) the wall was expanded and improved. Work continued periodically under various dynasties over the following nearly two thousand years, the most recent addition of a 1,000 km section beginning in 1571 CE.

4. The term *dynasty* probably refers to
   (1) hereditary rule by the same family
   (2) an empire
   (3) a popular leader
   (4) military government
   (5) military fortification

5. China was first unified as one country in
   (1) 475 BCE
   (2) 221 BCE
   (3) 206 BCE
   (4) 220 CE
   (5) 1571 CE

6. A popular myth is that the Great Wall of China can be seen from the moon. This is
   (1) true
   (2) uncertain
   (3) imprecise
   (4) false
   (5) yet to be verified

Questions 7–8 are based on the following passage.

The 18th century, known as the Enlightenment or Age of Reason, was a time of rapid economic, social, and political change. Industrialization had led to an increasingly wealthy middle class of manufacturers and merchants in societies where wealth and influence had belonged only to the landowning nobility. Despite poverty and harsh working conditions, urbanization and more efficient food production led to a population explosion that nearly doubled the population of Europe in a period of one hundred years. At the same time, philosophers, such as Rousseau and Voltaire, inspired by scientific advances, rejected ideas based on tradition and attempted to apply logic to social and political questions. Rousseau, for example, rejected the traditional idea of the divine right of kings, stating that they ruled only by the will of the governed. Although Enlightenment philosophers considered themselves a class of elite thinkers and intellectuals, their ideas focused on the rights of the individual and the equality of all people. Their ideas were among factors that contributed to the American and French Revolutions.

7. The Enlightenment took place during the
   (1) 1500s
   (2) 1600s
   (3) 1700s
   (4) 1800s
   (5) 1900s

8. The writers of the United States Declaration of Independence were probably influenced by
   (1) Enlightenment ideas
   (2) harsh working conditions
   (3) landowning nobility
   (4) British Parliament
   (5) tradition

Questions 9–10 are based on the following table.

Employment by Industry 2012
Prairie Provinces
(Rounded to nearest percent)

Sector	Manitoba	Saskatchewan	Alberta
Public Administration	6%	6%	4%
Agriculture	4%	7%	3%
Forestry, fishing, mining, oil & gas	1%	5%	8%
Utilities	1%	1%	1%
Construction	7%	8%	11%
Manufacturing	11%	5%	6%
Trade	15%	15%	15%
Transportation	6%	5%	5%
Finance	6%	6%	5%
Professional, scientific technical services	4%	5%	7%
Accommodation & Food Service	7%	6%	6%
Culture & Recreation	4%	4%	3%
Health Care	16%	13%	11%
Education	8%	8%	6%
Business, building & other support	3%	2%	3%

Source: Statistics Canada

9. In which province is the greatest percentage of the workforce employed in agriculture?
   (1) Manitoba
   (2) Saskatchewan
   (3) Alberta
   (4) Manitoba and Saskatchewan equally
   (5) All Prairie Provinces equally

10. The largest number of people in Alberta is employed in which sector?
    (1) Oil and gas
    (2) Finance
    (3) Health care
    (4) Trade
    (5) Manufacturing

ANSWERS AND ANALYSIS

1. **(1)** More countries in Africa have serious-to-alarming hunger index rates than on any other continent.

2. **(5)** The lowest rates of hunger are in industrialized countries

3. **(2)** As the population of Asia is four times that of Africa, the actual number of under-nourished people is greater.

4. **(1)** A dynasty refers to the succession of members of the same family who rule a country. This is evident in the passage about the Qin Dynasty, which was named for its founder.

5. **(2)** The passage states that King Qin Shihuang defeated the other states in 221 BCE and unified China.

6. **(4)** If it is a myth, it is not true. In fact, this story originated in 1938, long before people had been to the moon and was later disproved by moon landings. In fact, no human structures can be seen from the moon although many, including the Great Wall, can be seen from the international space station that orbits above the Earth.

7. **(3)** The 18th century means the 1700s, just as we live in the 2000s, but it is called the 21st century.

8. **(1)** The Declaration of Independence expresses the rights of the individual, for example, to life, liberty, and the pursuit of happiness.

9. **(2)** 7% of the workforce in Saskatchewan is employed in agriculture, as compared with 4% in Manitoba and 3% in Alberta.

10. **(4)** Trade is the largest employment sector in Alberta.

The New World

THINK ABOUT IT

Imagine you were a space explorer and discovered a new planet that was rich in natural resources. There were people who lived there who were different from any you had seen before. There may be gold, oil, and other minerals. There could be strange plants that are good to eat. The planet is very large and it would take many years to explore and discover all of its mysteries and wealth, but clearly there are resources there that can change the world. However, the planet is far away, and it is an expensive, difficult, and dangerous journey, and those who travel there would be far from home.

That is what it was like for the Europeans when they discovered the Americas. It was like discovering a new planet with resources and opportunities that could change the world and mean great wealth to the people and countries that controlled it. The result was exploration, adventure, settlement, and war.

IN THIS CHAPTER

After completing this chapter, you will be able to

→ INTERPRET PASSAGES ABOUT CANADA'S ABORIGINAL PEOPLES

→ INTERPRET INFORMATION ABOUT EARLY EXPLORERS

→ IDENTIFY THE ROLE OF CONFLICT BETWEEN FRANCE AND BRITAIN IN CANADIAN HISTORY

→ RESPOND TO QUESTIONS ABOUT COLONIZATION AND SETTLEMENT OF THE NEW WORLD

→ RECOGNIZE CONDITIONS THAT LED TO CANADIAN CONFEDERATION

→ READ AND RESPOND TO PASSAGES ABOUT CANADA'S FIRST PRIME MINISTER

CANADA'S ABORIGINAL PEOPLES

When European explorers first arrived in the new world, they found that people were already here, living on all parts of both North and South America. The Aboriginal peoples (meaning *first inhabitants*) had been here for many thousands of years and formed different tribes and nations with their own unique ways of life, languages, and cultures. Some groups were predominantly hunter-gatherers, some were nomads who followed the buffalo, while others were farmers.

Aboriginal peoples were very different from their European visitors. They did not have a centralized formal government in the way that Europeans were used to. Their societies were governed by unwritten laws and codes of conduct, established over many generations. They had no written language and agreements between individuals or tribes were made orally. They also did not have the same level of technology, and so European trade goods, such as axes, knives, needles, metal pots, and blankets were in much demand. The arrival of Europeans changed the Aboriginal way of life forever.

Although there were some instances of conflict between European settlers and Aboriginal peoples, strong economic and military alliances were formed, and Aboriginal tribes were allies of both sides in the North American war between the French and English, and in the American Revolution. In Canada, where economic growth and expansion were slower than in the United States, the violent confrontations portrayed in American films did not occur. Although some native land claims have yet to be resolved, Aboriginal people in Canada have had—and continue to have—a greater political influence and control of their destiny than their American counterparts.

Originally named *Indians* by Columbus when he landed in the Bahamas in 1492 because he thought he had reached the East Indies (the Philippines and other island groups in Eastern Asia), the term is seldom used today. In Canada, the constitution currently recognizes three groups of Aboriginal peoples:

1. **FIRST NATIONS**—formerly called *Indians*, including the various nations of eastern, central, and western Canada, generally located on lands called *reserves*
2. **INUIT**—indigenous people of Northern Canada
3. **MÉTIS**–descended from mixed Aboriginal and European parents

Aboriginal people currently make up more than 4% of the Canadian population in 600 recognized bands.

PRACTICE

Choose the best answer for each of the questions that come after the following passages and graphs:

Estimates about how long native peoples have lived in North America vary, as do theories about how they got here. Artifacts up to 12,000 years old have been found, and estimates place the arrival of Aboriginal peoples in North America between 12,000 and 30,000 years ago.

North American Aboriginal peoples are thought to be genetically related to the people of central Asia, in the Altai region of southern Russia, northern China, Mongolia, and Kazakhstan. The most common theory is that about 13,000 years ago, near the end of the last ice age, the level of the ocean was lower because of the large amount of polar ice. At that time, the lands that are now Russia and Alaska were connected by a land bridge in the area

<table>
<tr><td>TIP</td></tr>
</table>

The Canadian Constitution recognizes three categories of Aboriginal people: First Nations, Inuit, and Métis.

currently covered by the Bering Strait. People walked across the land bridge, following herds of animals. Gradually, many of the people migrated southward, spreading out to all corners of North and South America, developing different customs to suit their environment and even different languages.

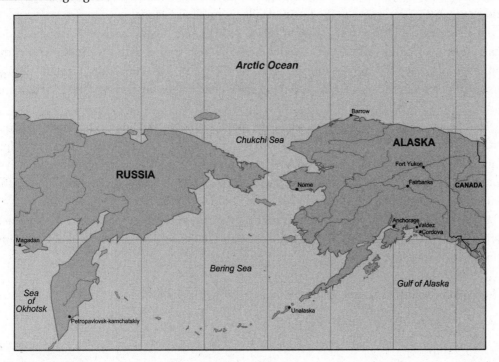

1. Aboriginal people have lived in North America for
   (1) 12,000 years
   (2) 13,000 years
   (3) 30,000 years
   (4) 50,000 years
   (5) an unknown period

2. Aboriginal peoples are thought to have come to the Americas by
   (1) canoe
   (2) boats formed from reeds
   (3) land bridge
   (4) ship across the Bering Sea
   (5) walking across the ice

Little is known about how the Haida came to inhabit their islands 130 km off the coast of British Columbia. Archeological evidence shows the islands were inhabited as long as 13,000 years ago, making the Haida people one of the oldest in North America. Evidence from 10,000 years ago indicates they had established a rich culture and were adept at harvesting plentiful sea life.

The Haida had a highly organized class structure within two clans, the Ravens and Eagles. Women married members of the opposite clan, and lineage—including things such as property rights—was traced through the mother.

The Haida are thought to be the first to build totem poles, recording lineage of family groups and events of the past. They constructed long houses from cedar planks and beams. They were a seafaring people, forming huge canoes that could hold 50 to 60 people from a single tree. They were also warriors, trading and raiding along the mainland coast for plunder and slaves, before returning to the fortified villages on their islands.

First contact with Europeans came in July 1774, when the Spanish vessel *Santiago*, under Juan Perez, was blown off course. Although the Spanish traded with the Haida who came out in canoes, they did not set foot on land. In 1787, a British ship under Captain George Dixon arrived at the islands. He named them the Queen Charlotte Islands, after his ship, and claimed them for Britain.

This began a period of trade for sea otter pelts, valuable in China. The trade was not entirely peaceful, and there were battles with traders, leading to the seizure of several ships. The Haida adapted quickly to European warfare and the use of captured canons and swivel guns. As the sea otter declined, so did trade. Ultimately, European disease decimated the Haida population, reducing their number from about 7,000 to 700 by the early 1900s.

Haida culture and art remain vibrant today. The Queen Charlotte Islands were renamed Haida Gwaii, meaning islands of the Haida people, in 2009, and became a national park and conservation area in 2010.

3. Haida Gwaii is the name for a
    (1) group of islands
    (2) tribe
    (3) ship
    (4) trading company
    (5) body of water

4. European trade with the Haida was primarily driven by Chinese demand for
    (1) curios
    (2) iron
    (3) copper
    (4) sea otter skins
    (5) new technology

5. The Haida were nearly destroyed by
    (1) violence
    (2) alcohol
    (3) trade
    (4) social trade
    (5) European diseases

The Iroquois Confederacy, also known as the Haudenosaunee, was a powerful alliance of five nations in the Great Lakes region (namely, the Mohawks, Oneidas, Onondagas, Cayugas, and Senecas) that was formed to end warfare between the tribes. The agreement, known as the Great Peace, was symbolized in part by the longhouse in which the people lived.

Longhouses varied in size, often as long as 60 metres long and 6 metres in width and height. Each longhouse was home to an extended family, or clan, and the size of the building was determined by the number of people. The house was constructed of poles set upright with branches across the top to form a curved roof. Bark shingles were sewn on the outside of the structure. Doors at each end were covered with furs and smoke holes (usually five to represent the five nations) were spaced down the length of the roof. Inside were areas designated for each family.

The Iroquois were a matriarchal society and membership in the clan was determined by the mother. The women were in charge of the longhouse, farming, and the distribution of food, and they selected which men would represent the clan in council. If a young man married, he would leave the longhouse to live with the family of his wife. Men were the hunters and warriors and representatives for their clans. In the early 1700s, a sixth tribe, the Tuscarora, were displaced by European expansion in North Carolina and were accepted into the alliance.

6. The group of people who lived together in a longhouse were
    (1) all of the Iroquois
    (2) one tribe
    (3) one clan
    (4) five tribes
    (5) one family

7. A matriarchal society is one in which leadership roles are played by
    (1) men
    (2) women
    (3) tribal leaders
    (4) a queen
    (5) priests

ANSWERS

1. **(5)** Estimates about how long native peoples have lived in North America vary.
2. **(3)** The most common theory is that they walked across the Bering Land Bridge, which existed near the end of the last ice age.
3. **(1)** Haida Gwaii is a group of islands, formerly known as the Queen Charlotte Islands, off the coast of British Columbia.
4. **(4)** Sea otter pelts were in great demand in China, leading to European trade with the Haida and the near-extinction of sea otters.
5. **(5)** Although all of these presented troubles for the Haida, it was European diseases that were most damaging and ravaged the population.
6. **(3)** The people who would live together in one longhouse were the members and families of one clan, or extended family.
7. **(2)** Lineage was traced through the mother and women were in charge of most areas of daily life.

CHALLENGE EXERCISE

Aboriginal peoples play an important role in Canada's past, present, and future. Using the Internet, local library, or other resources research Aboriginal peoples in your province or territory. What are some of the distinguishing features of their culture and language?

EARLY EXPLORERS

The continents of America are named for Amerigo Vespucci (1454–1512), who was an Italian explorer, navigator, and cartographer (map maker). Shortly after the return of Columbus, Vespucci was involved with several voyages on behalf of Spain and Portugal. He was the first to discover that the lands were a new continent and not, as Columbus had supposed, the east coast of Asia, which is why the Americas bear his name. He also discovered that the continents went much farther south than previously thought.

TIP

France and Britain were the primary European explorers and settlers of Canada and North America.

Although the French, and later the British, were the primary explorers of Canada and North America, the Spanish and Portuguese were also active explorers. Christopher Columbus sailed in Spanish ships and claimed the New World for Spain. Portugal was one of the most powerful seafaring nations. On Columbus's return, the Portuguese king claimed the discovered lands. To avoid dispute, the Pope divided the New World between Portugal and Spain in 1494, essentially drawing a line from top to bottom through this new part of the known world. Everything east of the line belonged to Portugal, which gave them the tip of Brazil. Everything west of the line belonged to Spain. Of course, Columbus had landed in the Bahamas, so no one knew North America was there. Spain and Portugal, whose powers were in decline, concentrated exploration in the south. France, England, and other countries ignored the Pope's decree and explored the north.

On the GED Social Studies Test, you may read information about some early explorers. The information could include stories of voyages, important discoveries, maps of routes, and the historical significance of discoveries. There were many people who helped in the discovery, exploration, and mapping of North America. You will learn about just a few of them in the practice exercises below.

PRACTICE

Choose the best answer for each of the questions that follow the passages.

Columbus was not the first European to discover America. Nearly 500 years before, Norse explorers had discovered and settled in Newfoundland, which they called Vinland. The Norse had already discovered Iceland and Greenland. Led by Leif Eriksson, a group of adventurers followed the route of previous Norse ships that had seen land after being blown off course in a storm. Eriksson sailed north from Greenland until sighting land, and then followed the coast down to Newfoundland.

Discovered in 1960, and then excavated and restored, L'Anse aux Meadows is the site of a Norse settlement established about 1000 CE at the tip of Newfoundland. Archeological evidence shows that the same site had previously been inhabited by indigenous peoples. Native artifacts were found dating back as far as 6,000 years, but none contemporary with the Norse habitation. Excavation of the site found the location of eight buildings of various sizes. Construction was probably of sod over a wooden frame and the buildings are typical of those used by the Norse people of the time. Smaller buildings of various sizes may have served as workshops, dwellings, or storage. One building, measuring 28.8 m by 15.6 m was the longhouse. Archeological evidence gives some information about their way of life. Researchers theorize that the settlement did not last for long because of the scarcity of game during the harsh winters.

L'Anse aux Meadows is a Canadian National Park and was declared a World Heritage Site in 1978. It is the only known Norse settlement in North America outside of Greenland.

1. The first European to establish a settlement in North America was
    (1) Christopher Columbus
    (2) Amerigo Vespucci
    (3) L'Anse aux Meadows
    (4) Indigenous peoples
    (5) Leif Eriksson

2. Evidence in this passage suggests that the Norse established their settlement by
    (1) invading an existing settlement
    (2) building on a site that had been settled in the past
    (3) building in a previously unsettled area
    (4) getting lost in a storm
    (5) searching for archeological evidence

3. L'Anse aux Meadows is important
    (1) only to Canadians
    (2) to Norse people
    (3) to all North Americans
    (4) to European historians
    (5) internationally

Spanish settlements in South America began as early as 1496, coming after the establishment of Santa Domingo in the Caribbean. Exploration and settlement of North America was a much slower process. Shortly after Columbus returned from his first voyage, King Henry VII of England commissioned the Italian navigator John Cabot (Giovanni Caboto) to lead a 1496–1497 expedition from Bristol, England, to the New World. The expedition landed in Newfoundland and is believed to be the first European landing in North America since the Vikings. Throughout the years that followed, there were many journeys to the New World, particularly for fish, but no permanent settlement was formed.

Another important early explorer was France's Jacques Cartier, who made his first journey in 1534. He explored the Gulf of St. Lawrence around northern New Brunswick, Prince Edward Island, and the entrance to St. Lawrence River in addition to making contact with the Iroquois. On a second voyage, he travelled farther down the St. Lawrence as far as present-day Montreal. In 1541, Cartier returned with instructions from the French king to establish a colony in the New World. The settlement was established, but because of scurvy and attacks by the Iroquois, it was abandoned in 1543. Cartier is remembered for mapping the St. Lawrence and naming the country Canada from the Iroquois word for village.

One of the most important early explorers of Canada was Samuel de Champlain. Champlain was a cartographer who accompanied a voyage to establish a French settlement in 1604. The explorers established their first colony on the small St. Croix Island in the St. Croix River, which runs between present day New Brunswick and Maine. During the winter, nearly half the crew died of scurvy or starvation, and the following summer, Champlain relocated the survivors to current Nova Scotia, where they established Port-Royal, which became the first permanent settlement in North America that wasn't founded by the Spanish. In 1608, Champlain established another settlement at the site of present-day Quebec City.

Samuel de Champlain is known as the "Father of New France." He was the first to thoroughly map Canada's east coast and to establish a permanent colony in North America.

4. The first attempted permanent settlement in North America was established by
   (1) Jacques Cartier
   (2) John Cabot
   (3) Samuel de Champlain
   (4) Henry VII
   (5) Leif Eriksson

5. The name of the country of Canada comes from
   (1) French
   (2) English
   (3) Iroquois
   (4) Norse
   (5) Italian

6. The first permanent settlement in North America was established in
   (1) Nova Scotia
   (2) New Brunswick
   (3) Maine
   (4) Quebec
   (5) Newfoundland

ANSWERS

1. **(5)** A Norse group led by Leif Eriksson discovered America 500 years before Columbus.
2. **(2)** Archeological evidence shows that the settlement was built on a site that had been settled numerous times in the past, but none contemporary with the Norse settlement.
3. **(5)** A world heritage site is a man-made site of outstanding international importance.
4. **(1)** Cartier's attempt at a permanent settlement along the St. Lawrence was abandoned because of scurvy and Iroquois attacks.
5. **(3)** The passage states that the name Canada comes from the Iroquois word for village.
6. **(1)** The passage states that the first permanent colony was at Port Royal in Nova Scotia.

CHALLENGE EXERCISE

What is the history of your community? Who were the first settlers? Where did they come from and how did they come there? What was the basis of the early economy?

FRANCE AND BRITAIN

The first 200 years of settlement and expansion in North America was a story of skirmishes and war between the French and English that often mirrored conflicts between the two nations in Europe. From their small settlements in Port Royal and Quebec, the French quickly expanded outward through the fur trade, which became the basis of the economy, and enabled them to form strong alliances with First Nations people, in particular with the Mi'kmaq and Maliseet people of Nova Scotia and New Brunswick (which the French called Acadia) and the Algonquin and Huron people of Quebec and Ontario.

In 1627, agriculture began to play an important role in New France. The feudal *seigneurial* system was introduced, in which large tracts of farm land were leased by seigneurs to habitants who worked the land. Nevertheless, emigration from France was slow. In total, only about 10,000 people came to settle and work the land. By 1663, there were about 16,000 French in North America, compared with nearly 70,000 British subjects. The French relied heavily on their First Nations allies in confrontations with the English.

The British in the New World focused initially on fishing off Newfoundland. Settlement took place along the coast farther south in what would later become the thirteen colonies. In the 1620s, large numbers of Puritans left England to seek religious freedom and settle in what is now Massachusetts, where they established farmlands. As more and more people came, seeking land that was not available in England, they displaced the First Nations inhabitants. In 1660, the King of England granted huge tracts of land in the interior of what is now Canada to the Hudson's Bay Company. The grant included the entire Hudson Bay region as well as modern day Manitoba and much of Saskatchewan and became the heart of the British fur trade. By 1760, two million British subjects lived from Newfoundland to Georgia.

PRACTICE

Choose the best answer for each of the questions that follow the next passages and maps.

The French and Indian War was the colonial portion of the Seven Years War fought in Europe from 1756 to 1763. It was the bloodiest and most widely fought American war in the 18th century, taking more lives than the American Revolution and involving people on three continents. The war was but one of many imperial struggles between the French and English over colonial territory and wealth in North America and in Europe, as well as a product of the localized rivalry between British and French colonists.

The war began in November 1753, when the band of men led by a young Virginia major named George Washington entered Ohio territory to deliver a message to a French captain demanding that French troops withdraw from the area. The demand was rejected. In 1754, Washington received permission to build a fort near the present site of Pittsburgh. In May, after Washington's troops clashed with local French forces, the English colonists surrendered the meagre fort they had built.

The incident set off a string of small battles, but it was not until May 1756 that the French and the English formally declared war.

By September 1760, the British controlled all of the North American frontier; the war between the two countries was effectively over. The 1763 Treaty of Paris, which also ended the Seven Years War in Europe, forced the French to surrender all of her American possessions to the British and the Spanish. The results of the war ended French political and cultural influence in North America. England gained massive amounts of land and vastly strengthened its hold on the continent. The war, however, also had other results. It badly eroded the relationship between England and Native Americans, and, though the war seemed to strengthen England's hold on the colonies, in reality it played a major role in the deteriorating relationship between England and its colonies that eventually led to the Revolutionary War.

TIP

War between the French and English in North America often mirrored conflicts between the two nations in Europe.

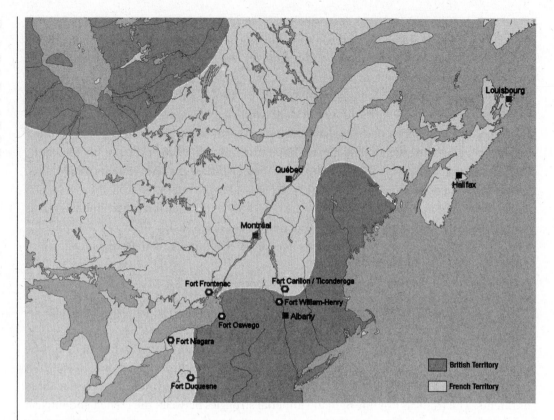

British Territory

French Territory

1. British forces in the Ohio were led by a(n)
   (1) French patriot
   (2) Native American
   (3) English-born gentleman
   (4) Future American president
   (5) American traitor

2. Based on information from the passage, British victory in North America was a contributing factor in
   (1) the French Revolution
   (2) the American Revolution
   (3) native land claims
   (4) greater economic ties with the colonies
   (5) the Seven Years War

3. After the Treaty of Paris, what country other than Britain had the largest territory in North America?
   (1) Spain
   (2) France
   (3) the United States
   (4) Russia
   (5) Portugal

The *seigneurial* system was the form of agricultural land ownership in New France in the St. Lawrence Lowlands, based in large part on the feudal system in place in France. Under the system, large rectangular tracts of land, 15 km in length and 5 km wide, were granted to important colonists, called seigneurs, who were usually former nobles or military officers. The narrow end of each tract was along the St. Lawrence River. The tracts were then subdivided into long narrow strips and leased to farmers, called habitants, who worked the land as part owners and paid rent and taxes to the seigneurs. A third group, called engagés, were laborers who came from France on three-year contracts to work on the farms.

The seigneurs had specific responsibilities. They had to sub-divide the land for the habitants. They were required to build a church and flour mill on the seigneury. They also had to pay taxes to the government based on the number of people living there and the amount of land being cultivated. The habitants also had specific duties. They were required to build a house and farm the land, to pay taxes to the seigneur, and to work several days each year for the seigneur for free.

In many ways, the seigneurial system worked well for everyone. It was an efficient way to organize and develop the land. Seigneurs benefited from the system with land, prestige, and income, although they had neither the wealth nor status of their counterparts in France. Habitants received substantial tracts of land, as well as greater income and independence than French peasants. Ninety percent of the residents of New France, with the exception of officials and clergy, lived on seigneuries.

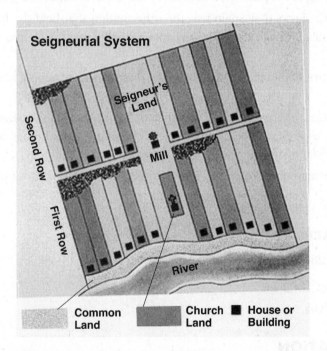

4. Three groups of people who lived under the seigneurial system were
   (1) nobles, seigneurs, habitants
   (2) military officers, habitants, engagés
   (3) priests, habitants, seigneurs
   (4) seigneurs, habitants, engagés
   (5) peasants, seigneurs, nobles

5. Critics say that one result of the seigneurial system was that villages were not able to develop because
    (1) government did not permit it
    (2) people did not have enough money
    (3) seigneurs and the church prevented it
    (4) the land was not fertile
    (5) houses were not close together

6. Based on the information, which of the following had the greatest wealth and influence in French society?
    (1) Seigneurs
    (2) Habitants
    (3) French nobles
    (4) Engagés
    (5) Peasants

ANSWERS

1. **(4)** They were led by Major George Washington, a future leader in the Revolutionary War and first president of the United States.
2. **(2)** According to the passage, it eventually led to the Revolutionary War.
3. **(1)** The map shows that Spain was the other nation that held the largest territory in North America. Russia's holdings were much smaller and the United States did not yet exist.
4. **(4)** Seigneurs, habitants, engagés were the three classes of people who lived under the system.
5. **(5)** In villages, houses are close together to form a community. Because of the way seigneuries were organized and because all habitants built homes on their land, the houses were far apart.
6. **(3)** The passage states seigneurs had neither the wealth nor status of counterparts in France.

CHALLENGE EXERCISE

Research the significance of the following:

1. The Plains of Abraham
2. Je me souviens

CONFEDERATION

The Dominion of Canada was formed on July 1, 1867, uniting the provinces of New Brunswick, Nova Scotia, and Canada (Ontario and Quebec). The union had taken several years of discussion and the Charlottetown and Quebec Conferences of 1864. The meetings were attended by representatives of the provinces, known today as the Fathers of Confederation. In contrast with the United States constitution, the agreements that were reached were legal in description. The new country would have a strong federal government and would maintain strong ties with Britain. Debts of the provinces would be assumed by the federal government and a railway would be built from Montreal to Halifax, connecting the Maritimes and central Canada.

Britain, who did not want the continued expense of providing military protection for the colonies, also supported the union. Following approval by provincial legislatures, Canadian representatives travelled to England for the Conference of London. In 1867, the British North America Act (BNA Act) officially created the country of Canada. Although Canada was now a separate country with its own government, it was still not completely independent. Britain retained control over foreign policy. In addition, the highest court of appeal was the Privy Council in Britain and the constitution was an act of British Parliament, which could only be amended in Britain. The Statute of Westminster in 1931 gave Canada full control of its destiny. In 1982, the constitution was patriated when a new constitution was passed by the Parliament of Canada. The Queen, however, remains the head of state of Canada through her representative the Governor General.

The dates Canadian provinces and territories entered confederation:

TIP

Canada became a country in 1867 with the union of New Brunswick, Nova Scotia, Ontario, and Quebec.

Province/Territory	Date
Quebec	1 July 1867
New Brunswick	1 July 1867
Nova Scotia	1 July 1867
Ontario	1 July 1867
Manitoba	15 July 1870
Northwest Territories	15 July 1870
British Columbia	20 July 1872
Prince Edward Island	1 July 1873
Yukon Territory	13 June 1898
Saskatchewan	1 September 1905
Alberta	1 September 1905
Newfoundland	31 March 1949
Nunavut	1 April 1999

On the GED Social Studies Test, some of the questions could be about the Canadian constitution. Passages may include information about the Fathers of Confederation or the Charlottetown and Quebec conferences, extracts from political speeches, or extracts from the BNA Act or Constitution of 1982. You do not need specific knowledge about the constitution to prepare for the test, but general knowledge of the constitution will help you interpret the passages.

PRACTICE

Choose the best answer for each of the questions at the end of the following passages.

In true Canadian form, the Confederation of 1867 was a peaceful exercise. Following the American and French Revolutions, other revolutions in South America and elsewhere had won independence for a number of smaller nations. Canada, however, maintained a close and loyal relationship with Britain. Confederation was partly driven by a desire for independence, but more so by practical internal and external factors, and was brought about by mutual agreement.

In 1840, Ontario and Quebec had been joined together to form the province of Canada. Each had an equal number of seats in the provincial legislature, which meant that most votes ended in a tie. Desire to end this political deadlock was one factor that contributed to confederation. The possibility of economic development and improved trade was another factor. Building a national railroad was one of the most important points of the proposed confederation because it would decrease isolation of the provinces and increase trade routes, as well as provide a means for movement of troops for mutual defense. The provinces of a unified Canada would also be better able to expand westward into the lands held by the Hudson's Bay Company.

Perhaps the most important external factor that provided motivation for confederation was mutual defense. The American Civil War, in which the British had given unofficial aid to the losing South, had recently ended. Residents of British North America were concerned about possible invasion. The American doctrine of manifest destiny held that the United States was destined to spread across the entire continent. Americans were also interested in the lands that were later to become western Canada. Another factor was raids into Canada by the Fenian Brotherhood, a group of Irish republicans based in the United States.

1. Unlike many other countries, Canada gained independence through
   (1) agreement
   (2) revolution
   (3) revolutions in other countries
   (4) fear
   (5) war

2. An external cause of confederation was
   (1) political deadlock
   (2) economic development
   (3) fenian raids
   (4) national railroad
   (5) expansion westward

3. Which of the following did the provinces feel was the greatest threat?
   (1) The United States
   (2) Isolation
   (3) Fenian raids
   (4) Political deadlock
   (5) British

Canada has different levels of government. The federal government, or Parliament of Canada, is responsible for matters affecting the whole country. Provincial and territorial governments, called *legislatures*, are responsible for matters in their specific regions. The 1867 Constitution Act, also called the British North America Act, specifies the powers of each level of government in section *VI. Distribution of Legislative Powers*.

The Act states: *It shall be lawful for the Queen, by and with the Advice and Consent of the Senate and House of Commons, to make Laws for the Peace, Order, and good Government of Canada, in relation to all Matters not coming within the Classes of Subjects by this Act assigned exclusively to the Legislatures of the Provinces.*

The Act lists the powers of the parliament, which include the following:

- Trade
- Unemployment insurance
- Any mode or system of taxation
- Postal service
- Defense
- Navigation and shipping
- Issuing money
- Banking
- Copyrights
- Indian reserves
- Marriage and divorce
- Criminal law
- Penitentiaries

Legislatures of the provinces and territories also have exclusive powers. These include the following:

- Direct taxation within the province
- Public lands and timber
- Prisons
- Hospitals
- Municipalities
- Solemnization of marriage
- Education
- Property and civil rights
- The administration of justice

4. Which of the following is a responsibility of the Parliament of Canada?
    (1) Hospitals
    (2) Public lands
    (3) Education
    (4) Defense
    (5) Property and civil rights

5. Which of the following is a responsibility of the legislatures?
   (1) Courts
   (2) Criminal law
   (3) Penitentiaries
   (4) Banking
   (5) Copyrights

6. According to the information given, who can pass laws about matters not listed in the act?
   (1) Legislatures
   (2) Parliament
   (3) The queen or king of England
   (4) Municipalities
   (5) The prime minister

ANSWERS

1. **(1)** The passage states that Canadian confederation was brought about by mutual agreement.

2. **(3)** Other answers are internal causes.

3. **(1)** Fenian raids had occurred and were a real danger, but the greatest perceived threat was United States expansion.

4. **(4)** The constitution gives the power over defense to the Parliament of Canada.

5. **(1)** Parliament is responsible for criminal law and penitentiaries, but legislatures are responsible for the administration of justice, which is the courts, except the supreme court.

6. **(2)** The Act states: *It shall be lawful for the Queen, by and with the Advice and Consent of the Senate and House of Commons, to make Laws...* In Canada, the queen or king of England does not really make laws. They are made by the House of Commons or Parliament.

TIP

Canada's first prime minister was Sir John A. MacDonald.

EARLY PRIME MINISTERS

In Canada, unlike the United States, people do not vote for the prime minister in an election. Instead, they vote for their member of parliament. The leader of the political party with the most members elected to parliament becomes prime minister.

The first, and one of the most famous, prime ministers of Canada was Sir John A. MacDonald. He was a colourful figure who drank too much and was an excellent public speaker. He was also a visionary. The former premier of the Province of Canada (Ontario and Quebec), MacDonald was one of the Fathers of Confederation. He served from 1867–1873 as prime minister. He was defeated by Canada's second prime minister, Alexander Mackenzie, who served from 1873–1878, but returned to power from 1878–1891. Topics on the GED Social Studies Test about early prime ministers may include passages about their accomplishments or extracts from political speeches. Because the speeches were given more than a century ago, the language is an older style.

PRACTICE

Choose the best answer for each of the questions about the following passages.

The following is an excerpt of a speech on January 1, 1865, by Sir John A. MacDonald to the Legislature of the Province of Canada (Ontario and Quebec). The subject is the discussions at the Quebec Conference with other provinces about joining together in confederation.

> *Now, as regards the comparative advantages of a Legislative and a Federal Union, I have never hesitated to state my own opinions. I have again and again stated in the House, that, if practicable, I thought a Legislative Union would be preferable. I have always contended that if we could agree to have one government and one parliament, legislating for the whole of these peoples, it would be the best, the cheapest, the most vigorous, and the strongest system of government we could adopt. But, on looking at the subject in the Conference, and discussing the matter as we did, most unreservedly, and with a desire to arrive at a satisfactory conclusion, we found that such a system was impracticable. In the first place, it would not meet the assent of the people of Lower Canada, because they felt that in their peculiar position—being in a minority, with a different language, nationality and religion from the majority, …their institutions and their laws might be assailed, and their ancestral associations, on which they prided themselves, attacked and prejudiced…. We found too, that though their people speak the same language and enjoy the same system of law as the people of Upper Canada, a system founded on the common law of England, there was as great a disinclination on the part of the various Maritime Provinces to lose their individuality, as separate political organizations… Therefore, we were forced to the conclusion that we must either abandon the idea of Union altogether, or devise a system of union in which the separate provincial organizations would be in some degree preserved….*
>
> *… The Conference having come to the conclusion that a legislative union, pure and simple, was impracticable, our next attempt was to form a government upon federal principles, which would give to the General Government the strength of a legislative and administrative union, while at the same time it preserved that liberty of action for the different sections which is allowed by a Federal Union. And I am strong in the belief— that we have hit upon the happy medium in those resolutions, and that we have formed a scheme of government which unites the advantages of both, giving us the strength of a legislative union and the sectional freedom of a federal union, with protection to local interests.*

1. In the speech, MacDonald describes two types of government: a legislative union with only one government for the country and a federal union. MacDonald supported the idea of a Legislative Union for all of the following reasons EXCEPT that it was
   (1) Cheapest
   (2) Strongest
   (3) Most practical
   (4) Best
   (5) Most vigorous

2. Lower Canada probably refers to
   (1) Ontario
   (2) Manitoba
   (3) Quebec
   (4) Nova Scotia
   (5) New Brunswick

3. The other provinces did not support the idea of a legislative union and preferred a federal union
   (1) because it is more simple
   (2) to have assent from Lower Canada
   (3) because it is more economical
   (4) because it is more efficient
   (5) to keep their individuality

ANSWERS

1. **(1)** In MacDonald's opinion, all of these reasons support a Legislative Union except practicality. At the conference, they found *that such a system was impracticable.*
2. **(3)** Lower Canada refers to Quebec, which has its own language and religion.
3. **(5)** The other provinces prefer a system with a federal government and provincial governments to protect their individuality.

CHALLENGE EXERCISE

When did your province or territory become part of confederation? Who was the first premier? What were the reasons that your province or territory joined confederation?

CHAPTER CHECK-UP

Complete these practice exercises and check the answers and analysis that follow. After you mark your work, review any topic in the chapter that you had trouble with or did not understand.

Questions 1–3 are based on the following information.

If we could travel back in time and visit this region [Arctic] about 8500 years ago, we would probably find a population living in small communities along the coastline of the Bering Land Bridge. We would have observed a way of life based on marine mammals and other species of animals, birds, and fish that were hunted along the shorelines and islands of the ice-free waters. During certain seasons of the year, we would have observed hunters and their families moving inland to hunt in the valleys and to fish in the freshwater lakes and rivers.

As the population in this area grew and new territory was needed, the settlements gradually spread north along the coast and inland using the large river valleys. Eventually these expanded north of the Seward Peninsula until they reached as far as the northern coast of

Alaska. This was a very different environment because during the winter the sea was covered by a thick layer of ice. It was here that a remarkable shift in the way of life took place as our ancestors developed the knowledge, skills, and technology needed to utilize the winter sea-ice environment to hunt marine mammals. This adaptation endures as one of the defining characteristics of Inuit culture from Alaska to Greenland.

These early groups that learned to live on the sea-ice must have been very successful hunters since it looks as though their population started to grow and eventually expand eastwards. As they did so, new settlements were created. This movement east took place about 5000 years ago by a people we refer to as the Sivullirmiut which means the first people. In our legends these early people were often called Tunnit.

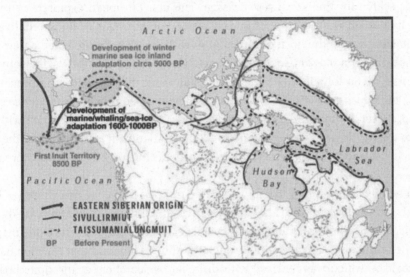

1. Information in this map and passage about Inuit origins shows that the Inuit came to North America
    (1) from Greenland
    (2) across the Bering Land Bridge
    (3) about 5,000 years ago
    (4) from Labrador
    (5) from Alaska

2. What defining characteristic of Inuit culture developed as settlements gradually spread north?
    (1) Changing language
    (2) Invention of canoe
    (3) Inuit sculpture
    (4) Movement east
    (5) Hunting the winter sea-ice

3. According to the information given, Inuit people now inhabit
   (1) Canada's north
   (2) Greenland
   (3) Hudson Bay
   (4) Alaska, Greenland
   (5) Alaska, Canada's north, Greenland

Questions 4–6 are based on the following information.

One of the great mysteries of Canada's north is the missing ships and men of Sir John Franklin's search for the Northwest Passage. The first European explorers to reach North America had sailed west in hope of finding a new route to Asia as an alternative to sailing south and east around the horn of Africa. After realizing they had reached a new world, not Asia, the search for a sea route across the top of North America to the Pacific continued.

The voyage of Sir John Franklin was one of many over the centuries. In a previous voyage, Franklin, an English rear-admiral, had successfully mapped much of the Arctic coastline. In May 1845, he set out from England with two ships, 24 officers, and 129 men with orders to search for the Northwest Passage. After crossing the Atlantic, it is thought that they wintered near Beechey Island above Baffin Island, well north of Hudson Bay, but they were never seen again.

It is generally believed that the ships became trapped in the ice near Beechey Island and most of the crew succumbed to starvation, scurvy, and illness, while others tried to walk out over the ice. Inuit who were interviewed several years later told of seeing white men, who did not ask them for help, walking south through the snow. They said that the men had resorted to cannibalism, which was received with disbelief by searchers at the time; however, evidence from three graves found on Beechey Island supports this conclusion.

Franklin was a popular figure at home and an extensive search was conducted for the lost ships, but they were never found. Even today, researchers continue to look for the remains of the Franklin expedition.

4. The Northwest Passage is a
   (1) sailing route from the Atlantic to Pacific
   (2) sailing route from British Columbia to Asia
   (3) sailing route from Europe to Africa
   (4) overland route on sea-ice
   (5) overland route southward from Hudson Bay

5. The Franklin expedition originated in
   (1) Canada's north
   (2) Baffin Island
   (3) Hudson Bay
   (4) England
   (5) United States

6. Based on information in the passage, what probably happened to the expedition?
   (1) They were attacked by natives.
   (2) They froze to death.
   (3) They became trapped in ice and starved.
   (4) The ships sank.
   (5) They became lost at sea.

Questions 7–9 are based on the following information.

Responsible Government is a term that has a unique meaning and history in Canada and precedes confederation. Originally, the colonies of British North America were each ruled by a Governor and an appointed legislative council. Each province also had an elected assembly, but the assemblies had no real power and were often not listened to by the governor and council. The result was frustration among the people of the colonies, and rebellions in Upper and Lower Canada in 1837 and 1838.

The British Government sent an investigator, Lord Durham, to determine the causes of the rebellion. Among his recommendations were the union of Upper and Lower Canada and a government that was responsible to the elected representatives of the people. The executive council would require the approval and confidence of the elected representatives. At first, governors resisted the idea. They were concerned about the possibility that their instructions from Britain and the will of the elected assemblies might sometimes be in conflict. In 1846, responsible government became a reality when the British government declared that they did not want to interfere in the decisions of the colonies.

Responsible government is still an important concept today. The descendent of the legislative council, the prime minister's cabinet, is responsible to the House of Commons. If they lose the confidence of the House, the government must resign.

7. Responsible government is considered to be an important factor in Canada's confederation without revolution because
   (1) the rebellions were put down
   (2) Upper and Lower Canada were unified
   (3) it gave people a voice in their government
   (4) it removed governors from the colonies
   (5) Canada became an independent nation

8. Before there was a representative government, who made decisions affecting the colonies?
   (1) The king
   (2) Governor and council
   (3) The people
   (4) Elected representatives
   (5) Prime minister

9. Based on this passage, if the minister of finance (a member of cabinet) presented a budget that was defeated by the House of Commons, what would happen?
    (1) He would be removed from cabinet.
    (2) He would prepare a new budget.
    (3) He would appeal to the Governor General.
    (4) The government must resign.
    (5) An investigation would be conducted.

Questions 10–12 are based on the following information.

Acadians are descendants of early French settlers in the Maritime Provinces of Nova Scotia and New Brunswick, which were then called Acadia. For the first 100 years of colonization, they lived under French rule, participating with their Mi'kmaq allies in numerous wars with the British in North America, which often mirrored the conflict between their parent countries in Europe. By the 1713 Treaty of Utrecht, Britain gained possession of New Brunswick and mainland Nova Scotia, while France retained Cape Breton and Fort Louisburg. Acadian settlers in British-controlled territories were allowed to keep their homes, but they were still perceived by the British as a threat, particularly in Nova Scotia. The British demanded that they swear an unconditional oath of loyalty to become British subjects.

The Acadians refused for several reasons. First, they were Catholic and the King of England was also the head of the protestant Anglican Church. Second, they were afraid that as British subjects, they might be required to fight against France if there were a war. Third, the Acadians feared that their Mi'kmaq allies would see them as traitors if they swore loyalty to Britain. Fourth, some of the Acadians still wanted to overthrow the British occupation. In the end, they promised to be neutral.

To appreciate what later occurred, one must understand that the British and French continued to fight in other parts of North America. Some Acadians did continue to participate, helping to supply Fort Louisburg in Cape Breton and participating in other conflicts, although most stayed neutral. In 1755, Governor Charles Lawrence and the Nova Scotia Legislative Council decided that the best way to minimize the threat was to deport them all, whether they had been neutral or not. In total, over 10,000 Acadians were loaded on ships and sent away with few of their belongings between 1755 and 1764. At first they were sent to the thirteen colonies; then they were sent back to France. Some found their way back to North America to Louisiana, which was then a colony of Spain, while others made their way to Quebec and northern New Brunswick.

In 1764, the British government permitted the Acadians to return to their homes. Many returned to find that their land had been taken over by British settlers. The event is known as the Acadian Expulsion. Well over 1,000 people died during the expulsion.

10. The British believed that the Acadians were a threat because of
    (1) their Catholic faith
    (2) their unique Acadian culture
    (3) the Treaty of Utrecht
    (4) their promise to be neutral
    (5) ongoing war in North America with the French

11. Based on the passage, all of the following are true EXCEPT
    (1) Acadians did not want to bear arms against France
    (2) The Treaty of Utrecht gave mainland Nova Scotia and New Brunswick to Britain
    (3) Many Acadians died during the expulsion
    (4) All Acadians remained neutral
    (5) Acadians refused to swear an oath of loyalty

12. The Expulsion of the Acadians is considered a black mark on Canadian history, probably because it involved
    (1) forcible deportation of innocent civilians
    (2) an order of the legislative council
    (3) an illegal deportation
    (4) their not being wanted in the thirteen colonies
    (5) some Acadians who still wanted to overthrow the British

ANSWERS

1. **(2)** The passage and map show that the Inuit ancestors crossed the Bering Land Bridge and established their first territory in Alaska about 8,500 years ago.

2. **(5)** Hunting marine sea mammals from winter sea-ice became a defining characteristic of Inuit culture

3. **(5)** The information given shows that Inuit people spread across the north from Alaska, through Canada's north and on to Greenland.

4. **(1)** The Northwest Passage is a sailing route from the Atlantic to the Pacific.

5. **(4)** The passage states that they set sail from England in 1845.

6. **(3)** The passage states that it is generally believed that they became trapped in ice and the crew succumbed to starvation, scurvy, and disease.

7. **(3)** The purpose of responsible government is to address the concerns of the people with a government that is responsible to their wishes.

8. **(2)** Before representative government, the governor and appointed council made most decisions.

9. **(4)** Even today, the cabinet is responsible and must have approval of the elected representatives.

10. **(5)** War with the French was still ongoing, so the French Acadians were considered a possible threat.

11. **(4)** Some Acadians did participate in actions against the British, but most remained neutral.

12. **(1)** The expulsion of the Acadians is considered a black mark because it was the forcible deportation of thousands of civilians based on their heritage, without regard to whether they were neutral or not. In addition, most lost their land and possessions, and many died.

Canadian Politics and Government

18

CONSTITUTION ACT

The constitution of Canada began with the British North America Act of 1867, an act of the Parliament of the United Kingdom (Britain) that established Canada as a nation and established the method of government and responsibilities and powers of different levels of government. Since that time, many documents have become part of the constitution, some from acts of parliament in the U.K. and some in Canada. These include various amendments to the BNA Act and the Statute of Westminster (U.K.), as well as acts such as the Manitoba Act of 1870, admitting other provinces into the confederation. In total, more than 30 acts and orders make up the Canadian constitution.

In 1982, the constitution was patriated (brought back to Canada) by the government of Canada, led by Prime Minister Pierre Trudeau, and supported by most of the provinces. The Constitution Act, 1982, which was an act of Canadian Parliament, was declared by Queen Elizabeth II in Ottawa on April 17 of that year. It includes the Constitution Act of 1867 (formerly the BNA Act).

The Constitution Act, 1982 contains a number of parts:

- Part 1—Canadian Charter of Rights and Freedoms
- Part 2—Rights of the Aboriginal Peoples of Canada
- Part 3—Equalization and Regional Disparities
- Part 4—Constitutional Conferences
- Part 5—Procedure for Amending the Constitution of Canada
- Part 6—Amendment to the Constitution Act, 1867
- Part 7—General

The former BNA Act and orders are still part of the constitution, but the names are changed. The complete acts of the constitution and all new names are listed in a schedule in the Constitution Act 1982.

On the GED Social Studies Test, you may be given questions that include excerpts from the Charter of Rights and Freedoms or another section of the Constitution Act, 1982, as well as some other constitutional document.

PRACTICE

Choose the best answer for each of the questions that come after the following excerpts.

PART VII
GENERAL

52. (1) The Constitution of Canada is the supreme law of Canada, and any law that is inconsistent with the provisions of the Constitution is, to the extent of the inconsistency, of no force or effect.

(2) The Constitution of Canada includes

(*a*) the Canada Act, 1982, including this Act;

(*b*) the Acts and orders referred to in the Schedule; and

(*c*) any amendment to any Act or order referred to in paragraph (*a*) or (*b*).

(3) Amendments to the Constitution of Canada shall be made only in accordance with the authority contained in the Constitution of Canada.

> **TIP**
>
> The constitution of Canada includes the Constitution Act 1867 (formerly the British North America Act), the Constitution Act of 1982, and other statutes and amendments.

1. Based on the excerpt from Part VII of the Constitution Act, 1982, if the Supreme Court found that part of a law violated a section of the Charter of Rights and Freedoms, then
    (1) the whole law would have no force
    (2) the part of the law that violated the Charter would have no force
    (3) the government must resign
    (4) the Charter would be changed
    (5) the Charter would not apply to that law

2. Based on the excerpt, you can conclude that the
    (1) Constitution has not changed since 1867
    (2) Constitution Act, 1982 replaces all former acts
    (3) Constitution can change in the future
    (4) Constitution can only be changed by British Parliament
    (5) Constitution has no force or effect

PART V
PROCEDURE FOR AMENDING THE CONSTITUTION OF CANADA

38. (1) An amendment to the Constitution of Canada may be made by proclamation issued by the Governor General under the Great Seal of Canada where so authorized by
    (*a*) resolutions of the Senate and the House of Commons; and
    (*b*) resolutions of the legislative assemblies of at least two-thirds of the provinces that have, in the aggregate, according to the then latest general census, at least fifty per cent of the population of the provinces.

(2) An amendment made under subsection (1) that derogates from the legislative powers, the proprietary rights or any other rights or privileges of the legislature or government of a province shall require a resolution supported by a majority of the members of each of the Senate, the House of Commons and the legislative assemblies required under subsection (1).

(3) An amendment referred to in subsection (2) shall not have effect in a province the legislative assembly of which has expressed its dissent thereto by resolution supported by a majority of its members prior to the issue of the proclamation to which the amendment relates unless that legislative assembly, subsequently, by resolution supported by a majority of its members, revokes its dissent and authorizes the amendment.

3. Part V of the Constitution Act, 1982, the amending formula, describes the conditions under which changes can be made to the constitution. According to the formula, changes to the constitution require approval of
    (1) House of Commons, Senate, and seven provinces
    (2) Governor General, House of Commons, Senate
    (3) House of Commons, Senate, and seven provinces with at least 50% of Canada's population
    (4) Governor General, House of Commons, Legislatures of all provinces
    (5) House of Commons, Senate, all provinces and territories

4. Under subsection (3), if one province votes against an amendment that takes away from its powers
   (1) the amendment will not pass
   (2) the amendment will apply to all provinces
   (3) the amendment must be passed
   (4) the government of that province must resign
   (5) the amendment will not apply to that province

ANSWERS

1. **(2)** The Constitution is the supreme law of Canada and overrides every other law. The section states that to the *extent of the inconsistency* a conflicting law will have no force or effect.

2. **(3)** The section states that it includes the Constitution Act of Canada, other acts listed in the schedule, and amendments that may be made in the future, so it is possible that it could change.

3. **(3)** The amending formula requires approval of House of Commons, Senate, and Legislatures of two-thirds of the provinces, representing 50% of Canada's population. Ontario and Quebec have more than 50%, so together have veto power.

4. **(5)** The section states the amendment *shall not have effect* in that province until such time as it is passed.

CHALLENGE EXERCISE

Use the Internet to search for the Constitution Act of Canada. Read Part 1: Canadian Charter of Rights and Freedoms. Which rights do you think are most important? Are there any rights you think are not important?

CANADIAN GOVERNMENT

TIP

The government of Canada is based on the British parliamentary system.

The federal government of Canada is a parliamentary system, which means that it is based on the structure of the government in Britain. A parliamentary government has different parts that provide checks and balances to help make sure the legislation passed is given proper consideration.

On the GED Social Studies Test, you will probably not be asked specific questions about the parliamentary system, but you do need to understand how it works to answer questions about Canadian civics and government.

PRACTICE

Choose the best answer for each of the questions that follow this passage.

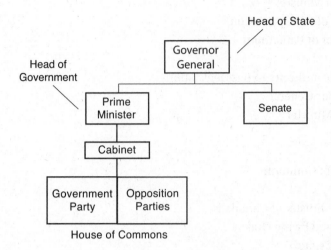

Parliamentary government, based on the British system, has three main parts: Head of State, House of Commons, and the Senate (in Britain, the House of Lords). The Head of State is the official head of the country. In England and Canada, it is the Queen. The Queen is a member of no political party and is neutral in political matters. In Canada, the Governor General is the representative of the Queen. The Head of State in Canada has no governmental authority; however, no legislation can become law until it is signed by the Queen or Governor General.

The House of Commons is composed of Members of Parliament elected from across the country. When the media speaks of parliament, they often mean the House of Commons. This is the part of the federal government that has real political and governing authority. Most representatives in the House of Commons are members of political parties. The political party that wins the most seats forms the government. Elected representatives from the other parties are the opposition, who have the important job of pointing out problems and holding the government accountable. The leader of the winning party is the prime minister, the head of government. The prime minister also selects representatives from the House of Commons to be part of an executive council called the Cabinet. Members of the Cabinet are called ministers, and each is responsible for a government department. Under Canada's representative government, the prime minister and cabinet are responsible to the House of Commons.

The third part of parliamentary government is the Senate. The members of the Senate are not elected. They are appointed by the Governor General, but the choice is made by the Prime Minister. Senators serve for life or until age 75. In theory, the fact they are not elected means they can be impartial. The Senate is known as the *house of second sober thought*. Their job is to point out problems in the bills passed by the House of Commons and send them back if changes are required. The Senate cannot completely stop a bill from being passed. Any bill that is passed three times by the House of Commons must be passed by the Senate. It will also be signed automatically by the Governor General and become law.

1. Which of the following is the representative of the Queen?
   (1) Governor General
   (2) Prime Minister
   (3) Cabinet Minister
   (4) Leader of the Opposition
   (5) Member of Parliament

2. Who has the authority to pass legislation?
   (1) Governor General
   (2) Prime Minister
   (3) Cabinet
   (4) Senate
   (5) House of Commons

3. The Prime Minister of Canada is
   (1) appointed by the Queen
   (2) head of state
   (3) a member of the opposition
   (4) an elected representative
   (5) a member of the Senate

Canada and the United States are both democracies, but their systems of government are very different.

Head of State and Head of Government: In the United States, these are the same person. In Canada, they are different. Although the Queen and Governor General have no governing authority, they do have certain powers (such as the ability to dissolve parliament or to refuse to dissolve parliament) that could be applied in extreme circumstances to prevent abuse of power by a prime minister. The president of the United States has no such counterbalance.

Houses of government: In the United States the two houses of government, Congress and Senate, are both elected. The result is often that one political party has a majority in one house, while another party has a majority in the other. Each concentrates on its own political agenda. The president is also elected directly and may be of a different political party than either chamber. Proponents argue that this results in compromise; however, it can also make it difficult to get things done. In Canada, the Senate is not elected and does not have to follow along party lines. In addition, the Canadian Senate may slow down, but cannot prevent, legislation from being passed.

Separation of powers: The United States has a separation of powers. That is, the president and other members of the executive branch are separate from the legislative bodies. They are not members of Congress (called the House) or the Senate and are not allowed to personally present legislation or answer questions in either chamber. In Canada, there is a concentration of powers. The prime minister and members of Cabinet are also members of the House of Commons. They introduce and explain legislation and answer questions.

Term of office: In the United States, the president serves for a fixed term. Although a president could be impeached for wrong-doing, presidential legislation and actions can be voted down repeatedly and the president will serve out the term. In Canada, the prime minister and cabinet are responsible to the House of Commons as representatives of the people. If legislation introduced by the government is defeated, the government falls and a new election is held. This seldom happens, but might occasionally occur in the case of a budget or other controversial legislation.

4. The head of government in the United States is the
   (1) Prime Minister
   (2) President
   (3) Governor General
   (4) Speaker of the House
   (5) Executive

5. Based on the information in the passage, one might conclude that
   (1) presidents have unlimited power
   (2) the Canadian senate should be elected
   (3) it can be difficult for a president to keep promises
   (4) presidents require a greater degree of accountability than prime ministers
   (5) the Governor General has no power

6. The perspective of the writer of this passage is that the
   (1) Canadian system is better than the American system
   (2) United States is not a true democracy
   (3) American system is superior to the Canadian system
   (4) American system requires reform
   (5) Canadian system requires reform

Canada has three levels of government with different responsibilities and powers.

1. **FEDERAL**—responsible for matters that affect the country as a whole, such as defense, employment, international affairs, and the economy
2. **PROVINCIAL/TERRITORIAL**—responsible for matters that affect the province, such as property and civil rights, hospitals, and schools
3. **MUNICIPAL**—responsible for local matters, such as property zoning, garbage collection, and public transportation

Provincial governments, like the federal government, receive their powers based on the Constitution Act of 1867. In many cases, the powers overlap. For example, the federal government is responsible for transportation among the provinces, such as the TransCanada Highway and railways. Provincial governments are responsible for transportation within the respective provinces.

The structure of provincial governments is similar to the federal government. Each provincial government includes a Lieutenant Governor, a representative of the crown. Like the Governor General, the Lieutenant Governors sign bills into law; however, their role is otherwise largely ceremonial. The provinces do not have a Senate, but only one house, whose members are elected. The elected house has different names in different provinces, including Legislative Assembly, House of Assembly, Provincial Parliament, or National Assembly. The political party that wins the most seats in the legislature governs. Its leader is the premier, who selects other members to form the cabinet.

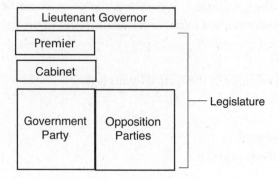

Territorial governments are similar to provincial governments, but have their own distinctions. The territories do not receive their power from the constitution, but from acts of the federal government. Canada's three territories, which make up 40% of the country's landmass but only 3% of the population, were governed for much of their history by the federal government. Over time, however, the federal government has allowed the territories to take on many of the same powers as the provinces.

The legislative assembly of the Yukon Territory is very similar to a provincial government, with the exception that instead of a Lieutenant Governor, there is a Commissioner, who is a representative of the federal government rather than the Queen. Legislatures of the Northwest Territories and Nunavut have a similar structure, but are unique in that they do not have a party system. Both territories employ a form that they call *government by consensus.* Candidates are elected as independents. At the first meeting of the legislature, the first order of business is for the representatives to elect from among their number a speaker of the house, premier, and cabinet. Government by consensus better represents the values of the Aboriginal peoples than an adversarial party system.

7. Based on the information in the passage, which of the levels of government is responsible for city parks.
   (1) Governor General
   (2) Federal
   (3) Provincial
   (4) Municipal
   (5) Federal, provincial, and municipal

8. Which of the following is a difference between provincial and territorial governments?
   (1) Legislative assembly
   (2) Premier
   (3) Cabinet
   (4) Elected members
   (5) Constitutional powers

9. Based on the information in this passage, you can conclude that the Northwest Territories and Nunavut have a
   (1) largely aboriginal population
   (2) small landmass
   (3) large population
   (4) strong sense of independence
   (5) Lieutenant Governor

At each level of government, Canadians vote for the people they want to represent them. Voters in Canada must be Canadian citizens who are at least 18 years of age on election day. They must also be on the voters list. Candidates in an election must meet similar requirements, and must be residents of the area they want to represent.

By law, a federal election must be held at least every five years on the third Monday of October on the fourth calendar year following the previous election. A prime minister may choose to have an election sooner by asking the Governor General to dissolve parliament and call for an election. A federal election could also be required if the government is defeated by a vote of non-confidence, which occurs if parliament votes against an important bill, such as acceptance of the throne speech or a budget. This shows that parliament has lost confidence in the government. Provincial elections must take place at least every five years. Timing of municipal elections varies.

For federal elections, Canada is divided into 338 electoral districts, also called *ridings*. Citizens in each riding elect one person to be their Member of Parliament (MP). Candidates usually run on behalf of political parties, but independent candidates can also run. For provincial elections, each province is divided into different ridings.

In municipal elections, there are no political parties. Voters elect a mayor and councillors to administer the municipality. There are different types of organization for municipal elections. Some municipalities have electoral districts called *wards* that each elect one or more councillors or aldermen. Other municipalities elect councillors at large or a combination of both.

Voting is a right of Canadian citizens, but it is also a responsibility. Democracy only works if all Canadians participate. In the 2011 federal election, only 61% of eligible voters cast a ballot.

House of Commons Seats by Province

Province/Territory	Population Estimate 2011	Electoral Seats
British Columbia	4,573,321	42
Alberta	3,779,353	34
Saskatchewan	1,057,884	14
Manitoba	1,250,574	14
Ontario	13,372,996	121
Quebec	7,979,663	78
New Brunswick	755,455	10
Nova Scotia	945,437	11
Prince Edward Island	145,855	4
Newfoundland & Labrador	510,578	7
Yukon	34,666	1
Northwest Territories	43,675	1
Nunavut	33,322	1
Total	**34,482,779**	**338**

Source: Elections Canada

10. Which of the following would result in a federal election?
    (1) A party serves a four-year term
    (2) The prime minister has a low popularity rating
    (3) The federal budget does not pass a vote
    (4) A financial scandal occurs in the senate
    (5) The government party is defeated in a provincial election

11. Which of the following is elected in a municipal election?
    (1) Mayor
    (2) Prime Minister
    (3) Premier
    (4) Member of parliament
    (5) Member of provincial parliament

12. Based on information in the table, the principle that underlies the distribution of seats in the House of Commons could best be described as
    (1) representation by area
    (2) representation by economic strength
    (3) equal representation
    (4) representation by population
    (5) representation by state

ANSWERS

1. **(1)** The Governor General is the Queen's representative in Canada.
2. **(5)** Only the House of Commons can pass legislation.
3. **(4)** The Prime Minister is also an elected member of the House of Commons.
4. **(2)** The president is both Head of State and Head of Government
5. **(3)** One can conclude that it may be difficult for a president to keep promises because the president is often of a different political party than the Congress and Senate.
6. **(1)** The passage presents perceived weaknesses of the United States system, followed by contrasting benefits of the Canadian system.
7. **(4)** Municipal government is responsible for local matters, such as city parks and recreation.
8. **(5)** Both provincial and territorial governments have legislative assemblies with elected members, premier, and cabinet. Only the provinces derive their powers from the constitution while territories derive theirs from Ottawa.
9. **(1)** The populations of both territories are largely aboriginal, which is reflected in their choice of government by consensus.
10. **(3)** When an important bill, such as the budget, does not pass, it is considered a vote of non-confidence.
11. **(1)** Mayors are part of a municipal government.
12. **(4)** Although there are other considerations, the Canadian system is primarily based on the principle of representation by population as evidenced by the larger number of seats in provinces with a greater population.

CHALLENGE EXERCISE

New Canadians must write a test before becoming citizens. The tests ensure they know about Canadian government and rights and responsibilities of citizens. Materials to prepare for the test are some of the best sources about Canadian civics and government. On the Internet, search for "Discover Canada: The Rights and Responsibilities of Citizenship."

CANADIAN JUSTICE

The Canadian justice system affects every aspect of our daily lives, from employment laws to transport of hazardous material to the criminal code and traffic laws. There are two kinds of law: criminal law (an act against society) and civil law (personal disputes). Both federal and provincial governments have a role in Canadian justice.

Under the constitution, the federal government is the only one with authority to make criminal laws, which are found in various federal acts, such as the *Criminal Code of Canada*, *Controlled Drugs and Substances Act*, and *Competition Act*. However, the constitution gives the provinces responsibility for the administration of justice, so most courts are provincial courts. In addition, the provinces have responsibility for civil and property laws, as well as things like traffic laws and provincial fishing, wildlife, and game laws. Over all the statutes and regulations of every level of government is the constitution, particularly the Charter of Rights and Freedoms, which is the supreme law of the land.

TIP

The government of Canada is responsible for the criminal code and other laws that affect the country as a whole. The provinces have responsibility for civil and property laws and administration of justice.

On the GED Social Studies Test, some topics may include Canadian justice, in particular, extracts from landmark decisions of the Supreme Court. You do not need to know about any specific court cases or law, but a good understanding of how Canadian justice works will help prepare you to answer questions on the test.

PRACTICE

Choose the best answer for each of the questions that pertain to the following passages.

The court system in Canada has four levels. At the lowest level is the provincial or territorial court, which hears less-serious criminal proceedings, traffic offenses, family law cases (except divorce), and cases involving provincial or territorial regulations. Small claims court is also a provincial court. In addition, serious criminal matters appear first in provincial court for a preliminary inquiry before proceeding to the final level of the court system.

The second level is the provincial or territorial *superior* court. These courts are known variously in different provinces as the Court of Queen's Bench, Superior Court, or Provincial Supreme Court. Superior Courts preside over law suits, as well as trials of the more-serious criminal offenses.

If one party in a civil case (law suit) or in a criminal case is dissatisfied with the decision of a provincial or superior court, an appeal can be made to the third level, the provincial court of appeals. The court of appeals is different from the lower-level courts because there is no jury and there is more than one judge. In most cases there are three. The court of appeal does not generally hold trials or hear witnesses. Their job is to review proceedings and hear arguments to determine if an error has been made. They can set aside or overturn a decision or order a new trial. The provincial court of appeal may also hear constitutional questions.

The Supreme Court of Canada is Canada's highest court and the final court of appeal in all areas of Canadian law. Applications to the Supreme Court must first have exhausted all other levels of appeal. The Supreme Court consists of nine judges, including the Chief Justice. The Supreme Court can decide which cases it will hear. Decisions of the court are extremely important for all Canadians. Although government makes laws, it is the courts that decide how the law works.

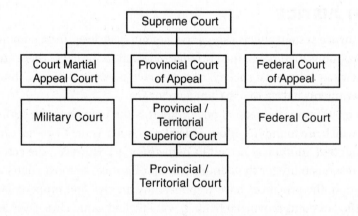

1. One difference between a Provincial Court of Appeal and a Provincial Court is that the Provincial Court of Appeal
   (1) does not hear criminal cases
   (2) does not hear civil cases
   (3) does not have judges
   (4) does not hear arguments
   (5) does not conduct trials

2. Federal Courts are Superior Courts that only hear cases involving matters specifically identified in federal statutes, such as tax violations, copyright laws, or citizenship appeals. To file a Supreme Court appeal to a decision of the Federal Court, an appellant must
   (1) first appeal to the Federal Court of Appeal
   (2) first appeal to Parliament
   (3) first appeal to the Provincial Court of Appeal
   (4) submit a notice of appeal to the Supreme Court
   (5) submit a notice of appeal to the Provincial Court of Appeal

3. A serious criminal proceeding begins first in
   (1) Provincial Court
   (2) Provincial Superior Court
   (3) Provincial Supreme Court
   (4) Provincial Court of Appeal
   (5) Supreme Court

The law can be divided into two broad categories. The first is public offenses, in which a person is accused of an offense against society as specified by the criminal code or other statute. In such cases, the people are represented by the Crown. Criminal cases have names such as *Her Majesty the Queen vs. John Doe*. The second category involves a private dispute between two parties, called a civil case. Government legislation can be a relevant component of civil disputes; however, Canadian law still relies heavily on traditions passed down from our European heritage.

In all provinces and territories except Quebec, common law is the basis for many decisions. The common law originated in Britain hundreds of years ago. It is based on *precedent*, meaning what has been done or decided before. Under common law, when a judge has made a decision and given an explanation in one case, that decision may be referenced in later, similar cases. The precedent will stand unless overruled by a higher court. Over time, common law has evolved into established principles of law.

Civil cases in Quebec follow an entirely different system, guaranteed by the Constitution and in existence since 1866; it is known as the Quebec Civil Code. The civil code has its origins in the Roman Empire, which first collected all laws together in one book. Numerous other countries have followed this example, which also served as the basis for the Napoleonic code, which was the first organization of French law and continues to underlie it today.

4. An example of a precedent is
    (1) a government regulation
    (2) an earlier court decision
    (3) a quote from a Canadian politician
    (4) a federal statute
    (5) a private dispute between two parties

5. A criminal offense in Quebec would be prosecuted under
    (1) the common law
    (2) provincial legislation
    (3) the Criminal Code of Canada
    (4) the Quebec Civil Code
    (5) the Napoleonic Code

6. A trial in which one person sues another for breach of contract is an example of a
    (1) criminal case
    (2) crown prosecution
    (3) public offense
    (4) civil case
    (5) precedent

ANSWERS

1. **(5)** The Provincial Court of Appeals, unlike the lower courts, does not conduct trials.
2. **(1)** Applications to the Supreme Court must first have exhausted all other levels of appeal. The graphic shows that the first level of appeal is the Federal Court of Appeal.
3. **(1)** Serious criminal matters appear first in provincial court for a preliminary inquiry.
4. **(2)** A precedent is a decision that was made before in a similar case.
5. **(3)** Criminal cases are prosecuted under the Criminal Code of Canada or other federal statutes.
6. **(4)** In law, the word *civil* can have two meanings, both used in the passage. It can refer to a private dispute between two parties as described in this question, or to the civil code used in Quebec.

CANADIAN ECONOMY

TIP

The economy refers to the financial activity of a country.

The term *economy* refers to the financial activity of a country, including its production of goods, use of resources, monetary systems, banking, industries and employment, and the distribution of wealth. On the GED Social Studies Test, there may be questions on a wide variety of Canadian and general economy topics, such as consumer spending, banking systems, unemployment, and national debt. The ability to read and understand passages and to interpret information from charts, graphs, and tables will be paramount in your responses to such questions.

PRACTICE

Choose the best answer for each of the questions that pertain to the following passages and graphics:

The law of supply and demand is an economic theory that relates the price of goods to the demand of consumers and the available supply. The idea is that if a product in demand is scarce, people will pay more for it, but as the price increases, fewer people will want to buy it. There are four basic principles:

1. If the demand for a product increases, but the supply stays the same, the price will increase.
2. If the demand for a product decreases, but the supply stays the same, the price will decrease.
3. If the supply of a product decreases, but the demand stays the same, the price will increase.
4. If the supply of a product increases, but the demand stays the same, the price will decrease.

Theoretically, supply will adjust to the point where price and demand intersect.

Supply and Demand

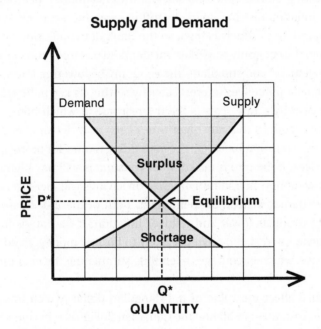

1. Based on information in the graph, you can conclude that
   (1) as price increases, supply decreases
   (2) as price increases, supply increases
   (3) as price increases, demand increases
   (4) as supply decreases, price decreases
   (5) supply and demand are always equal

2. In 1973, the Organization of Petroleum Exporting Countries (OPEC) issued an oil embargo, limiting the supply to the United States and other countries. We can conclude that a probable result of the embargo was
   (1) higher gas prices
   (2) lower gas prices
   (3) lower demand for gas
   (4) higher supply of gas
   (5) an oil surplus

3. Based on information in the passage and graphic, you can conclude that when there is high unemployment
   (1) there is a shortage of workers
   (2) there is greater demand for workers
   (3) labour unions are more likely to go on strike
   (4) people will demand higher wages
   (5) people will work for lower wages

One bank in Canada does not have accounts, mortgages, or credit cards. The Bank of Canada is a crown corporation and its role is to safeguard the economic health of Canada. To do so, it impacts the inflation rate in Canada by influencing interest rates. When the economy is strong, the demand for products is high, so the Bank of Canada slows demand by raising interest rates. When the economy is weaker, the demand for products is lower, so the Bank of Canada increases demand and stimulates the economy by lowering interest rates.

The Bank of Canada influences interest rates by setting its key policy rate, also known as the target for the overnight rate. This is the interest rate at which banks borrow from one another. The bank examines this rate eight times each year. Raising and lowering the rate influences the interest rate that banks charge for lending money for mortgages, car loans, and other lending services. If the rate is raised, then consumers will pay higher interest and are less likely to borrow money. In addition, interest on savings will increase, which encourages consumers to save money instead of spending it. Both of these decrease spending, which brings demand for products lower and reduces inflation. If the rate is lowered, then consumers will pay lower interest and are more likely to borrow money. In addition, interest on savings will decrease, which encourages spending, stimulating the economy and increasing demand.

Interest rates also affect the value of the Canadian dollar, which impacts demand and inflation. When interest rates are higher, the Canadian dollar rises in value. This increases the price of Canadian exports, slowing the economy, while decreasing the cost of imports. By the same reasoning, low interest rates reduce the value of the Canadian dollar, which increases the cost of imports but lowers the cost of exports, which stimulates employment and growth.

Adjusting interest rates to maintain growth and slow inflation is a careful balancing act. The target of the Bank of Canada is to maintain the interest rate at 2%. Since the 2% target was introduced in 1995, the inflation rate in Canada has averaged close to the target.

4. During 2012 and 2013, the Bank of Canada maintained a key policy rate of 1%. This suggests that the economy
   (1) had high inflation
   (2) was in a period of high demand
   (3) was strong
   (4) was slow
   (5) had high interest rates for personal savings

5. When the value of the Canadian dollar is high, it results in
   (1) lower prices for domestic goods
   (2) a 2% inflation rate
   (3) decreases in the cost of Canadian exports
   (4) higher prices for imported goods
   (5) lower prices for imported goods

6. If the inflation rate in Canada were high, the Bank of Canada might respond by
   (1) lowering the key policy rate
   (2) raising the key policy rate
   (3) asking Parliament to set new economic policy
   (4) decreasing mortgage rates
   (5) increasing mortgage rates

Economic indicators are statistics about selected economic activities that suggest trends in the overall health of the economy. Especially during difficult economic times, economists, politicians, and consumers pay close attention to economic indicators for signs of economic recovery. Some important economic indicators that you will hear about on the news include housing starts, unemployment, and consumer price index.

Housing starts show the number of new homes that are being built. A greater number of housing starts indicates consumer confidence through purchasing of new homes. It also indicates employment opportunities in the construction industry and is a good overall indicator of economic activity. Unemployment is another important indicator of economic health. The consumer price index is a measure of inflation, showing the cost of common products that consumers purchase on a regular basis.

7. Which of the following could be an indicator of economic growth?
   (1) High unemployment
   (2) Few new housing starts
   (3) Increase in the consumer price index
   (4) Economists
   (5) Economic indicators

ANSWERS

1. **(2)** Looking at the supply line, you can see that quantity increases with price.

2. **(1)** Limited supply meant that quantity was less than demand, so price increased.

3. **(5)** When there is high unemployment, the supply of labour exceeds the demand. People are willing to work for less money because jobs are hard to find.

4. **(4)** A low interest rate suggests that the Bank of Canada was striving to stimulate a slow economy.

5. **(5)** When the Canadian dollar is high, it is worth more in other countries, which means that imported goods are cheaper.

6. **(2)** If inflation were high, the Bank of Canada would raise interest rates to decrease spending and demand.

7. **(3)** An increase in the consumer price index can indicate an increase in the demand for goods, which shows economic growth.

CANADIAN PRIME MINISTERS

On the GED Social Studies Test, some questions may be about Canadian prime ministers. You do not have to know all the Canadian prime ministers to respond to the questions, but some are more famous than others and learning about any of them will help as you study.

	Term of office 1867–1873 1878–1891	Sir John A. MacDonald	Canada's first prime minister
	Term of Office 1896–1911	Sir Wilfred Laurier	First French Canadian prime minister
	Term of Office 1921–1926 1926–1930 1935–1948	William Lyon Mackenzie King	Prime minister during World War II

	Term of Office 1957–1963	John Diefenbaker	Canada's largest majority, before Brian Mulroney
	Term of Office 1963–1968	Lester B. Pearson	Awarded the Nobel Peace Prize and considered father of United Nations peacekeeping
	Term of Office 1968–1979 1980–1984	Pierre Trudeau	Patriated the Canadian Constitution
	Term of Office 1984–1993	Brian Mulroney	Canada's largest majority, signed the North American Free Trade Agreement (NAFTA), and introduced Goods and Services Tax (GST)
	Term of Office 1993–1993	Kim Campbell	Canada's first female prime minister

Some questions about Canadian prime ministers or politics may include political cartoons. In most instances, you do not need to recognize the prime minister, and questions will involve interpreting clear national or international political or social issues. Other questions may include passages from historic speeches or information about the prime minster or accomplishments.

CHALLENGE EXERCISE

Search the Internet or library to learn about the position of prime minister of Canada. Who is the prime minster of Canada today? What political party does the prime minister represent? What issues or scandals surround the prime minister's term in office? Who is the premier of your province and what political party does he or she represent?

PRACTICE

Choose the best answer for each of the questions that follow the next passages and political cartoons.

1. Based on this art we can conclude that the speech from the throne
   (1) was a turning point in Canadian history
   (2) was not popular with Canadians
   (3) ignored the issue of Senate reform
   (4) focused on environmental issues
   (5) outlined important government reforms

Statement on the introduction of the Official Languages Bill, October 17, 1968
Hon. Mr. TRUDEAU (Prime Minister):

Mr. Speaker:

Many of the bills which are placed before members of this House are concerned with a specific problem, or a single occupation, or one region of the country. The Official Languages Bill is a reflection of the nature of this country as a whole, and of a conscious choice we are making about our future.

Canada is an immense and an exciting country, but it is not an easy country to know. Even under modern conditions, it is a long and expensive trip from St. Johns to Vancouver, or from Windsor to Inuvik. The great differences of geography, history and economics within our country have produced a rich diversity of temperament, viewpoint and culture.

This is easy to state, and it has been repeated in hundreds of patriotic speeches; but without the direct experience which has not been available to most Canadians, it is difficult to appreciate it fully.

The most important example of this diversity is undoubtedly the existence of the two major language groups, both of which are strong enough in numbers and in material and intellectual resources to resist the forces of assimilation. In the past this underlying reality of our country has not been adequately reflected in many of our public institutions.

2. Based on information in the passage, you can conclude that Canada has had two official languages since about
   (1) 1867
   (2) 1968
   (3) 1975
   (4) 1986
   (5) 2001

3. The speaker says that although Canada has a rich diversity, it is difficult for most Canadians to appreciate it fully because of
   (1) the great diversity of temperament, viewpoint, and culture
   (2) the great differences of geography, history, and economics
   (3) the number of people
   (4) two language groups
   (5) the large size of the country

4. The speaker's argument is that
   (1) government services should reflect Canadian diversity
   (2) Canada should have one official language
   (3) Canada is too large
   (4) Canadians are patriotic
   (5) the cost of travel makes it difficult to know all of Canada

CRUSHED!

5. This political cartoon from 1884 shows Prime Minister Sir John A. MacDonald seated at the top. Based on the cartoon, you can conclude that MacDonald's government
   (1) did not care about ordinary people
   (2) was unpopular
   (3) was oppressive
   (4) was a majority that overrode opposition parties in the house
   (5) used illegal means to maintain public support

I welcome you to an historic occasion. For the first time, the majority of the nations of the world will agree to ban a weapon which has been in military use by almost every country in the world. For the first time, a global partnership of governments, international institutions and non-governmental groups has come together—with remarkable speed and spirit—to draft the treaty we will sign today. For the first time, those who fear to walk in their fields, those who cannot till their lands, those who cannot return to their own homes—all because of landmines—once again can begin to hope.

For all of them, for all of us, this is a day we will never forget.

The work of many nations, groups and individuals has brought us to this moment. The International Committee of the Red Cross, whose surgeons have seen too many bodies shattered by landmines, offered early leadership. The International Campaign to Ban Landmines drove the cause with their enthusiasm and commitment. The late Princess of Wales seized the attention of the world when she exposed the human cost of landmines. And Secretary-General Kofi Annan showed courageous leadership. He recognized that the Ottawa process embodied a solemn commitment made by 156 UN members in 1996. A pledge to "pursue vigorously an effective, legally-binding international agreement to ban the use, stockpiling, production, and transfer of anti-personnel landmines."

At the first G-7 Summit I attended as Prime Minister, in Naples in 1994, I raised the Canadian concern over the landmine epidemic. In 1995, our foreign minister, André Ouellet committed Canada to the cause of banning landmines. And in 1996, Lloyd Axworthy brought new energy, commitment and new urgency to world action. He convened a conference in Ottawa because we were not satisfied with what had been done to end the extermination in slow motion caused by landmines.

We knew that it was not good enough to end the landmine epidemic at some distant future date. Not with a hundred million mines planted all over the world. Not with thousands of innocent civilians—men, women and children—dying every year. We knew we had to act. And we did.

At the end of that October conference, on behalf of Canada, Lloyd Axworthy challenged the world to return here just fourteen months later to sign a treaty banning the use, transfer, production and stockpiling of anti-personnel landmines. His challenge marked a breakthrough. A breakthrough that has led directly to this historic moment. Back then, we believed if only a handful of countries came to sign, it would be an achievement. Today and tomorrow, more than 100 countries will sign this treaty.

—The Right Honorable Jean Chrétien, Ottawa, December 3, 1997

6. Based on the information in this passage, who created public awareness of the suffering caused by landmines?
   (1) The late Princess of Wales
   (2) The Secretary-General
   (3) The International Committee of the Red Cross
   (4) The prime minister
   (5) Lloyd Axworthy

7. What great achievement is about to take place?
   (1) Awareness of suffering caused by landmines
   (2) A conference to discuss landmines
   (3) A G-7 Summit
   (4) A fundraising event for anti-landmine campaign
   (5) An international agreement to ban landmines

8. According to the speech, who played a leading role in bringing about the achievement?
   (1) The late Princess of Wales
   (2) The United Nations
   (3) The Government of Canada
   (4) The International Committee of the Red Cross
   (5) The Prime Minister

ANSWERS

1. **(3)** In the graphic, Senate Reform is the big elephant in the room, a figure of speech meaning an issue that is not being properly addressed.

2. **(2)** The Official Languages Act, which formalized Canada's two official languages, was introduced in 1968 and passed in 1969.

3. **(5)** The speaker says Canada is a hard place to know because it is a long and expensive trip from one part to another.

4. **(1)** Trudeau argues that the diversity of our country has not been reflected in public institutions.

5. **(4)** MacDonald is depicted atop a majority government that rolls over the opposition members.

6. **(1)** Chrétien credits the late Princess of Wales, Lady Diana, with seizing the moment to turn the attention of the world to the human cost of land mines.

7. **(5)** More than 100 nations will sign an agreement to ban landmines.

8. **(3)** According to the speech, the Government of Canada played an important role in the treaty, beginning with the prime minister at the G-7 summit and commitment by Foreign Minister Ouellet, and culminating with the challenge by Lloyd Axworthy.

CHAPTER CHECK-UP

Complete these practice exercises, and check the answers and analysis that follow. After you mark your work, review any topic in the chapter that you had trouble with or did not understand.

Questions 1–3 are based on the following information.

The role of Canada's Minister of Finance is an unenviable one. An important member of the cabinet with great influence on financial policy, the minister often bears the blame in the public eye for cutbacks in funding or increases in taxes. Nevertheless, several former Ministers of Finance have gone on the become Prime Minister.

The role of the minister, as the head of the Department of Finance, is to report to Parliament on economic matters, such as the activities of the Bank of Canada, the state of the Canada Pension Plan, and updates about petroleum and gas taxes. One of the most important functions of the Minister of Finance is the preparation and delivery of the annual budget, which reviews the government's income and expenditures and makes projections for the coming year, including expected revenues, expenses, tax changes, and debt level.

One interesting Canadian tradition is that the Minister of Finance usually wears a new pair of shoes when delivering the budget speech. Although this is a fairly recent tradition, no one really knows who began it or what it signifies.

1. The passage indicates that the Minister of Finance often wears new shoes to deliver the budget speech because
    (1) it is a tradition
    (2) it is an important function
    (3) it represents prosperity
    (4) he or she hopes to become prime minister
    (5) British ministers of finance do the same

2. The role of the Minister of Finance is unenviable because he or she
    (1) will never become prime minister
    (2) has little influence
    (3) must prepare the budget
    (4) is blamed for unpopular financial decisions
    (5) must report to Parliament

3. The Minister of Finance is responsible to Parliament to provide information about all of the following EXCEPT
    (1) government expenditures
    (2) revenues
    (3) national debt
    (4) foreign affairs
    (5) changing interest rates

Questions 4 and 5 are based on the following passage.

If the only thing that mattered in the relations between the people and the government was the possession of power, the government would, of course, be free to do as it pleases. That is what obtains under a dictatorship. No account is taken of the will of the people. It is on that principle that the Nazi, Italian and Japanese dictators are acting today. Under democratic government, however, quite as important as the possession of power is its exercise in accordance with the will of the people.

When those who hold representative and responsible positions have given a definite promise to the people, they have created an obligation to act in accordance with that promise, until the people are again consulted. Such an obligation may not be binding according to law, but as an obligation it is no less sacred.

There are those, I know, who make light of what they call "political promises." It will, I think, be generally agreed that a political platform or programme is one thing; a definite and concrete promise or pledge is quite another. Because of circumstances, a government may, without breaking faith, fail to carry out, to the letter, its full programme. No change in circumstances could, however, justify a government in ignoring a specific pledge to the people, unless it was clear that the safety of the nation was immediately involved, and there was no possibility of consulting the people.

—The Right Honourable William Lyon Mackenzie King
Address on the National Security Plebiscite, April 7, 1942

4. In the first paragraph, the speaker describes
    (1) the difference between Canada and its enemies
    (2) the constitution of Canada
    (3) Canada's obligations to its allies
    (4) the importance of possessing power
    (5) the ability of government to do as it pleases

5. The speaker's purpose in this quotation is to explain
    (1) problems with other nations
    (2) the importance of democracy
    (3) why governments must keep their promises
    (4) the will of the people
    (5) government's legal obligations

6. According to King, the government cannot be blamed for
    (1) breaking a specific promise
    (2) failing to carry out its full program
    (3) not consulting the people
    (4) not keeping political promises
    (5) doing as it pleases

Questions 7 and 8 are based on the following information.

In 2003–2004 in Ontario, taxation revenues comprised the largest category of revenue for the provincial government. Of the $69.5 billion in Provincial revenue expected in 2003–2004, $49.9 billion or about 72% was expected to be derived from taxation revenue. Three revenue sources within this category—Personal Income Tax, Retail Sales Tax, and Corporations Tax—account for 58% of total revenue. The Province also collected a number of other taxes such as Gasoline and Fuel Taxes, Tobacco Tax, Employer Health Tax, and Land Transfer Tax. However, the government also had many expenses and was expected to have a total deficit in excess of $5.6 billion.

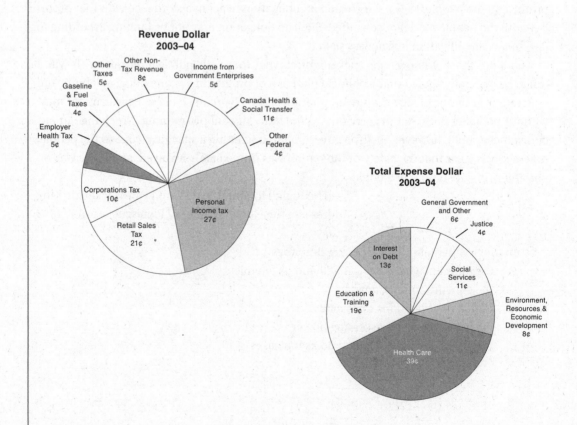

7. Which of the following was Ontario's greatest source of non-tax revenue from 2003–2004?
   (1) Personal Income Tax
   (2) Retail Sales Tax
   (3) Gasoline and Fuel Taxes
   (4) Income from Government Enterprises
   (5) Health and Social Transfers

8. Which of the following provided Ontario with the least amount of revenue from 2003-2004?
   (1) Personal Income Tax
   (2) Retail Sales Tax
   (3) Gasoline and Fuel Taxes
   (4) Income from Government Enterprises
   (5) Health and Social Transfers

9. The largest amount of the provincial income is expended on
   (1) Education and training
   (2) Social services
   (3) Interest on debt
   (4) Health care
   (5) Justice

10. The attitude of the cartoon towards Prime Minister Harper and U.S. President Obama is
    (1) critical of environmental policy
    (2) critical of close relationship
    (3) critical of complaints by environmentalists
    (4) supportive of environmental policy
    (5) supportive of continued clean energy negotiation

ANSWERS

1. **(1)** The last paragraph of the passage states clearly that the practice of wearing new shoes to deliver the budget speech is an interesting Canadian tradition.

2. **(4)** The first paragraph relates that the Minister of Finance often bears the blame for unpopular cutbacks or tax increases.

3. **(4)** In the second paragraph, you learn that the Minister of Finance prepares budget reports on financial issues, but no mention is made of foreign affairs, which would be under a different department and minister.

4. **(1)** The first paragraph describes the difference between a democratic government, such as Canada's, which considers the will of the people, and a dictatorship that does as it pleases. The nations mentioned were Canada's enemies at the time of this speech, during World War II.

5. **(3)** The purpose of the quotation is to explain why governments should keep their promises.

6. **(2)** According to King, the government cannot be blamed if changing circumstances mean that it cannot carry out its full platform, but it is obligated to keep specific promises.

7. **(5)** Transfers from the federal government for health and social services were the largest source of non-tax income at 11%.

8. **(3)** Gasoline and fuel taxes provided the least amount of income, listed at 4%.

9. **(4)** Health care accounts for thirty-nine cents of every dollar, by far the largest expenditure.

10. **(1)** The cartoon criticizes Obama and Harper, who are depicted atop piles of dirty energy sources.

Canada and the 20th Century

19

THINK ABOUT IT

In 1900, Canada was a young country of five million people, and had expanded to stretch from sea to sea to sea. It had recently completed a national railroad. Although a sovereign dominion, the constitution was an act of British Parliament, which still controlled foreign affairs, and Canada had little or no international presence.

By the year 2000, Canada, with a population of 30 million, had gained one of the highest standards of living and strongest economies in the world. A completely independent country with our own constitution, Canada is internationally respected for diplomacy, peacekeeping, and international affairs. The twentieth century was the time when Canada came into its own.

IN THIS CHAPTER

On the GED Social Studies Test, there may be questions involving the events of the 20th century. Canada was involved in and affected by the same international events as other nations, events that have shaped today's world. Canada fought in both world wars, suffered during the Great Depression, and experienced the Cold War. Canada was one of the founding countries of the United Nations, championed human rights, and was instrumental in establishing United Nations Peacekeeping.

After completing this chapter, you will be able to

→ **RESPOND TO QUESTIONS ABOUT CANADA AT WAR**

→ **IDENTIFY THE IMPACT OF THE GREAT DEPRESSION ON THE CANADIAN ECONOMY**

→ **DESCRIBE CHARACTERISTICS OF OTHER POLITICAL SYSTEMS**

→ **DEFINE THE COLD WAR**

→ **IDENTIFY PAST AND PRESENT ISSUES OF CANADIAN UNITY**

TIP

Questions may include newspaper articles, maps, charts, photographs, or other types of information about wars of the 20th century.

CANADA AT WAR

In the 20th century, Canada participated in two world wars, as well as several other military conflicts, and participated in United Nations Peacekeeping activities. Canadians can truly be proud of the men and women of our armed forces who have given and sacrificed so much in the cause of peace.

WORLD WAR I (1914–1918)—A result of military buildup and complex alliances, the war began when Austria-Hungary invaded Serbia in retaliation for the assassination of the heir to the throne, Archduke Ferdinand. Although centred in Europe, the conflict drew in other countries from around the world. Participants were in two opposing alliances. The Allies included Britain, France, Russia, Canada, the United States, and many other countries. The Central Powers included Austria-Hungary, Germany, the Ottoman Empire (Turkey), as well as others. Early in the conflict, advances of the Central Powers were stopped and both sides dug many kilometres of trenches to protect their territory. The next four years were a slow, costly process of trench warfare in which thousands of men lost their lives to advance only a few hundred metres. In total, seventy million men were involved in the war, including 625,000 Canadians, which was a huge number for a country of only eight million people. More than nine million combatants died, of which 67,000 were Canadian; another 173,000 Canadian soldiers were injured.

WORLD WAR II (1939–1945)—The war began in 1939 when Nazi Germany, under leader Adolf Hitler, invaded Poland. Spanning Europe, Asia, the South Pacific, and Northern Africa, the conflict involved all of the world's major powers and more than 100 million soldiers. Participants were in two opposing alliances. The Allies were Britain, France, Canada, Russia, the United States, and many others. The Axis powers included primarily Germany, Italy, and Japan. This war was different from all of those that preceded it because of the influence of technology. Tanks and airplanes, which were now capable of carrying bombs and travelling great distances, changed the face of war. The German strategy of blitz-krieg—rapid offensives through the quick movement of troops, tanks, and planes—was a revolution in warfare that soon had much of Europe within the Nazi grasp. No one knows exactly how many people were killed, but estimates range between 60 and 85 million. This included approximately 25 million soldiers and 40 to 55 million civilians, including 6 million Jews exterminated in Nazi death camps. More than one million Canadians fought in World War II. Approximately 45,000 Canadian soldiers were killed and 98,000 injured.

KOREAN CONFLICT (1950–1953)—At the end of World War II, the Korean Peninsula, previously conquered by Japan, was divided between the Soviet Union (Russia) in the north and the United States in the south. The north established a communist government, supported by Russia and China. The south established a democratic government, supported by the United States and the United Nations. Conflict between north and south erupted into war in 1950 when North Korea unexpectedly invaded. With authorization from the United Nations, an alliance of sixteen democratic countries, including the United States and Canada, sent troops to support South Korea. North Korea was supported by Chinese troops. More than 27,000 Canadians fought in the Korean Conflict. 516 were killed and 1500 injured.

GULF WAR 1 (1990–1991)—The Persian Gulf War was a result of tensions between the Middle Eastern countries of Iraq and Kuwait. Iraq had long believed that Kuwait, one of the richest countries in the world, should be part of Iraq and that their oil field was part of the Iraqi oil field. In 1990, Iraq invaded and took control of (annexed) Kuwait. A coalition of 35 United Nations countries, led by the United States, responded with military force. This war was different from those that had gone before because it consisted of massive air strikes, followed by movement of tanks and men. No Canadians were killed in the Gulf War.

Questions about world conflicts on the GED Social Studies Test will usually be about the conflicts in general, not just Canada's role. Understanding Canada's role, however, is a good way to learn about the conflicts. Questions about wars might include newspaper articles, maps, charts, photographs, or other types of information.

PRACTICE

Choose the best answer for each of the questions that come after the following passage.

Canadian soldiers at Vimy Ridge.

The Battle of Vimy Ridge, during the conflict known as The Great War, is considered a turning point in Canada's history as a nation. The ridge was a seven-kilometre stretch of high ground in France that was held by the Central Powers and overlooked Allied lines. Previous attempts to dislodge the German troops emplaced there had been repulsed with heavy casualties. A plan was made in which Canadian troops would storm the ridge. This would be the first time that all four Canadian divisions would fight together.

There were months of careful planning. The Canadian soldiers were each trained with specialties as machine gunners, grenade throwers, and riflemen. Mining engineers dug tunnels towards the ridge to get troops safely to their starting points. A devastating artillery barrage by more than a thousand guns would cover their advance.

On April 9, 1917, at 5:30 a.m., the Canadian divisions began their advance. Moving upward through mud and climbing through trenches and shell holes in the face of heavy machine gun fire, the Canadians continued. By noon of the first day, much of the ridge had been taken and by the following day, it lay entirely in Canadian control.

Not only careful planning, but also the bravery and determination of the Canadian force secured the victory. Four soldiers were awarded the Victoria Cross for acts of individual bravery, such as single-handed charges against machine gun emplacements. Of these heroes, only one survived the war. More than one hundred thousand Canadians fought at Vimy Ridge. More than 3,500 were killed and 7,000 injured.

The success of Vimy Ridge was one of the greatest victories of the war. It also established a sense of national pride among Canadians at home and established Canada's reputation during the war as an elite military force. In 1922, the government of France gave Vimy Ridge to Canada as thanks for Canadian soldiers killed in France. It is now the site of the Canadian Vimy Ridge Memorial.

1. The Battle of Vimy Ridge took place in
    (1) France
    (2) Germany
    (3) Canada
    (4) Great Britain
    (5) United States

2. Based on the passage and photograph, you can conclude that Canadian forces advanced
    (1) under cover of night
    (2) through a wooded area
    (3) hidden from sight by trenches and shell holes
    (4) in the open over rough terrain
    (5) in tanks and motorized vehicles

3. According to the passage, which of the following is a result of the Battle of Vimy Ridge?
    (1) Victory over Germany
    (2) Crossroads in Canada's development as a nation
    (3) End of the War
    (4) Freedom for the French
    (5) Defeat of Allied forces

4. The Battle of Vimy Ridge was a part of
    (1) the Korean conflict
    (2) the Gulf War
    (3) the Crimean War
    (4) World War I
    (5) World War II

In the early years of the Second World War, the Axis powers moved swiftly. Japan had captured much of Asia, including large parts of China and the Korean Peninsula. In Europe, Germany and Italy controlled most of the continent, as well as northwest Africa. Canada continued to send troops to support the war effort and, more importantly, sent convoys of ships carrying supplies to England.

As in the early years of World War I, the United States preserved a policy of isolationism. While President Franklin Delano Roosevelt quietly supported the allied war effort, believing that the United States would ultimately be drawn in, the American people believed it was a European war and wished to remain apart from the political and military conflict.

On December 7, 1941, Japan launched a surprise attack against the United States Naval Base at Pearl Harbor, Hawaii. The attack killed more than 2,100 U.S. servicemen, sank 21 ships, and destroyed 180 airplanes. The American people were so outraged by the attack that they abandoned the policy of isolationism and declared war on Japan on December 8. America was now embroiled in World War II, and its economic power and military might helped turn the course of the war.

5. Based on the information in the passage, *isolationism* means a policy of
    (1) remaining separate from conflict in Europe
    (2) selling to both sides in a military conflict
    (3) remaining apart from the affairs of others
    (4) avoiding war unless attacked
    (5) not engaging in trade with other countries

6. Based on the information in the passage, which of the following countries was not among the Allies prior to the attack on Pearl Harbor?
    (1) United States
    (2) England
    (3) Canada
    (4) Australia
    (5) South Africa

7. Based on information in the passage, which of the following was a European Axis power?
    (1) England
    (2) Italy
    (3) China
    (4) Canada
    (5) Japan

ANSWERS

1. **(1)** The passage states that Vimy Ridge is in France and that it was later given to Canada by the French government.

2. **(4)** In the photograph there is no cover and the terrain is muddy, with barbed wire, shell holes, and rough ground.

3. **(2)** Although an important battle, it was not the end of the war. The passage states that it was a turning point in Canada's history as a nation and established the reputation of Canadian troops and a sense of national pride.

4. **(4)** The battle took place in 1917 and involved the Allies and Central Powers, including Germany, which shows it was World War 1.

5. **(3)** Isolationism is a political policy of remaining apart from the affairs of other nations.

6. **(1)** The United States did not enter the war until the day after the attack.

7. **(2)** Italy and Japan were both Axis powers, but Japan is located in Asia as suggested in the passage.

CHALLENGE EXERCISE

What was D-day and what role did Canada play? Use the Internet to research the topic.

THE GREAT DEPRESSION

The First World War was followed by a period known as the *Roaring Twenties* in Canada, the United States, and the United Kingdom (Britain). It was a time of economic prosperity. People spent lavishly. There were automobiles, movies with sound, telephones, and electricity. Free from the horrors of war, people celebrated life. There was huge industrial growth and demand for consumer goods. It was an age of jazz, parties, and a dance called the Charleston.

In 1929, the stock market crashed as stock prices plummeted. Although the market recovered somewhat, people had lost confidence in the economy. They saved their money instead of spending. Sudden decline in demand for goods and services led to lowering prices and unemployment. This period, known as the Great Depression, was a worldwide economic collapse that extended for ten years until the start of the Second World War. It was a period of massive unemployment, low prices, and business collapse. Many people lost their homes and farms. It is a time remembered by images of homeless men travelling by way of railroad boxcars from place to place in search of work, hoping to send any earnings home to families they could no longer support. Canada was one of many countries that suffered under the Great Depression.

TIP

The Great Depression was a worldwide economic collapse from 1929 to the start of World War II.

PRACTICE

Choose the best answer for each of the questions that follow the next passages and images.

1. The men in this photograph from the Great Depression are probably
   (1) protesting low wages
   (2) unemployed
   (3) lobbying for better working conditions
   (4) protesting discrimination against immigrants
   (5) demanding solutions to the problem of homeless people

The Great Depression was felt all across Canada, but the Prairie Provinces suffered particular hardship. Despite record wheat harvests in Canada, demand for exports of wheat were low and prices plunged. Farmers began stockpiling wheat in hopes that prices would improve, but competing exports from other countries maintained a surplus on the world market. Demand remained low and prices plummeted to less than a third of their former value. However, many farmers had incurred debt, during the prosperity of the 1920s, for land, equipment, and better homes—debts they could no longer pay.

On top of the crash of world prices came a savage drought. In 1931, there was little rain, only roaring wind. 1936 and 1937 were among the hottest and driest summers on record, again with little rain and high winds. Without crops to anchor it, topsoil that had been over-worked by years of poor farming practices, simply blew away. Unable to grow crops, earn a living, or pay their debt, many farmers simply gave up. Thousands of family farms were abandoned.

2. Based on information in this passage, the prairies were hard hit by the depression because of
   (1) poor harvests
   (2) worldwide wheat surplus
   (3) flood
   (4) stock market crash
   (5) political interference

3. Which of the following actions could reduce the likelihood of the same situation happening again?
   (1) Stockpiling wheat supplies
   (2) Reducing wheat production
   (3) Increasing wheat production
   (4) Improved weather services
   (5) Diversification of crops

4. This is a photograph of a "Bennett Buggy," named for Prime Minister R.B. Bennett who served from 1930 to 1935. The photo depicts
   (1) transportation for people who cannot afford gas
   (2) farmers abandoning their homes
   (3) plowing the fields
   (4) early eco-conscious car
   (5) typical country life on the prairies

5. The name the Bennett Buggy shows that people
   (1) respected the Canadian prime minister
   (2) hoped for financial relief from the prime minister
   (3) respected a traditional way of life
   (4) blamed the government for financial problems
   (5) blamed the United States for financial problems

ANSWERS

1. **(2)** During the Great Depression, there was high unemployment. The sign in the picture shows the men want to live in one place, not wander to look for jobs.

2. **(2)** According to the passage there was a surplus on the world market that led to low prices.

3. **(5)** By diversifying crops, farmers would be less subject to falling prices for one crop.

4. **(1)** Because the horses are attached to a car during the Great Depression, it is logical to assume that the drivers could not afford gas.

5. **(4)** By naming the vehicle for the prime minister, people showed their displeasure with the government. Bennett Buggies were common on the Canadian prairies during the Depression.

POLITICAL SYSTEMS

There are as many different political systems as there are countries. Every nation is a little different. There are also many terms to describe different types of government. Canada, for example, is a monarchy. We have a Queen. We are also a representative democracy, a nation with elected representatives. We could, perhaps, best be described as a constitutional monarchy, a form of government with a monarch who acts as head of state within a constitution that includes an elected parliament.

Some other terms to describe political systems include dictatorship, junta, theocracy, and socialism. A dictatorship is a rule by one person. There are still many dictatorships in the world, such as North Korea. In a dictatorship, even if there is a house of government, one person really holds all the power. A junta (pronounced *hoonta*) is a government by a small group of military leaders, which usually follows a military overthrow of the government.

Theocracy is a rule by religious leaders. In the present day, Islamic states are the most likely to include religious influence in government. Iran is currently the only true theocracy, with an Islamic head of state who wields more power than the elected president.

Socialism is a system, somewhat related to communism, in which the means of production and distribution of goods is owned by the government so that wealth is shared or more evenly distributed. Many industrialized countries and political parties include some socialist policies. For example, unemployment insurance, Medicare, and welfare all represent socialist values.

Imperialism refers to a conglomerate in which one country conquers and rules others. A good example is the Roman Empire. Rome conquered and ruled many other countries. They maintained governors and a military presence in subjected lands that were all bound to the policies of Rome. Colonialism is a similar term, in which a country establishes settlements in ungoverned lands. The Canadian provinces, for example, were once colonies of Britain.

During the 20th century, democracy, communism, and fascism were political systems that had the greatest influence on world events. Capitalism is also a term used to describe countries such as Canada and the United States. This is primarily an economic term to describe a country in which businesses are run by private owners to achieve a profit, rather than being owned by the government, but democracies are also capitalist societies.

TIP

Democracy, communism, and fascism had a great influence on the 20th century.

On the GED Social Studies Test, you may or may not be asked specific questions about political systems; however, you do need a basic knowledge of political systems to understand some of the topics on the test.

PRACTICE

Choose the best answer for each of the questions that follow the table and passages.

	Democracy	Communism	Fascism
Definition	A system of government in which all eligible citizens have an equal voice	A system of government in which all citizens contribute according to their ability and receive according to their need	A system in which all citizens submit themselves to the greater good of the state and/or race.
Government	Participatory, usually through elected representatives who can be removed, at the will of the people, in the next election	In theory, there is no leader or government. People work together for the common good. In practice, there is a one-party system with one leader who wields dictatorial power	One supreme dictator who is often synonymous with the state
Philosophy	Every individual is created equal and has equal right to participate in the decisions of the state	All individuals should share equally in wealth and no one is better or should have more than anyone else	The state is glorious and the efforts of all citizens should serve the state
Economic system	Capitalism, including private ownership of businesses and corporations that operate for the purpose of earning profit	The economy is controlled by the state and everyone has an equal share	Businesses are privately owned, but follow the direction of the state
Private property	Encouraged	None	Permitted
International view	Generally encourages democracy and capitalism in other countries to promote international trade	International movement that seeks to spread communism to other countries	Other nations are not important except as they can benefit or be conquered by the state
Examples	Canada, Britain, United States	Former Soviet Russia (USSR Union of Soviet Socialist Republics), China, Cuba	Nazi Germany, WW2 Italy under Mussolini

1. Based on the information in the table, which of the following statements is best representative of fascism?
   (1) The empire that will last for 1,000 years.
   (2) Government is by the people and for the people.
   (3) Workers of the world, throw off your chains.
   (4) Everyone should share equally in the wealth of the nation.
   (5) God save the Queen.

2. Based on the information in the table, which of the following statements is best representative of democracy?
   (1) The state is the absolute. Individuals and groups are relative.
   (2) All within the state, nothing outside the state, nothing against the state.
   (3) The truth is that people are tired of liberty.
   (4) One person, one vote.
   (5) Inactivity is death.

3. Based on the information in the table, which of the following statements is best representative of communism?
   (1) Profit is king.
   (2) Abolish all private property.
   (3) Government is subject to the will of the people.
   (4) Elections belong to the people.
   (5) Government is where 51% of the people take away the rights of the other 49%.

Politicians, policies, and political parties are often described as *left-wing*, *right-wing*, or *moderate*. What is meant by these terms? As with everything, the terms are relative and often depend on the perspective of the critic. Furthermore, many individuals and parties support some policies that come from both sides of the political spectrum. In addition, there are different degrees of the left and right political spectrum.

From an economic perspective, left-wing parties traditionally support taxation and government spending to support social programs and re-distribute wealth. They support labour unions, industry regulation, and government programs to create work. Their philosophy of personal taxation involves higher tax rates for higher incomes, redistributing the wealth from rich to poor. In terms of social policy, left-wing is traditionally associated with progressive values and supports criminal rehabilitation, pro-choice, gay rights, and gun control.

Right-wing economic policy traditionally favours lower taxes, smaller government, and economic restraint. They support corporate interests, minimal regulation, and allowing lower taxes to stimulate economic growth and create jobs. Their policy of personal taxation favours a common tax rate for everyone, regardless of income. Right-wing social policy focuses on traditional values. It is typically tough on crime, pro-life, in favour of traditional family values, and anti-gun control.

The terms *centrist* or *moderate* are used to describe individuals, parties, or policies. The terms refer to the middle of the political spectrum, neither far-left nor far-right. What constitutes moderate, however, changes as society changes and depends on personal perspective.

4. Which of the following ideologies would be to the furthest left of the political spectrum?
   (1) Fascism
   (2) Monarchy
   (3) Democracy
   (4) Dictatorship
   (5) Communism

5. Which of the following is most likely to be a right-wing policy?
   (1) Increased sales taxes
   (2) Gun registry
   (3) Balanced budget
   (4) Medicare
   (5) Wealthy people should pay more

ANSWERS

1. **(1)** Fascism glorifies the state.
2. **(4)** The other answers are based on sayings of fascist leader Benito Mussolini.
3. **(2)** Under communism, everybody owns everything and there is no private property. The remaining choices are all based on statements about democracy.
4. **(5)** Communism is to the extreme left of the political spectrum. We know this from the passage by its description of the left as supporting redistribution of wealth. Fascism is to the extreme right.
5. **(3)** All of the others would be left-wing policies. Right-wing is described as favouring lower taxes, smaller government, and economic restraint. Although it is not stated in the passage, left-wing supporters typically see no problem with government debt or spending, which may produce social or economic benefit.

THE COLD WAR

Today, much is said about the pressures people face, especially youth. We live in a world of rapidly changing technology and social change. However, the pressures of today are no greater than those of the second half of the 20th century, when people lived with constant awareness of the possibility of nuclear destruction of the world.

The Cold War refers to a period that lasted from 1945, at the end of World War II, until 1989. It was a time of tension between the democratic countries of the North Atlantic Treaty Organisation (NATO), led by the United States, and the communist countries of the Warsaw Pact, led by the Soviet Union (USSR). The two sides did not come to direct war, although they fought a war of propaganda and political influence. The world became divided into two armed camps with thousands of nuclear missiles on each side aimed at the other, capable of destroying all life on earth several times over. Fortunately, China, the most populous communist country in the world, was not an ally of the Soviet Union and so an uneasy balance of power was maintained.

Flags of the United States and Soviet Union

PRACTICE

Choose the best answer for each of the questions that follow the passage:

Following the Bolshevik revolution of 1917 and the subsequent civil war in Russia, the revolutionaries gained control of the country and formed its first communist government. The victorious Red Army assisted communists in other countries of the former Russian Empire to seize control of their governments. Soon these countries were combined to form one gigantic country, the Union of Soviet Socialist Republics, under the rule of the communist Russian government in Moscow.

In 1939, at the start of the Second World War, Russian leader Joseph Stalin signed a non-aggression pact with Nazi Germany, keeping the Soviet Union out of the war. In 1941, however, the Germans launched a surprise invasion. German troops advanced rapidly into Russia, pushing back the poorly equipped and poorly trained Soviet troops until the coming of winter. In the face of long supply lines and the harsh Russian winter, the Germans were pushed back. Soviet troops drove the Germans back into Europe, occupying countries that had formerly been conquered by Germany and now fell under communist control.

By the end of the Second World War, the Soviet Union had expanded its borders and established communist governments in liberated countries. With the war ended, the Soviet Union retained the territories it had taken. Theoretically independent nations, the eight communist Eastern Bloc countries remained under the control of Moscow. In 1955, the countries were joined in a mutual defense treaty called the Warsaw Pact, under the leadership and direction of the USSR. The Warsaw Pact was a response to the North Atlantic Treaty Organisation (NATO), led by the United States, which was established for common defense against the advance of communism.

EASTERN BLOC AREA
BORDER CHANGES
1938 TO 1948

USSR 1938

Annexed or
Expanded SSRs

Satellite States

New Satellite
State Land

— 1938 Borders
— New Borders

1. The Bolsheviks were
   (1) Polish
   (2) German
   (3) democratic
   (4) communist
   (5) Czarist

2. Based on information in this passage, the non-aggression pact meant
   (1) Soviet Union would not resist German attack
   (2) Germany and Soviet Union would not attack one another
   (3) Soviet Union would allow Germany to attack Europe
   (4) Soviet Union and Germany would attack NATO
   (5) Germany would not attack the Soviet Union

3. Which of the following was a satellite state of the Soviet Union?
   (1) Poland
   (2) Latvia
   (3) United States
   (4) Russia
   (5) Nazi Germany

The North Atlantic Treaty Organisation (NATO), is an alliance of military cooperation and mutual defense that was established in 1949 by 12 founding nations, including the United States, Canada, England, and France. The organization was originally established to serve three primary purposes. First, NATO would discourage Soviet expansion in Europe and ensure the security of democratic nations. Second, the organization would prevent a resurgence of the national military fervour of fascism in Europe. Finally, the nations of Europe were devastated in the aftermath of the war. Nearly 20 million civilians had died in addition to 17 million soldiers. Whole cities had been bombed into oblivion and governments and the economies were in ruins. NATO would assist in the political reintegration of the redeveloping countries into the world scene.

Over the years, NATO's role has changed several times in response to world events and the number of member nations has grown. Since the end of the Cold War, fall of the Berlin Wall, and disintegration of Russian communism and the Soviet Union, several former East Bloc communist countries including Poland, Hungary, and the Czech Republic have joined NATO. In the contemporary post-9-11 era, the role of NATO has again changed, protecting the security of member nations through peacekeeping, combatting terror, and guarding the freedom of individuals around the world from violent extremism, sometimes even from their own governments.

4. Member countries of NATO have which form of government?
   (1) Dictatorship
   (2) Communist
   (3) Democratic
   (4) Terrorist
   (5) Fascist

5. NATO is primarily a
   (1) military alliance
   (2) political alliance
   (3) economic alliance
   (4) civilian organization
   (5) soviet

ANSWERS

1. **(4)** The Bolsheviks were the Russian Social Democratic (communist) Party.
2. **(2)** Germany and the Soviet Union would not attack one another.
3. **(1)** On the map, Poland is indicated as one of the satellite countries.
4. **(3)** Twelve democratic countries established NATO, primarily to resist expansion of the communist Soviet Union.
5. **(1)** Although it also has political implications, NATO is primarily a military alliance, whose very presence deterred Soviet expansion in the 20th century.

CHALLENGE EXERCISE

Use the Internet to search for information about the Berlin Wall. What was it? Who built it and why? What did it mean when the wall was torn down?

TIP

Possible
separation of
Quebec has
been a recurring
issue of national
unity.

CANADIAN UNITY

Throughout Canada's history, there have been movements for separation in different Canadian provinces. From the Anti-Confederation Party of Nova Scotia in 1867 to the Alberta First Party today, there have been those who want their province to separate from the rest of Canada. The strongest secessionist feelings, however, have always been in Quebec with its unique language, culture, and history.

PRACTICE

Choose the best answer for each of the questions that follow the next passage.

Quebec has always considered itself sovereign and distinct from the rest of the country. The provincial legislature, for example, is called the National Assembly. Quebec license plates have the saying "Je me souviens" (I will remember), which means that French Quebecers will never forget their unique language, culture, and heritage. Quebec has always had a unique place in confederation with more control over taxation, immigration, and other areas than the rest of the provinces, and it remains the only one that has not ratified the Constitution Act.

In 1970, the FLQ Crisis took place in Quebec. A group called the Front de liberation du Quebec kidnapped two political prisoners, Quebec Minister of Labour Pierre Laporte and British Trade Commissioner James Cross in Montreal, murdering Laporte and holding Cross for more than 60 days, while demanding complete independence for Quebec. In response to the crisis, the government of Quebec requested intervention of the federal government. Prime Minister Pierre Trudeau activated the War Measures Act in response, which gave the federal government broad powers to maintain security and order, the only time the act was ever activated during peacetime.

In the province of Quebec, people were horrified by the kidnapping and murder. The FLQ crisis took away any support in the province for violent revolution; however, it did not dampen the aspiration for independence. In 1976, the Parti Québécois under René Lévesque won the provincial election on a platform of separation from Canada. In 1980, a referendum was held to ask the people if they wanted to separate from Canada, but the proposal was defeated by 60% of the voters. In 1995, a second referendum was held. Again, the proposal was defeated, but this time the result was much closer.

Today, national unity remains an issue. There is still a strong sense of national pride and independence among the French in Quebec. The focus of political attention for most people, however, is issues that are common to all Canadians, such as jobs and the economy.

1. Based on information in the passage, you can conclude that the FLQ crisis was considered a(n)
   (1) act of civil disobedience
   (2) political crisis
   (3) popular political movement
   (4) terrorist threat
   (5) foreign invasion

2. Based on information in the passage, you can conclude that the majority of Quebecers
   (1) did not support Quebec independence
   (2) do not speak French as a first language
   (3) supported the FLQ
   (4) do not consider Quebec distinct
   (5) want the federal government to solve their problems

3. Premier René Lévesque could be described as a
   (1) Separatist
   (2) Terrorist
   (3) Federalist
   (4) Monarchist
   (5) Soldier

The Meech Lake Accord was a set of constitutional amendments agreed upon by the federal and provincial governments on 30 April 1987. It would have granted the provinces greater control over immigration and Supreme Court appointments, a veto over constitutional changes, and increased control over federal spending in areas of provincial jurisdiction, such as education and health care. It would also have recognized Quebec as a distinct society within Canada. The Accord had to be approved by Parliament and all provincial legislatures within three years.

As the 1990 deadline approached, there was heated public debate about adopting the Accord. The premier of Newfoundland and Labrador, Clyde Wells, was a vocal opponent. Elected two years after the Accord was negotiated, Wells argued that Meech Lake would give Quebec greater legislative powers than the other provinces, make it almost impossible to enact future constitutional reforms, and undermine federal funding to Canada's poorer provinces. The federal government countered that defeating the Accord would threaten national unity by reviving the separatist movement in Quebec. In the end, Meech Lake failed when the ratification deadline passed without the necessary support from Newfoundland and Labrador and Manitoba.

The debate surrounding Meech Lake and its ensuing failure created a political backlash in Quebec. As separatist sentiments increased in Quebec, Canada's first ministers negotiated a second package of proposed constitutional amendments in 1992. Known as the Charlottetown Accord, it was largely a second version of Meech Lake. Unlike Meech Lake, however, it had to be approved by the Canadian people in a national referendum instead of ratified by provincial legislatures.

Although the Accord received a majority of votes in Newfoundland and Labrador, New Brunswick, Prince Edward Island, Ontario, and the Northwest Territories, it was opposed by the other provinces, particularly Quebec.

4. If it had been passed, the Meech Lake Accord would have resulted in
   (1) separation of Quebec
   (2) separation of Newfoundland and Labrador
   (3) Quebec ratification of the constitution
   (4) increased federal funding
   (5) a threat to national unity

5. One way that the Charlottetown Accord was different from the Meech Lake Accord is that
   (1) it was passed
   (2) it required approval of all provinces
   (3) it was subject to a general vote of the people
   (4) it was not a constitutional amendment
   (5) it did not recognize Quebec as a "distinct society"

6. The people of which province did not support the Charlottetown Accord?
   (1) Prince Edward Island
   (2) New Brunswick
   (3) Newfoundland and Labrador
   (4) Ontario
   (5) Quebec

ANSWERS

1. **(4)** We know that the FLQ crisis was considered a terrorist threat because the Quebec government asked the federal government to intervene and the war measures act was activated.

2. **(1)** Although separatist sentiment was strong, the majority of Quebecers did not vote for separation.

3. **(1)** Lévesque was leader of the Parti Québécois, which ran on a platform of separation from Canada.

4. **(3)** Approval of the Meech Lake Accord by all provinces, including Quebec, would have made the province a signatory to the constitution.

5. **(3)** Unlike Meech Lake, the Charlottetown Accord was voted on in a referendum, which is a vote by all of the eligible voters.

6. **(5)** Voters in all the provinces listed approved the accord except Quebec. Prairie and western provinces voters also did not support the accord.

CHAPTER CHECK-UP

Complete these practice exercises, and check the answers and analysis that follow. After you mark your work, review any topic in the chapter that you had trouble with or did not understand.

Questions 1–3 are based on the following information.

The Cold War reached its most critical moment during a 13-day period in October 1962. The United States had placed nuclear missiles in Turkey aimed at the Soviet capital of Moscow. The United States had also launched a failed attempt to overthrow Fidel Castro's new communist government in Cuba. In response to these acts, Soviet leader Nikita Khrushchev made a secret proposal to Castro to install Soviet nuclear missiles in Cuba, only 100 km from Florida on the mainland United States. Construction of the missile sites began.

United States intelligence services discovered the plan and sent a spy plane to confirm the presence of nuclear missiles in Cuba with photographic evidence. President John F. Kennedy announced that America would not allow nuclear missiles in Cuba and demanded that they be removed. He sent a fleet of warships to blockade Cuba. NATO countries were also put on alert in case of an attack.

During the days that followed, the world held its breath on the brink of nuclear war. Publicly, Khrushchev denounced the U.S. blockade of international waters and airspace. Two Soviet ships attempted to run the blockade. U.S. warships were instructed to fire warning shots against further attempts and then to open fire. A U.S. spy plane was shot down by Soviet missiles.

Behind the scenes, the two sides continued to negotiate with assistance from the United Nations Secretary General. An agreement was eventually reached. The Soviet Union would remove the missiles. In return, the United States agreed never again to invade Cuba. Secretly, the U.S. also agreed to remove their nuclear missiles from Turkey.

1. Which of the following was not a cause of the Cuban missile crisis?
   (1) United States missiles in Turkey
   (2) Russian missiles in Cuba
   (3) United States invasion of Cuba
   (4) Cuban proximity to the United States
   (5) the Cuban Revolution

2. The term *blockade* means
   (1) to surround an area to prevent people and goods from entering and exiting
   (2) an official ban on trade
   (3) a threat or penalty for disobedience
   (4) resistance or open defiance
   (5) bold opposition to a military force

3. The Cuban Missile Crisis was the first instance in which Mutually Assured Destruction (MAD) was an important factor in negotiations. MAD could have meant
   (1) conflict with the United Nations
   (2) the end of the world
   (3) conflict between the United States and Cuba
   (4) heavy losses on both sides
   (5) the end of the cold war

4. This cartoon about the second Quebec referendum suggests that
   (1) Quebec will have another referendum
   (2) Quebec and Canada are enemies
   (3) Quebec and Canada will never agree
   (4) Quebec still has a strong separatist spirit
   (5) Quebec and Canada will negotiate an agreement

Questions 5–8 are based on the following information.

July 6, 1944 is a day that will always be remembered in world history. It was D-Day, the largest sea invasion in history, in which the Allies would attempt to re-establish a toe hold in continental Europe and free it from Nazi occupation. At 6 a.m., Allied ships off-shore began bombardment of the beaches and Axis defensive positions.

   The invasion took place along an eighty kilometre strip of shoreline in Normandy, France. Over 5,000 ships and landing craft, 150,000 soldiers, 50,000 vehicles, and 11,000 airplanes would take part. Five beaches were targeted for the landing. The United States would land at Omaha Beach and Utah Beach to the west. The Canadians would land at Juno Beach, and the British would strike at Gold Beach and Sword Beach.

At 7:35 a.m. the attack on Juno Beach began. 14,000 Canadian troops of the 3rd Canadian Infantry division attacked the shores, battling against fierce German opposition in entrenched strongholds. At first, casualties were heavy, but the Canadians continued to advance. Within two hours, the beachhead was secured. Canadian reinforcements were landed and they moved inland to capture nearby towns and strategic objectives, including an airfield and railway line. In total, 340 Canadians were killed and more than 570 injured in the attack.

All of the allied landings were successful against fierce German resistance. Because of the sheer number of men, vehicles, and equipment, there was confusion and communication difficulty once the troops were ashore. Not all of the objectives of the day were achieved, but the Allies had established a firm position from which they would not be dislodged. The invasion marked a turning point in the war, leading ultimately to victory and the liberation of Europe.

Canadian troops landing on D-Day.

5. D-Day was an important battle during
   (1) the Korean War
   (2) the French-German War
   (3) the Great War
   (4) World War I
   (5) World War II

6. The D-Day landing was important because
   (1) the Germans wanted to establish a beachhead
   (2) the coast of Normandy was a German stronghold
   (3) the Allies wanted to conquer Europe
   (4) the Axis powers had conquered continental Europe
   (5) Britain was in danger of being invaded

7. Canadian forces on D-Day seized
   (1) Juno Beach
   (2) Sword Beach
   (3) Omaha Beach
   (4) Gold Beach
   (5) Utah Beach

8. The D-Day invasion took place in
   (1) Germany
   (2) United States
   (3) France
   (4) Britain
   (5) Canada

Questions 9–12 are based on the following information.

Why Canadian Unity?
(Extract from a speech to the London School of Economics 1998)

It is easy to imagine the reaction throughout the world if Canada were to break up. It would be said that this defunct federation had died from an overdose of decentralization and tolerance—in short, from an overdose of democracy. "Don't be as tolerant, decentralized and open as Canada was, or else your minorities will turn against you, threaten the unity of your country, and even destroy it". That's what would be said.

I entered politics precisely because I want to hear the opposite point of view. I want countries throughout the world to say: "We can have confidence in our minorities, and allow them to develop in their own way, because they will make our country stronger, just as Quebec makes Canada stronger".

Canadians are modest folk, who have no idea how much the debate on the unity of their country is universal in scope. If a country so blessed as Canada fails to stay together, Canadians will have sent a most unfortunate message to the rest of the world at the dawn of the new century.

Indeed, Canadians are now debating what could be the most important question of the next century: how to enable different populations to live together within the same country. And while it is true that Canadians are talking about it calmly and peacefully, we have seen elsewhere that things often go very much awry.

Since the end of the Cold War, the number of conflicts within states has greatly exceeded the number of conflicts between states, according to a commission of the Carnegie Corporation, which has identified 233 ethnic or religious minorities that are calling for improvements to their legal and political rights.

And so we must promote plural identities. Let every Quebecer be able to say: "I am a Quebecer and a Canadian, and I refuse to choose between the two".

In Canada, we often talk about the "two solitudes" to describe the difficulties between Francophones and Anglophones. We have forgotten that this expression is taken from a letter by Rilke, who was trying to express love, rather than isolation. "Love consists in this, that two solitudes protect, and touch, and greet each other," wrote the poet, expressing this dual quest for autonomy and sharing, for defining oneself and opening up to others, which is necessary both for relations between persons and relations between populations.

9. The subject of this speech is primarily
    (1) English-French relations in Canada
    (2) Canadian unity as an example to the world
    (3) treatment of minorities
    (4) problems with Canadian democracy
    (5) Quebec separatism

10. According to the speech, since the Cold War ended, the majority of wars have been
    (1) civil wars
    (2) world wars
    (3) wars between states
    (4) wars over oil
    (5) wars caused by terrorism

11. The speaker thinks that countries, like Canada, with diverse people groups can preserve national unity and peace by
    (1) civil war
    (2) separation
    (3) taking a democratic approach
    (4) respecting and valuing all cultures
    (5) decentralization of government

12. Canada is often described as a "cultural mosaic." This term means a country in which
    (1) diverse languages and cultures assimilate into one cohesive group
    (2) diverse languages and cultures co-exist
    (3) different types of art, literature, and music are appreciated
    (4) different languages and cultures live in isolation from one another
    (5) diversity is protected in the constitution

ANSWERS

1. **(5)** The Cuban revolution installed a communist government, which contributed to the U.S. invasion attempt, but was not a direct cause of the crisis.

2. **(1)** The blockade surrounded Cuba to prevent materials of war from entering.

3. **(2)** Mutually assured destruction through nuclear war could have meant the end of life on earth.

4. **(3)** The cartoonist shows that although Quebec and the rest of Canada are friends, they still do not agree about many things.

5. **(5)** The date was 1944, during World War II.

6. **(4)** Germany and the Axis powers had conquered continental Europe, and the allied forces had no base on the continent from which to fight back.

7. **(1)** Canadians landed at Juno Beach.

8. **(3)** The beaches were located in Normandy, France.

9. **(2)** The speaker sees Canada as an example to the world of how different cultures can peacefully come together, while preserving their own identity.

10. **(1)** The greatest number of conflicts have been among differing cultural, religious, and language groups, within countries.

11. **(4)** The speaker says that diverse cultures within a society should protect, trust, and greet each other.

12. **(2)** Canada is proud of being a cultural mosaic, a country that preserves and promotes diversity, which we feel makes us a stronger society. The term is often used in contrast with the United States description of itself as a "melting pot," made up of diverse languages and cultures that lose their identity and assimilate to become American.

Canada and the World

20

THINK ABOUT IT

The three largest economies in the world, based on their gross domestic product (GDP) are:

1. European Union
2. United States
3. China

The three strongest military powers in the world are:

1. United States
2. Russia
3. China

Canada has a much smaller economy than some countries (although we are ranked 11th in GDP) and a much smaller military. Nevertheless, Canada often plays an important role in world affairs.

What is Canada's relationship with other countries that have larger economies and greater military power? What is Canada's role in world affairs?

IN THIS CHAPTER

The GED Social Studies Test will contain questions about international events, world trade, the environment, and other issues that concern Canada and our world.

After completing this chapter, you will be able to

→ **RESPOND TO QUESTIONS ABOUT RESOURCES AND INDUSTRY IN CANADA AND OTHER NATIONS**

→ **DESCRIBE ENVIRONMENTAL ISSUES AFFECTING CANADA AND THE WORLD**

→ **DESCRIBE THE RELATIONSHIP BETWEEN CANADA AND THE UNITED STATES**

→ **IDENTIFY CANADA'S ROLE IN WORLD AFFAIRS**

→ **RESPOND TO QUESTIONS ABOUT GLOBAL MARKETS AND FOREIGN TRADE**

RESOURCES AND INDUSTRY

Every country has industries and resources that are the basis of its economy—that provide jobs for citizens, tax revenue for governments, and exports for foreign trade. Economies can be made up of different industries.

- **NATURAL RESOURCES**—materials and substances that are found in the environment, such as forestry, fisheries, mining, oil, and agriculture
- **MANUFACTURING**—mass production of goods, such as automobile and other industrial factories
- **SERVICE**—providing primarily intangible services—rather than the production of durable goods—such as fast food restaurants, entertainment, sales, transport, distribution
- **KNOWLEDGE**—service industries in which the services require specifically learned skills and expertise, such as the traditional professions of accounting, law, or medicine, communications, technology, banking and finance.

Over the past half-century, the structure of economies has changed. Advanced economies, such as Canada and the United States, are based increasingly on knowledge, and the high-paying jobs of today and the future are based on intellectual and information capacities.

PRACTICE

Choose the best answer for each of the questions that follow this next passage.

Saudi Arabia has an oil-based economy with strong government controls over major economic activities. It possesses about 17% of the world's proven petroleum reserves, ranks as the largest exporter of petroleum, and plays a leading role in OPEC. The petroleum sector accounts for roughly 80% of budget revenues, 45% of GDP, and 90% of export earnings. Saudi Arabia is encouraging the growth of the private sector in order to diversify its economy and to employ more Saudi nationals. Diversification efforts are focusing on power generation, telecommunications, natural gas exploration, and petrochemical sectors. Over 5 million foreign workers play an important role in the Saudi economy, particularly in the oil and service sectors, although Riyadh is struggling to reduce unemployment among its own nationals. Saudi officials are particularly focused on employing the country's large youth population, which generally lacks the education and technical skills the private sector needs. Riyadh has substantially boosted spending on job training and education, most recently with the opening of the King Abdallah University of Science and Technology—Saudi Arabia's first co-educational university. As part of its effort to attract foreign investment, Saudi Arabia acceded to the World Trade Organization in 2005. The government has begun establishing six "economic cities" in different regions of the country to promote foreign investment and plans to spend $373 billion between 2010 and 2014 on social development and infrastructure projects to advance Saudi Arabia's economic development.

Source: Central Intelligence Agency *The World Factbook*

1. The economy of Saudi Arabia is based on
   (1) natural resources
   (2) manufacturing
   (3) services
   (4) knowledge industries
   (5) diverse industries

2. Many of the skilled jobs in Saudi oil and service sectors go to
   (1) youth
   (2) Saudi nationals
   (3) university students
   (4) foreign workers
   (5) women

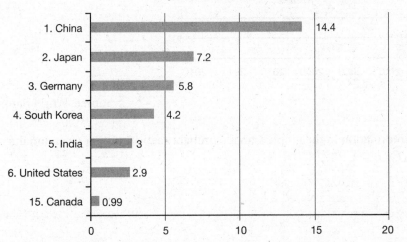

Top Car Manufacturing Nations (2011)

Total passenger car production in millions

3. Based on the chart, we can conclude that the majority of automobiles in the world are made in
   (1) Africa
   (2) Asia
   (3) Europe
   (4) North America
   (5) Australia

4. Although ranked 6th in passenger-car production, the United States is second in total automobile production. This probably means that the United States
   (1) is one of the largest producers of commercial vehicles
   (2) is one of the largest producers of aircraft
   (3) exports more passenger cars than it imports
   (4) is not technologically advanced in auto production
   (5) has less demand for passenger vehicles

Gross Domestic Product (GDP) is the total dollar value of all of the goods and services produced in an economy each year. It is also an important economic indicator, used to measure the health of an economy. An economy that is healthy should grow every year. Often, you may hear economists talk about change in the GDP to say how much the economy is growing.

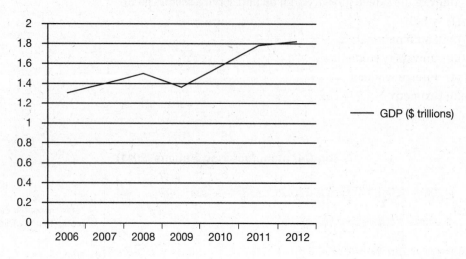

Canadian GDP ($ trillions)

Source: World Bank

5. Based on the information in the graph, Canada probably experienced a recession during which year?
   (1) 2007
   (2) 2008
   (3) 2009
   (4) 2011
   (5) 2012

6. The greatest period of economic growth was between
   (1) 2006–2007
   (2) 2007–2008
   (3) 2008–2009
   (4) 2010–2011
   (5) 2011–2012

ANSWERS

1. **(1)** According to the passage, the Saudi economy is based primarily on oil, which is a natural resource.

2. **(4)** According to the passage, many jobs go to foreign workers because Saudi youth often lack the education and technical skills.

3. **(2)** Four of the top five countries on the chart are in Asia.

4. **(1)** To be second in total production, the United States must be a leader in production of other automobiles. In fact, it is the world leader in commercial vehicle production, such as cars, trucks, taxis, buses, vans, and delivery vehicles.

5. **(3)** GDP goes down in 2009, indicating a period of negative economic growth.

6. **(4)** Although none of these years show great economic growth, the line goes up most steeply between 2010 and 2011.

CHALLENGE EXERCISE

Research on the Internet, or use other resources, to find out more about the economy of your province or territory. What are the three largest industry sectors?

THE ENVIRONMENT

The environment is an extremely important global concern. Countries may be starting to understand that the environmental conditions in one country have an impact on all others. Effects of air pollution, oil spills, or nuclear contamination, for example, can often be felt far across the world from where they occurred.

Environmental issues are a common topic of discussion at international meetings of world governments, along with human rights, world trade, and the global economy. Agreement can often be difficult to reach, but there is increasing awareness that we must act to protect our planet from ourselves.

TIP

Environmental issues are a global concern.

PRACTICE

Choose the best answer for each of the questions that follow these next passages.

What Is the Impact of the BP Oil Spill?

Growing global demand for oil and dwindling traditional supplies have led to a surge in deep-water exploration and drilling. In the United States alone, deep-water wells now account for more than 30% of domestic oil production. Although drilling technology has advanced rapidly, some scientists are concerned that safety measures have not. The April 2010 explosion of British Petroleum's Deepwater Horizon drilling rig in the Gulf of Mexico may have proved them right. The event resulted in the largest accidental marine oil spill in history.

In total, nearly 200 million gallons of oil and 2 million gallons of chemical dispersants were released into the Gulf during the incident. In addition to threatening sea life, large amounts of oil washed up onto beaches and coastal marshes, threatening fisheries and tourism. Sea birds and animals were coated in oil. Toxins from the spill may also have been carried by ocean currents to other regions.

Although there may no longer be visible oil on the surface of the Gulf, the long-term effects of the accident are not known, making it difficult to plan restoration efforts. Oil on the ocean floor and in coastal wetlands is likely to persist for years. In addition, the Gulf of Mexico is a delicate ecosystem, and it is difficult to predict how it will be affected. One concern is the toxic effects on eggs and larval organisms of species breeding at the time and the ripple effect it could have on the food web. Another concern is that ocean bacteria, which feed hungrily to break down the oil, deplete oxygen in the water of the region, threatening other species. Scientists and environmentalists will observe population fluctuations and other environmental impacts for the next several decades. Politicians and economists will count the long-term economic costs of environmental damage and of impact on commercial fisheries, outdoor recreation, and tourism.

1. On April 20, 2010, a British Petroleum deep-sea oil well exploded in the Gulf of Mexico off the coast of Mississippi, beginning the largest marine oil spill in history. Based on information in the passage, damage from the spill
   (1) is limited to the Gulf of Mexico
   (2) has been cleaned up
   (3) also affects coastal areas
   (4) was not as serious as expected
   (5) only affected birds and mammals

2. It is difficult to make restoration plans because
   (1) the spill was at sea
   (2) not all the impacts are known
   (3) there were too many birds and animals affected
   (4) the spill was a long time ago
   (5) oil is on the ocean floor

3. If the oil's toxicity hit egg and larval organisms, the possible consequence could be
   (1) reduced herring populations
   (2) visible oil on the surface
   (3) damage to wetlands and beaches
   (4) wiping out the entire species
   (5) disruption of the entire ecosystem

The Kyoto Protocol is an international agreement that was signed in Kyoto, Japan in 1997, as a part of the United Nations Framework Convention on Climate Change (UNFCC). The agreement involved 191 industrialized and developing nations and the European Union, all of whom made legally-binding commitments to reduce greenhouse gas emissions to pre-1990 levels by 2012 and further reductions by 2020. The protocol also recognized that developed countries are the ones who have created the current problem because of two centuries of industrialization, and they placed a higher burden on developed countries.

Some important absences from the Kyoto Accord are the United States and Canada. The United States originally signed the agreement, but did not ratify it and has made no commitment. Canada signed the agreement and it was ratified in the House of Commons; however, in 2011 the country formally withdrew from the agreement. The reason for the withdrawal was that Canada had not put in place measures to meet their targets and would have been subject to $14 billion in penalties. The Canadian government did, however, design their own new target to reduce emissions by 17% from 2005 levels by the year 2020, a much lower standard than the Kyoto Protocol.

4. The purpose of the Kyoto Protocol is to combat
   (1) global warming
   (2) industrialization
   (3) smog
   (4) fuel consumption
   (5) high energy costs

5. The Canadian government withdrew from the Kyoto Protocol because
   (1) the United States had not ratified it
   (2) Canada does not care about environmental protection
   (3) of lobbying by industry
   (4) Canada would not meet the target
   (5) Canada is a developing country

On March 11, 2011, the largest earthquake to ever hit Japan occurred approximately 70 kilometres off the Japanese coast. As a result of the quake, a tsunami raced towards shore. More than 18,000 people died in the initial quake and following tsunami, and nearly 7,000 were injured.

One of the longest lasting impacts of the great quake was the resulting disaster at the Fukushima Nuclear Power Plant. Fortunately, three of the plant's six reactors were in shutdown at the time of the quake. When it struck, the remaining reactors began automatically to shut down and coolant was pumped in, powered by electric generators. Less than an hour later, the tidal wave struck, flooding the generators and resulting in a nuclear meltdown, the worst nuclear disaster since Chernobyl in 1986.

The immediate and future impacts for Japan of the disaster are great. Billions of dollars have already been spent on a cleanup that is expected to take nearly 40 years. Water that flooded the reactors must be removed and safely disposed of and hundreds of thousands of tons of contaminated soil. People living near Fukushima are also expected to have a higher chance of thyroid and other cancers.

The full extent of the environmental impact is not known, and the effects are continuing and could have global consequences. The international community learned more than two years later that several hundred tons of contaminated water each day was still leaking into the ocean. How far this will be carried and what lasting damage has been done is unknown. Investigations have shown that, despite the magnitude of the quake, the incident was foreseeable, preventable, and the result of human error. It has caused other countries to re-examine their own nuclear power programs, safety protocols, and whether nuclear power is the best alternative to meet future needs.

6. Based on information in the passage, the Fukushima nuclear disaster was the result of
   (1) an earthquake
   (2) a tsunami
   (3) human error
   (4) faulty design
   (5) flood

7. An international environmental concern is
   (1) radioactive fallout from the atmosphere
   (2) radioactive water in the ocean
   (3) radioactive soil
   (4) cancer
   (5) cost of cleanup

8. One impact for Canada of the Fukushima disaster could be
   (1) research into alternative energy sources
   (2) abandonment of the nuclear energy program
   (3) radioactive contamination of the Pacific coast
   (4) condemnation of Japanese response to the crisis
   (5) financial aid to Japan

ANSWERS

1. **(3)** Oil had also washed onto beaches and coastal wetlands.
2. **(2)** It is difficult to know how to respond because not all the problems are known yet.
3. **(5)** If a generation of one species were damaged or wiped out, it would disrupt the food web and all the animals and plants that depend on one another in the ecosystem.
4. **(1)** The protocol reduces greenhouse gas emissions, which contribute to global warming.
5. **(4)** The Canadian government believed that they would not meet the targets set by the protocol and would be subject to heavy financial penalties.
6. **(3)** Although an earthquake and tsunami were the immediate cause, investigation showed that the effects such events would have was foreseeable and preventable, the result of human error.
7. **(2)** Continued leaking of radioactive water into the ocean could have far-reaching environmental effects.
8. **(1)** The passage states that the accident has caused other countries to consider whether nuclear power is the best alternative for needs.

CANADA AND THE U.S.

Many Canadians have good friends or family across the border. Although we do not always agree, we share many common policies and international interests.

PRACTICE

Choose the best answer for each of the following questions.

Balance of trade is the difference between the value of goods and services a country exports and the value of that which it imports. If a country exports more than it imports, it is called a trade surplus. It means more money is coming into the economy than going out. If a country imports more than it exports, it is a trade deficit. For countries, as well as for families, spending more than you earn results in debt and a poor financial outlook.

The United States has historically been Canada's largest trading partner and currently accounts for more than 50% of Canada's international trade. Canada generally preserves a trade surplus with the United States. In July 2013, for example, Canada's exports to the U.S. stood at just over 30 billion dollars and imports at over 26 billion dollars.

As Canada's global trading partners have increased in the past few decades, the United States accounts for less of our country's international trade. Canada's overall trade deficit for July 2013 stood at 1.3 billion dollars, driven primarily by imports of crude oil, transportation equipment, and auto parts as well as decreased European demand for Canadian imports.

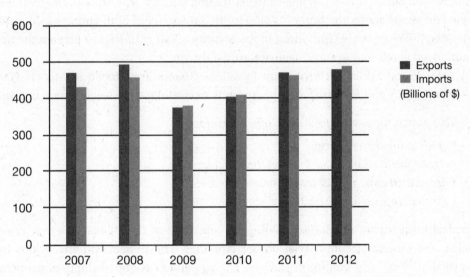

Canada World Trade

Source: Statistics Canada

1. Balance of trade could be defined as
   (1) exports minus imports
   (2) exports plus imports
   (3) the total value of goods produced by a country
   (4) trade between Canada and the United States
   (5) trade between Canada and the world

2. In which year, represented on the chart, did Canada have the greatest trade deficit?
   (1) 2007
   (2) 2008
   (3) 2009
   (4) 2011
   (5) 2012

3. If the Canadian dollar were low, what likely impact would it have on the balance of trade with the United States?
   (1) Decrease demand for Canadian exports
   (2) Increase Canadian demand for U.S. imports
   (3) No impact on balance of trade
   (4) Canada is more likely to have a trade deficit
   (5) Canada is more likely to have a trade surplus

Canada and the United States have the longest undefended border in the world, also the busiest. More than 300,000 people each day cross the border for business, shopping, or travel or to visit family or friends.

The United States is also Canada's largest trading partner. The smooth bilateral flow of people and goods across the border is vital to the prosperity of both countries. Monitoring the border, however, is also important to the security of our countries to prevent the flow of unauthorized goods and to stand against terrorist threats.

In 2011, Prime Minister Harper and President Obama announced an *Action Plan on Perimeter Security and Economic Competitiveness*. According to the Government of Canada:

> *This plan is focused on four areas of cooperation:*
> - *Addressing threats early;*
> - *Trade facilitation, economic growth and jobs;*
> - *Integrated cross-border law enforcement; and*
> - *Critical infrastructure and cyber-security*

Critical infrastructure includes building new facilities at the Windsor-Detroit crossing, which is the busiest of commercial border crossings. The project will create jobs in the construction phase and long-term staffing. The agreement is one example of cooperation between the two countries for security and trade.

Source: Foreign Affairs Canada

4. Based on information in this passage, "bilateral" probably means
   (1) friendly
   (2) secure
   (3) unprotected
   (4) two-way
   (5) shared

5. Based on information in the passage, we conclude that the main purpose of the plan announced in December 2011 was
   (1) infrastructure development
   (2) border security
   (3) preventing terrorism
   (4) job creation
   (5) preventing smuggling

6. Which of the following does not seem to be related to the other items in the agreement?
   (1) Trade facilitation
   (2) Addressing threats
   (3) Cross-border law enforcement
   (4) Cyber-security
   (5) Critical infrastructure

The United States and Canada are close military allies who work together in defense of North America, as well as in NATO and United Nations' peacekeeping and security forces. In 2001, following the 9/11 attacks on the World Trade Center, the United States Government demanded that the Taliban government of Afghanistan hand over al-Qaeda leader Osama bin Laden, who was thought to be in hiding in that country. When the Taliban refused to do so without evidence of his involvement in the attack, the United States with the United Kingdom and other allies invaded.

Canada did not play a significant role in the initial attack although, as a member of North Atlantic Treaty Organisation (NATO), it viewed the attack on the United States as an attack on itself. The Taliban government was quickly overthrown; however, it was not defeated, as most supporters escaped to Pakistan or rural and mountainous regions from which they carried out a guerilla war against foreign troops and the newly installed civilian government. In response, the United Nations established an International Security Assistance Force (ISAF) to provide security for the country and train Afghan security forces to provide their own security for the future. In 2003, NATO took over responsibility for the ISAF.

While the United States initially provided the bulk of security forces, Canada and 43 other allied countries also contributed, particularly when the U.S. later made an additional commitment to the invasion and security of Iraq. Canada was one of the largest contributors to security of Afghanistan, helping to maintain order, train security forces, and battle insurgents. In total, over 41,000 Canadians served in Afghanistan, more than 155 were killed and 1,800 wounded.

7. Canada and the United States are both
   (1) military superpowers
   (2) allies of the Taliban
   (3) members of NATO
   (4) terrorist countries
   (5) opposed to the Muslim countries

8. According to the passage, Canada's role in Afghanistan was primarily to
   (1) oppose the United States
   (2) fight the Taliban
   (3) maintain security
   (4) capture Osama bin Laden
   (5) carry out guerilla warfare

ANSWERS

1. **(1)** Balance of trade is the difference between exports and imports.
2. **(5)** In 2012, exports were significantly lower than imports.
3. **(5)** A low Canadian dollar means that Canadian goods are cheaper and exports increase. At the same time, the cost of importing foreign goods is higher, so demand for imports will decrease.
4. **(4)** Bilateral means having two sides. A bilateral border and bilateral trade go both ways.
5. **(2)** All items are mentioned or implied, but all contribute to border security between the two countries.
6. **(4)** Unlike the other items listed, cyber-security does not relate directly to border security.
7. **(3)** Both are members of NATO, an alliance formed during the Cold War, which has since expanded its membership. Member countries are committed to mutual defense.
8. **(3)** Canada's initial involvement was as part of the United Nations International Security Assistance Force to provide security for the country.

CANADA IN WORLD AFFAIRS

Many people in the world have some knowledge of the United States. They know who the president is. They have heard of Washington, New York, Los Angeles, and other major cities. They are familiar with U.S. sports heroes and movie stars. They know very little about Canada.

Internationally, many people have heard of Toronto, but seldom our other cities. They do not know who the prime minister is, the size of the country, or our history. They know little about our music, literature, or culture.

Yet Canada's reputation is known and favourably regarded by ordinary people in many countries. We have a reputation as peacemakers, a people who treat others with respect, and who care about others. That reputation has slipped somewhat in recent years, partly as a result of our slow response to global environmental issues and decrease in foreign aid. Nevertheless, because of our economy, diplomacy, military security, and technology, Canada is among the top ten influential countries in the world.

PRACTICE

Choose the best answer for each of the questions that follow.

Canadians have long been aware of the favourable international reputation of their country. Indeed, that reputation has been long held and much deserved. Canada has been a leader in promotion of human rights throughout the world. The government of Canada was a driving force behind the international treaty to ban landmines, which was signed in Ottawa. Canada has also been a leader in the United Nations, creating the modern concept of UN peacekeeping and participating in formation of the International Criminal Court. However, there is evidence that Canada's reputation is slipping.

In a 2010 speech in Toronto, the executive director of Human Rights Watch, Kenneth Roth, spoke of the decline of Canada's moral voice in the world. He said that although we are a small country the values we historically exhibited in world affairs meant that, "Canada punched above its weight. It was a nation to be contended with".

Roth continued by saying as follows:

It is thus with considerable sadness that I see Canada in recent years shying away from being a strong moral voice on international issues. Like most Western nations, Canada contributes few peacekeepers.

Ottawa seems to have abandoned concepts that it once promoted, such as the responsibility to protect people facing mass atrocities. When HRW sought a governmental partner to lead our recent campaign to ban cluster munitions, we had to go to Norway, instead of Canada.

The Canadian government is the only Western one to let its citizens languish in Guantanamo.

The government tried to cover up and deny allegations that Canadian soldiers surrendered Afghan detainees knowing that would likely be tortured.

The government endorsed a free trade agreement with Colombia even though hundreds of Colombian trade unionists had been murdered with impunity.

Once a government that regularly stood with victims of human rights abuse, Canada, these days, mostly stands aside.

1. According to the passage, which of the following is a positive contribution that Canada made to world affairs?
   (1) Surrendering Afghan detainees
   (2) Ban on cluster munitions
   (3) Reduction in peacekeepers
   (4) U.N. peacekeeping
   (5) Free trade with Colombia

2. According to the passage, Canada's influence formerly came from
   (1) values
   (2) military strength
   (3) political alliances
   (4) financial aid
   (5) strong legal system

3. The attitude of the speech towards the Canadian government is
   (1) angry
   (2) neutral
   (3) critical
   (4) fearful
   (5) supportive

Canada is a member of the G8. Formed in 1975 as the G6, the group consists of the world's leading industrialized economies and originally consisted of the United States, France, Britain, Germany, Japan, and Italy. Canada was admitted in 1976 and Russia in 1998. Leaders of the countries meet every year to discuss and form agreements about transnational issues, such as macroeconomic policies, international trade, and relations with developing countries.

In 2012, one issue that came before the G8 was that of developing international standards for tax transparency and disclosure of foreign ownership by multi-national countries, an issue that is seen as critical to economies of developing countries, particularly in Africa. One economist estimates that some of the world's poorest nations lose twice as much money in taxes as they receive in foreign aid because large corporations avoid paying taxes and often hide foreign ownership through shell companies. Global standards for reporting would give these countries the information they need to force these companies to pay their rightful taxes and set one standard so that companies don't have to report in different ways in different countries.

Canada has been seen as slow to support this issue, which has come as a surprise to many. According to Canadian officials, Canada does support the agenda of transparency. However, because of the structure of the Canadian political and tax systems, any new rules will also need support of the provinces. Some critics believe that Canada's slow response is based on the idea that having a competitive tax system is important to attracting multinational companies to our country.

4. Which of the following was the last country to join the G8?
   (1) United States
   (2) Russia
   (3) Canada
   (4) France
   (5) Germany

5. Based on information in this passage, we can conclude that multinational companies are able to avoid paying their rightful taxes in developing countries because
   (1) companies do not earn as much money
   (2) the countries do not try to collect
   (3) the countries prefer to receive foreign aid
   (4) companies have locations in many countries
   (5) companies hide financial information

6. Based on the information in the passage, we might conclude that Canada's slow acceptance of the issue is based on a philosophy of
   (1) support for multinational companies
   (2) non-involvement in the economy
   (3) Canada first
   (4) support for poor countries
   (5) minimizing bureaucracy

ANSWERS

1. **(4)** The other choices are negative.
2. **(1)** The passage says that it was values that informed Canada's dealings with the world and gave Canada a strong moral voice in world affairs.
3. **(3)** The speaker criticizes the Canadian government for no longer taking a strong moral stance.
4. **(2)** Russia was admitted in 1998.
5. **(5)** The call for transparency and disclosure of ownership is to combat secrecy and make information available.
6. **(3)** This is the only choice supported by the passage. One suggestion is that reluctance may be based for a competitive tax system to attract investment in Canada.

GLOBAL MARKETS AND FOREIGN TRADE

During the early and mid-twentieth century, the approach to foreign trade and economic development in most countries was based on tariffs and duties. Goods manufactured in other countries were subject to import duties when they came into the country. This made the price of foreign goods more expensive, which encouraged purchases of domestic products and growth of manufacturing. Today, advanced economies are global in outlook and are based less on manufacturing and more on the service and knowledge industries. Canada has entered into free-trade agreements with a number of countries, which reduces or eliminates tariffs, opening up foreign markets to Canadian goods and services and enabling imports of cheaper goods. This allows Canada access to much larger markets for products and services that we offer competitively and gives consumers access to lower prices. Foreign trade now accounts for more than 65% of Canada's GDP, the second-highest level in the G8.

PRACTICE

Choose the best answer for each of the questions that follow the next passages.

Free-trade agreements enable Canadian businesses to be competitive in foreign markets. Elimination of import tariffs and other trade barriers puts Canadian companies on even terms with local businesses so that they can offer competitive prices in foreign markets. Canada currently has trade agreements with over ten countries and is pursuing similar agreements with many more.

Each free-trade agreement varies in its terms and provisions and may not include all industry sectors. Recent negotiations have included additional provisions, such as labour mobility, intellectual property, and investment.

1. Which of the following provisions of a free trade agreement could give Canadian workers access to foreign jobs?
   (1) Labour mobility
   (2) Intellectual property
   (3) Investment
   (4) Elimination of tariffs
   (5) Elimination of quotas

2. The benefit to Canada of free trade agreements is that they give Canadian businesses
   (1) advantages over foreign businesses in partner countries
   (2) advantages in Canadian markets
   (3) equality with foreign businesses in Canadian markets
   (4) special tax benefits in foreign markets
   (5) equality with foreign businesses in partner countries

3. Based on information in the passage, we conclude that if Canada has a free trade agreement with another country
   (1) all Canadian businesses will benefit equally
   (2) foreign goods will be cheaper than Canadian goods
   (3) Canadian businesses will be less competitive abroad
   (4) only some Canadian businesses may benefit
   (5) Canadian intellectual property will be protected

The North American Free Trade Agreement (NAFTA), signed by Prime Minister Brian Mulroney, Mexican President Carlos Salinas, and U.S. President George H.W. Bush, came into effect on January 1, 1994. Since 1993, NAFTA has generated economic growth and rising standards of living for the people of all three member countries. By strengthening the rules and procedures governing trade and investment throughout the continent, NAFTA has proved to be a solid foundation for building Canada's future prosperity.

Canada's merchandise trade with its NAFTA partners reached nearly $626.3 billion in 2008. Canadian merchandise exports to the United States grew at a compounded annual rate of almost 6.3% between 1993 and 2008. Canada's bilateral trade with Mexico was close to $23.8 billion in 2008. Approximately 80% of Canada's total merchandise exports were destined to our NAFTA partners in 2008. Total merchandise trade between Canada and the United States more than doubled between 1993 and 2008. Trade between Canada and Mexico has more than quadrupled over the same period.

Trade in services has also increased under NAFTA. Canada's trade in services with the United States and Mexico has doubled from $42.9 billion in 1993 to $86.5 billion in 2005. Our trade in services with the United States reached $91.3 billion in 2008, up from $42.3 billion in 1993. Two-way trade in services between Canada and Mexico reached $1.8 billion in 2006.

In turn, the enhanced economic activity and production in the region have contributed to the creation of jobs for Canadians. One in five jobs in Canada is related in part to trade. More than 4.3 million net new jobs have been created in Canada between 1993 and 2008.

For Canadians, it is important that trade and investment liberalization proceed hand-in-hand with efforts to protect the environment and improve working conditions. Under NAFTA, our three countries have been able to introduce the successful approach of parallel environmental and labour cooperation agreements.

4. NAFTA is an agreement between which of the following countries?
   (1) Canada, United States
   (2) Canada, Mexico
   (3) Canada, United States, European Union
   (4) United States, Mexico, European Union
   (5) Canada, United States, Mexico

5. Canada's greatest economic activity under NAFTA is
   (1) export of services to the United States
   (2) export of goods to the United States
   (3) export of services to Mexico
   (4) export of goods to Mexico
   (5) import of goods from Mexico

6. Based on the information in the passage, which of the following is true of NAFTA?
   (1) Reduced environmental protection requirements
   (2) Reduced Canadian trade in services
   (3) Improved labour conditions in Mexico
   (4) Loss of Canadian jobs to Mexico
   (5) Loss of Canadian jobs to the United States

ANSWERS

1. **(1)** Labour mobility has to do with restrictions on geographic or occupational movement of workers.

2. **(5)** Free-trade agreements eliminate barriers and put foreign and local businesses on equal footing.

3. **(4)** The passage indicates that all free-trade agreements are different and relate to different industry sectors, not all industry sectors.

4. **(5)** The agreement is between the three countries that make up North America.

5. **(2)** According to the passage, of the $626.3 billion of trade in 2008, only $23.8 billion was with Mexico and $91.3 billion was trade in services with the U.S. The majority, therefore, was in trade of merchandise.

6. **(3)** According to the passage, one purpose of the agreement is to improve working conditions.

CHAPTER CHECK-UP

Complete these practice exercises, and check the answers and analysis that follow. After you mark your work, review any topic in the chapter that you had trouble with or did not understand.

Questions 1–4 are based on the following information.

The Universal Declaration of Human Rights (UDHR), which was adopted by the UN General Assembly on 10 December 1948, was the result of the experience of the Second World War. With the end of that war, and the creation of the United Nations, the international community vowed never again to allow atrocities like those of that conflict to happen again. World leaders decided to complement the UN Charter with a road map to guarantee the rights of every individual everywhere. The document they considered, and which would later become the Universal Declaration of Human Rights, was taken up at the first session of the General Assembly in 1946. The Assembly reviewed this draft Declaration on Fundamental Human Rights and Freedoms and transmitted it to the Economic and Social Council "for reference to the Commission on Human Rights for consideration . . . in its preparation of an international bill of rights". The Commission, at its first session early in 1947, authorized its members to formulate what it termed "a preliminary draft International Bill of Human Rights". Later the work was taken over by a formal drafting committee, consisting of members of the Commission from eight States, selected with due regard for geographical distribution.

The Commission on Human Rights was made up of 18 members from various political, cultural and religious backgrounds. Eleanor Roosevelt, widow of American President Franklin D. Roosevelt, chaired the UDHR drafting committee. With her were René Cassin of France, who composed the first draft of the Declaration, the Committee Rapporteur Charles Malik of Lebanon, Vice-Chairman Peng Chung Chang of China, and John Humphrey of Canada, Director of the UN's Human Rights Division, who prepared the Declaration's blueprint. But Mrs. Roosevelt was recognized as the driving force for the Declaration's adoption.

The entire text of the UDHR was composed in less than two years. At a time when the world was divided into Eastern and Western blocks, finding a common ground on what should make the essence of the document proved to be a colossal task. By its resolution 217 A (III) of 10 December 1948, the General Assembly, meeting in Paris, adopted the Universal Declaration of Human Rights.

1. What was the inspiration for the United Nations Declaration of Human Rights?
   (1) Communist domination of Eastern Europe
   (2) A legacy for Franklin D. Roosevelt
   (3) Creation of the United Nations
   (4) Treaty of Paris
   (5) Atrocities committed in World War II

2. Based on information from the passage, we can conclude that the United Nations had their first meeting in
   (1) 1946
   (2) 1947
   (3) 1948
   (4) 1950
   (5) 2010

3. What role did a Canadian play in preparation of the document?
   (1) Member of the committee
   (2) Lobbied for approval
   (3) Wrote the document
   (4) Obtained Canada's support
   (5) Chaired the committee

4. The United Nations Declaration of Human Rights was drafted and approved during
   (1) World War II
   (2) The Cold War
   (3) World War 1
   (4) The Korean conflict
   (5) The Great Depression

Questions 5–7 are based on the following information.

China is one of the largest and fastest-growing economies in the world. With the largest population on earth, the country has undergone rapid urbanization and growth in GDP, to emerge as the world's fourth largest economy and a power in global trade. Despite its Communist government's poor record on human rights, many nations are competing to establish closer economic relations with China, including Canada.

China is Canada's fourth largest trading partner. Exports to China include communications, transportation, and aerospace technology, but consist primarily of products such as ore, woodpulp and paper, fruits and grains, wood and wood products. Canada imports primarily manufactured goods, such as electronics, toys, furniture, clothes, and plastic articles. Although Canada exports billions of dollars in goods to China, we import more than twice as much. The government of Canada hopes to increase Canadian penetration into the Chinese market, seeing vast potential in over a billion potential customers.

5. Based on information from the passage, we can conclude that in trade with China, Canada has a
   (1) trade deficit
   (2) trade surplus
   (3) balance of trade
   (4) competitive advantage
   (5) larger market

6. Based on information from the passage, Canada's exports to China consist primarily of
   (1) manufactured goods
   (2) technology
   (3) airplanes
   (4) natural resources
   (5) knowledge services

7. Based on information in the passage, what is the most likely reason that some people might protest increased trade with China?
   (1) Human rights record
   (2) China is too large a market
   (3) The Chinese economy grows too rapidly
   (4) Size of the Chinese population
   (5) Difficulty of transportation

Questions 8–10 are based on the following information.

The Copenhagen Accord is an agreement on climate change that was drafted by the United States and agreed upon by a small number of countries, including Canada, in 2009. Although the accord endorses the Kyoto Protocol, it has significant differences from that document, which was agreed upon by 190 countries. The Copenhagen Accord is not a legally binding document and has no penalties if targets are not met. Unlike Kyoto, countries set their own targets to reduce emissions rather than striving to reduce them below 1990 levels. Canada, for example, has targeted a reduction by 17% from 2005 levels by 2020, as compared with commitments by the European Union, Russia, Japan, and Ukraine to a significant reduction over 1990 levels. As one of the world's top ten polluters, this commitment by Canada is seen sceptically by critics. Nevertheless, the accord represents at least some environmental commitment by Canada, which withdrew from Kyoto, and the United States, which had set no targets under Kyoto.

In part, the Copenhagen Accord reads as follows:

"1. We underline that climate change is one of the greatest challenges of our time. We emphasise our strong political will to urgently combat climate change in accordance with the principle of common but differentiated responsibilities and respective capabilities. To achieve the ultimate objective of the Convention to stabilize greenhouse gas concentration in the atmosphere at a level that would prevent dangerous anthropogenic interference with the climate system, we shall, recognizing the scientific view that the increase in global temperature should be below 2 degrees Celsius, on the basis of equity and in the context of sustainable development, enhance our long-term cooperative action to combat climate change. We recognize the critical impacts of climate change and the potential impacts of response measures on countries particularly vulnerable to its adverse effects and stress the need to establish a comprehensive adaptation programme including international support".

8. Based on information from this passage, it is likely that world response to Canada's participation in the Copenhagen Accord would be
   (1) supportive
   (2) tentative
   (3) enthusiastic
   (4) understanding
   (5) critical

9. In comparison with the Kyoto Protocol, the Copenhagen Accord has
   (1) more signatory countries
   (2) no legal effect
   (3) stricter targets
   (4) greater world support
   (5) no targets

10. Based on the information in the passage, we can conclude that the countries believe that climate change is
    (1) a theory
    (2) a fact
    (3) untrue
    (4) unimportant
    (5) unstoppable

Questions 11–12 are based on the following information.

With no chromium deposits of its own, China is the largest importer of chrome ore and the largest exporter of chrome goods.

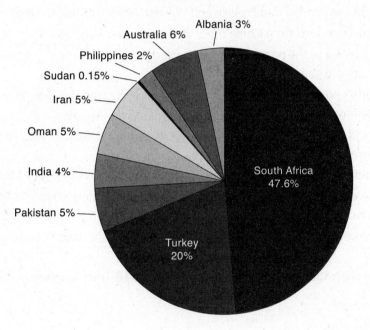

China-imported chrome ore by countries in 2012

Albania 3%
Australia 6%
Philippines 2%
Sudan 0.15%
Iran 5%
Oman 5%
India 4%
Pakistan 5%
South Africa 47.6%
Turkey 20%

11. Based on this information, we can conclude that the largest producer of chromium in the world is
    (1) Pakistan
    (2) Turkey
    (3) China
    (4) South Africa
    (5) Australia

12. Based on the information in the chart, from which country does China import the least amount of chrome ore?
    (1) Sudan
    (2) India
    (3) Albania
    (4) Philippines
    (5) Oman

ANSWERS

1. **(5)** The passage states that the inspiration for the declaration was to ensure that the atrocities of World War II would never be repeated.

2. **(1)** The passage states that the first meeting of the General Assembly was in 1946.

3. **(3)** The passage states that Canadian John Humphrey prepared the document blueprint, no doubt based on the discussions and input from the committee.

4. **(2)** One achievement was that the document was drafted and approved at a time when the world was divided into Eastern and Western blocks, during the cold war.

5. **(1)** Canada imports from China more than it exports, which is a trade deficit.

6. **(4)** According to the passage, Canada's exports consist primarily of ores, wood products, fruits and grains, all natural resources

7. **(1)** China's poor record on human rights is a likely reason that people would object to increased trade.

8. **(5)** World opinion of Canada is critical for abandoning the Kyoto Protocol and adopting a lower standard.

9. **(2)** Unlike the Kyoto Protocol, the Copenhagen Accord is not legally binding.

10. **(2)** The extract from the Accord clearly states the signatory countries believe climate change to be the greatest challenge of our time.

11. **(4)** China has no deposits of its own, but imports the largest amount from South Africa.

12. **(1)** The chart shows that China imports less than 1% from Sudan.

Social Studies—
Practice Test

Directions: The GED Social Studies Test **includes 50 multiple-choice questions. Do not spend more than 70 minutes on the test.**

The practice test includes multiple-choice questions based on reading passages, maps, cartoons, photographs, tables, charts, and graphs. The information on the test represents global social studies topics. Some questions are about specifically Canadian topics.

The Social Studies test does not require specific knowledge of nations, political figures, or world events. The questions test your ability to read and interpret information, including skills in comprehension, application, analysis, and synthesis. A good general knowledge of social studies can also help you to interpret the information on the test.

Record your responses on the answer sheet that follows. For each question, mark the numbered space that corresponds with your answer choice.

EXAMPLE

Top 5 Nickel-Producing Countries 2011

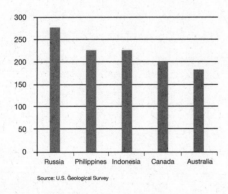

Source: U.S. Geological Survey

Based on this graphic, which country is the fourth-largest producer of nickel?

(1) Russia

(2) Philippines

(3) Canada

(4) Indonesia

(5) Australia

In this example, apply your ability to interpret the bar graph to recognize that Canada has the fourth-highest level of production. Fill in answer space 3 on the answer sheet.

ANSWER SHEET
Social Studies Practice Test

1. ① ② ③ ④ ⑤
2. ① ② ③ ④ ⑤
3. ① ② ③ ④ ⑤
4. ① ② ③ ④ ⑤
5. ① ② ③ ④ ⑤
6. ① ② ③ ④ ⑤
7. ① ② ③ ④ ⑤
8. ① ② ③ ④ ⑤
9. ① ② ③ ④ ⑤
10. ① ② ③ ④ ⑤
11. ① ② ③ ④ ⑤
12. ① ② ③ ④ ⑤
13. ① ② ③ ④ ⑤
14. ① ② ③ ④ ⑤
15. ① ② ③ ④ ⑤
16. ① ② ③ ④ ⑤
17. ① ② ③ ④ ⑤
18. ① ② ③ ④ ⑤
19. ① ② ③ ④ ⑤
20. ① ② ③ ④ ⑤

21. ① ② ③ ④ ⑤
22. ① ② ③ ④ ⑤
23. ① ② ③ ④ ⑤
24. ① ② ③ ④ ⑤
25. ① ② ③ ④ ⑤
26. ① ② ③ ④ ⑤
27. ① ② ③ ④ ⑤
28. ① ② ③ ④ ⑤
29. ① ② ③ ④ ⑤
30. ① ② ③ ④ ⑤
31. ① ② ③ ④ ⑤
32. ① ② ③ ④ ⑤
33. ① ② ③ ④ ⑤
34. ① ② ③ ④ ⑤
35. ① ② ③ ④ ⑤
36. ① ② ③ ④ ⑤
37. ① ② ③ ④ ⑤
38. ① ② ③ ④ ⑤
39. ① ② ③ ④ ⑤
40. ① ② ③ ④ ⑤

41. ① ② ③ ④ ⑤
42. ① ② ③ ④ ⑤
43. ① ② ③ ④ ⑤
44. ① ② ③ ④ ⑤
45. ① ② ③ ④ ⑤
46. ① ② ③ ④ ⑤
47. ① ② ③ ④ ⑤
48. ① ② ③ ④ ⑤
49. ① ② ③ ④ ⑤
50. ① ② ③ ④ ⑤

SOCIAL STUDIES

Complete the practice test, and then check the answers and analysis that follow. After you mark your work, review any topics you had trouble with or did not understand.

Questions 1–4 are based on the following passage.

Louis Riel was born in 1844 in the Red River Colony in what is now Manitoba. The population was made up largely of the descendants of European fur traders and First Nations mothers. The majority, including Riel, were French-speaking Métis.

In 1869, the Hudson's Bay Company sold vast land, including the Red River territory, to the government of Canada. While negotiations between the company and the Canadian government took place, Canadian and American settlers began to arrive. Concerns of the existing inhabitants to protect their lands and culture were heightened when the Canadian government appointed a lieutenant governor and sent land survey crews to resurvey the territory.

The Métis and other concerned residents seized control of Fort Garry and united under Louis Riel to establish a provisional government, which expelled the surveyors, prevented arrival of the lieutenant governor, and negotiated with Canada for entry into Confederation. A group of armed settlers, intent on overthrowing the provisional government were rounded up and imprisoned. One particularly vocal individual, Thomas Scott of Ontario, was tried and executed, an act that galvanized public opinion in Canada against Riel and ultimately led to his downfall.

The rights of the people of the Red River Colony were recognized in 1870 by the federal government in the Manitoba Act, creating the province of Manitoba. A peaceful military force was sent by Ottawa to assume control. As a result of outrage in Ontario over Scott's death, Riel was not granted amnesty and was forced into exile. He was elected to Parliament three times, but was never able to return to take his seat.

Despite assurances, many Métis soon found themselves deprived of lands and rights, and many moved farther west. In 1885, Riel returned to champion the rights of the Métis in Saskatchewan. This conflict, known as the Northwest Rebellion, led to his arrest and execution for treason.

1. The main issue of the Red River Rebellion was
   (1) the life of Louis Riel
   (2) expelling surveyors
   (3) rights of the Métis in Saskatchewan
   (4) entry into Confederation
   (5) protecting property rights and culture

2. Who controlled Manitoba before 1869?
   (1) The Hudson's Bay Company
   (2) Louis Riel
   (3) The Red River Colony
   (4) The government of Canada
   (5) The Métis

3. If Riel's government had not executed Thomas Scott, it is probable that
   (1) military force would not have been sent
   (2) Riel would have become a member of Parliament
   (3) the Métis would not have moved farther west
   (4) the Manitoba Act would not have been passed
   (5) settlers would not have come

4. The modern principal of which Riel would most approve, based on his political ideas as seen in the Red River Rebellion, is
   (1) might makes right
   (2) separation of church and state
   (3) environmentalism
   (4) imperialism
   (5) land claims settlements

Questions 5–7 are based on the following passage.

Mongolia, to the north of China, was the birthplace of one of the largest empires in history. Dwarfing the Roman Empire of old, at its height, the Mongol Empire covered nearly all of Asia, extending from Eastern Europe and through much of Russia, all of China and North and South Korea to the Pacific.

Genghis Khan was born with the name *Temujin* about 1162 CE, a younger son of the leader of a nomadic Mongol tribe. The Mongols were made up of a number of tribes that wandered the grassy Mongol plains searching for the best grazing for their horses, cattle, and other animals. There was no unity among the tribes, who often raided one another. His father died while Temujin was still a child, and his tribe, refusing to be led by someone so young, abandoned his mother and their family, so that he grew up in poverty.

By the age of 16, Temujin had assumed his place at the head of his father's tribe and married the daughter of another tribal leader, forming an alliance. He gradually assumed more power through alliances with other tribes and through conquest. He won the loyalty of his followers and even those he conquered by rewarding people based on their accomplishments, rather than on their family ties. By the end of his life in 1227, he had become the great Mongol Khan, successfully uniting the Mongol tribes into a great military force that conquered all of central Asia, including much of China. Following his death, his sons continued the expansion throughout the continent.

In addition to conquest, Genghis Khan had numerous other accomplishments. He brought peace among Mongol people by uniting the tribes. He oversaw the creation and introduction of a written language for his people and established a code of law. He established a government based more on accomplishment than heredity. Largely through conquest, he introduced the Mongol people to art and culture and international trade. Conquest also brought in a variety of tradespeople and craftsmen.

5. Based on information in the passage, we can conclude that a nomadic tribe is one that
   (1) is based on agriculture
   (2) is warlike
   (3) has advanced art and culture
   (4) wanders from place to place
   (5) has no leaders

6. Based on information in the passage, we can conclude that in addition to being a military leader, Genghis Khan was a skilled
   (1) politician
   (2) artist
   (3) scholar
   (4) lawyer
   (5) farmer

7. Based on information in the passage, the Mongol Empire under Genghis Khan included all of
   (1) Asia
   (2) Central Asia
   (3) Southern Asia
   (4) Europe
   (5) Eastern Europe

Questions 8–10 are based on the following information.

There is one international bank in the world whose goal is not to make profit but to combat poverty. It is the World Bank, officially a part of the United Nations, which provides loans and expertise for a wide range of projects in developing countries. World poverty has been reduced significantly since the 1980s, but there are still more than one billion people worldwide who live in a state of abject poverty, a situation that the World Bank describes as, *morally unacceptable given the resources and technology we have available today.* At the same time, the gap in money and opportunities between rich and poor is getting wider, especially in developing countries. The World Bank wants to raise the standard of living and income potential for everyone, not just a privileged few.

The overall goal of the World Bank is a world that is free of poverty. Many people in affluent countries, such as Canada, have little understanding of what poverty means in some other countries. Many people throughout the world, if they can find work at all, will receive less than $1.25 per day. The World Bank hopes to decrease this number to less than 3% of the world's population by 2030.

Without access to education, healthcare, and basic infrastructure (roads, running water, sewerage, schools, hospitals, communications, and environmental controls) these people can have no hope to change their present or their future. These are the types of projects that the World Bank funds through loans to developing countries. Often, the loans come with conditions that require changes to economic or social policy. In 2012 alone, the World Bank provided more than 30 billion dollars in loans.

8. The primary role of the World Bank is to
   (1) give loans
   (2) earn profit
   (3) provide economic expertise
   (4) reduce poverty
   (5) promote human rights through economic sanctions

9. Which of the following projects is most likely to receive funding by a World Bank loan?
   (1) Student loans in Canada
   (2) Military equipment in Syria
   (3) Food banks in the United States
   (4) Auto plant in Uganda
   (5) Educational development in Ethiopia

10. Which of the following philosophies best reflects the goals and activities of the World Bank?
    (1) Shared prosperity
    (2) The rich should pay for the poor
    (3) Charity begins at home
    (4) Survival of the fittest
    (5) Poverty can be overcome by hard work

Questions 11–13 are based on the following information.

Canadian Charter of Rights and Freedoms
Equality Rights

Section 15
(1) Every individual is equal before and under the law and has the right to the equal protection and equal benefit of the law without discrimination and, in particular, without discrimination based on race, national or ethnic origin, colour, religion, sex, age or mental or physical disability.
(2) Subsection (1) does not preclude any law, program or activity that has as an object the amelioration of conditions of disadvantaged individuals or groups including those that are disadvantaged because of race, national or ethnic origin, colour, religion, sex, age or mental or physical disability.

11. The passage above is
    (1) a declaration of the Supreme Court
    (2) part of the Constitution of Canada
    (3) part of the Canadian Labour Code
    (4) part of the preamble to the Constitution
    (5) a set of government regulations

12. This section of the charter provides
    (1) freedom of religion
    (2) freedom of expression
    (3) special laws and programs
    (4) recognition of diversity
    (5) equality under the law

13. This section of the charter would prohibit all of the following EXCEPT
    (1) a government jobs program for young people
    (2) restricting enrolment in the armed forces to ages 18–24
    (3) targeting a particular race for police investigation
    (4) refusing a fair trial based on religion
    (5) denying a government job to a disabled person

Questions 14–17 are based on the following passage.

On the morning of Friday, November 8, 2013, category 5 Typhoon Haiyan descended on the Philippines. A typhoon is like a hurricane, but stronger, and occurs in the Pacific Ocean, blowing towards Asia. It brings with it heavy rains and strong winds that often push high waves before them. When it reached land at the small city of Tacloban, Haiyan was a storm of unparalleled magnitude bringing 400 mm of rain, sustained winds of 235 kmph, gusts of 275 kmph, and waves 15 metres high.

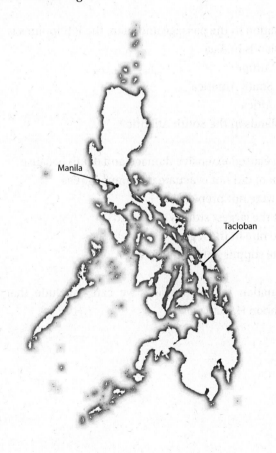

With advance warning, the government in Manila had evacuated hundreds of thousands of people in the path of the storm to shelters in schools, government buildings, and churches, but the structures were no match for the power of the storm. The city of Tacloban, population 220,000, directly in the path of the storm, was virtually flattened. Millions of people were affected by the storm. As many as 10,000 people were killed and 630,000 left homeless. In the aftermath, aid workers struggled to reach the affected areas. Hundreds of corpses lay in the streets of Tacloban and other communities, while looting erupted and violence threatened. The biggest challenges faced by relief workers were to get aid to the worst affected areas, most importantly to obtain clean drinking water, and to maintain order.

The international community was quick to express sympathy and support. The United Nations called for $301 million in aid. Australia pledged $9 million, New Zealand $1 million. The government of Canada pledged to match contributions by Canadian citizens to registered charities up to a total of $5 million. The United States immediately pledged $100,000 in aid, as well as troops and equipment to help in transportation and rescue efforts. China also pledged $200,000.

14. One difference between a hurricane and a typhoon is
    (1) rain
    (2) location
    (3) high winds
    (4) waves
    (5) destruction

15. Based on information in the passage and map, the Philippines is
    (1) a group of islands in Asia
    (2) an island in Europe
    (3) a country in South America
    (4) a country in Africa
    (5) a group of islands in the South Atlantic

16. Typhoon Haiyan caused extensive damage and death because
    (1) the government did not evacuate threatened areas
    (2) aid workers were not prepared
    (3) it was one of the largest storms on record
    (4) typhoons are rare in the region
    (5) of inadequate supplies of drinking water

17. Based on information in the passage, we can conclude that international aid in response to Typhoon Haiyan was
    (1) rapid
    (2) abundant
    (3) sympathetic
    (4) withheld
    (5) insufficient

Questions 18–20 are based on the following passage.

Although known for peacekeeping and friendliness, Canada has seen its share of political debate. On February 15, 1965, the Canadian flag, with its red maple leaf on a white background with two red panels at the sides, was flown for the first time as Canada's official flag. It had been a long time in coming.

For more than 40 years, a new Canadian flag was one of the most contentious issues in politics. Since Confederation in 1867, the official flag had been Britain's Union Jack. Canada needed a flag as a symbol of its independence and diverse heritage. Attempts had been made under several Prime Ministers to arrive at a solution. Many people felt that the new flag should include the Union Jack. Others insisted that it should not.

When Lester Pearson became Prime Minister in 1963, he promised Canadians a new flag, but everyone had a different idea. When the final design was presented to Parliament, it was debated for nearly six months before the government introduced closure and it was passed. Truly, the flag that has become a symbol of peace throughout the world had a stormy beginning.

18. This passage deals chiefly with
    (1) political debate in Canada
    (2) Canadian peacekeeping
    (3) the Canadian flag debate
    (4) Canada's reputation for peace
    (5) Canada's independence and diverse heritage

19. According to this passage, people who suggested designs for a new flag were usually
    (1) honoured
    (2) misunderstood
    (3) criticized
    (4) forgotten
    (5) elected Prime Ministers

20. Which statement is true according to the passage?
    (1) Canadians are patriotic.
    (2) Canadians did not like the Union Jack.
    (3) Parliament is unable to make decisions.
    (4) Canadians have many cultural and national origins.
    (5) The Canadian flag is over 100 years old.

Questions 21–24 are based on the following passage.

At the end of World War II, much of Eastern Europe had fallen behind the iron curtain of communist domination and Soviet control. Nowhere was this more evident than Berlin. Germany, at the end of the war, was divided into four zones controlled by each of the four major allied powers: the Soviet Union, United States, Britain, and France. The city of Berlin, although located entirely within the Soviet zone, was also divided into four. The original intent was that the country would be reconstructed and unified, so that it could once again become self-sustaining.

Tensions between the Soviets under leader Joseph Stalin and the other allied powers grew as it became evident that the Soviets had no intention of reconstructing and withdrawing from the conquered territory. While West Germany was once again united with a democratically elected government and market economy, East Germany remained a puppet of Russia under communist rule.

Over the succeeding years, several million East Germans fled across the open borders to freedom in the west. In the early 1950's, barbed wire and guard patrols effectively closed the border between east and west, leaving Berlin as the most accessible point for escape. In 1961, the East German government constructed the Berlin Wall, which ran through the centre of the city and around to completely enclose West Berlin. It consisted of high cement walls and guard towers. On the East German side was a wide area of barren ground known as the *death strip*. For nearly thirty years, the Berlin Wall prevented unauthorized access to the west and made West Berlin an island in communist territory.

The fall of the Berlin Wall was sudden and unexpected. In 1988 and 1989 communist governments in Eastern European countries were weakening as well as developing a new spirit of tolerance. Suddenly, on November 9, 1989, the East German government announced that border checkpoints with West Germany were open. In disbelief, East Germans approached the wall and found that it was true. Thousands of people on both sides rushed to the wall in celebration, many people chipping away at the wall with hammers and other tools. The remainder of the wall was removed with heavy equipment the following year. On October 3, 1990, Germany was restored as a single unified state.

21. The Berlin Wall separated West Berlin from
    (1) East Berlin
    (2) West Germany
    (3) East Germany
    (4) Soviet Union
    (5) France

22. The purpose of the Berlin Wall was to
    (1) demonstrate Soviet power
    (2) protect against invasion
    (3) prevent smuggling
    (4) keep people out
    (5) keep people in

23. The term *iron curtain* probably refers to
    (1) political, physical, and military separation of communist countries
    (2) the Berlin Wall
    (3) democratically elected government and market economy
    (4) prevention of escape from communist countries
    (5) barriers to German reunification

24. The reunification of Germany was made possible by
    (1) World War II
    (2) the fall of the Berlin Wall
    (3) the influence of the United States
    (4) a collapse of European communism
    (5) a celebration of thousands of people

Questions 25–27 are based on the following information.

Traditionally, Canadians have regarded themselves as not overly patriotic. Not that they don't love their country, but there are few flags on the front lawns or patriotic speeches by action heroes on TV. Indeed, what could a country whose national symbols are a beaver and a leaf have to be proud of?

Yet while Canadian national pride may be quiet, it runs deep. Canadians travelling overseas sew small flags on their clothing because we know the high regard in which our nation is held. We know who held the line when poison gas was first used in World War I, and we remember Vimy Ridge and the Somme. We know who invented basketball, and we remember the 1972 Summit Series of Hockey. It was Canadians who smuggled six American diplomats out of Iran in 1980, and Canadians invented the snowmobile and the zipper.

The red maple leaf may not have the grandeur of an eagle or a lion, but it stands for peace, courage, and innovation.

25. According to the passage, Canadians
    (1) have little to be proud of
    (2) are not very patriotic
    (3) boast about their country
    (4) are quietly patriotic
    (5) have strong national symbols

26. Who held the line when poison gas was first used in World War I?
    (1) Americans
    (2) Canadians
    (3) Iranians
    (4) Germans
    (5) Diplomats

27. A good title for this passage might be
    (1) "Canada's National Symbols"
    (2) "Remember the Canada Cup"
    (3) "Proud to Be Canadian"
    (4) "The Red, White, and Blue"
    (5) "The Lion and Eagle"

Questions 28–30 are based on the following information.

Protecting the American people from terrorist threats is the reason the Department of Homeland Security (DHS) was created, and remains our highest priority. Our vision is a secure and resilient nation that effectively prevents terrorism in ways that preserve our freedom and prosperity.

Understanding Evolving and Emerging Threats

Terrorist tactics continue to evolve, and we must keep pace. Terrorists seek sophisticated means of attack, including chemical, biological, radiological, nuclear, and explosive weapons, as well as cyber-attacks. Threats may come from abroad or be homegrown.

We must be vigilant against new types of terrorist recruitment as well, by engaging communities at risk being targeted by terrorist recruiters.

Improving Terrorism Prevention

The Department's efforts to prevent terrorism are centered on a risk-based, layered approach to security in our passenger and cargo transportation systems and at our borders and ports of entry. It includes new technologies to

- Detect explosives and other weapons
- Help protect critical infrastructure and cyber networks from attack
- Build information-sharing partnerships

We do this work cooperatively with other federal, state, local, tribal, and territorial law enforcement as well as international partners.

Source: United States Department of Homeland Security. "Preventing Terrorism Overview."

28. The United States Department of Homeland Security exists to
    (1) prevent terrorism
    (2) conduct espionage against other countries
    (3) conduct espionage against U.S. citizens
    (4) research terrorist methodologies
    (5) protect American financial interests

29. Based on information in the passage, we can conclude that threats to United States security involve people who
    (1) come from other countries
    (2) come from the United States
    (3) cross the border from Canada
    (4) have sophisticated technology
    (5) come from the United States and other countries

30. Homeland Security's efforts are focused on
    (1) public buildings
    (2) transportation systems
    (3) explosives detection
    (4) information sharing
    (5) vigilante justice

Questions 31–33 are based on the following information.

On September 11, 2001, a three-pronged terrorist attack took place against the United States, directed at targets in New York City and Washington, D.C. Nineteen al-Qaeda terrorists succeeded in hijacking four commercial airliners in-flight. Using pilot training they had obtained in flight schools in the United States, the terrorists turned the planes towards their targets.

At 8:46 a.m. the first plane crashed into the north tower of the World Trade Center in New York. At 9:03 a.m., while millions around the world watched on live television, the second plane struck the south tower. Less than an hour later, the towers would collapse. At 9:37 a.m. a third plane struck the Pentagon in Washington. At 10:03 a.m., the hijackers crashed the fourth plane into a field in Pennsylvania to avoid being overcome by passengers who had turned on their captors and were trying to break into the cockpit.

Immediately after the attacks, the United States suspected al-Qaeda and its leader, Osama bin Laden. This was not an isolated incident. Bin Laden had been implicated in other terrorist attacks over the previous decade although nothing had ever been done. He was known to be closely allied with the Taliban government of war-torn Afghanistan, where he had set up headquarters and terrorist training camps.

9/11 was a day that changed the world. It launched the global war on terror and the worldwide manhunt for Bin Laden, which ended with his death in 2011. It resulted in the invasion of Afghanistan, which drew in other U.S. allies, and the invasion of Iraq. It led to atrocities against Iraqi prisoners transported by the United States to their base at Guantanamo Bay, Cuba. It led to the deaths of civilians and of thousands of allied troops who remained in Afghanistan and Iraq to restore order.

The events of 9/11 turned the attention of North Americans for the first time to the reality of terrorism. It resulted in the capture or death of many terrorist leaders and serious harm to their organisations. It also led to greater global cooperation in combating terror, both on the ground and through sharing intelligence.

31. According to the information in the passage, the weapons that terrorists used against the World Trade Center were
    (1) explosives
    (2) missiles
    (3) tanks
    (4) airplanes
    (5) fighter jets

32. Before the attacks, al-Qaeda leader Osama bin Laden was
    (1) unknown to intelligence organisations
    (2) an internationally wanted criminal
    (3) known to have committed other attacks
    (4) active in Saudi politics
    (5) a member of the CIA

33. Canadian troops were sent to Afghanistan because Canada
    (1) is an ally of the United States
    (2) protested against terrorist attacks
    (3) was afraid of attacks on Canadian soil
    (4) wanted Afghanistan's oil
    (5) opposed the Taliban's record on human rights

Questions 34–37 are based on the following information.

In 1958, an idea called the Phillips Curve was introduced to explain the relationship between unemployment and inflation. Under the theory, when the rate of inflation in an economy is high, unemployment is low because there is more money in the economy. By the same logic, when inflation is low, unemployment will be high because there is less money in the economy and less demand for goods and services, which results in lower production and fewer jobs. For many years, this idea influenced government economic policy, and it is still influential today.

In the 1970s, it became apparent that the Phillips Curve was not entirely accurate as Canada experienced a period of both high unemployment and high inflation. The government of the day, under Pierre Trudeau, introduced legislation to control both wages and prices. In the recession of 2010 to 2012, the model was again disproved when the country experienced low inflation but growing unemployment. Nonetheless, the Phillips Curve has become ingrained into the traditional wisdom of governments who attempt to combat employment through increasing the amount of money in the economy.

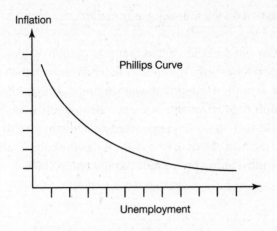

Inflation

Phillips Curve

Unemployment

34. The term *high inflation* means
   (1) high prices
   (2) low prices
   (3) low wages
   (4) high wages
   (5) high unemployment

35. Based on the Phillips Curve, unemployment in an economy would be higher if the inflation rate were
   (1) 6%
   (2) 5%
   (3) 4%
   (4) 3%
   (5) 2%

36. Following the Phillips Curve, which action might a government take to reduce high unemployment?
   (1) Increase interest rates
   (2) Reduce interest rates
   (3) Reduce government spending
   (4) Cut jobs in the civil service
   (5) Increase taxes

37. The relationship between unemployment and inflation in the Phillips Curve could be described as
   (1) parallel
   (2) corresponding
   (3) inverse
   (4) equivalent
   (5) matching

Questions 38–39 are based on the following information.

Free trade between Canada and the United States is not a new idea. In the late 1800s and early 1900s, it was called *reciprocity*. In the 1891 federal election, the Liberal Party of Canada proposed reciprocity with the United States as an alternative to the protectionist policies of conservative Sir John A. MacDonald, but was defeated at the polls. In 1911, the Liberal government, which was then in power, negotiated an agreement with the United States, but was again defeated in the next election. Ironically, it was the conservatives who finally implemented the Canada-United States Free-Trade Agreement in 1988.

THE CERTAIN RESULT OF A RECIPROCITY HOLE IN THE LINE FENCE

W. S. JOHNSTON & CO'Y. LIMITED. PRINTERS. TORONTO

Feeding on Canadian raw materials?

38. The cartoon suggests that reciprocity would mean
    (1) Canada and the United States would both benefit
    (2) Canada could access U.S. markets
    (3) Canada could profit from export of raw materials
    (4) the United States would take Canadian raw materials
    (5) Canada would buy U.S. raw materials

39. Duties and taxes on imported goods are an example of
    (1) protectionist policies
    (2) reciprocity
    (3) Liberal policies
    (4) Conservative policies
    (5) free trade

Questions 40–42 are based on the following information.

Canadians are accustomed to thinking of their government as a three-party system. However, throughout the years, a number of political parties representing particular regions, issues, or points of view have come and gone. At the provincial level, several have even formed governments.

In the federal election of 2004, a total of nine registered parties fielded candidates. These included the Bloc Quebecois, Canadian Action Party, Communist Party of Canada, Conservative Party of Canada, Liberal Party of Canada, Marijuana Party, Marxist-Leninist Party of Canada, and New Democratic Party.

Nor must we forget that the three major national parties, despite the common view, also represent distinct philosophies.

40. Which of the following could best be described as a single-issue party?
     (1) Bloc Quebecois
     (2) Liberal Party of Canada
     (3) Conservative Party of Canada
     (4) New Democratic Party
     (5) Green Party

41. Which of the following parties is least likely to form the Government of Canada?
     (1) Bloc Quebecois
     (2) Liberal Party of Canada
     (3) Conservative Party of Canada
     (4) New Democratic Party
     (5) Green Party

42. Which of the following parties is most likely to support lower taxes and fewer government programs?
     (1) Bloc Quebecois
     (2) Liberal Party of Canada
     (3) Conservative Party of Canada
     (4) New Democratic Party
     (5) Green Party

Questions 43–45 are based on the following information

The Day of the Dead is a celebration that officially takes place on November 2, but actually runs from the evening of October 31 until November 2 each year. Although Mexican in origin, the holiday, which is similar in some ways to North America's Halloween, has spread to other Latin and non-Latin countries throughout the world—including Brazil, the United States, and the Philippines—and there are similar traditions in South Korea and other Asian, African, and European countries.

The belief is that the gates of heaven open on the evening of October 31, so that the souls of the dead can come in. Families traditionally make alters in their homes, often out of paper, to honour departed loved ones. These alters are decorated with candy skulls, marigolds, and favourite foods and mementos of the departed. Families gather around alters to feast and pray for their dead loved ones. There are cardboard skeletons, lots of noise, and funny stories are told about the people from when they were alive. The purpose is to wake up the dead souls and make them feel welcome and honoured.

November 1 is the day when the souls of young children and infants are honoured. Traditions vary in different regions of Mexico and throughout the world. In some areas, the day is marked by visits from neighbours to the families of children who have died. November 2 is the day that adults are remembered. It is not uncommon for families to picnic at the cemetery to spend time with the loved ones they have lost. Outside of Mexico, the day is often celebrated with parades that feature costumes and marigolds. Parades are commonly found in Spain and throughout the United States.

43. The Day of the Dead is closely tied to the North American celebration of
    (1) Thanksgiving
    (2) Remembrance Day
    (3) Labor Day
    (4) Halloween
    (5) Christmas

44. The Day of the Dead could be described as a time of
    (1) sadness
    (2) happiness
    (3) fear
    (4) anger
    (5) remembrance

45. The Day of the Dead is celebrated in
    (1) Mexico
    (2) Europe
    (3) Spain
    (4) the United States
    (5) many countries

Questions 46–47 are based on the following passage.

In 1776, thirteen North American colonies rebelled against British rule with the Declaration of Independence followed by the American Revolutionary War. The question is often asked, why did Canadians not join the revolution? There are many answers.

In the first place, the Canadian colonies were generally not as populous, nor as prosperous as their American counterparts, especially on the east coast. Their closest trading relationships were with Britain, and the economy and security relied heavily on the influx of British military. They were not as heavily affected by new British tariffs and taxes as the thirteen colonies. In the second place, even at that time, the personality of Canadian colonists was different from Americans. They were less independent and more content with British rule.

In the third place, both the Americans and British recognized that French Quebec was the only colony with the population and potential to sway the conflict. The Americans first sent a delegation and then invaded Quebec, attacking Montreal, hoping to stir up French resentment against Britain and bring Quebec into the union. The Americans, led by Benedict Arnold, were instructed not to molest the countryside or ordinary citizens but to limit their attack to Montreal. However, the Americans miscalculated. The Quebecois had no greater love for the American colonists who had fought against them on the side of the British in the Seven Years War than they did for Britain. In addition, the Quebec Act of 1774 had guaranteed language and cultural rights under continued British Rule. After the attack on Montreal was repelled by British troops, Quebec remained primarily neutral for the remainder of the conflict.

46. Based on the information in the passage, how many colonies originally formed the United States?
    (1) 6
    (2) 13
    (3) 17
    (4) 50
    (5) 52

47. One reason that Quebec did not support the Revolutionary War is
    (1) the Quebec Act
    (2) loyalty to Britain
    (3) loyalty to America
    (4) prosperity of Quebec
    (5) British military presence

Questions 48–50 are based on the following passage.

The concept for the European Union began after the Second World War as a means of establishing long-term peace and mutual prosperity in Europe. It began as a trade agreement in 1958 between Belgium, Germany, France, the Netherlands, Italy, and Luxembourg. Since that time, it has expanded to become a political, as well as economic, alliance, with 28 members in 2013. The change in name from European Economic Community to European Union in 1993 reflects the change.

The European Union is built primarily on treaties that have been approved by all member governments. It also includes a number of supranational agencies, including the European Council, European Parliament, and courts, although preserving the sovereignty of member states and the ability of their governments to rule themselves. One key piece of legislation, passed in 2009, is the Charter of Fundamental Rights, approved by all member countries, which commits all to a standard of human rights. The European Union has also eliminated trade barriers between countries, provided for mobility rights, and established the Euro as a common currency.

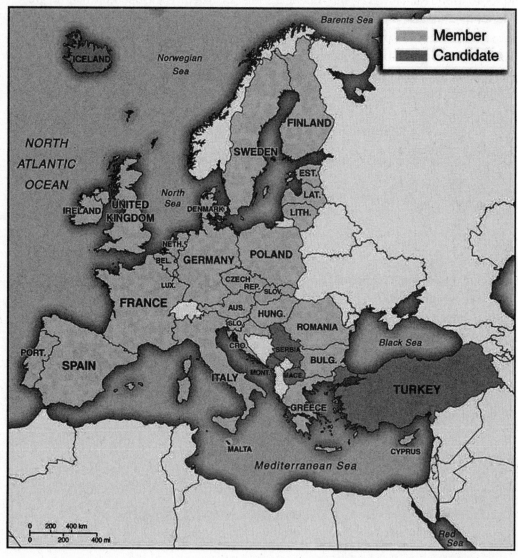

Source: CIA *The World Factbook*

48. At the time of writing, which of the following was not a full member of the European Union?
    (1) United Kingdom
    (2) Finland
    (3) Turkey
    (4) Spain
    (5) Italy

49. The original purpose of the European Union was to
    (1) reduce trade barriers
    (2) increase business opportunities
    (3) ensure human rights
    (4) prevent war
    (5) create a single European government

50. The continent of Europe is bounded on one side by the Atlantic Ocean and the other by the
    (1) Pacific Ocean
    (2) North Sea
    (3) Norwegian Sea
    (4) Indian Ocean
    (5) Mediterranean Sea

SOCIAL STUDIES ANSWERS AND ANALYSIS

ANSWERS

1. **(5)**		16. **(3)**		31. **(4)**		46. **(2)**
2. **(1)**		17. **(5)**		32. **(3)**		47. **(1)**
3. **(2)**		18. **(3)**		33. **(1)**		48. **(3)**
4. **(5)**		19. **(3)**		34. **(1)**		49. **(4)**
5. **(4)**		20. **(4)**		35. **(5)**		50. **(5)**
6. **(1)**		21. **(3)**		36. **(2)**		
7. **(2)**		22. **(5)**		37. **(3)**		
8. **(4)**		23. **(1)**		38. **(4)**		
9. **(5)**		24. **(4)**		39. **(1)**		
10. **(1)**		25. **(4)**		40. **(5)**		
11. **(2)**		26. **(2)**		41. **(1)**		
12. **(5)**		27. **(3)**		42. **(3)**		
13. **(1)**		28. **(1)**		43. **(4)**		
14. **(2)**		29. **(5)**		44. **(5)**		
15. **(1)**		30. **(2)**		45. **(5)**		

Interpret Your Results

Test Area	Questions	Recommended Minimum Score	Your Score
History	1, 2, 3, 4, 5, 6, 7, 21, 22, 23, 24, 31, 32, 33, 38, 39, 46, 47	13	
Geography	14, 15, 16, 17, 43, 44, 45	5	
Civics and Government	11, 12, 13, 18, 19, 20, 25, 26, 27, 28, 29, 30, 40, 41, 42	10	
Economics	8, 9, 10, 34, 35, 36, 37, 48, 49, 50	7	
Total		35	

Check your answers and calculate how you scored in each test area. If you scored less than the recommended minimum score in any test area, you should review topics in the relevant chapters.

ANSWER ANALYSIS

1. **(5)** Métis and other residents were concerned for their property and culture when Canada sent land survey crews and American settlers began to arrive.

2. **(1)** In 1869, the Hudson's Bay Company sold the land to Canada.

3. **(2)** Although elected to Parliament, Riel was unable to take his seat as he was not granted amnesty for the execution.

4. **(5)** Originally concerned to protect Métis land and culture, Riel would likely sympathize with land claims of other aboriginal peoples.

5. **(4)** The tribe wandered, searching for the best grazing for their livestock.

6. **(1)** In addition to conquest, Genghis Khan increased his influence through marriage, conquest, and winning the loyalty of his followers.

7. **(2)** The map clearly depicts Central Asia and the passage states he had conquered Central Asia by his death.

8. **(4)** The goal of the World Bank is to combat poverty.

9. **(5)** The passage speaks of the importance of access to education, healthcare, and infrastructure to promote the possibility for change.

10. **(1)** The passage does not suggest charity, but a moral responsibility for all to share in the prosperity of our world.

11. **(2)** The Charter of Rights and Freedoms is part of the Constitution Act, 1982 and the supreme law of Canada.

12. **(5)** The excerpt begins by stating that every individual is equal under the law.

13. **(1)** Section (2) permits programs to assist disadvantaged groups, such as unemployed youth.

14. **(2)** Although a typhoon is often stronger, both have rain, wind, and waves. A typhoon, however, occurs in the Pacific Ocean blowing towards Asia.

15. **(1)** The map shows a group of islands and we know that typhoons blow towards Asia.

16. **(3)** The storm is described as being of unparalleled proportions.

17. **(5)** The UN requested $301 million. The amounts pledged are far less.

18. **(3)** Although the other topics are mentioned, the passage is primarily about the flag debate.

19. **(3)** The passage shows there was much disagreement, so new ideas would have had critics.

20. **(4)** Canada needed a flag to represent its diverse heritage.

21. **(3)** West Berlin was located entirely within East Germany and surrounded by the wall.

22. **(5)** The wall was built in response to people fleeing communist East Germany.

23. **(1)** Although a physical barrier, the wall was more than that and also represented the ideological and military separation.

24. **(4)** The fall of the Berlin Wall and reunification of Germany were possible because of the decline of European communism.

25. **(4)** The passage shows Canadians as proud, but not ones to brag about their country.

26. **(2)** The passage is about Canadian patriotism.

27. **(3)** The passage is about Canadian patriotism.

28. **(1)** Homeland Security was created to protect the American people from terrorist threats.

29. **(5)** Threats may come from abroad or be homegrown.

30. **(2)** The department's approach focuses on passenger and cargo transportation, as well as borders.

31. **(4)** Terrorists hijacked commercial flights and flew them into their targets.

32. **(3)** The passage states he was implicated in other attacks.

33. **(1)** The passage states that the invasion drew in other U.S. allies.

34. **(1)** We deduce the meaning because the passage talks about prices and demand for goods and services.

35. **(5)** On the graph, we can see that when inflation is lower (closer to the bottom), unemployment is higher (farther to the right).

36. **(2)** The government might reduce interest rates, which discourages savings and encourages people to borrow money and buy. This puts more money in the economy.

37. **(3)** It is inverse because they are opposite.

38. **(4)** The cartoon shows the United States hogging the raw materials in the trough.

39. **(1)** Protectionist policies were the opposite of reciprocity.

40. **(5)** Although they have positions on other issues, the Green Party, as its name suggests, is primarily concerned with environmentalism.

41. **(1)** The Bloc Quebecois only has candidates in Quebec and could not form a government.

42. **(3)** Traditionally, conservatives support less government involvement in the economy. Responses to these questions require general knowledge of Canadian politics.

43. **(4)** The passage says it is similar to Halloween, and it is held at the same time.

44. **(5)** People feast, pray, and tell stories to remember their loved ones.

45. **(5)** Although originating in Mexico, it is celebrated in many countries around the world.

46. **(2)** It was a rebellion of thirteen American colonies.

47. **(1)** French Quebec did not love the British or Americans, but had received a degree of cultural and linguistic independence from the Quebec Act.

48. **(3)** On the map, Turkey is shown as a candidate, but not yet a full member.

49. **(4)** The concept began after World War II to establish long-term peace and prosperity in Europe.

50. **(5)** The map shows the Atlantic to the east and Mediterranean to the south. The Norwegian Sea is part of the Atlantic, and the Pacific and Indian Oceans do not border the EU.

Mathematics

Math Review

21

PLACE VALUE

Words are formed with letters and numbers are formed with digits. The position that a digit occupies in a number tells you how many ones, tens, hundreds, thousands and so on that the number contains. Study the chart below and memorize the place value names.

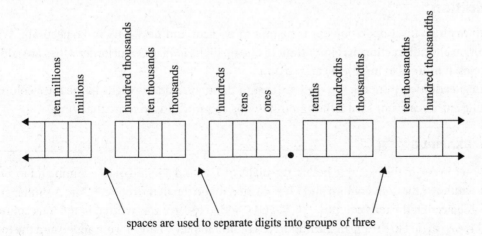

spaces are used to separate digits into groups of three

If you read the number 25 430, you state *twenty-five thousand, four hundred thirty*. The 2 is in the ten thousands position, the four is in the hundreds position, and so on.

➡ EXAMPLE 1 _____

Write out the number 12 620. Name the place value for the underlined digit.

Solution

Twelve thousand, six hundred twenty

6 is in the hundreds position.

➡ EXAMPLE 2 _____

Write out the number 704 102. Name the place value for the underlined digit.

Solution

Seven hundred four thousand, one hundred two

4 is in the thousands position.

PRACTICE

Write out each number in word form. Name the place value for the underlined digit.

1. 760
2. 25 332
3. 6 345 003
4. 2 315
5. 350 500

ANSWERS

1. Seven hundred sixty. 6 is in the tens position.
2. Twenty five thousand, three hundred thirty two. 3 is in the hundreds position.
3. Six million, three hundred forty five thousand, three. 3 is in the hundred thousands position.
4. Two thousand, three hundred fifteen. 2 is in the thousands position.
5. Three hundred fifty thousand, five hundred. 5 is in the ten thousands position

WHOLE-NUMBER OPERATIONS

Addition

With mathematical operations, it is helpful to be neat and necessary to be accurate. With addition and subtraction, it is important to line up digits in place value order. Ones are added to ones, hundreds to hundreds, and so on.

Begin addition from the top digit farthest to the right. Add the digits in the ones column, noting any to carry forward if the amount in this column adds to more than nine.

➡ EXAMPLE _____

As you can see in the example below, the digits of 4, 2, and 5 in the ones column add to 11. 1 was written in the ones column and 1 was carried to the top of the tens column. A similar step was followed in the tens column. 1, 5, 7, and 6 added to 19. 9 was written in the tens column and 1 was carried to the top of the hundreds column. Finally, 1 and 1 were added and the total of 2 was written in the hundreds column.

$$\begin{array}{r} 1\ 1 \\ 154 \\ 72 \\ +65 \\ \hline 291 \end{array}$$

To *sum* means to add values. The mathematical operation of addition is such a foundational skill that it is important to memorize basic addition facts. If you need practice beyond the following five questions, purchase some flashcards or look up additional practice problems online.

PRACTICE

Find the sum for the following addition problems.

1. $\begin{array}{r} 123 \\ 67 \\ +201 \\ \hline \end{array}$
2. $\begin{array}{r} 71340 \\ 2301 \\ +\ \ 67 \\ \hline \end{array}$
3. $\begin{array}{r} 1523 \\ 6741 \\ +\ 8910 \\ \hline \end{array}$
4. $1230450 + 54567 + 2341$

ANSWERS

1. 391
2. 73 708
3. 17 174
4. 1 287 358

Subtraction

Again, it is important to line up digits in place value order. Ones are subtracted from ones, hundreds from hundreds, and so forth.

Begin subtraction from the top digit farthest to the right using the column method as with addition.

➡ EXAMPLE 1 _____

Subtract $\begin{array}{r} 457 \\ -\ 35 \\ \hline 422 \end{array}$

The result of subtracting 35 from 457 is 422. The answer to a subtraction problem is called a *difference*.

➡ EXAMPLE 2 _____

Subtract $\begin{array}{r} 531 \\ -\ 46 \\ \hline \end{array}$

This problem becomes more complicated. How do you subtract 6 from 1? That is, how can you subtract a larger number from a smaller number? To do this, you must borrow from the place-value column to the left. To subtract 6 from 1, you must borrow one group of ten from the tens column. This reduces the 3 to a 2 and a small 1 is listed at the top of the ones column.

Subtract $\begin{array}{r} 2\ 1 \\ 531 \\ -\ 46 \\ \hline \end{array}$

By borrowing, you are now subtracting 6 from 11. However, notice that you will again run into a similar problem in the tens column. You are trying to subtract 4 from the remaining 2. Once again, you will need to borrow – this time from the hundreds column.

Subtract
```
  4 12 1
  531
 – 46
 ----
  485
```

By borrowing, you found the difference between 46 and 531 to be 485. You can always check this answer through addition.

Check
```
  485
 + 46
 ----
  531
```

➡ EXAMPLE 3 _____

Subtract
```
  2003
 – 522
```

You can subtract 2 from 3 in the ones column; however, you will need to borrow in order to subtract in the tens and hundreds column.

Subtract
```
  1 9 1
  2003
 – 522
```

As there were zeroes in the tens and hundreds columns, you had to move all the way to the thousands place value to borrow. Effectively you reduced 20 to 19 and placed one full group of ten in the tens column.

Subtract
```
   1 9 1
   2003
  – 522
  -----
   1481
```

By borrowing, you found the difference between 522 and 2003 to be 1481.

Check
```
  1481
 + 522
 -----
  2003
```

PRACTICE

Find the difference for the following subtraction problems.

1. 753   2. 1432   3. 12300   4. 10001 – 789   5. 127350 – 2245
  – 42   – 560   – 1450

ANSWERS

1. 711
2. 872
3. 10 850
4. 9 212
5. 125 105

Multiplication

Continue to use the column method with multiplication problems as well. Always place the largest number on top.

The ability to complete quick *mental multiplication* problems will be key to your success in a number of the GED problems. Brush up on your multiplication/times tables by purchasing some flashcards or looking up additional practice problems online.

➡ **EXAMPLE 1** _____

Multiply   251

          × 12

          502 → 502 is the product of 2×251

    2 510 → 2510 is the product of 10×251

    3 012 → By adding 502 and 2510, you find the final product of 3 012

The result of a multiplication problem is a *product*.
Again, you work through the problem from right to left.

➡ **EXAMPLE 2** _____

Multiply   405

         × 213

    1 215 → 1 215 is the product of 3×405

    4 050 → 4 050 is the product of 10×405

  81 000 → 81 000 is the product of 200×405

  86 265 → By adding 1 215, 4 050 and 81 000, you find the final product.

86 265 is the product of multiplying 405 by 213.

PRACTICE

Find the product for the following multiplication problems.

1. 51
  × 13

2. 845
  × 102

3. 416
  × 37

4. 3104
  × 560

5. 4560
  × 75

ANSWERS

1. 663
2. 86 190
3. 15 392
4. 1 738 240
5. 342 000

Division

Long division has often been considered the most difficult of the four basic mathematical operations. In order to divide, one must also be able to multiply and subtract. Again, neatness and accuracy will go a long way in ensuring your success.

➡ **EXAMPLE 1** _____

$$
\begin{array}{r}
72 \\
4\overline{)288} \\
\end{array}
$$

DIVISOR ⟶ $4\overline{)288}$ ⟵ DIVIDEND
       72 ⟵ QUOTIENT
      −28
       08
       −8
        0

The result of a division problem is called a *quotient*. The number used to divide is called the *divisor* and the value being divided is called the *dividend*.

➡ **EXAMPLE 2** _____

Divide 1250 by 7. This example is illustrated step-by-step.

   0178
$7\overline{)1250}$
 −7
  55
 −49
   60
   56
    4 ⟵ REMAINDER

(**STEP 1**) 7 does not go into 1. Write 0 above.

(**STEP 2**) 7 goes into 12 once. Write 1 above.

(**STEP 3**) $1 \times 7 = 7$. Write 7 below 12 and subtract.

(**STEP 4**) 7 does not go into 5. Bring down the next number, 5.

(**STEP 5**) 7 goes into 55 seven times. Write 7 above.

(**STEP 6**) $7 \times 7 = 49$. Write 49 below 55 and subtract.

(**STEP 7**) 7 does not go into 6. Bring down the next number, 0.

(**STEP 8**) 7 goes into 60 eight times. Write 8 above.

(**STEP 9**) $8 \times 7 = 56$. Write 56 below 60 and subtract.

(**STEP 10**) 4 is the *remainder*. If numbers do not divide evenly, there will be an amount left over. This is the remainder. It will always be less than the divisor.

Check: $178 \times 7 +$ remainder $4 = 1250$

Division can be illustrated in three different ways. Example 2 can be written:

$$1250 \div 7 \quad \text{or} \quad \frac{1250}{7} \quad \text{or} \quad 7\overline{)1250}$$

In all three examples, you would say "Divide 1250 by 7". Note that the fraction bar "—" indicates an operation of division. The value on top is divided by the value on bottom.

PRACTICE

Find the quotient for the following division problems.

1. $11\overline{)132}$ 3. $6\overline{)724}$ 5. $1311 \div 8$ 7. $\dfrac{224}{14}$

2. $7\overline{)78}$ 4. $42\overline{)2130}$ 6. $275 \div 25$ 8. $\dfrac{2160}{20}$

ANSWERS

1. 12   3. 120 r4   5. 163 r7   7. 16

2. 11 r1   4. 50 r30   6. 11   8. 108

ORDER OF OPERATIONS

Given the calculation $10 - 4 \times 2$, is the correct answer 12 or 2? That is, do you subtract 4 from 10 and multiply the result by 2; or, do you multiply 4 by 2 and subtract the product from 10?

With mathematical calculations, you need a list of guidelines that must be followed implicitly in order to achieve a consistent answer. These guidelines are referred to as the *order of operations.*

B	**BRACKETS**	If there are brackets, perform all operations within the brackets first.
E	**EXPONENTS**	
D	**DIVISION**	} Complete division and multiplication from left to right
M	**MULTIPLICATION**	
A	**ADDITION**	} Complete addition and subtraction from left to right
S	**SUBTRACTION**	

TIP

The acronym BEDMAS (although meaningless as a word) is a helpful way to remember the order in which to complete mathematical operations.

Given these guidelines, you now know that the answer to the $10 - 4 \times 2$ is 2. Simplifying in the correct order the question becomes $10 - 8 = 2$.

Brackets

Brackets, or parentheses, are a very crucial part of mathematical expressions and algebraic equations. They indicate order and help to protect or isolate parts of the expression or equation. There are three common sets of symbols that serve to protect:

( ) Parentheses
{ } Braces
[ ] Brackets

No matter what set of symbols is used, always simplify within them first.

➡ EXAMPLE 1 _____

Simplify 17 + 2(46 + 3)

Solution

17 + 2(49)   Notice that the operation between a number and a bracket is
17 + 98   multiplication. 2 is multiplied by 49.
115

➡ EXAMPLE 2 _____

Simplify $\dfrac{25(6-4)}{5}$

Solution

$\dfrac{25(2)}{5}$

$\dfrac{50}{5}$

10

Remember that the fraction line means division.

➡ EXAMPLE 3 _____

Three people went out to dinner. Two had the $19.99 dinner special and the third person
had a chicken salad for $13.95. They shared a bottle of wine that cost $34. If they split the bill
equally before tipping, how much would each pay?

Solution

$\dfrac{2(19.99)+13.95+34}{3} = \dfrac{87.93}{3} = \$29.31$

Exponents

Exponents are small numbers written in superscript to a base number. They indicate that a
number is being raised to a certain power. The most common exponents are 2 and 3. When
a value is raised to the power of 2, that value is being *squared*. When a value is raised to the
power of 3, that value is being *cubed*.

➡ EXAMPLE 1 _____

Simplify 5^2

Solution
$5^2 = 5 \times 5 = 25$

➡ **EXAMPLE 2** _____

Simplify 4^3

Solution

$4^3 = 4 \times 4 \times 4 = 64$

QUICK CALCULATOR POINTER

There is a button on your calculator, x^2, that will square any value.

There is another button on your calculator, x^y, that will allow you to enter alternate powers such as 3.

Try it!

$5\,\boxed{x^2}$ Did you get 25?

$4\,\boxed{x^y}\,3$ Did you get 64?

PRACTICE

Simplify the following expressions using Order of Operations.

1. $12 + 6(3 \times 2)$

2. $2^2 + 3^3 \times 4$

3. $3\left(\dfrac{12 \div 2}{3}\right)$

4. $25 \div 5 + 3(6^2 - 4)$

5. $35 - 3(10 - 8)(2)$

6. $3^2 + 2^2 - (100 \div 10)$

7. $\dfrac{9 + 2(8)}{5}$

8. $(4 \times 6) + (3 \times 2) + (18 \div 2)$

ANSWERS

1. $12 + 6(3 \times 2) = 12 + 6(6) = 12 + 36 = 48$

2. $2^2 + 3^3 \times 4 = 4 + 27 \times 4 = 4 + 108 = 112$

3. $3\left(\dfrac{12 \div 2}{3}\right) = 3\left(\dfrac{6}{3}\right) = 3(2) = 6$

4. $25 \div 5 + 3(6^2 - 4) = 25 \div 5 + 3(36 - 4) = 25 \div 5 + 3(32) = 5 + 96 = 101$

5. $35 - 3(10 - 8)(2) = 35 - 3(2)(2) = 35 - 12 = 23$

6. $3^2 + 2^2 - (100 \div 10) = 9 + 4 - (10) = 13 - 10 = 3$

7. $\dfrac{9 + 2(8)}{5} = \dfrac{9 + 16}{5} = \dfrac{25}{5} = 5$

8. $(4 \times 6) + (3 \times 2) + (18 \div 2) = (24) + (6) + (9) = 30 + 9 = 39$

ESTIMATING

There is not one correct way to estimate; however, it is an important mathematical skill as it gives you an approximation of the correct answer. It gives you a sense, on a gut level, what number or range of numbers will be correct. In some real world situations an estimated answer is as accurate as you need to make your calculation. For example, if you have only $20 to spend on groceries, you would likely estimate how much the five items in your grocery cart are going to cost to ensure that the total is not greater than $20. It is not important to know the exact value, just a close estimate.

Use the following guidelines when estimating:

- Round numbers. Round to the nearest whole number that is easy to work with.

  27×11 could be estimated as $30 \times 10 = 300$

- Choose numbers that work well together.

  $148 \div 9$ could be estimated as $150 \div 10 = 15$

- Use a whole number to estimate fractions and decimals.

  $\frac{7}{8} + 0.75$ could be estimated as $1 + 1 = 2$

CHALLENGE EXERCISE

Visit a grocery store or drug store and purchase about ten items. Estimate the total for your bill to the nearest dollar. How accurate was your estimate?

PROBLEM SOLVING

The majority of GED problems—and in fact the majority of real-world mathematical problems—will be presented in words. Learning to interpret word problems and translate them into mathematical operations is an important skill. Study the following chart and familiarize yourself with the words and their mathematical meanings.

Addition (+)	Subtraction (−)	Multiplication (×)	Division (÷)
Sum	Difference	Product	Quotient
Plus	Subtract	Times	Share
More than	Less than	Twice	Per
Increased by	Decreased by	Of	Average
Total			

TIP

Some words can be translated into either multiplication or division. If you have "half of twenty", you can think about that as (20 × ½) or as (20 ÷ 2).

➥ **EXAMPLE 1** _____

Nick is training for a marathon. He ran 7.8 km on Monday, 10.5 km on Tuesday and again on Thursday. He also completed a long 21 km run on Sunday. How many kilometres did he run in total this week?

Solution

Did you notice the word *total*? This indicates that the operation involved is adding.

$$
\begin{array}{r}
7.8 \\
10.5 \\
10.5 \\
+21 \\
\hline
49.8 \text{ km in total.}
\end{array}
$$

➡ EXAMPLE 2

To maintain a healthy weight, women are directed to consume approximately 2100 calories a day and men approximately 2750 calories a day. What is the difference between a man's daily caloric intake and a woman's?

Solution

Did you notice the word *difference*? This indicates that the operation involved is subtracting.

$$
\begin{array}{r}
2750 \\
-2100 \\
\hline
650 \quad \text{A man consumes approximately 650 calories/day more than a woman.}
\end{array}
$$

➡ EXAMPLE 3

One extra-large pizza contains 12 slices. If three boys equally share the pizza, how many pieces do they each get?

Solution

Did you notice the word *share*? This indicates that the operation involved is division.

$12 \div 3 = 4$ pieces of pizza each.

Multi-step Problems

When you are required to use more than one operation to find an answer, you may need to break the solving down into smaller steps.

➡ EXAMPLE 1

Alicia received the following amounts for babysitting during the month of December: $29, $20, $37.50, $35, and $21. She babysat for 15 hours in total during December. What was Alicia's average hourly babysitting rate?

Solution

(STEP 1) Calculate the total of Alicia's earnings through addition.

$$29 + 20 + 37.5 + 35 + 21 = \$142.50$$

(STEP 2) Calculate the average hourly rate through division.

$$\$142.50 \div 15 = \$9.50$$

Alicia receives, on average, $9.50 per hour.

EXAMPLE 2

Every month, the Smiths pay a home mortgage of $1250 and utilities in the amount of $445. What is the cost of these expenses for one year?

Solution

STEP 1 Calculate the total monthly expenses through addition.

$$\$1250 + \$445 = \$1695/\text{month}$$

STEP 2 Calculate the annual cost of these expenses through mulitiplication.

$$\$1695 \times 12 = \$20\,340$$

The Smiths spend $20 340 every year on mortgage and utilities.

Setup Problems

Throughout the GED test, you will be asked to choose an answer that illustrates the setup of a multi-step word problem. You will not be asked to solve or find the solution; rather you are being asked to choose the calculation that is set up correctly (using order of operations).

EXAMPLE

Three friends are sharing the cost of a weekend vacation. They spent $360 on accommodation, $145 on food and $80 on gas. Which of the following expressions represents the amount that each person will need to contribute to cover the costs equally?

(1) $(360)(145)(80) \div 3$

(2) $(360 + 145 + 80) \div 3$

(3) $(3)(360 + 145 + 80)$

(4) $\dfrac{(360)-(145)-(80)}{3}$

(5) $(3)(360) + 3(145) + 3(80)$

Solution

The answer is (2). It is the only expression that first finds the total and then divides by the three people sharing the expenses.

Not Enough Information Is Given

Again, throughout the GED test you will occasionally see that one of the choices to the multiple-choice questions is "Not enough information is given". This is a legitimate answer and may in fact be the correct answer if the question is misleading or fails to provide enough information to complete a calculation. The fact that this choice sometimes exists emphasizes the need to read every problem carefully—noting the information that has been supplied and being confident about what is being asked.

→ EXAMPLE _____

Fabric is advertised on sale as "two metres for the price of one". Patricia is making identical bridesmaid dresses that each requires 3.5 metres of fabric. How much will Patricia spend on fabric to make three dresses?

    (1) $15.75
    (2) $10.50
    (3) $21.00
    (4) $63.00
    (5) Not enough information is given.

Solution

The answer is (5). You are not given the price per metre of the fabric.

PRACTICE

Solve the following word problems.

1. 142 students attend a community college. Every student spends $24 per course to cover the cost of technology fees. If each student takes 3 courses each, how much money is collected in technology fees?

2. Over a one week period there are 275 cans of vegetables received at a local food bank. If these cans have to be evenly shared among 55 family boxes, how many cans of vegetables does each family receive?

3. Tracy has four children. The two oldest children each receive an allowance of $15/week. The two younger children each receive an allowance of $12/week. How much should Tracy budget for allowances each year? (Remember that there are 52 weeks per year).

4. Four friends go to a hockey game and decide to split the cost of the event evenly. They purchase four tickets at $47/each, two posters at $12/each and food and beverage that costs $36 in total. Which of the following expressions represents the amount that each person will need to contribute?

    (1) $(47 + 12) + 36 \div 4$
    (2) $4(47) + (12) + (36)$
    (3) $\dfrac{(47) + (12) + (36)}{4}$
    (4) $\dfrac{4(47) + 2(12) + (36)}{4}$
    (5) Not enough information is given.

5. The distance between two towns is 150 kilometres. Cary's vehicle averages 20 km per litre of gas. How much would Cary spend on gas if he made a return trip between these two towns?

   (1) $30.00
   (2) $15.00
   (3) $7.50
   (4) $22.50
   (5) Not enough information is given.

ANSWERS

1. $10 224   3. $2 808   5. (5)
2. 5 cans   4. (4)

CHAPTER CHECK-UP

1. What place value does 5 occupy in the number 45 321?
   (1) Ones
   (2) Tens
   (3) Hundreds
   (4) Thousands
   (5) Ten Thousands

2. Place the following six numbers in order from largest to smallest.

   | 215 | 2 101 | 251 | 1 987 | 999 | 521 |

(1)	521	999	215	1 987	2 101	251
(2)	215	251	521	999	1 987	2 101
(3)	2 101	1 987	999	521	251	215
(4)	1 987	2 101	521	999	215	251
(5)	2 101	1 987	999	251	215	521

3. Using order of operations, simplify the expression $\dfrac{57-5(3+2)}{2}$

   (1) 64
   (2) 110
   (3) 32
   (4) 16
   (5) 130

4. Using order of operations, simplify the expression $(11 - 2^3) + (12 \div 6)(4)$
   (1) 25
   (2) 32
   (3) 27
   (4) 13
   (5) 11

5. In one year, Brianne spends $9000 on rent and $5400 on food. How much does Brianne spend monthly on rent?

   (1) $800
   (2) $750
   (3) $850
   (4) $900
   (5) Not enough information is given

6. The Robertson family purchased a home in 2010 for $475,550. They sold it two years later for $468 475. How much money did they lose on this real estate deal?

   (1) $6 050
   (2) $7 075
   (3) $8 410
   (4) $9 000
   (5) Not enough information is given

7. 250 children attend an elementary school. There are 10 classes at the school, kindergarten through grade 7. How many children attend kindergarten?

   (1) 10
   (2) 30
   (3) 20
   (4) 25
   (5) Not enough information is given

8. Brian is training for a bike race. He cycled for 2 hours on Monday, 1 hour on Tuesday, 4 hours on Thursday and a total of 6 hours on the weekend. If Brian continues to train exactly the same number of hours for 8 weeks, which of the following expressions represent the total number of hours Brian will cycle in this time period?

   (1) $\dfrac{2+1+4+6}{8}$

   (2) $(2)(1)(4)(6)(8)$

   (3) $8(2 + 1 + 4 + 6)$

   (4) $8(2 - 1 - 4 - 6)$

   (5) Not enough information is given

9. Lucy purchased 6 loaves of bread. If her family consumes 1 loaf of bread every two days, how long will her purchase last?

   (1) 6 days
   (2) 1 week
   (3) 24 days
   (4) 12 days
   (5) 9 days

10. Jason won $4500 on a lottery. He feels generous and decides to give it all away by sharing it equally among his six siblings. How much will each sibling receive?
    (1) $600
    (2) $500
    (3) $450
    (4) $900
    (5) $750

ANSWERS

1. **(4)** Thousands

2. **(3)** 2 101   1 987   999   521   251   215

3. **(4)** $\dfrac{57-5(3+2)}{2}=\dfrac{57-5(5)}{2}=\dfrac{57-25}{2}=\dfrac{32}{2}=16$

4. **(5)** $(11-2^3)+(12\div6)(4)=(11-8)+(2)(4)=(3)+(8)=11$

5. **(2)** $\$9000\div12=\$750$

6. **(2)** $\$475\ 550-\$468\ 475=\$7\ 075$

7. **(5)** You are not given information about how many children are in each class.

8. **(3)** First, find the hours cycled in one week by adding $(2+1+4+6)$ and multiply by 8 weeks.

9. **(4)** If they consume 1 loaf every 2 days, they will consume 6 loaves in 12 days. Multiply $(6)(2)=12$.

10. **(5)** To *share equally* complete an operation of division. $\$4\ 500\div6=\$750$

Decimals

22

THINK ABOUT IT

Surprisingly, the modern method of writing decimal values was only invented and commonly practiced for the past 500 years. In terms of Math History, this is a relatively recent event! Certainly, it was necessary to have a numerical system that provided an opportunity to express quantities that are less than one. A quantity less than one can be expressed as a fraction, such as ½, or it can be expressed as a decimal fraction, such as 0.5. Fortunately for us, the decimal system we use is built on a base of ten and is actually rather easy to understand.

IN THIS CHAPTER

After completing this chapter, you will be able to

- → **ORDER DECIMAL FRACTIONS**
- → **ROUND DECIMAL FRACTIONS**
- → **ADD, SUBTRACT, MULTIPLY, AND DIVIDE DECIMAL FRACTIONS**
- → **TRANSLATE AND SOLVE WORD PROBLEMS THAT INCLUDE DECIMAL FRACTIONS**

PLACE VALUE

Place value was presented in the previous chapter. Remember that the position that a digit occupies in a number tells you its place value. So far, you have reviewed the place value to the left of the decimal place. In this chapter, you will focus on the place value of the digits to the right of the decimal place.

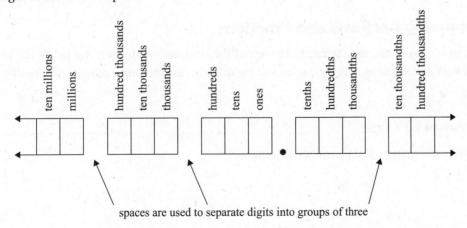

spaces are used to separate digits into groups of three

In this system with a base of ten, if a number contains a decimal it is called a *decimal fraction*. The digits to the right of the decimal point indicate quantities less than one. Similar to fractions, decimals are used to illustrate a part of a whole.

For example, three tenths can be expressed using the fraction $\frac{3}{10}$ or the decimal value of 0.3.

The way money is notated is perhaps one of the most commonly recognized uses of the decimal. The quarter can be written as 25¢ or as $0.25. You know the value of a quarter to be 25 out of 100 cents in a dollar.

Decimals and Fractional Equivalents

The place value name indicates what number will be in the denominator of the fractional equivalent. A number that terminates in the tenths position will have the number 10 in the denominator of an equivalent fraction. A number that terminates in the thousandths position will have the number 1000 in the denominator of an equivalent fraction.

TIP

Simplifying a fraction involves reducing it to lowest terms. Refer to Chapter 24 for more information on this topic.

➡ **EXAMPLE 1** _____

Write the equivalent fraction for 0.15. Remember to fully simplify the fraction.

Solution

$$0.15 = \frac{15}{100} = \frac{3}{20}$$

The decimal 0.15 terminated in the hundredths position. The denominator is 100. The fraction can be simplified.

➡ **EXAMPLE 2** _____

Write the equivalent fraction for 0.2347. Remember to fully simplify the fraction.

Solution

$$0.2347 = \frac{2\,347}{10\,000}$$

The decimal 0.2347 terminated in the ten thousandths position. The denominator is 10 000. The fraction did not simplify.

Comparing Decimals and Fractions

With whole numbers, the farther to the left of the decimal one moves, the larger the value. With decimal fractions, the farther to the right of the decimal one moves, the smaller the value.

➡ **EXAMPLE 1** _____

Given 0.005 and 0.2, which number is smaller?

Solution

0.005 is smaller than 0.2

  The first number represents five thousandths.

  The second number represents two tenths.

➡ EXAMPLE 2_____

Given 0.075 and $\frac{3}{10}$, which number is smaller?

Solution

When comparing numbers it is best to use the same format. That is, compare fractions to fractions or decimals to decimals.

  Convert both to decimals.

  Compare 0.075 to 0.3

  0.075 is smaller than 0.3

It is more involved, but you can also convert both expressions to similar fractions.

  $0.075 = \dfrac{75}{1\,000}$ Notice that the decimal terminated in the thousandths position. The value in the bottom of the fraction is 1 000.

  $\dfrac{3}{10} \times \dfrac{100}{100} = \dfrac{300}{1\,000}$ You can clearly see that $\dfrac{300}{1\,000}$ is larger than $\dfrac{75}{1\,000}$.

Zeroes and Decimals

For accuracy, it is good practice to write a zero before the decimal point; however, it is not required. It is also possible to write zeroes to the right of the decimal number without changing its value.

0.2 = 0.20 = 0.200 = 0.200 0 etc.

But be careful!

$0.2 \neq 0.02$ The symbol $\neq$ means "does not equal"

0.2 is equivalent to two tenths.

0.02 is equivalent to only two hundredths. It is a much smaller quantity. Putting zeroes between the decimal point and the digits does change its value.

  Another way to think about this is to ask yourself, "is $0.20 the same as $0.02?" No, it is not. One number represents 20¢ and the other is only 2¢. Looking at decimals in terms of money makes good sense.

TIP

The symbol $\neq$ means "does not equal".

PRACTICE

1. Write the fraction equivalent of the following decimals. Simplify all fractions.
   a. 0.12
   b. 2.15
   c. 0.005
   d. 1.001
   e. 4.5

2. Arrange the following sets of decimals from smallest to largest.
   a. 2.5   1.67   0.89   2.45   2.01
   b. 10.2   10.18   10.0   10.01   10.001

ANSWERS

1. a. $\frac{12}{100} = \frac{3}{25}$ c. $\frac{5}{1\,000} = \frac{1}{200}$ e. $\frac{45}{10} = \frac{9}{2}$ or $4\frac{1}{2}$

   b. $\frac{215}{100} = \frac{43}{20}$ or $2\frac{3}{20}$ d. $\frac{1\,001}{1\,000}$ or $1\frac{1}{1\,000}$

2. a. 0.89   1.67   2.01   2.45   2.5
   b. 10.0   10.001   10.01   10.18   10.2

ROUNDING

In real-world problems, it is often adequate to know an approximate value. Generally, you would not say that you ran 5.356 kilometres—even if your GPS watch shows that exactly. You would likely tell your friend that you ran just over 5 kilometres. You have rounded the distance to the nearest kilometre.

Other units of measurement need to be more accurate. Money, for example, is generally expressed to two decimal places. That is, money figures are rounded to the nearest hundredth. $345.678 would be rounded to $345.68.

The steps to rounding any decimal fraction are as follows:

a. Underline the digit to which the number is being rounded.
b. Look to the digit immediately to the right. If the number is 5 or more, add 1 to the underlined value. Round up. If the number is 4 or less, leave the underlined value as is.
c. Change all the remaining digits that follow the underlined digit to zeroes.

➡ EXAMPLE 1

Round 1.45 to the nearest tenth.

Solution

1.4̲5   The digit to the right of 4 is 5. Round 4 up to 5.

1.4̲5 ≈ 1.5

TIP

The symbol ≈ is often used to indicate "approximately equal to."

➥ EXAMPLE 2

Round 2.614 to the nearest hundredth.

Solution

2.6<u>1</u>4   The digit to the right of 1 is 4. Leave 1 as 1.

2.6<u>1</u>4 ≈ 2.61

➥ EXAMPLE 3

Round 14.999 to the nearest tenth.

Solution

This is slightly more complicated. Rounding 9 up creates the value of 10 which is then carried to the next place value to the left.

14.<u>9</u>99   The digit to the right of 9 is 9. Round 9 up to 10. Carry to the ones place.

14.<u>9</u>99 ≈ 15.0   It is important that we leave a 0 in the tenth position to show that the value is accurate to this place value.

PRACTICE

1. Round the following numbers to the nearest hundredth.
   a. 0.125
   b. 2.0678
   c. 1.0344
   d. 2.601
   e. 0.009

2. Round the following numbers to the nearest tenth.
   a. 3.45
   b. 0.99
   c. 4.54
   d. 0.02
   e. 15.27

3. Round the following numbers to the nearest whole number.
   a. 15.2
   b. 4.56
   c. 3.999
   d. 0.33
   e. 112.7

ANSWERS

1. a. 0.13   b. 2.07   c. 1.03   d. 2.60   e. 0.01

2. a. 3.5   b. 1.0   c. 4.5   d. 0.0   e. 15.3

3. a. 15   b. 5   c. 4   d. 0   e. 113

ADDING AND SUBTRACTING DECIMALS

The directions for adding and subtracting decimals are essentially the same as for adding and subtracting whole numbers covered in Chapter 21. Neatness and accuracy are keys to success. It is important to line up digits in place value order. Ones are added to ones, tenths are added to tenths and so on.

Begin addition and subtraction from the top digit farthest to the right. When adding, remember to carry forward if the amount in this column adds to more than nine. When subtracting, remember to borrow if the value being subtracted is greater than the value directly above.

➡ EXAMPLE 1 _____

Add 123.45 + 210.1 + 67.89

Solution

$$
\begin{array}{r}
1\,1\,1\,1 \\
123.45 \\
210.10 \\
+\ \ 67.89 \\
\hline
401.44 \\
\end{array}
$$

➡ EXAMPLE 2 _____

Subtract 37.45 from 110.05

Solution

$$
\begin{array}{r}
0\,9\,1 \\
1\cancel{1}0.05 \\
-\ \ 37.45 \\
\hline
72.60 \\
\end{array}
$$

➡ EXAMPLE 3 _____

Quinn had a quarter, a dime, two loonies, and a nickel. How much money does he have altogether?

Solution

$$
\begin{array}{r}
1 \\
0.25 \\
0.10 \\
2.00 \\
+\ \ 0.05 \\
\hline
\$2.40 \\
\end{array}
$$

PRACTICE

1. Find the sum of each.
   a. 65.25 + 110.1
   b. 16.5 + 0.67 + 13.1
   c. 213.4 + 365.89
   d. 45.67 + 2.75 + 3.11
   e. 1 001.5 + 11.22 + 76.009

2. Find the difference of each.
   a. 120 − 25.65
   b. 3 850 − 625.5
   c. 0.5 − 0.002
   d. 75.2 − 3.4
   e. 3.79 − 2.25

3. Susan had $10. She purchased a coffee for $1.75 and a muffin for $1.95. How much did Susan have after making these purchases?

ANSWERS

1. a. 175.35   b. 30.27   c. 579.29   d. 51.53   e. 1 088.729

2. a. 94.35   b. 3 224.5   c. 0.498   d. 71.8   e. 1.54

3. $6.30

MULTIPLYING DECIMALS

Again, the process for multiplying decimal fractions is very similar to the process covered in Chapter 21 – Multiplying Whole Numbers. It is important to review these steps mentally (without a calculator). Although you may be able to use a calculator on a portion of the GED test, you will be expected to memorize basic multiplication products. If necessary, review a times table or create flash cards to help reinforce basic multiplication results.

The only difference between multiplying decimal fractions and whole numbers is that great care must be taken in determining where to place the decimal point in the final product. The answer will have the total of all the decimal places in each factor.

➡ EXAMPLE 1

Multiply 12.5×0.51

Solution

$$
\begin{array}{r}
12.5 \quad \text{1 decimal place} \\
\times \ 0.51 \quad \text{2 decimal places} \\
\hline
125 \\
6\,250 \\
\hline
6.375 \quad \text{The final product will have 3 decimal places}
\end{array}
$$

➡ EXAMPLE 2 _____

Robin earns $752.25 each week. How much will Robin earn in one year? (Remember that there are 52 weeks in a year).

Solution

$$
\begin{array}{r}
752.25 \quad \text{2 decimal places} \\
\times \quad 52 \\
\hline
150450 \\
3761250 \\
\hline
39\,117.00 \quad
\end{array}
$$

The final product will have 2 decimal places.
Robin earns $39 117 in a year.

PRACTICE

1. Find the product of each.
    a. 245.1×13.45
    b. 16×25.50
    c. 10.02×1002
    d. 20.5×1.5
    e. 721×3.4

2. Cassandra walks a 6.75 km route six times a week. How many kilometres does she walk in one week?

3. A recipe calls for 1.5 teaspoons of vanilla. If you were tripling the recipe, how much vanilla would you need?

ANSWERS

1. a. 3 296.595   b. 408   c. 10 040.04   d. 30.75   e. 2 451.4

2. Cassandra walks 40.5 km in a week.

3. You would need 4.5 teaspoons.

DIVIDING DECIMALS

Although the steps for dividing decimal fractions are very similar to the steps involved in long division of whole numbers, extra care must be taken with regards to the position of the decimal point.

Before beginning the process of long division, you must first ensure that the divisor is a whole number. If the divisor is a decimal fraction, it must be converted to a whole number by multiplying by a factor of ten.

EXAMPLE 1

Divide $10.45 \div 2.5$

Solution

$$(10)\ 2.5\overline{)10.45}\ (10)$$

$$
\begin{array}{r}
4.18 \\
25\overline{)104.50} \\
-100 \\
\hline
45 \\
-25 \\
\hline
200 \\
200 \\
\hline
0
\end{array}
$$

Multiply both the divisor and the dividend by ten. This will move the decimal point one place to the right in both the divisor and dividend.

Next, place the decimal point in the quotient directly above the decimal point in the dividend.

Continue to follow the same division steps as described in Chapter 21.

EXAMPLE 2

Divide $12 \div 0.7$

Solution

$$(10)\ 0.7\overline{)12.}\ (10)$$

$$
\begin{array}{r}
17.142 \\
7\overline{)120.000} \\
-7 \\
\hline
50 \\
-49 \\
\hline
10 \\
-7 \\
\hline
30 \\
-28 \\
\hline
20 \\
-14 \\
\hline
6
\end{array}
$$

Multiply both the divisor and the dividend by ten. This will move the decimal point one place to the right in both the divisor and dividend.

Next, place the decimal point in the quotient directly above the decimal point in the dividend.

Continue to follow the same division steps as described in Chapter 21.

In this example, the process seems endless as we do not seem to reach a remainder of zero. In general, the quotient is rounded to an appropriate place value. In this example, we have rounded to the nearest hundredth.

$$12 \div 0.7 \approx 17.14$$

➥ EXAMPLE 3

Divide   52.4 ÷ 0.125

Solution

(1000) 0.1 2 5 ⌒)52.4 ⌒ (1000)

$$
\begin{array}{r}
419.2 \\
125\overline{)52400.000} \\
-500\downarrow \\
\overline{240} \\
-125\downarrow \\
\overline{1150} \\
-1125\downarrow \\
\overline{250} \\
-250 \\
\overline{0}
\end{array}
$$

Multiply both the divisor and the dividend by a thousand. This will move the decimal point three places to the right. Note that extra zeroes were added in the dividend.

Next, place the decimal point in the quotient directly above the decimal point in the dividend.

Divide as in the preceding examples.

➥ EXAMPLE 4

Kristie purchased 1.5 dozen dinner rolls for $3.74. How much would 1 dozen cost?

Solution

1.5⌒)3.74⌒

$$
\begin{array}{r}
2.493 \approx 2.49 \\
15\overline{)37.400} \\
-30\downarrow \\
\overline{74} \\
\underline{60}\downarrow \\
140 \\
-135\downarrow \\
\overline{50} \\
-45 \\
\overline{5}
\end{array}
$$

1 dozen rolls would cost approximately $2.49.

PRACTICE

1. Find the quotient of each.
   a. 165.6 ÷ 72
   b. 75 ÷ 1.2
   c. 110.5 ÷ 0.47 (Round to the nearest hundredth)
   d. 125.75 ÷ 0.25
   e. $\frac{78}{11}$ (Round to the nearest hundredth)

2. Ryan drinks 8.5 litres of water over 4.5 days. If he continues at this rate, what would his daily average intake be rounded to one decimal place?

ANSWERS

1. a. 2.3   b. 62.5   c. 235.11   d. 503   e. 7.09

2. Ryan drinks approximately 1.9 litres of water each day.

CHAPTER CHECK-UP

1. One coin measures 1.26 cm across. Another coin measures 0.85 cm. How much larger is the first coin across than the second?
   (1) 1.41 cm
   (2) 1.48 cm
   (3) 1.07 cm
   (4) 2.11 cm
   (5) 0.41 cm

2. The gas tank of Henry's car holds 52.5 L of gasoline. Henry used all of that gas to travel 315 km. Calculate the km/L of gasoline for Henry's car.
   (1) 6 km/L
   (2) 16 km/L
   (3) 0.6 km/L
   (4) 60 km/L
   (5) 262.5 km/L

3. Tracy is making four identical bridesmaids' dresses. Each dress requires 4.4 metres of fabric, and the fabric Tracy picked costs $24.49 per metre. What is the total cost for the material for all four dresses (before taxes)?
   (1) $407.76
   (2) $215.51
   (3) $115.56
   (4) $431.02
   (5) Not enough information is given

4. Five babies were born on the same day. Their birth weights were recorded as follows. Order the babies from smallest to largest based on their birth weights.

Colin	4.245 kg
Chris	4.334 kg
Linda	3.876 kg
Lucy	3.921 kg
Ana	3.088 kg

(1) Linda	Lucy	Ana	Chris	Colin
(2) Colin	Chris	Ana	Lucy	Linda
(3) Ana	Linda	Lucy	Colin	Chris
(4) Chris	Colin	Lucy	Linda	Ana
(5) Lucy	Ana	Colin	Chris	Linda

5. Oliver visits the candy store and purchases 0.45 kg of licorice and 0.89 kg of chocolate. The price for licorice is $4.99/kg and the price of bulk chocolate is $23.99/kg. How much did Oliver pay for his purchases? Round your answer to the nearest hundredth.
   (1) $28.59
   (2) $28.60
   (3) $28.98
   (4) $23.60
   (5) $23.59

6. Samantha asks the salesclerk to cut 6.5 metres of rope at a hardware store. When she gets home she measures the rope herself and discovers it only measures 5.75 metres. How much rope was she shorted?
   (1) 1.25 m
   (2) 1.0 m
   (3) 0.75 m
   (4) 0.50 m
   (5) 0.25 m

7. Gas is advertised at $1.21/litre. Laura buys 62.5 litres. How much will Laura spend on fuel?
   (1) $74.98
   (2) $75.63
   (3) $75.00
   (4) $75.62
   (5) $62.50

8. Kevin was given $400 to spend on clothes. He purchases a pair of jeans for $64.75, a sweater for $45, and a winter coat for $185.50. His bill also indicates that he paid $20.68 in tax. How much money will Kevin have left after this purchase?
   (1) $315.93
   (2) $117.07
   (3) $91.74
   (4) $48.70
   (5) $84.07

9. A candy store owner has 4.65 kg of candy. If she shares the candy evenly among 5 bags, how much candy will each bag contain?
   (1) 0.47 kg
   (2) 1 kg
   (3) 0.87 kg
   (4) 0.93 kg
   (5) 2.33 kg

10. Cassie owes her parents $2 450.85. She would like to pay them back in even installments over the next 12 months. How much will she pay each month?

    (1) $245.09
    (2) $204.24
    (3) $210.12
    (4) $223.25
    (5) $200.10

ANSWERS

1. **(5)** Subtract. $1.26 - 0.85 = 0.41$ cm

2. **(1)** Divide. $315 \div 52.5 = 6$ km/L

3. **(4)** Multiply. $(4)(4.4)(24.49) = \$431.02$

4. **(3)** Compare place value.

5. **(4)** Complete three calculations. Multiply $(0.45)(4.99) = \$2.25$ for licorice. Multiply $(0.89)(23.99) = \$21.35$ for chocolate. Together they cost: $\$2.25 + \$21.35 = \$23.60$

6. **(3)** Subtract. $6.5 - 5.75 = 0.75$ m

7. **(2)** Multiply. $1.21 \times 62.5 = \$75.63$

8. **(5)** Complete two calculations. Add $\$64.75 + \$45 + \$185.50 + \$20.68 = \$315.93$. Subtract $\$400 - \$315.93 = \$84.07$

9. **(4)** Divide. $4.65 \div 5 = 0.93$ kg

10. **(2)** Divide. $\$2 450.85 \div 12 = \$204.24$

The Metric System

23

THINK ABOUT IT

The metric system was initially developed during the French Revolution; however, in 1960 the world agreed upon the International System of Units, which is known simply as SI. The system was fully adopted by Canada in 1970. The SI is the simplest system of measurement ever invented because, like our number system, it is based on the number 10 and units can be expressed as decimal fractions.

IN THIS CHAPTER

After completing this chapter, you will be able to

→ **IDENTIFY METRIC UNITS**

→ **CONVERT METRIC UNITS**

→ **ESTIMATE METRIC UNITS**

→ **SELECT APPROPRIATE UNITS OF MEASUREMENT**

Common Base Units

Quantity	Unit	Symbol
Length & distance	metre	m
Mass & weight	gram	g
Volume or Capacity	litre	L

MEASURING LENGTH AND DISTANCE

As you can see in the preceding chart, the basic unit of measurement for length and distance is the metre. If you stretch your arm out beside you, a metre is about the distance from the tip of your nose to the tip of your hand outstretched.

If you are measuring a distance much smaller than a metre, such as the length of a hem on a pair of pants that need to be shortened, you would likely measure using the centimetre. A centimetre is about the width of a standard pen. There are 100 centimetres in every metre.

If you are measuring a distance much larger than a metre, such as the distance between Toronto and Ottawa, you would likely measure using kilometres. A kilometre is 1000 metres.

In the words **centi**metre and **kilo**metre there are short prefixes that have been added to the base unit of the metre. A centimetre is one one-hundreth (0.01) of a metre and a kilometre is one thousand (1000) times larger than a metre. These prefixes can be added to any of the base unit lists in the chart: metre, gram and litre.

It is important to memorize some of the most common prefixes and their values.

Prefix	Symbol	Meaning (multiply base unit by)
mega	M	1 000 000
kilo	k	1 000
hecto	h	100
deca	da	10
deci	d	0.1
centi	c	0.01
milli	m	0.001

Combinations of the prefixes and base units are generally abbreviated into commonly used symbols. It would also be helpful to familiarize yourself with the following table.

Length/Distance	m	Metre
	mm	Millimetre
	cm	Centimetre
	km	Kilometre
Volume/Capacity	L	Litre
	mL	Millilitre
Mass/Weight	g	Gram
	mg	Milligram
	kg	Kilogram

Selecting Appropriate Units of Measurement

In general, the units of measurement are given within a mathematical problem. However, sometimes the units given in the word problem will not necessarily match up with the units of measurement in the answer. Deciding what unit is most appropriate involves determining whether something can be described in terms of the base or whether units of measurement much larger or much smaller must be used.

➡ **EXAMPLE 1**

For each item, determine the letter of the most reasonable unit of measurement.

1. The height of a refrigerator
   a. centimetre (cm)
   b. metre (m)
   c. kilometre (km)

2. The distance around your wrist
   a. centimetre (cm)
   b. metre (m)
   c. kilometre (km)

3. The amount of pop in a large jug
   a. millilitre (mL)
   b. litre (L)
   c. kilolitre (kL)

4. Your body mass
   a. milligram (mg)
   b. gram (g)
   c. kilogram (kg)

Solution

Remember that the question asked was *what is the most reasonable unit of measurement?* There is not necessarily one correct answer, but the answers listed are the most reasonable.

1. The height of a refrigerator would be measured in metres (m).

2. The distance around your wrist would be measured in centimetres (cm).

3. The amount of pop in a large jug would be measured in litres (L).

4. Your body mass would be measured in kilograms (kg).

PRACTICE

1. Determine the most reasonable unit of measure for the width across a loonie coin.
   a) millimetre (mm)
   b) centimetre (cm)
   c) metre (m)

2. Determine the most reasonable unit of measure for the mass of a cat.
   a) milligram (mg)
   b) gram (g)
   c) kilogram (kg)

3. Determine the most reasonable unit of measure for the amount of gas your car will hold.
   a) millilitre (mL)
   b) litre (L)
   c) kilolitre (kL)

4. Determine the most reasonable unit of measure for the height of a bookcase.
   a) centimetre (cm)
   b) metre (m)
   c) kilometre (km)

5. Determine the most reasonable unit of measure for the amount of liquid in a bottle of cough syrup.
   a) millilitres (mL)
   b) litres (L)
   c) kilolitre (kL)

ANSWERS

1. **(b)** cm

2. **(c)** kg

3. **(b)** L

4. **(b)** m

5. **(a)** mL

CONVERTING METRIC UNITS OF MEASUREMENT

The most common prefixes are *kilo, centi* and *milli*. Notice that all prefixes are based on the number *ten*. Each prefix increases or decreases the size of the unit ten times. If you relate these prefixes to the place-value chart in Chapters 21 and 22, it is really quite easy to convert from one unit of measurement to another. It is just a matter of moving the decimal point!

millions	hundred thousands	ten thousands	thousands	hundreds	tens	units	tenths	hundredths	thousandths
Mega			kilo	hecto	deca	BASE	deci	centi	milli
M			k	h	da	metre	d	c	m
						litre			
						gram			

Moving the decimal point to the left involves using larger units of measurement. Moving the decimal point to the right involves using smaller units of measurement. Remember that one kilometre is a thousand times larger than one metre. One millimetre is a thousand times smaller than a metre.

EXAMPLE 1

Convert 4.8 kilograms to grams.

Solution

The question is 4.8 kg = _____ g?

The prefix *kilo* means 1000. To convert, multiply 4.8 by 1 000 or simply move the decimal point three places to the right.

$$4.8 \text{ kg} \times 1\,000 = \textbf{4 800 g} \quad \text{OR} \quad 4.800 \text{ kg} = \textbf{4800 g}$$

Note on the conversion line below, to change from the prefix *kilo* to the *base* unit (gram) it is necessary to move the decimal 3 places to the right.

mega, ___, ___, kilo, hecto, deca, Base, deci, centi, milli

EXAMPLE 2

The length of a standard hockey arena is 61 metres. How many centimetres is that?

Solution

The question is 61 m = _____ cm?

Find the starting unit (metre) on the line below. Count the number of places right to the ending unit (centimetre). Move the decimal point the same number of places in the same direction (two places right).

mega, ___, ___, kilo, hecto, deca, Base, deci, centi, milli

61.00 m = 6100 cm

EXAMPLE 3

An 8-fluid-ounce glass of water is equivalent to approximately 250 ml of water. How many litres is that?

Solution

The question is 250 mL = _____ L?

Find the starting unit (milli) on the line below. Count the number of places left to the ending base unit (litre). Move the decimal point the same number of places in the same direction (three places left).

mega, ___, ___, kilo, hecto, deca, Base, deci, centi, milli

250 mL = 0.250 L

PRACTICE

1. Convert the following.
   a) 0.450 kilograms (kg) = _____ grams (g)
   b) 315 centimetres (cm) = _____ metres (m)
   c) 0.14 Megalitres (ML) = _____ litres (L)
   d) 76.5 millilitres (mL) = _____ litres(L)
   e) 345 decimetres (dm) = _____ kilometres (km)
   f) 420 grams (g) = _____ milligrams (mg)
   g) 725 metres (m) = _____ kilometres (km)

ANSWERS

1. a) 0.450 kilograms (kg) = **450** grams (g)
   b) 315 centimetres (cm) = **3.15** metres (m)
   c) 0.14 Megalitres (ML) = **140 000** litres (L)
   d) 76.5 millilitres (mL) = **0.0765** litres(L)
   e) 345 decimetres (dm) = **0.0345** kilometres (km)
   f) 420 grams (g) = **420 000** milligrams (mg)
   g) 725 metres (m) = **0.725** kilometres (km)

CHALLENGE EXERCISE

Select a room in your home such as your bedroom or living room. Using a carpenter's tape measure, measure the width and length of this room in centimetres. Convert your result to millimetres, metres, and kilometres.

IMPERIAL MEASUREMENTS

In Canada we officially use the metric system of measurement. However, you may notice a few of the GED questions refer to units other than metres, litres, and grams. Although Canadians *officially* use the metric system, in common-day language we still may refer to feet (ft.), inches (in.), and pounds (lb.) (instead of metres, centimetres, and grams). These are imperial units of measurement from the old British system of measurement.

For example, you probably know your height in feet and inches and your body mass in pounds. Not all Canadians know their own height in metres or their weight in kilograms!

On the GED® test, you will not need to convert between imperial and metric units of measurement, but it would be helpful to be familiar with these equivalencies.

Length	1 foot (ft.) = 12 inches (in.)	1 inch is about 2.54 cm
Mass	1 pound (lb.) = 16 ounces (oz.)	1 pound is about 0.5 kg
Volume	1 gallon = 4 quarts (qt.)	1 gallon is about 3.8 L

CHALLENGE EXERCISE

Using the chart above, determine your weight in kilograms and your height in metres.

CHAPTER CHECK-UP

1. For exercise, Ruth walked around a very large park four times. The park was 1 200 metres around. In total, how far did Ruth walk?
    - (1) 48 km
    - (2) 480 km
    - (3) 480 m
    - (4) 4.8 m
    - (5) 4.8 km

2. Brad was prescribed a cough medication and was told to take 50 mL of medication every day. In litres, how much medication does Brad consume in seven days?
    - (1) 0.035 L
    - (2) 0.35 L
    - (3) 3.5 L
    - (4) 35 L
    - (5) Not enough information is given

3. What is the most reasonable unit of measure for the thickness of this book?
    - (1) milligram (mg)
    - (2) metre (m)
    - (3) millimetre (mm)
    - (4) centimetre (cm)
    - (5) millilitre (mL)

4. On average, a Canadian child drinks about 550 grams of soft drink per day. In a thirty day month, how much soft drink does the average Canadian child drink?
    - (1) 165 kg
    - (2) 1650 g
    - (3) 16.5 kg
    - (4) 1.65 kg
    - (5) 1 650 000 g

5. Patricia lost 45 pounds in one year. On average, how many pounds did Patricia lose each month?
    - (1) 12.5 lbs
    - (2) 10.75 lbs
    - (3) 4.5 lbs
    - (4) 3.75 lbs
    - (5) Not enough information is given

ANSWERS

1. **(5)** Multiply 1 200 × 4 = 4 800 metres. Convert to kilometres by moving the decimal point three places left. 4 800 m = 4.8 km.

2. **(2)** Multiply 50 × 7 = 350 mL. Convert millilitres to litres by moving the decimal point three places left. 350 mL = 0.35 L

3. **(4)** Centimetres.

4. **(3)** Multiply 550 × 30 = 16 500 g. Convert grams to kilograms by moving the decimal point three places left. 16 500 g = 16.5 kg

5. **(4)** Divide. 45 ÷ 12 = 3.75 pounds.

Fractions

24

THINK ABOUT IT

The word fraction comes from the Latin word *fractio*, which means to fracture or break. It sounds painful and for many students, the study of fractions has been just that—painful! But it doesn't have to be. In this chapter, you will learn what fractions are and a few basic steps involved in simplifying, adding, subtracting, multiplying, and dividing fractions.

IN THIS CHAPTER

After completing this chapter, you will be able to

→ **UNDERSTAND FRACTION NOTATION**

→ **CONVERT BETWEEN FRACTIONS AND DECIMALS**

→ **CREATE EQUIVALENT FRACTIONS**

→ **SIMPLIFY FRACTIONS**

→ **ADD, SUBTRACT, MULTIPLY, AND DIVIDE FRACTIONS**

→ **SOLVE REAL-WORLD PROBLEMS**

FRACTION FACTS

A fraction is a number that expresses a part of a whole or a part of a group. If you read six of eleven chapters in a book, you have read $\frac{6}{11}$ of the book.

A fraction is always made of two numbers. The top number is called the *numerator* and the bottom number is called the *denominator*.

$$\frac{6}{11} \begin{array}{l} \rightarrow \text{Numerator} \\ \rightarrow \text{Denominator} \end{array}$$

➡ EXAMPLE 1

This example is easy to visualize. Suppose a pie is cut into five equal pieces and you eat two of them. Then you can say that you ate two-fifths or $\frac{2}{5}$ of the pie.

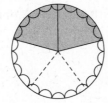

The following rectangle is divided in ten equal parts. What fraction of the rectangle is shaded?

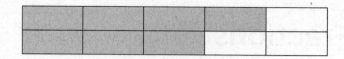

Solution

Seven of the ten parts are shaded: $\frac{7}{10}$ which is read as *seven-tenths*.

FRACTION TYPES

There are three basic types of fractions that you should be familiar with.

- **PROPER FRACTIONS** express values that are less than one. Their numerators are less than their denominators. For example: $\frac{2}{3}$, $\frac{3}{4}$ and $\frac{1}{20}$.

- **IMPROPER FRACTIONS** express values that are equal to or greater than one. Their numerators are greater than or equal to their denominators. For example: $\frac{7}{5}$, $\frac{8}{8}$, and $\frac{13}{12}$.

- **MIXED NUMBERS** are made up of a whole number and a proper fraction. Mixed numbers always express values that are greater than one. For example: $2\frac{1}{3}$, $4\frac{2}{5}$, and $12\frac{4}{9}$.

➡ **EXAMPLE 1** _____

The circles shown below have been divided into three equal parts. The shaded part can be described by the improper fraction $\frac{10}{3}$ or by the mixed number $3\frac{1}{3}$.

➡ **EXAMPLE 2** _____

The boxes shown below have been divided into four equal parts. Write the improper fraction that represents the shaded part. Then write this fraction as a mixed number.

Solution

13 of the "parts" have been shaded. Write this as $\frac{13}{4}$ (improper) or as $3\frac{1}{4}$ (mixed).

CONVERTING BETWEEN IMPROPER FRACTIONS AND MIXED NUMBERS

In the previous example and practice questions, you can visually understand the equivalence between the improper fraction and mixed number. Any amount equal to or greater than one can be written in either an improper or mixed format.

To convert from improper fraction to a mixed number, follow these steps:

a. Think of the fraction line as a line of division. Ask yourself how many times does the denominator divide evenly into the numerator?

b. Write the whole number result as the whole number part of the mixed number. The remainder is written over the original denominator. This is the fractional part of the mixed number.

➡ EXAMPLE 1

Convert the improper fraction $\frac{11}{3}$ to a mixed number.

Solution

a. Ask "how many times will 3 divide evenly into 11?"

$$
\begin{array}{r}
3 \\
3\overline{\smash{)}11} \\
-9 \\
\hline
2 \quad \text{REMAINDER}
\end{array}
$$

The result is that 3 divides evenly into 11 three times, with 2 as a remainder.

b. Write the whole number first and the remainder over the denominator. $\frac{11}{3} = 3\frac{2}{3}$

➡ EXAMPLE 2

Convert the improper fraction $\frac{17}{4}$ to a mixed number.

Solution

a. Ask "how many times does 4 divide evenly into 17?"

$$
\begin{array}{r}
4 \\
4\overline{\smash{)}17} \\
-16 \\
\hline
1 \quad \text{REMAINDER}
\end{array}
$$

The result is that 4 divides evenly into 17 four times, with 1 as a remainder.

b. Write the whole number first and the remainder over the denominator. $\frac{17}{4} = 4\frac{1}{4}$

Converting Between Mixed Numbers and Improper Fractions

It is also helpful to convert from a mixed number to an improper fraction.

To convert from a mixed number to an improper fraction, follow these steps:

a. Multiply the whole number of the mixed number by the denominator of the fraction.

b. Add the numerator to the result calculated in step a.

c. Write the total in the numerator over the original denominator.

➡ EXAMPLE 1

Convert the mixed number $2\frac{3}{4}$ to an improper fraction.

Solution

  a. $2 \times 4 = 8$

  b. $3 + 8 = 11$

  c. $\dfrac{11}{4}$

➡ EXAMPLE 2

Convert the mixed number $10\frac{2}{7}$ to an improper fraction.

Solution

  a. $10 \times 7 = 70$

  b. $2 + 70 = 72$

  c. $\dfrac{72}{7}$

PRACTICE

1. Write the fraction that describes the shaded regions.

  a.

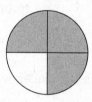

  b.

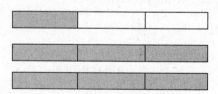

  c.

2. Write as mixed numbers.

  a. $\dfrac{9}{4}$

  b. $\dfrac{32}{5}$

  c. $\dfrac{12}{12}$

  d. $\dfrac{29}{7}$

  e. $\dfrac{50}{4}$

3. Write as improper fractions.

   a. $3\frac{4}{5}$

   b. $14\frac{3}{10}$

   c. $6\frac{2}{7}$

   d. $2\frac{5}{9}$

   e. $21\frac{7}{10}$

ANSWERS

1. a. $\frac{3}{4}$ b. $\frac{13}{2}=6\frac{1}{2}$ c. $\frac{7}{3}=2\frac{1}{3}$

2. a. $\frac{9}{4}=2\frac{1}{4}$ b. $\frac{32}{5}=6\frac{2}{5}$ c. $\frac{12}{12}=1$ d. $\frac{29}{7}=4\frac{1}{7}$ e. $\frac{50}{4}=12\frac{2}{4}=12\frac{1}{2}$

3. a. $3\frac{4}{5}=\frac{19}{5}$ b. $14\frac{3}{10}=\frac{143}{.10}$ c. $6\frac{2}{7}=\frac{44}{7}$ d. $2\frac{5}{9}=\frac{23}{9}$ e. $21\frac{7}{10}=\frac{217}{10}$

Converting Between Fractions and Decimals

In Chapter 23 you learned to convert decimals to fractions with an understanding of place value. To convert a fraction to a decimal, it is simply a process of division. Fractional notation is another way of expressing division in which the numerator is divided by the denominator.

➡ **EXAMPLE 1** _____

Convert $\frac{5}{6}$ to a decimal.

Solution

Can be rewritten as $5 \div 6$.

Either using your calculator or completing long division ($6\overline{)5}$), we find $\frac{5}{6} = 0.833\,33$

In general you would round this value to two decimal places. $\frac{5}{6} = 0.83$

➡ **EXAMPLE 2** _____

Convert $\frac{3}{8}$ to a decimal.

Solution

$\frac{3}{8}$ can be rewritten as $3 \div 8$.

Either using your calculator or completing long division ($8\overline{)3}$), you find $\frac{3}{8} = 0.375$

PRACTICE

1. Convert the following fractions to decimals. Round to two decimal places.

   a. $\dfrac{2}{3}$ d. $\dfrac{10}{12}$ g. $\dfrac{20}{30}$ j. $\dfrac{4}{9}$

   b. $\dfrac{4}{5}$ e. $\dfrac{31}{35}$ h. $10\dfrac{1}{2}$

   c. $\dfrac{3}{4}$ f. $\dfrac{4}{7}$ i. $3\dfrac{1}{8}$

ANSWERS

1.   a. 0.67   b. 0.8   c. 0.75   d. 0.83   e. 0.89   f. 0.57   g. 0.67   h. 10.5   i. 3.13   j. 0.44

EQUIVALENT FRACTIONS

In each of the following diagrams, one half of the shape is shaded.

 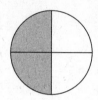 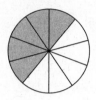

TIP

Equivalent fractions have the same value, even though they look different.

Therefore, you can conclude that $\dfrac{1}{2} = \dfrac{2}{4} = \dfrac{5}{10}$. These are called *equivalent fractions* because they all represent the same value.

In general, fractions are always reduced to their lowest terms. A fraction is said to be in the lowest terms when the numerator and the denominator are no longer divisible by a common number.

REDUCING TO LOWEST TERMS

To reduce a fraction to lowest terms, follow these steps:

a. Identify the Greatest Common Factor (GCF). Ask yourself, "What is the largest number that divides evenly into both the numerator and denominator?"

b. Factor both the numerator and denominator using the GCF.

c. Cancel the GCF and leave your answer in lowest terms.

➡ **EXAMPLE 1** _____

Reduce $\dfrac{12}{36}$ to lowest terms.

Solution

$$\frac{12}{36} = \frac{\overset{1}{\cancel{12}} \times 1}{\underset{1}{\cancel{12}} \times 3} = \frac{1}{3}$$

➡️ **EXAMPLE 2**_____

Reduce $\frac{51}{85}$ to lowest terms.

Solution

$$\frac{51}{85} = \frac{\overset{1}{\cancel{17}} \times 3}{\underset{1}{\cancel{17}} \times 5} = \frac{3}{5}$$

QUICK CALCULATOR POINTER

Remember that the fraction button on your calculator, $a\frac{b}{c}$, can be helpful working with and reducing fractions.

Try it. Enter the following on your calculator and hit the = key. The fraction has been reduced to lowest terms for you.

$$27 \boxed{a\frac{b}{c}} 120 = \qquad \text{Did you get 9/40?}$$

PRACTICE

1. Reduce the following fractions to lowest terms.

   a. $\frac{10}{20}$ d. $\frac{21}{21}$ g. $\frac{16}{48}$ j. $2\frac{21}{56}$

   b. $\frac{18}{27}$ e. $\frac{35}{45}$ h. $3\frac{6}{18}$

   c. $\frac{33}{77}$ f. $\frac{28}{49}$ i. $14\frac{26}{39}$

ANSWERS

1. a. $\frac{1}{2}$ b. $\frac{2}{3}$ c. $\frac{3}{7}$ d. $\frac{1}{1}$ e. $\frac{7}{9}$ f. $\frac{4}{7}$ g. $\frac{1}{3}$ h. $3\frac{1}{3}$ i. $14\frac{2}{3}$ j. $2\frac{3}{8}$

ADDING AND SUBTRACTING FRACTIONS

In order to add or subtract fractions, the denominator of each expression must be exactly the same. If the denominators are the same, it is just a matter of combining the numerators and simplifying the expression.

For example: $\frac{1}{8} + \frac{3}{8} = \frac{4}{8} = \frac{1}{2}$

The fractions $\frac{1}{8}$ and $\frac{3}{8}$ have a common denominator of 8.

If the denominators are not the same, we must first convert the fractions to equivalent expressions by *creating a common denominator.*

For example: Add $\frac{2}{3}$ and $\frac{1}{4}$

$$\frac{2}{3} = \frac{2 \times 4}{3 \times 4} = \frac{8}{12}$$
$$+ \frac{1}{4} = \frac{1 \times 3}{4 \times 3} = \frac{3}{12}$$
$$\frac{11}{12}$$

Notice that the process of changing $\frac{2}{3}$ to $\frac{8}{12}$ is the reverse of the process for reducing fractions to lowest terms.

The following examples include a description of the steps involved in converting to a common denominator.

➡ EXAMPLE 1

Subtract $\frac{5}{6} - \frac{3}{8}$

Solution

STEP 1 Determine the *lowest common denominator* (LCD). Ask yourself, "What is the lowest number that 6 and 8 both divide evenly into?" To determine this value, consider multiples of the larger number. Multiples of 8 are 8, 16, 24, 32, 40, and so on. Does 6 divide evenly into any of these numbers? Yes! 6 divides evenly into 24. 24 is the LCD.

STEP 2 Convert each fraction to contain the LCD.

$$\frac{5}{6} = \frac{5 \times 4}{6 \times 4} = \frac{20}{24}$$

$$\frac{3}{8} = \frac{3 \times 3}{8 \times 3} = \frac{9}{24}$$

STEP 3 Complete the operation of subtraction. Reduce the fraction to lowest terms.

$$\frac{20}{24} - \frac{9}{24} = \frac{11}{24}$$

➡ EXAMPLE 2

$\frac{1}{2} + \frac{3}{5} - \frac{1}{3}$

Solution

STEP 1 Determine the lowest common denominator (LCD). Ask yourself, "What is the lowest number that 2, 5 and 3 both divide evenly into?" To determine this value, consider multiples of the largest number. Multiples of 5 are 5, 10, 15, 20, 25, 30, 25, 40, 45, etc. Do 2 and 3 both divide evenly into any of these numbers? Yes. 2 and 3 both divide evenly into 30. 30 is the LCD.

STEP 2 Convert each fraction to contain the LCD.

$$\frac{1}{2} = \frac{1 \times 15}{2 \times 15} = \frac{15}{30}$$

$$\frac{3}{5} = \frac{3 \times 6}{5 \times 6} = \frac{18}{30}$$

$$\frac{1}{3} = \frac{1 \times 10}{3 \times 10} = \frac{10}{30}$$

STEP 3 Complete the operations of addition and subtraction. Reduce the fraction to lowest terms.

$$\frac{15}{30} + \frac{18}{30} - \frac{10}{30} = \frac{23}{30}$$

PRACTICE

1. Add or subtract the following fraction as indicated. Remember to reduce to lowest terms where possible.

   a. $\frac{1}{5} + \frac{2}{5}$

   d. $\frac{4}{7} - \frac{3}{14}$

   g. $5\frac{3}{10} + 4\frac{7}{15}$

   j. $2\frac{1}{3} + \frac{5}{6} - 1\frac{2}{3}$

   b. $\frac{9}{15} - \frac{5}{10}$

   e. $\frac{5}{8} + \frac{5}{24}$

   h. $\frac{5}{6} - \frac{1}{3} + \frac{5}{12}$

   c. $\frac{3}{20} + \frac{5}{8}$

   f. $3\frac{3}{4} - 2\frac{1}{4}$

   i. $\frac{7}{11} + \frac{1}{2} - \frac{3}{22}$

ANSWERS

1. a. $\frac{3}{5}$ b. $\frac{1}{10}$ c. $\frac{31}{40}$ d. $\frac{5}{14}$ e. $\frac{5}{6}$ f. $1\frac{1}{2}$ g. $9\frac{23}{30}$ h. $\frac{11}{12}$ i. 1   j. $1\frac{1}{2}$

CHALLENGE EXERCISE

Most kitchens are equipped with a set of six or seven nested measuring cups. Create a common denominator and see how many cups of flour you would have in total if each measuring cup was filled to capacity.

MULTIPLYING FRACTIONS

Suppose there was $\frac{1}{2}$ of a pizza left over and it had to be shared among 3 friends. Each person would get $\frac{1}{3}$ of $\frac{1}{2}$ the original pizza. How much of the original pizza would they each receive?

In arithmetic, the word *of* means to multiply. To find the solution to this problem we would need to multiply $\frac{1}{3}$ by $\frac{1}{2}$.

Fortunately, multiplying fractions is a much easier process than adding or subtracting. When multiplying fractions, one simply multiplies the numerator by the numerator and the denominator by the denominator.

➡ EXAMPLE 1 _____

$\dfrac{2}{3} \times \dfrac{4}{5}$

Solution

$\dfrac{2}{3} \times \dfrac{4}{5} = \dfrac{2 \times 4}{3 \times 5} = \dfrac{8}{15}$

➡ EXAMPLE 2 _____

Multiply $1\dfrac{2}{3} \times 3$

Solution

First, write both numbers as improper fractions, and then multiply numerators and denominators.

$$1\dfrac{2}{3} \times 3 = \dfrac{5}{3} \times \dfrac{3}{1} = \dfrac{5 \times 3}{3 \times 1} = \dfrac{15}{3} = 5$$

In general, the steps to follow when multiplying fractions are

a. Rewrite any mixed numbers as improper fractions.
b. Multiply numerator by numerator and denominator by denominator.
c. Simplify fully.

It is sometimes easier to simplify, by cancelling common factors, before multiplying. You can cancel common factors within the fraction but also diagonally across the $\times$ symbol. Study the example below.

➡ EXAMPLE 3 _____

Multiply $\dfrac{6}{18} \times 2\dfrac{4}{10}$

Solution

$$\dfrac{6}{18} \times 2\dfrac{4}{10} = \dfrac{6}{18} \times \dfrac{24}{10} = \dfrac{2 \times 3 \times 4 \times 6}{3 \times 6 \times 2 \times 5} = \dfrac{\overset{1}{2} \times \overset{1}{3} \times 4 \times \overset{1}{6}}{\underset{1}{3} \times \underset{1}{6} \times \underset{1}{2} \times 5} = \dfrac{4}{5}$$

➡ EXAMPLE 4 _____

Multiply $\dfrac{5}{27} \times \dfrac{18}{15}$

Solution

$$\dfrac{5}{27} \times \dfrac{18}{15} = \dfrac{\overset{1}{5}}{3 \times \underset{1}{9}} \times \dfrac{2 \times \overset{1}{9}}{\underset{1}{5} \times 3} = \dfrac{2}{9}$$

PRACTICE

1. Multiply the following fraction as indicated. Always remember to reduce to lowest terms where possible.

    a. $\frac{1}{4} \times \frac{3}{5}$ d. $2\frac{3}{4} \times 1\frac{1}{2}$ g. $\frac{8}{3} \times \frac{27}{24}$

    b. $\frac{9}{14} \times \frac{7}{18}$ e. $\left(\frac{5}{6}\right)\left(3\frac{1}{4}\right)\left(\frac{2}{15}\right)$ h. $12 \times \frac{4}{5}$

    c. $1\frac{2}{3} \times \frac{3}{8}$ f. $\frac{7}{10} \times 3$

2. Susan spent $\frac{1}{4}$ of her $1\frac{1}{2}$ hour water aerobics class in the hot tub. How long was Susan in the hot tub?

3. Dave glued four $\frac{1}{8}$ inch thick boards together. How thick was his finished project?

ANSWERS

1. a. $\frac{3}{20}$ b. $\frac{1}{4}$ c. $\frac{5}{8}$ d. $4\frac{1}{8}$ e. $\frac{13}{36}$ f. $\frac{21}{10}$ or $2\frac{1}{10}$ g. 3 h. $\frac{48}{5}$ or $9\frac{3}{5}$

2. Susan spent $\frac{3}{8}$ of an hour in the hot tub.

3. The project was $\frac{1}{2}$ inch thick.

DIVIDING FRACTIONS

All fraction division questions can be rewritten as fraction multiplication questions. Dividing by any number is the same as multiplying by the reciprocal of that same number. This is true for whole numbers or for fractions.

If you had ten dollars and divided the money between two people, each person would receive 5 dollars. Notice that $10 \times \frac{1}{2} = \frac{10}{2} = 5$. $\frac{1}{2}$ is the reciprocal of 2.

In general the steps to follow when dividing fractions are:

a. Reciprocate the divisor (the second fraction).
b. Change the operation to multiplication.
c. Multiply numerator by numerator and denominator by denominator.
d. Simplify fully.

➡ **EXAMPLE 1** _____

$\frac{2}{3} \div \frac{1}{2}$

Solution

$\frac{2}{3} \div \frac{1}{2} = \frac{2}{3} \times \frac{2}{1} = \frac{4}{3}$ or $1\frac{1}{3}$

TIP

To "reciprocate" or "invert" a fraction means the same as "flipping" the fraction.

Divide $1\frac{3}{4}$ by 5

Solution

First, write both numbers as improper fractions and then multiply by the reciprocal of the divisor.

$$1\frac{3}{4} \div 5 = \frac{7}{4} \times \frac{1}{5} = \frac{7}{20}$$

PRACTICE

1. Divide the following fractions as indicated. Always remember to reduce to lowest terms where possible.

   a. $\frac{5}{8} \div \frac{1}{8}$ c. $2\frac{1}{2} \div \frac{1}{4}$ e. $\frac{11}{12} \div \frac{2}{3}$ g. $\frac{5}{7} \div 3$

   b. $10 \div \frac{4}{5}$ d. $\frac{10}{12} \div 2$ f. $3\frac{1}{4} \div \frac{1}{2}$ h. $\frac{3}{8} \div \frac{1}{6}$

2. Review all the basic operations with fractions. Simplify the following.

   a. $\frac{3}{8} + \frac{1}{8}$ c. $\frac{4}{7} \times \frac{21}{28}$ e. $1\frac{2}{3} + 4\frac{4}{6}$ g. $\frac{8}{9} \div 3$

   b. $2 \div \frac{1}{2}$ d. $\frac{5}{6} - \frac{7}{9}$ f. $3\frac{1}{2} \times 4$ h. $\left(\frac{4}{5} - \frac{1}{3}\right)\left(\frac{7}{10}\right)$

ANSWERS

1. a. 5   c. 10   e. $\frac{11}{8} = 1\frac{3}{8}$ g. $\frac{5}{21}$

   b. $\frac{25}{2} = 12\frac{1}{2}$ d. $\frac{5}{12}$ f. $\frac{13}{2} = 6\frac{1}{2}$ h. $\frac{9}{4} = 2\frac{1}{4}$

2. a. $\frac{1}{2}$ c. $\frac{3}{7}$ e. $6\frac{1}{3}$ g. $\frac{8}{27}$

   b. 4   d. $\frac{1}{18}$ f. 14   h. $\frac{49}{150}$

QUICK CALCULATOR POINTER

The fraction button on your calculator, $a\frac{b}{c}$, can be very helpful calculating all basic operations with fractions.

Try it. Enter the following on your calculator and hit the = key. Remember that the calculator will automatically reduce to lowest terms.

$2\dfrac{1}{4}+\dfrac{2}{3}$

Solution

$2\ \boxed{a\dfrac{b}{c}}\ 1\ \boxed{a\dfrac{b}{c}}\ 4 + 2\ \boxed{a\dfrac{b}{c}}\ 3 =$ Did you get 2 ⌐ 11 ⌐ 12? This is the same as $2\dfrac{11}{12}$.

CHALLENGE EXERCISE

Study a clock. Express the following minutes as a fraction of an hour: 20 minutes, 15 minutes, 22 minutes, 40 minutes, and 55 minutes. Reduce every fraction fully.

CHAPTER CHECK-UP

1. Convert the following three fractions to common denominators and order them from smallest to largest.

   $\dfrac{2}{5}\quad \dfrac{3}{10}\quad \dfrac{9}{20}$

   (1) $\dfrac{6}{20}\quad \dfrac{8}{20}\quad \dfrac{9}{20}$

   (2) $\dfrac{9}{20}\quad \dfrac{8}{20}\quad \dfrac{6}{20}$

   (3) $\dfrac{3}{10}\quad \dfrac{4}{10}\quad \dfrac{5}{10}$

   (4) $\dfrac{2}{5}\quad \dfrac{3}{5}\quad \dfrac{9}{5}$

   (5) $\dfrac{2}{5}\quad \dfrac{3}{10}\quad \dfrac{9}{20}$

2. Louise sells chocolate chip cookies by the dozen. On average she sells $5\dfrac{1}{3}$ dozen cookies each day. How many dozen cookies does she sell in a week?

   (1) 448

   (2) $36\dfrac{2}{3}$

   (3) $\dfrac{110}{3}$

   (4) $12\dfrac{1}{3}$

   (5) $37\dfrac{1}{3}$

3. Michelle and Justin were pruning their 14 apple trees. If Justin pruned $6\frac{3}{4}$ trees, how many did Michelle prune?

(1) $7\frac{3}{4}$

(2) $7\frac{1}{4}$

(3) $6\frac{1}{4}$

(4) $7\frac{1}{2}$

(5) $6\frac{3}{4}$

4. Susan purchases 6 metres of fabric to make placemats. Each placemat requires $\frac{3}{8}$ metres of fabric. How many placemats will Susan be able to make?
(1) 10
(2) 6
(3) 12
(4) 16
(5) Not enough information is given

5. There are 125 students at a small elementary school. $\frac{1}{5}$ of the students contract chicken pox. How many students did not contract the disease?

(1) $\frac{3}{5}$

(2) $\frac{4}{5}$

(3) 50
(4) 100
(5) 25

6. A bouquet of flowers contained a dozen roses. $\frac{2}{3}$ of the roses were pink and the rest were red. How many pink roses are there?
(1) 12
(2) 10
(3) 8
(4) 6
(5) 4

7. Sarah walked $4\frac{1}{2}$ km one day, $5\frac{1}{4}$ km the next day, and $6\frac{1}{3}$ km on the third day. How many kilometres did Sarah walk in total?

(1) $11\frac{3}{9}$

(2) $16\frac{1}{12}$

(3) $12\frac{1}{6}$

(4) $13\frac{1}{12}$

(5) $15\frac{1}{2}$

8. Irene had $3\frac{3}{4}$ metres of fabric that she wanted to cut into three equal lengths. How long will each piece measure?
   (1) 1.25 m
   (2) 1.1 m
   (3) 2.25 m
   (4) 0.75 m
   (5) 1.75 m

9. A small backyard measured $10\frac{3}{4}$ metres by $6\frac{1}{2}$ metres. How much greater was the length than the width?

(1) 10.75 m
(2) 6.50 m
(3) 3.75 m
(4) 4.25 m
(5) 4.50 m

10. The typical college year is approximately 36 weeks long. College students spend, on average, about $3\frac{4}{5}$ days a week in school. Which expression tells how many days a year an average college student spends in school?

(1) $\dfrac{36 \times 3\frac{4}{5}}{7}$

(2) $36 \times 3\frac{4}{5}$

(3) $36 \div 3\frac{4}{5}$

(4) $36 + 3.75$

(5) Not enough information is given.

ANSWERS

1. **(1)** $\frac{2}{5} = \frac{8}{20}$ compared to $\frac{3}{10} = \frac{6}{20}$ compared to $\frac{9}{20}$

2. **(5)** Multiply. $5\frac{1}{3} \times 7 = \frac{16}{3} \times \frac{7}{1} = \frac{112}{3} = 37\frac{1}{3}$

3. **(2)** Subtract. $14 - 6\frac{3}{4} = \frac{14}{1} - \frac{27}{4} = \frac{56}{4} - \frac{27}{4} = \frac{29}{4} = 7\frac{1}{4}$

4. **(4)** Divide. $6 \div \frac{3}{8} = \frac{6}{1} \times \frac{8}{3} = \frac{48}{3} = 16$

5. **(4)** Two-part question. First, multiply. $125 \times \frac{1}{5} = \frac{125}{5} = 25$. Therefore, 25 students contracted chicken pox. Second, subtract. $125 - 25 = 100$

6. **(3)** Multiply. $12 \times \frac{2}{3} = \frac{24}{3} = 8$

7. **(2)** Add. $4\frac{1}{2} + 5\frac{1}{4} + 6\frac{1}{3} = 4\frac{6}{12} + 5\frac{3}{12} + 6\frac{4}{12} = 15\frac{13}{12} = 16\frac{1}{12}$

8. **(1)** Divide. $3\frac{3}{4} \div 3 = \frac{15}{4} \times \frac{1}{3} = \frac{15}{12} = 1\frac{1}{4}$. Convert to a decimal. $1\frac{1}{4} = 1.25$

9. **(4)** Subtract. $10\frac{3}{4} - 6\frac{1}{2} = 10\frac{3}{4} - 6\frac{2}{4} = 4\frac{1}{4}$. Convert to a decimal. $4\frac{1}{4} = 4.25$

10. **(2)**

Percentages

25

THINK ABOUT IT

The word percent comes from the Latin phrase *per centum*, and essentially means *parts per hundred* or *out of one hundred*. For example, if you achieve 75% on a test, you answered 75 out of 100 questions correctly. Percent is indicated by the symbol %.

If you were to answer every question on the GED test correctly, you would achieve 100%. In general, 100% is the highest score you can achieve; however, if bonus marks are given, it may be possible to achieve more than 100%. If you answered every question correctly and were given five extra marks for the bonus question, you would achieve 105%. In real-world problems, it is possible to achieve more than 100%.

Not only are percent problems common in our everyday world, but percent problems are a frequent part of the GED test problems.

IN THIS CHAPTER

After completing this chapter, you will be able to

→ **UNDERSTAND PERCENT NOTATION**

→ **CONVERT BETWEEN FRACTIONS, DECIMALS, AND PERCENTS**

→ **SOLVE WORD PROBLEMS THAT INCLUDE PERCENTS**

→ **EVALUATE SIMPLE INTEREST PROBLEMS**

→ **CALCULATE PERCENTAGE INCREASES AND DECREASES**

CONVERTING BETWEEN PERCENTS, DECIMALS, AND FRACTIONS

Percent, or percentages, are closely related to fractions and decimals. The following are all equivalent:

$$15\% = 0.15 = \frac{15}{100}$$

Each expression indicates 15 per one hundred, or fifteen hundredths. They are all equal in value but expressed in different ways.

CONVERTING PERCENTS TO DECIMALS

- Rewrite the numeral without the % symbol
- Multiply the number by 0.01 or simply move the decimal point two places left.

➡ EXAMPLE 1 _____

Convert 15% to a decimal.

Solution
 a.   15.
 b.   Multiply by 0.01 (or move the decimal two places to the left) = 0.15

➡ EXAMPLE 2 _____

Convert 27.5% to a decimal.

Solution
 a.   27.5
 b.   Multiply by 0.01 (or move the decimal two places to the left) = 0.275

➡ EXAMPLE 3 _____

Convert 8% to a decimal.

Solution
 a.   8
 b.   Multiply by 0.01 (or move the decimal two places to the left) = 0.08
      (Note that a zero was added to occupy the tenths position).

➡ EXAMPLE 4 _____

Convert 112.75% to a decimal.

Solution
 a.   112.75
 b.   Multiply by 0.01 (or move the decimal two places to the left) = 1.127 5

CONVERTING DECIMALS TO PERCENTS

To convert from decimal to percent, simply reverse the process.

 ■ Multiply the number by 100 or move the decimal point two places right.
 ■ Add the % symbol to the numeral.

➡ EXAMPLE 1 _____

Convert 0.25 to a percent.

Solution
 a.   Multiply by 100 (or move the decimal two places to the right) = 25
 b.   Add the % symbol. 25%

➡ EXAMPLE 2 _____

Convert 2.45 to a percent.

Solution
   a. Multiply by 100 (or move the decimal two places to the right) = 245
   b. 245%

➡ EXAMPLE 3 _____

Convert 0.06 to a percent

Solution
   a. $0.06 \times 100 = 6$
   b. 6%

PRACTICE

1. Convert the following to decimals.

a.	36%	d.	1.5%	g.	15.45%	j.	64.5%
b.	45%	e.	115%	h.	0.25%		
c.	76%	f.	250%	i.	2.25%		

2. Convert the following decimals to percents.

a.	0.66	d.	0.378	g.	0.001 5	j.	0.6
b.	1.34	e.	2.2	h.	5.08		
c.	0.08	f.	0.75	i.	0.07		

ANSWERS

1.

a.	0.36	d.	0.015	g.	0.154 5	j.	0.645
b.	0.45	e.	1.15	h.	0.002 5		
c.	0.76	f.	2.50	i.	0.022 5		

2.

a.	66%	d.	37.8%	g.	0.15%	j.	60%
b.	134%	e.	220%	h.	508%		
c.	8%	f.	75%	i.	7%		

CONVERTING PERCENTS TO FRACTIONS

- Rewrite the numeral without the % symbol
- Multiply the number by $\frac{1}{100}$
- Reduce the fraction to lowest terms.

➡ EXAMPLE 1 _____

Convert 15% to a fraction.

Solution

  a. 15.

  b. Multiply by $\dfrac{1}{100} = \dfrac{15}{100}$

  c. Reduce to lowest terms. $\dfrac{15}{100} = \dfrac{3}{20}$

➡ **EXAMPLE 2** _____

Convert 27.5% to a fraction.

Solution

  a. 27.5

  b. Multiply by $\dfrac{1}{100} = \dfrac{27.5}{100} = \dfrac{275}{1\,000}$ (So as not to mix decimal and fraction formats, both numerator and denominator were multiplied by ten)

  c. Reduce to lowest terms.

      $\dfrac{275}{1\,000} = \dfrac{11}{40}$

➡ **EXAMPLE 3** _____

Convert 8% to a fraction.

Solution

  a. 8

  b. Multiply by $\dfrac{1}{100} = \dfrac{8}{100}$

  c. Reduce to lowest terms. $\dfrac{8}{100} = \dfrac{2}{25}$

Converting Fractions to Percents

When converting from a fraction to a percent, it is generally easier to first convert the fraction to a decimal and then convert the decimal to a percent.

- Divide the numerator by the denominator.
- If necessary, round to the nearest one-hundredth position.
- Convert the decimal to percent by moving the decimal point two places right and adding the % symbol.

➡ **EXAMPLE 1** _____

Convert $\dfrac{3}{4}$ to a percent.

Solution

  a. $3 \div 4 = 0.75$

  b. 0.75

  c. 75%

➡ EXAMPLE 2

Convert $\frac{3}{8}$ to a percent.

Solution
a. $3 \div 8 = 0.375$
b. 0.375
c. 37.5%

➡ EXAMPLE 3

Convert $\frac{4}{7}$ to a percent.

Solution
a. $4 \div 7 = 0.571\,428\,571$
b. 0.57
c. 57%

➡ EXAMPLE 4

Convert to a percent. $3\frac{1}{3}$

Solution
a. First convert to an improper fraction. $\frac{10}{3}$. $10 \div 3 = 3.333\,333\,33$
b. 3.33
c. 333%

PRACTICE

1. Convert the following percents to fractions. Simplify fully.

a. 45%	d. 10.5%	g. 2.75%	j. 7.5%
b. 72%	e. 4.8%	h. 0.4%	
c. 5%	f. 225%	i. 110%	

2. Convert the following fractions to percents.

a. $\frac{2}{3}$ c. $\frac{7}{10}$ e. $3\frac{8}{21}$

b. $\frac{5}{8}$ d. $2\frac{4}{5}$

ANSWERS

1. a. $\frac{9}{20}$ d. $\frac{21}{200}$ g. $\frac{11}{400}$ j. $\frac{3}{40}$

   b. $\frac{18}{25}$ e. $\frac{6}{125}$ h. $\frac{1}{250}$

   c. $\frac{1}{20}$ f. $\frac{9}{4}$ i. $\frac{11}{10}$

2. a. 67%   c. 70%   e. 338%

   b. 62.5%   d. 280%

CHALLENGE EXERCISE

Survey about 20 people. Ask each person their shoe size. Determine the percentage of people that wear size 7, size 8, size 9, and so on, based on this small sample size.

Comparing and Ordering Percents, Decimals, and Fractions

You may be familiar with the phrase "you can't compare apples to oranges". Similarly, it is difficult to compare numbers written in one format to numbers written in a different format. In part, learning how to convert between formats is helpful for making comparisons.

➡ EXAMPLE 1 _____

If you were told that Susan ran 1.375 kilometres and Tracy ran $1\frac{5}{13}$ kilometres, it would be difficult to say confidently who ran the greater distance without first converting the numerals to the same format. You could convert both to decimals or both to fractions. In general, comparing decimals seems to be easier to understand.

Solution

Convert $1\frac{5}{13}$ to a decimal.

$$1\frac{5}{13} = 1.384\ 615\ 385$$

Therefore, Tracy ran approximately 1.385 kilometres which is farther than the 1.375 kilometres that Susan ran.

➡ EXAMPLE 2 _____

Convert the following numbers all to decimals and then order them left to right from smallest to largest.

$$0.125 \quad 12.45\% \quad \frac{2}{11}$$

Solution

0.125 is already in decimal form.

Convert 12.45% to a decimal.
12.45% = 0.1245

Convert $\frac{2}{11}$ to a decimal. $\frac{2}{11}$ ~0.181 818 181

From smallest to largest: 12.45%　　0.125　　$\frac{2}{11}$

PRACTICE

1. John read 72% of the newspaper, Frank read $\frac{5}{8}$ of the newspaper, and Scott read 0.7 of the newspaper. Who read the most?

2. Trish completed $\frac{3}{4}$ of the questions on her homework. John completed 75% of the same assignment. Who completed the fewest number of questions.

3. Which of the following is the smallest value?
   a. 0.123
   b. $\frac{3}{11}$
   c. 12%
   d. $\frac{2}{11}$

ANSWERS

1. John read the most. 72% is greater than $\frac{5}{8}$ = 62.5% and also greater than 0.7 = 70%.

2. They both completed the same. $\frac{3}{4}$ = 75%

3. 12%. 12% = 0.12 which is smaller than 0.123 and smaller than $\frac{3}{11}$ = 0.273 and smaller than $\frac{2}{11}$ = 0.182

SOLVING PERCENT PROBLEMS USING PROPORTIONS

Percent problems, no matter how difficult, solve for only one of the following three unknown values:

- An unknown part (the total and percent will be known)
- An unknown total (the part and percent will be known)
- An unknown percent (the part and total will be known)

The following proportion holds true for all percent problems:

$$\frac{\text{part}}{\text{total}} = \frac{\% \text{ percent}}{100}$$

The words *is* and *of* are helpful in identifying the part from the whole. You can expand the proportion and write it as follows:

$$\frac{\text{is}}{\text{of}} = \frac{\text{part}}{\text{total}} = \frac{\% \text{ percent}}{100}$$

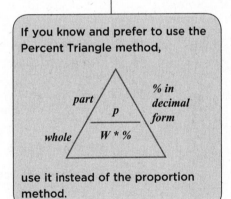

If you know and prefer to use the Percent Triangle method,

use it instead of the proportion method.

➡ EXAMPLE 1 _____

What is 45% of 200?

Solution

a. Set up the proportion. The percentage amount is always written in fraction form, over 100. The value that follows the word *of* indicates it is the total. The value before or after the word *is* indicates it is the part.

$$\frac{x}{200} = \frac{45}{100}$$

b. Solve the proportion. Use the variable x in place of the unknown and then cross multiply and divide.

$$\frac{x}{200} = \frac{45}{100}$$

$$(100)(x) = (200)(45)$$

$$100x = 9000$$

$$x = \frac{9000}{100}$$

$$x = 90$$

c. State the solution. 90 is 45% of 200.

➡ **EXAMPLE 2**

23 is what percent of 69?

Solution

a. Set up the proportion.

$$\frac{23}{69} = \frac{\text{percent?}}{100}$$

b. Solve the proportion. Use the variable x in place of the unknown and then cross multiply and divide.

$$\frac{23}{69} = \frac{x}{100}$$

$$(69)(x) = (23)(100)$$

$$69x = 2300$$

$$x = \frac{2300}{69}$$

$$x = 33.3333$$

c. State the solution. 23 is 33.3% of 69.

➡ **EXAMPLE 3**

Susan was told that her $200 represented 40% of the total winnings. How much was the total winnings?

Solution

a. Set up the proportion.

$$\frac{200}{\text{total?}} = \frac{40}{100}$$

b. Solve the proportion. Use the variable x in place of the unknown and then cross multiply and divide.

$$\frac{200}{x} = \frac{40}{100}$$

$$(40)(x) = (200)(100)$$

$$40x = 20000$$

$$x = \frac{20000}{40}$$

$$x = 500$$

c. State the solution. The total winnings are $500.

➡ EXAMPLE 4 _____

Fifteen students received a final grade of "B" or higher. There were twenty students in the class. What percent of students received a grade of "B" or higher?

Solution
a. Set up the proportion. In this problem it may be more difficult to determine the part and the whole as the helpful words; *is* and *of* are not used. Read the problem carefully.

$$\frac{15}{20} = \frac{\text{percent?}}{100}$$

b. Solve the proportion. Use the variable x in place of the unknown and then cross multiply and divide.

$$\frac{15}{20} = \frac{x}{100}$$

$$(20)(x) = (15)(100)$$

$$20x = 1500$$

$$x = \frac{1500}{20}$$

$$x = 75$$

c. State the solution. 75% of the students received a grade of "B" or higher.

PRACTICE

1. 20% of 12 is what number?

2. 6 is what percent of 25?

3. 63 is 15% of what number?

4. What is 12.5% of 60?

5. 70 is what percent of 50?

6. 11 is $27\frac{1}{2}$ % of what number?

7. Debbie got 82% on a test that was out of 75. What score did Debbie get?

8. Seven out of twenty-five teenagers have tried smoking by the age of sixteen. What percent is this?

9. Cheryl donated 12% of her total earnings to charity last year. If Cheryl donated $6600 to charity, how much did she earn?

10. An invoice from a hotel shows that $29.75 was charged as a room tax. The room rate was $175. What is the room tax rate?

ANSWERS

1. 2.4

2. 24%

3. 420

4. 7.5

5. 140%

6. 40

7. Debbie received 61.5 marks out of 75.

8. 28% of teens have tried smoking by the age of sixteen.

9. Cheryl earned $55,000.

10. The room tax rate is 17%.

PERCENT INCREASE AND DECREASE

Percent is often used to express an increase or decrease in value. For example, you may read that the unemployment rate has decreased by 1.2% or that the cost of living has increased by 2.5%.

Finding a percentage increase or decrease is a three-step process:

- Determine the amount of increase or decrease (this involves subtraction).
- Set up the following proportion.

$$\frac{\text{Increase or Decrease Amount}}{\text{Original Amount}} = \frac{\text{percent}}{100}$$

- Solve the proportion by cross multiplying and dividing.

➡ **EXAMPLE 1** _____

Ron's rent recently increased from $550 to $600. What was the percent increase?

Solution

a. $600 − $550 = $50

b. $\dfrac{\$50}{\$550} = \dfrac{x}{100}$

c. $x = 9\%$ Ron's rent increased by 9%

→ **EXAMPLE 2** _____

Gas prices decreased from $1.20/litre to $1.15/litre. What percent did gas prices decrease?

Solution

a. $1.20 − $1.15 = $0.05

b. $\dfrac{\$0.05}{\$1.20} = \dfrac{x}{100}$

c. Gas prices decreased by 4%

PRACTICE

1. Tania's hourly wage increased from $24.75 to $25.50. What is the percent increase?

2. Jeans, originally priced at $80, are on sale for $60. What is the percent decrease?

3. In 1959 the cost of one bottle of Coke was 5 cents. Today, a bottle of Coke can cost $1.10. By what percentage has the price of a bottle of Coke increased?

4. Darren weighed 210 pounds at the beginning of January. By the end of February, his weight was down to 199.5 pounds. By what percentage did his body mass decrease?

5. A precious stone was originally valued at $12 200. Ten years later it was reappraised and valued at $13 725. What is the percentage increase in the precious stone's value?

ANSWERS

1. 3% increase.

2. 25% decrease.

3. 2100% increase!!! (Remember that 5 cents is equal to $0.05)

4. 5% decrease.

5. 12.5%

CHALLENGE EXERCISE

On average, there are about 2066 hours of sunshine in Toronto in a given year. Research online how many hours of sunshine a city close to you receives (if you live in Toronto, choose another major city some distance away). Is it more or less? What is the percentage difference?

SIMPLE INTEREST

Simple interest is the amount of interest paid solely on the amount of money borrowed or lent. This original amount borrowed or lent is called the *principle*. Problems involving simple interest are common real-world situations that require an understanding of percent.

To solve problems involving simple interest, we use the following formula: $I = Prt$

Where I = Interest earned, in dollars

P = Principle amount invested, in dollars

r = Rate of interest, expressed as a percent and converted to a decimal

t = Time, in years

TIP

Simple Interest Formula:
Interest = (Principle)(Rate)(Time)

➥ EXAMPLE 1 _____

Brian invested $5000 in a guaranteed Canada Savings Bond (CSB). The bond earned a rate of 2.5% over three years. How much simple interest did it earn in that time?

Solution

First, convert 2.5% to a decimal. 2.5% = 0.025
Next, using the formula, solve for I

$$I = (\$5000)(0.025)(3)$$
$$I = \$375$$

➥ EXAMPLE 2 _____

John has a CSB in the amount of $500. It earns 3% every year. If John cashes the savings bond in after 200 days, how much will he earn in interest?

Solution

First, convert 3% to a decimal. 3% = 0.03

In this problem, we also need to determine the fraction of the year that the money was invested.

$$\frac{200}{365} = 0.55 \text{ year}$$

Next, using the formula, solve for I

$$I = (\$500)(0.03)(0.55)$$
$$I = \$8.25$$

PRACTICE

1. Janet borrows $25,000 at 5.5%. How much interest will Janet owe on the loan in 10 years?

2. At the age of 25, Josh invested $2,000 in a bond that was generating 3% simple interest annually. How much interest will this bond earn by the time Josh is 45?

3. Department store credit cards can charge 28% annual interest on outstanding bills. If you owe $250 on your credit card, how much interest will you pay in one month?

ANSWERS

1. $13 750

2. $1 200

3. $5.83

CHALLENGE EXERCISE

Look at a credit card or utility bill that you receive. What percent of interest is charged? Assuming simple interest, calculate how much interest would accumulate in a year on your current balance if you did not make any payments.

SOLVING MULTISTEP PERCENT PROBLEMS

Many real-world problems involving percents combine many of the types of problems illustrated earlier in this chapter. The steps you need to follow to solve these problems will depend on the situation. It is important to read the problem carefully and break it down into more manageable parts. The math involved in each part will be no more difficult than any of the previous examples.

➡ **EXAMPLE 1** _____

Before Christmas, winter coats were marked as 25% off the original sales price. After Christmas, winter coats were further discounted an additional 20% off the last sales price. If a winter coat was originally priced at $250, what would the final sales price be after Christmas?

Solution

(STEP 1) Determine the discount and the price before Christmas.
$250 × 25% = $250 × 0.25 = $62.50 discount
$250 − $62.50 = $187.50 sales price before Christmas

(STEP 2) Determine the discount and the price after Christmas.
$187.50 × 20% = $187.50 × 0.20 = $37.50 further discount
$187.50 − $37.50 = $150

The final sales price after Christmas would be $150.

➡ **EXAMPLE 2** _____

There is a bulk sale on toilet tissue at the local grocery store. Every package costs $7.99. If you purchase ten or more packages at the same time, you receive an additional 10% discount. How much would it cost to purchase 12 packages?

Solution

(STEP 1) Determine the original cost of 12 packages.
$7.99 × 12 = $95.88

(STEP 2) Determine the discount and the sales price.
$95.88 × 10% = $95.88 × 0.10 = $9.59 discount
$95.88 − $9.59 = $86.29

The final sales price for 12 packages is $86.29

CHAPTER CHECK-UP

1. Which of the following is not equal to 7.4?

    (1) $\frac{37}{5}$

    (2) 740%

    (3) 7.4%

    (4) $\frac{740}{100}$

    (5) $7\frac{4}{10}$

2. Arrange in order from smallest to largest

    $$0.375 \quad 37.55\% \quad \frac{3}{7} \quad 1.38 \quad \frac{5}{8}$$

    (1) $\frac{3}{7}$ 1.38 $\frac{5}{8}$ 0.375   37.55%

    (2) 37.55% $\frac{3}{7}$ 0.375 $\frac{5}{8}$ 1.38

    (3) 1.38 $\frac{5}{8}$ $\frac{3}{7}$ 37.55%   0.375

    (4) 0.375   37.55% $\frac{3}{7}$ $\frac{5}{8}$ 1.38

    (5) 37.55%   0.375 $\frac{3}{7}$ 1.38 $\frac{5}{8}$

3. By 6 pm, Troy had consumed 76% of his daily caloric allowance of 2 500 calories. How many calories did Troy have left to consume after 6 pm?

    (1) 500

    (2) 900

    (3) 1 600

    (4) 1 900

    (5) 600

4. The original price of a pillow is y dollars. Pillows are discounted by 30%. Which of the following expression indicates the discounted price of four pillows?

    (1) $4y - 0.3(4y)$

    (2) $30\%(4y)$

    (3) $0.30y$

    (4) $70\%(y)$

    (5) Not enough information is given

5. Stock ABC has increased by 21% in three months. If it was originally valued at $15.75 per stock, what is its value after the increase?
   (1) $36.75
   (2) $19.06
   (3) $12.40
   (4) $15.61
   (5) $3.31

6. Melanie was pleased to receive 90% on her last Biology quiz. The quiz was comprised of fifty one-mark questions. How many questions did Melanie get right?
   (1) 40
   (2) 48
   (3) 43
   (4) 45
   (5) 50

7. In a random survey of 120 children, it was found that 10% of the children had red hair, 45% had brown hair, 20% had blonde hair and the rest had black hair. How many children had black hair?
   (1) 60
   (2) 50
   (3) 40
   (4) 30
   (5) Not enough information is given.

8. If Jeff borrowed $4 800 at a simple interest rate of 7.5%, how much interest would Jeff owe after 2 years?
   (1) $7 200
   (2) $360
   (3) $720
   (4) $550
   (5) $4 080

ANSWERS

1. **(3)** $\frac{37}{5} = 7.4$, $740\% = 7.4$, $7.4\% = 0.074$, $\frac{740}{100} = 7.4$, $7\frac{4}{10} = 7.4$

2. **(4)**

3. **(5)** Find 76% of 2 500 = 1 900 calories consumed. Therefore, he has 2 500 – 1 900 = 600 calories left to consume.

4. **(1)** Four times the original price less four times 30% of the original price.

5. **(2)** $15.75 + 21\%($15.75) = $19.06

6. **(4)** Solve $\frac{x}{50} = \frac{90}{100}$

7. **(4)** Subtract 100% – 10% – 45% – 20% = 25% have black hair. Solve $\frac{x}{120} = \frac{25}{100}$

8. **(3)** Interest = ($4 800)(0.075)(2)

Rate, Ratio, and Proportion

26

It is Thanksgiving and you have been asked to bring the turkey to the family dinner. You find that, on average, most guests require about 0.75 kilograms of uncooked turkey each. If there are fifteen guests invited to Thanksgiving dinner, what size of turkey should you purchase?

This everyday-life problem can be solved using a *proportion*. A proportion is made up of two equal fractions.

$$\frac{0.75 \text{ kilograms of turkey}}{1 \text{ person}} = \frac{\text{how many kilograms of turkey?}}{15 \text{ people}}$$

You solved percent proportion problems in the previous chapter. The same approach can be used for a wide variety of real-world problems.

IN THIS CHAPTER

After completing this chapter, you will be able to

→ **COMPUTE UNIT RATES**

→ **UNDERSTAND RATIO**

→ **UNDERSTAND PROPORTION**

→ **UNDERSTAND SCALE DRAWINGS**

→ **UNDERSTAND PROBABILITY**

RATIO

A *ratio* is simply a comparison of two or more things having the same units. For example, when preparing a homemade window cleaner, one mixes 1 cup of vinegar to 8 cups of water. Both the vinegar and water are measured in the same unit—cups. Ratios can be expressed in three different ways.

- In words: one to eight

- As a fraction: $\frac{1}{8}$

- With a colon: 1:8

TIP

Ratios, like fractions, should always be reduced to lowest terms.

Rate

A *rate* is a ratio in which there is a comparison of two things expressed with different units. For example, a person takes 90 minutes to walk 10 kilometres. For clarity, a rate is often expressed as a unit rate in which one of the parts being compared has a quantity of 1. As a unit rate, this person walks the equivalent of 1 kilometre every 9 minutes. Determining unit rates is also a matter of solving a proportion.

$$\frac{90 \text{ minutes}}{10 \text{ kilometers}} = \frac{\text{how many minutes?}}{1 \text{ kilometer}}$$

Solving Proportions

When rates or ratios are set equal to one another, the equation that results is called a *proportion*. As long as you know three parts of the proportion, you can solve for the missing part. To solve it, you rely on the cross-product rule.

You must take care when setting up the proportion equations. The terms in each rate or ratio must be written in the same order. It is helpful to use words or labels to identify what quantity is expressed in the numerator and what quantity is expressed in the denominator.

➡ EXAMPLE 1 _____

Tania was paid $100 for 8 hours of work. How much is Tania paid per hour? (This problem asks you to find the unit rate per one hour).

Solution

a. Set up the proportion, using words or symbols to indicate the units used.

$$\frac{\$100}{8 \text{ hours}} = \frac{\$?}{1 \text{ hour}}$$

b. Solve the proportion. Use the variable x in place of the unknown and then cross multiply and divide.

$$\frac{100}{8} = \frac{x}{1}$$
$$(8)(x) = (100)(1)$$
$$8x = 100$$
$$x = \frac{100}{8}$$
$$x = 12.50$$

c. State the solution. Tania earns $12.50 per hour.

➡ EXAMPLE 2 _____

15 is to 6 as 4 is to what number?

Solution

a. Set up the proportion, using words or symbols to indicate the units used. (In this problem, no units are used).

$$\frac{15}{6} = \frac{4}{?}$$

b. Solve the proportion. Use the variable x in place of the unknown and then cross-multiply and divide.

$$\frac{15}{6} = \frac{4}{x}$$

$$(15)(x) = (6)(4)$$

$$15x = 24$$

$$x = \frac{24}{15}$$

$$x = 1.6$$

c. State the solution. 15 is to 6 as 4 is to 1.6.

➡ EXAMPLE 3 _____

If a truck travels 180 kilometres on 20 litres of gas, how many litres will it take to travel 500 kilometres? How far does the truck travel on 1 litre of gas (that is, what is the unit rate)?

Solution

This is a two-part problem.

Part 1.

a. Set up the proportion, using words or symbols to indicate the units used.

$$\frac{180 \text{ km}}{20 \text{ L}} = \frac{500 \text{ km}}{? \text{ L}}$$

b. Solve the proportion. Use the variable x in place of the unknown and then cross-multiply and divide.

$$\frac{180}{20} = \frac{500}{x}$$

$$(180)(x) = (20)(500)$$

$$180x = 10\ 000$$

$$x = \frac{10\ 000}{180}$$

$$x = 55.6$$

c. State the solution. It will take 55.6 litres of gas to travel 500 km.

Part 2.

a. Solve the same proportion, this time to find the unit rate.

$$\frac{180 \text{ km}}{20 \text{ L}} = \frac{? \text{ km}}{1 \text{ L}}$$

$$\frac{180}{20} = \frac{x}{\text{L}}$$

$$(20)(x) = (180)(1)$$

$$20x = 180$$

$$x = \frac{180}{20}$$

$$x = 9$$

b. State the solution. The truck travels 9 km on 1 litre of gas.

→ EXAMPLE 4

Thirty people lined up in front of an ice cream truck were surveyed and it was found twenty people preferred chocolate ice cream to vanilla. If you were serving ice cream to 120 children at a large birthday party, how many children would you expect to order vanilla ice cream instead of chocolate?

Caution! This is still a proportion problem, but you must read the information very carefully and complete an extra step.

Solution

a. First, determine how many people in the original survey preferred vanilla ice cream. If twenty out of thirty people preferred chocolate, that means only ten preferred vanilla.

    30 in total – 20 prefer chocolate = 10 prefer vanilla

b. Set up the proportion, using words or symbols to indicate the units used.

$$\frac{10 \text{ prefer vanilla}}{30 \text{ total}} = \frac{? \text{ order vanilla}}{120 \text{ total}}$$

c. Solve the proportion. Use the variable x in place of the unknown and then cross-multiply and divide.

$$\frac{10}{30} = \frac{x}{120}$$

$$(30)(x) = (10)(120)$$

$$30x = 1\,200$$

$$x = \frac{1\,200}{30}$$

$$x = 40$$

d. State the solution. 40 children will order vanilla ice cream.

PRACTICE

1. It takes 6 hours to drive 570 kilometres. How long does it take to drive 285 kilometres?

2. Brittany earned \$475 after working $3\frac{1}{2}$ days. How much would Brittany earn if she worked 10 days at the same pay rate?

3. There is a sale at the local grocery store. Boxes of macaroni and cheese are advertised as \$10.20/dozen. How much would one box cost?

4. 45 people attend a staff meeting. 27 are men, the rest are women. What is the ratio of women to men (reduced to lowest terms).

5. Laurence works in a pharmacy. The pharmacy fills 340 prescriptions in an 8.5 hour day. On average, how many prescriptions are filled every hour?

ANSWERS

1. 3 hours   3. $0.85   5. 40

2. $1 357.14   4. $\frac{2}{3}$

CHALLENGE EXERCISE

Go to a grocery store and locate a large bag of flour, a large bag of sugar, a large bag of cat food, and a large bag of potatoes. Determine the unit rate (price per kg) for each of these items.

SCALE DRAWINGS

Another type of real-world problem involving proportion is scale drawings. Drawing something to scale implies that the drawing has the same shape as the real object but not the same size. However, the measurements are proportionate to the real object. The scale is clearly stated on the drawing and it indicates a comparison between the drawing measurement and the actual measurement.

For example, at the bottom of a map you may see a scale similar to the following.

1 centimetre = 1 kilometre (1:100 000)

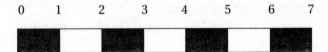

This scale tells you that for every centimetre measured on the drawing there is an equivalency to 1 kilometre in actual distance.

Some scale drawings do not indicate the units of measurement.

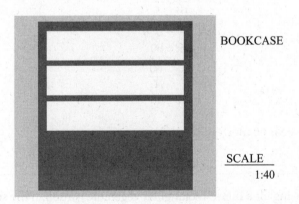

BOOKCASE

SCALE
1:40

The scale noted is 1:40. It doesn't matter what unit of measurement you use, the actual measurement will be 40 times bigger. If it measures 1 inch on the paper, it will measure 40 inches in actuality. If it measures 1 cm on the paper, it will measure 40 cm in actuality.

➡ EXAMPLE 1

Douglas fir trees are the second tallest conifers in the world. How tall is this Douglas fir tree, given the scale below.

Scale: 1 cm = 10 metres

Solution

Measure the drawing using a centimetre ruler.

From bottom to top, you can determine the tree is approximately 6 cm.

Solve the proportion.

$$\frac{1 \text{ cm}}{10 \text{ m}} = \frac{6 \text{ cm}}{? \text{ m}}$$

$$\frac{1}{10} = \frac{6}{x}$$

$$(1)(x) = (10)(6)$$

$$1x = 60$$

$$x = \frac{60}{1}$$

$$x = 60$$

The Douglas fir tree is 60 metres tall.

➡ EXAMPLE 2

Below is a scale drawing for a raised rectangular vegetable garden. If the scale is 1:35, find the actual length of the garden. Express your answer in metres.

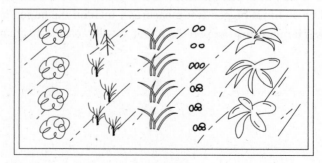

Scale: 1:35

Solution

Measure the length using a ruler. Again, you are using centimetres

From left to right, you determine the length is 8.5 cm.

Solve the proportion.

$$\frac{1}{35} = \frac{8.5 \text{ cm}}{? \text{ cm}}$$

$$\frac{1}{35} = \frac{8.5}{?}$$

$$(1)(x) = (35)(8.5)$$

$$1x = 297.5$$

$$x = \frac{297.5}{1}$$

$$x = 297.5$$

The garden is 297.5 cm in length. Expressed in metres, this is 2.975 metres.

PRACTICE

1. Given a scale of 1 cm = 1 kilometre, what is the distance between town A and town B?

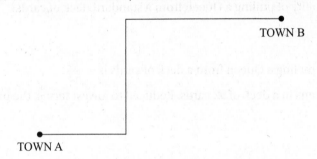

TOWN B

TOWN A

2. Given a scale of 1 cm = $\frac{1}{2}$ metre, what is the length of the van shown below?

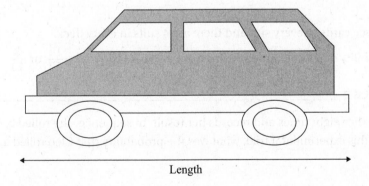

Length

ANSWERS

1. 9.5 km
2. 4.5 m

CHALLENGE EXERCISE

Locate a map of Canada. Study the scale given on the map. Using a ruler and the scale, determine the actual distances between Vancouver and Calgary and also between Halifax and Winnipeg.

UNDERSTANDING PROBABILITY

Probability is defined as the likelihood that something will occur. It is often expressed as a ratio.

$$\text{The probability that something will occur} = \frac{\text{number of likely outcomes}}{\text{total number of outcomes}}$$

Probability can be expressed as a ratio, a fraction, a decimal or a percent. The probability of winning \$2 in a lottery could be expressed in the following ways:

$$1{:}4 \quad \text{or} \quad \frac{1}{4} \quad \text{or} \quad 0.25 \quad \text{or} \quad 25\%$$

➡ **EXAMPLE 1** _____

What is the probability of pulling a Queen from a standard deck of cards?

Solution

The probability of pulling a Queen from a deck of cards is $= \frac{4}{52}$.

There are 4 Queens in a deck of 52 cards. Reduced to lowest terms, the probability of such an event is $= \frac{1}{13}$

➡ **EXAMPLE 2** _____

What is the probability of pulling any face card from a single deck?

Solution

There are 3 face cards in every suit and there are 4 suits in every deck.

The probability of pulling any face card from a deck of cards is $= \frac{12}{52}$ or $\frac{3}{13}$.

➡ **EXAMPLE 3** _____

Cleo rolls the dice eight times and records her result. In sequence, she rolled 2, 5, 1, 2, 4, 4, 2, and 6. Given this experimental trial, what was the probability that Cleo rolled a 2?

Solution

Cleo made 8 rolls in total. She rolled a 2 three times. The probability of rolling a 2 in this experiment can be expressed as $\frac{3}{8}$ or 37.5%

MEAN, MEDIAN, AND MODE

Mean, median, and mode are the three most common kinds of averages that you must be familiar with for the GED exam.

Mean is likely the average you are most familiar with. To calculate the mean, you simply add up all the numbers and divide by the total number of values.

Median is the middle value within a list of numbers. To determine the median, line up all the numbers from smallest to largest. The value in the middle is the median.

Mode is the value that appears most frequently within a group of numbers.

TIP

If you are asked to find an average of a group of values, it is the same as being asked to find the mean.

➡ EXAMPLE 1

Find the mean, median, and mode of the following numbers:

$$11 \quad 12 \quad 14 \quad 10 \quad 11 \quad 13 \quad 9 \quad 17 \quad 11$$

Solution

a. Order the numbers from smallest to largest. There are 9 values.

$$9 \quad 10 \quad 11 \quad 11 \quad 11 \quad 12 \quad 13 \quad 14 \quad 17$$

b. To calculate the mean, add all the numbers together and divide by 9.

$$\frac{9+10+11+11+11+12+13+14+17}{9} = 12$$

The mean is 12.

c. The median is the middle number.

$$9 \quad 10 \quad 11 \quad 11 \quad (11) \quad 12 \quad 13 \quad 14 \quad 17$$

The median is 11.

d. The mode is the number that appears most frequently.

$$9 \quad 10 \quad 11 \quad 11 \quad 11 \quad 12 \quad 13 \quad 14 \quad 17$$

The mode is 11 (it is the only number to appear three times).

➡ EXAMPLE 2

Stephanie receives 58%, 64%, 85%, 52%, 82% and 70% on six quizzes she completes in her Math class. What is her mean score? What is her median score?

Solution

To find the mean score

a. Add all the values together: 58 + 64 + 85 + 52 + 82 + 70 = 411
b. Divide the sum by the total number of tests she completed: 411 ÷ 6 = 68.5
   Stephanie's mean score is 68.5%

To find the median score we look for the middle number. In this situation, it is slightly more complicated than in Example 1 because Stephanie wrote an even number of tests. In fact, there is no exact middle number! In this instance, find the mean of the *two* middle numbers:

a. Line the numbers up in order: 52 58 64 70 82 85
b. The two middle numbers are 64 and 70
c. Add these middle numbers together and divide by 2: $64+70 = 134 \div 2 = 67$
   Stephanie's median score is 67%

PRACTICE

1. What is the probability of rolling a 4 when you roll one die?

2. What is the probability of pulling an ace card from a deck of cards?

3. At a hockey game, Robyn purchases 10 draw tickets. Only 400 tickets are sold. What is the probability Robyn will win expressed as a percent?

4. Sabrina works as a waitress and earns the following tips:

   Monday—$47   Tuesday—$53
   Friday—$87   Saturday—$92

   What is the mean value of tips Sabrina earns over these four shifts?

5. Seven students receive the following grades on an English exam:

   66%   89%   63%   75%   89%   52%   91%

   What is the median score? What is the mode?

ANSWERS

1. $\dfrac{1}{6}$

2. $\dfrac{4}{52} = \dfrac{1}{13}$

3. $\dfrac{10}{400} = 0.025 = 2.5\%$

4. $69.75

5. The median score is 75%. The mode is 89%.

CHAPTER CHECK-UP

1. There are 150 mg of medication in a 100 L liquid. How much liquid is needed to obtain 600 mg of medication?
   (1) 120 mL
   (2) 150 mL
   (3) 200 mL
   (4) 400 mL
   (5) Not enough information is given.

2. Abagail earns $63 for delivering 126 papers. At the same rate, how much would she earn if she delivered 200 papers?

   (1) $65
   (2) $70
   (3) $80
   (4) $95
   (5) $100

3. Adrian drives 250 kilometres in 2.5 hours. What is Adrian's speed in km/hr?

   (1) 25 km/hr
   (2) 90 km/hr
   (3) 100 km/hr
   (4) 110 km/hr
   (5) 95 km/hr

4. A 13.6 kg bag of dog food is on sale for $27.97. What is the unit price (per kg) for this brand of dog food?

   (1) $2.06
   (2) $1.03
   (3) $2.80
   (4) $1.36
   (5) $2.56

5. The scale for the box drawn below is 1 cm = 2 feet. What is the *actual* height of the box?

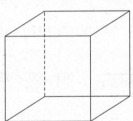

   (1) 6 feet
   (2) 3 feet
   (3) 0.5 feet
   (4) 3 cm
   (5) 6 cm

6. David purchases a box of mandarin oranges. He had to discard 3 rotten oranges from the box, which contained 24 oranges in total. Given this one trial, what is the probability that you will pick a rotten orange from a full box?

   (1) $\dfrac{24}{3}$

   (2) $\dfrac{1}{8}$

   (3) 24%

   (4) 3%

   (5) 8%

7. Kathy runs on a treadmill five times a week. She records the following times in one week:

Monday: 30 minutes
Wednesday: 45 minutes
Friday: 32 minutes
Saturday: 50 minutes
Sunday: 24 minutes

On a daily basis, what is Kathy's mean time spent running?
(1) 181 minutes
(2) 32 minutes
(3) 36.2 minutes
(4) 32.2 minutes
(5) 24 minutes

8. Which of the following group of numbers has a mean of 14, a median of 13 and a mode of 12?

(1)	11	12	13	14	15
(2)	8	9	10	11	12
(3)	10	11	12	12	12
(4)	12	12	13	16	17
(5)	12	12	13	14	15

ANSWERS

1. **(4)** Solve. $\dfrac{150 \text{ mg}}{100 \text{ mL}} = \dfrac{600 \text{ mg}}{x}$ $(600)(100) \div 150 = 400$ mL

2. **(5)** Solve. $\dfrac{\$63}{126 \text{ papers}} = \dfrac{x}{200 \text{ papers}}$ $(63)(200) \div 126 = \$100$

3. **(3)** Solve. $\dfrac{250 \text{ km}}{2.5 \text{ hr}} = \dfrac{x}{1 \text{ hr}}$ $(250)(1) \div 2.5 = 100$ km/hr

4. **(1)** Divide. $\$27.97 \div 13.6 = \$2.06$/kg

5. **(1)** It measures about 3 cm. If every cm = 2 feet, 3 cm = 6ft.

6. **(2)** $\dfrac{3 \text{ chances}}{24 \text{ total}} = \dfrac{1}{8}$ There is a 12.5% probability of picking a rotten orange.

7. **(3)** Add $30 + 45 + 32 + 50 + 24 = 181$ and divide by 5 = 36.2 minutes

8. **(4)** Mean: $(12 + 12 + 13 + 16 + 17) \div 5 = 14$. The middle number (median) is 13. And 12 occurs most frequently (mode).

Geometric Measurement

27

THINK ABOUT IT

Geometry is the study of points, lines, planes, and space. It is a very interactive and visual mathematical study and there are a great number of practical applications.

On the GED exam, you can expect to see questions about lines and angles as well as questions regarding the perimeter, area, and volume of triangular, rectangular, and circular shapes. You will be provided with a formula sheet so it is not necessary to memorize all of the geometric formulas presented in this chapter; however, it is important to know which formula to use in different situations.

IN THIS CHAPTER

After completing this chapter, you will be able to

→ **UNDERSTAND LINES AND ANGLES**

→ **CALCULATE PERIMETER AND AREA, USING FORMULAS, FOR THE FOLLOWING SHAPES: TRIANGLE, CIRCLE, SQUARE, AND RECTANGLE**

→ **DETERMINE THE VOLUME OF A CYLINDER, CONE, AND PYRAMID**

→ **APPLY THE PYTHAGOREAN THEOREM**

LINES

A picture of a line is drawn below. Similar to the number line, arrows are drawn at both ends to show that the line continues on forever in both directions. You name lines by indicating two points on this line (in this case A and B) and drawing a double-headed arrow above the letters.

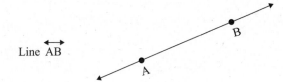

A ray is a "half line". One end has a finite endpoint and it extends forever in one direction (indicated by the arrow on the opposite end). You name rays by beginning with the endpoint and drawing a single-headed arrow above the letters.

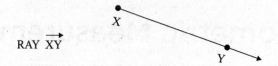

Intersecting and Parallel Lines

When two lines cross one another, they are said to *intersect*. Generally, you name the point of intersection and assign it a letter.

When two lines never intersect, they are called *parallel* lines. The symbol ‖ means *parallel to*. Study the example below.

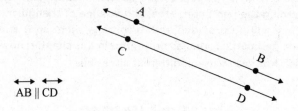

ANGLES

An angle is formed whenever two rays have a common endpoint. This common point is also called the *vertex*.

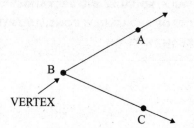

The angle above can be named in several different ways. It may be called ∠ABC or ∠CBA. The symbol ∠ means angle. The vertex is always listed in the middle of the three letters.

In the following example, there is only a letter listed at the vertex. You would name this angle, ∠x. On the GED, you may also see the notation m∠x which means *the measure of* ∠x.

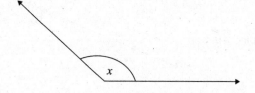

Angles are commonly measured in *degrees*. The symbol for degrees is a small circle. For example, 45° as illustrated in the following example. There is a 45° gap or spread that exists between the two rays.

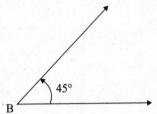

Naming Angles

You will be required to know the following types, or categories, of angles.

RIGHT ANGLE: Measures 90° exactly. The square symbol shown indicates it is a 90° angle.

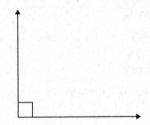

ACUTE ANGLE: Measures between 0° and 90°

OBTUSE ANGLE: Measures between 90° and 180°

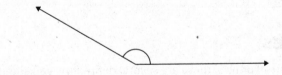

STRAIGHT ANGLE: Measures 180° exactly.

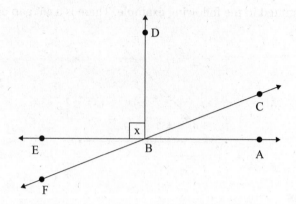

1. Refer to the diagram above to answer the following questions.
   a. What is the measurement of ∠x
   b. What type of angle is ∠ABC?
   c. What type of angle is ∠ABD?
   d. What type of angle is ∠ABF?
   e. What type of angle is ∠ABE?
   f. What type of angle is ∠EBC?
   g. What other angle has the same measurement as ∠x?

ANSWERS

1. a. 90°
   b. Acute angle
   c. Right angle
   d. Obtuse angle
   e. Straight angle
   f. Obtuse angle
   g. ∠ABD or ∠DBA

PAIRS OF ANGLES

When working with pairs of angles, there are several definitions you should be familiar with. When the sum of the measure of two angles is 90°, the angles are complementary.

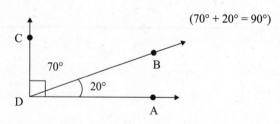

(70° + 20° = 90°)

When the sum of the measure of two angles is 180°, the angles are *supplementary*.

$$(35° + 145° = 180°)$$

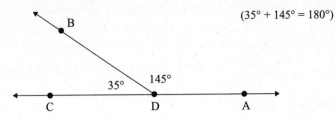

When two lines intersect, the angles on opposite sides of the intersection point are called *vertically opposite angles.*

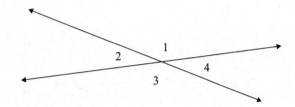

- ∠1 and ∠2 are supplementary.
- ∠3 and ∠4 are also supplementary.
- m∠1 ≅ m∠3.When angles have equal measurement they are *congruent.* The symbol ≅ means congruent.
- m∠2 ≅ m∠4.These angles are also congruent.
- Vertically opposite angles are always congruent.

➡ **EXAMPLE**

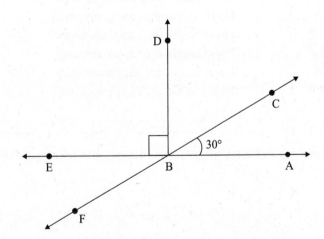

Given the drawing above, determine the measurement of the following

∠*CBD*

∠*DBE*

∠*EBF*

∠*FBA*

Solution

$\angle CBD = 60°$	Because $\angle CBD$ and $\angle ABC$ are complementary
$\angle DBE = 90°$	Because $\angle DBE$ is marked with a square symbol
$\angle EBF = 30°$	Because $\angle EBF$ and $\angle ABC$ are vertically opposite
$\angle FBA = 150°$	Because $\angle EBF$ and $\angle FBA$ are supplementary

TRANSVERSALS

A *transversal* is a line that intersects two or more lines. In this section, you will look specifically at a transversal that intersects parallel lines.

Study the following illustration.

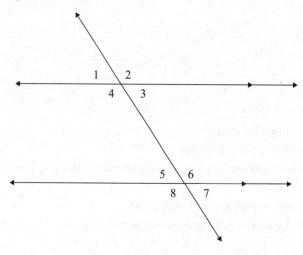

$\angle 1 = \angle 3 = \angle 5 = \angle 7$	These four angles are congruent
$\angle 2 = \angle 4 = \angle 6 = \angle 8$	These four angles are congruent
$\angle 1 + \angle 2 = 180°$	These angles are supplementary
$\angle 4 + \angle 3 = 180°$	These angles are supplementary
$\angle 5 + \angle 6 = 180°$	These angles are supplementary
$\angle 8 + \angle 7 = 180°$	These angles are supplementary

➡ **EXAMPLE** _____

M and N are parallel lines and $\angle 1 = 40°$. What are the measurements of all the other angles?

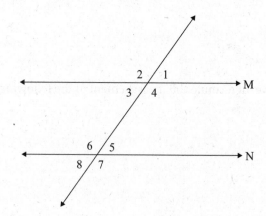

Solution

$\angle 2 = 140°$	Because $\angle 1$ and $\angle 2$ are supplementary
$\angle 3 = 40°$	Because $\angle 3$ and $\angle 1$ are congruent
$\angle 4 = 140°$	Because $\angle 4$ and $\angle 2$ are congruent
$\angle 5 = 40°$	Because $\angle 5$ and $\angle 1$ are congruent
$\angle 6 = 140°$	Because $\angle 5$ and $\angle 6$ are supplementary
$\angle 7 = 140°$	Because $\angle 6$ and $\angle 7$ are congruent
$\angle 8 = 40°$	Because $\angle 5$ and $\angle 8$ are congruent

PRACTICE

1. Calculate the missing angles, marked x and y, in the figures that follow.

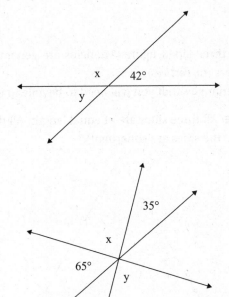

2. Line A is parallel to line B. $\angle 1 = 120°$ Determine the measurements of all the other angles.

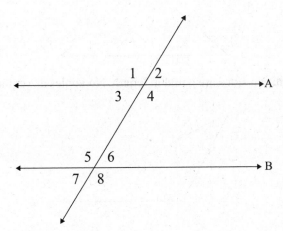

TRIANGLES

A triangle is an enclosed, three-sided figure. Triangles are generally named by the letters assigned to the three corners (or *vertices*).

There are four types of triangles that you will need to be able to identify and name.

EQUILATERAL TRIANGLE: All three sides are of equal length. All three angles measure 60°. (The marks indicate that the sides are congruent).

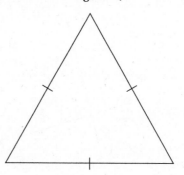

ISOSCELES TRIANGLE: Two sides are equal in length. Two angles are equal.

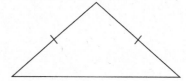

SCALENE TRIANGLE: No sides are equal in length. No angles are equal.

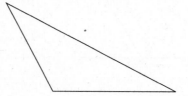

RIGHT TRIANGLE: One angle measures exactly 90°. The square symbol indicates it is a 90° angle. Also note that the longest side, directly opposite the 90° has been labelled with the special name, *hypotenuse*.

TIP

To bisect an angle means to "cut in half".

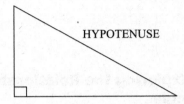

HYPOTENUSE

PRACTICE

Referring to the triangles types and their descriptions, respond to the following.

1. In △*ABC* below, what is the measure of ∠*C*?

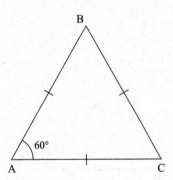

2. What type of triangle is △*ABC* above?

3. In △*XYZ* below, ∠*X* = 40°, ∠*Y* = 90°, ∠*Z* = 50°. What type of triangle is it?

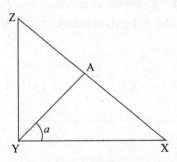

4. *YA* bisects ∠*XYZ* above. What is the measure of ∠*a*?

5. △*ABC* below is a scalene triangle. ∠*B* = 50°, ∠*A* = 20°. *CD* bisects ∠*ACB*. What is the measure of ∠*x*?

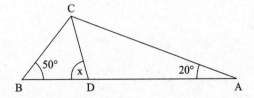

Isosceles Triangles—Exploring the Relationship Between Sides and Angles

The definition of an isosceles triangle states that two angles are equal and two sides are equal. In fact, it is the sides directly opposite the two equal angles that are also equal.

➡ **EXAMPLE 1** _____

Given $\triangle ABC$:

a. Determine the measurement of $\angle C$
b. Find BC

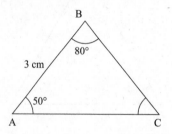

Solution

Knowing that all angles in a triangle add to 180° and given $\angle A = 50°$ and $\angle B = 80°$, $\angle C$ must equal 50°. This confirms that it is an isosceles triangle.

Given $AB = 3$ cm, BC must also $= 3$ cm. Remember that the sides directly opposite equal angles are also equal.

a. $\angle C = 50°$
b. $BC = 3$ cm

➡ **EXAMPLE 2** _____

Find x in the figure below.

Solution

The length AB is the distance from the centre of the circle to the edge (the *radius*). The radius remains constant to any point on the circle. Therefore, BC must be the same length as AB.

Given that you can now confirm there are two equal sides in the triangle, you can confidently state that it is an isosceles triangle. As such, the two angles opposite the equal length sides must also be equal.

Answer: $x = 60°$

Right Triangles—Exploring the relationship between sides and angles (Pythagorean Theorem)

The relationship between the length of sides and the measurement of angles is also unique for right triangles.

ANGLES: One angle will always measure 90°. Therefore the sum of the remaining two angles will also equal 90°. $\angle A + \angle B = 90°$

SIDES: A very famous mathematician, Pythagoras of Samos, determined the length of the hypotenuse squared was equivalent to the sum of the square of the lengths of the two remaining sides. It sounds confusing but it can be summarized into a simple formula known as the Pythagorean Theorem. This formula is provided for you on the formula sheet.

$$c^2 = a^2 + b^2$$

where c represents the hypotenuse; a and b represent the lengths of the other two sides.

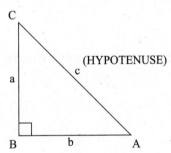

➡ EXAMPLE 1

What is the length of AB?

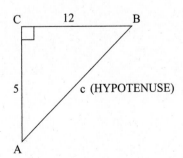

Solution

In this example, you are solving for the length of the hypotenuse, side c.

Substitute into the formula and simplify. It will not matter which side you use as a and b; however, standard labelling is such that the side opposite an angle is assigned the same small letter.

$$c^2 = a^2 + b^2$$
$$c^2 = (12)^2 + (5)^2$$
$$c^2 = 144 + 25$$
$$c^2 = 169$$
$$\sqrt{c^2} = \sqrt{169}$$
$$c = 13$$

➡ **EXAMPLE 2** _____

What is the length of XY?

What is the measure of $\angle Z$?

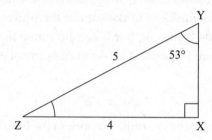

Solution

Solve for XY. It is not the hypotenuse. It can be either a or b in the formula.

$$c^2 = a^2 + b^2$$
$$(5)^2 = (4)^2 + b^2$$
$$25 - 16 = b^2$$
$$9 = b^2$$
$$\sqrt{9} = \sqrt{b^2}$$
$$b = 3$$

$$XY = 3$$

Solve for $\angle Z$.

$90° - 53° = 37°$

$\angle Z = 37°$

CHALLENGE EXERCISE

Was Pythagoras of Samos correct? Test his theory. Create a right triangle on the floor of your living room or classroom. Using masking tape, mark out a very large triangle, making sure that one angle measures 90°. To do this, place a book or something square in one corner. The tape should line up with one side and the bottom of the book. Next, using a tape measure or metre stick, measure all three sides. Substitute the lengths into the formula: $c^2 = a^2 + b^2$. When simplified, the left and right sides of the equation should balance or be very close to one another (there may be some room for error as the measurements are not likely exact).

PRACTICE

1. In the following triangle, find $\angle B$

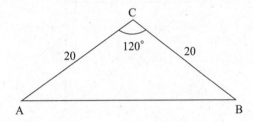

2. In the following triangle, $\angle X = \angle Y$. Find XZ

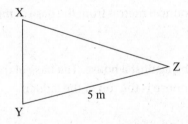

3. In the following drawing, $AB = BC$ and $\angle C = 70°$. Find $\angle DAB$

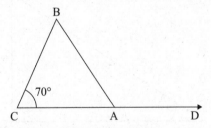

4. Find the measurement of $\angle x$ in the next drawing.

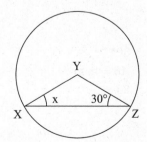

5. In the following triangle, find *AB*

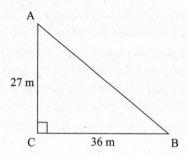

6. In the next triangle, find *XZ*

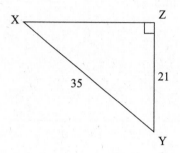

7. A 15-metre telephone pole forms a 90° angle with the ground. It is supported by a length of wire staked into the ground 6 metres from the base of the pole. To one decimal place, how long is the wire?

8. A 5-metre ladder is leaning against a house. The base of the ladder is 3 metres from the house. How high up the house is the top of the ladder?

9. In the following triangle, find *XZ* and ∠*Z*

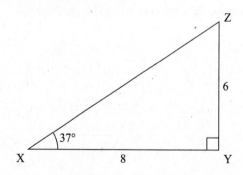

ANSWERS

1. 30°
2. 5 m
3. 110°

4. 30°
5. *AB* = 45 m
6. 28

7. 16.2 m
8. 4 m
9. 10; ∠*Z* = 53°

PERIMETER

The *perimeter* is the distance around a figure. It is the sum of the lengths of all the sides or the total distance around a circular or curved shape. The perimeter of a circle is called its *circumference*.

TIP

It may be helpful to make a photocopy of the formula sheet. It will be referenced heavily in the following sections.

➡️ **EXAMPLE 1** _____

Find the perimeter of the following triangle.

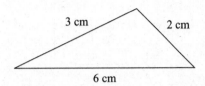

Solution

Add the lengths of each side together.

$$P = a + b + c \quad P = 3 \text{ cm} + 2 \text{ cm} + 6 \text{ cm} = 11 \text{ cm}$$

Always answer with correct units.
The perimeter of the triangle is 11 cm.

➡️ **EXAMPLE 2** _____

Find the perimeter of the following rectangle.

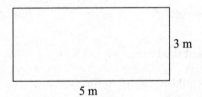

Solution

Recognizing that the measure of length will be the same on both sides and that the measure of width will also be the same on both sides, you could simply add the lengths of each side together. Alternatively, you can use the formula $P = 2(l) + 2(w)$. Substitute values for length (l) and width (w) and simplify. Again, answer with correct units.

$$P = 2(5 \text{ m}) + 2 \,(3 \text{ m}) = 10 \text{ m} + 6 \text{ m} = 16 \text{ m}$$

The perimeter of the rectangle is 16 m.

➡️ **EXAMPLE 3** _____

Brian is fencing his perfectly square backyard. He measures one side and determines it is 24 metres long. How much fencing will he need to purchase to ensure his backyard is properly fenced?

Solution

If you are not provided with a picture, it is helpful to make a quick sketch. Again, you can simply add together the measure of each side or use the formula for the perimeter of a square:

$$P = 4(s)$$

The perimeter of the square is 96 m. Brian will need 96 m of fencing.

24 metres

Circles

There are some unique and important concepts about circles. Before calculating the circumference, you must first familiarize yourself with the following diagram and definitions.

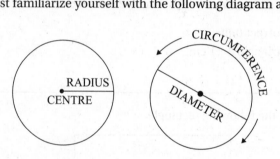

CENTRE: The exact middle of the circle.

RADIUS (r): The distance from the centre to the edge.

DIAMETER (d): The distance of a straight line that travels through the centre and connects two points on the edge. Diameter is twice the length of the radius. *d* = *2r*

CIRCUMFERENCE: The distance around the circle. The formula for the circumference of a circle is $C = \pi d$.

Notice that this formula includes the letter π = *pi*. Pronounced just like *pie*, this is a letter from the Greek alphabet. It is used in a number of formulas and represents a value of approximately 3.14. Memorize this amount. If you are doing a calculation with your calculator, you can also enter the value by pressing SHIFT EXP . 3.14 will generally be accurate enough for the calculations on the GED exam; however, π is actually a number whose decimal equivalency never terminates. It is truly an irrational number!

TIP

π = 3.14
Memorize
this value.

➡ **EXAMPLE 1** _____

Find the circumference of the circle below.

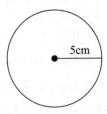

Solution

In the preceding figure, you are only provided with the length of the radius.

First, calculate the diameter. $d = 2r$

$$d = 2(5 \text{ cm}) = 10 \text{ cm}$$

Next, calculate the circumference using the formula $C = \pi d$

$$C = (3.14)(10 \text{ cm}) = 31.4 \text{ cm}$$

PRACTICE

1. Find the perimeter of the following.

   a.
   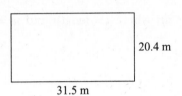

   c.

   b.
   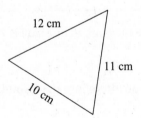

   d.
   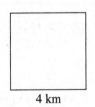

2. Deborah would like to sew ribbon on the edge of a circular tablecloth. She measures the distance from edge to edge, across the centre, to be 5 metres. How much ribbon should she purchase? (Round your answer to the nearest whole metre.)

ANSWERS

1. a. 103.8 m   b. 33 cm   c. 12.56 m   d. 16 km
2. 16 m of ribbon.

AREA

Area is essentially the size of a surface. Area can also be defined as the amount of space inside the boundary of a two dimensional object such as a rectangle or circle.

The result of calculating area will include units that are squared. There are three commonly accepted ways to express this result:

$$25 \textbf{ square} \text{ metres} = 25 \text{ metres } \textbf{sq.} = 25 \text{ m}^2$$

Don't get confused! The square mentioned in the answer isn't related to the shape. You use *square* (sq) when stating the area of any shape—even a circle. The square in the answer has to do with the fact that area is a two-dimensional measurement.

➡ **EXAMPLE 1** _____

Find the area of the following rectangle.

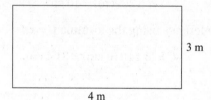

3 m

4 m

Solution

Using the formula for the area of a rectangle, $A = lw$, **where** l = **length and** w = **width**, substitute and simplify.

$A = (4)(3) = 12$
The area of the rectangle is 12 m².

➡ **EXAMPLE 2** _____

David wants to know the area of his square animal pen. The measure of one side is 7 metres.

Solution

If helpful, draw a quick sketch of this square shape. Then, substitute into the formula for the area of a square. $A = s^2$, where s = side length.

$A = (7)^2 = 49$
The area of the animal pen is 49 m².

➡ **EXAMPLE 3** _____

Find the area of the face of the clock below. The radius measures 6 inches.

Solution

Use the formula for the area of a circle. $A = \pi r^2$, where $\pi = 3.14$ and $r = $ radius.

$A = (3.14)(6)^2 = 113.04$

The area of the clock face is 113.04 sq. inches.

Triangles

There are some very unique and important concepts about triangles. Before calculating the area of this shape, you must first familiarize yourself with the diagrams and definitions that follow.

TIP

Height is a vertical measurement perpendicular to the base. It is measured "top to bottom".

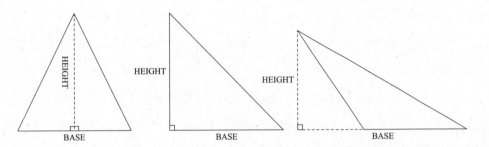

The formula for the area of a triangle is $A = \frac{1}{2}$ **(base)(height).** This is notated $A = \frac{1}{2} \, bh$. Remember that when two letters (variables) are right next to one another, you complete an operation of multiplication.

➡ **EXAMPLE 1** _____

Find the area of the triangle below.

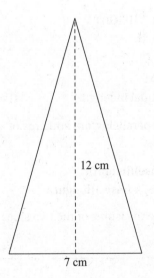

12 cm

7 cm

Solution

Substitute into the formula for the area of a triangle.

$A = \frac{1}{2} \, bh$

$A = \frac{1}{2} \, (7)(12) = 42$

The area of the triangle is 42 cm^2.

➡ EXAMPLE 2 _____

The height of a triangular sail is 3 metres longer than its base. Determine an algebraic expression for the area of the sail.

Solution

Draw a quick sketch to confirm your understanding of the problem. Label the height and the base. Remember that "3 metres longer" implies an operation of addition.

   Substitute into the formula.

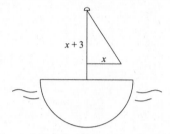

$A = \frac{1}{2} \, bh$

$A = \frac{1}{2} \, (x)(x + 3)$ sq. metres. This could also be written $A = \frac{1}{2} \, (x^2 + 3x)$ m^2.

Parallelogram and Trapezoid

Although much less common, you should still be familiar with these two geometric shapes. Study the diagrams below.

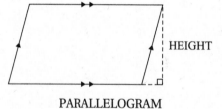

PARALLELOGRAM
(Opposite sides parallel and equal in length)

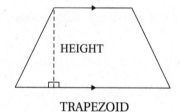

TRAPEZOID
(Pair of opposite sides are parallel)

   The formulas for the area of a parallelogram and area of a trapezoid are very similar to the area of a triangle formula.

   Area of a Parallelogram = (base)(height).
   Area of a Trapezoid = ½ (base$_1$ + base$_2$)(height).

Note that base$_1$ + base$_2$ are the measures of the two sides that run parallel to one another.

➡ EXAMPLE _____

Find the area of the following shape.

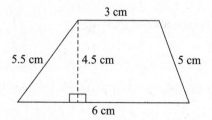

Solution

Not all shapes will be labelled or described. You need to know the characteristics of a given shape so that you can identify the shape above as a trapezoid. Substitute the measurements into the formula and simplify.

$A = \frac{1}{2}(b_1 + b_2)(h)$
$A = \frac{1}{2}(6 + 3)(4.5) = 20.25$
The area of the trapezoid is 20.25 cm^2

PRACTICE

1. Find the area of the following shapes.
   a.

   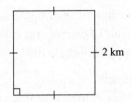

   2 km

   b.

   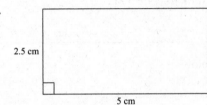

   2.5 cm

   5 cm

   c.

   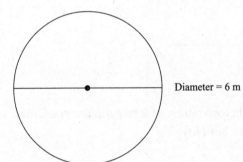

   Diameter = 6 m

   d.

   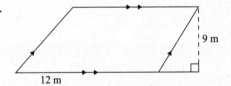

   9 m

   12 m

2. Margaret needs new linoleum for her kitchen. She measures the length of the room and finds it to be 6 metres. The width is 2 metres shorter. How much linoleum will she need to purchase to cover the entire surface?

3. What would be the area of a square tablecloth that covers a table and drapes 15 cm below the table on each side? The table measures 150 cm on each side.

ANSWERS

1. a. 4 km²   b. 12.5 cm²   c. 28.26 m²   d. 108 m²
2. 24 sq. metres
3. 32, 400 cm² or 3.24 m²

CHALLENGE EXERCISE

Determine how many square metres of carpet you would need to re-carpet your own living room.

VOLUME

Volume is the measure of the amount of space inside a three-dimensional figure such as a rectangular prism, a sphere, a cylinder, or a pyramid. The result of calculating volume will include units that are cubed. Again, there are a few common ways to notate this:

$$25 \text{ cubic metres} = 25 \text{ cu. metres} = 25 \text{ m}^3$$

Capacity is a related idea. *Capacity* refers to the amount of liquid measurement an object can hold. For example, the capacity of your fuel tank may be 50 L.

➡ EXAMPLE 1 _____

Find the volume for the rectangular container below.

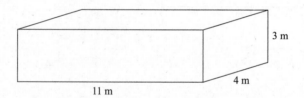

Solution

Substitute measurements into the formula for volume of a rectangular container: $V = lwh$; where l = **length**, w = **width** and h = **height**. Simplify.

$$V = lwh$$
$$V = (11)(4)(3) = 132$$

The volume of the rectangular container is 132 m³.

➡ EXAMPLE 2 _____

Find the volume for the cylinder below.

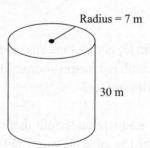

Solution

Substitute measurements into the formula for volume of a cylinder: $V = \pi r^2 h$, where $\pi = 3.14$, $r = $ **radius** and $h = $ **height**. Simplify.

$V = \pi r^2 h$
$V = (3.14)(7)^2(30) = 4\ 615.8$

The volume of the cylinder is $4\ 615.8$ m³.

➡ **EXAMPLE 3** _____

A shipping crate has the shape of a cube. Each edge measures 4 metres. What is the volume of the shipping crate in cubic metres?

Solution

Draw a quick sketch for clarity. Then substitute measurements into the formula for volume of a cube: $V = s^3$

$V = (4)^3 = 64$

The volume of the shipping crate is 64 m³.

PRACTICE

1. Find the volume of the following shapes.

   a.

   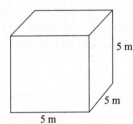

   5 m
   5 m
   5 m

   b.

   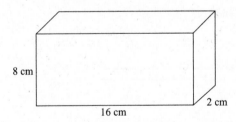

   8 cm
   2 cm
   16 cm

   c. This is a square pyramid. The formula to calculate the volume of a square pyramid is on the formula sheet. Familiarize yourself with the figure.

   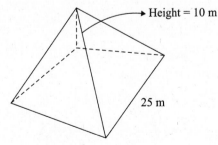

   Height = 10 m
   25 m

2. The Smiths just built a pool for their backyard. It measures 15 m long by 6 m wide by 2 m deep. Calculate the capacity (volume) of the pool in cubic metres.

ANSWERS

1. a. 125 m³   b. 256 cm³   c. 2 083 m³
2. The capacity of the pool is 180 m³.

CHALLENGE EXERCISE

A sugar cube measures about 1.5 cm along each edge. Using sugar cubes, build a rectangular box (container) that measures 162 cm³. How many sugar cubes did you need to create this shape?

CHAPTER CHECK-UP

1. Peter draws an angle that is supplementary to 125°. What kind of angle is it and what does it measure?
    (1) Obtuse, 125°
    (1) Right, 90°
    (3) Acute, 55°
    (4) Straight, 180°
    (5) Acute, 35°

2. Below is a diagram for a living room and small den. If both rooms are to be carpeted with luxury carpet that costs $35 per square metre, how much would it cost to purchase carpet for both rooms?

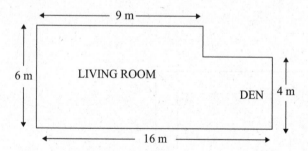

LIVING ROOM — 9 m, 6 m
DEN — 4 m
16 m

    (1) $3360
    (2) $820
    (3) $3125
    (4) $2870
    (5) $1975

3. Which expression indicates the maximum volume of the water tank in the following diagram?

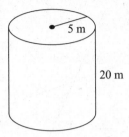

(1) $3.14(20 \times 5^2)$ m^3

(2) $(3.14 \times 20 \times 5)$ m^3

(3) $\frac{1}{2}(20 \times 5)$ m^3

(4) $(20 \div 5^2)(3.14)$ m^3

(5) $3.14 + (20 + 5^2)$ m^3

4. In the next diagram $\angle ABD$ is a straight angle. If the measure of $\angle x = 32°$, what would $\angle CBE$ measure?

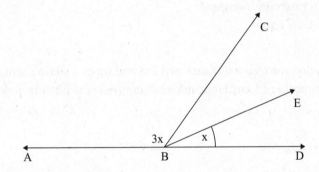

(1) $3x + 32°$

(2) $180° - (3x + 32°)$

(3) $3x - (180° - 32°)$

(4) $90° + 3x + 32°$

(5) Not enough information is given.

5. In the following diagram, *AB* is parallel to *CD* and $\angle 1 = 130°$. Which of the following cannot be true?

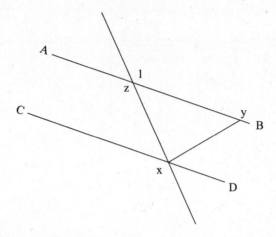

(1) $\triangle xyz$ is a right triangle
(2) $\triangle xyz$ is a scalene triangle
(3) $\triangle xyz$ is an equilateral triangle
(4) $\triangle xyz$ is an isosceles triangle
(5) $\angle 1$ and $\angle z$ are equal

6. A hiker walks due west for a distance of 5 km and turns a sharp corner right and walks due north for another 12 km. How many kilometres is the hiker from his starting point?
(1) 17 km
(2) 13 km
(3) 7 km
(4) 34 km
(5) Not enough information is given.

7. Which of the following expressions would describe the perimeter of the shape below?

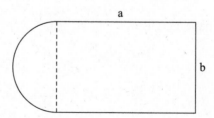

(1) $\frac{1}{2}\pi ab$

(2) $a + b + \pi b$
(3) $2a + 2b$
(4) $2a + b + \frac{1}{2}\pi b$

(5) $(2a)(b)(\frac{1}{2}\pi b)$

8. Triangle *ABC* is a right triangle. Which of the following must be an obtuse angle?

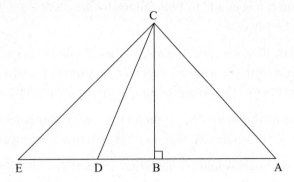

(1) ∠*EDC*
(2) ∠*EBC*
(3) ∠*DBC*
(4) ∠*AEC*
(5) ∠*DBA*

9. Study the figures below. How are the areas of the triangle and rectangle related?

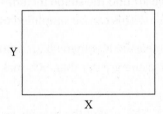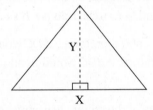

(1) The area of the triangle is twice the area of the rectangle.
(2) The area of the rectangle is four times bigger than the area of the triangle.
(3) The area of the rectangle is equal to the area of the triangle.
(4) The area of the triangle and rectangle are not related.
(5) The area of the triangle is half the area of the rectangle.

10. If *AC* is perpendicular to *CB* and ∠*CBD* = 140°, then ∠*A* equals what?

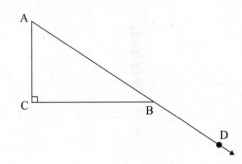

(1) 140°
(2) 50°
(3) 40°
(4) 90°
(5) 60°

ANSWERS

1. **(3)** Supplementary angles add to 180°. Subtract. 180° − 125° = 55°. This is an angle less than 90°. It is an acute angle.

2. **(4)** First calculate the total area. The area of the living room is (9m)(6m) = 54 m². The area for the den is (7m)(4m) = 28 m². Together, they total 82 m². Next, you multiply the total area by the price of the carpet per square metre: (82m²)($35) = $2870.

3. **(1)** The formula for the volume of a cylinder is $V = \pi r^2 h$. You can multiply in any order. Substituting in, $V = (3.14)(5)^2(20)$. Option 1 has all terms, just in a different order.

4. **(2)** The unknown angle would be the difference between 180° and the other known angles.

5. **(3)** $\triangle xyz$ cannot be an equilateral triangle as each angle would need to measure 60°. You know that the measure of angle supplementary to $\angle 1 = 50°$ and this angle is contained within the triangle.

6. **(2)** Solve using the Pythagorean Theorem. $c^2 = a^2 + b^2$. $c^2 = (12)^2 + (5)^2$. $c^2 = 169$. $c = 13$ km.

7. **(4)** This is an irregular shape. The distance around the shape includes three sides of a rectangle and ½ a circle. Add $a + b + a + \frac{1}{2}\pi b$. This can be simplified to $2a + b + \frac{1}{2}\pi b$.

8. **(1)** $\angle DBC = 90°$; therefore, $\angle BDC$ would measure less than 90°. It is supplementary to $\angle EDC$; therefore, $\angle EDC$ would need to measure greater than 90°, making it an obtuse angle.

9. **(5)** The area of the rectangle is equal to XY. The area of the triangle is $\frac{1}{2}XY$.

10. **(2)** $\angle CBD$ is supplementary with $\angle CBA$ which makes $\angle CBA = 40°$. All three of the angles within the triangle add to 180°. Subtract: 180° − 90° − 40° = 50°

Integers

28

INTEGERS

The numbers that have been used in the earlier chapters, 0 and all positive numbers such as 1, 2, 3, and so on, are known as *natural numbers*. These represent positive values, such as the number of dollars in your bank account or the number of degrees above zero when expressing temperature.

Every natural number has an opposite, such as –1, –2, –3, and so on. The set of 0, natural numbers, and their opposites are called *integers*. These integers are also known as signed numbers.

All of the integers have a position on the number line.

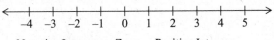

Negative Integers   Zero   Positive Integers

The positive integers are all to the right of zero and can be preceded by the positive sign (+), such as +1, +2, +3, or can be written without the positive sign, such as 1, 2, 3. The negative integers are all to the left of zero and must be preceded by the negative sign (–), such as –1, –2, –3. Zero is neither positive nor negative.

A *rational number* is any number that can be expressed as a quotient, or fraction, such as $\frac{a}{b}$, of two integers as long as b does not equal to zero. Rational numbers include whole numbers, integers, fractions, and decimals fractions. All *rational numbers* can be positioned on the number line. For example, $-2\frac{1}{2}$ lies midway between –2 and –3, while 3.5 lies midway between 3 and 4.

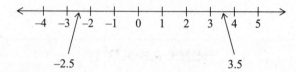

GRAPHING A NUMBER

Any number can be represented as a point on the number line. To graph a number means to locate its place on a number line.

➡ **EXAMPLE 1** _____

Graph –4.8

Solution

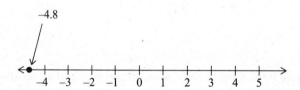

➡ **EXAMPLE 2** _____

Graph $\frac{13}{4}$ = 3.25

Solution

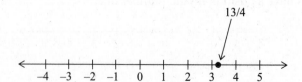

PRACTICE

1. Graph –1.7

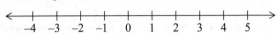

2. Graph $\frac{15}{4}$

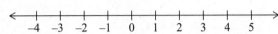

3. Graph $-2\frac{3}{5}$

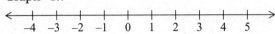

ANSWERS

1. Graph –1.7

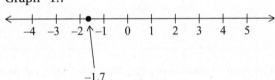

2. Graph $\frac{15}{4}$

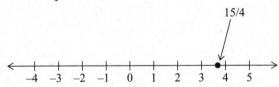

3. Graph $-2\frac{3}{5}$

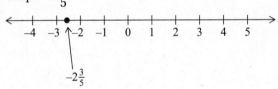

REAL NUMBERS AND ORDER

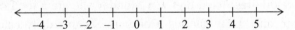

The numbers on the number line always increase to the right; therefore a number on the right is always larger than a number on the left.

Use the following symbols to compare the position and value of real numbers.

   =   is equal to
   <   is less than
   ≤   is less than or equal to
   >   is greater than
   ≥   is greater than or equal to

Using these symbols, <, >, or =, you can write:

$-6 < -5$	negative six *is less than* negative five
$\dfrac{2}{3} < \dfrac{11}{13}$	two thirds *is less than* eleven thirteenths
$-4 > -7$	negative four *is greater than* negative seven
$0 > -3.7$	zero *is greater than* negative three point seven

➡ EXAMPLE 1

Compare each pair of numbers below using <, >, or =.

a. -3 ? -2

b. 0 ? -6

c. -6 ? $-5\dfrac{1}{2}$

d. 4.6 ? 7.2

Solution

a. $-3 < -2$

b. $0 > -6$

c. $-6 < -5\dfrac{1}{2}$

d. $4.6 < 7.2$

➡ EXAMPLE 2

The cost of a plumbing repair as quoted by Paul's Plumbing is $2 250, while Perfect Pipes gave a quote of $1 750. Compare the two job quotes using a standard symbol.

Solution

$2\ 250 > \$1\ 750$

PRACTICE

1. Compare each pair of numbers below using <, > or =.

   a. -2.5 _____ -2.8

   b. 8 _____ 10

   c. $-\dfrac{1}{2}$ _____ 0.5

   d. 5 _____ 0

   e. $-\dfrac{3}{4}$ _____ -0.75

   f. 3.75 _____ 3.57

2. Susan is on a calorie-restricted diet. On Monday she ate a total of 1410 calories. On Tuesday she ate only 1150 calories. Compare Susan's daily calorie intake using a standard symbol.

ANSWERS

1. a. $-2.5 > -2.8$

   b. $8 < 10$

   c. $-\dfrac{1}{2} < 0.5$

   d. $5 > 0$

   e. $-\dfrac{3}{4} = -0.75$

   f. $3.75 > 3.57$

2. $1410 > 1150$

ADDING AND SUBTRACTING INTEGERS

It is helpful to visualize the number line when you are adding and subtracting signed numbers (integers). Essentially, the (+) positive sign means to move right on the number line and the (–) negative sign means to move left. It becomes more complicated when you are adding or subtracting a (–) negative number so it is helpful to memorize some guidelines.

Adding Signed Numbers

1. When adding two positive values together: simply combine the values. The result will be positive.
2. When adding two negative values together: consider the values without their sign and combine them. The result will be negative.
3. When adding values that are opposite in sign: consider the numbers without their signs and subtract the smaller from the larger. The result will always have the same sign as that of the *larger* number.
4. When adding more than two values together: follow the above three rules, combining two integers at a time until you've reached your answer.

➡ EXAMPLE 1 _____

Add 6 + 2

Solution

6 + 2 = +8

➡ EXAMPLE 2 _____

Add –3 + (–2)

Solution

–3 + (–2) = –5

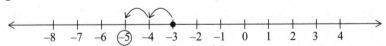

➡ EXAMPLE 3 _____

Add 10 + (–3)

Solution

10 + (–3) = +7

➡ EXAMPLE 4 _____

Add 4 + (–12) + (–3) + 5

Solution

4 + (–12) = –8 + (–3) = –11 + 5 = –6

Subtracting Signed Numbers

1. Change every subtraction to addition by adding the opposite of the subtracted number. Another way to simplify this rule is to recognize that if the signs are the same, such as (–) and (–), change the operation to addition (+). If the signs are different, such as (–) and (+), change the operation to subtraction (–).

   Both versions of this guideline are illustrated below.

2. Follow the rules of addition.

➡ **EXAMPLE 1** _____

Subtract 8 – 5

Solution

$8 + (–5) = +3$

Add the opposite of +5

➡ **EXAMPLE 2** _____

Subtract –3 – (–6)

Solution

$–3 + 6 = +3$

The signs were the same (–) (–), operation was (+)

➡ **EXAMPLE 3** _____

Subtract 16 – (+4)

Solution

$16 – 4 = 12$

The signs were different (–) (+), operation was (–)

➡ **EXAMPLE 4** _____

Subtract 10 – (–2) – (+3) – (–5)

Solution

$10 + 2 – 3 + 5 = 14$

QUICK CALCULATOR POINTER

There is a button on your calculator, +/–, that will change the sign of values.
To enter –5 in your calculator, press 5 and then press +/–
   Try combining these integers: 4 + (–2) – (–10) by pressing 4 ⊞ 2 +/– ⊟ 10 +/– =
Did you get 12?

Although you can combine signed values using your calculator, you still need to memorize the rules because many GED questions do not allow you to use your calculator!

PRACTICE

1. Simplify the following:

   a. $3 + (-2)$

   b. $-14 + 10$

   c. $-27 + (-5) + 40 + (-3)$

   d. $15 + (-1) + 14$

   e. $-11 - (-4)$

   f. $-7 - (5)$

   g. $12 - (+3) - 6$

   h. $8 - (2) - (-3) - (+5)$

   i. $-1.5 - (-2.5) + (-4.5)$

   j. $\dfrac{1}{3} - \left(-\dfrac{5}{6}\right) + \dfrac{2}{3}$

ANSWERS

1. a. 1

   b. −4

   c. 5

   d. 28

   e. −7

   f. −12

   g. 3

   h. 4

   i. −3.5

   j. $\dfrac{11}{6}$

MULTIPLYING AND DIVIDING INTEGERS

Not only are the rules for multiplying and dividing signed numbers less complicated than for adding and subtracting, but the rules are identical for both operations of multiplication and division.

1. A positive value multiplied or divided by another positive value is always a positive result.
2. A positive value multiplied or divided by a negative value (or vice versa) is always a negative result.
3. A negative value multiplied or divided by a negative value is always a positive result.

You can simplify these rules even more:

1. $(+)(+) = (+)$
2. $(+)(-) = (-)$
3. $(-)(-) = (+)$

➡ **EXAMPLE 1** _____

Multiply
$(-3)(2)$

Solution

$(-3)(2) = -6$
Opposite signs, negative result

➡ **EXAMPLE 2** _____

Multiply $(-8)(-10)$

Solution

$(-8)(-10) = +80$
Same signs, positive result

➡ EXAMPLE 3_____

Multiply 2(–4)(–5)(3)

Solution

2(–4) = –8(–5) = + 40(3) = +120

As we did with addition and subtraction, simplify the expression two numbers at a time (left to right).

➡ EXAMPLE 4_____

Divide $\dfrac{-10}{-5}$

Solution

$\dfrac{-10}{-5} = +2$

Same signs, positive result

Example 5

Divide $\dfrac{27}{-3}$

Solution

$\dfrac{27}{-3} = -9$

Opposite signs, negative result

PRACTICE

1. Simplify the following:

    a. (–6)(–11)

    b. (3)(–2)(4)

    c. $-10\left(\dfrac{2}{5}\right)$

    d. –20 ÷ (–4)

    e. $\dfrac{-49}{-7}$

    f. (2 – 10)(–8)

    g. $\dfrac{-25}{5}$

    h. [(–2)(–16)] ÷ (–4)

    i. (–6 + 10)(–1 – 7)

    j. $\dfrac{16-10}{-3}$

ANSWERS

1. a. 66

    b. –24

    c. –4

    d. 5

    e. 7

    f. 64

    g. –5

    h. –8

    i. –32

    j. –2

REVISITING EXPONENTS AND ORDER OF OPERATIONS

Exponents and Order of Operations (BEDMAS) were introduced in Chapter 21. At the time, you only considered examples with positive natural numbers. In the examples below, consider all the operations with signed numbers. You will soon see how important it is to protect signed numbers with brackets.

➡️ **EXAMPLE 1** _____

Simplify and compare -2^2 and $(-2)^2$

Solution

There is a very subtle difference between these two expressions; however, remember that order of operations states to simplify exponents before multiplying.

The first expression -2^2 can be rewritten as -1×2^2 which equals -4.

The second expression $(-2)^2$ makes it clear that -2 is being squared. The result is $+4$.

➡️ **EXAMPLE 2** _____

Simplify $2^3 - 3(10 - 3^2) + 2(4)^2$

Solution

$8 - 3(10 - 9) + 2(16)$
$8 - 3(1) + 2(16)$
$8 - 3 + 32$
37

TIP

BEDMAS is an acronym for Brackets, Exponents, Division, Multiplication, Addition and Subtraction.

➡️ **EXAMPLE 3** _____

Simplify $10 + 2(3^2 - 2^2) - 9$

Solution

$10 + 2(9 - 4) - 9$
$10 + 2(5) - 9$
$10 + 10 - 9$
11

PRACTICE

1. Simplify the following:

   a. $(16 - 9)^2$

   b. $2 - 3(2)^3$

   c. $(3 + 7) - 2(4)^2$

   d. $2^3 - (12) + 5(2)^2$

   e. $-2(10 - 20)(-1)^2$

   f. $20 - 5(3^2 - 2^2)$

   g. $\dfrac{4^2 - 3^2}{14}$

   h. $[3 - (10 + 2)] - 1^3$

   i. $7 + 3 \times 4 + 27 \div 3$

   j. $\dfrac{25 \div 5 + 3^2}{2^3}$

SQUARE ROOTS

TIP

To access any of the second functions on your calculator that appear in yellow above the buttons, you must first press SHIFT.

When you were introduced to exponents, you were also introduced to a button on your calculator: $\boxed{x^2}$

You may have noticed that above this button there is a yellow symbol that looks like $\sqrt{}$. This is the square root symbol. *Taking the square root* of some number is the opposite of *squaring* some number. When you see an expression such as $\sqrt{36}$, you are being asked to find a number that when multiplied by itself will equal 36. When simplified, $\sqrt{36} = 6$.

It is helpful to be familiar with the following common squares. They are also called *perfect squares*.

$1^2 = 1$	$2^2 = 4$	$3^2 = 9$	$4^2 = 16$
$5^2 = 25$	$6^2 = 36$	$7^2 = 49$	$8^2 = 64$
$9^2 = 81$	$10^2 = 100$	$11^2 = 121$	$12^2 = 144$

➡ **EXAMPLE 1** _____

Find $\sqrt{49}$ without using a calculator.

Solution

Ask yourself, What number times itself equals 49?

You know that $7 \times 7 = 49$ or that $7^2 = 49$

Therefore, the $\sqrt{49} = 7$

➡ **EXAMPLE 2** _____

Find $\sqrt{40}$ without using a calculator.

Solution

Ask yourself, What number times itself equals 40?

There is no whole number answer to this question. In fact, most square roots are not whole numbers. You can find the more exact answer to this question using a calculator, or you can approximate the answer, without using a calculator, by thinking about common squares.

You know that $6 \times 6 = 36$ and that $7 \times 7 = 49$.

Therefore, the $\sqrt{40}$ is between 6 and 7.

➡ **EXAMPLE 3** _____

Find $\sqrt{40}$ using a calculator.

Solution

To find the exact answer to this question, enter the following on your calculator:

$$40 \;\boxed{\text{SHIFT}}\;\boxed{x^2}$$

You will see 6.32455532 in the display. Likely you would be directed to round this value to the nearest tenth or hundredth position on a GED exam question.

$$\sqrt{40} \approx 6.32$$

PRACTICE

1. Simplify without a calculator.

    a. $\sqrt{16}$ c. $-\sqrt{4}$ e. $2\sqrt{25}$

    b. $\sqrt{81}$ d. $\sqrt{55}$

2. Simplify with a calculator. Round to the nearest hundredth.

    a. $\sqrt{20}$ b. $\sqrt{300}$

ANSWERS

1. a. 4   c. −2   e. 10

    b. 9   d. Between 7 and 8

2. a. $\sqrt{20} \approx 4.47$ b. $\sqrt{300} \approx 17.32$

SCIENTIFIC NOTATION

The most accurate way of expressing very large or very small numbers is with scientific notation. Fortunately, scientific notation is easy to understand as it works with a base of 10, just as our decimal system does.

Although scientific notation is not used a great deal within GED questions, you will likely be asked to convert to scientific notation or expand from scientific notation.

Scientific notation is written $N \times 10^y$, where a positive y indicates a large number and a negative y indicates a small number.

➡ EXAMPLE 1 _____

The distance from the Earth to the Sun is approximately 149 600 000 km. Express this number in scientific notation.

Solution

    a. There is always only one digit in front of the decimal point in proper scientific notation. Move the decimal point from the end of this number to position it between 1 and 4.

    b. Count the number of places that the decimal point was moved left. In this case it moved 8 places left.

149 600 000.

TIP

When you use your calculator for the square root function and you get a result with decimals that go on and on, without any pattern, the answer is only an approximation. A number like this is called an *irrational number*.

c. Express the answer in scientific notation as 1.496×10^8 km.

➡ EXAMPLE 2

The mass of a hydrogen atom is about 0.00000000000000000000000017 g. Express this number in scientific notation.

Solution
a. Move the decimal point from the front of this number to position it between 1 and 7.
b. Count the number of places that the decimal point was moved right. In this case it moved 24 places right.

$$0.\underbrace{00000000000000000000000017}_{\curvearrowright}$$

c. Express the answer in scientific notation as 1.7×10^{-24} g.

➡ EXAMPLE 3

Express in scientific notation: 754 000 000 000 kg

Solution
7.54×10^{11} kg

➡ EXAMPLE 4

Express in scientific notation: 0.0000567 km

Solution
5.67×10^{-5} km

PRACTICE

1. Express in proper scientific notation.
    a. 210 000 000 cm
    b. 0.0045 kg
    c. 5 100 000 000 000 km
    d. 0.00000078 g
    e. 2450×10^3 litres

ANSWERS

1. a. 2.1×10^8 cm
    b. 4.5×10^{-3} kg
    c. 5.1×10^{12} km
    d. 7.8×10^{-7} g
    e. 2.450×10^6 litres

CHALLENGE EXERCISE

Research online the distance between the earth and the moon. Next, research the distance between the earth and the sun. Working with the distances you found online, how much further is it to the sun than the moon—expressed in scientific notation?

CHAPTER CHECK-UP

1. Of the following, which statement is NOT true?
   (1) $-10 \leq -4$
   (2) $12 < -14$
   (3) $-1 > -5$
   (4) $3 \geq 1$
   (5) $-21 < 14$

2. Determine $\sqrt{144}$
   (1) 10
   (2) 12
   (3) 15
   (4) 20
   (5) 25

3. Simplify $3^3 - 2(-10) + 4(2)^2$
   (1) 63
   (2) 45
   (3) 23
   (4) −20
   (5) −52

4. Simplify $\dfrac{(-2)(-4)}{2^2 + 6^2}$
   (1) $\dfrac{1}{5}$
   (2) $1\dfrac{2}{5}$
   (3) $\dfrac{6}{11}$
   (4) $-\dfrac{2}{5}$
   (5) −5

5. Which point on the number line below represents the closest approximation to $\sqrt{30}$?

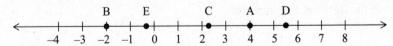

   (1) A
   (2) B
   (3) C
   (4) D
   (5) E

6. The average person sleeps about 250 000 hours over their total lifetime. Expressed in scientific notation, how many *minutes* does a person sleep in a lifetime?
   (1) 150×10^2 minutes
   (2) 2.5×10^5 minutes
   (3) 1.5×10^{-7} minutes
   (4) 1.5×10^7 minutes
   (5) Not enough information is given.

7. Evaluate $(6 \times 10^5) \div (3 \times 10^2)$
   (1) 20
   (2) 200
   (3) 2000
   (4) 1800
   (5) 180

8. The distance between two stars is 470 000 000 000 000 km. What is this number expressed in scientific notation?
   (1) 470×10^4 km
   (2) 4.7×10^{12} km
   (3) 4.7×10^{-10} km
   (4) 4.7×10^1 km
   (5) 4.7×10^{14} km

ANSWERS

1. **(2)** $12 < -14$ is not true. 12 is to the right of –14 on the number line.

2. **(2)** $\sqrt{144} = 12$. This is a common square root that you should memorize.

3. **(1)** $3^3 - 2(-10) + 4(2)^2 = 27 + 20 + 4(4) = 27 + 20 + 16 = 63$

4. **(1)** $\dfrac{(-2)(-4)}{2^2 + 6^2} = \dfrac{8}{4 + 36} = \dfrac{8}{40} = \dfrac{1}{5}$

5. **(4)** $\sqrt{30}$ is between $\sqrt{25}$ and $\sqrt{36}$ which means $\sqrt{30}$ is between 5 and 6.

6. **(4)** Multiply. $250\,000 \times 60 = 15\,000\,000 = 1.5 \times 10^7$

7. **(3)** Expand the numbers and divide. $(6 \times 10^5) \div (3 \times 10^2) = 600\,000 \div 300 = 2\,000$.

8. **(5)** Move the decimal 14 places left.

Charts, Graphs, and Statistical Data

29

THINK ABOUT IT

What are the trends in current weather patterns? What predictions are being made about the stock market? How many people in Canada are living below the poverty line? These are very different questions about a diverse range of topics but all can be answered through an analysis of data. Data analysis and the ability to read and understand charts, graphs, and tables are skills that are tested frequently on the GED Math exam. These skills are used extensively in all sciences, as well as in business professions and a variety of other careers.

Fortunately, the actual math involved in data analysis is generally very straightforward. Data analysis generally involves finding specific numerical information, calculating averages, and determining differences.

IN THIS CHAPTER

After completing this chapter, you will be able to

→ **UNDERSTAND TABLES**

→ **UNDERSTAND BAR AND LINE GRAPHS**

→ **UNDERSTAND PIE CHARTS**

→ **INTERPRET DATA**

TABLES

Likely, without even realizing it, you analyze data on a regular basis. Choosing items from a menu board in a café, determining the time that the next bus arrives, and reading food labels are all examples of the analysis of information presented in a table. Several questions can be posed about the same table.

EXAMPLE 1

Study the table below and respond to the following questions:

Vancouver—Victoria Ferry Schedule

Leave Tsawwassen (Vancouver)		Leave Swartz Bay (Victoria)	
7:00 am	Daily	7:00 am	Daily
9:00 am	Daily	9:00 am	Daily
11:00 am	Daily	11:00 am	Daily
1:00 pm	Daily	12:00 pm	Feb 7 only
2:00 pm	Fri & Sun only except Feb 9	1:00 pm	Daily
3:00 pm	Daily	3:00 pm	Daily
5:00 pm	Daily	4:00 pm	Fri & Sun only except Feb 9
6:00 pm	Fri & Sun only	5:00 pm	Daily
7:00 pm	Daily	7:00 pm	Daily
9:00 pm	Daily	9:00 pm	Daily

1. How many ferries run daily between Vancouver and Victoria?
2. What is the last ferry you can catch from Victoria (Swartz Bay)?
3. Which ferry operates on Feb 7 only?

Solution

1. 8. Count the number of ferries that state "daily". There are 8 in both columns.
2. The last ferry to leave Victoria (Swartz Bay) is 9:00 pm.
3. The ferry leaving Victoria at 12:00 pm.

EXAMPLE 2

Study the data below and respond to the following questions:

Nutrition Facts	
Per 1 burger (130g)	
Amount	% Daily Value
Calories 200	
Fat 9 g	14 %
Saturated Fat 2 g + Trans Fat 1 g	15 %
Cholesterol 70 mg	
Sodium 800 mg	33 %
Carbohydrate 4 g	1 %
Fibre 0 g	0 %
Sugars 0 g	
Protein 25 g	
Vitamin A 0 % Vitamin C 0 %	
Calcium 4 % Iron 2 %	

Chicken Burger

Nutrition Facts	
Per 1 burger (130g)	
Amount	% Daily Value
Calories 340	
Fat 27 g	42 %
Saturated Fat 2 g + Trans Fat 2 g	70 %
Cholesterol 70 mg	
Sodium 330 mg	14 %
Carbohydrate 3 g	1 %
Fibre 0 g	0 %
Sugars 3 g	
Protein 24 g	
Vitamin A 0 % Vitamin C 0 %	
Calcium 2 % Iron 30 %	

Beef Burger

1. Which burger has more calories? How many more?
2. Consider the % daily allowance of fat in a beef burger. How many grams of fat should one consume daily?
3. How many chicken burgers would someone have to eat to fully use up their daily sodium intake?

Solution

1. The beef burger has 140 calories more than the chicken burger. Calculate this through subtraction: 340 calories – 200 calories = 140 calories.

2. 64.3 grams. This is a percent proportion problem. Solve: $\dfrac{27g}{?g} = \dfrac{42}{100}$.

   Multiply (27) (100) and divide by 42.

3. Three. The chart shows that 33% of the daily allowance for sodium occurs in one chicken burger. Two burgers would provide 66% and three burgers would provide 99%.

PRACTICE

Pleasantville Community College Continuing Studies Courses		
Course	Course Fee	Maximum Enrollment
Introduction to Guitar	$150	12
Watercolour Painting	$95	8
M.S. Word, Level I	$210	16
Occupational First Aid, Level I	$110	18
Learn Spanish for Fun	$65	25

Use the chart above to answer the following questions.

1. How many more students can take Spanish than the Watercolour Painting course?
2. If twelve students register for the Occupational First Aid course, how much revenue will the college collect?
3. If all classes are full, what is the total enrollment for all classes?
4. How much more expensive is the Guitar course than the Spanish course?
5. What is the average fee charged for a Continuing Studies course?

ANSWERS

1. 17
2. $1 320
3. 79
4. $85
5. $126 (Reminder: Finding averages was illustrated in Chapter 26)

BAR GRAPHS

A bar graph is a convenient way of illustrating comparison. The bars can run either horizontally or vertically; however, in either case one can quickly see what value may be larger or smaller than another. Read the labels on the axes carefully. Understand what data is being represented and what it means.

➡ **EXAMPLE** _____

The bar graph below illustrates the number of calories an average person would burn in one hour of activity. Various parts of the graph have been labelled. Familiarize yourself with these terms and answer the following questions:

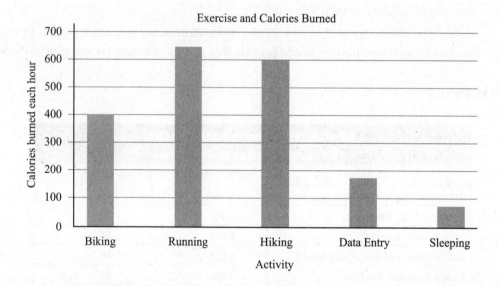

1. Which activity burns the most calories?

2. If an average person ran for one hour and then went for a $2\frac{1}{2}$-hour hike, how many calories would she burn all together?

3. Biking burns how many more calories per hour than sleeping?

Solution

1. It is easy to see that running burns the most calories. The bar is the highest.

2. First determine how many calories are burned each hour by these activities. It is helpful to use a ruler or piece of paper to line up the top of the bar with the values on the left. Running burns approximately 650 calories and hiking burns 600 calories. Now, determine the total for one hour of running and $2\frac{1}{2}$ hours hiking:

   $(1)(650) + (2\frac{1}{2})(600) = 2\,150$ calories.

3. Approximate the calories burned for each activity. Biking is approximately 400 and sleeping is about 80. The difference between the two is $400 - 80 = 320$ calories.

PRACTICE

Use the graph below to answer the following questions.

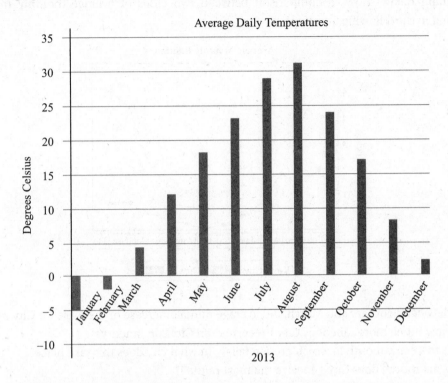

1. On average, how much warmer is it in June than February?
2. How many months achieved an average daily temperature higher than 15° but less than 25°?
3. Consider the three warmest months. What is the average daily temperature over this three-month period?
4. Between which two consecutive months is there the greatest change in daily average temperature?

ANSWERS

1. About 25° warmer in June than February.
2. 4. May, June, September, and October.
3. 28° average over July, August and September.
4. Between October and November.

CHALLENGE EXERCISE

Over the course of one week, record the number of minutes you spend watching television each day. Construct a column chart with days of the week along the horizontal axis and minutes plotted along the vertical axis.

LINE GRAPHS

Line graphs are commonly used to show change over time with some measure on the horizontal scale and another on the vertical scale. If the graph illustrates more than one line, it is important to study the key to understand what information is represented.

The graph below shows a comparison between two cities of average monthly rainfall. Respond to the following questions.

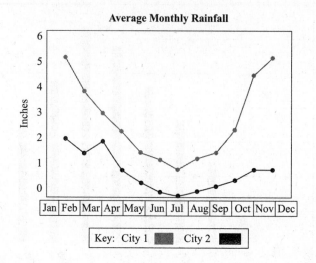

1. Between February and March, did average rainfall increase or decrease for City 2?
2. How much more rain does City 1 receive than City 2 in January?
3. Is there any month in which no rain falls?   In what city does this take place?
4. What month does City 1 receive the most rainfall?
5. Over the entire year, how much rain does City 2 experience?

Solution

1. It increased. The line is rising.
2. 3 inches. Find the difference between 5 inches and 2 inches.
3. No rain falls in City 2 in July.
4. There is not one exact month. In both January and December, City 1 experiences 5 inches of rainfall.
5. 10.5 inches. Evaluate each data point and total the rainfall quantities for each month.

PRACTICE

The graph below represents the value of a vehicle over time. Respond to the following questions.

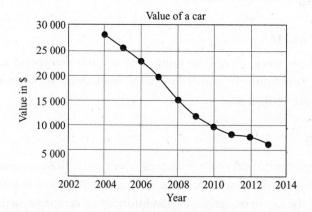

1. How many data points are on the graph?
2. What is the title of the vertical axis?
3. Over time, did the value of the car increase or decrease?
4. In 2008, what was the value of the car?
5. What is the change in the vehicle's value over the entire time period?

ANSWERS

1. 10
2. "Value in $"
3. The value decreased.
4. $15 000
5. $21 000 approximately.

PIE CHARTS

Pie charts, or circle graphs, are commonly used to show relative sizes of data. Often the percent of each quantity is included on the graph. These charts are appropriately named because they resemble a pie that has been sliced into pieces. Pie charts are sometimes more difficult to analyze for exact data values (in comparison to column or bar charts); however, they are useful for general comparison of parts.

➡ EXAMPLE

This pie chart illustrates the expenses a student attending community college incurs in one year.

TIP

The entire circle (or pie) equals 100%.

Community College Expenses

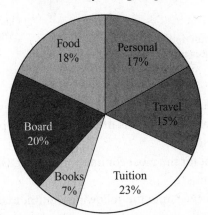

1. Which is the greatest expense for a community college student?
2. If total college expenses were $20 000, how much did books cost?
3. Food, room, and travel equate to what percent of total expenses?
4. If total college expenses were $25 000 a year, on average, how much did this student spend on travel every month?

Solution

1. The greatest expense is tuition at 23%.

2. Books cost $1 400. Solve using a percent proportion. $\frac{x}{20\,000} = \frac{7}{100}$. Multiply (7)(20 000) and divide by 100 = $1 400.

3. 53%. Add 18%+20%+15%

4. Travel costs $312.50 a month. Find this amount by solving a percent proportion. $\frac{x}{25\,000} = \frac{15}{100}$. Multiply (15)(25 000) and divide by 100 = $3 750. Next divide the yearly amount by 12 to get the monthly amount, $3 750 ÷ 12 = $312.50

PRACTICE

This pie chart illustrates the type of treatments at a medical centre recorded in one month.

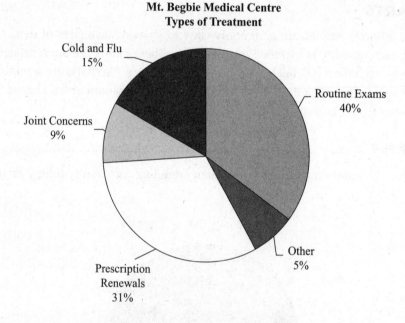

Mt. Begbie Medical Centre
Types of Treatment

1. What is the second-least-common treatment this month?
2. If there were 400 patient visits in this month, how many patients saw a doctor about cold and flu symptoms?
3. Routine exams account for the most common treatment. Of the 400 patient visits, how many were routine exams?
4. If percentages remain the same the following month, and 184 patients come to the clinic to either have their prescription renewed or inquire about joint concerns, how many patients come to the clinic for a routine exam that month?

ANSWERS

1. Joint Concerns.
2. 60 patients.
3. 160 patients.
4. 184 patients. (The total % for prescription renewals and joint concerns equals the % for routine exams).

CHALLENGE EXERCISE

Create a monthly budget of your expenses. Determine the percentage of your total budget that you spend on each category. Build a pie chart to illustrate your budget. If you are comfortable with a spreadsheet program such as M.S. Excel, you could create the pie chart electronically.

CHAPTER CHECK-UP

Questions 1 and 2 refer to the following chart.

International Shipping Rates	
1 kg–3 kg	$15.00
3.1 kg–5 kg	$20.00
Over 5 kg	$22.50

1. If a customer is shipping a 2.9 kg package from Toronto to New York, how much would it cost?

   (1) $5.00
   (2) $15.00
   (3) $20.00
   (4) $22.50
   (5) Not enough information is given.

2. Another customer has multiple packages. He wants to ship three 2-kg parcels to Hong Kong and one 4.2-kg parcel to Switzerland. How much will it cost him altogether?
   (1) $55
   (2) $60
   (3) $65
   (4) $72.50
   (5) $85

Questions 3 and 4 refer to the bar chart below.

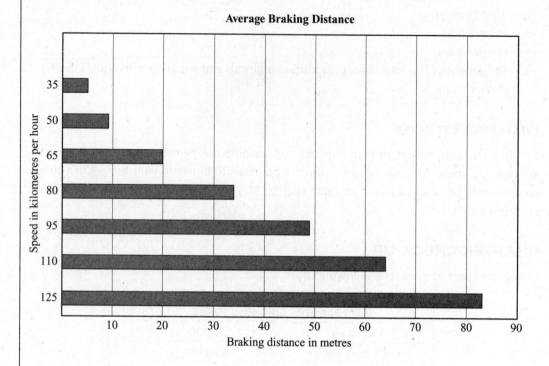

Average Braking Distance

3. What is the braking distance for a vehicle travelling 95 km/hr?

   (1) 32 m
   (2) 84 m
   (3) 63 m
   (4) 50 m
   (5) 48 m

4. What speed is a car travelling that travels a braking distance of 20 metres?

   (1) 50 km/h
   (2) 65 km/h
   (3) 80 km/h
   (4) 95 km/h
   (5) 110 km/h

Questions 5 and 6 refer to the following pie chart.

Popular Vacation Destinations

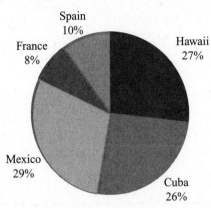

5. If 2 700 people were surveyed, how many people prefer to travel to Cuba?

    (1) 1 298 people
    (2) 270 people
    (3) 260 people
    (4) 702 people
    (5) 980 people

6. If there was a sudden seat sale to Europe and the percentage of people that originally preferred Mexico reduced to 19% (with the remaining 10% now choosing France), what is the new percent of travellers now preferring to travel to France?

    (1) 8%
    (2) 10%
    (3) 18%
    (4) 19%
    (5) 9%

7. Use the line graph that follows to determine the rate of travel in kilometres per hour.

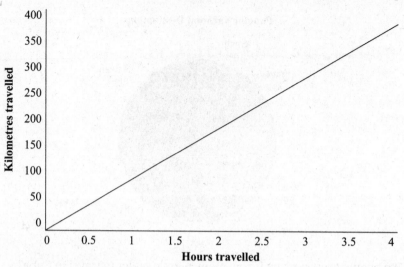

(1) Less than 70 km/hr
(2) Between 70 and 75 km/hr
(3) Between 80 and 85 km/hr
(4) Between 90 and 100 km/hr
(5) Not enough information is given.

ANSWERS

1. **(2)**

2. **(3)** Calculate (3)($15) + (1)($20) = $65

3. **(5)**

4. **(2)**

5. **(4)** Solve $\dfrac{x}{2\,700} = \dfrac{26}{100}$. Multiply (26)(2 700) and divide by 100 =

6. **(3)** Add 10% + 8% = 18%

7. **(4)** Divide the total distance travelled by the total time: 375 km ÷ 4 hours = 93.75 km/hr

Linear Equations and Inequalities

30

THINK ABOUT IT

"Why do we need to learn algebra?" This is a common question for many students. The rules and guidelines for working with numbers are complicated enough, why introduce letters or variables into the mix as well? It is a difficult question to fully answer, but mathematicians will ask you to be patient and believe that algebra is the very foundation for understanding the world around us. Very complicated theories, such as Einstein's theory of special relativity, can be explained and understood using algebra. How a spacecraft orbits the Earth can also be understood, in large part, using algebra. Algebra can be challenging, but never boring; it can help you understand a vast array of fascinating topics.

IN THIS CHAPTER

After completing this chapter, you will be able to

→ **IDENTIFY LIKE TERMS**
→ **EVALUATE ALGEBRAIC EXPRESSIONS**
→ **SOLVE LINEAR EQUATIONS**
→ **SOLVE LINEAR INEQUALITIES**
→ **TRANSLATE AND SOLVE ALGEBRAIC WORD PROBLEMS**

ALGEBRAIC EXPRESSIONS AND TERMS

In algebra, a **variable** is used to represent an unknown value. Common variables used are x and y; however, any letter or symbol could be used to indicate that some value is unknown.

An **algebraic expression** combines variables, mathematical operations, and integers. $2x - 3y + 10$ is an example of an algebraic expression.

An **algebraic term** is comprised of up to three elements:

- A sign (+ or −)
- A value (assumed to be 1 if not shown)
- A variable or combination of variables

The signed value is also referred to as the **coefficient**.

In the algebraic expression above, there are three terms: $+2x$, $-3y$ and $+10$.
Notice that a term does not need a variable, as is the case with $+10$.

How many terms are there in the following expression? What is the coefficient of the third term?

$$-7a + 4ab - 3b + 5$$

Solution

There are four terms.
The coefficient of the third term is –3.

Collecting Like Terms

Like terms have the same variable, or combination of variables, raised to the same power. Remember that the value in front of the variable is called the coefficient. Coefficients can be combined through addition and subtraction just as values can be combined through addition and subtraction. When *collecting like terms* you combine the coefficients but do not change the variables.

➡ **EXAMPLE 1**

Simplify the following algebraic expression by collecting like terms.

$$2x - 3y + 4 - 5x + 10$$

Solution

Identify like terms:
$2x$ and $-5x$ are like terms. Combined, you get $-3x$
$+4$ and $+10$ are like terms. Combined, you get $+14$
$-3y$ is not like any other term.

The expression simplified is $-3x - 3y + 14$

➡ **EXAMPLE 2**

Simplify the following algebraic expression by collecting like terms.

$$7ab - 3a + 15ab + 8a$$

Solution

$7ab$ and $+ 15ab$ are like terms. Combined, you get $+22ab$
$-3a$ and $+ 8a$ are like terms. Combined, you get $+5a$

The expression simplified is $22ab + 5a$

Removing Brackets

Many algebraic expressions and equations include brackets. Brackets are used to protect the order of mathematical operations. When simplifying expressions and solving equations, brackets must be removed. To remove brackets you simply *distribute across* the brackets. To distribute, you complete an operation of multiplication.

➥ EXAMPLE 1 _____

Simplify $2(x - 12)$

Solution

Each term within the brackets must be multiplied by the term directly in front of the bracket.

$$2(x) + 2(-12) = 2x - 24$$

➥ EXAMPLE 2 _____

Simplify $-1x(3x + 4y - 10)$

Solution

This example is slightly more complicated. Notice from the answer that when we multiply $-1x(3x)$ the result is $-3x^2$. Not only did you multiply the coefficients but you also added the exponents above x. Remember if no exponent is shown, it is assumed to be 1.

$-1x(3x + 4y - 10)$
$= (-1x)(3x) + (-1x)(4y) + (-1x)(-10)$
$= -3x^2 - 4xy + 10x$

➥ EXAMPLE 3 _____

Simplify $2x(12x - 4) - 3x - 5$

Solution

$2x(12x - 4) - 3x - 5$
$= 24x^2 - 8x - 3x - 5$ Remember to collect like terms.
$= 24x^2 - 11x - 5$

PRACTICE

1. Simplify each expression by removing brackets and collecting like terms.

    a. $10m - 7n - 6n$
    b. $3(7x - 11)$
    c. $-2(5a + 3) + 8a$
    d. $7x(2x + 12)$
    e. $2(10x - 4) - 3(x - 5)$

ANSWERS

1. a. $10m - 13n$
    b. $21x - 33$
    c. $-2a - 6$
    d. $14x^2 + 84x$
    e. $17x + 7$

EVALUATING ALGEBRAIC EXPRESSIONS

When you replace a variable by a known quantity you are evaluating the algebraic expression.

This process involves substituting the known number for the variable (or variables) and simplifying the expression using *order of operations*.

➡ **EXAMPLE 1** _____

Evaluate $2x - 7y$ when $x = -2$ and $y = 3$

Solution

a. Substitute the given values for the variables. It is helpful to protect any values substituted with brackets.

$2(-2) - 7(3)$

b. Follow order of operations to simplify.

$-4 - 21 =$
-25

➡ **EXAMPLE 2** _____

Evaluate $-3a^2 + 5b + 3$ when $a = -4$ and $b = 2$

Solution

a. Substitute the given values for the variables.

$-3(-4)^2 + 5(2) + 3$

b. Follow order of operations to simplify.

$-3(16) + 10 + 3 =$
$-48 + 10 + 3 =$
-35

PRACTICE

1. Evaluate the following expressions.
   a. $2x - 5y$ when $x = -2$ and $y = 3$
   b. $-1a^2 + 11b$ when $a = -5$ and $b = 2$
   c. $-2(x + 4) + 4y$ when $x = 0$ and $y = -5$
   d. $x^2 + 5x - 6$ when $x = 4$
   e. $\dfrac{(x+4)^2}{y}$ when $x = 2$ and $y = -3$

ANSWERS

1. a. -19
   b. -3
   c. -28
   d. 30
   e. -12

EQUATIONS

An equation is a statement that indicates that two mathematical expressions are equal. Equality is indicated with the = symbol. Equations are the foundation of algebra, and examples of equations can be found in a wide range of studies such as commerce, physics, and chemistry.

This next section focuses on the steps involved in solving linear equations. There are some very basic steps to follow when solving linear equations. Not every step will be necessary every time; however, it is helpful to be systematic and follow the same approach with every equation. The ultimate goal in solving an equation is to find a number for the variable that makes the statement of equality true.

When given a simple equation such as $x + 5 = 12$, you likely can see the answer needs to be 7. You know that $7 + 5 = 12$. The left and right side of this equation are balanced and the statement of equality is true. The variable x represents the number 7.

SOLVING LINEAR EQUATIONS

The Addition and Subtraction Principles

The *addition principle* states that if you add the same number to both sides of an equation the equation remains true. Similarly, the *subtraction principle* states that if you subtract the same number from both sides of an equation, the equation remains true. You can use these principles to help isolate a variable.

 **EXAMPLE 1** _____

Solve $x - 10 = 15$

Solution

To isolate x in this equation you must do the opposite operation to subtraction. That is, you must add.

$$x - 10 = 15$$
$$x - 10 + 10 = 15 + 10 \qquad \text{Add 10 to both sides}$$
$$x = 25$$

Check by substituting the value for x back into the original equation.

$$x - 10 = 15$$
$$(25) - 10 = 15$$

EXAMPLE 2 _____

Solve $y + 7.5 = 12.5$

Solution

To isolate y in this equation you must do the opposite operation to addition. That is, you must subtract.

$$y + 7.5 = 12.5$$
$$y + 7.5 - 7.5 = 12.5 - 7.5 \qquad \text{Subtract 7.5 from both sides}$$
$$y = 5$$

Check by substituting the value for *y* back into the original equation.

$$y + 7.5 = 12.5$$
$$(5) + 7.5 = 12.5$$

Another way of illustrating these principles is to simply move terms to the other side of the = sign. If a term changes sides of the equation, it must also change sign.

➡ **EXAMPLE 3** _____

Solve $x + \dfrac{1}{4} = \dfrac{2}{3}$

Solution

To isolate *x* in this equation, move ¼ to the other side of the equation.

$$x + \frac{1}{4} = \frac{2}{3}$$
$$x = \frac{2}{3} - \frac{1}{4}$$
$$x = \frac{8}{12} - \frac{3}{12}$$
$$x = \frac{5}{12}$$

When $\dfrac{1}{4}$ moves to the right side of the equation, it changes sign. It becomes $-\dfrac{1}{4}$.

A common denominator of 12 was created in order to subtract the two fractions. Check by substituting the value for *x* back into the original equation.

$$x + \frac{1}{4} = \frac{2}{3}$$
$$\left(\frac{5}{12}\right) + \frac{1}{4} = \frac{2}{3}$$
$$\frac{5}{12} + \frac{3}{12} = \frac{8}{12}$$

The Multiplication and Division Principles

The *multiplication principle* states that if you multiply both sides of an equation by the same value, the solution to the equation will remain unchanged. Similarly, the *division principle* states that if you divide both sides of an equation by the same value, the solution to the equation will remain unchanged. You also can use these principles to help isolate a variable.

➡ **EXAMPLE 1** _____

Solve $4x = 24$

Solution

To isolate x in this equation you must do the opposite operation to multiplication. That is, you must divide.

$$4x = 24$$

$$\frac{4x}{4} = \frac{24}{4} \qquad \text{Divide both sides by 4}$$

$$x = 6$$

Check by substituting the value for x back into the original equation.

$$4x = 24$$

$$4(6) = 24$$

➡ EXAMPLE 2

Solve $\dfrac{x}{3} = 12$

Solution

To isolate x in this equation you must do the opposite operation to division. That is, you must multiply.

$$\frac{x}{3} = 12$$

$$(3)\frac{x}{3} = 12(3) \qquad \text{Multiply both sides by 3. The 3 cancels on the left}$$

$$x = 36$$

Check by substituting the value for x back into the original equation.

$$\frac{x}{3} = 12$$

$$\frac{36}{3} = 12$$

➡ EXAMPLE 3

Solve $1.5y = 60$

Solution

$$1.5y = 60$$

$$\frac{1.5y}{1.5} = \frac{60}{1.5} \qquad \text{Divide both sides by 1.5}$$

$$y = 40$$

Check by substituting the value for y back into the original equation.

$$1.5y = 60$$

$$1.5(40) = 60$$

Multistep Equations

It is often necessary to use more than one principle when solving an equation. It is best to be systematic and follow these steps in the same order every time. You may not need every step but it is important to follow the order exactly as shown.

   a.   Remove brackets.
   b.   Collect like terms.
   c.   Use the addition and subtraction principles to isolate the variable term.
   d.   Use the multiplication and division principles to isolate the variable.
   e.   Check.

➡ EXAMPLE 1

Solve $2x + 4x - 10 = 8$

Solution

$$2x + 4x - 10 = 8 \qquad \text{Collect like terms.}$$
$$6x - 10 = 8$$
$$6x = 8 + 10 \qquad \text{Move 10 to the right side of the equation. } -10 \text{ becomes } +10$$
$$6x = 18$$
$$\frac{6x}{6} = \frac{18}{6} \qquad \text{Divide both sides by 6.}$$
$$x = 3$$

Check by substituting the value for x back into the original equation.

$$2x + 4x - 10 = 8$$
$$2(3) + 4(3) - 10 = 8$$
$$6 + 12 - 10 = 8$$

➡ EXAMPLE 2

Solve $3(y - 4) = 27$

Solution

$$3(y - 4) = 27 \qquad \text{Remove brackets}$$
$$3y - 12 = 27$$
$$3y = 27 + 12 \qquad \text{Move 12 to the right side of the equation. } -12 \text{ becomes } +12$$
$$3y = 39$$
$$\frac{3y}{3} = \frac{39}{3} \qquad \text{Divide both sides by 3.}$$
$$y = 13$$

Check by substituting the value for y back into the original equation.

$$3(y - 4) = 27$$
$$3((13) - 4) = 27$$
$$3(9) = 27$$

Solve $3(x + 5) - 2x = 12 + 8$

Solution

$$3(x + 5) - 2x = 12 + 8$$
$$3x + 15 - 2x = 12 + 8 \qquad \text{Remove brackets.}$$
$$1x + 15 = 20$$
$$1x = 20 - 15$$
$$x = 5$$

Collect Like Terms.

Move 15 to the right side of the equation. +15 becomes –15

Check by substituting the value for x back into the original equation.

$$3(x + 5) - 2x = 12 + 8$$
$$3((5) + 5) - 2(5) = 12 + 8$$
$$3(10) - 10 = 12 + 8$$
$$30 - 10 = 20$$

PRACTICE

1. Solve the following one-step equations.

   a. $x + 5 = 17$
   b. $2y = 12$
   c. $a - 4 = 20$
   d. $\frac{3}{4}y = 21$
   e. $4.5 + x = 16.5$

2. Solve the following multi-step equations.

   a. $5x - 25 = 2x + 5$
   b. $2(x + 3) = 27$
   ◆ c. $4(a - 7) = 2 + 2a$
   d. $5y - 10 + 2(3y - 4) = 26$
   e. $7x - \frac{1}{2} = 2x + \frac{1}{4}$

ANSWERS

1. a. $x = 12$
   b. $y = 6$
   c. $a = 24$
   d. $y = 28$
   e. $x = 12$

2. a. $x = 10$
   b. $x = 10.5$
   c. $a = 15$
   d. $y = 4$
   e. $x = 0.15$

The "point" of
the arrow is
directed towards
the smaller
quantity. The
open side of the
arrow is directed
towards the
larger quantity.

INEQUALITIES

Statements of inequality indicate comparison. One side of the equation is greater than, less than, or perhaps equal to the other. Equations of inequality are not necessarily in balance; however, you still perform the exact same steps to isolate the variable.

Familiarize yourself with the following signs of inequality:

>	**Greater Than.**	For example, $20 > 10$
<	**Less Than.**	For example, $5 < 7$
≥	**Greater Than or Equal To**	For example, $20 \geq 15$. $20 \geq 20$ is also a true statement.
≤	**Less Than or Equal To**	For example, $5 \leq 12$. $5 \leq 5$ is also a true statement.

$2x < 100$ is an inequality that means 2 times a number is less than 100.

$x \geq 16.8$ is an inequality that means x represents any number greater than or equal to 16.8.

By graphing an inequality on the number line, you can see that there are infinite values that satisfy an inequality.

➡ **EXAMPLE 1** _____

Graph the solution set for the inequality $x \leq 5$.

Solution

The solution set for this inequality includes 5 and all values less than 5. Fill in the circle at 5 to indicate that 5 is a part of the solution set.

➡ **EXAMPLE 2** _____

Graph the solution set for the inequality $x > -2$.

Solution

The solution set for this inequality does not include –2 but includes all values greater than –2. You leave the circle empty at –2 to indicate that -2 is not a part of the solution set.

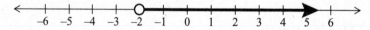

Solving Inequalities

The steps involved with solving inequalities are identical to the steps involved in solving linear equations. There is only one important exception: If you multiply or divide an inequality by a negative number, you must change the direction of the inequality sign. This takes place in Example 2 below.

➡ **EXAMPLE 1** _____

Solve $6x - 2 \leq 26$

Solution

$$6x - 2 \le 26$$
$$6x \le 26 + 2$$
$$6x \le 28$$
$$\frac{6x}{6} \le \frac{28}{6} \qquad \text{Move 2 to the right side of the inequality. } -2 \text{ becomes } +2$$
$$x \le \frac{14}{3} \qquad \text{Divide both sides by 6}$$

Simplify to lowest terms. The number must be less than or equal to $\frac{14}{3}$

Check by substituting the value for x back into the original inequality.

$$6x - 2 \le 26$$
$$6\left(\frac{14}{3}\right) - 2 \le 26$$
$$\frac{84}{3} - 2 \le 26$$
$$28 - 2 \le 26$$

➡ EXAMPLE 2

Solve $-9x > 33 + 2x$

Solution

$$-9x > 33 + 2x$$
$$-9x - 2x > 33 \qquad \text{Move } 2x \text{ to the left side of the inequality. } +2x \text{ becomes } -2x$$
$$-11x > 33$$
$$\frac{-11x}{-11} < \frac{33}{-11}$$
$$x < -3 \qquad \text{Collect like terms.}$$

Divide both sides by -11 and change the direction of the inequality sign.

The number must be less than -3.

Check by substituting the value for x back into the original inequality. Choose any number less than -3. The value -4 has been used to check.

$$-9x > 33 + 2x$$
$$-9(-4) > 33 + 2(-4)$$
$$36 > 33 - 8$$
$$36 > 25$$

PRACTICE

1. Graph the solution set for the following inequalities.

   a. $x > 3$

   b. $x \le -2$

2. Solve the following inequalities.

    a. $2(x+4) \leq 12$ e. $20(2x+3) \leq 100$

    b. $\frac{1}{3}x \geq 10$ f. $\frac{3(3x)+6}{10} \geq 3$

    c. $-3(x-4) > 3$ g. $18 > 3(y-6)$

    d. $4x - 5x + 10 > 8$ h. $12x - 5 \geq 4x + 1$

ANSWERS

1. a.

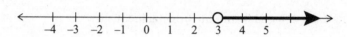

  b.

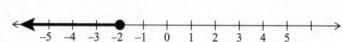

2.

    a. $x \leq 2$ f. $x \geq \frac{8}{3}$

    b. $x \geq 30$

    c. $x < 3$ g. $12 > y$

    d. $x < 2$

    e. $x \leq 1$ h. $x \geq \frac{3}{4}$

SOLVING WORD PROBLEMS

Now that you have reviewed the mechanics of solving equations, you can turn again to real world problems. The majority of problems presented in the GED Math Test will be word problems, and you have already had practice solving proportion and ratio problems using an algebraic approach. In this section, you are going to explore other types of algebraic problems that involve translating words into algebraic expressions and equations. Remember the chart presented in Chapter 21:

Addition (+)	Subtraction (−)	Multiplication (x)	Division (÷)
Sum	Difference	Product	Quotient
Plus	Subtract	Times	Share
More than	Less than	Twice	Per
Increased by	Decreased by	Of	Average
Total			

TRANSLATING TO ALGEBRAIC EXPRESSIONS AND EQUATIONS

In general, just as you would read a sentence from left to right, you can translate a word-problem sentence and convert to variables, integers and operations from left to right. Substitute x (or some other variable) into the expression for quantities that are unknown. This is often the quantity or amount to which other parts are being compared or related. The order in which addition and multiplication occurs is not significant; however, the order in which terms are written for subtraction and division is crucial.

➡ EXAMPLE 1

Translate the following into an algebraic expression:

Six more than twice some number

Solution

a. Identify the unknown amount and assign it a variable. You don't know what the "some number" is. Name it x.

b. Read from left to right, replacing words with numbers and words with operations.

~~Six more than twice some number~~

    6   +   2 (x)

The expression is $6 + 2x$

➡ EXAMPLE 2

Translate the following into an algebraic expression:

Four less than a number divided by two

Solution

a. Identify the unknown amount and assign it a variable. You don't know what the "number" is. Name it x.

b. Read from left to right, replacing words with numbers and words with operations. *Extra care must be taken with this example.* Although the phrase starts with *four less than*, the subtraction must follow the *a number divided by two*.

The expression is $\frac{x}{2} - 4$

➡ EXAMPLE 3

Translate the following into an algebraic equation:

The sum of two consecutive integers is 25.

Solution

a. You don't know what the first "integer" is. Name it x. The next consecutive integer would be $x + 1$

b. *Sum* means to add and the word *is* indicates equal to.

The equation is $x + (x + 1) = 25$

➡ EXAMPLE 4

Translate the following into an algebraic equation and solve:

Together Kathy and Amber collect 15 kg of apples. Kathy collects four times as much as Amber. How many kilograms does Amber collect?

Solution

a. You don't know what Amber collected. Name this quantity x. Kathy collected four times this amount. Name this quantity $4x$.

b.   *Together* means to add.
     The equation is $x + 4x = 15$

c.   Solve the equation
     $$x + 4x = 15$$
     $$5x = 15$$
     $$\frac{5x}{5} = \frac{15}{5}$$
     $$x = 3$$

d.   Interpret and state the solution:
     Amber collected 3 kg. Kathy collected four times as much, which is 12 kg.

e.   Check it. Together did they collect 15 kg? Yes.
     $3 \text{ kg} + 12 \text{ kg} = 15 \text{ kg}$

PRACTICE

1. Translate the following phrase to an algebraic expression: The quotient of some number and seven is increased by twenty-five.

2. Translate the following phrase to an algebraic equation: The product of two consecutive numbers is 30. Do not solve.

3. Caryn is y years old. How old will she be in twenty years? Translate to an algebraic equation. Do not solve.

4. Every week Tess earns $1 100. She estimates that she pays out F for food, G for transportation, E for entertainment and S for savings. How much does she net per week – expressed as an algebraic expression?

5. Solve. Six times a number less ten is equal to two times the same number plus four. What is the number?

6. A 12-inch submarine sandwich is cut into two pieces. The first piece is half as long as the second piece. How long are the pieces?

7. Solve. Kari purchased three pairs of shoes. The first pair was two times the cost of the second pair. The third pair was $40 less than the second pair. Her total purchase was $280. How much did the first pair of shoes cost?

8. The length of the second side of a triangle is twice that of the first. The third side is 5 cm less than the second. The perimeter of the triangle measures 40 cm. Find the length of each side.

ANSWERS

1. $\frac{x}{7} + 25$

2. $x(x + 1) = 30$

3. $y + 20$

4. $1\,100 - (F + G + E + S)$

5. The number is 3.5

6. The first piece is 4 inches long and the second piece is 8 inches long.

7. The first pair of shoes cost $160

8. The first side measures 9 cm, the second measures 18 cm, and the third measures 13 cm.

CHAPTER CHECK-UP

1. What is the perimeter of the following rectangle?

$2a + b + c$ (left side)

$5a + 2b$ (bottom)

   (1) $14a + 6b + 2c$
   (2) $7a + 3b + c$
   (3) $14a - 6b - 2c$
   (4) $7a^2 + 3b^2 + c^2$
   (5) $(14a)(6b)(2c)$

2. Evaluate $(x^2 - 4)(2x - y)$ when $x = -3$ and $y = 4$.

   (1) 130
   (2) 100
   (3) −130
   (4) −50
   (5) 50

3. Given the equation $-2(3x - 6) = 2x + 4$, solve for x.
   (1) $x = 2$
   (2) $x = -1$
   (3) $x = 1$
   (4) $x = 3$
   (5) $x = -4$

4. Given the inequality $8y - 32 \geq 64$, solve for y.
   (1) $y \geq 2$
   (2) $y \geq 12$
   (3) $y \leq 12$
   (4) $y \geq 6$
   (5) $y \leq 6$

5. Moriah and Quinn go to a movie theatre. Each child pays x dollars for admission. A small popcorn costs y dollars and a medium soft drink costs z dollars. Moriah purchases a small popcorn and a medium drink. Quinn purchases a medium drink. Which of the following expressions represents the total of what both children spent?

   (1) $\dfrac{2x + 2y + 2z}{2}$
   (2) $(x)(y)(z)$
   (3) $x + y + z$
   (4) $2(x + y + z)$
   (5) $2x + y + 2z$

6. Kim and Kari earn money delivering papers. If Kim earns twice as much as Kari and the two girls earn a total of $84, how much did Kari earn?

   (1) $56
   (2) $28
   (3) $42
   (4) $21
   (5) Not enough information is given.

7. A rug has a perimeter of 15 metres. The length is 1.5 metres more than the width. Find the dimensions of the rug.
   (1) The width is 6.75 m; the length is 8.25 m
   (2) The width is 4.5 m; the length is 3 m
   (3) The width is 3 m; the length is 4.5 m
   (4) The width is 4 m; the length is 10 m
   (5) Not enough information is given.

8. A room is l m long, w m wide, and h m high. Which of the following expressions represents the number of square metres of wallpaper needed to paper the four walls of the room?

   (1) $\frac{1}{2}(lh) + \frac{1}{2}(wh)$
   (2) $4(l + w + h)$
   (3) $(lwh) \div 2$
   (4) $2(lwh)$
   (5) $2(lh) + 2(wh)$.

ANSWERS

1. **(1)** Collect like terms. $14a + 6b + 2c$

2. **(4)** $(x^2 - 4)(2x - y) = ((-3)^2 - 4)(2(-3) - (4)) = (9 - 4)(-6 - 4) = (5)(-10) = -50$

3. **(3)** $-2(3x - 6) = (2x + 4)$
    $$-6x + 12 = 2x + 4$$
    $$-6x - 2x = 4 - 12$$
    $$\frac{-8x}{-8} = \frac{-8}{-8}$$
    $$x = 1$$

4. **(2)** $8y - 32 \geq 64$
    $$8y \geq 64 + 32$$
    $$\frac{8y}{8} \geq \frac{96}{8}$$
    $$y \geq 12$$

5. **(5)** $2x + y + 2z$

6. **(2)** $x + 2x = 84$
    $$3x = 84$$
    $$\frac{3x}{3} = \frac{84}{3} \quad \text{Kari earns \$28 and Kim earns 2(\$28) = \$56.}$$
    $$x = 28$$

7. **(3)** $2(x) + 2(x + 1.5) = 15$
    $$2x + 2x + 3 = 15$$
    $$4x = 15 - 3 \quad \text{Width is 3m, length is 3m +1.5m = 4.5 m.}$$
    $$\frac{4x}{4} = \frac{12}{4}$$
    $$x = 3$$

8. **(5)** To wallpaper all four walls, you will need the area of each wall. The area of the longer walls will = (Length)(Height). The area of the two end walls will equal (Width)(Height). There are two long walls and two end walls. $A = 2(lh) + 2(wh)$

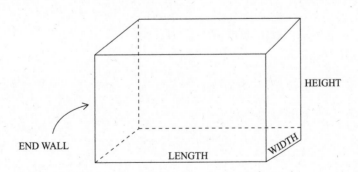

END WALL

HEIGHT

LENGTH

WIDTH

Quadratics

31

THINK ABOUT IT

The path that an emergency flare travels through the air can be mathematically described by the quadratic function. As the following graph illustrates, a quadratic equation produces a parabolic shape. You can visualize a flare traveling in a similar parabolic path where h represents the height the flare reaches over a period of time (t).

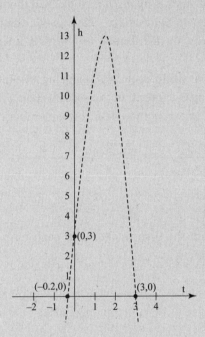

IN THIS CHAPTER

After completing this chapter, you will be able to

→ **WRITE QUADRATIC EXPRESSIONS**

→ **FACTOR QUADRATIC EXPRESSIONS**

→ **SOLVE QUADRATIC EQUATIONS**

QUADRATIC EXPRESSIONS

A quadratic expression contains a variable that is raised to the power of two, or *squared*. Although not tested extensively on the GED exam, quadratic equations occur in many real-world situations and it is important that you are familiar with quadratic expressions and equations on a basic level.

CHALLENGE EXERCISE

The shape of a satellite dish is parabolic and the curve can be described with a quadratic expression. What other objects travel in a parabolic path? Research quadratics and parabolas online. Find at least three more common objects that travel in a path that can be described with a quadratic expression.

Multiplying Factors with Two Terms

Recall in the previous chapter that the first step to complete when solving linear equations was to remove brackets. You did this by *distributing across* the brackets, or by completing a process of multiplication. Remember that $2(x - 12)$ was equivalent to $2x - 24$.

This multiplication process, or distributive property, is followed no matter how many terms are being combined.

When there are two terms within each bracket being combined, every term in the first bracket must be multiplied by every term in the second. This process is sometimes referred to as "FOIL". FOIL is simply an acronym to help you remember the steps involved:

➡ **EXAMPLE 1** _____

Multiply $(x + 10)(x - 8)$

Solution

a. Multiply each term within the first bracket with each term in the second using FOIL. You will create four products.

F	First	$(x + 10)(x - 8)$	$(x)(x) = x^2$
O	Outside	$(x + 10)(x - 8)$	$(x)(-8) = -8x$
I	Inside	$(x + 10)(x - 8)$	$(+10)(x) = +10x$
L	Last	$(x + 10)(x - 8)$	$(+10)(-8) = -80$

b. Collect like terms.

$$x^2 - 8x + 10x - 80 =$$
$$x^2 + 2x - 80$$

c. The result is $x^2 + 2x - 80$

➥ EXAMPLE 2 _____

Multiply $(x-4)(x-3)$

Solution

a. Multiply each term within the first bracket with each term in the second bracket.

F	First	$(x-4)(x-3)$	$(x)(x) = x^2$
O	Outside	$(x-4)(x-3)$	$(x)(-3) = -3x$
I	Inside	$(x-4)(x-3)$	$(-4)(x) = -4x$
L	Last	$(x-4)(x-3)$	$(-4)(-3) = +12$

b. Collect like terms.

$x^2 - 3x - 4x + 12 =$
$x^2 - 7x + 12$

c. The result is $x^2 - 7x + 12$

➥ EXAMPLE 3 _____

Multiply $(x-5)(x+5)$

Solution

a. $(x-5)(x+5) = x^2 + 5x - 5x - 25$

b. Collect like terms.

$x^2 - 5x - 5x - 25 =$
$x^2 - 25$

c. The result is $x^2 - 25$

All three examples resulted in answers that are quadratic expressions. The variable is raised to the power of two. In other words, the variable is squared.

PRACTICE

1. Multiply and simplify.
    a. $(x-3)(x+2)$
    b. $(x+10)(x+5)$
    c. $(x-3)(x-3)$
    d. $(x+4)(x-7)$
    e. $(x-12)(x+13)$

ANSWERS

1. a. $x^2 - 1x - 6$
    b. $x^2 + 15x + 50$
    c. $x^2 - 6x + 9$
    d. $x^2 - 3x - 28$
    e. $x^2 + x - 156$

FACTORING

Factoring is the reverse process of distribution. Rather than multiplying to combine, you divide to break terms down into lower terms. For example, you can factor the value 12 as 2×6 or 3×4. You use factoring to help simplify expressions and it can also be used to help solve quadratic equations.

 EXAMPLE 1 _____

Factor $7x - 49$

Solution

There are two terms in the expression $7x - 49$

Ask yourself, "What divides evenly into both terms?"

Both terms are divisible by 7. 7 is called the common factor.

$$\frac{7x - 49}{7} = 7(x - 7)$$

Rather than distributing the 7 across the bracket through a process of multiplication, 7 was "removed" from the expression through division. The common factor of 7 was placed in front of the bracket in order for the expression to remain equivalent.

 EXAMPLE 2 _____

Factor $3x^2 - 12x$

Solution

There are two terms in the expression $3x^2 - 12x$.

Ask yourself, "What divides evenly into both terms?"

Both terms are divisible by 3 and also by x. $3x$ is the common factor.

$$\frac{3x^2 - 12x}{3x} = 3x(x - 4)$$

The common factor, $3x$, was placed in front of the bracket and each term in the expression was divided by $3x$.

 EXAMPLE 3 _____

Factor $x^2 + 6x + 8$

Solution

This is more difficult to factor. There is not a common factor. That is, there is no number or variable that divides evenly into all three terms. Rather, you must follow a process which is the reverse of FOIL.

Ask yourself, "What two numbers **multiply** to 8 (the third term) and **add** to 6 (the value in front of x)?"

The possible combination of factors for 8 are:

$$1 \times 8 \qquad\qquad 1 + 8 = 9$$
$$2 \times 4 \qquad\qquad 2 + 4 = 6$$

TIP

**Factoring:
The process of
finding what
to multiply
together to get
an expression.**

The values that multiply to 8 and add to 6 are 2 and 4.

$$x^2 + 6x + 8 = (x + 4)(x + 2)$$

You can check factoring by FOILing. $(x + 4)(x + 2) = x^2 + 4x + 2x + 8 = x^2 + 6x + 8$

➡ EXAMPLE 4

Factor $x^2 - 3x - 40$

Solution

Ask yourself, "What two numbers multiply to –40 and add to –3?"

There are many combinations of factors that multiply to –40. They are:

-1×40	$-1 + 40 = 39$
-2×20	$-2 + 20 = 18$
-4×10	$-4 + 10 = 6$
-5×8	$-5 + 8 = 3$
1×-40	$1 + -40 = -39$
2×-20	$2 + -20 = -18$
4×-10	$4 + -10 = -6$
5×-8	$5 + -8 = -3$

Whew! It can take a long time but it is important to try all combinations until you find one that works. The values that multiply to –40 and add to –3 are 5 and –8.

$$x^2 - 3x - 40$$
$$(x + 5)(x - 8)$$

You can check factoring by FOILing. $(x + 5)(x - 8) = x^2 + 5x - 8x - 40 = x^2 - 3x - 40$

PRACTICE

1. Factor the following algebraic expressions.
   a. $15x - 20$
   b. $6x^2 - 3x$
   c. $x^2 + 7x + 12$
   d. $x^2 - 5x + 6$
   e. $x^2 - x - 72$
   f. $x^2 - 36$
   g. $x^2 - 14x + 40$
   h. $x^2 + 16x + 64$

ANSWERS

1. a. $5(3x - 4)$
   b. $3x(2x - 1)$
   c. $(x + 4)(x + 3)$
   d. $(x - 2)(x - 3)$
   e. $(x - 9)(x + 8)$
   f. $(x - 6)(x + 6)$
   g. $(x - 4)(x - 10)$
   h. $(x + 8)(x + 8)$

SOLVING QUADRATIC EQUATIONS

There are several different methods to solve quadratic equations. You will only consider the method of factoring at this time.

Remember that quadratic expressions have a variable that is squared. When an equation contains a quadratic expression, the squared variable indicates that there can be up to 2 unique solutions. Just as the goal in solving linear equations was to find a value for the variable that would make the equation true (and balanced), the goal in solving quadratic equations is to find the value or values that will make the equation true.

➡ EXAMPLE 1

Solve $x^2 + 5x = 14$

Solution

a. **Set the equation equal to zero.** Move all terms to one side of the equation and write the expression in descending order. The squared term is always first, the linear term second and the constant last.

$$x^2 + 5x = 14$$
$$x^2 + 5x - 14 = 0$$

b. **Factor the quadratic expression.** What two numbers multiply to –14 and add to 5?

$$x^2 + 5x - 14 = 0$$
$$(x + 7)(x - 2) = 0$$

c. **Set each factor equal to zero and solve for the variable.** This step relies on the zero principle. If two factors multiply to zero, then either the first or the second factor must itself equal zero.

$$(x + 7) = 0$$
$$x = -7 \text{ and}$$
$$(x - 2) = 0$$
$$x = 2$$

d. **Check.** Both numbers should check into the original equation.

$$x^2 + 5x = 14 \qquad\qquad x^2 + 5x = 14$$
$$(-7)^2 + 5(-7) = 14 \qquad (2)^2 + 5(2) = 14$$
$$49 - 35 = 14 \qquad\qquad 4 + 10 = 14$$

The solutions are –7 and 2.

➡ EXAMPLE 2

Solve $x^2 - 4x = -4$

Solution

a. **Set the equation equal to zero.**

$$x^2 - 4x = -4$$
$$x^2 - 4x + 4 = 0$$

b. **Factor the quadratic expression**. What two numbers multiply to +4 and add to –4?

$$x^2 - 4x + 4 = 0$$
$$(x-2)(x-2) = 0$$

c. **Set each factor equal to zero and solve for the variable**.

$$(x-2) = 0$$
$$x = 2 \text{ and}$$
$$(x-2) = 0$$
$$x = 2$$

d. **Check**. Notice that both numbers are exactly the same. Only check once.

$$x^2 - 4x = -4$$
$$(2)^2 - 4(2) = -4$$
$$4 - 8 = -4$$

The solution is 2.

PRACTICE

1. Solve for x.

   a. $x^2 + 6x + 8 = 0$
   b. $x^2 - 2x - 15 = 0$
   c. $x^2 + 7x = -12$

   d. $x^2 - 49 = 0$
   e. $x^2 - 7x = 30$

ANSWERS

1. a. $x = -4, x = -2$
   b. $x = 5, x = -3$
   c. $x = -4, x = -3$

   d. $x = -7, x = 7$
   e. $x = 10, x = -3$

CHALLENGE EXERCISE

Another strategy for solving quadratic equations is by using a formula. Solve by substituting into the Quadratic Formula: $x = \dfrac{-b \pm \sqrt{b^2 - 4ac}}{2a}$, where a is the coefficient of the square (x^2) term, b is the coefficient of the linear (x) term, and c is the constant. Solve again the five equations above using the quadratic formula and fully simplify. The $\pm$ symbol in front of the radical means that one answer will be calculated by adding the perfect square and the second answer will be calculated by subtracting the perfect square. If calculated correctly, the answers will be exactly the same as those you found by factoring.

WORKING BACKWARDS

As the steps involved in solving quadratic equations are quite time-consuming, it may sometimes be easier to *work backwards* when given a multiple-choice question. You can simply substitute the numbers given back into the equations to see if they check. Essentially, you are just completing step d from the process described above.

➡ **EXAMPLE** _____

What are the possible values for x if $x^2 - 8x = 20$?
(1) $x = 4, x = 5$
(2) $x = -2, x = -10$
(3) $x = 1, x = 20$
(4) $x = 10, x = -2$
(5) $x = -5, x = -4$

Solution

If one number in the pair fails, the option is not correct. It is often easier to substitute positive values into the equation, so begin with them where possible.

Option 1: $(4)^2 - 8(4) = 20$?
$16 - 32 \neq 20$ False

Option 2: $(-2)^2 - 8(-2) = 20$?
$4 + 16 = 20$ True. This is correct, so test the other number in the pair.

Option 3: $(-10)^2 - 8(-10) = 20$?
$100 + 80 \neq 20$ False. This number did not work so option (2) is not the correct answer. However, you now know that -2 works, so look for another pair with that answer.

Option 4: $(-10)^2 - 8(10) = 20$?
$100 - 80 = 20$ True. This is correct and you know that $x = -2$ is also correct.
                   The correct answer is (4)

PRACTICE

1. What are the possible values for x if $x^2 + 11x + 24 = 0$?
    (1) $x = 2, x = 12$
    (2) $x = 3, x = 8$
    (3) $x = -3, x = -8$
    (4) $x = -4, x = -6$
    (5) $x = 1, x = 24$

2. In the equation $2x^2 + 5x = 12$, what is one possible value for x?

    (1) $x = 3$

    (2) $x = 1$

    (3) $x = 2$

    (4) $x = -1$

    (5) $x = -4$

3. In the equation $4x^2 = 25$, what is one possible value for x?

    (1) $x = 4$

    (2) $x = 2.5$

    (3) $x = 5$

    (4) $x = -1.5$

    (5) $x = -2$

ANSWERS

1. (3)
2. (5)
3. (2)

CHAPTER CHECK-UP

1. Multiply and simplify: $(x - 12)(x + 4)$

    (1) $x^2 + 16x + 48$

    (2) $x^2 + 10x + 8$

    (3) $x^2 - 12x + 4$

    (4) $x^2 - 8x - 48$

    (5) $x^2 + 4x - 12$

2. Factor $x^2 - 10x - 39$.

    (1) $(x - 10)(x - 39)$

    (2) $(x - 5)(x - 5)$

    (3) $(x - 13)(x + 3)$

    (4) $(x - 1)(x + 39)$

    (5) $(x + 39)(x + 1)$

3. Solve for x given $x^2 - 9x + 20 = 0$.

    (1) $x = 2$, $x = 10$

    (2) $x = 1$, $x = 20$

    (3) $x = -2$, $x = -7$

    (4) $x = -8$, $x = -1$

    (5) $x = 4$, $x = 5$

4. In the equation $2x^2 + x - 10 = 0$, what is one possible value for x?
   (1) $x = 1$
   (2) $x = 4$
   (3) $x = -3$
   (4) $x = 2$
   (5) $x = 0$

5. Which of the following is an algebraic expression that represents the area of the following rectangle?

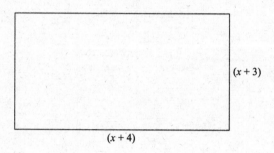

   (1) $x^2 + 2x + 5$
   (2) $x^2 + 7x + 12$
   (3) $x^2 - 5x + 2$
   (4) $x^2 + 3x + 10$
   (5) $x^2 + 10x - 7$

ANSWERS

1. **(4)** $(x - 12)(x + 4) = x^2 + 4x - 12x - 48 = x^2 - 8x - 48$

2. **(3)** $x^2 - 10x - 39 = (x - 13)(x + 3)$ You can check this answer by FOILing

3. **(5)** Solve.

   $x^2 - 9x + 20 = 0$
   $(x - 4)(x - 5) = 0$
   $x - 4 = 0$ and $x - 5 = 0$
   $x = 4$ and $x = 5$

4. **(4)** $2x^2 + x - 10 = 0$
   $2(2)^2 + 2 - 10 = 0$ 2 is the only value that makes the equation true.
   $2(4) + 2 - 10 = 0$
   $8 + 2 - 10 = 0$

5. **(2)** Multiply the length by the width. $(x + 3)(x + 4) = x^2 + 4x + 3x + 12 = x^2 + 7x + 12$

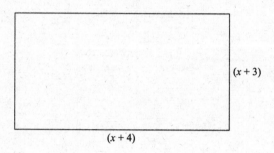

Coordinate Graphs

32

THINK ABOUT IT

There is a familiar saying that states a *picture is worth a thousand words*. This saying certainly rings true with mathematical graphs. You were first introduced to graphs in Chapter 29 and it was quickly apparent that graphs are valuable because they provide a visual representation of what can be quite complicated data. In fact, algebraic problems can be solved graphically and graphs can also be used to validate and check problems that have been solved algebraically.

IN THIS CHAPTER

After completing this chapter, you will be able to

→ **LOCATE POINTS ON A COORDINATE GRAPH**

→ **DETERMINE THE DISTANCE BETWEEN POINTS**

→ **GRAPH LINEAR EQUATIONS USING A TABLE OF VALUES**

→ **DETERMINE THE SLOPE OF A LINE**

→ **TRANSLATE UNIT RATES**

→ **FIND *X*- AND *Y*-INTERCEPTS**

→ **DETERMINE THE EQUATION OF A LINE**

GRAPHING POINTS ON A COORDINATE GRID

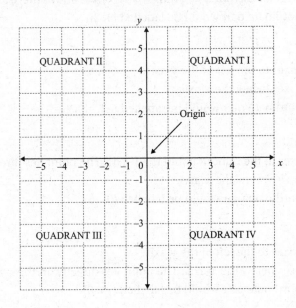

The figure above is called a Cartesian coordinate system. The system consists of two real number lines intersecting through zero at right angles. The horizontal number line is the *x-axis* and the vertical number line is the *y-axis*. As labelled above, the point of intersection is referred to as the *origin*.

Every point in this system can be labelled as an ordered pair of coordinates: (*x*-coordinate, *y*-coordinate).

➡ **EXAMPLE** _____

Given the graph below, name the coordinate pair for points *A*, *B*, *C* and *D*.

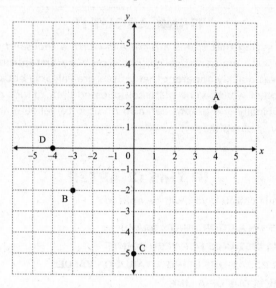

TIP

Coordinate pairs are always listed alphabetically (x,y)

Solution

Point *A*:

1. The first point in the coordinate pair is the *x*-coordinate. It measures how far right or left of the *y*-axis the point is. Point *A* is **+4** boxes to the right of the *y*-axis.
2. The second point in the coordinate pair is the *y*-coordinate. It measures how far up or down from the *x*-axis the point is. Point *A* is **+2** boxes above the *x*-axis.
3. Point *A* as a coordinate pair would be labelled (4, 2).

Point *B*:

1. Point *B* is **–3** boxes to the left of the *y*-axis.
2. Point *B* is **–2** boxes below the *x*-axis.
3. Point *B* as a coordinate pair would be labelled (–3, –2).

Point *C*:

1. Point *C* is **0** boxes to the right or left of the *y*-axis. The point lies directly on the *y*-axis.
2. Point *C* is **–5** boxes below the *x*-axis.
3. Point *C* as a coordinate pair would be labelled (0, –5).

Point *D*:

1. Point *D* is **–4** boxes to the left of the *y*-axis.
2. Point *D* is **0** boxes below the *x*-axis. The point lies directly on the *x*-axis.
3. Point *D* as a coordinate pair would be labelled (–4, 0).

PRACTICE

1. Name the coordinates of the five points labelled on the Cartesian grid below.

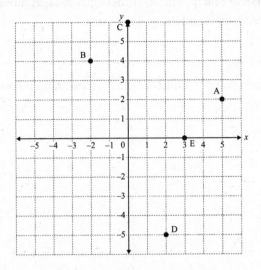

ANSWERS

1. Point A: (5, 2)
2. Point B: (–2, 4)
3. Point C: (0, 6)
4. Point D: (2, –5)
5. Point E: (3, 0)

FINDING THE DISTANCE BETWEEN POINTS

Finding the distance between points is a very simple operation. It is essentially the same as measuring the distance between points using a ruler; however, the "ruler" you use in these situations are the grid lines marked on the graph. If no lines are shown, it is not much more difficult. Instead you will visualize lines and use the values in the coordinate pairs to determine distance.

➡ **EXAMPLE 1** _____

Find the distance between Points *A* and *B* labelled in the graph below.

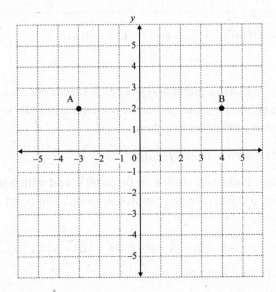

Solution

Both Point A and Point B lay on the same parallel line. Simply begin on Point A and count the boxes that you move right to reach Point B. From $(-3, 2)$ to $(4, 2)$ move 7 boxes right.

The distance between Point A and Point B is 7 units.

➡ EXAMPLE 2 _____

Find the distance between Points C and D labelled in the graph below.

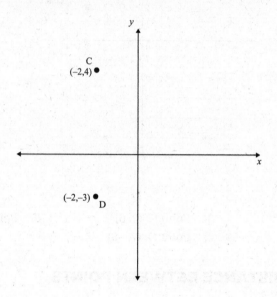

Solution

The grid lines no longer exist in this example, but we can see that Point C and Point D lay on the same vertical line. The fact that the x-coordinates are the same confirms this.

To determine the distance, focus on the y-coordinates and find the difference between the values. The y-coordinate for Point C is $+4$. The y coordinate for Point D is -3. The difference in these values can be determined through subtraction: $4 - (-3) = 4 + 3 = 7$.

The distance between Point C and Point D is 7 units.

➡ EXAMPLE 3 _____

Find the distance between point A $(5, 2)$ and point B $(-3, -4)$.

Solution

In this example, you do not have a graph and you can see from the coordinates given that the numbers do not sit on either the same vertical or horizontal line. To solve this problem, use a formula that is provided on the formula sheet:

$$\text{Distance between points} = \sqrt{(x_2 - x_1)^2 + (y_2 - y_1)^2}$$

It does not matter which point you choose to be point 1 and which one you choose to be point 2. In this example, you will consider point A as point 1 and point B as point 2.

Substitute and simplify:

$$\sqrt{(-3-5)^2 + (-4-2)^2} = \sqrt{(-8)^2 + (-6)^2} = \sqrt{64+36} = \sqrt{100} = 10$$

The distance between point A and point B is 10 units.

PRACTICE

1. Using the graph below, find the distance between the following set of points.

   a. *A* and *B*   c. *B* and *C*

   b. *C* and *D*   d. *D* and *A*

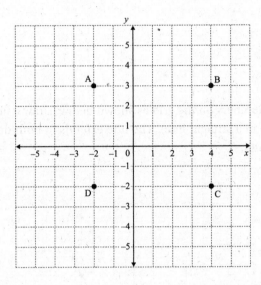

2. Determine the distance between Point *M* (4, 6) and Point *N* (–2, 1). Round to one decimal place.

ANSWERS

1. a. 6   b. 6   c. 5   d. 5
2. 7.8 units

GRAPHING LINEAR EQUATIONS

An equation with two variables that are raised to a power of 1, such as *x* and *y*, are called linear equations. If the variable is raised to a power other than 1, the line will not be straight and the function is not linear (remember the parabolic shape introduced in the previous chapter?). There are a number of different ways of graphing a linear equation. You will explore the method that relies on a table of values.

 **EXAMPLE 1** _____

Graph $y = 2x - 4$

Solution

1. Create a table of values by choosing numbers for *x*. Use a minimum of three values. In this example, the numbers are given.

X	Y
3	
1	
–1	

TIP

To draw a line, you only need two points but it is recommended that you use a minimum of three for accuracy.

2. Substitute each *x* value into the equation given and simplify for *y*. Complete the chart.

If $x = 3$ $y = 2(3) - 4$ $y = 2$

If $x = 1$ $y = 2(1) - 4$ $y = -2$

If $x = -1$ $y = 2(-1) - 4$ $y = -6$

X	Y
3	2
1	-2
-1	-6

3. Plot the pairs of numbers on the grid as shown below. Draw a line through them (they should all line up in a straight line). The line extends in both directions so arrows are placed on either end.

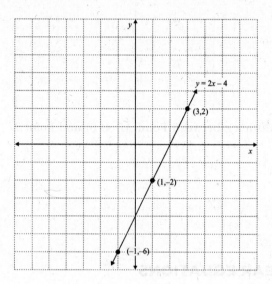

➡ **EXAMPLE 2**

Graph $y = -1x + 3$

Solution

1. The values for *x* are given; however, you can choose any three numbers that would fit on the grid.

X	Y
2	
0	
-2	

2. Substitute each *x* value into the equation given and simplify for *y*. Complete the chart

If $x = 2$ $y = -1(2) + 3$ $y = 1$

If $x = 0$ $y = -1(0) + 3$ $y = 3$

If $x = -2$ $y = -1(-2) + 3$ $y = 5$

X	Y
2	1
0	3
−2	5

3. Plot the pairs of numbers and draw a line through them, extending the line in both directions.

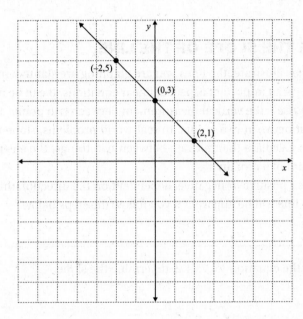

PRACTICE

Graph the following three equations on the grids provided.

  a. $y = 2x - 2$ b. $y = -2x + 1$ c. $y = \dfrac{1}{2}x - 1$

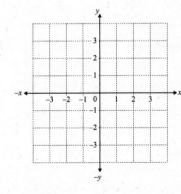 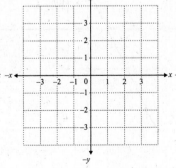 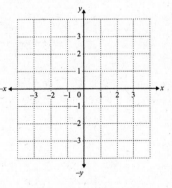

ANSWERS

a. $y = 2x - 2$

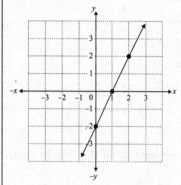

b. $y = -2x + 1$

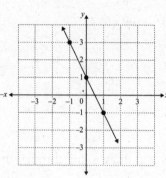

c. $y = \frac{1}{2}x - 1$

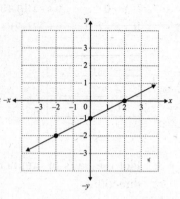

DETERMINING THE SLOPE OF THE LINE

TIP

slope = $\dfrac{\text{rise}}{\text{run}}$

As these last examples illustrate, the lines you are graphing are slanted, making a *slope*. The steepness of this line is an important aspect of linear equations. It can be measured as a ratio of rise to run, where *rise* is the vertical measurement between two points and *run* is the horizontal measurement between two points. In real-world problems, slope is very meaningful and is often used to calculate the unit rate between two things, the steepness of a flight of stairs or even the slant of a roof line.

Slope can be either positive or negative, dependent on the direction that the line is pointing. The sign on the line will be apparent if you follow the steps below.

➡ **EXAMPLE 1** _____

Given the graph for the equation $y = 2x + 2$, determine the slope.

Solution

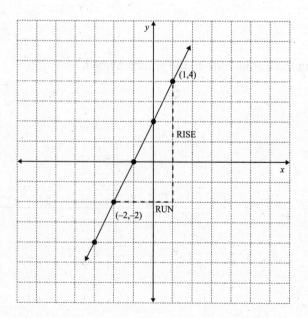

Any two points can be chosen to determine slope. In this example, they are (1, 4) and (–2,–2).
   Visually, move right from (–2,–2) until you are directly below (1, 4). The **run** is 3 units.
   Now, move up from this position until you reach (1, 4). The **rise** is 6 units.

$$\text{slope} = \frac{rise}{run} = \frac{6}{3} = +2$$

Notice that the value in front of x in the original equation is also +2.

➡ EXAMPLE 2

Determine the slope for a line that passes through points A (–3,4) and B (2, –1).

Solution

There is no graph provided in this example and there is no need to create one. You can also find slope using a simple formula. This formula is provided for you on the formula sheet.

$$\text{Slope } (m) = \frac{y_2 - y_1}{x_2 - x_1} \quad \text{given points } (x_1, y_1) \text{ and } (x_2, y_2)$$

It does not matter which point you use as the first or second but you must be consistent in your choice when you substitute into the formula. In the calculation below, Point *A* was assigned one and Point *B* was two.
   Substitute into the formula and simplify.

$$\text{Slope } (m) = \frac{-1-(4)}{2-(-3)} = \frac{-5}{5} = -1$$

TIP

It is common practice to assign the variable *m* for the slope of a line.

PRACTICE

1. Given the graph below, determine the slope of the line.

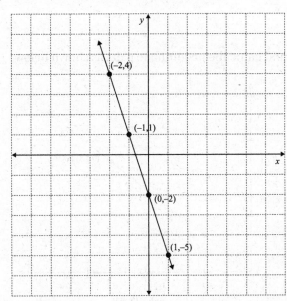

2. Find the slope of the lines that passes through the following pair of points on a graph.
    a.   (–3, 4) and (3, –2)
    b.   (–5, –1) and (5, 5)
    c.   (–1, 4) and (3, –5)
    d.   (–3, –2) and (4, 5)

TIP

The slope of
a perfectly
horizontal line is
equal to zero.

ANSWERS

1. $m = -3$
2. a. $m = -1$ b. $m = \frac{3}{5}$ c. $m = \frac{-9}{4}$ d. $m = +1$

APPLICATIONS OF SLOPE

When the line graphed represents real-world quantities, the slope can be interpreted as a unit rate (refer back to Chapter 26). Study the example below.

➡ **EXAMPLE** _____

The graph represents the distance a jogger ran over a period of time. Determine the jogger's speed in km/hr.

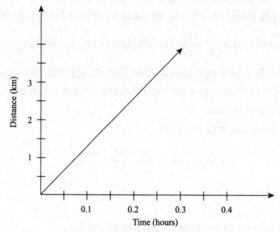

Solution

a.   Plot two points and name their coordinate pairs as shown below.

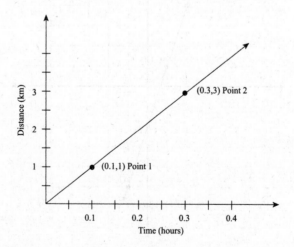

b.   Calculate slope using $(m) = \dfrac{y_2 - y_1}{x_2 - x_1} = \dfrac{3 - (1)}{0.3 - (0.1)} = \dfrac{2}{0.2} = 10$ km/hr

PRACTICE

1. Given the graph below, determine the unit rate (beats/minute).

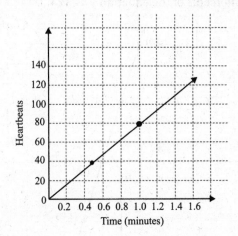

2. Given the graph below, determine the unit rate (km/hour).

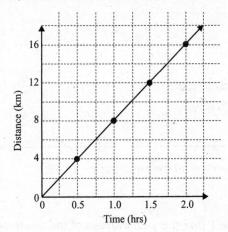

ANSWERS

1. 80 beats/minute.
2. 8 km/hr

CHALLENGE EXERCISE

Collect data and plot a graph to determine the rate of your movement per minute. Walk, run, ride a bike, or drive a car. Every 15 minutes, record how far you have gone. Do this over a period of 1½ hours. You will have 6 data points in the format (time, distance). Plot these points and calculate the slope, which can then be expressed as a unit rate.

THE *X*- AND *Y*-INTERCEPTS OF A LINE

The *x*-intercept of a line is the point where the graph crosses the *x*-axis. The *y*-intercept of a line is the point where the graph crosses the *y*-axis. These points can be named visually if a graph is provided; however, they can also be determined algebraically.

➡ **EXAMPLE 1**

Determine the x- and y-intercepts of the equation $y = -3x + 3$.

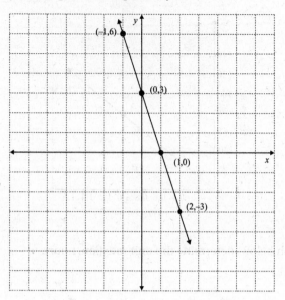

Solution

The x-intercept, as labelled, is $(1, 0)$.

The y-intercept, as labelled, is $(0, 3)$.

➡ **EXAMPLE 2**

Determine the x and y-intercepts of the equation $y = 4x - 5$.

Solution

Did you notice in example 1 that the y-coordinate of the x-intercept is 0? This will always be the case as the intercept occurs where the line crosses the x-axis. To solve algebraically, substitute 0 for y and solve for x:

$$y = 4x - 5$$
$$0 = 4x - 5$$
$$\frac{5}{4} = \frac{4x}{4}$$
$$1.25 = x$$

The x-intercept is $(1.25, 0)$

Did you notice in example 1 that the x-coordinate of the y-intercept is 0? This will always be the case as the intercept occurs where the line crosses the y-axis. To solve algebraically, substitute 0 for x and solve for y:

$$y = 4x - 5$$
$$y = 4(0) - 5$$
$$y = 0 - 5$$
$$y = -5$$

The y-intercept is $(0, -5)$

PRACTICE

1. Find the x- and y-intercepts for the following equations.
   a. $y = -3x + 2$
   b. $y = 4x + 7$
   c. $y = -\frac{1}{2}x - 1$
   d. $y = x - 5$
   e. $y = -8x + 10$

ANSWERS

1. Find the x- and y-intercepts for the following equations.
   a. x-intercept: $(\frac{2}{3}, 0)$ y-intercept: $(0, 2)$
   b. x-intercept: $(-1.75, 0)$ y-intercept: $(0, 7)$
   c. x-intercept: $(-2, 0)$ y-intercept: $(0, -1)$
   d. x-intercept: $(5, 0)$ y-intercept: $(0, -5)$
   e. x-intercept: $(1.25, 0)$ y-intercept: $(0, 10)$

DETERMINING THE EQUATION OF THE LINE

Linear equations can be written in many formats; however, the most convenient form for graphing purposes and for understanding slope and intercepts is the slope-intercept equation form:

$y = mx + b$, where m = the slope of the line and the point $(0, b)$ is the y-intercept.

➡ EXAMPLE 1 _____

Determine the slope and y-intercept of the equation $y = -2x + 4$.

Solution

As the equation is already written in the slope-intercept form, slope and y-intercept can be determined without calculation.

Slope $(m) = -2$ (The coefficient of x)
y-intercept = $(0, 4)$ (The constant, b, at the end of the equation)

➡ EXAMPLE 2 _____

What is the slope and y-intercept for $y = -\frac{2}{3}x - 11$?

Solution

Slope $(m) = -\frac{2}{3}$ (The coefficient of x)

y-intercept = $(0, -11)$ (The constant, b, at the end of the equation)

⇨ EXAMPLE 3 _____

Determine the slope and *y*-intercept for $3x + y = 6$.

Solution

In this example, the equation is not already written in the slope-intercept form. Simply rearrange the equation.

> $3x + y = 6$
> $y = -3x + 6$
> Slope $(m) = -3$ (The coefficient of *x*)
> *y*-intercept $= (0, +6)$ (The constant, *b*, at the end of the equation)

⇨ EXAMPLE 4 _____

Given the following graph, determine the slope, the *y*-intercept and the equation of the line.

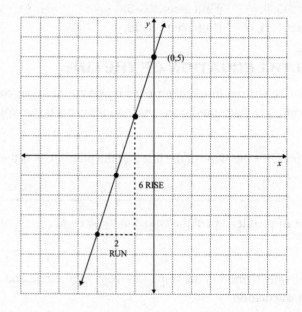

Solution

You work backwards with this type of question. Visually, you can see the *y*-intercept and using the slope formula we can calculate the slope. After determining these values, you simply back-substitute into the slope-intercept equation: $y = mx + b$

> The *y*-intercept is $(0, 5)$
> The slope $= +3$
> The equation of the line is $y = 3x + 5$

PRACTICE

1. Find the slope and y-intercept for the following equations.

    a. $y = 2.5x + 4.5$

    b. $y = -4x - 7$

    c. $y = -\frac{1}{2}x - \frac{1}{5}$

    d. $y - 4x = 12$

    e. $5x - 10 + y = 0$

2. Find the equation of the line graphed on the grid below.

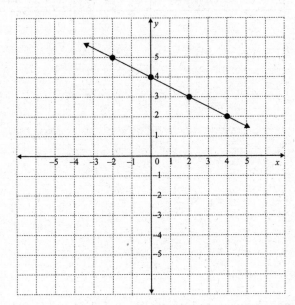

ANSWERS

1. a. $m = 2.5$; y-intercept $(0, 4.5)$

    b. $m = -4$; y-intercept $(0, -7)$

    c. $m = -\frac{1}{2}$; y-intercept $(0, -\frac{1}{5})$

    d. $y - 4x = 12$ $\qquad m = 4$; y-intercept $(0, 12)$
        $y = 4x + 12$

    e. $5x - 10 + y = 0$ $\quad m = -5$; y-intercept $(0, 10)$
        $y = -5x + 10$

2. $y = -\frac{1}{2}x + 4$

CHAPTER CHECK-UP

1. Which of the following is the y-intercept of a line drawn through *M* and *N*?

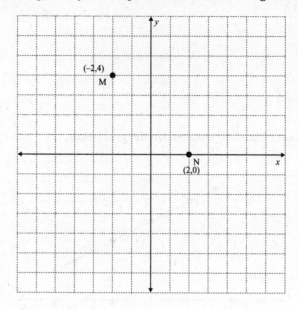

(1) (0, –2)

(2) (0, 2)

(3) (0, 3)

(4) $(0, \frac{1}{2})$

(5) (2, 0)

2. What is the distance between two points labelled (2, 5) and (5, 9)?

(1) 21 units

(2) 9 units

(3) 4 units

(4) 5 units

(5) 7 units

3. What is the slope of a line that passes through (–1, –3) and (2, 4)?

(1) $m = \frac{3}{7}$

(2) $m = \frac{7}{3}$

(3) $m = \frac{1}{2}$

(4) $m = \frac{-4}{3}$

(5) $m = \frac{-1}{4}$

4. Robyn graphed three points, as shown on the grid below. The three points form the corners of a rectangle. What are the coordinates of the fourth point required to complete this rectangle?

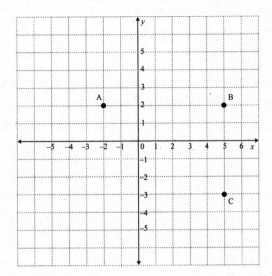

(1) (3, 2)

(2) (−3, 2)

(3) (2, 3)

(4) (−2, −3)

(5) (2, −3)

5. What is the equation of the line shown on the graph below?

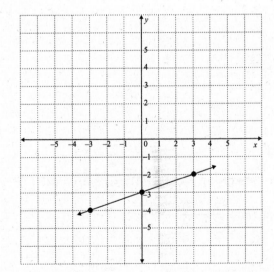

(1) $y = \frac{1}{3}x - 3$

(2) $y = -3x + 1$

(3) $y = 2x - 3$

(4) $y = \frac{4}{3}x + 2$

(5) $y = 4x + 7$

6. Determine the slope of the line given the equation $y + 4x + 7 = 0$.
   (1) $m = 7$
   (2) $m = 4$
   (3) $m = -4$
   (4) $m = -7$
   (5) $m = 1$

7. The following graph relates the consumption of gasoline to the distance travelled by the car. What is the unit rate (km/L) for this vehicle?

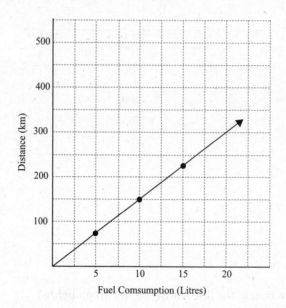

   (1) 23 km/L
   (2) 21 km/L
   (3) 20 km/L
   (4) 18 km/L
   (5) 15 km/L

ANSWERS

1. **(2)**

2. **(4)** Simplify. $\sqrt{(5-2)^2 + (9-5)^2} = \sqrt{(3)^2 + (4)^2} = \sqrt{9+16} = \sqrt{25} = 5$

3. **(2)** Simplify. Slope $(m) = \dfrac{4-(-3)}{2-(-1)} = \dfrac{7}{3}$

4. **(4)**

5. **(1)** Determine the slope by determining the rise and run between two points. The y-intercept is $(0, -3)$. Substitute into the slope-intercept equation $y = mx + b$.

6. **(3)** Set the equation into the slope-intercept form. $y = -4x - 7$. The slope is the coefficient of x.

7. **(5)** Determine the slope and simplify fully.

Function Concepts

33

THINK ABOUT IT

Functions are algebraic and numeric descriptions of the actions you do every single day. The action of throwing a ball in the air can be described by a function. A function can be used to determine something as simple as the interest accrued in a savings account, and as complicated as the path travelled by a space shuttle. Functions are an essential mathematical key to help explain the world around us!

IN THIS CHAPTER

After completing this chapter, you will be able to

→ **DEFINE A FUNCTION**

→ **EVALUATE A FUNCTION**

→ **GRAPH A FUNCTION**

→ **PERFORM THE VERTICAL LINE TEST**

WHAT IS A FUNCTION?

You have already worked with functions in the previous Math chapters—you just didn't call them that. Functions are nothing more than a set of rules that describe the relationship between two things. In Chapter 31 and Chapter 32 you studied linear and quadratic functions both algebraically and also graphically. The graphs clearly illustrated the relationship between the two variables. Remember the graph that illustrated the height a flare travelled over a certain period of time (Chapter 31)? What about the graph that illustrated the distance travelled by a jogger over a period of time (Chapter 32)? Although the first graph was curved and the second one was straight, they both are considered functions. There are thousands of different functions in a wide variety of mathematical studies, such as calculus, commerce, and physics. For the purpose of preparation for the GED exam, it is only necessary to explore some introductory concepts and basic terminology with regard to functions. However, if you explore mathematics further, functions will certainly be a big part of your studies.

EVALUATING A FUNCTION

Evaluating a function follows the same process as evaluating all algebraic expressions. Substitute for the variable and follow the rules of order of operations to fully simplify.

The only difference is that equations may now be presented in function notation. The notation $f(x)$ is used in place of y.

The notation
f(*x*) is
commonly used
instead of *y* in
equations that
are functions.

Previously, the directions may have been:

Given $y = 3x + 5$, find y if $x = 3$.

We would substitute for x and simplify.

$y = 3(3) + 5 = 14$

Now, the directions may look like:

Given $f(x) = 3x + 5$, find $f(3)$.

You do exactly the same thing as we did above, $f(3) = 3(3) + 5 = 14$, and we get the same result. The value inside the brackets is what x represents.

➡ EXAMPLE 1

Given $f(x) = -2x + 12$, find $f(2)$, $f(1)$, $f(0)$ and $f(-3)$.

Solution

$f(2) = -2(2) + 12 = -4 + 12 = 8$

$f(1) = -2(1) + 12 = -2 + 12 = 10$

$f(0) = -2(0) + 12 = 0 + 12 = 12$

$f(-3) = -2(-3) + 12 = 6 + 12 = 18$

➡ EXAMPLE 2

Given $f(x) = x^2 - 4$, find $f(2)$, $f(1)$, $f(0)$ and $f(-3)$.

Solution

$f(2) = (2)^2 - 4 = 4 - 4 = 0$

$f(1) = (1)^2 - 4 = 1 - 4 = -3$

$f(0) = (0)^2 - 4 = 0 - 4 = -4$

$f(-3) = (-3)^2 - 4 = 9 - 4 = 5$

PRACTICE

1. Given $f(x) = 6x - 1$, find $f(5)$, $f(-2)$, and $f(-4)$
2. Given $f(x) = x^3$, find $f(5)$, $f(2)$, and $f(-2)$
3. Given $f(x) = x^2 - 2x + 3$, find $f(4)$, $f(1)$, and $f(-1)$

ANSWERS

1. $f(5) = 29$, $f(-2) = -13$, and $f(-4) = -25$
2. $f(5) = 125$, $f(2) = 8$, and $f(-2) = -8$
3. $f(4) = 11$, $f(1) = 2$, and $f(-1) = 6$

GRAPHING A FUNCTION

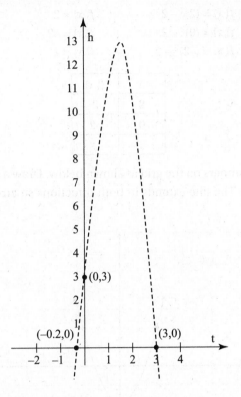

All functions can be graphed on a Cartesian coordinate system. The system, which has two axes, allows for easier comparison between two things.

Input values (*the independent variable*) are generally plotted horizontally and the output values (*the dependent variable*) are generally plotted vertically.

Consider again the curved graph above that illustrates the path of a flare, and you can see that time (input) is plotted along the horizontal axis and height (output) is plotted vertically. Time is the "control" variable and height is what is changing over time.

➡ EXAMPLE 1 _____

Graph $f(x) = x^2 - 2$. This is a quadratic function.

Solution

1. Create a table of values. You can choose values or they will be provided for you.

X	Y
2	
0	
−2	

2. Substitute each x value into the equation given and simplify for $f(x)$. Complete the chart

If $x = 2$ $f(x) = (2)^2 - 2$ $f(x) = 2$

If $x = 0$ $f(x) = (0)^2 - 2$ $f(x) = -2$

If $x = -2$ $f(x) = (-2)^2 - 2$ $f(x) = 2$

X	$f(x)$
2	2
0	-2
-2	2

3. Plot the pairs of numbers on the grid as shown below. Draw a smooth curve to connect these three points. The line extends in both directions so arrows are placed on either end.

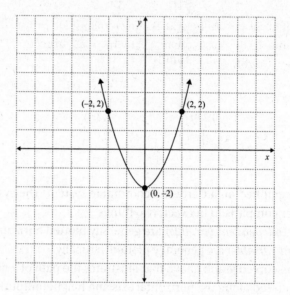

➡ **EXAMPLE 2**

Graph $f(x) = \sqrt{x}$. This is a square root function.

Solution

1. Create a table of values.

X	$f(x)$
9	
4	
0	
-2	

2. Substitute each x value into the equation given and simplify for $f(x)$. Complete the chart

If $x = 9$ $f(x) = \sqrt{9}$ $f(x) = 3$

If $x = 4$ $f(x) = \sqrt{4}$ $f(x) = 2$

If $x = 0$ $f(x) = \sqrt{0}$ $f(x) = 0$

If $x = -2$ $f(x) = \sqrt{-2}$ It is not possible to take the square root of a negative number.

X	$f(x)$
9	3
4	2
0	0
-2	Error

3. Plot the pairs of numbers on the grid as shown below. Draw a smooth curve to connect these three points. In this case, the line extends in one direction only. It begins at zero and extends to the right.

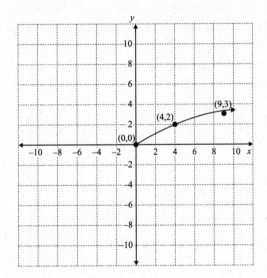

PRACTICE

Graph the following three equations on the grids provided.

a. $f(x) = x^2 - 3$

b. $f(x) = \sqrt{x} - 1$

c. $f(x) = x^3$

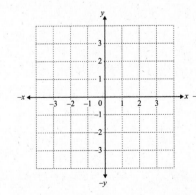

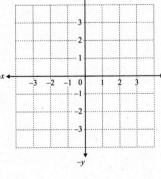

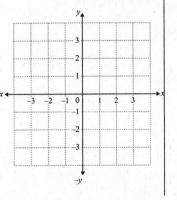

ANSWERS

a. $f(x) = x^2 - 3$

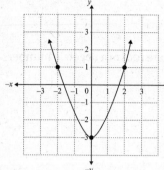

b. $f(x) = \sqrt{x} - 1$

c. $f(x) = x^3$

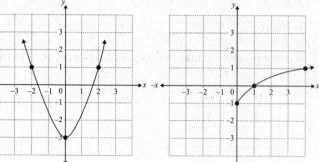

THE VERTICAL LINE TEST

In order for the relationship between the input and output variables to be defined as a function, there must be only one, and exactly one, y-value that corresponds to each given x-value. The easiest way to see if an equation meets this definition is to look at its graph to see if it passes the *vertical line test*. If a vertical line intersects a graph only once, then the graph represents a function. If a vertical line intersects the graph more than once, it is not a function. Consider the examples below.

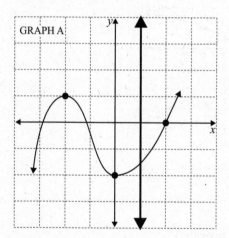

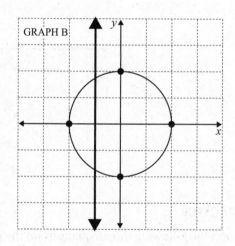

Graph *A* passes the vertical line test; therefore, it is a function. Graph *B* fails the test. It is not a function.

EXAMPLE

Using the vertical line test, determine if the graph below is a function.

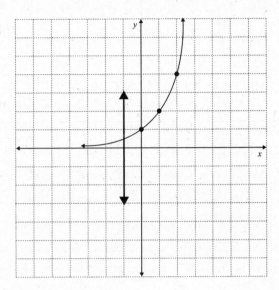

Solution

Yes. This is a function. (It is the exponential function $f(x) = 2^x$)

CHAPTER CHECK-UP

1. Given $f(x) = x^2 + 3$, find $f(-2)$
   (1) 0
   (2) 3
   (3) 7
   (4) 9
   (5) 1

2. Which of the following functions would make $f(1) = 5$ a true statement?
   (1) $f(x) = x^3$
   (2) $f(x) = x^2 + 4$
   (3) $f(x) = \sqrt{x-1}$
   (4) $f(x) = \dfrac{2}{x}$
   (5) $f(x) = 2x - 3$

3. The graph below can be represented by which function?

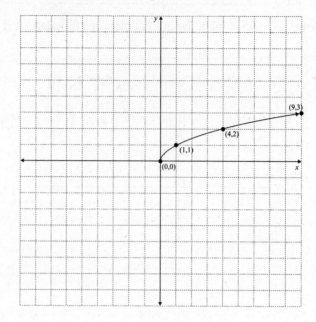

(1) $f(x) = x$
(2) $f(x) = x^2$
(3) $f(x) = x^3$
(4) $f(x) = \sqrt{x}$

(5) $f(x) = \dfrac{1}{x}$

4. Which of the following statements are true?
   a. Very few functions exist.
   b. The notation $f(x)$ can be used in any equation in place of x.
   c. A linear equation is not a function.
   d. The output variable is the independent variable.
   e. The vertical line test helps to determine if an equation is a function.

ANSWERS

1. **(3)** Given $f(x) = (-2)^2 + 3 = 4 + 3 = 7$

2. **(2)** $f(x) = x^2 + 4;\ f(1) = (1)^2 + 4 = 5$

3. **(4)** This is a square root function.

4. **(e)** The rest of the statements are false.

Math—Practice Test

EXAMPLE

If a grocery store bill totaling $15.75 is paid with a $20.00 bill, how much change should be returned?

(1) $5.26
(2) $4.75
(3) $4.25
(4) $3.75
(5) $3.25

The correct answer is $4.25; therefore, answer space 3 would be marked on the answer sheet.

FORMULA SHEET

AREA (A) FORMULAS

Square	$A = s^2$	Where s = side
Rectangle	$A = lw$	Where l = length, w = width
Parallelogram	$A = bh$	Where b = base, h = height
Triangle	$A = \frac{1}{2} bh$	Where b = base, h = height
Trapezoid	$A = \frac{1}{2}(b_1 + b_2)h$	Where b_1 and b_2 = base, h = height
Circle	$A = \pi r^2$	Where π = 3.14, r = radius

PERIMETER (P) FORMULAS

Square	$P = 4s$	Where s = side
Rectangle	$P = 2l + 2w$	Where l = length, w = width
Triangle	$P = a + b + c$	Where a, b, and c are the sides
Circle	$C = \pi d$	Where π = 3.14, d = diameter, and C = circumference (perimeter of a circle)

VOLUME (V) FORMULAS

Cube	$V = s^3$	Where s = side
Rectangular Container	$V = lwh$	Where l = length, w = width, and h = height
Cylinder	$V = \pi r^2 h$	Where π = 3.14, r = radius and h = height
Square Pyramid	$V = \frac{1}{3} b^2 h$	Where b = area of the base, h = height
Cone	$V = \frac{1}{3} \pi r^2 h$	Where π = 3.14, r = radius, and h = height

GRAPHING

Distance between two points	$d = \sqrt{(x_2 - x_1)^2 + (y_2 - y_1)^2}$	
Slope of a line	$m = \frac{y_2 - y_1}{x_2 - x_1}$	Where (x_1, y_1) and (x_2, y_2) are two points in a plane.

PROBABILITY

Mean	$mean = \frac{x_1 + x_2 + \ldots + x_n}{n}$	Where x's are the numbers in a series and where n = total number of values in the series.
Median		The point in an ordered set of numbers at which half of the numbers are above and half of the numbers are below this value.

MISCELLANEOUS

Pythagorean Theorem	$c^2 = a^2 + b^2$	Where c = hypotenuse and a and b are the legs of a right triangle.
Simple Interest	$i = prt$	Where i = interest, p = principal, r = rate, and t = time
Distance/Rate/Time	$d = rt$	Where d = distance, r = rate, and t = time

ANSWER SHEET
Math Practice Test

1. ① ② ③ ④ ⑤
2. ① ② ③ ④ ⑤
3. ① ② ③ ④ ⑤
4. ① ② ③ ④ ⑤
5. ① ② ③ ④ ⑤
6. ① ② ③ ④ ⑤
7. ① ② ③ ④ ⑤
8. ① ② ③ ④ ⑤
9. ① ② ③ ④ ⑤
10. ① ② ③ ④ ⑤
11. ① ② ③ ④ ⑤
12. ① ② ③ ④ ⑤
13. ① ② ③ ④ ⑤
14. ① ② ③ ④ ⑤
15. ① ② ③ ④ ⑤
16. ① ② ③ ④ ⑤
17. ① ② ③ ④ ⑤
18. ① ② ③ ④ ⑤
19. ① ② ③ ④ ⑤
20. ① ② ③ ④ ⑤

21. ① ② ③ ④ ⑤
22. ① ② ③ ④ ⑤
23. ① ② ③ ④ ⑤
24. ① ② ③ ④ ⑤
25. ① ② ③ ④ ⑤
26. ① ② ③ ④ ⑤
27. ① ② ③ ④ ⑤
28. ① ② ③ ④ ⑤
29. ① ② ③ ④ ⑤
30. ① ② ③ ④ ⑤
31. ① ② ③ ④ ⑤
32. ① ② ③ ④ ⑤
33. ① ② ③ ④ ⑤
34. ① ② ③ ④ ⑤
35. ① ② ③ ④ ⑤
36. ① ② ③ ④ ⑤
37. ① ② ③ ④ ⑤
38. ① ② ③ ④ ⑤
39. ① ② ③ ④ ⑤
40. ① ② ③ ④ ⑤

41. ① ② ③ ④ ⑤
42. ① ② ③ ④ ⑤
43. ① ② ③ ④ ⑤
44. ① ② ③ ④ ⑤
45. ① ② ③ ④ ⑤
46. ① ② ③ ④ ⑤
47. ① ② ③ ④ ⑤
48. ① ② ③ ④ ⑤
49. ① ② ③ ④ ⑤
50. ① ② ③ ④ ⑤

MATHEMATICS, PART I

You will have 45 minutes to complete this section. You may use a Casio fx-260 calculator. You may refer to the Formula Sheet.

1. Which of the following statements is false?

   (1) $\dfrac{1}{3} = \dfrac{17}{51}$

   (2) $0.2\% = 0.002$

   (3) $\dfrac{3}{5} = 60\%$

   (4) $200\% = 0.200$

   (5) $\dfrac{1}{8} = 0.125$

2. In one year the average housing price in a city increased dramatically from $425,000 to $561,000. What was the percent of increase?

   (1) 32%
   (2) 24%
   (3) 28%
   (4) 30%
   (5) Not enough information is given.

3. Trish purchases 6.5 metres of ribbon for a craft project. She cuts the ribbon into 25 cm lengths. How many pieces of ribbon will she have?

   (1) 162.5 pieces
   (2) 76 pieces
   (3) 26 pieces
   (4) 260 pieces
   (5) 76.5 pieces

4. Which of the following functions would make $f(11) = 3$ a true statement?

   (1) $f(x) = x^2 - 3$
   (2) $f(x) = 5x + 2$
   (3) $f(x) = \sqrt{x - 2}$
   (4) $f(x) = 3x^2$
   (5) $f(x) = x^3$

5. What is the slope of a line that passes through (–5, –10) and (3, 12)?

   (1) $\dfrac{4}{11}$

   (2) $\dfrac{11}{4}$

   (3) -1

   (4) $\dfrac{-1}{2}$

   (5) 11

6. Given the equation $x^2 - 3x - 10 = 0$, which of the following give(s) a complete solution of the equation?

    (1) 1 and 2
    (2) –2 and 5
    (3) –5
    (4) –2
    (5) 2 and –5

7. The graph below represents the solution to which of the following inequalities?

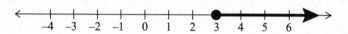

    (1) $2x \geq 10$
    (2) $x + 2 \geq 5$
    (3) $3x \leq 15$
    (4) $x - 3 \leq 6$
    (5) $-2x > 12$

8. The following graph shows the distribution of students at Career Start College. If 2000 students attend this college, how many students are enrolled in the Trades?

CAREER START COLLEGE

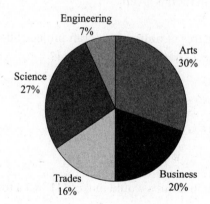

    (1) 160
    (2) 316
    (3) 220
    (4) 260
    (5) 320

9. The mass of Earth is about 6×10^{21} metric tons. The mass of Jupiter is about 1.908×10^{24} metric tons. Expressed in scientific notation, the mass of Jupiter is how much bigger than the mass of Earth?

    (1) 1.902×10^{24} metric tons
    (2) 1.902×10^{21} metric tons
    (3) 7.902×10^{45} metric tons
    (4) 4.092×10^{3} metric tons
    (5) 4.092×10^{24} metric tons

10. In the triangle below, what is the length, in metres, of side *AC*?

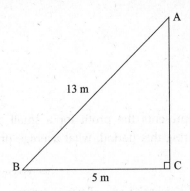

(1) 10 m
(2) 4 m
(3) 14 m
(4) 26 m
(5) 12 m

11. If $3x + 5 = 35$, then $\frac{3}{5}x$ is equal to
(1) 4
(2) 5
(3) 10
(4) 6
(5) –2

12. The graph below relates the salary earned to the hours worked for a service technician at a garage. What is the technician's hourly wage?

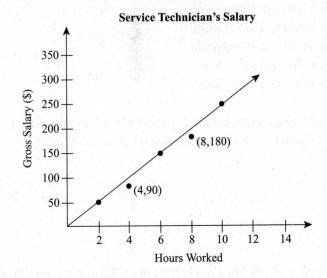

(1) $12.50/hr
(2) $17.50/hr
(3) $21.00/hr
(4) $22.50/hr
(5) $24.00/hr

13. Given $f(x) = 2x^2 + 1$, find $f(-3)$
    (1) −11
    (2) −35
    (3) 37
    (4) −17
    (5) 19

14. The following graph represents the profit for a small craft company over the first six months in 2013. During this period, what average profit or loss has the business generated?

Caroline's Crafts - Revenue Report

    (1) Between $3500 and $3800 profit
    (2) Between $4000 and $4500 profit
    (3) Between $4800 and $5000 profit
    (4) Between $4000 and $5000 loss
    (5) Between $3200 and $3600 loss

15. The volume of a single sugar cube is 2.25 cm³. If a rectangular box of sugar cubes measures 15 cm by 5cm by 3cm, how many sugar cubes can it hold?
    (1) 225
    (2) 200
    (3) 150
    (4) 100
    (5) 75

16. On average, Jane walks 20 km a week. How many kilometres does Jane walk in a year?
    (1) 2400 km
    (2) 1040 km
    (3) 1400 km
    (4) 840 km
    (5) 960 km

17. At a big-box store, Gwen purchases a package of paper towels that is sold in multiples of 8. The sale price is $22 for the bundle. What is the cost of a single roll of paper towels?
    (1) $2.50
    (2) $1.50
    (3) $2.20
    (4) $1.75
    (5) $2.75

18. If $\angle 1 = 28°$ and $\angle 2 = 3(\angle 1)$, then $\angle 3$ equals

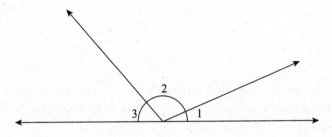

    (1) 84°
    (2) 96°
    (3) 68°
    (4) 86°
    (5) 180°

19. Mr. Walters invests $20,000 in bonds that pay simple interest at the rate of 7.5% annually. How much interest will Mr. Walters earn in 3 years?
    (1) $5 500
    (2) $4 500
    (3) $1 500
    (4) $150 000
    (5) $50 000

20. In the line segment AC below, the ratio of $AB:BC = 5:2$. If $AB = 40$ centimetres, what is the length of BC?

    (1) 2 cm
    (2) 4 cm
    (3) 16 cm
    (4) 8 cm
    (5) 20 cm

21. Tim works at an accounting office and processes tax returns. It is the busy season and he has seventy-five returns still left to complete. He began the week with 90 tax returns. What fraction of his work has he already completed?

(1) $\frac{1}{6}$

(2) $\frac{75}{90}$

(3) $\frac{1}{4}$

(4) $\frac{1}{5}$

(5) $\frac{1}{90}$

22. Provincial sales tax on goods and services is 7%. Preparing for school, Chris purchases 3 binders at $3.45/each, two packages of pens for $4.99/each and a scientific calculator for $22.99. How much tax does Chris pay on his purchase?
(1) $4.30
(2) $17.10
(3) $21.94
(4) $10.05
(5) $3.03

23. What is Janet's mean grade if she received 72%, 82%, 67%, 90% and 75% on the first five Math quizzes she wrote?
(1) 75.8%
(2) 78.2%
(3) 77.2%
(4) 81%
(5) 71.5%

24. A cell phone plan advertises that the cost for service is a flat $42 fee plus an additional 10 cents for every text message sent or received. Which of the following functions represents what a customer would pay in one month if she makes x number of texts.
(1) $42(0.10x)$
(2) $42 + $10x$
(3) $42.10x$
(4) $42 + $0.10x$
(5) $42 - $10x$

25. Joan borrows $240 from her sister. She paid back $\frac{1}{3}$ of the total after one week and then paid back $\frac{1}{2}$ of the remaining amount the following week. How much does she still owe?

(1) $80
(2) $100
(3) $120
(4) $40
(5) $60

MATHEMATICS, PART II

You will have 45 minutes to complete questions 26–50. You may NOT use a calculator. You may refer to the Formula Sheet.

26. Wayne has 3.75-kg of dog food to share among his five dogs. How much food will each dog receive?
    (1) 0.55 kg
    (2) 0.65 kg
    (3) 0.85 kg
    (4) 0.75 kg
    (5) 0.45 kg

27. What is the equation of the line shown in the graph below?

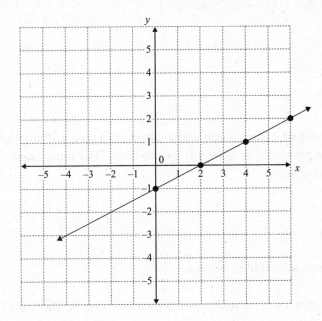

    (1) $y = \frac{1}{2}x - 3$

    (2) $y = -2x - 3$

    (3) $y = \frac{1}{2}x$

    (4) $y = 2x$

    (5) $y = \frac{1}{2}x - 1$

28. Which of the following algebraic expressions represents the area of the figure below?

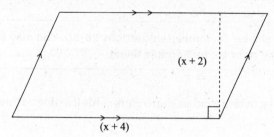

(1) $x^2 + 2x + 4$
(2) $x^2 - 6x - 8$
(3) $x^2 + 1x + 2$
(4) $x^2 + 6x + 8$
(5) $x^2 - 8x + 6$

29. Evaluate $2x^2(3y - 4)$ given $x = 2$ and $y = -1$.
(1) 12
(2) 65
(3) −28
(4) −56
(5) −8

30. Linda is prescribed a medication and is directed to take a 20 mg dose every 4 hours, over a 16-hour period. She does this for five days. How much medication does Linda consume altogether?
(1) 760 mg
(2) 400 mg
(3) 1 280 mg
(4) 500 mg
(5) Not enough information is given.

31. The ages of Tania, Tracy, and Kim are consecutive integers. The sum of their ages is 108. Which of the following equations may be used to find their ages:
(1) $(x)(x + 1)(x + 2) = 108$
(2) $(x) + (x + 1) + (x + 2) = 108$
(3) $(x) - (x + 1) - (x + 2) = 108$
(4) $(x) + (2x) + (3x) = 108$
(5) $\dfrac{x + 2x + 3x}{3} = 108$

Question 32 refers to the nutrition label below.

Nutrition Facts		
Serving Size 5 oz. (144g)		
Servings per Container 4		
Amount Per Serving		
Calories 310	**Calories** from Fat 100	
		% Daily value*
Total Fat 15g		21%
Saturated Fat 2.6g		17%
Trans Fat 1g		
Cholesterol 118g		39%
Sodium 560mg		28%
Total Carbohydrate 12g		4%
Dietary Fiber 1g		4%
Sugars 1g		
Protein 24g		
Vitamin A 1%	**Vitamin C** 2%	
Calcium 2%	**Iron** 5%	

* Percent Daily Values are based on a 2000
Calorie dirt. Your daily values may be higher
or lower, depending on your calorie needs:

	Calories	2,000	2,500
Total Fat	Less than	65g	80g
Saturated Fat	Less than	20g	25g
Cholesterol	Less than	300mg	300mg
Sodium	Less than	2,400mg	2,400mg
Total Carbohydrate		300g	375g
Dietary Fiber		25g	30g

Calories per gram

Fat 9 · Carbohydrate 4 · Protein 4

32. If someone ate the entire container of food, how many calories would she consume?

(1) 310

(2) 1 550

(3) 1 240

(4) 620

(5) Not enough information is given.

33. Which point on the number line below represents the closest approximation to $\sqrt{18}$?

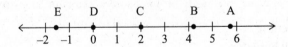

(1) A

(2) B

(3) C

(4) D

(5) E

34. Simplify $10 - 2(7 - 5) + 4(6)$

(1) 3

(2) 15

(3) 38

(4) 30

(5) 40

35. What is the perimeter of the figure below?

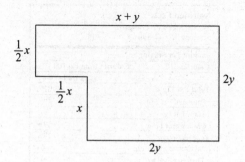

(1) $2x + 4y$

(2) $3x + 5y$

(3) $4x + 6y$

(4) $4x + 2y$

(5) $5x + 3y$

36. The graph below illustrates what type of function?

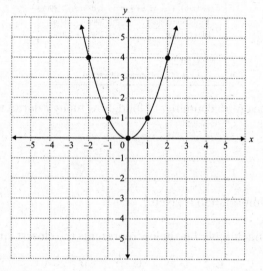

(1) Linear Function

(2) Exponential Function

(3) Quadratic Function

(4) Square Root Function

(5) Cubic Function

37. On a can of orange concentrate, the directions state to mix four cans of water with one can of concentrate. How many cans of water would be added to $2\frac{1}{2}$ cans of concentrate?

(1) 8 cups

(2) $4\frac{1}{2}$ cups

(3) 10 cups

(4) $6\frac{3}{4}$ cups

(5) 6 cups

38. Jennifer is purchasing furniture online. She finds a sofa she likes and reads on the photograph a scale of 1 cm: 2 feet. Jennifer measures the picture and notes that the length of the sofa is 4 cm. How long is the actual sofa?

    (1) 400 cm
    (2) 2 feet
    (3) 4 feet
    (4) 8 feet
    (5) 10 feet

39. Mary graphed two points, as shown on the grid below. The points represent two corners of a right triangle. Which one of the following points would complete Mary's right triangle?

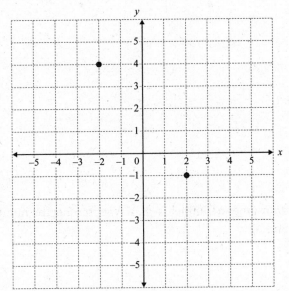

    (1) (–2, 0)
    (2) (4, 3)
    (3) (–1, –2)
    (4) (–2, –1)
    (5) (0, 0)

40. In one week Laura watched 6 hours of television more than Melanie. Rachelle watched 2 hours less than Laura and 4 hours more than Melanie. How many hours of television did Melanie watch that week?

    (1) 3 hours
    (2) 4 hours
    (3) 5 hours
    (4) 6 hours
    (5) Not enough information is given.

41. At a riding stable there are three identical circular exercise arenas arranged similar to the following diagram. Which of the following expressions represents the total area of all three arenas?

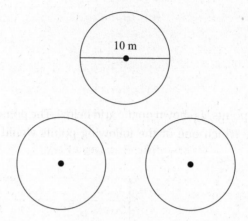

10 m

(1) $3\pi(5)^2$

(2) $3\pi(10)$

(3) $\frac{1}{3}\pi(25)$

(4) $3\pi(10)^3$

(5) πr^2

42. Seven less than four times a number is 33. If N represents the number, which equation can be used to find N?

(1) $33 = 4N - 7$

(2) $33 = 7 - 4N$

(3) $7 + 4N = 33$

(4) $4N \div 7 = 33$

(5) $33 - 7 = 4N$

43. A candy jar contains 5 red jelly beans, 4 blue jelly beans, 6 green jelly beans, and 3 yellow jelly beans. What is the probability of choosing a green jelly bean?

(1) $\frac{5}{18}$

(2) $\frac{2}{9}$

(3) $\frac{1}{6}$

(4) $\frac{1}{3}$

(5) $\frac{1}{2}$

44. Mr. Bailey purchases 2 pounds of nails from the hardware store for his woodworking students. Every pound contains 180 nails. If Mr. Bailey has 20 students and he shares the nails between them equally, how many nails does each student receive?
    (1) 36 nails
    (2) 18 nails
    (3) 9 nails
    (4) 6 nails
    (5) 5 nails

Question 45 is based on the following chart.

Overweight Baggage Fees

Region	Weight	Fees (per bag)
North America	51–70 lbs	$100
	71–100 lbs	$200
Europe	51–70 lbs	$125
South America	51–70 lbs	$75
	71–100 lbs	$200

45. A family moving to Brazil has three overweight bags weighing 52 lbs, 65 lbs, and 80 lbs. How much will they pay in additional baggage fees?
    (1) $150
    (2) $350
    (3) $200
    (4) $275
    (5) $250

46. Wild salmon is priced at $6.48 for 2 kilograms. Which of the following could be used to find out how much 4.5 kgs would cost at the same price per kilogram.

    (1) $\dfrac{2}{\$6.48} = \dfrac{?}{4.5}$

    (2) $\dfrac{\$6.48}{2} = \dfrac{4.5}{?}$

    (3) $\dfrac{2}{\$6.48} = \dfrac{4.5}{?}$

    (4) $\dfrac{2}{4.5} = \dfrac{?}{\$6.48}$

    (5) $\dfrac{4.5}{2} = \dfrac{\$6.48}{?}$

Question 47 refers to the diagram below.

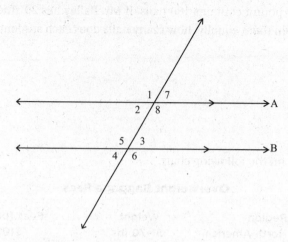

47. What is the measurement of angle ∠1 given ∠3 = 55°?
    (1) 125°
    (2) 55°
    (3) 35°
    (4) 135°
    (5) 100°

48. Which of the following fractions is not equivalent to $\frac{20}{24}$?

    (1) $\frac{10}{12}$

    (2) $\frac{5}{6}$

    (3) $\frac{40}{48}$

    (4) $\frac{4}{6}$

    (5) $\frac{100}{120}$

49. A snail crawls 250 mm. What fraction of a metre has the snail crawled?

    (1) $\frac{1}{5}$

    (2) $\frac{1}{4}$

    (3) $\frac{1}{2}$

    (4) $\frac{3}{4}$

    (5) $\frac{5}{4}$

50. The graph below can be represented by which function?

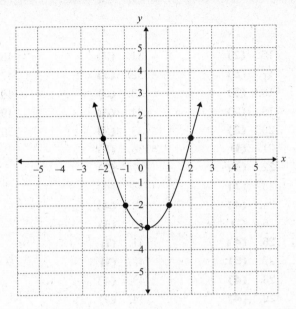

(1) $f(x) = x^2 - 3$

(2) $f(x) = x^3$

(3) $f(x) = 2x - 1$

(4) $f(x) = \sqrt{x}$

(5) $f(x) = 2^x$

ANSWERS

1.	**(4)**	16.	**(2)**	31.	**(2)**	46.	**(3)**
2.	**(1)**	17.	**(5)**	32.	**(3)**	47.	**(1)**
3.	**(3)**	18.	**(3)**	33.	**(2)**	48.	**(4)**
4.	**(3)**	19.	**(2)**	34.	**(4)**	49.	**(2)**
5.	**(2)**	20.	**(3)**	35.	**(2)**	50.	**(1)**
6.	**(2)**	21.	**(1)**	36.	**(3)**		
7.	**(2)**	22.	**(5)**	37.	**(3)**		
8.	**(5)**	23.	**(3)**	38.	**(4)**		
9.	**(1)**	24.	**(4)**	39.	**(4)**		
10.	**(5)**	25.	**(1)**	40.	**(5)**		
11.	**(4)**	26.	**(4)**	41.	**(1)**		
12.	**(4)**	27.	**(5)**	42.	**(1)**		
13.	**(5)**	28.	**(4)**	43.	**(4)**		
14.	**(3)**	29.	**(4)**	44.	**(2)**		
15.	**(4)**	30.	**(2)**	45.	**(2)**		

Interpret Your Results

Test Area	Questions	Recommended Minimum Score	Your Score
Numbers and Basic Operations	9, 17, 26, 29, 33, 34, 44	5	
Fractions and Measurements	3, 16, 21, 25, 30, 37, 38, 43, 46, 48, 49	7	
Decimals and Percents	1, 2, 19, 22	3	
Data Analysis	8, 12, 14, 23, 32, 45	4	
Algebra	4, 5, 6, 7, 11, 13, 24, 27, 31, 35, 36, 39, 40, 42, 50	10	
Geometry	10, 15, 18, 20, 28, 41, 47	4	
Total			

Check your answers and calculate how you scored in each test area. If you scored less than the recommended minimum score in any test area, you should review topics in the relevant chapters.

ANALYSIS

1. **(4)** 200% = 2.0

2. **(1)** Find the difference between \$561 000 – \$425 000 = \$136 000. Compare the difference to the original price:

$$\frac{136000}{425000} = \frac{x}{100}$$
$$(136000)(100) \div 425000 = 32\%$$

3. **(3)** Convert 6.5 m to cm by multiplying by 100 = 650 cm. Divide 650 cm by 25 cm = 26 pieces.

4. **(3)** Substitute in and evaluate each function for $x = 11$. The only function to simplify properly is

$$f(x) = \sqrt{x-2}$$
$$f(11) = \sqrt{11-2}$$
$$f(11) = \sqrt{9}$$
$$f(11) = 3$$

5. **(2)** Solve using the slope formula on the formula page.

$$m = \frac{y_2 - y_1}{x_2 - x_1}$$
$$m = \frac{12 - (-10)}{3 - (-5)}$$
$$m = \frac{22}{8}$$
$$m = \frac{11}{4}$$

6. **(2)** Either work backwards or solve by factoring.
$$x^2 - 3x - 10 = 0$$
$$(x - 5)(x + 2) = 0$$
$$x - 5 = 0 \text{ and } x + 2 = 0$$
$$x = 5, x = -2$$

7. **(2)** The graph illustrates a solution where $x \geq 3$. Equation (2) simplifies to this inequality.
$$x + 2 \geq 5$$
$$x \geq 5 - 2$$
$$x \geq 3$$

8. **(5)** Find 16% of 2000.

$$\frac{16}{100} = \frac{?}{2000}$$
$$(16)(2000) \div 100 = 320$$

9. **(1)** Subtract. $(1.908 \times 10^{24}) - (6 \times 10^{21}) = 1.902 \times 10^{24}$

10. **(5)** Solve using the Pythagorean Theorem (on the formula sheet).

$c^2 = a^2 + b^2$

$13^2 = 5^2 + b^2$

$169 - 25 = b^2$

$144 = b^2$

$b = \sqrt{144} = 12$

11. **(4)** First solve for x in the first equation.

$3x + 5 = 35$

$3x = 35 - 5$

$\dfrac{3x}{3} = \dfrac{30}{3}$

$x = 10$

Next, substitute this value into the expression $\left(\dfrac{3}{5}\right)(x)$.

$$\dfrac{3x}{5} = \dfrac{3(10)}{5} = 6$$

12. **(4)** Choose either point. Divide the Gross Salary by the Hours Worked.

$$180 \div 8 = \$22.50$$

13. **(5)** Substitute into the function, given $x = -3$, and simplify.

$f(x) = 2x^2 + 1$

$f(-3) = 2(-3)^2 + 1$

$f(-3) = 2(9) + 1$

$f(-3) = 19$

14. **(3)** Add the revenue amounts from each month. Approximate as accurately as possible. $2000 + 1750 + 1200 + 600 + (-500) + (-200) = \$4850$

15. **(4)** Find the volume of the rectangular box using the formula on the formula sheet. Volume $= LWH = (15)(5)(3) = 225$ cm^3. Next, divide the total volume by the volume of one cube. $225 \div 2.25 = 100$

16. **(2)** Solve the proportion. $\dfrac{20}{1} = \dfrac{?}{52}$ $(20)(52) \div 1 = 1040$

17. **(5)** Find the unit price. $\$22 \div 8 = \$2.75$

18. **(3)** If $\angle 1 = 28°$, then $\angle 2 = 3(28°) = 84°$ and $\angle 3 = 180° - 28° - 84° = 68°$.

19. **(2)** Substitute into the simple interest formula on the formula sheet.

$i = prt$

$i = (20000)(0.075)(3)$

$i = \$4500$

20. **(3)** Solve the proportion. $\dfrac{5}{2} = \dfrac{40}{?}$ $(2)(40) \div 5 = 16$

21. **(1)** First find the difference between the returns Tim had to start and the number of returns he has remaining. $90 - 75 = 15$. Next, compare this difference to the original amount.

$$\dfrac{15}{90} = \dfrac{1}{6}$$

22. **(5)** First, calculate how much Chris spent. $(3)(\$3.45) + (2)(4.99) + 22.99 = \$43.32$.

Next, find 7% of this amount.

$$\frac{7}{100} = \frac{?}{43.32} \qquad (7)(43.32) \div 100 = \$3.03$$

23. **(3)** Find the mean using the formula on the formula sheet.

$$\frac{72+82+67+90+75}{5} = 77.2\%$$

24. **(4)** The monthly charge includes the flat rate of $42 plus (+) 10 cents per text. Convert 10 cents to a dollar amount by dividing by 100. Therefore, $42 + \$0.10x$ is the correct function.

25. **(1)** First find $\frac{1}{3}$ of $240 = \$80$. Subtract $\$240 - \$80 = \$160$. Next find $\frac{1}{2}$ of $160 = \$80$. Finally, subtract $\$160 - \$80 = \$80$.

26. **(4)** Divide 3.75 kg by 5 = 0.75 kg.

27. **(5)** Determine both the slope and y-intercept and substitute into the slope-intercept equation ($y = mx + b$). The y-intercept is $(0,-1)$ and the slope is $+\frac{1}{2}$. The slope can be calculated by looking at the rise and run between two points.

28. **(4)** This is a parallelogram. Refer to the formula sheet for the area formula.

$$A = (\text{base})(\text{height}).\ A = (x + 4)(x + 2) = x^2 + 2x + 4x + 8 = x^2 + 6x + 8$$

29. **(4)** Substitute and simplify using order of operations.
$2x^2(3y - 4) =$
$2(2)^2(3(-1) - 4) =$
$2(4)(-3 - 4) =$
$2(4)(-7) =$
-56

30. **(2)** Read carefully. Taking a dose every 4 hours over 16 hours means that Linda will take 4 doses daily. She does this for five days. $(5)(4) = 20$ doses. Finally $(20)(20\text{ mg}) = 400$ mg.

31. **(2)** Consecutive integers go up by one, such as $x, x + 1$, etc. The sum of these numbers indicates addition.

32. **(3)** Calories per serving are 310. There are 4 servings per container.

$$(310)(4) = 1\ 240 \text{ calories.}$$

33. **(2)** $\sqrt{18}$ is between $\sqrt{16}$ and $\sqrt{25}$ which means the value is between 4 and 5.

34. **(4)** Substitute and simplify using order of operations.
$10 - 2(7 - 5) + 4(6)$
$10 - 2(2) + 24$
$10 - 4 + 24$
$6 + 24$
30

35. **(2)** Collect like terms. $x + x + \frac{1}{2}x + \frac{1}{2}x = 3x$ and $2y + 2y + y = 5y$

36. **(3)** You must be able to recognize basic function shapes.

37. **(3)** Solve the proportion. $\frac{4}{1} = \frac{?}{2.5}$ $(4)(2.5) \div 1 = 10$

38. **(4)** Solve the proportion. $\frac{1 \text{ cm}}{2 \text{ ft}} = \frac{4 \text{ cm}}{?}$ $(4)(2) \div 1 = 8$ feet

39. **(4)** Visually test each point. It must be directly below $(-2, 4)$ and also directly left of $(2, -1)$. Point $(-2, -1)$ is the only one that satisfied this requirement.

40. **(5)** You are given how the hours compare between the three girls; however, you are not given a starting point quantity. We need more information to determine how many hours of televison Melanie watched.

41. **(1)** Consider the area of a circle formula on the formula sheet. $A = \pi r^2$. The radius is half the measurement of the diameter; therefore $\frac{1}{2}(10) = 5$ m. You need three times the area. Expression 1 satisfies all requirements.

42. **(1)** Translate into an algebraic equation. *Seven less than* is subtraction and *four times* is multiplication. Likely you may write the equation $4N - 7 = 33$; however, the (1) equation is equivalent.

43. **(4)** First determine the total number of jelly beans in the jar by adding $5 + 4 + 6 + 3 = 18$. Next, compare as a fraction the number of green jelly beans to the total and simplify. $\frac{6}{18} = \frac{1}{3}$

44. **(2)** Determine the total number of nails. Every pound contains 180 nails and Mr. Bailey purchases 2 pounds = 360 nails. Next divide the total by the number of students.

$$360 \div 20 = 18$$

45. **(2)** Brazil is in South America. Referencing the table, calculate

$$(2)(\$75) + (1)(\$200) = \$350$$

46. **(3)** Set up the proportion keeping units aligned. $\frac{2 \text{ kg}}{\$6.48} = \frac{4.5 \text{ kg}}{?}$

47. **(1)** $\angle 1$ and $\angle 3$ are supplementary. Subtract: $180° - 55° = 125°$

48. **(4)** Equivalent fractions reduce to the same decimal. Another way to test equivalency is to ensure that the fraction (numerator and denominator) is being divided or multiplied by the same value.

49. **(2)** Convert 250 mm to metres by dividing by 1 000. 250 mm = 0.25 m. Next convert 0.25 m to an equivalent fraction. $\frac{25}{100} = \frac{1}{4}$

50. **(1)** You may immediately recognize the graph as quadratic and option (1) is the only quadratic equation. However, if you don't recognize this right away you can test coordinates from each point to see if they simplify into the equation properly.

Acknowledgements

The authors gratefully acknowledge the kindness of all organizations concerned with the granting of permission to reprint passages, charts, graphics, and photographs used in this book.

The copyright holders and publishers of quoted materials are listed below.

Language Arts Reading—Diagnostic test, Passage for Questions 1–5: from *The Tipping Point*, by Malcom Gladwell. Little, Brown and Company, 2000.

Language Arts Reading—Diagnostic test, Poem for Questions 6–11: *"The Road Not Taken,"* by Robert Frost. 1915.

Language Arts Reading—Diagnostic test, Passage for Questions 12–17: from *The Good Earth*, by Pearl S. Buck, 1931.

Language Arts Reading—Diagnostic test, Passage for Questions 18–22: from *The Town House*, by Tish Cohen, Harper Collins, 2007.

Language Arts Reading—Diagnostic test, Drama passage for Questions 28–32: from *Hedda Gabler*, by Henrik Ibsen. 1891.

Language Arts Reading—Diagnostic test, Passage for Questions 33–36: from *The Little Prince*, by Antoine de Saint Exupéry. 1943.

Language Arts Reading—Diagnostic test, Poem for Questions 37–40: *The Power of the Dog*, by Rudyard Kipling.

Science Diagnostic test, Passage and graphic for Questions 4–6: *What is Cancer?*, from the National Cancer Institute. *www.cancer.gov.*

Science Diagnostic test, Data for the graph of greenhouse gas emissions based on information from Environment Canada. *www.ec.gc.ca*

Science Diagnostic test, Passage for Questions 19–20. Originally published on Universe Today. www.universetoday.com

Science Diagnostic test, Data for the table of calories per day for Questions 22–24. Adapted from information from the U.S. Department of Agriculture. *www.cnpp.usda.gov*

Science Diagnostic test, Passage for Questions 41–43: adapted from information from the World Wildlife Fund blog. *http://blog.wwf.ca/blog/2012/04/08/canadian-polar-bear-populations/*

Social Studies Diagnostic test, Map for Questions 30–31: from Wikipedia. GNU free Documentation License. *http://en.wikipedia.org/wiki/File:World_Nominal_GDP_2010.svg*

Social Studies Diagnostic test, Cartoon for Questions 35–36: from Wikipedia Commons. *http://commons.wikimedia.org/wiki/File:Napoleon_Complex.jpg?uselang=en-ca*

Social Studies Diagnostic test, Passage and Map for Questions 47–48: CIA *World FactBook*.

Chapter 4, Passage for Topic Sentences Question 2: from *www.newfoundlandlabrador.com*

Chapter 4, Passage for Topic Sentences Question 4: extracted from "Luck vs. Talent vs. Skill." *Forbes*. 13 July 2009.

Chapter 4, Passage for Topic Sentences Question 5: adapted from Fitts, Maribeth. "Juicy Fruits: Pick Fresh Peaches and Pears." *Canadian Gardening Magazine* (online).

Chapter 5, Passage for Thesis Statement Question 3: from *Angler's Paradise–Sooke, B.C.,* by Ray Bone, SportfishingBC.com.

Chapter 10, Practice with Fiction, Passage for Questions 1–5: from "The Oval Portrait," by Edgar Allan Poe. 1850.

Chapter 10, Practice with Fiction, Passage for Questions 6–10: from "The People on the Shore" in *Dinner Along the Amazon*, by Timothy Findley. Penguin Books, 1984.

Chapter 10, Practice with Fiction, Passage for Questions 11–15: from "The Window" in *Mrs. Golightly and Other Stories*, by Ethel Wilson. McClelland and Stewart, 1990.

Chapter 10, Practice with Poetry, Poem for Questions 1–4: "There's Been a Death in the Opposite House," by Emily Dickinson.

Chapter 10, Practice with Poetry, Poem for Questions 5–8: "In Flanders Fields," by John McCrae.

Chapter 10, Practice with Poetry, Poem for Questions 9–12: "What Is so Great about Birthdays?" by Robert William Service.

Chapter 10, Practice with Poetry, Poem for Challenge Exercise: "With rue my heart is laden," by A.E. Houseman.

Chapter 10, Practice with Drama, Passage for Questions 1–5: from "Still Stands the House" by Gwen Pharis Ringwood. Samuel French Publishers, 1939

Chapter 10, Practice with Drama, Passage for Questions 6–9: from "Desire Under the Elms" by Eugene O'Neill. 1924.

Chapter 10, Reading for Application, Poem for Questions 5–6: "Song." by Christina Rossetti, 1848.

Chapter 10, Chapter Check-up, Passage for Questions 1–4: from *The English Patient*, by Michael Ondaatje. MacLelland and Stewart, 1992.

Chapter 11, Conclusions and Inferences, Passage for Questions 1–4: from "The Corner of X and Y Streets," *Golightly and Other Stories*, by Ethel Wilson, MacMillan, 1961.

Chapter 11, Conclusions and Inferences, Poem for Questions 10–12: "On Shakespeare" by John Milton, 1632.

Chapter 11, Cause and Effect, Passage for Questions 1–2: from *The Backwoods of Canada*, by Catharine Parr Traill, 1836.

Chapter 11, Cause and Effect, Passage for Questions 3–4: from "When Twilight Falls on the Stump Lots," by Sir Charles G.D. Roberts, 1902.

Chapter 11, Cause and Effect, Passage for Questions 5–6: from "The Green Drake" by A. E. Coppard.

Chapter 11, Characterization, Passage for Questions 1–3: from "A White Heron" by Sarah Orne Jewett.

Chapter 11, Characterization, Passage for Questions 4–5: from "The Necklace" by Guy de Maupassant, 1884.

Chapter 11, Characterization, Passage for Questions 6–8: from *Water for Elephants* by Sara Gruen, Harper Collins, 2006.

Chapter 11, Supporting Details, Passage for Questions 1–2: from *The History of Emily Montague* by Frances Brooke, 1769.

Chapter 11, Passage for Supporting Details, Passage for Questions 3–5: from a book review of Mordecai Richler's *The Incomparable Atuk,* by Aaron C. Brown, *CanadianBookReview. wordpress.com.*

Chapter 11, Mood and Tone, Passage for Questions 1–2: from "The Oval Portrait," by Edgar Allen Poe.

Chapter 11, Mood and Tone, Passage for Questions 3–5: from "Snow" in *Over Prairie Trails* by Frederick Philip Grove.

Chapter 11, Mood and Tone, Passage for Questions 6–8: from "Louise" in *Cosmopolitans* by W. Somerset Maugham (London: Heinemann, 1936).

Chapter 11, Chapter Check-up, Passage for Questions 8–11: from *The Order of Good Cheer* by Bill Gaston, Anansi Press, 2009.

Chapter 11, Chapter Check-up, Poem for Questions 12–15: "My Last Duchess" by Robert Browning. 1842.

Chapter 12, What Is Synthesis? Passage for Questions 1–5: from "A Note on Modernism" by Sir Charles G.D. Roberts, 1931.

Chapter 12, Organizational Structure. Passage for Question 2: from "The Fiery Wooing of Mordred," in *Young Men in Spats*, by P.G. Wodehouse.

Chapter 12, Organizational Structure. Poem for Question 4: from "A Valediction: Forbidding Mourning," by John Donne, 1611.

Chapter 12, Organizational Structure. Passage for Question 5: from *The Backwoods of Canada* by Catharine Parr Traill, 1836.

Chapter 12, Coordinate Information. Passage for Practice 1: from "The Ghost," in *A Moment of Time*, by Richard Hughes.

Chapter 12, Coordinate Information. Passage for Questions 1–3: from "The Substance of the Story" by Edith Ronald Mirrielees.

Chapter 12, Coordinate Information. Poem for Questions 4–5: from "The Cremation of Sam McGee," by Robert W. Service, 1907.

Chapter 12, Perspective and Purpose. Passage for Questions 5–6: from "The Rocking Horse Winner," by James Joyce, 1926.

Chapter 12, Compare and Contrast. Poem for Questions 1–2: *Sonnet 18*, by William Shakespeare.

Chapter 12, Compare and Contrast. Passage for Questions 3–5: from "A Glance in the Mirror" by Ernest Butler, in *Thanks for Listening: Stories and Short Fictions by Ernest Butler*. Ed. Marta Dvorak. Canada: Wilfred Laurier Press, 2004.

Chapter 12, Integrate Information. Passage for Questions 1–3: from *Call of the Wild*, by Jack London, 1903.

Chapter 12, Integrate Information. Poem for Question 4: "So We'll Go No More A-Roving," by Lord Byron, 1817.

Chapter 12, Chapter Check-Up, Passage for Questions 1–3: from "The Open Boat," by Stephen Crane, 1897.

Chapter 12, Chapter Check-Up, Poem for Questions 4–7: "When I have fears that I may cease to be," by John Keats, 1848.

Progress Check, Passage for Questions 1–7: from *The Importance of Being Earnest*, by Oscar Wilde, 1895.

Progress Check, Passage for Questions 8–12: from *All That Matters*, by Wayson Choy, Doubleday Canada, 2004.

Progress Check, Poem for Questions 13–15: from "Ode: Intimations of Immortality from Recollections of Early Childhood," by William Wordsworth, 1815.

Language Arts Reading–Practice test, Poem for Instructions: "How Happy is the Little Stone," by Emily Dickinson.

Language Arts Reading–Practice test, Passage for Questions 1–5: from a book review of Margaret Lawrence's *The Stone Angel*, by Alexandra Lucas.

Language Arts Reading–Practice test, Passage for Questions 6–11: from *Les Canadiens*, by Rick Salutin and Ken Dryden, Talonbooks.

Language Arts Reading–Practice test, Passage for Questions 12–18: from "Travels in Ceylon," *Running in the Family* by Michael Ondaatje. MacLelland and Stewart, 1982.

Language Arts Reading–Practice test, Poem for Questions 23–27: "A Summer Evening," by Archibald Lampman, 1896.

Language Arts Reading–Practice test, Passage for Questions 28–32: from "Literature in a New Country," *Scotchman's Return and Other Essays*, by Hugh MacLennan.

Language Arts Reading–Practice test, Poem for Questions 33–36: "Stopping by Woods on a Snowy Evening," by Robert Frost, 1922.

Language Arts Reading–Practice test, Passage for Questions 37–40: from *The Book of Negroes*, by Lawrence Hill, Harper Collins, Canada, 2007.

Chapter 15, The Earth, Chart for Questions 5–6 based on data from: Source Natural Resources Canada, *http://www.earthquakescanada.nrcan.gc.ca/historic-historique/map-carte-eng.php*

Science–Practice Test, Passage for Questions 24–25 based on information from: "Genetic Limits on Evolution in Invasive Species," by Spencer Barrett and Lain Martyn, *http://csee-scee.ca/wp-content/uploads/2012/04/invasive-plants_En-MR.pdf*

Science–Practice Test, Passage for Questions 28–30 based on information from: Stem Cell Network, *http://www.stemcellnetwork.ca/index.php?page=what-are-stem-cells&hl=eng*

Science–Practice Test, Passage for Questions 45–47 based in part on information from: "Understanding the Canadian Shield." *http://www.canadianshieldfoundation.ca/?page_id=39* downloaded 22 Sept 2013.

Chapter 16, The World, Data, Passage, and Map for Questions 1–5: from CIA *World FactBook*.

Chapter 16, Regions in Canada, Map for Questions 1–4: from Natural Resources Canada, *http://geogratis.gc.ca/api/en/nrcan-rncan/ess-sst/dcdd5e21-8893-11e0-8ea0-6cf049291510.html*. Canadian Open Government License.

Chapter 16, Chapter Check-Up. Map for Questions 1–3, von Grebmer, K., C. Ringler, M. W. Rosegrant, T. Olofinbiyi, D. Wiesmann, H. Fritschel, O. Badiane, M. Torero, Y. Yohannes, J. Thompson, C. von Oppeln, and J. Rahall. 2012. *2012 Global Hunger Index—The Challenge of Hunger: Ensuring Sustainable Food Security under Land, Water, and Energy Stresses*. "Global

Hunger Index Scores by Security" map. Bonn, Germany: Welthungerhilfe; Washington, DC: International Food Policy Research Institute; Dublin, Ireland: Concern Worldwide.

Chapter 17, Canada's Aboriginal Peoples. Passage for Questions 6–7 based in part on information from: *http://www.canadahistory.com/sections/eras/new%20france/The%20 Iroquois.html, http://www.nysm.nysed.gov/IroquoisVillage/constructiontwo.html, and http://en.wikipedia.org/wiki/Iroquois*

Chapter 17, Early Prime Ministers, Passage for Questions 1–3. Speech by Sir John A. MacDonald. Public Domain. 1865.

Chapter 17, Chapter Check-Up. Passage and Map for Questions 1–3 from: Inuit Tapiriit Kanatami, *www.ITK.ca.* Used with Permission.

Chapter 17, Chapter Check-Up. Passage for Questions 7-9 based in part on information from: *http://www.canadiana.ca/citm/specifique/responsable_e.html*

Chapter 18, Canadian Justice, Passage for Questions 4–6 based in part on information from *http://www.justice.gc.ca/eng/csj-sjc/*

Chapter 18, Canadian Prime Ministers. Photograph of Prime Minister Sir John A. MacDonald. National Archives. Public Domain.

Chapter 18, Canadian Prime Ministers. Photograph of Prime Minister Sir Wilfred Laurier. Library and Archives Canada. Public Domain.

Chapter 18, Canadian Prime Ministers. Photograph of Prime Minister William Lyon Mackenzie King. Library and Archives Canada. Public Domain.

Chapter 18, Canadian Prime Ministers. Photograph of Prime Minister John Diefenbaker. Library and Archives Canada. Public Domain.

Chapter 18, Canadian Prime Ministers. Photograph of Prime Minister Lester B. Pierson. Wikimedia.com. Public Domain.

Chapter 18, Canadian Prime Ministers. Photograph of Prime Minister Pierre Trudeau. Library and Archives Canada. Used with permission.

Chapter 18, Canadian Prime Ministers. Photograph of Prime Minister Brian Mulroney. Government of the United States. Public Domain.

Chapter 18, Canadian Prime Ministers. Photograph of Prime Minister Kim Campbell, by Denise Grant.

Chapter 18, Chapter Check-Up. Passage and Charts for Questions 7–8 from: Government of Ontario, Ministry of Finance. Used with permission.

Chapter 19, Canadian Unity. Passage for Questions 4–6, from: "Meech Lake," by Jenny Higgins, Newfoundland and Labrador Heritage Web Site. Used with permission.

Chapter 19, Chapter Check-Up. Passage for Questions 9–12, from: "Why Canadian Unity." Reproduced with the permission of the Privy Council Office, 2014.

Chapter 20, Resources and Industry. Passage for Questions 1–2, from: Central Intelligence Agency *The World Factbook.*

Chapter 20, Canada and the U.S., Passage for Questions 4–6, based on information from: Source Foreign Affairs Canada

Chapter 20, Global Markets and Foreign Trade, Passage for Questions 1–3, based on information from: Source Foreign Affairs Canada

Chapter 20, Global Markets and Foreign Trade, Passage for Questions 4–6, based on information from: Source Foreign Affairs Canada

Chapter 20, Chapter Check-Up. Passage for Questions 1–4, from: United Nations. © (2014) United Nations. Reprinted with the permission of the United Nations.

Chapter 20, Chapter Check-Up. Chart for Questions 11–12, from: *www.mining-bulletin.com* Used with permission.

Social Studies–Practice Test, Passage for Questions 28–30, from: "Preventing Terrorism Overview," United States Department of Homeland Security.

Social Studies–Practice Test, Passage and Map for Questions 48–50, from: Central Intelligence Agency, *The World Factbook*.

Every effort has been made to trace the copyright holders of items appearing in the book, and we apologize in the event of any unintentional omissions. We would be pleased to insert the appropriate acknowledgments in any subsequent edition of this publication.

Index

Russian Revolution, 607, 611–612, 685
Rutherford, Ernest, 502–503

S

Scale drawings, 821–824
Scalene triangle, 836
Science test
  diagnostic examination, 55–79
  Earth. *See* Earth
  life science. *See* Life science
  overview of, 469–470
  physical science. *See* Physical science
  practice test, 567–589
  skills needed for, 469
  space science. *See* Space science
Scientific notation, 867–868
Secondary consumers, 526
Second Continental Congress, 609
Sedimentary rock, 562
Seigneurs, 628, 631
Self-pollination, 535
Semi-colon, 266–267
Senate, 649, 650
Sentence(s)
  clauses, 148–151
  complex, 174–177
  compound, 168–174
  improper coordination and subordination in, 178
  modifiers used in, 204–206
  nouns, 135–138, 140–141
  parallelism in, 200–204, 226
  predicates, 154–157
  pronouns, 138–141
  run-on, 194–200
  simple, 165–168
  structure of, 187–214
  subject of, 151–153
  supporting, 222–225
  topic, 215–222
  transition, 247
  verbs. *See* Verb(s)
Sentence fragment, 187–193
Separation of powers, 650
Service industry, 698
Sexual reproduction, 535
Signed numbers
  addition of, 861
  subtraction of, 861–863
Simile, 374
Simple interest, 811–813
Simple predicate, 154–156
Simple sentence, 165–168
Simple subject, 151–153

Single replacement reaction, 482
Singular nouns, 137, 282, 293
Singular verb, 294–296
Skeletal system, 530
Slope-intercept, 923
Slope of the line
  applications of, 920–921
  determining of, 918–920
Socialism, 681
Social Studies test
  aboriginal peoples, 622–625
  Age of Revolution, 607–612
  atlases, 595–599
  Britain, 628–632
  Canada. *See* Canada
  diagnostic examination, 81–106
  early civilizations, 603–606
  early explorers, 626–627
  France, 628–632
  maps, 595–599
  practice test, 719–744
  regions of Canada, 612–614
  subjects covered on, 593–594
Solar system, 545–548
Solid, 479
Somatic nervous system, 532
Sound energy, 492
Soviet Union, 685
Space science
  description of, 541–545
  solar system, 545–548
  universe, 545–548
Spanish settlements, 627
Spatial order, 428
Species, 526
Specific gravity, 474
Spelling
  of contractions, 280–281
  of homonyms, 283–285
  of possessives, 281–283
Square roots, 866–867
St. Lawrence River, 627, 631
Stalin, Joseph, 685
Stamp Act, 609
Statute of Westminster, 633
Straight angle, 831
Stratosphere, 554
Sub-dividing paragraphs, 228–230
Subduction, 549
Subject
  compound, 153–154, 295
  simple, 151–153
  verb agreement with, 293–297
Subordinate clause, 150–151
Subtraction
  of decimals, 768–769

description of, 749–751, 756
  of fractions, 791–793
  of integers, 861–863
Subtraction principle, 887–888
Sun, 543, 546, 548
Sunlight, 528
Superior court, 656
Supplementary angles, 833
Supply and demand, law of, 659
Supporting details, 407–409
Supporting sentences, 222–225
Supreme Court, 656
Survival of the fittest, 518
Swells, 559
Synonym, 226
Synthesis, reading
  coordination of information, 431–435
  definition of, 425
  description of, 425–428
  integration of information, 440–442
  organizational structure, 428–431
  perspective, 435–438
  purpose, 435–438
Synthesis reaction, 482

T

Tables, 871–873
Taliban, 707
Teeth, 523
Tense, 297–299
Territorial government, 651–652
That, 175
Theocracy, 681
Thermodynamics, 529
Thermosphere, 554
Thesis statement, 236–239, 318–322
Title of essay, 330
Tone, 411–414
Topic of essay, 317–322
Topic sentence, 215–222
Topographical map, 595
Trade deficit, 704
Trade surplus, 704
Trait, 514
Transform plates, 549
Transition word, 246–247
Transparency, 710
Transversals, 834–836
Trapezoid, 848–850
Treaty of Paris (1763), 629
Triangles
  area of, 847–848
  types of, 836–844
Tropopause, 555